Lecture Notes in Artificial Intelligence   11742

Subseries of Lecture Notes in Computer Science

Series Editors

Randy Goebel
  University of Alberta, Edmonton, Canada
Yuzuru Tanaka
  Hokkaido University, Sapporo, Japan
Wolfgang Wahlster
  DFKI and Saarland University, Saarbrücken, Germany

Founding Editor

Jörg Siekmann
  DFKI and Saarland University, Saarbrücken, Germany

More information about this series at http://www.springer.com/series/1244

Haibin Yu · Jinguo Liu ·
Lianqing Liu · Zhaojie Ju ·
Yuwang Liu · Dalin Zhou (Eds.)

Intelligent Robotics and Applications

12th International Conference, ICIRA 2019
Shenyang, China, August 8–11, 2019
Proceedings, Part III

Springer

Editors
Haibin Yu
Shenyang Institute of Automation
Shenyang, China

Jinguo Liu
Shenyang Institute of Automation
Shenyang, China

Lianqing Liu
Shenyang Institute of Automation
Shenyang, China

Zhaojie Ju
University of Portsmouth
Portsmouth, UK

Yuwang Liu
Shenyang Institute of Automation
Shenyang, China

Dalin Zhou
University of Portsmouth
Portsmouth, UK

ISSN 0302-9743   ISSN 1611-3349 (electronic)
Lecture Notes in Artificial Intelligence
ISBN 978-3-030-27534-1   ISBN 978-3-030-27535-8 (eBook)
https://doi.org/10.1007/978-3-030-27535-8

LNCS Sublibrary: SL7 – Artificial Intelligence

This Springer imprint is published by the registered company Springer Nature Switzerland AG
The registered company address is: Gewerbestrasse 11, 6330 Cham, Switzerland

Preface

On behalf of the Organizing Committee, we welcome you to the proceedings of the 12th International Conference on Intelligent Robotics and Applications (ICIRA 2019), organized by Shenyang Institute of Automation, Chinese Academy of Sciences, co-organized by Huazhong University of Science and Technology, Shanghai Jiao Tong University, and the University of Portsmouth, technically co-sponsored by the National Natural Science Foundation of China and Springer, and financially sponsored by Shenyang Association for Science and Technology. ICIRA 2019 with the theme of "Robot Era" offered a unique and constructive platform for scientists and engineers throughout the world to present and share their recent research and innovative ideas in the areas of robotics, automation, mechatronics, and applications.

ICIRA 2019 was most successful this year in attracting more than 500 submissions regarding the state-of-the-art development in robotics, automation, and mechatronics. The Program Committee undertook a rigorous review process for selecting the most deserving research for publication. Despite the high quality of most of the submissions, a total of 378 papers were selected for publication in six volumes of Springer's *Lecture Notes in Artificial Intelligence* a subseries of *Lecture Notes in Computer Science*. We sincerely hope that the published papers of ICIRA 2019 will prove to be technically beneficial and constructive to both the academic and industrial community in robotics, automation, and mechatronics. We would like to express our sincere appreciation to all the authors, participants, and the distinguished plenary and keynote speakers.

The success of the conference is also attributed to the Program Committee members and invited peer reviewers for their thorough review of all the submissions, as well as to the Organizing Committee and volunteers for their diligent work. Special thanks are extended to Alfred Hofmann, Anna Kramer, and Volha Shaparava from Springer for their consistent support.

August 2019

Haibin Yu
Jinguo Liu
Lianqing Liu
Zhaojie Ju
Yuwang Liu
Dalin Zhou

Organization

Honorary Chairs

Youlun Xiong   Huazhong University of Science and Technology, China

Nanning Zheng   Xi'an Jiaotong University, China

General Chair

Haibin Yu   Shenyang Institute of Automation, Chinese Academy of Sciences, China

General Co-chairs

Kok-Meng Lee   Georgia Institute of Technology, USA

Zhouping Yin   Huazhong University of Science and Technology, China

Xiangyang Zhu   Shanghai Jiao Tong University, China

Program Chair

Jinguo Liu   Shenyang Institute of Automation, Chinese Academy of Sciences, China

Program Co-chairs

Zhaojie Ju   The University of Portsmouth, UK

Lianqing Liu   Shenyang Institute of Automation, Chinese Academy of Sciences, China

Bram Vanderborght   Vrije Universiteit Brussel, Belgium

Advisory Committee

Jorge Angeles   McGill University, Canada

Tamio Arai   University of Tokyo, Japan

Hegao Cai   Harbin Institute of Technology, China

Tianyou Chai   Northeastern University, China

Jie Chen   Tongji University, China

Jiansheng Dai   King's College London, UK

Zongquan Deng   Harbin Institute of Technology, China

Han Ding   Huazhong University of Science and Technology, China

Xilun Ding	Beihang University, China
Baoyan Duan	Xidian University, China
Xisheng Feng	Shenyang Institute of Automation, Chinese Academy of Sciences, China
Toshio Fukuda	Nagoya University, Japan
Jianda Han	Shenyang Institute of Automation, Chinese Academy of Sciences, China
Qiang Huang	Beijing Institute of Technology, China
Oussama Khatib	Stanford University, USA
Yinan Lai	National Natural Science Foundation of China, China
Jangmyung Lee	Pusan National University, South Korea
Zhongqin Lin	Shanghai Jiao Tong University, China
Hong Liu	Harbin Institute of Technology, China
Honghai Liu	The University of Portsmouth, UK
Shugen Ma	Ritsumeikan University, Japan
Daokui Qu	SIASUN, China
Min Tan	Institute of Automation, Chinese Academy of Sciences, China
Kevin Warwick	Coventry University, UK
Guobiao Wang	National Natural Science Foundation of China, China
Tianmiao Wang	Beihang University, China
Tianran Wang	Shenyang Institute of Automation, Chinese Academy of Sciences, China
Yuechao Wang	Shenyang Institute of Automation, Chinese Academy of Sciences, China
Bogdan M. Wilamowski	Auburn University, USA
Ming Xie	Nanyang Technological University, Singapore
Yangsheng Xu	The Chinese University of Hong Kong, SAR China
Huayong Yang	Zhejiang University, China
Jie Zhao	Harbin Institute of Technology, China
Nanning Zheng	Xi'an Jiaotong University, China
Weijia Zhou	Shenyang Institute of Automation, Chinese Academy of Sciences, China
Xiangyang Zhu	Shanghai Jiao Tong University, China

Publicity Chairs

Shuo Li	Shenyang Institute of Automation, Chinese Academy of Sciences, China
Minghui Wang	Shenyang Institute of Automation, Chinese Academy of Sciences, China
Chuan Zhou	Shenyang Institute of Automation, Chinese Academy of Sciences, China

Publication Chairs

Yuwang Liu   Shenyang Institute of Automation, Chinese Academy
                      of Sciences, China
Dalin Zhou   The University of Portsmouth, UK

Award Chairs

Kaspar Althoefer   Queen Mary University of London, UK
Naoyuki Kubota   Tokyo Metropolitan University, Japan
Xingang Zhao   Shenyang Institute of Automation, Chinese Academy
                      of Sciences, China

Special Session Chairs

Guimin Chen   Xi'an Jiaotong University, China
Hak Keung Lam   King's College London, UK

Organized Session Co-chairs

Guangbo Hao   University College Cork, Ireland
Yongan Huang   Huazhong University of Science and Technology,
                      China
Qiang Li   Bielefeld University, Germany
Yuichiro Toda   Okayama University, Japan
Fei Zhao   Xi'an Jiaotong University, China

International Organizing Committee Chairs

Zhiyong Chen   The University of Newcastle, Australia
Yutaka Hata   University of Hyogo, Japan
Sabina Jesehke   RWTH Aachen University, Germany
Xuesong Mei   Xi'an Jiaotong University, China
Robert Riener   ETH Zurich, Switzerland
Chunyi Su   Concordia University, Canada
Shengquan Xie   The University of Auckland, New Zealand
Chenguang Yang   UWE Bristol, UK
Tom Ziemke   University of Skövde, Sweden
Yahya Zweiri   Kingston University, UK

Local Arrangements Chairs

Hualiang Zhang   Shenyang Institute of Automation, Chinese Academy
                      of Sciences, China
Xin Zhang   Shenyang Institute of Automation, Chinese Academy
                      of Sciences, China

Contents – Part III

Continuum Mechanisms and Robots

Unmanned Underwater Vehicles

Parallel Robotics

Human-Robot Collaboration

Swarm Intelligence and Multi-robot Cooperation

Adaptive and Learning Control System

Wearable and Assistive Devices and Robots for Healthcare

Nonlinear Systems and Control

Marine Bio-inspired Robotics and Soft Robotics: Materials, Mechanisms, Modelling, and Control

Parameter Optimization of Eel Robot Based on NSGA-II Algorithm

AnFan Zhang[1]([✉]), Shugen Ma[2], Bin Li[3], MingHui Wang[3], and Jian Chang[3]

[1] Faculty of Marine Science and Technology,
Hainan Tropical Ocean University, Sanya, China
zhangaf@hntou.edu.cn
[2] Department of Robotics, Ritsumeikan University, Shiga-ken 525-8577, Japan
[3] State Key Laboratory of Robotics, Shenyang Institute of Automation,
Chinese Academy of Sciences, Shenyang, China

Abstract. In order to obtain an efficient gait, this paper studies the swimming efficiency of underwater eel robot in different gaits. The optimal gait parameters combination of three gaits is studied by using Non-dominated Sorting in Genetic algorithm (NSGA-II). The relationship between input power and velocity in different gait patterns is analyzed, and the optimal gait parameters combination in each gait patterns is obtained. The simulation results show that the new gait only need less input power than the serpentine gait in the same velocity, and the new gait has faster velocity compared to the eel gait using the same joint input power. Finally, the above founds have further verified by experiments. The experiments have proved that the new gait has higher swimming efficiency. Besides, It is found that both the optimal gait amplitude and optimal phase shift exist in both the new gait and the serpentine gait.

Keywords: Parameter optimization · Gait pattern · NSGA-II · Eel robot

1 Introduction

High efficiency gait will help the energy utilization of the robot and prolong the working time of the robot. One approach to obtain an efficient gait is by deriving an analytical solution of the optimal gait. However, the eel robot system is a highly coupled and the number of the system states increases with the increase of the number of modules, which makes it difficult to obtain the analytical solution of the optimal gait. An even more main approach called numerical analysis method [1–3] can be divided into two approaches according to the models of robot and usually contains a serial of assumptions [4]. One is based on CPG model. The amphibious snake-like robot adopted a gradient-free online Powell method combined with CPG model to obtain the optimal gait [5]. The advantages of this method are low computational cost and fast speed, but the parameters of CPG model lack physical significance. The other is the gait optimization based on the

© Springer Nature Switzerland AG 2019
H. Yu et al. (Eds.): ICIRA 2019, LNAI 11742, pp. 3–15, 2019.
https://doi.org/10.1007/978-3-030-27535-8_1

dynamic model, and the physical meaning of the model parameters is obvious. This paper mainly studies the optimal gait problem based on the dynamic model of underwater eel-like robot.

The eel-like robot belongs to a chain-like structure robot without a fixed base. There are many related studies on gait optimization of chain-structured robot without fixed base on land or amphibious [5–9]. It can be divided into two categories. The first type uses optimal control method to obtain optimal gait. Ostrowski [2] elaborated the gait selection and optimal control of nonholonomic motion system with Lie group symmetry. Lagrange reduction theory was used to simplify the optimal control problem. Optimal control technology was used to study the optimal gait and gait shifting, but the computational cost of this technology is high. In order to reduce the computational complexity, Cortes [10] studied the optimal control and gait selection of dynamic systems with group symmetry. The truncated basis function with periodic input was used to obtain the solution of the approximate optimal control problem, but only the approximate optimal gait of eel-like robot was studied. The second method is to obtain the optimal gait parameter combination by using optimization algorithm. Parodi [11] used Lyapunov method to design the controller to ensure that the body shape converges to local curvature. The locally optimized gait parameters ensured rapid system response and efficient propulsion. The evaluation indicator was used to evaluate the energy and rapid response ability.

In [12,13],The NSGA-II algorithm was used to analyze the optimal gait parameter combination of land snake-like robot, and only serpentine gait pattern was analyzed, no attention is paid to other gait patterns. The optimal gait amplitude parameter was concentrated around $\alpha \sim 30°$ and the optimal gait phase shift was concentrated around $\beta \sim 70°$ of land snake-like robot are obtained. Compared with the force that the robot receives on the land, hydrodynamic force that the robot receives under water is more complex, its feasible gait space is more diverse than the terrestrial environment, and the solution space to be searched is larger. In [1], the Particle Swarm Optimization (PSO) and genetic algorithm (GA) were used to optimize the parameter combination of serpentine gait. Multi-objective optimization algorithm MOO was adopted to optimize the gait parameters combination of serpentine gait [3]. Kelasidi [14] studied the relationship between gait parameters, forward speed and power consumption in two gaits (eel gait and serpentine gait), and found that the power consumption COST per unit mass decreased with the increase of modules, but the average power used cannot reflect the change of instantaneous power.

This paper analyzes the relationship between the input power, velocity and gait parameters of the underwater eel robot in new gait (found in [15]), eel gait, serpentine gait. The advantages and disadvantages of the new gait are emphatically analyzed compared with the other two gaits. The energy efficiency of the three gait is analyzed and compared by using the dynamic model in non-inertial frame and the multi-objective optimization algorithm NSGA-II. The analytical dynamic model based on non-inertial frame is used to calculate dynamics, which can effectively reduce the computation time of dynamics. The multi-objective optimization NSGA-II algorithm is used to effectively reduce the calculation time and quickly find the Pareto frontier, so as to improve the calculation efficiency. The two optimal objectives are the minimum power input and the maximum velocity. Taking the sum of the maximum input power plus absolute value as input power can effectively prevent the situation of excessive instantaneous power. The simulation results show that the eel-like robot with the new gait consumes less power than that of the serpentine gait and eel gait at the same speed, and has faster speed at the same input power. Finally, experiments verify the efficiency of the new gait, and the relationship between the average speed and the gait amplitude and the phase shift in the new gait and serpentine gait is analyzed.

2 The Dynamic Model of the Eel Robot

In this paper, the dynamic model in [17] is adopted, which is based on a special non-inertial system. Considering only two-dimensional motion, it is assumed that the eel robot is buoyancy-gravity equilibrium, and that the robot is a slender body with circular cross-section.

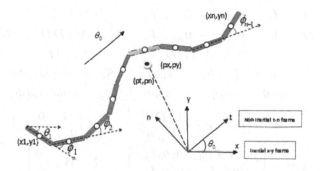

Fig. 1. The prototype of underwater Eel-like robot and its kinematic parameters.

The kinematics of the planar eel robot is presented and illustrated in Fig. 1 consisting of n links of length $2l$ interconnected by $n-1$ active joints. The robot is defined with respect to the fixed global frame, $x - y$, and is still defined with respect to the non-inertial $t - n$ frame, and both of them share the same origin (Fig. 1). Each link has the same mass m, moment of inertia $\frac{1}{3}ml^2$ and the $x_i - y_i$ frame attached to the mass center of each link. The mathematical symbols are described in Table 1. The joint angle vector is defined as $\phi = [\phi_1, \phi_2, ..., \phi_{n-1}]^T$, and absolute angle in global frame is defined as $\theta = [\theta_1, ...\theta_n]^T$, orientation angle is defined as $\theta_0 = \frac{1}{n}\sum_1^n \theta_i$. Correspondingly absolute angle in t-n frame is $\Phi = [\Phi_1, ...\Phi_n]^T$. The direction of the t axis is along eel robot tangential or forward direction, and the direction of the n axis is along the normal direction of the robot. $\theta_0 \in R$ stands for the global frame orientation and is expressed with respect to the global x axis with counterclockwise positive direction. Other coefficients are defined by

Table 1. Definition of mathematical terms

Symbol	Definition
n	The number of links
m	Link mass
θ	Absolute angle vector in global frame
ϕ	Joint angle vector
θ_0	Orientation angle of Eel robot
$\boldsymbol{\theta}$	Absolute angle vector in global frame
$\boldsymbol{\phi}$	Joint angle vector
$\boldsymbol{\Phi}$	Absolute angle vector in t-n frame
α	Gait amplitude
ω	Gait frequency
β	Phase shift
γ	The offset of the joint angle

$$A = [I_{n-1}, 0_{n-1}] + [0_{n-1}, I_{n-1}] \qquad e = [1 \ldots 1]^T$$
$$D = [I_{n-1}, 0_{n-1}] - [0_{n-1}, I_{n-1}] \quad K = A^T(DD^T)^{-1}D$$
$$V = A^T(DD^T)^{-1}A \qquad J = JI_{n,n}$$
$$\sin \boldsymbol{\Phi} = [\sin \Phi_1, \ldots, \sin \Phi_n]^T \quad S_{\boldsymbol{\Phi}} = diag(\sin(\boldsymbol{\Phi}))$$
$$\cos \boldsymbol{\Phi} = [\cos \Phi_1, \ldots, \cos \Phi_n]^T \quad C_{\boldsymbol{\Phi}} = diag(\cos(\boldsymbol{\Phi}))$$
$$W_c = [B_m, e] = \begin{bmatrix} D \\ e^T/n \end{bmatrix}^{-1} \quad E = \begin{bmatrix} e & 0_{n \times 1} \\ 0_{n \times 1} & e \end{bmatrix}$$
$$R_{2n \times 2n} = \begin{bmatrix} \cos \theta_0 I_{n,n} & \sin \theta_0 I_{n,n} \\ -\sin \theta_0 I_{n,n} & \cos \theta_0 I_{n,n} \end{bmatrix} \quad \theta = W_c \begin{bmatrix} \phi \\ \theta_0 \end{bmatrix}.$$

The fluid force model adopted in this dynamic model considers linear resistance, additional mass force effect, non-linear resistance and fluid moment. The acceleration of the CM in t-n frame can be expressed as

$$\begin{bmatrix} \dot{v}_t \\ \dot{v}_n \end{bmatrix} = -M_p \begin{bmatrix} u_n e^T S_{\boldsymbol{\Phi}}^2, -u_n e^T S_{\boldsymbol{\Phi}} C_{\boldsymbol{\Phi}} \\ -u_n e^T S_{\boldsymbol{\Phi}} C_{\boldsymbol{\Phi}}, u_n e^T C_{\boldsymbol{\Phi}}^2 \end{bmatrix} (\begin{bmatrix} lK^T S_{\boldsymbol{\Phi}} \ddot{\boldsymbol{\Phi}} + lK^T C_{\boldsymbol{\Phi}} \dot{\boldsymbol{\Phi}}^2 \\ -lK^T C_{\boldsymbol{\Phi}} \ddot{\boldsymbol{\Phi}} + lK^T S_{\boldsymbol{\Phi}} \dot{\boldsymbol{\Phi}}^2 \end{bmatrix}$$
$$+ \begin{bmatrix} +2\dot{\theta}_0 lK^T C_{\boldsymbol{\Phi}} \dot{\boldsymbol{\Phi}} + \dot{\theta}_0^2 * lK^T \cos \boldsymbol{\Phi} + \ddot{\theta}_0 lK^T \sin \boldsymbol{\Phi} \\ +2\dot{\theta}_0 lK^T S_{\boldsymbol{\Phi}} \dot{\boldsymbol{\Phi}} + \dot{\theta}_0^2 * lK^T \sin \boldsymbol{\Phi} + \ddot{\theta}_0 lK^T \cos \boldsymbol{\Phi} \end{bmatrix}) + M_p \begin{bmatrix} e^T f_{D,t} \\ e^T f_{D,n} \end{bmatrix} + \begin{bmatrix} +v_n \dot{\theta}_0 \\ -v_t \dot{\theta}_0 \end{bmatrix} \quad (1)$$

where $M_p = \begin{bmatrix} nm + u_n e^T S_{\boldsymbol{\Phi}}^2, -u_n e^T S_{\boldsymbol{\Phi}} C_{\boldsymbol{\Phi}} \\ -u_n e^T S_{\boldsymbol{\Phi}} C_{\boldsymbol{\Phi}}, nm + u_n e^T C_{\boldsymbol{\Phi}}^2 \end{bmatrix}^{-1}$. The torque equations for all links are expressed in matrix form as

$$J\ddot{\boldsymbol{\Phi}} + M_{\boldsymbol{\Phi}}\ddot{\boldsymbol{\Phi}} - \boldsymbol{\tau} + M_{\boldsymbol{\Phi}} e\ddot{\theta}_0 + W_{\boldsymbol{\Phi}}\dot{\boldsymbol{\Phi}}^2 + W_{\boldsymbol{\Phi}} e\dot{\theta}_0^2$$
$$+ 2W_{\boldsymbol{\Phi}}\dot{\boldsymbol{\Phi}}\dot{\theta}_0 + K_{Dt}f_{Dt} + K_{Dn}f_{Dn} = D^T u \quad (2)$$

where $M_\Phi, W_\Phi, K_{Dt}, K_{Dn}$ are defined as

$$M_\Phi = ml^2 S_\Phi V S_\Phi + ml^2 C_\Phi V C_\Phi + u_n l^2 K_1 K^T S_\Phi + u_n l^2 K_1 K^T C_\Phi,$$
$$W_\Phi = ml^2 S_\Phi V C_\Phi + ml^2 C_\Phi V S_\Phi + u_n l^2 K_1 K^T C_\Phi - u_n l^2 K_2 K^T S_\Phi,$$
$$A_1 = S_\Phi K S_\Phi^2 + C_\Phi K S_\Phi C_\Phi, K_{Dt} = u_n l^2 A_1 e e^T m11 - u_n l^2 A_2 e e^T m21 - l S_\Phi K,$$
$$K_1 = A1 + u_n A_1 e e^T (m12 S_\Phi C_\Phi - m11 S_\Phi^2) - u_n A_2 e e^T (m22 S_\Phi C_\Phi - m21 S_\Phi^2),$$
$$K_2 = A2 - u_n A_1 e e^T (m11 S_\Phi C_\Phi - m12 C_\Phi^2) + u_n A_2 e e^T (m21 S_\Phi C_\Phi - m22 C_\Phi^2),$$
$$A_2 = S_\Phi K S_\Phi C_\Phi + C_\Phi K C_\Phi^2, K_{Dn} = u_n l^2 A_1 e e^T m12 - u_n l^2 A_2 e e^T m22 + l C_\Phi K.$$

In summary, the equations of motion for the underwater eel robot are given by Eqs. (1) and (2). By introducing the state variables

$$x = [\phi^T, \theta_0, p_x, p_y, \dot{p}_x, \dot{\theta}_0, \dot{\phi}^T, v_t, v_n]^T \in R^{2n+4}$$

the model of the Underwater Eel Robot in state space form is rewritten as $\dot{x} = f(x, u)$. For further details, please see [17].

3 The Optimization Goal Description and Multi-objective Optimal Method

3.1 Gait Patterns

There are many gaits for eel robot. Firstly, the definition of general gait is given.

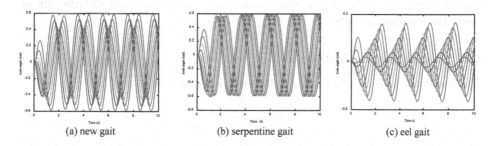

(a) new gait   (b) serpentine gait   (c) eel gait

Fig. 2. Gait patterns.

$$\phi_j = \alpha g(n, i) \sin(\omega t + (j - 1)\beta) + \gamma \tag{3}$$

where gait amplitude α, gait frequency ω, and phase shift β are considered to decision variables. Different $g(n, i)$ means different gait pattern. The phase offset γ control the direction of swimming. Figure 2 shows the pictures of all the joint angle varies with time in three gait patterns.

The new gait is a new gait pattern found in the tangential velocity tracking of eel robot based on iterative learning control [15]. See Fig. 2(a). This gait is characterized by smaller amplitudes near the center of mass and larger amplitudes farther away from the center of mass. In our previous work [15], we found that new gait always occurs at high speed. The gait is defined as follows

$$\phi_j = \begin{cases} \alpha \frac{(n+2-j)}{(n+1)} \sin(\omega t + (j-1)\beta) + \gamma, j < n/2 \\ \alpha \frac{(2+j)}{(n+1)} \sin(\omega t + (j-1)\beta) + \gamma, j > n/2 \end{cases}$$

Serpentine gait is considered to have high propulsion efficiency and is the most commonly gait pattern in various literature [14, 16], see Fig. 2(b), is defined as follows.

$$\phi_j = \alpha \sin(\omega t + (j-1)\beta) + \gamma, j = 1...n-1. \tag{4}$$

The eel gait is inspired by Bio-eel's swimming, see Fig. 2(c). This gait is characterized by smaller head amplitude and larger tail amplitude. Each joint angle is defined as follows

$$\phi_j = \alpha \frac{n-j}{n+1} \sin(\omega t + (j-1)\beta) + \gamma, j = 1...n-1. \tag{5}$$

The new gait have not been analyzed in detail in previous literatures. There is no comparison between the advantages and disadvantages of the new gait compared to other gaits. Therefore, this paper analyzes the three gait patterns mentioned above. In these gaits, the same range of gait parameters can be constrained as follows.

$$0 \le \alpha \le 1.4, 0 \le \omega \le \pi, 0 \le \beta \le \pi.$$

Since the linear relationship between gait frequency ω and velocity has been confirmed by most literatures, we mainly focus on the optimal distribution of the other two parameters.

3.2   Evaluation Indicator

The indicator to evaluate the gait efficiency is defined as

$$J_1 = \frac{P_{min}}{v_t} \tag{6}$$

where P_{min} is a function representing the input power of all joints. v_t is the velocity of robot.

The smaller the indicator J_1, the higher the efficiency. If the index is optimized directly, it is easy to cause the velocity to approach zero. Therefore, we decompose the indicator into two objectives, and then optimize it by multi-objective optimization algorithm. The optimal parameters α, β, ω are obtained under the objective of minimum input power and maximum speed. After the optimization is completed, this indicator is used to evaluate the efficiency. The input power of all joints is

$$P_{in} = \sum_{i=1}^{n-1} \tau \dot{\phi}$$

Different from other literature, this paper takes the sum of the maximum input power plus absolute value as the input power evaluation function, which can effectively prevent the situation of excessive instantaneous power. The specific optimization objective function is expressed as follows.

$$V_{min} = -\max_{t \in [t_0, t_1]} \{v_t(t)\} \tag{7}$$

$$P_{min} = \min_{i=1,...n-1} \text{sum} \left(\max_{t \in [t_0, t_1]} |\tau(t). * \dot{\phi}(t)^T| \right) \tag{8}$$

where v_t is the tangential velocity of eel-like robot. The initial time and end time are represented by t_0, t_1 respectively. $\tau(t)$ is the input joint torque. $\dot{\phi}$ is the joint angular velocity. Vector dot product is denoted by .*.

It is necessary to select a multi-objective optimization algorithm which can converge to the pareto surface quickly due to the complexity of the dynamics and the long time to obtain numerical solutions. In this paper, NSGA-II algorithm is used to optimize the parameters of eel-like robot. This algorithm does not require initial values and can reach the optimal solution at a faster speed. It is a non-dominated sorting genetic algorithm with elite strategy, which can obtain Pareto surface faster for complex models. The non-dominated sorting genetic algorithm NSGA-II is proposed based on the Pareto sorting idea.

4   Simulation and Experiment

The dynamics was calculated using ode45 solver in Matlab with a relative and absolute error tolerance of 10^{-6}, and the number of modules n is set to 8. The control gain of the PD controller in the simulation is designed as $K_p = 200, K_d = 100$. Initial states are set to zero. The NSGA-II algorithm used a crossover probability of 0.9, a mutation probability of 0.1, a population of 200, and an evolutionary algebra of 200.

The fluid parameters were set as $\rho = 1000\,\text{kg/m}^3$, $C_M = 1, C_f = 0.03, C_D = 2, C_a = 1, \lambda_1 = 7.1905 \times 10^{-4}, \lambda_2 = 1.5 \times 10^{-3}, \lambda_3 = 7.1526 \times 10^{-5}$. For a cylindrical body immersed in a flow with a Reynolds number of approximately $Re = 10^5$. The normal drag coefficient for the environmental force was set to $c_n = 9.3750$, and the tangential drag coefficient was set to $c_t = 0.2209$, and the added mass coefficient was set to $u_n = 0.5522, u_t = 0$.

4.1   Analysis of Optimization Results

According to Pareto set obtained by NSGA-II, it is found that optimal phase shift of eel gait is near 0.5 rad, and the optimal amplitude of eel gait is mainly around 0.5 rad. Optimal phase shift of serpentine gait is near 0.5 rad, and the optimal amplitude serpentine gait is mainly 0.1–0.5 rad. The optimization results of serpentine gait are consistent with the paper [12,13]. The optimal phase shift of new gait is also near 0.5 rad.

The optimization results are shown in Fig. 3, which describe the relationship between the optimized velocity and the input power of the three gait pattern.

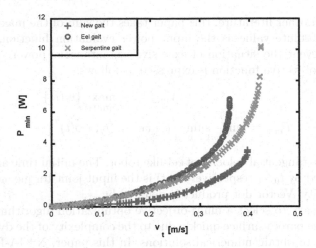

Fig. 3. Velocity vs input power.

In Fig. 3, the points corresponding to the same velocity of those gait patterns are taken, and the corresponding efficiency of each gait are obtained in Table 2. Eel-like robot with the new gait has smaller input power at the same speed. At the same input power, eel-like robot with the new gait has faster speed. It can be seen that the new gait is more efficient (J_1 is smaller). Although the new gait has higher energy efficiency, its maximum speed can only reach 0.3961 m/s. More higher speed can be provided by the serpentine gait.

Table 2. Optimal gaits and corresponding gait parameters

Gait	$v_t/(m/s)$	$P_{min}/(W)$	α	β	ω	J_1
Serpentine gait	0.299	2.342	0.265	0.329	1.857	7.83
Eel gait	0.297	2.76	0.413	0.553	3.064	9.293
New gait	0.299	1.242	0.367	0.388	1.931	4.154

In summary, compared with serpentine gait and eel gait, the new gait consumes less power at the same speed and has faster speed at the same input power. Compared with serpentine gait and eel gait, the new gait has higher swimming efficiency. Next, the serpentine gait and the new gait will be analyzed in detail.

4.2   Simulation and Experimental Analysis

In order to analyze the efficiency of serpentine gait and new gait, and the influence of amplitude and phase shift on velocity. This section uses the 3D motion capture system VXtrace to obtain real-time location. All the experimental equipment is shown in Fig. 4. Motion capture system VXtrace is composed of C-trace scanner, Calibration rod, Maxshot and Controller. The system can accurately and timely measure the position and direction of the reflecting target in space. The visual range of C-Track 780 is $7.8\,\mathrm{m}^3$, the horizontal visual range is trapezoidal, and the sampling frequency of C-Track 780 is set to $29\,\mathrm{Hz}$.

Fig. 4. Experimental equipments.

The robot consists of 8 modules, the total length is $1.6\,\mathrm{m}$ and the total mass is $6.75\,\mathrm{Kg}$ (see Fig. 5). The robot is completely submerged in water, and the robot moves in the horizontal plane. O-ring and silicone are used to ensure the sealing of the robot. Each modular universal unit MUU has two degrees of freedom of pitch and yaw.

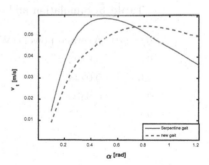

Fig. 5. The underwater eel robot.   **Fig. 6.** Velocity vs amplitude.

In order to obtain the forward velocity of the robot, the Savitzky-Golay filter in MATLAB is used to estimate the velocity of the robot. The window length of the filter is set to 19, and the mean filter method is used when the filter is invalid. The most important feature of this filter is that it can keep the shape and width of the signal unchanged while filtering out the noise. In addition, the initial state of the experiment is consistent.

Velocity Vs Amplitude. In Fig. 6, the simulation of the two gaits is obtained by changing the amplitude under the condition of constant frequency (0.5 Hz) and phase (0.8 rad). The simulation results show that speed of both gaits increases and then decreases with the increase of the amplitude. The new gait and serpentine gait exists the optimal amplitude to maximize the velocity. After repeated experiments, these points near the optimal amplitude of the serpentine gait and new gait are selected as Tables 3 and 4. Table 4 shows that in the new gait, as the increase of the amplitude, the power consumption P_{in} increases, the average power increases, the swimming efficiency decreases (J_1 increases), and there is an optimal amplitude to maximize the average speed of the experiment. Compared to Table 3 and 4, At the same input power, the experimental average speed of serpentine gait is lower than that of new gait, and the average input power of new gait is lower than that of serpentine gait (except for $\alpha = 0.8$). When the average speed is the same, the J_1 of the new gait is lower than that of the serpentine gait, so the efficiency of the new gait is higher. There is a slight difference between the individual results of the experiment ($\alpha = 0.8$) and the simulation results. The possible reason is that the robot was subject to extra resistance produced by dragging of wires due to the large swing of the tail. In addition, the actual shape different from the simulation hypothesis. In fact, the simulation model can not fully reflect some characteristics of the actual prototype. For example, the simulation robot is completely symmetrical, while the robot prototype is not completely symmetrical. The simulation assumes that the cross-section of the prototype is a cylinder, while the actual cross-section of the prototype is not a complete cylinder.

Table 3. Simulation and experimental of serpentine gait

$\alpha/(rad)$	Average power/(W)	Average speed/(m/s)	J_1
0.5	0.0193	0.0197	0.9797
0.6	0.0244	0.0234	1.0427
0.7	0.0304	0.0208	1.4615
0.8	0.0375	0.0258	1.4535

Table 4. Simulation and experimental of new gait

$\alpha/(rad)$	Average power/(W)	Average speed/(m/s)	J_1
0.5	0.0149	0.0179	0.8324
0.6	0.0190	0.0197	0.9645
0.7	0.0235	0.0242	0.9711
0.8	0.0285	0.0178	1.6011

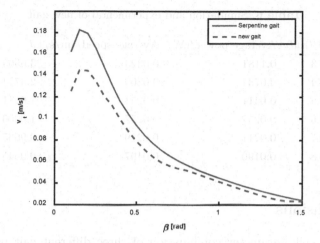

Fig. 7. Velocity vs phase shift.

Velocity vs Phase Shift. The influence of phase shift on velocity is analyzed by changing phase shift under the condition of constant amplitude (0.6 rad) and frequency (0.5 Hz). The variation trend of velocity with phase shift is shown in Fig. 7. It can be seen that the phase shift between the two gaits also has an optimal value (near 0.2–0.3 rad). Several points are selected from the figure, and the experimental result of the serpentine gait and new gait are shown in Tables 5 and 6 respectively. The average power is decreasing with the increase of phase shift by analysing the Tables 5 and 6. In addition, as the phase shift increases, the indicator J_1 of the new gait decreases, and the efficiency of the new gait increases. Comparing simulation and experiment, it is found that optimal phase of the new gait and the serpentine gait exists for maximum speed. Overall, the experimental results are consistent with the optimization results of the NSGA-II algorithm.

Table 5. Simulation and experimental of serpentine gait

$\beta/(rad)$	Average power/(W)	Average speed/(m/s)	J_1
0.3	0.1842	0.0287	6.4181
0.4	0.1380	0.0256	5.3906
0.5	0.0905	0.0284	3.1866
0.6	0.0554	0.0270	2.0519
0.7	0.0346	0.0218	1.5872
0.8	0.0244	0.0234	1.0427

Table 6. Simulation and experimental of new gait

$\beta/(rad)$	Average power/(W)	Average speed/(m/s)	J_1
0.3	0.1181	0.0323	3.6563
0.4	0.0734	0.0309	2.3754
0.5	0.0411	0.0254	1.6181
0.6	0.0257	0.0257	1.0000
0.7	0.0211	0.0219	0.9635
0.8	0.0190	0.0197	0.9645

5   Conclusions

The optimal gait parameter combination of three different gait patterns was analyzed by multi-objective optimization algorithm NSGA-II to obtain high efficiency swimming gait, and the swimming efficiency of three gait patterns was evaluated by efficiency indicator J_1. The simulation results show that the new gait has faster speed at the same input power, and consumes less input power at the same speed. That is, the new gait has higher swimming efficiency than the serpentine gait and eel gait. Then, experiments are carried out to verify that the new gait is more efficient. In addition, optimal gait amplitude and the optimal phase shift exist that make the velocity maximum in both the new gait and the serpentine gait. In future research, we will analyze the influence of additional resistance caused by dragging wires.

References

1. Wiens, A.J., Nahon, M.: Optimally efficient swimming in hyper-redundant mechanisms: control, design, and energy recovery. Bioinspir. Biomim. **7**(4), 046016 (2012)
2. Ostrowski, J.P., Desai, J.P., Kumar, V.: Optimal gait selection for nonholonomic locomotion systems. Int. J. Robot. Res. **19**(3), 225–237 (1999)
3. Tesch, M., Schneider, J., Choset, H.: Expensive multiobjective optimization for robotics. In: IEEE International Conference on Robotics and Automation, pp. 973–980. IEEE (2013)
4. Guo, X., Ma, S., Li, B., Wang, M., Wang, Y.: Optimal turning gait for a three-link underwater robot. In: 2015 IEEE International Conference on Cyber Technology in Automation, Control, and Intelligent Systems, IEEE-CYBER 2015, pp. 1321–1326 (2015)
5. Kohannim, S., Iwasaki, T.: Optimal turning gait for mechanical rectifier systems with three dimensional motion. In: 53rd IEEE Conference on Decision and Control, pp. 5862–5867 (2014)
6. Reviewed, P., Oscillations, O.: Optimal Oscillations and Chaos Generation in Biologically-Inspired Systems. University of California Los Angeles (2016)
7. Kanso, E., Marsden, J.E.: Optimal motion of an articulated body in a perfect fluid. In: Proceedings of the 44th IEEE Conference on Decision and Control, and the European Control Conference, CDC-ECC 2005 (2005)

8. van Rees, W.M., Gazzola, M., Koumoutsakos, P.: Optimal morphokinematics for undulatory swimmers at intermediate Reynolds numbers. J. Fluid Mech. **775**, 178–188 (2015)
9. Crespi, A., Ijspeert, A.J.: Online optimization of swimming and crawling in an amphibious snake robot. IEEE Trans. Robot. **24**(1), 75–87 (2008)
10. Corts, J.: Optimal gaits for dynamic robotic locomotion. Int. J. Robot. Res. **20**(9), 707–728 (2001)
11. Parodi, O., Lapierre, L., Jouvencel, B.: Optimized gait generation for Anguilliform motion. In: OCEANS 2006 - Asia Pacific, pp. 1–8 (2006)
12. Wei, W., Deng, G.Y.: Optimization and control of NSGA-II in snake like robot. Comput. Eng. **38**(8), 137–140 (2012)
13. Mehta, V.: Optimal gait analysis of snake robot dynamics. Coe. Psu. Edu. (2007)
14. Kelasidi, E., Pettersen, K.Y., Gravdahl, J.T.: Energy efficiency of underwater snake robot locomotion. In: Control and Automation, pp. 1124–1131. IEEE (2015)
15. Zhang, A., Ma, S., Li, B., Wang, M.: Tracking control of tangential velocity of eel robots based on iterative learning control. Robot **40**(06), 3–12 (2018)
16. Lapierre, L., Jouvencel, B.: Path following control for an eel-like robot. In: Europe Oceans 2005, Brest, France, vol. 1, no. 1, pp. 460–465 (2005)
17. Zhang, A., Ma, S., Li, B., Wang, M., Wang, Y.: Modeling and simulation of an underwater planar eel robot in non-inertial frame. In: The 7th Annual IEEE International Conference on CYBER Technology in Automation, Control, and Intelligent Systems (2016)

A Novel Dual-Drive Soft Pneumatic Actuator with the Improved Output Force

Shoufeng Liu[1], Fujun Wang[1(✉)], Guanwei Zhang[1], Zhu Liu[1],
Wei Zhang[1], Yanling Tian[1,2], and Dawei Zhang[1]

[1] Key Laboratory of Mechanism Theory and Equipment Design
of Ministry of Education, School of Mechanical Engineering, Tianjin University,
Tianjin 300054, China
wangfujun@tju.edu.cn
[2] School of Engineering, University of Warwick, Coventry CV4 7AL, UK

Abstract. This paper presents a novel dual-drive soft pneumatic network actuator consisting of a series of chambers made of elastomeric material, an inextensible bottom layer (paper), the rigid parts, the tendon, and coffee granular cavity. The soft actuator is the most important part when establishing soft robotic systems and can be used to make the soft gripper. The fabrication process of the soft actuator is presented. The proposed actuator has the design of the decreasing chamber height, which is beneficial to improving the output force and the contact area with the object. The proposed actuator has a cavity filled with coffee granular in the bottom, which improves the contact area and grasping stability. The tendon-pneumatic dual-drive and rigid parts between the adjacent chambers increase the force of the soft actuator. The bending angle model of the soft actuator is established briefly based on the elongation of the spacing layer and the contact layer of the soft actuator. The experiments prove that the proposed actuator has the significant improved output force.

Keywords: Soft actuator · Decreasing chamber height · Rigid parts ·
Coffee granular cavity · Tendon-pneumatic dual-drive

1 Introduction

Soft robots [1, 2] have developed rapidly due to the advantages of easy manufacturing, low manufacturing cost, inherent compliance, and safety interaction. Soft robots have become an important branch of robotics field. Soft robots have wide application prospects in the fields of human-robot interaction [3], end-grasping [4, 5], narrow space operation [6], post-operative rehabilitation [3], minimally invasive surgery [6] and so on. Robotic grippers play an important role in robot operation. The traditional rigid gripper has high manufacturing cost, complex mechanical structure, and complex control system. The rigid gripper has low adaptability in grasping different objects and cannot safely grasp soft and fragile objects, which limits the further application of robots [4, 5]. Soft gripper made from soft material has attracted wide attention. With the development of industry, kinds of objects need to be grasped. Soft grippers have great advantages in grasping soft, fragile objects, and objects of irregular shapes and different sizes [4, 5].

Soft actuators are the most important part of making the soft gripper. One of the most common actuation methods employed in soft robots is soft pneumatic actuators

© Springer Nature Switzerland AG 2019
H. Yu et al. (Eds.): ICIRA 2019, LNAI 11742, pp. 16–25, 2019.
https://doi.org/10.1007/978-3-030-27535-8_2

(SPAs) [2]. The existing SPAs include pneumatic network actuators (PneuNets) [7], fiber reinforced actuators [8] and McKibben actuators [9].

Because of the inherent compliance of the soft actuator, the output force is relatively small. At present, many studies are devoted to improving the output force of the soft actuator. Glick *et al.* [4] designed a soft actuator with gecko-inspired adhesive to increase the output force. There is a group of soft pneumatic actuators that use jamming [10] or layer jamming [11, 12] as a mechanism for enhancing output force. Recently, a kind of directly 3D printed soft actuators [3] are developed. They can be easily and rapidly manufactured using an affordable open source FDM 3D printer, with the characteristic of high rigidity, large output force and low durability. Besides, the tendon actuation applied to the soft material also has the large force [13–16]. The rigid parts between the chambers of the PneuNets will enhance the output force [17].

In this paper, a novel dual drive soft pneumatic network actuator is designed. The soft actuator has the decreasing chamber height, a cavity filled with coffee granular in the bottom, and the tendon-pneumatic actuation and rigid parts between the adjacent chambers. These designs can improve the output force of the soft actuator and the grasping ability of the soft gripper made of the soft actuator.

The rest of the paper is organized as follows: Sect. 2 presents the design of the soft actuator; In Sect. 3, the bending angle modeling of the soft actuators are established; In Sect. 4, the fabrication process of the soft actuators is presented; Experimental results are presented in Sect. 5; Finally, Sect. 6 draws the conclusion.

2 The Design of the Soft Actuator

The proposed soft actuator consists of a series of chambers and channels made from elastomeric material, including the top main body (elastomer), the bottom inextensible elastomer embedding an inextensible paper, the rigid parts between the adjacent chambers, the tendon, and coffee granular cavity as shown in Fig. 1.

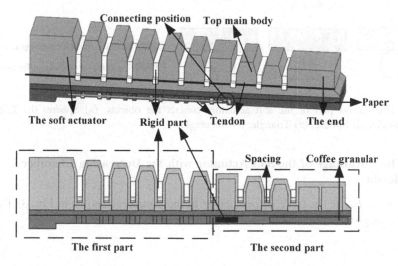

Fig. 1. The schematic mechanism of the proposed actuator

The first part of the soft actuator is inflated and the second part is not inflated acting as the compliance structure [5]. When the chamber of the actuator is inflated, the side wall of the chamber expands, and the length of the spacing layer becomes larger. The paper at the bottom of the actuator restrains the expansion at the bottom of the actuator (the length of the inextensible layer of actuator is unchanged), which makes the actuator bend. A larger output force will be obtained by using a tendon drive. The connection position of the tendon drive is shown in Fig. 1.

2.1   The Compliance of the Soft Actuator

Soft actuators made from soft materials have a relatively high compliance. When touching flexible or fragile objects, soft actuators cannot damage them. However, soft actuators still have a certain degree of hardness when touching objects, due to the relatively thick bottom layer. The bottom cavity of the second part of the actuator designed in this paper contains a certain number of coffee granular, which can make the actuators softer.

The second part of the soft actuator acts as the compliance structure and has the high compliance when contacting the objects [5]. The actuator with the rigid parts between the adjacent chambers, the second part of the soft actuator acting as the compliance structure, and the coffee granular structure can have good performance in contacting the objects as shown in Fig. 2. Due to the design of the coffee granular stricture, the actuator can adapt to different shapes of objects, while improves the contact area with the object and improving the grasping stability and ability of the soft gripper (see Fig. 2(a–c)). In contrast, ordinary actuators have smaller contact area and lower grasping stability when adapting to different shapes of objects (see Fig. 2(d–f)).

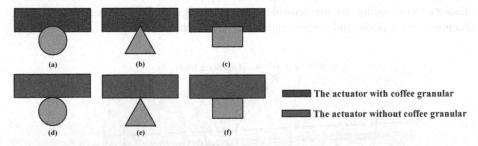

Fig. 2. The second part of the soft actuators contact the objects. (a) Sphere. (b) Triangle. (c) Rectangle. (d) Sphere. (e) Triangle. (f) Rectangle

2.2   The Advantage of the Soft Actuator with the Decreasing Chamber Height

The tip force F_{tip} is the force perpendicular to the ground as shown in Fig. 3. The tip force F_{tip} is given by

$$F_{tip} = F \sin \theta, \tag{1}$$

where F is the contact force and θ is the contact angle between the actuator and the object.

Because the curvature of the actuator with the constant chamber height is constant everywhere, the contact angle θ of the end of the actuator is relatively smaller when it contacts the object as shown in Fig. 3(a). Based on (1), the tip force F_{tip} of the actuator is small. The curvature of the actuator with the decreasing chamber height is decreasing gradually, and the contact angle θ of the end of the actuator is larger when it contacts the object as shown in Fig. 3(b). Based on (1), the tip force F_{tip} of the actuator is larger. Besides, the end of the actuator with the decreasing chamber height has smaller curvature and larger contact area with the object, therefore it is suitable for grasping application, which will have high grasping stability.

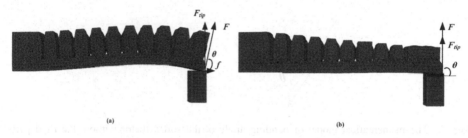

Fig. 3. The contact force of the soft actuators at the applied pressure of 20 kPa. (a) The soft actuator with the constant chamber height. (b) The soft actuator with the decreasing chamber height.

2.3   The Output Force Improvement of the Actuator

When the actuator is inflated, the chamber wall will expand, resulting in mutual extrusion of the adjacent chambers, which increases the bending angle and output force of the actuator. The extrusion of the chamber can be increased and air energy can be made full use by adding removable rigid parts between the adjacent chambers. Rigid parts can be removed while not need too much force and bending angle.

The bottom of the actuator contains rigid plate which is poured into the bottom of each chamber to connect the tendon. A tendon is connected to the rigid plate (the connecting position between the first part and second part of the actuator) as shown in Fig. 1. The connecting position design is to make full use of the compliance of the second part of the actuator and pull smoothly. Pulling the tendon will increase the force of the connecting position. The single point pull is adopted instead of the traditional pulling through the bottom passage, which avoids the large resistance between the tendon and the bottom passage. If the actuation is tendon alone, the actuator will be deformed severely and unable to bend effectively due to the multi-chamber design of the actuator. The tendon-pneumatic dual-drive will increase its output force under normal bending conditions. Combining with the coffee granular, in the meanwhile, the designs can meanwhile increase the contact area with the object while increasing the output force of the actuator.

3   Bending Angle Modeling of the Soft Actuator

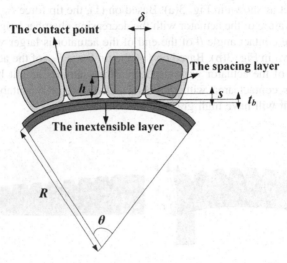

Fig. 4. The mathematical model of bending angle of the soft actuator without the rigid parts between the adjacent chambers

For the inextensible layer of the soft actuator as shown in Fig. 4,

$$R\theta = l, \tag{2}$$

where l is the length of the soft actuator, R is the curvature radius of the soft actuator.

The maximum displacement δ of the chamber lateral wall can be obtained, but it is difficult to get the displacement of the chamber lateral wall in the spacing layer. In order to solve the problem conveniently, a proportional coefficient k is set. For the spacing layer of the soft actuator without added rigid parts,

$$\theta(R + t_b + s) = l + 2(n - 1)\frac{\delta}{k}. \tag{3}$$

For the soft actuator with added rigid parts between the adjacent chambers, the maximum displacement δ of the chamber lateral wall in the contact layer can be obtained, ignoring extrusion deformation of the chambers and rigid parts,

$$\theta\left(R + t_b + \frac{h}{2}\right) = l + 2(n - 1)\delta, \tag{4}$$

where s is the spacing height of the soft actuator, h is the height between the contact point and the bottom, n is the number of the chamber, and k is the proportional coefficient.

Combining (2) and (3),

$$\theta = \frac{2(n-1)\frac{\delta}{k}}{t_b + s}. \tag{5}$$

Combining (2) and (4),

$$\theta = \frac{2(n-1)\delta}{t_b + h}. \tag{6}$$

From (5), the bending angle θ of the soft actuator without the rigid parts between the adjacent chambers is inversely proportional to the thickness t_b of the inextensible layer at the bottom of the soft actuator and the height s of the spacing. From (6), the bending angle θ of the soft actuator with the rigid parts between the adjacent chambers is inversely proportional to the thickness t_b of the inextensible layer at the bottom of the soft actuator and the height h between the contact point and the bottom. The bending angle θ is proportional to the number n of chambers and the side wall elongation δ of the soft actuator. The side wall maximum displacement δ of the soft actuator is related to the side wall thickness, width and height of the inner chamber. The proportional coefficient k is related to the spacing height s.

4 Fabrication of the Soft Actuator

A commercially available material Dragon skin 30 silicone rubber (Dragon skin 30, smooth-on Inc., America) is used to make the soft actuator [12]. The multistep fabrication process of the soft actuator is illustrated where all molds can be used repeatedly [12].

Step 1, the molds are made by 3D printing where the material is PLA filament, and the top molds are assembled as shown in Fig. 5(a). The bottom layer mold, rigid parts, and coffee granular mold are assembled as shown in Fig. 5(b).

Step 2, component A and B of Dragon skin 30 silicone rubber is mixed at a weight ratio of 1:1, and then fully mixed evenly with a glass rod. The mixed silicone rubber is put into a vacuum chamber for degassing for about 10 min.

Step 3, the silicone rubber after degassing is slowly poured into the assembled top mold and then pour the same silicone rubber in the bottom layer molds until the half height.

Step 4, place the two poured molds at the room temperature for about 6 h (the room temperature is favorable to the cure of the better soft actuator), then demold and take out the cured main body.

Step 5, then lay a piece of paper and then pour silicone rubber to fill the bottom layer mold and place the cured main body alignment on the bottom molds after the silicone rubber in the half the height of bottom layer molds is cured.

Step 6, place the poured mold in an oven at 65 °C for about 20 min, then demold and take out the cured actuator.

Step 7, when the actuator is assembled and cured, insert the needle tube into the vent positions of the actuator (favorable to sealing, preventing leakage). Then the air tube is fed into the actuator.

Step 8, carry out the bending experiment to observe whether the actuator has the air leakage. If the air leaks, fill it up. The cured soft actuator is shown in Fig. 6.

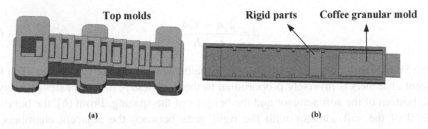

Fig. 5. The molds. (a) The assembled top molds. (b) The assembled bottom layer molds

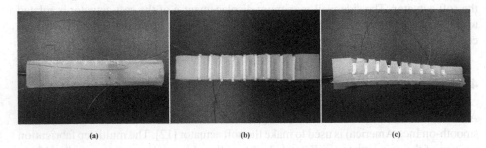

Fig. 6. The cured dual-drive soft actuator viewed from (a) bottom, (b) top, (c) side

5   Experiments

5.1   The Compliance Experiments

The compliance of the soft actuator is tested. The coffee granular structure improves the bottom flexibility of the actuator so that it can adapt to the irregularity of the object, as shown in Fig. 7. When the bottom of the soft actuator touches the object, the actuator will depend on the fluidity of the coffee granular to adapt to the shape of the object, which increase the contact area. The grasping stability of the soft gripper is closely related to the contact area with the objects. The soft gripper made by the soft actuator with coffee granular structure will have good grasping stability and adaptability.

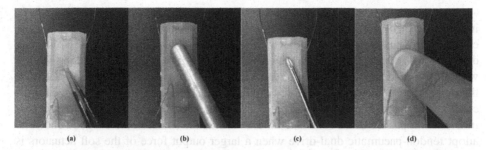

Fig. 7. (a) The tweezers. (b) The cylinder. (c) The screwdriver. (d) The human finger

5.2 The Output Force Experiments

The output force of the soft actuators is tested. The experimental setup is shown in Fig. 8(a), the output force of chamber 5 (the tendon drive position) is tested. This is because the first part is inflated and the second part is not inflated, the output force of chamber 5 is important parameter. Four experiments are carried out on actuators without the rigid parts, actuators with the rigid parts, actuators driven by 3 N and 4 N tendon pulls and air pressure. The average value is obtained and the experimental results are shown in Fig. 8(b). Rigid parts will increase the output force of the actuator, and the output force of the actuator will also be increased by using tendon-pneumatic dual-drive. The output force of tendon-pneumatic dual-drive will increase with the increase of the tendon pull force, which can expand the output force range of the actuator. At the applied pressure of 30 kPa, the output force increases by 56.3%, 86%, 25.8% correspondingly.

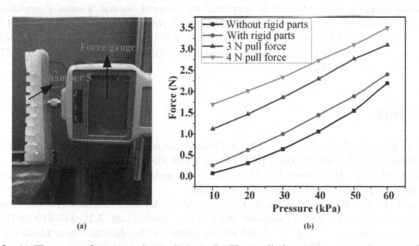

Fig. 8. (a) The output force experimental setup. (b) The applied pressure versus the output force of the chamber 5

The output force of pneumatic actuator is limited, this is because the output force increases with the increase of air pressure. Too much air pressure will make the chamber of actuator expand too much, which will lead to the decrease of its life and destruction. The tendon drive can increase its output force without affecting its life without too much pressure. According to the needed output force of the soft actuator, the magnitude of the tendon pull force can be chosen. As an easy-to-install and easy-to-control driving mode, tendon drive will greatly compensate for the limitation of inherent compliance of the soft material of the actuator. Therefore, it is a good choice to adopt tendon-pneumatic dual-drive when a larger output force of the soft actuators is needed.

6 Conclusion

This paper presents the mechanical design, the bending angle modeling, fabrication process, and experiments of a novel dual-drive soft actuator. The soft actuator has the decreasing chamber height, a cavity filled with coffee granular in the bottom, and the tendon-pneumatic dual-drive and rigid parts between the adjacent chambers. The experiments prove that these designs improve the output force and the contact area with the object. The mathematical model of bending angle of the soft actuator without the rigid parts between the adjacent chambers is established.

The tendon-pneumatic dual-drive design will have a significant improvement on the output force and cannot affect the life of the soft actuator. The tendon-pneumatic dual-drive mode can be adopted when a larger output force of the soft actuators is needed. The soft actuator is suitable to make the soft gripper, which can improve the grasping stability and ability.

Acknowledgement. This research is supported by National Natural Science Foundation of China (Grant nos. 51675376, 51675371 and 51675367). National Key R&D Program of China (nos. 2017YFB1104700, 2017YFE0112100, and 2016YFE0112100), Science & Technology Commission of Tianjin Municipality (Grant no. 18PTZWHZ00160), China-EU H2020 MNR4SCell (no. 734174).

References

1. Lee, C., et al.: Soft robot review. Int. J. Control Autom. Syst. **15**(1), 3–15 (2017)
2. Trimmer, B.: Soft robots. Curr. Biol. **23**(15), R639–R641 (2013)
3. Yap, H., Ng, H., Yeow, C.: High-force soft printable pneumatics for soft robotic applications. Soft Robot. **3**(3), 144–158 (2016)
4. Glick, P., Suresh, S.A., Ruffatto, D., Cutkosky, M., Tolley, M.T., Parness, A.: A soft robotic gripper with gecko-inspired adhesive. IEEE Robot. Autom. Lett. **3**(2), 903–910 (2018)
5. Zhou, J., Chen, S., Wang, Z.: A soft-robotic gripper with enhanced object adaptation and grasping reliability. IEEE Robot. Autom. Lett. **2**(4), 2287–2293 (2017)
6. Ranzani, T., Gerboni, G., Cianchetti, M., Menciassi, A.: A bioinspired soft manipulator for minimally invasive surgery. Bioinspir. Biomim. **10**(3), 035008 (2015)

7. Mosadegh, B., et al.: Pneumatic networks for soft robotics that actuate rapidly. Adv. Funct. Mater. **24**(15), 2163–2170 (2014)
8. Nikolov, S., Kotev, V., Kostadinov, K., Wang, F., Liang, C., Tian, Y.: Model-based design optimization of soft fiber-reinforced bending actuators. In: Proceedings of the IEEE 3M-NANO, pp. 136–140 (2016)
9. Chun, C., Hannaford, B.: Measurement and modeling of McKibben pneumatic artificial muscles. IEEE Trans. Robot. Autom. **12**(1), 90–102 (1996)
10. Li, Y., Chen, Y., Yang, Y., Wei, Y.: Passive particle jamming and its stiffening of soft robotic grippers. IEEE Trans. Robot. **33**(2), 446–455 (2017)
11. Kim, Y.J., Cheng, S., Kim, S., Iagnemma, K.: A novel layer jamming mechanism with tunable stiffness capability for minimally invasive surgery. IEEE Trans. Robot. **29**(4), 1031–1042 (2013)
12. https://softroboticstoolkit.com/. Accessed 27 Apr 2019
13. Manti, M., Hassan, T., Passetti, G., D'Elia, N., Laschi, C., Cianchetti, M.: A bioinspired soft robotic gripper for adaptable and effective grasping. Soft Robot. **2**(3), 107–116 (2015)
14. Camarillo, D.B., Milne, C.F., Carlson, C.R., Zinn, M.R., Salisbury, J.K.: Mechanics modeling of tendon-driven continuum manipulators. IEEE Trans. Robot. **24**(6), 1262–1273 (2008)
15. Mutlu, R., Yildiz, S.K., Alici, G., Panhuis, M.I.H., Spinks, G.M.: Mechanical stiffness augmentation of a 3D printed soft prosthetic finger. In: IEEE International Conference on Advanced Intelligent Mechatronics (AIM), pp. 7–12 (2016)
16. Al Abeach, L.A.T., Nefti-Meziani, S., Davis, S.: Design of a variable stiffness soft dexterous gripper. Soft Robot. **4**(3), 274–284 (2017)
17. Park, W., Seo, S., Bae, J.: A hybrid gripper with soft material and rigid structures. IEEE Robot. Autom. Lett. **4**(1), 65–72 (2019)

Research on Motion Evolution of Soft Robot Based on VoxCAD

Yueqin Gu[1], Xuecheng Zhang[1,2], Qiuxuan Wu[1(✉)], Yancheng Li[1],
Botao Zhang[1], Farong Gao[1], and Yanbin Luo[1]

[1] Hangzhou Dianzi University, Hangzhou 310018, China
wuqx@hdu.edu.cn
[2] Zhejiang Tsinghua Institute of flexible Electronic Technology, Jiaxing, China

Abstract. The shape changes of soft organisms demonstrate the survival rules in the evolution of self life. It is important for the transform control of soft robots about how to envolve suitable for the shape demands. In this paper, the compositional pattern producing networks (CPPN) algorithm was used to evolve soft robot. By taking simple random functions as genotype inputs, the functions can be weighted combinations to generate the desired phenotype, which mapping relationship between genotypes and phenotypes can be achieved. The VoxCAD simulation software was used to build the three-dimensional topological structure of soft robot and the evolution process of the virtual life was realized by using the specific rule shape to simulate the real environment. The evolutionary analysis of the four-legged walking soft robot was carried out in the simulation experiment, which the effectiveness of the method was verified.

Keywords: Compositional pattern producing networks · VoxCAD · Genotype · Phenotype · Four-legged walking

1 Introduction

Inspired by nature, the exploitation of evolutionary robots can compensate for the deficiency of rigid robots to some extent. Evolutionary robots simulate the natural law of "natural selection, survival of the fittest" in Darwin's theory of evolution which can adapt to different environment by evolving and changing their shape in a restricted environment [1]. This flexible autonomous robot's shape, control and sensory system can be collaboratively optimized for different tasks and environment to achieve a purpose of adaptating to the environment. Sims et al. [2] studied the characteristics of soft evolutionary robots by setting different environmental attributes. Clune et al. [3] found that CPPN is obviously faster than direct coding in coding ability by analyzing soft robots with various materials. With more materials were added, the motion performance will be improved obviously. Cheney et al. [4] used CPPN evolutionary algorithm to

H. Yu et al. (Eds.): ICIRA 2019, LNAI 11742, pp. 26–37, 2019.
https://doi.org/10.1007/978-3-030-27535-8_3

optimize virtual organisms in the research of soft robots, which enabled the evolved soft robots to move through fixed holes. Kriegman et al. [5] put forward the minimum life growth model by analyzing the evolution of life, pointing out that the body of robot would change continuously in its life cycle. Corucci et al. [6] was inspired by the evolution of nature, and proposed a effective method to adaptive and intelligent soft robot. Woolley et al. [7] evolved octopus-like tentacles by evolutionary algorithm through the study of octopus wrist arm in nature, which can move in any direction. Lessin et al. [8] combined the biology of completely rigid bones and soft muscle tissue by developing and reusing the functions of simulation software system. The complex and effective simulation muscles could be evolved to drive the rigid skeleton, which provide ideas for the evolution of soft robots [9–11].

Currently, most of the research on evolutionary soft robots focusing on the realization of simple motion, such as land crawling, swimming in water and so on [12–14]. But there is little research on the way of multi-legged walking and the regularity of walking [15,16]. In this paper, inspired by the leg-walking animals in nature, taking the four-legged walking soft robot as the evolutionary direction and the improved evolutionary algorithm is used to operate the evolution of soft robots. Through simple random function is used as the genotype input to generate the phenotype of the four-legged walking soft robots. Then the simulation analysis is carried out in VoxCAD simulation software, so that the four-legged walking effect can be obtained intuitively. The experimental analysis of the four-legged walking soft robot provides a idea for the gait analysis of the evolutionary multi-legged soft robot in the future.

2   Analysis of Evolutionary Algorithm for Soft Robot

2.1   Basic Principles of CPPN

CPPN is a new compositional pattern development algorithm, which can represent complex repetitive patterns in cartesian coordinate space. Different between most generation and growth coding, CPPN can realize its basic function without explicitly simulating growth or partly interaction. The phenotype is treated as a function of n, the expression level is the function output of the coding phenotype about each coordinate in the space, which a simple one-dimensional function combination can be given to generate a pattern with multiple rules, as shown in Fig. 1 below. Firstly, given the input x, an asymmetric primary function is generated, and then the function is combined with symmetric function (F_1) and periodic function (F_2) to generate segments with opposite polarity.

At the same time, for multiple input functions, the desired results can also be generated by using CPPN. For example, the bilateral symmetry can be established by using Gauss function, and the discrete segments of the main part can be established by adopting sine and cosine function. Then these special functions are weighted and combined, and a new mapping relationship can be obtained.

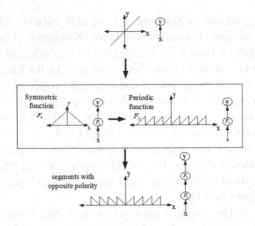

Fig. 1. A function diagram of simple combined gradient

2.2 Analysis of Multi-objective Evolutionary Algorithm

The multi-objective evolutionary algorithm adopted in this paper is realized on the basis of CPPN by modifying different function types and adjusting corresponding weights. In order to make evolution more focused, two individuals were randomly selected from each generated individual, and the high fitness value was used as the dominator to operate the genetic operator. To make the effect of walking more obvious, different individuals can be built at the beginning of the program, and the new individual is introduced into the running program to cover the existing duplicate individuals. In the gait analysis of four-legged walking robot, in order to improve the evolution rate of voxels and increase the evolutionary algebra. When the individual is initialized, the size of voxel is set to $7 * 7 * 7$ and 15 individuals are selected from each generation to participate in crossover and mutation operations. The evolutionary regularity is shown in Fig. 2 below.

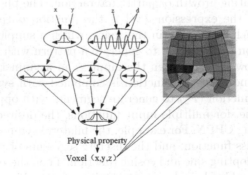

Fig. 2. Phenotype structure of the four-legged walking

As can be seen from Fig. 2 above, when given different input parameters (x, y, z), sinusoidal functions and Gauss functions can be generated, and then weighted combinations of these functions can generate periodic functions, symmetric functions and so on. Finally, the phenotypic structure with pace gait can be generated by weighted composition, which can be regarded as a mixture of two Gauss functions. The flow chart of the algorithm is shown in Fig. 3 below.

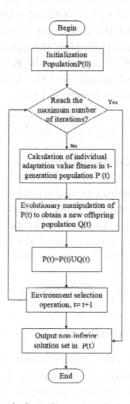

Fig. 3. A flow diagram of algorithm

3   Experimental Method of Evolutionary Soft Robots

3.1   Evaluation of Experimental Objectives and Fitness

In this paper, the walking distance of the evolved soft robot is taken as the objective function of the experiment. In the program, we choose the fastest moving individual in the specified simulation time as best one. The fastest individual of each generation is saved as the optimal individual, and then the optimality is regarded as the initial individual of the next generation. Finally, the evolution is not completed until the arrival of the running time or the termination of the number of iterations. The final selected individual is regarded as the best individual in the program, and the selection has the longest motion distance.

Assessment of fitness is a measure of individual survival opportunities under certain environmental conditions, which it is important for evolutionary computation. The function of fitness is the core of evolutionary computation. In the design of evolutionary processes that can perform simple walking tasks. The function of fitness is the limiting factor in the process of evolutionary. It is usually expressed as the evaluation of the optimal adaptive value of offspring, and the function of fitness can detect the difference of adaptability among individuals of evolutionary population, thus reflecting the survival of the fittest.

The function of fitness in this paper can be defined: assuming that the distance between the optimal individual and the geometric center at the end of evolution is represented, it can be concluded that:

$$d = \sqrt{(x - x_0)^2 + (y - y_0)^2 + (z - z_0)^2} \tag{1}$$

In the above formula (1), the coordinates (x, y, z) indicate the actual running position of the individual, and (x_0, y_0, z_0) indicate the center position coordinates. Then define two parameters p and m, where p indicates the number of non-empty voxels in the evolution of the individual, and m indicates the size of the total voxel space. At the beginning, the parameter m can be set to the experiment (such as setting the voxel space and size is $7*7*7$), so the following Eq. (2) fitness function expression can be obtained:

$$fitness = f(d) = d \times (1 - \frac{p}{m}) \tag{2}$$

3.2 The Major Step of Experiment

In this paper, the voxel phenotype is represented as a network, and the relative coordinates of the voxel are taken as the input. In order to inquire about the voxel, the input layer of the network is composed of four nodes, which can encode the relative Cartesian coordinate system and polar radius of the voxel. The network is updated through a series of hidden nodes to output the real value of the node. The main methods and implementation steps are as follows:

(1) Activation function

In the CPPN algorithm, in order to make the generated soft robot have a certain complexity, a variety of shapes are evolved, a variety of activation functions are added to the nodes, and a new phenotype is generated by multiplying the weights among the activation functions. The activation functions used in this paper are as follows:

Sigmoid function:

$$f(x) = \frac{2}{1 + e^{-x}} - 1, -1 \leq x \leq 1 \tag{3}$$

Positive_Sigmoid function:

$$p(x) = (1 + f(x)) \cdot \frac{1}{2} = \frac{1 - e^{-x}}{2(1 + e^{-x})}, -1 \leq x \leq 1 \tag{4}$$

Inverted_Sigmoid function:

$$I(x) = \frac{1}{f(x)} = \frac{1 + e^{-x}}{1 - e^{-x}}, -1 \leq x < 0, 0 < x \leq 1 \tag{5}$$

Neg_Square function:

$$n(x) = -x^2, -1 \leq x \leq 1 \tag{6}$$

Sinc function:

$$g(x) = \sin(x), -\pi \leq x \leq \pi \tag{7}$$

(2) The Selection of Individual

In the experiment, the selection problem of Individual is based on pareto optimal algorithm which is similar to the traditional roulette selection method. The greater the fitness value, the greater the probability of being selected. If all pareto optimal solutions generated in the $P(t)$ generation have the best fitness, then they can be selected into the $P(t + 1)$ generation, the better individuals will be retained. The formula for calculating the selection probability is as follows (8):

$$P_i = \frac{f_i}{\sum\limits_{i=1}^{N} f_i} among i = 1, 2, \ldots, N \tag{8}$$

Among them, f_i represents the fitness value of chromosome i, and the number of individuals in which it is located is N, and P_i represents the probability of being selected.

(3) The Crossover of Individual

In the experiment, multiple individuals perform crossover operations. Assuming that a individuals participate in the crossover, and a new individuals can be obtained. The crossover method is defined as follows: for selected a parent individuals $X_i (1 \leq i \leq a)$, the number of a individuals $r_1, r_2, \ldots, r_a$ was randomly extracted from the equal distribution of 0 to 1 at a time, and a new individuals $X_i{'}$ was generated, so you know:

$$X_i{'} = \frac{\sum\limits_{j=1}^{a} r_j X_i}{a} \tag{9}$$

Because the value of the random sequence of equal distribution of $r_1, r_2, \ldots, r_a$ is taken infinite values and the new individual is also infinite, the diversity of the population can be obviously enhanced and the computational efficiency can be improved.

(4) The Mutation of Individual

In standard genetic algorithm, in order to achieve universal search in solution space. When the binary position is flipped, A small mutation probability P_m is set to introduce the lack of genes into the population. In this paper, when multi-objective mutation is carried out, the value of mutation probability is dynamically changed through the ranking values of the parent and the offspring, which has large randomness.

4   Experimental Analysis of Four-Legged Walking Soft Robot

In the experimental analysis of evolutionary soft robot, this paper takes four-legged walking as the object of study. Compared with bipedal walking, four-legged soft robot has better stability in the process of walking, with a variety of different motion regularities, and their motion patterns is closer to those of natural organism. Therefore, the soft robot evolved in this experiment is composed of four legs. The voxel size is $7 * 7 * 7$, and the total voxel is composed of 343 small voxels. First, when initializing the parameters, 15 individuals are defined for each generation. Five phenotypes are selected from 15 individuals and selected from the first generation in Fig. 4 below:

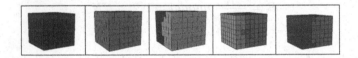

Fig. 4. Phenotypic chart of the first generation of individuals

The fifteen individuals generated in the first generation were used as new populations for cross-mutation operation, and five individuals were still selected from the crossed populations as shown in Fig. 5 below:

Fig. 5. Intersection of individual phenotype

Since individual voxels were relatively small in the initial definition, the evolutionary algebra was set to 1000 generations in the experiment to observe the evolutionary results. After 11 h of running, the evolution ended. The final evolutionary algebra was 848 generations. Five individual phenotypes were selected from 848 generations as shown in Fig. 6.

Fig. 6. Optimal individual of population

During the evolution process, the individual fitness value will change with the evolutionary algebra. When there is no optimal fitness value in some generations, it will continue to evolve until the optimal fitness value appears. In the evolution process of 1000 generations, 15 individuals are defined to run 20 times independently in each generation, and the relationship between the fitness curve of the optimal individuals and algebra is obtained as shown in Fig. 7. The algebra of the optimal individuals in the following figure: gen0, gen10, gen45, gen68, gen139, gen189, gen211, gen270, gen343, gen387, gen432, gen490, gen580, gen641, gen712, gen746, gen790, gen807, gen822, gen848.

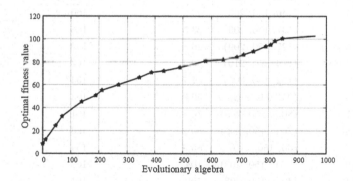

Fig. 7. Optimal fitness value of individual

The optimal individuals evolved from 848 generations are taken as the research objects to analyze their motion states. This part of the simulation is still running in VoxCAD, and the motion time is defined as 20 s. Therefore, the voxel changes at different times can be obtained as shown in Fig. 8 below.

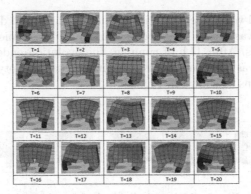

Fig. 8. Voxels change with time

The Fig. 8 above shows the voxel color changes of a soft robot that has evolved voxels at different times. The relationship between displacement and coordinates with time can also be shown in the table below. Taking the time interval of 1 s, the displacement changes in 20 s can be obtained as Table 1 below:

Table 1. Diagram of displacement versus time

Time t (s)	Coordinate	Displacement d (mm)	Speed v (mm/s)
0	(150, 150, 210)	0	0
1	(146, 150, 202)	20.3	160
2	(137, 150, 203)	23.5	168
3	(127, 150, 209)	26.8	159
4	(113, 150, 210)	39.4	162
5	(102, 150, 203)	51.7	154
6	(95, 150, 208)	56.9	163
7	(80.5, 150, 209)	70.8	161
8	(70.9, 150, 209)	80.2	163
9	(65, 150, 210)	85.9	154
10	(47.9, 150, 203)	104	168
11	(42.2, 150, 208)	109	161
12	(33.3, 150, 210)	117	168
13	(25.5, 150, 206)	126	158
14	(13.4, 150, 206)	138	171
15	(1.8, 150, 210)	149	169
16	(−11.7, 150, 207)	162	170
17	(−20.4, 150, 210)	171	169
18	(−26, 150, 210)	176	171
19	(−38.9, 150, 210)	189	168
20	(−54.2, 150, 210)	205	170

From the data in the table, the soft robot can be approximately regarded as a straight line motion in the process of motion, and the longest distance in the process of motion is 205 mm, Therefore, the variation of displacement and velocity with time in 20 s can be obtained as shown in Figs. 9 and 10 below:

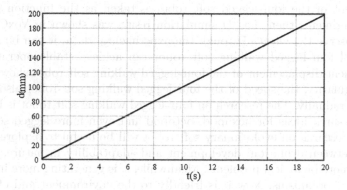

Fig. 9. Displacement versus time curve

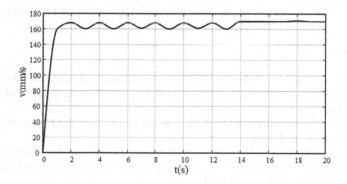

Fig. 10. Velocity versus time curve

For the four-legged walking soft robot, the displacement increases with time, and the approximately moves in a straight line in the process of motion. In the initial operation, the body and four-legged of the evolved four-legged robot are composed of soft materials. The center of gravity is unstable because of the soft four-legged, so there will be fluctuations. But with the increase of the motion time, the velocity of the motion gradually approaches to the uniform motion. In the process of program simulation, firstly, the motion structure of the evolutionary algorithm is defined by using the compositional pattern generation network algorithm, in other words, it evolves a four-legged-like soft robot. Secondly, the output of the evolutionary algorithm is simulated in VoxCAD to observe its motion state.

5 Summary

In this paper, the four-legged soft robot with walking characteristics is evolved by adopting the improved compositional pattern generation network algorithm which inspired by the walking mode of four-legged organisms in nature. The displacement of the four-legged soft robot is taken as the function of fitness in the experiment, then the 3D simulation result was shown in VoxCAD software to observe the effect. Through the experimental data, it can be seen that the evolved four-legged walking soft robot can achieve stable operation, and the movement displacement of the four-legged walking soft robot shows a linear motion regularity, the speed of the four-legged walking soft robot also tends to be stable gradually. The research on four-legged walking soft robot is helpful to provide research ideas for hexapod, octopod and even more legged soft robot. Also, The research on evolutionary soft robot will be useful to explore the relationship between evolution, development and adaptability in nature, and help us clarify more biological problems. Meanwhile, it is generating more interesting evolutionary organisms. Now it is friendly to the environment and efficient to perform tasks, so that soft robots really with the "wisdom" of human beings and solve problems intelligently.

Acknowledgement. This work reported here was supported by the Key Projects of Science and Technology Plan of Zhejiang Province (Grant No. 2019C04018).

References

1. Sanan, S., Moidel, J., Atkeson, C.G.: A continuum approach to safe robots for physical human interaction. In: International Symposium on Quality of Life Technology, June 2011
2. Turk, M.G.: Proceedings of the 21st Annual Conference on Computer Graphics and Interactive Techniques (1994)
3. Cheney, N., MacCurdy, R., Clune, J., Lipson, H.: Unshackling evolution: evolving soft robots with multiple materials and a powerful generative encoding. ACM SIGEVOlution **7**(1), 11–23 (2014)
4. Cheney, N., Bongard, J., Lipson, H.: Evolving soft robots in tight spaces. In: Proceedings of the 2015 Annual Conference on Genetic and Evolutionary Computation, pp. 935–942. ACM, July 2015
5. Kriegman, S., Cheney, N., Corucci, F., Bongard, J.C.: A minimal developmental model can increase evolvability in soft robots. In: Proceedings of the Genetic and Evolutionary Computation Conference, pp. 131–138. ACM, July 2017
6. Corucci, F.: Evolutionary developmental soft robotics: towards adaptive and intelligent soft machines following nature's approach to design. In: Laschi, C., Rossiter, J., Iida, F., Cianchetti, M., Margheri, L. (eds.) Soft Robotics: Trends, Applications and Challenges. BIOSYSROB, vol. 17, pp. 111–116. Springer, Cham (2017). https://doi.org/10.1007/978-3-319-46460-2_14
7. Woolley, B.G., Stanley, K.O.: Evolving a single scalable controller for an octopus arm with a variable number of segments. In: Schaefer, R., Cotta, C., Kołodziej, J., Rudolph, G. (eds.) PPSN 2010. LNCS, vol. 6239, pp. 270–279. Springer, Heidelberg (2010). https://doi.org/10.1007/978-3-642-15871-1_28

8. Lessin, D., Risi, S.: Soft-body muscles for evolved virtual creatures: the next step on a bio-mimetic path to meaningful morphological complexity. In: Proceedings of the European Conference on Artificial Life 13, pp. 604–611. MIT Press, Cambridge, July 2015
9. Stanley, K.O.: Compositional pattern producing networks: a novel abstraction of development. Genet. Program Evolvable Mach. 8(2), 131–162 (2007)
10. Auerbach, J.E., Bongard, J.C.: Evolving CPPNs to grow three-dimensional physical structures. In: Proceedings of the 12th Annual Conference on Genetic and Evolutionary Computation, pp. 627–634. ACM, July 2010
11. Cheney, N., Lipson, H.: Topological evolution for embodied cellular automata. Theor. Comput. Sci. 633, 19–27 (2016)
12. Hiller, J.D., Lipson, H.: Evolving amorphous robots. In: ALIFE, pp. 717–724, August 2010
13. Arita, T., Joachimczak, M., Ito, T., Asakura, A., Suzuki, R.: ALife approach to eco-evo-devo using evolution of virtual creatures. Artif. Life Robot. 21(2), 141–148 (2016)
14. Stanley, K.O., D'Ambrosio, D.B., Gauci, J.: A hypercube-based encoding for evolving large-scale neural networks. Artif. Life 15(2), 185–212 (2009)
15. Cubes, M.: A high resolution 3D surface construction algorithm. In: Proceedings of the 14th Annual Conference on Computer Graphics and Interactive Techniques, pp. 163–169. Association for Computing Machinery, New York, July 1987
16. Clune, J., Lipson, H.: Evolving three-dimensional objects with a generative encoding inspired by developmental biology. In: ECAL, pp. 141–148, June 2011

A Gecko-Inspired Robot Employs Scaling Footpads to Facilitate Stable Attachment

Zhongyuan Wang[1,2(✉)], Kebo Deng[1], Qingyao Bian[2,3],
and Zhendong Dai[2]

[1] The 28th Research Institute of China Electronics Technology
Group Corporation, Nanjing 210007, People's Republic of China
wangzy051@163.com
[2] Institute of Bio-inspired Structure and Surface Engineering,
Nanjing University of Aeronautics and Astronautics,
Nanjing 210016, People's Republic of China
[3] College of Automation Engineering,
Nanjing University of Aeronautics and Astronautics,
Nanjing 210016, People's Republic of China

Abstract. This paper presents the design of a legged robot with different scale of footpad that can climb with full balanced weight and on vertical surface. The adhesion performance, footpad scaling and body dynamics are explored and discussed in this paper. Results show that the robot chose a more crawling gait can maintain stability when climb with full balanced weight. Wall climbing experiments show that a gecko-inspired design principle of footpad can obtain a reliable climbing performance. The robot with different size of footpads also provides a good platform to better understand the scaling and biomechanics of surface attachment in climbing robot.

Keywords: Legged robot · Adhesion performance · Balanced weight ·
Wall climbing · Scaling

1 Introduction

The extraordinary locomotory abilities of geckos, insects and spiders, which are attributed to striking adhesive setae segmented into scansors or pads on the undersides of the toes or legs, have been well-known for many centuries [1]. The outstanding climbing performances of animals inspired the engineers and researchers for the design of artificial systems, such as adhesive materials, which in turn enabled the construction of climbing robots that can climb smooth walls and ceiling [2–4].

Inspired by hairy footpads of various animals in nature, fiber arrays with different end shapes such as mushrooms, asymmetric spatulae and concave structures have been developed [5–11]. By using the fibrillar surfaces, several robotic prototypes with tank-like treads and rotary legs have been reported. Mini Whegs robot [12] was equipped with mushroom-shaped adhesive microstructure (MSAMS) made of polyvinyl siloxane (PVS), using four mulit-spoke wheel-leg appendages. This 100–120 g heavy robot easily

© Springer Nature Switzerland AG 2019
H. Yu et al. (Eds.): ICIRA 2019, LNAI 11742, pp. 38–47, 2019.
https://doi.org/10.1007/978-3-030-27535-8_4

climbs smooth vertical and even inverted surfaces. Waalbot [13], equipped with rotating compliant legs, can climb on smooth vertical walls using angled polyurethane fiber arrays.

Due to the limitation of the mechanism these robots can only work on relatively flat areas of the surface using relatively uniform motion pattern. However, legged climbing robots may increase their potential to adapt their gaits to uneven surfaces and allow for more instantaneous control of stability, if we can push or pull them effectively during the intermittent contact with the substrate at each step. Several groups have developed legged robots that use dry adhesives and capable of such a contact formation/breakage control [14–16]. One of the most impressive robots is the Stickybot [17], which utilizes a special footpad with directional polymer stalks (DPS) to effectively climb vertical surfaces, such as glass, plastic, and polished wood panels.

One of the key issues for the design of adhesive pad is the scaling of adhesion, in term of length and area scaling [18]. Length scaling will occur when the separation process is confined to a region smaller than the contact area [19]. It also occurs when peeling as the forces are proportional to the width elastic tape [20]. Area scaling will occur when stress are uniformly distributed the contact area. When gecko climb on incline surface, as the substrate became steeper, more adhesion forces are involved [21]. This means that the animal may use a strategy of change 'size': use more contact area for adhesion or perform a larger force per area but maintain a certain contact area. Furthermore, the observation that geckos alter forelimbs and hindlimbs orientation or inter-angle of digits [22, 23], indicate that the animal can change 'shape' of footpad to facilitate adhesion. For legged robots, study the scaling of footpad can help understand what kind of scale is the optimization choice when cope with different environments.

Another issue for climb in animal kingdom is control adhesion to maintain safety and stability. For example, geckos control attachment and detachment via shear forces, by pulling their legs towards or pushing their legs away from the body to maintain the center of mass (COM) close to the substrate, preventing detachment from the substrate [24]. By varying gait characteristics or joint movement, geckos can move in different habitats [25]. However, it seems that all these robots use a stationary foot manner for locomotion. Legged climbing robot involves the controlled application of forces during the leg-substrate contact and release, in order to propel the body forwards. When the legged robot climb on different surfaces (e.g. from ground to wall), different foot manner should be employed to cope with these surfaces. One interesting question is that, if the robot use only one foot manner, by employing its adhesive system to cope with different environments. What risks will be involved and how to overcome such a risk?

IBSS_Gecko is a legged mechanism for a gecko-inspired robot, which is first introduced by Dai and Sun (Fig. 1) [26]. The robot consists of a rigid body and four legs. The mass of the robot is about 400 g, while the length and width is 240 mm and 100 mm, respectively. Each leg has two linkages and three degree of freedoms (three motors). Three motors drive the leg to move it in the three-dimensional space. An integrated flexure in the foot (ball hinge and four springs) allows for up to 20 degrees of pitch, roll and yaw misalignment to obtain alignment and full contact with substrate. This design largely reduces required precision of footpad's trajectory and greatly increases the adaptability of the robot to different surfaces. Here, we introduce IBSS_Gecko robot as a platform for testing influence of footpad size, shape and foot manner.

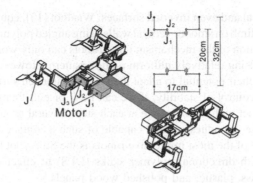

Fig. 1. Computer-aided design diagrams showing mechanical structure: each leg has three motors, responsible for joint rotations (J1, J2, J3). An integrated flexure in the foot (ball hinge and four springs, J) allows for up to 20 degrees of pitch, roll and yaw misalignment to obtain alignment and full contact with substrate.

This paper is organized in the following manner. Section 2 briefly reviews the biomechanics of a gecko climbing on a surface. Based on the biological principle in micro and macro scales, we develop a gecko-inspired footpad. The manner of footpad with strong attachment and easy-removal properties is designed and tested in Sect. 3. Furthermore, experiments on the IBSS_Gecko on the challenged condition-reduced gravity is designed, analyzed and discussed in Sect. 4. Finally, conclusions and future work are reported in Sect. 5.

2 Adhesion Performance of Footpad

The footpad consists of two parts: adhesive and backing layer. The adhesive is attached to the back side of the backing layer, so that it can prevent the adhesive from deforming irreversibly. While adhesion contact is the critical issue for climb robot, adhesion force analysis is required. The scaling for critical adhesive force capacity is found to be [28].

$$F_A \propto \sqrt{G\frac{A}{C}} \qquad (1)$$

where G is the effective work of adhesion, A is contact area and C is system compliance.

To achieve maximum force capacity, load on the footpad should be applied evenly to obtain full engagement with substrate. To make an active control of foot plane alignment, at least five active degrees of freedom are required. More degrees of freedom means more motors result in heavy weights and complex control. Three active DOF and three passive DOF satisfy the basic demand of footpad loading and robot loco-motion: Three active DOF can make sure footpad move to the specified location (point) and three passive DOF can offset the misalignment of the limitation of active DOF. While area scaling occurs at the level of the whole pad (uniform load distribution across the whole adhesive pad), the size of the footpad is largely influencing the adhesive performance. In order to understand effect of the size on adhesion performance, adhesive samples (MSAMS) which are mounted in 3 different shapes (pad 1: ca 4 cm × 1 cm, pad 2: ca 1 cm × 4 cm, pad 3: ca 2 cm × 2 cm) with the same area is used. Here we use a thickness of 1 mm and elastic modulus of 6.0 MPa polyvinylchloride plate as backing layer.

The performance is measured using a custom force platform in a manner previously discussed [27]. A two-dimensional force sensor is used to measure the forces between foot and substrate. A plastic square (ca 8 cm × 8 cm) is fixed on the top of the sensor to mimic foot/substrate contact surface. The forces along the y-axis are termed lateral forces and along the z-axis are termed normal forces. The force senor functions as simple cantilever beams in a metal H-shaped arrangement. Forces are measured from the deflection of the cantilever beams by foil strain gauges glued to the beams. The resolution of the sensor for each direction is 2 mN; the natural frequency for the x-, y- and z-axis is 1397 Hz, 4023 Hz and 8256 Hz, respectively. The data are logged, using a custom-built data acquisition device at a frequency of 100 Hz.

Contact failure forces are measured to test the adhesion performance of the footpad with different shape. Figure 2b shows force vs time for an example trial of the foot. The foot starts with a preload force (z direction) of the adhesive, the footpad move upward unless the normal force attains zero. Then the footpad is dragged in y and z directions respectively, unless adhesion failure occurs. We obtain lateral pull off force (y direction) and normal pull off force (z direction) respectively. All the data are calculated by averaging the forces which repeated seven times each time.

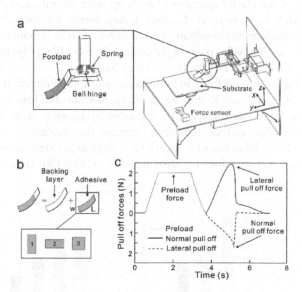

Fig. 2. Schematics of a. set-up of force platform b. design of footpad shape. Pad 1: ca 4 cm × 1 cm, Pad 2: ca 1 cm × 4 cm, Pad 3: ca 2.0 cm × 2.0 cm. Wide (W) × Length (L). c. A typical example of adhesion performance of pad 2.

For both lateral and normal force, the magnitude increases as preload increases up until a saturation point is reached, as shown in Fig. 3. The maximum normal force is about 2N, so the maximum pressure is 2×10^3 N m^{-2}. However, the maximum pressure of the adhesive itself is about 6×10^4 N m^{-2} [10]. This means that only an amount of fibers are contacted with substrate. Although a shorter width will result in a smaller peeling strength according to Kendall's peeling model [20], the results here show that a longer length (pad 3) will lead to a smaller maximum pressure. For the design of footpad size for climb, both the length and width should be considered.

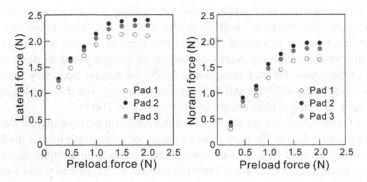

Fig. 3. Relationship between preload force and pull off force with different footpad shape.

The elastic modulus of the backing layer is also very important [27–29]. In order to understand effect of the elastic modulus of backing layer on adhesion performance in details, five backing layer is used. Contact failure forces are measured to test the adhesion performance of the footpad with different elastic modulus (1: 2.1 MPa polyvinylchloride, 2: 3.5 MPa polyvinylchloride, 3: 6.0 MPa polyvinylchloride, 4: 7.6 MPa Silicone rubber, 5: 12 MPa hard rubber). Sample 1, 2 and 3 with lower elastic modulus have a higher pull off force in both lateral and normal direction than sample 4 and 5. However, Sample 1 and 2 with lower elastic modulus has lower pull force than sample 3. As we know, a lower elastic modulus of backing layer which permits conformation to smaller surface radii can increase the maximum adhesion force. However, a low elastic modulus of backing layer lead to the deformation, result in a smaller real contact area and does not distribute forces well [30] (Fig. 4).

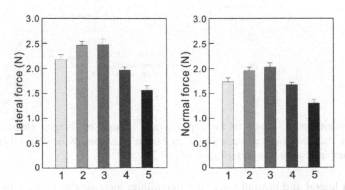

Fig. 4. Maximum pull off force of the footpad with different back layer (1: 2.1 MPa polyvinylchloride, 2: 3.5 MPa polyvinylchloride, 3: 6.0 MPa polyvinylchloride, 4: 7.6 MPa Silicone rubber, 5: 12 MPa hard rubber).

3 Adhesion Performance of Footpad

To understand how body dynamic of gecko is employed to facilitate adhesion, we use balloons to balanced gecko's body weight. A force measurement array (FMA) was used to measure ground reaction force of each leg [31]. The FMA consisted of 24 separates, custom-built three-dimensional force sensors, arranged in three rows and eight columns with each sensor having a glass cover-slip (ca 30 mm × 30 mm × 0.8 mm with ca 1 mm clearance gap) on top, resulting in a tiled strip of ca 250 mm × 90 mm measurement area. We defined the y-axis as the left-right axis in the plane of the platform and point to the locomotion direction and the forces along the y-axis were termed here as fore-aft forces. The x-axis was defined perpendicular to the y-axis and was also in the plane of the platform and termed as lateral forces. The z-axis was defined perpendicular to the xy-plane and termed as normal forces. A digital video camera (Olympus i-SPEED 3, 1280 × 1024 pixels) was synchronized with the force recordings from side view at a sampling frequency of 500 Hz. A mirror was mounted at an angle next to the FMA, giving the other side view of the gecko. The camera ran in synchrony with the data acquisition using a common starting pulse from a manual switch (Fig. 5).

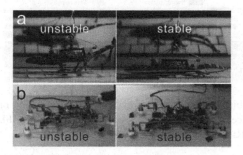

Fig. 5. a. Gecko walk on the platform with balanced force show that the animal is in an unstable state with a standing posture and a stable posture with a crawling posture. b. Robot wall on a glass surface with body weight is balanced fully show that a more crawling gait is more stable.

The balloons were held by hand at the initial time. Then the hand was removed slightly and gradually to let the animal run on the platform. Once body weight is balanced, adhesion should be employed and body dynamic should be adjusted to overcome the pith, roll and yaw moment generate by the balloons. Experimental results show that the gecko is pulled by the balloons result in a standing posture at the beginning. The animal swings its footpad to adjust its posture to overcome the pith roll yaw moment generate by the balloons. As a result, the footpad generates a large peak adhesion force and the animal suffers in an extremely unstable condition. Next, the animal adjusts its posture to a crawling behavior rapidly and walking on the substrate stably. At this instance, the peak adhesion force decreases to a small magnitude.

The strategy of shift the position of center of mass to promote stability can provide initial inspiration for the development of new capabilities in legged climbing robots: walking with body weight is fully balanced. When body weight is balanced by the balloons, adhesion should be introduced to balance pitch roll and yaw moment which generated by the balloons. When the footpad applies a loading force to the contact surface, the J1 joint is rotated to meet the requirement of engaging every adhesive fiber contact with substrate. However, this will raise the COM and making greatly increase the overturning moment. Meanwhile, raise the COM also will increases the risk of peel off. When such a posture is used to move forward, the robot's body is shook and the footpad is even peeled off. So here J1 joint is rotated reversely to reduce the body height during stance phase. Robot experiment is performed in glass surface, helium balloons which are fixed on the center of mass of the robot were used to balance body weight (Fig. 6). The size of footpad is 2.0 cm × 2.5 cm. Result show that the robot can walk on the glass surface stably.

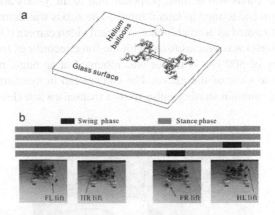

Fig. 6. The robot climbing under reduced gravity. b. Robot climbing on a glass surface with body weight fully balanced. Photos show different legs in swing phase. FL: Front left, HL: Hind left, FR: Front right, HR: Hind right.

To test whether a low COM position will result in a stable performance, robot experiment with same gait but different initial COM height (35 mm, 40 mm, 45 mm) is performed. When the robot walks with an initial COM height of 35 mm, it is stable. When the height adds to 40 mm, it becomes unstable. Once the height adds to 45 mm, the body is shook and even slip on the substrate.

Here, the gecko and robot nestle up to the contact surface to maintain stable when walking with fully balanced force. A higher cling angle (θ) may result in detachment occurs due to the force vector angle exceeds a critical detachment angle. Furthermore, a higher cling angle reduces the attachment reliability due to the overturning moment caused by the COM away from the substrate.

4 Climbing on the Wall: Employ Footpad with Different Size to Facilitate Adhesion

Dynamics of Gecko climbing on wall reveals that front legs pull toward, while hind legs push away to balance the overturning impulse moment [21, 24]. The adhesion force generate by front leg is significant higher that the hind leg, about 1.6 time larger in front leg than in hind leg [21]. For legged robot climb on vertical surface, a same size of front pad hind pad will largely increase the peeling force by using flat or fiber adhesive. Here, we assume that adhesion force (F) proportional to contact area (A) (geometric similarity, $F \propto a^3$, $A \propto a^2$ so $F \propto A^{2/3}$), so the area of front footpad (8.0 cm × 3.5 cm) is about 1.4 time larger than the hind footpad (5.0 cm × 4.0 cm). We design an alternating tripod gait for the legged robot. At any time, the robot is clinging by three feet, and the two of them are front feet. Four cylinders are attached to the back of body to reduce pitch back form the wall (Climbing experiment is performed by using MSAMS adhesive on glass surface; results show that the robot can climb on vertical surface stably (Fig. 7).

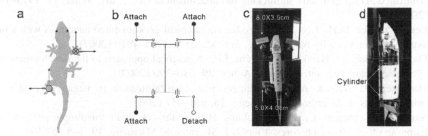

Fig. 7. a. Dynamical of gecko running on vertical surface. b. An alternating tripod gait for the legged robot. At any time, the robot is clinging by three feet, and the two of them are front feet. c. The area of front footpad (8.0 cm × 3.5 cm) is about 1.4 time larger than the hind footpad (5.0 cm × 4.0 cm). d. Cylinders is attached to the back of body to reduce pitch back form the wall.

5   Conclusions and Future Work

This paper presents the biologically inspired design of the footpad scaling and body dynamical for a legged climbing robot. The experimental tests show that the robot can climb under zero gravity and vertical glass surface. The major contribution of this work is the application of footpad scaling and body dynamical to the legged robot, and the demonstration of the feasibility and reliability of this design. To the best of our knowledge, the legged robot, both climbing with full balanced force and vertical surface, was demonstrated here for the first time.

Further optimization of the robot is planned to improve its performance in climbing on vertical and inverted surfaces during a dynamical trotting gait. Furthermore, scaling also depend on the size of the robot itself (body weight, body area). Footpad scaling is only discussing on different condition here, more work should involve to better understanding of 'scaling'.

References

1. Arzt, E., Gorb, S., Spolenak, R.: From micro to nano contacts in biological attachment devices. Proc. Natl. Acad. Sci. **100**, 10603–10606 (2003)
2. Cutkosky, M.R., Kim, S.: Design and fabrication of multi-material structures for bioinspired robots. Philos. Trans. R. Soc. A: Math. Phys. Eng. Sci. **367**, 1799–1813 (2009)
3. Gorb, S.N., Sinha, M., Peressadko, A., Daltorio, K.A., Quinn, R.D.: Insects did it first: a micropatterned adhesive tape for robotic applications. Bioinsp. Biomim. **2**, S117 (2007)
4. Sitti, M., Fearing, R.S.: Synthetic gecko foot-hair micro/nano-structures for future wall-climbing robots. In: International Conference on Robotics and Automation (ICRA 2003) Taipei, Taiwan (2003)
5. Campo, D.A., Greiner, C., Alvarez, I., Arzt, E.: Patterned surfaces with pillars with controlled 3D tip geometry mimicking bio-attachment devices. Adv. Mater. **19**, 1973–1977 (2007)
6. Lee, D.Y., Lee, D.H., Lee, S.G., Cho, K.: Hierarchical geckoinspired nanohairs with a high aspect ratio induced by nanoyielding. Soft Matter **8**, 4905–4910 (2007)
7. Davies, J., Haq, S., Hawke, T., Sargent, J.P.: A practical approach to the development of a synthetic gecko tape. Int. J. Adhes. Adhes. **29**, 380–390 (2009)
8. Haefliger, D., Boisen, A.: Three-dimensional microfabrication in negative resist using printed masks. J. Micromech. Microeng. **16**, 951–957 (2006)
9. Sameoto, D., Menon, C.: Direct molding of dry adhesives with anisotropic peel strength using an offset lift-off photoresist mold. J. Micromech. Microeng. **19**, 1–5 (2009)
10. Gorb, S., Varenberg, M., Peressadko, A., Tuma, J.: Biomimetic mushroom-shaped fibrillar adhesive microstructure. J. R. Soc. Interface **4**, 271–275 (2007)
11. Kim, S., Sitti, M.: Biologically inspired polymer microfibers with spatulate tips as repeatable fibrillar adhesives. Appl. Phys. Lett. **89**, 261911 (2006)
12. Daltorio, K.A., et al.: Mini-whegs TM climbs steep surfaces using insect-inspired attachment mechanisms. Int. J. Robot. Res. **28**, 285–302 (2009)
13. Murphy, M.P., Kute, C., Mengüç, Y., Sitti, M.: Waalbot II: adhesion recovery and improved performance of a climbing robot using fibrillar adhesives. Int. J. Robot. Res. **30**, 118–133 (2011)
14. Unver, O., Uneri, A., Aydemir, A., Sitti, M.: Geckobot: a gecko inspired climbing robot using elastomer adhesives. In: International Conference on Robotics and Automation (ICRA 2006), Orlando, USA (2016)
15. Li, Y., Ahmed, A., Sameoto, D., Menon, C.: Abigaille II: toward the development of a spider-inspired climbing robot. Robotica **30**, 79–89 (2012)
16. Henrey, M., Ahmed, A., Boscariol, P., Shannon, L., Menon, C.: Abigaille-III: a versatile, bioinspired hexapod for scaling smooth vertical surfaces. J. Bionic Eng. **11**, 1–17 (2014)
17. Kim, S., Spenko, M., Trujillo, S., Heyneman, B., Santos, D., Cutkosky, M.R.: Smooth vertical surface climbing with directional adhesion. IEEE Trans. Robot. **24**, 65–74 (2008)
18. Labonte, D., Walter, F.: Scaling and biomechanics of surface attachment in climbing animals. Philos. Trans. R. Soc. B: Biol. Sci. **370**, 20140027 (2015)
19. Spolenak, R., Gorb, S., Gao, H., Arzt, E.: Effects of contact shape on the scaling of biological attachment. Proc. R. Soc. A: Math. Phys. Eng. Sci. **460**, 1–15 (2005)
20. Kendall, K.: Thin-film peeling: the elastic term. J. Phy. D Appl. Phys. **8**, 1449–1452 (1975)
21. Wang, Z., Dai, Z., Ji, A., Ren, L., Xing, Q., Dai, L.: Biomechanics of gecko locomotion: the patterns of reaction forces on inverted, vertical and horizontal substrates. Bioinsp. Biomim. **10**, 016019 (2015)

22. Birn-Jeffery, A.V., Higham, T.E.: Geckos significantly alter foot orientation to facilitate adhesion during downhill locomotion. Biol. Lett. **10**, 20140456 (2014)
23. Zhuang, M.V., Higham, T.E.: Arboreal day geckos (Phelsuma madagascariensis) differentially modulate fore-and hind limb kinematics in response to changes in habitat structure. PloS One **11**, e0153520 (2016)
24. Autumn, K., Hsieh, S.T., Dudek, D.M., Chen, J., Chitaphan, C., Full, R.J.: Dynamics of geckos running vertically. J. Exp. Biol. **209**, 260–272 (2006)
25. Birn-Jeffery, A.V., Higham, T.E.: Geckos decouple fore-and hind limb kinematics in response to changes in incline. Front. Zool. **13**, 1 (2016)
26. Dai, Z., Sun, J.: A biomimetic study of discontinuous-constraint metamorphic mechanism for gecko-like robot. J. Bionic Eng. **4**, 91–95 (2007)
27. Wang, Z., Dai, Z., Yu, Z., Shen, D.: Optimal attaching and detaching trajectory for bio-inspired climbing robot using dry adhesive. In: International Conference on Advanced Intelligent Mechatronics (AIM 2014) France (2014)
28. Bartlett, M.D., Croll, A.B., King, D.R., Paret, B.M., Irschick, D.J., Crosby, A.J.: Looking beyond fibrillar features to scale gecko-like adhesion. Adv. Mater. **24**, 1078–1083 (2012)
29. Blum, F.D., Metin, B., Vohra, R., Sitton, O.C.: Surface segmental mobility and adhesion-effects of filler and molecular mass. J. Adhes. **82**, 903–917 (2006)
30. Zhou, M., et al.: The extended peel zone model: Effect of peeling velocity. J. Adhes. **87**, 1045–1058 (2011)
31. Asbeck, A., et al.: Climbing rough vertical surfaces with hierarchical directional adhesion. In: International Conference on Robotics and Automation (ICRA 2009) (2009)

Measurement Method of Underwater Target Based on Binocular Vision

Xiufen Ye[(⊠)] and Hao Chen

Harbin Engineering University, Harbin, China
{yexiufen, chenhao666}@hrbeu.edu.cn

Abstract. Traditional measurement methods are obtained by calculating the global disparity map. The accuracy of these methods is low and the speed is slow. Under the condition of uneven illumination, low contrast and obvious noise, they can't meet the measurement requirements well. An underwater image enhancement method based on Contrast Limited Adaptive Histogram Equalization and image weighting fusion is proposed. For the measurement of underwater target, only two matching points are solved in the algorithm design, which improves the accuracy and speed of underwater ranging. The idea of coarse-to-fine matching is adopted, that is, the SAD algorithm is used in matching area to complete the coarse matching such that the matching windows can be determined firstly. Then the stereo matching algorithm based on NCC and Census fusion is used to decide the final matching point. The algorithm is insensitive to light and can extract edges and corners better. Finally, three-dimensional reconstruction is carried out to restore the three-dimensional coordinates of the endpoints to be measured, and the real size can be obtained by calculating the Euclidean distance between the two points. The experimental results show that the algorithm runs fast and robustly without calculating the disparity of the whole image, and the results meet the accuracy requirements.

Keywords: Binocular vision · Image enhancement · Algorithmic fusion · Stereo matching

1 Introduction

The development direction of modern ranging system tends to be intelligent, which provides a broad application platform for stereo vision ranging [1]. As passive ranging, stereo vision technology does not need to send any signal to the target. It only needs to collect image pairs through image sensors. Through the recognition and monitoring of image information, the intellectualization of ranging system can be effectively improved [2]. Therefore, the research of real-time ranging system based on stereo vision technology has certain application value.

Underwater image has the characteristics of blur, color deviation and low visibility, so underwater image enhancement is particularly important for subsequent measurement tasks. In this paper [3], a dark channel priori model is proposed to identify underwater environment and an underwater reflection model is used to obtain enhanced images. This method combines the dark channel prior model with the underwater

© Springer Nature Switzerland AG 2019
H. Yu et al. (Eds.): ICIRA 2019, LNAI 11742, pp. 48–59, 2019.
https://doi.org/10.1007/978-3-030-27535-8_5

diffusion model, and has good performance. But it can't deal with the difference of local brightness distribution caused by underwater auxiliary lighting. In [4], an underwater image restoration method based on underwater image imaging model is proposed, which is suitable for underwater images with different tones. Although the enhancement effect is very bright, in fact, sometimes there will be color saturation, which does not conform to the real situation. Li et al. [5] defogged the blue-green channel of the image, corrected the red channel, and finally adjusted the restored underwater image using an adaptive exposure algorithm. To a certain extent, this method removes the chromatic aberration, enhances the contrast of the image and restores the real underwater image. However, it not only improves the contrast, but also increases the influence of noise and reduces the details of the image, and has little enhancement effect on the bluish-green image. Aiming at the problems of over-enhancement and lack of local details in existing underwater image enhancement methods, this paper proposes an underwater image enhancement method based on Contrast Limited Adaptive Histogram Equalization (CLAHE) and image weighted fusion.

In the field of underwater measurement, paper [6] adopts BM algorithm for stereo matching. This method needs to calculate the global disparity map for a long time, and the obtained values are global optimum rather than local optimum. In this paper [7], an improved SIFT feature matching algorithm is proposed, which achieves good matching accuracy. However, this algorithm can only calculate the distance between the camera and the object under test, rather than the distance between two points on the object. Paper [8] uses improved NCC for matching, but this method can't completely over-come the situation of uneven illumination and unclear features under water. Aiming at the low accuracy and slow speed of the existing matching methods, this paper proposes a local matching algorithm which matches only two points to be measured.

Firstly, the underwater image enhancement method based on CLAHE and image weighted fusion is proposed to enhance the image. In addition, for the measurement of underwater target size, only two matching points are solved in the algorithm design. In the matching algorithm, the SAD algorithm is used for coarse matching, and then the NCC and Census fusion stereo matching algorithm is used to find the best matching point. Finally, three-dimensional reconstruction is carried out to calculate the two-point Euclidean distance to obtain the true size.

2   Underwater Image Enhancement

The rugged surface of the seabed and the limited illumination ability of the auxiliary light make it very easy for bright and shaded areas to appear. The bright area has abundant light and good visual effect. However, the contrast and gray level of the shadow area are low, which makes the details of the object difficult to recognize. Therefore, enhancing shadow area information is the main goal.

In view of this situation, CLAHE [9] can effectively improve the local contrast. After enhanced by CLAHE algorithm, the local area may be stained due to excessive enhancement. To solve this problem, an underwater image enhancement algorithm based on CLAHE and weighted average fusion is proposed. The flow chart of underwater image enhancement algorithm is shown in Fig. 1.

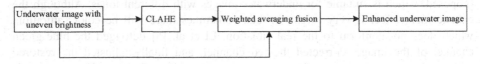

Fig. 1. Flow chart of underwater image enhancement algorithm

2.1   CLAHE Algorithm

The histogram equalization algorithm maps the gray level of the input image to the corresponding gray level of the output image through the conversion function. However, when processing the whole image, the algorithm can only increase the overall contrast of the image. After projection, the gray level of dark area is still low, and the gray level of bright area is still high. The internal information of dark and bright regions has not been significantly enhanced, so the basic histogram equalization has limited ability to enhance local images.

In order to solve the problem of noise sensitivity, this paper uses CLAHE algorithm, which greatly improves the image contrast. By setting contrast threshold, the histogram of image blocks is cut and redistributed, and then histogram equalization is processed. The enhanced image is obtained by linear interpolation between blocks. However, when the local area has very low contrast, that is, when the gray level distribution of the pixels is highly concentrated, the local area may produce color spots.

This paper presents a method of fusing the original image with the enhanced image of CLAHE. Compared with the original image, the information of shadow region is enhanced obviously, and the problem of color spot is improved to some extent.

2.2   Image Fusion Based on Weighted Average

Adding the original image information to the enhanced image of CLAHE algorithm can correct the enhanced image and achieve the purpose of desalinating the color spots. Because the gray level distribution of the original image is similar to that of the enhanced image, the fused target image still has a high definition.

The original image is A and the enhanced image obtained by CLAHE algorithm is B. Because image B is enhanced by image A, the image size is the same, all of them are $M \times N$, and the new image after fusion is recorded as P. The process of weighted average fusion of A and B source images can be expressed as follows:

$$P(m, n) = \omega_1 A(m, n) + \omega_2 B(m, n) \qquad (1)$$

In formula (1), m represents the row index of the pixels in the image, $m = 1, 2, ..., M$. n represents the column index of the pixels in the image, $n = 1, 2, ..., N$.

When multi-images are fused, the signal-to-noise ratio of fused images can be improved. Image noise is an unpredictable random error, which acts on the interference signal in image information. Histogram equalization results in color spots which obviously do not conform to the definition of noise. According to the interference effect on the image, the color spot can be regarded as a directional noise in a broad sense. In this paper, the effect of weighted average fusion on image noise is used to simulate its effect on color spots.

Assuming that there are M noisy images, $g_i(m, n)$ is the nth noisy image:

$$g_i(m,n) = f(m,n) + \eta_i(m,n) \tag{2}$$

Whereas, $f(m, n)$ represents the source image and $\eta_i(m, n)$ represents the zero-mean random noise.

For the convenience of calculation, the average fusion is adopted, that is, w_1 and w_2 are all 0.5 in formula (2). M noisy images are fused averagely, and the fused image $\bar{g}(m,n)$ is:

$$\bar{g}(m,n) = \frac{1}{M} \sum_{i=0}^{M} g_i(m,n) \tag{3}$$

Expectations of formula (3):

$$E\{\bar{g}(m,n)\} = f(m,n) \tag{4}$$

Variance of formula (4):

$$\sigma^2_{\bar{g}(m,n)} = \frac{1}{M} \sigma^2_{\eta(m,n)} \tag{5}$$

Formula (5) shows that after weighted average fusion, the variance of fusion image is reduced to 1/M of the variance of source image. Weighted average fusion can smooth the image and effectively reduce the interference of noise to the image. CLAHE algorithm improves image contrast without changing the logical relationship of gray levels between pixels. Therefore, the light and dark areas before and after enhancement remain the same in distribution. The contrast diagrams of various image enhancement algorithms are shown in Fig. 2.

The evaluation indexes of various image enhancement algorithms are shown in Table 1. It is clear that the results of our method techniques are much better than other methods. Gamma correction image has the highest gray average and the lowest PSNR value, indicating that the it has been over-enhanced. The CLAHE algorithm with the highest meangradient also enhances the noise we least want to see.

Generally, after image enhancement by our method, the contrast and details of the image have been significantly improved. In some areas where the gray level of the pixels is highly concentrated, the probability of obvious color spots is reduced, and the over-enhancement of the image is greatly restrained.

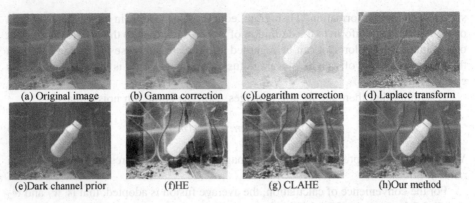

(a) Original image   (b) Gamma correction   (c)Logarithm correction   (d) Laplace transform

(e)Dark channel prior   (f)HE   (g) CLAHE   (h)Our method

Fig. 2. The contrast diagrams of various image enhancement algorithms

Table 1. Comparison of algorithm evaluation index of underwater image scene

Methods	Entropy	Gray average	Meangradient	MSE	PSNR
Original	6.668	49.322	7.402	-	-
Gamma correction	6.831	81.914	8.367	1104.07	17.701
Logarithm correction	6.302	**173.482**	8.597	15559.4	6.211
Laplace transform	7.313	131.369	21.593	549.46	20.731
Dark channel prior	6.672	44.722	7.567	760.965	19.317
HE	7.516	128.652	26.823	9069.18	8.555
CLAHE	7.547	95.872	**28.489**	3309.81	12.933
Ours	**7.593**	71.225	18.012	**81.633**	**29.012**

3 Target Dimension Measurement Method

3.1 Principle of Binocular Measurement

In binocular cameras, the image taken by the left camera is called the left view, and the image taken by the right camera is called the right view.

For point P (X, Y, Z) in space, after projection by left and right cameras, image points $P1$ $(x1, y1)$ and $P2$ $(x2, y2)$ are formed in left and right views respectively, and $y1 = y2$. If the center of the picture is (Cx, Cy), f is the focal length of the camera. The distance between binocular lens $C1$ and $C2$ is called the baseline distance as B. The parallax calculation is shown in Formula (6).

$$d = x1 - x2 \tag{6}$$

Using the principle of polar geometry, the coordinates of point P can be restored according to the following formulas:

$$\begin{bmatrix} X \\ Y \\ Z \end{bmatrix} = \frac{B}{d} \begin{bmatrix} 1 & 0 & -c_x \\ 0 & 1 & -c_y \\ 0 & 0 & f \end{bmatrix} \begin{bmatrix} x_1 \\ y_1 \\ 1 \end{bmatrix} \tag{7}$$

In order to measure the distance between two points in space, we only need to calculate the three-dimensional coordinates of two points, and then use the Euclidean distance formula to get the length of two points (Fig. 3).

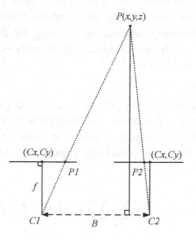

Fig. 3. Schematic diagram of binocular measurement

3.2 Basic Flow of Binocular Measurement

Binocular ranging mainly includes the following steps:

Camera Calibration. The binocular camera lenses are calibrated by Zhang Zhengyou's double calibration algorithm. The internal parameters of the camera and the relative rotation and translation parameters of the binocular camera are determined by taking many calibration board images with binocular cameras.

Image Rectification. Left and right views can be aligned by using Bouguet epipolar constraint algorithm with calibration parameters [10].

Stereo Matching. In the left view, we select two endpoints $A1$ and $B1$, and automatically determine two 20 * 20 block templates with $A1$ and $B1$ as the centers. SAD algorithm is used to match the corresponding size area in the right view. Then the matching points $A2$ and $B2$ with the greatest similarity to $A1$ and $B1$ are calculated using the algorithm of NCC and Census fusion [11] in the region (see Sect. 3.3 for details).

Three-Dimensional Reconstruction. According to the matching point pairs (*A1, A2*) and (*B1, B2*), the three-dimensional coordinates of points *A* and *B* are recovered by formula (7). The real distance between *A* and *B* can be obtained by using Euclidean distance.

3.3   Stereo Matching

The most common method of stereo matching is disparity map calculation method [12]. But disparity map calculation usually finds the optimal value of global energy function, so disparity map calculation takes a long time, and the value obtained is global optimum rather than local optimum. Considering that only the disparity of two endpoints needs to be calculated in length measurement, the disparity of measurement points can be calculated directly by local method.

SAD Rough Matching
SAD algorithm is a template matching algorithm based on gray value of pixels. It has the characteristics of simple calculation and no complex multiplication and division operation. It is suitable for preliminary screening of multi-level processing. So we use SAD algorithm to find the quasi-matching region in rough matching. The SAD matching cost function is as follows:

$$D_{SAD}(x,y) = \sum_{i=1}^{m} \sum_{j=1}^{n} |S_{xy}(i,j) - T(i,j)| \tag{8}$$

The basic idea of the algorithm is to sum the absolute value of the difference between the corresponding values of each pixel, and then evaluate the similarity of two image blocks. The minimum sum of absolute values is the region that matches the template best.

Similarity Calculation
For point p_1 on the left view, the corresponding matching point p_2 on the right view satisfies the following formula:

$$p_2 = min(\rho(I_1(\Omega_r(p_1)), I_2(\Omega_r(p_2)))) \tag{9}$$

Whereas $\Omega_r(p_1)$ represents the neighborhood with p_1 as the center and r as the radius, $I_n(x)$ represents the gray value of the corresponding region of x. $\rho(f, g)$ is used to calculate the similarity between f and g regions. In this paper, NCC and Census are used to calculate similarity:

$$\rho(f,g) = \alpha * \varepsilon(f,g) + (1 - \alpha) * \varphi(f,g) \tag{10}$$

Where α is the weight coefficient $\varepsilon(f,g)$, and $\varphi(f,g)$ are normalized by *NCC(f, g)* and *Census(f, g)*, respectively.

The output value of *NCC(f, g)* ranges from [−1, 1], while that of *Census(f, g)* ranges from $[0, r^2]$. We use the normalization method Min-Max Normalization to transform the original data linearly so that the result values are mapped between [0, 1]. The conversion function is as follows:

$$x_{out} = \frac{x - min}{max - min} \tag{11}$$

Where *max* is the maximum value of sample data and *min* is the minimum value of sample data.

NCC is an algorithm for calculating the correlation between two sets of data based on statistics. For an image, the *RGB* values of all pixels can be regarded as a set of data. If it has a subset that matches another set of data, its NCC value is 1, indicating high correlation; if NCC value is −1, it means completely unrelated. Then the matching degree between them is calculated by normalized correlation measure formula. The formula of *NCC(f, g)* is as follows:

$$NCC(f, g) = \frac{(f - \bar{f}) \bullet (g - \bar{g})}{\sigma_f \sigma_g} \tag{12}$$

Among them, $\bar{f}$ is the expectations of f, and σ_f is the standard deviations of f. It is the same with g.

The calculation formula of *Census(f, g)* is as follows:

$$Census(f, g) = Hamming(\eta(f), \eta(g)) \tag{13}$$

Suppose m is the central pixel of f and n is the other location pixels of f. It represents the return value of $f(n)$ compared with $f(m)$. If $f(n)$ is larger than $f(m)$, return one, otherwise return zero. Then these zeros and ones are joined together to form strings. The Census similarity can be calculated by using the corresponding strings of f and g as bitwise XOR. The calculation process is shown in Fig. 4.

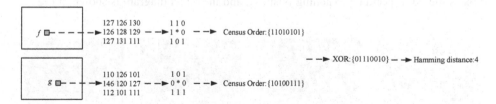

Fig. 4. Census calculation process

The flow chart of stereo matching algorithm is shown in Fig. 5, where *p1* is the input point and *p2* is the matching point.

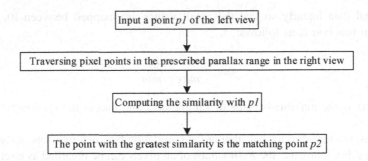

Input a point $p1$ of the left view

↓

Traversing pixel points in the prescribed parallax range in the right view

↓

Computing the similarity with $p1$

↓

The point with the greatest similarity is the matching point $p2$

Fig. 5. Basic flow of matching algorithm

4   Experiments and Results Analysis

In this paper, a stereo camera of type 3D-1MP02-V92 is used as the experimental equipment. The calibration is carried out underwater with a calibration board. The original and corrected images are shown in Fig. 6.

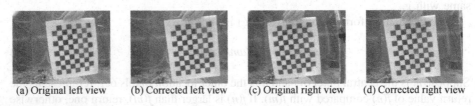

(a) Original left view   (b) Corrected left view   (c) Original right view   (d) Corrected right view

Fig. 6. Contrast image before and after image calibration

The image of the object to be measured is captured by binocular method underwater. The original image and the enhanced image are matched respectively. The red box is the corresponding matching position, and the effect diagram is shown in Fig. 7.

(a) Matching result of original image   (b) Matching result of enhanced image

Fig. 7. Contrast image of matching effect before and after image enhancement (Color figure online)

According to Fig. 7, the matching area is selected in the left view of the original image, and the correct rough matching result is not obtained. The calibration board can't be completely match in the original image, but can be matched correctly in the enhanced image by our method. Thus, image enhancement can greatly improve the accuracy of underwater ranging.

In order to verify the validity of the proposed method, the calibration board and bottle are measured underwater. Then some traditional match algorithms [13] are used for comparison. Several experimental positions are shown in Fig. 8, and the measurement results and errors are shown in Table 2. In the experiment, the neighborhood radius $r = 5$ and the weight $\alpha = 0.5$.

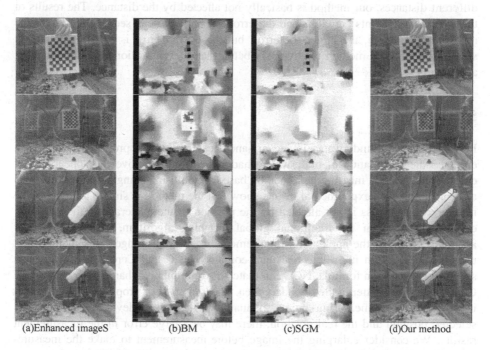

| (a)Enhanced imageS | (b)BM | (c)SGM | (d)Our method |

Fig. 8. Measuring the contrast images of calibration board

Table 2. Measuring results (mm)

Method	Length	Actual length	Running time (ms)	Error	Proportion%
BM	-	56.6	-	-	-
SGM	-	56.6	-	-	-
Our method	56.1	56.6	**82.6**	1.5	**0.9**
BM	-	200.0	-	-	-
SGM	208.6	200.0	86.7	8.6	4.3
Our method	196.5	200.0	**79.6**	**3.5**	**1.7**
BM	235.2	221.5	76.7	13.7	6.2
SGM	233.4	221.5	79.7	11.9	5.4
Our method	217.6	221.5	**75.9**	**3.9**	**1.8**
BM	238.8	221.5	**75.8**	17.3	7.8
SGM	230.6	221.5	83.7	9.1	4.1
Our method	216.7	221.5	76.3	**4.8**	**2.2**

From the experimental results, it can be seen that the calibration board can't be matched perfectly and the length measured by BM or SGM. Both of them are global optimum rather than local optimum, and are greatly affected by illumination and pixel value. BM and SGM methods also have unsatisfactory results in measuring the length of bottles. Because of the poor matching effect of the bottle mouth position, the final measurement error of most of them is more than 5%.

Due to the characteristics of NCC and Census, our algorithm can match well in the calibration board with repetitive textures. For the measurement of the same object at different distances, our method is basically not affected by the distance. The results of the two measurements are close and the error is small. We can see that the larger the measurement length, the larger the error, but the overall error is still in a relatively small range. So our method is obviously better than these traditional global matching algorithms.

5   Conclusion

In this paper, an underwater image enhancement method is proposed, which can enhance the information of underwater shadow area and improve the appearance of color spots. A target measurement method based on multi-matching algorithm fusion is also proposed. The experimental results show that the method is simple to operate, the measurement process is not affected by the position of the camera, and the matching effect is better than the traditional global matching algorithm. The measurement accuracy can meet the application requirements in a certain range. This method first uses SAD for rough matching, and then combines NCC and Census to form a new similarity calculation formula. NCC can match the illumination change area well, while Census performs better in the boundary area. The limitation of proposed method is that it needs to select measuring points manually. If there is a deviation between the selected position and the real position, there may be a large error in the measurement results. We consider enlarging the image before measurement to make the measurement as accurate as possible. How to choose more accurate measurement points is the next research goal.

Acknowledgements. This work was supported by the State Key Program of National Natural Science Foundation of China (Grant No. 61633004), the National Natural Science Foundation of China (Grant No. 41876100), the National key research and development program of China (Grant No. 2018YFC0310102 and 2017YFC0306002), the Development Project of Applied Technology in Harbin (Grant No. 2016RAXXJ071) and the Fundamental Research Funds for the Central Universities (Grant No. HEUCFP201707).

References

1. Huang, P.C., Jiang, J.Y., Yang, B.: Research status and progress of binocular stereo vision. Opt. Instrum. **39**(4), 81–86 (2017)
2. Bai, X., Yang, Y.Z., Han, F.Y.: Research on measuring method of plane geometric dimensions of parts based on computer vision. Machinery **55**(8), 81–83 (2017)

3. Xie, K., Pan, W., Xu, S.X.: An underwater image enhancement algorithm for environment recognition and robot navigation. Robotics **7**(1), 14 (2018)
4. Song, W., Wang, Y., Huang, D.M., He, Q., Wang, Z.H.: Combining background light fusion and underwater dark channel prior with color balancing for underwater image enhancement. Pattern Recognit. Artif. Intell. **31**(9), 86–98 (2018)
5. Li, C.Y., Quo, J.C., Pang, Y.W., Chen, S.J. Wang, J.: Single underwater image restoration by blue-green channels dehazing and red channel correction. In: IEEE International Conference on Acoustics. IEEE (2016)
6. Guo, S.X., Chen, S.Z., Liu, F.G., Ye, X.F., Yang, H.B.: Binocular vision-based underwater ranging methods. In: 2017 IEEE International Conference on Mechatronics and Automation (ICMA). IEEE (2017)
7. Sheng, M.W., Zhou, H., Huang, H., Qin, H.D.: Study on an underwater binocular vision ranging method. J. Huazhong Univ. Sci. Technol. (Nat. Sci. Ed.) **46**(8), 93–98 (2018)
8. Shi, X.C., Wang, X.J.: A ranging method in AUV underwater docking by binocular vision. Comput. Meas. Control **16**(10), 1460–1462 (2008)
9. Archie, M., Himanshu, J.: Novelty in image reconstruction using DWT and CLAHE. Int. J. Image Graph. Signal Process. (IJIGSP) **9**(5), 28–34 (2017)
10. Wang, H., Xu, Z.W., Xie, K., Li, J., Song, C.L.: Binocular measuring system based on OpenCV. J. Jilin Univ. (Inf. Sci. Ed.) **32**(2), 188–194 (2014)
11. Zou, J.G., Wan, Y., Meng, L.Y.: A new Stereo matching algorithm based on adaptive weight SAD algorithm and census algorithm. Bull. Surv. Mapp. **11**, 11–15 (2018)
12. Si, L.P., Wang, Q., Xiao, Z.L.: Matching cost fusion in dense depth recovery for camera-array via global optimization. In: 2014 International Conference on Virtual Reality and Visualization (ICVRV 2014), Shenyang, China, pp. 180–185 (2014)
13. Huang, S.M., Bi, Y.W., Xu, X.: Research and implementation of binocular Stereo matching algorithms. J. Ludong Univ. (Nat. Sci. Ed.) **34**(1), 25–30 (2018)

Robot Intelligence Technologies and System Integration

Method on Human Activity Recognition Based on Convolutional Neural Network

Zhang Haibin[(⊠)] and Naoyuki Kubota[(⊠)]

Faculty of Systems Design, Tokyo Metropolitan University, Tokyo, Japan
zhang-haibin@ed.tmu.ac.jp, kubota@tmu.ac.jp

Abstract. In order to improve the accuracy of human activity recognition based on smart device, we proposed a recognition method based on convolutional neural network. We preprocess the raw acceleration data and input the processed data directly into the convolution neural network to do local feature analysis. After processing, we get the characteristic output result, which can be directly inputted into the SoftMax classifier, which can recognize five activity, such as walking, running, going downstairs, going upstairs and standing. By comparing the experimental results, the recognition rate of different experimenters is 84.8%, which proves that the method is effective.

Keywords: Human activity recognition · Deep learning · Convolutional neural network

1 Introduction

With the continuous improvement of people's living standards and the pressure of work, people are increasingly in need of a healthy lifestyle. Sports that are good for health have become the focus of attention. The sports management system can urge people to maintain a certain amount of exercise every day and provide information such as heartbeat and blood pressure. Therefore, information technology and smart-wearing device have developed rapidly. With the continuous advancement of information science and smart device, sensor-based human behavior recognition has begun to enter the social stage. It collects sensor data in real time, performs data preprocessing, and judges the user's current activity status through data analysis and calculation, such as smart home system, the elderly safety recognition system. At present, the portable smartphone has built-in acceleration, gyroscope, magnetometer, direction sensor and other sensors, which can produce different data for different situation. For example, acceleration sensor can generate different and accurate three-dimensional acceleration data for different behaviors such as walking, running, upstairs and downstairs. The more and more accurate 3D acceleration data makes it possible to apply for behavior recognition based on portable smartphones.

© Springer Nature Switzerland AG 2019
H. Yu et al. (Eds.): ICIRA 2019, LNAI 11742, pp. 63–71, 2019.
https://doi.org/10.1007/978-3-030-27535-8_6

2 Related Work

2.1 Deep Learning

Deep learning is a new research field in machine learning theory. Its motivation is to build and simulate the neural network of human brain for analysis and learning. It imitates the mechanism of human brain to interpret data. It is a kind of unsupervised learning. At present, deep learning has achieved great success in image recognition, voice recognition, natural language processing and other fields.

In 2013, Chen Xianchang et al. used 60,000 handwritten data to train 10,000 handwritten data by improving the convolution neural network model for handwritten character recognition. The experimental results show that the recognition rate reaches 92%. In 2008, Zhao Zhihong et al. applied convolutional neural network to license plate character recognition, and achieved 98.68% recognition rate. In 2012, Abdel-Hamid et al. applied convolutional neural network to the recognition system of sound signals, and achieved a better recognition rate.

2.2 Behavior Recognition

There have been a number of studies on human behavior recognition at home and abroad. The early research is wearable computing, that is, the sensor is fixed in a specific location for human behavior and gesture recognition.

In 2004, MIT Media Laboratory used accelerometers carried by five positions of human body to identify 20 common behaviors in daily life, continuously collected sensor data from different parts of human body, and used pattern recognition to recognize user behavior perception, using different classifiers for average, motion energy, frequency domain entropy, etc. The test results show that the recognition is accurate.

In 2010, Wang Xichang et al. placed accelerometer on the upper limb, and applied the three-axis acceleration information to the recognition of upper limb movements, and obtained a relatively ideal recognition accuracy.

With the popularity of smart phones all over the world, human behavior recognition based on smart phones has rapidly begun to rise and achieved rapid development. Human behavior recognition of smartphones can be regarded as a classification problem, where the input data are time domain signals and the output results are the corresponding categories of classification labels. Qualcomm Grokop et al. placed the mobile phone in different parts of the human body, including pockets, trouser pockets and hands for binary recognition, and obtained 92.6% and 66.8% recognition rates. Chen et al. chose to fuse accelerometer and GPS information for traffic pattern recognition, which was used to distinguish whether the vehicle was in action or not. As a result, it was difficult to distinguish whether the vehicle was in static or not.

3 Introduction Deep Learning Theory

Convolutional neural network is a kind of deep learning network, which includes convolution layer and pooling layer. It first carries out convolution process and then pooling process. The output of the convolution layer is the input of the pooling layer, and the result of the pooling layer is the input of the next convolution layer. The key part of convolution neural network is shown in Fig. 1.

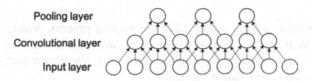

Fig. 1. Key component of CNN

3.1 Convolutional Layer

From the understanding of the local receptive field of biological vision cells, the convolutional neural network uses a local filter to perform the convolution process, that is, taking the local submatrix of the input and the local filter for inner product operation, and outputting the result as a convolution output matrix. The value of the corresponding dimension. In order to form a better data representation, the convolution layer provides a plurality of such partial filters to form a plurality of output matrices, each output matrix having a size of $(N - m + 1)$, and the detailed operation process is as shown in Eq. (1).

$$X_I^{l,j} = f\left(b_j + \sum_{a-1}^{m} w_a^j x_{i+a-1}^{l-1,j} \right) \tag{1}$$

Among them, l in $X_i^{l,j}$ denotes the lth convolution layer, i denotes a value of the ith convolution output matrix, j denotes the number of the corresponding output matrix, 0 to N from left to right, and N denotes the number of convolution output matrices. F denotes a non-linear function, and sigmoid function is used here. As shown in Fig. 1, the results of the first input layer as input term at the first position of the output matrix under the action of the first filter layer are shown in Formula (2).

$$X_1^{1,1} = f\left(b_1 + w_1^{1,1} x_1^{0,1} + w_2^{1,1} x_2^{0,1} + w_3^{1,1} x_3^{0,1} \right) \tag{2}$$

3.2 Pooling Layer

The pooling layer of CNN is a process that further reduces the dimensions of the matrix without destroying the intrinsic link of the data. The pooling layer can be constructed by the average structure or the maximum value. This experiment uses an average structure, so the experimental pool layer can also be called the mean pool layer. The input of the mean cell layer is derived from the convolution layer of the previous layer, and the output is used as the input layer for the convolution of the next layer. The mean value pool uses local averaging to reduce the dimension. The detailed operation process is as shown in Eq. (3).

$$X_i^{l,j} = \frac{1}{N} \times \left(\sum_{i-1,j-1}^{n} x_{x,j} \right) \tag{3}$$

where $X_i^{l,j}$ represents a local output after the pooling process, which is obtained by averaging the local small matrix of the previous layer size $n \times n$. The mean pooling process used in this experiment is implemented by a $1/n$ square matrix and a $n \times n$ square matrix called convolution function.

4   Introduction Recognition Model Based on Deep Learning

4.1   Data Collecting System

The experiment is carried out by MATLAB, involving processes such as data acquisition system processes, data processing based on convolutional neural networks, and SoftMax classifiers for classification.

In this paper, based on Android 5.0 system, the smart phone with ARM processor is used as the hardware platform. The lightweight behavior data collector can collect the acceleration information in real time.

The behavioral data of 15 users, aged from 20 to 50, were collected, including 5 people aged 20 to 30, 8 people aged 30 to 40 and 2 people aged 40 to 50. They basically covered the smartphone user group. The collected behavioral information was divided into five categories, including static standing, walking, running, upstairs and downstairs. The location of the user's mobile phone is as follows: bag, trouser pocket and hand. Each user collects acceleration information for each action and position for 10 times, each time for 10 s. The total data collected by the whole project group is 2 250 groups, of which 450 groups are for one behavior, and 750 groups are for each location, as listed in Tables 1 and 2.

Table 1. Samples number of different behaviors

Behaviors	Number of samples
Stay	450
Walk	450
Run	450
Upstairs	450
Downstairs	450
Total	2250

Table 2. Samples number of different wearing position

Wearing position	Number of samples
Pocket	750
Hand	750
Bag	750
Total	2250
Pocket	750
Hand	750

4.2   Data Processing Based on Convolutional Neural Network

The whole experimental process in this paper includes the preprocessing of data, the convolutional neural network processing of data and the SoftMax classification process. The specific experimental data processing process is shown in Fig. 2.

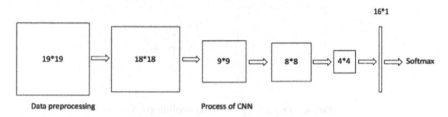

Fig. 2. Model of convolution neural network

4.3   Explanation of Convolutional Neural Network

The experiment is carried out using the data collected by the above data acquisition system. The input data needs to be pre-processed before the input convolutional neural network is trained and tested. The acquired data first processes a matrix $a = (a_x, a_y, a_z)$ of size 120×3, where a_x represents the acceleration information in the x-direction of the cell phone coordinate system, and a_y represents the acceleration in the direction of the phone coordinate system y. Information, a_z represents the acceleration information in the z direction of the phone coordinate system. In the experiment, the matrix a is first changed into the row vector b of 1×360 according to the phone coordinate system x, y, z, and then the last item in the a z is added to the row vector b to form a row vector c of 1×361. Finally, the row vector c is processed into a 19×19 matrix d. The specific variation is as shown in Fig. 3, where Δ represents a x, $\bigcirc$ represents a y, and $\square$ represents a z.

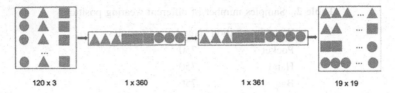

Fig. 3. Explanation of convolution neural network

After the preprocessing process, the data enters the first convolutional layer of the convolutional neural network. The convolution window size is 2 × 2, and there are 6 such convolution windows with different values, thus obtaining 6 different convolutions. Mapping matrix, each matrix size is 18 × 18. The intermediate processing includes the convolution process of the local convolution window and the processing of the sigmoid function. The processing of the convolution process is shown in Fig. 4.

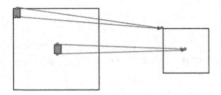

Fig. 4. Processing of the convolution layer

After passing through the first layer of the convolutional neural network, the data enters the pooling layer. The method of processing data by the pooling layer has the maximum mode and the average mode. The maximum mode is to use the maximum value of the local small matrix as the output of the mapping layer. The average method is to use the average value of the local small matrix as the output of the mapping layer. In this paper, the sampling process of the pooling layer is performed by means of the average value. The processing in the experiment is done by convolving a convolution window with the matrix to be processed, where each value of the convolution function is 1/n, where n is the total number of elements in the convolution window. The size of the matrix after the pooling layer processing in the experiment became 9 × 9. The data passes through the pooling layer of the second layer of the convolutional neural network and enters the convolution process of the third layer. The convolution window of the third layer has 12, the convolution window size is 2 × 2, and the output of the third layer is 12 different 8 × 8 matrices, wherein each matrix is obtained by convolving the matrix with the corresponding convolution window according to a certain rule in the pooling layer of the second layer of the convolutional neural network, as shown in Table 3. Column. The output of the first convolutional layer of the third layer is obtained by convolving the first three matrices with the first convolution window and then summing them. The specific process of convolution is the same as that of the first layer of the convolutional neural network. Like the product process, the other processes are the same as above. After passing through the third layer of the pooling layer, the data enters the fourth layer of the convolutional neural network. The processing of the fourth layer is the same as that of the second layer of the convolutional neural network.

4.4 Classification Model Based on Softmax

After the data processing of the convolutional neural network, the data is processed into a $16 \times 1 \times 12$ column matrix, which is input to the SoftMax classifier for separation. SoftMax classifier maps the signals to be separated to the corresponding behavior label. During training, the signal is subjected to a data processing process of the convolutional neural network to obtain a classification result, which is compared with the corresponding label data to calculate the corresponding relative error, and convolution window in the convolutional neural network is continuously corrected by training a certain number of times. The weights cause the relative error to decrease, and finally converge, and then the test set is input into the network for test classification. The training time in this paper is 2000, and the resulting classification error curve is shown in Fig. 5.

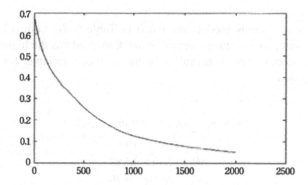

Fig. 5. Training error curve of convolution neural network

5 Experimental Result

The research group uses the multi-classification algorithm to perform behavior recognition, which is BP neural network, SVM algorithm and convolutional neural network. Two methods were used for testing separately. (1) Sample set test. Based on the sample, 450 samples is taken for testing, and the results showed that the accurate rate of the convolution network is 92%. (2) Cross-validation. The whole sample is randomly divided into 3 parts averagely, 2 of them for training, and 1 for testing. That is, 300 samples is randomly selected for training, and the remaining 150 samples is tested. Among them, 5 kinds of behaviors are randomly taken 30 samples. Cross-validation method has lower accuracy than sample test sets, but with classification accuracy closer to unlabeled samples. The results and accuracy of cross-validation experiments are listed in Tables 3 and 4.

Table 3. Specific experiment result

Activity	Run	Walk	Stay	Upstairs	Downstairs
Run	28	2	0	0	0
Walk	2	21	0	4	3
Stay	0	0	30	0	0
Upstairs	0	3	0	27	0
Downstairs	0	3	0	6	21

Table 4. Recognition rates of various behavior

Behaviors	(%)
Stay	100
Walk	70
Run	93.3
Upstairs	90
Downstairs	70

The accuracy of various models are listed in Table 5. By comparing the experimental accuracy rate, convolutional neural network method has the highest recognition rate. Therefore, convolutional neural network is more suitable for multi-feature behavior recognition.

Table 5. Accuracy of various models

	(%)	(%)
MVP	52.11	65.83
	58.09	75.76
	92	84.7

6   Conclusion and Future Work

6.1   A Subsection Sample

In conclusion, aiming at five kinds of daily behavior, this paper collects the acceleration information of user's behavior by putting mobile phones in three different positions, and classifies the collected data according to three different methods. Compared with the traditional BP neural network and SVM, the convolutional neural network does not need the artificial feature selection process and has a higher recognition rate, which accuracy can reach 84.7%. However, for three similar behaviors, walking, upstairs and downstairs, the recognition rate is lower compared with running and standing, which are easy to distinguish.

References

1. Zeng, M., Nguyen, L.T.: Convolutional neural networks for human activity recognition using mobile sensors. In: Mobile SCASE, pp. 197–205 (2014)
2. Abdel-Hamid, O., Mohamed, A.R., Jiang, H., et al.: Applying convolutional neural networks concepts to hybrid NN-HMM model for speech recognition. In: IEEE International Conference on Acoustics, Speech and Signal Processing (ICASSP), pp. 4277–4280. IEEE (2012)
3. Bagci, U., Bai, L.: A comparison of Daubechies and Gabor wavelets for classification of mr images. In: 2007 International Conference on Signal Processing and Communications, ICSPC 2007, pp. 676–679. IEEE (2007)
4. Bengio, Y.: Learning deep architectures for AI. Found. Trends Mach. Learn. 2(1), 1–127 (2009)

A Web Based Security Monitoring and Information Management System for Nursing Homes

Ying Li, Ying Xu, Yi Lv, and Junchen Wang[✉]

Beihang University, Beijing, China
wangjunchen@buaa.edu.cn

Abstract. With the accelerated aging of the population and the continuous emergence of robotic equipment, the level of intelligent monitoring of nursing homes faces new challenges. This paper proposes an intelligent security monitoring and information management system based on the actual environment of the nursing home. This network monitoring system integrating intelligent sensor terminal and intelligent assistant robot equipment. The system can monitor the elderly's urine in bed, ambulation, falling, position and accidents in the washroom in real time, and notify the caregiver in time; Regularly record the blood pressure, blood oxygen, heart rate physiological parameters of the elderly, and the interactive information between the intelligent bath chair, smart wheelchair, rehabilitation robot and the elderly in the nursing home, can storage the basic information of the elderly to reduce the difficulty of nursing staff, and at the same time provides convenience for the elderly.

Keywords: Security monitoring · Information management system · Nursing home

1 Introduction

The trend of population aging is gradually emerging in developed and developing countries around the world. China, as the world's largest population, the problem of population aging is gradually attracting social attention. According to the 2017 Data Analysis Center, as of 2017, more than 11.83% of chinese population is aged 65 or older. How to provide a healthy and comfortable old-age environment for the elderly, provide a full range of care for the elderly, become a problem for many nursing homes and old-age care institutions. In the early years, Harvard's Code Blue system [1], based on the early Zigbee technology, set up a wireless sensor network for ECG, blood oxygen, and acceleration sensors. It can monitor the ECG, blood oxygen, and fall alarms of the elderly in the LAN, through the zigbee network. Send information to the monitoring center. Trinugroho et al. [2] proposed a real-time network health monitoring system based on enterprise service bus, which can realize telemedicine by using portable wireless sensors to read vital signs and Internet technologies in wireless body area networks. It is proposed to meet the requirements of real-time remote recording of vital signs, but it is not suitable for occasions where there are many people in the nursing home and the activity space is large. Zhu et al. [3] proposed a network-based

© Springer Nature Switzerland AG 2019
H. Yu et al. (Eds.): ICIRA 2019, LNAI 11742, pp. 72–81, 2019.
https://doi.org/10.1007/978-3-030-27535-8_7

automatic sleep monitoring system for nursing homes. The sensor under the mattress was used to record the respiration rate, heart rate, and physical activity of the elderly at night, and then to assess the quality of sleep of the elderly. However, this system is only suitable for the evaluation of the quality of sleep of the elderly at night, and cannot achieve the full angle of attention for the elderly.

Based on the above research [4–7], integrated and integrated monitoring system becomes a trend this paper proposes an intelligent network monitoring system, which collects basic physiological parameter information of the elderly through intelligent robot equipment, dangerous detection sensor terminals and physiological parameter collection equipment.

2 System Design

Combined with the actual environment of the nursing home, the overall plan of the wireless network security monitoring system was formulated. From the perspective of the ward and the user, the functional requirements of the safety monitoring system are clarified. Based on the overall scheme, the dangerous state detection alarm terminal scheme, wireless network communication scheme and safety guarding information management are designed according to the system function.

Combined with the actual environment of the nursing home, the overall plan of the wireless network security monitoring system was formulated. From the perspective of the ward and the user, the functional requirements of the safety monitoring system are clarified. Based on the overall scheme, the dangerous state detection alarm terminal scheme, wireless network communication scheme and safety guarding information management are designed according to the system function.

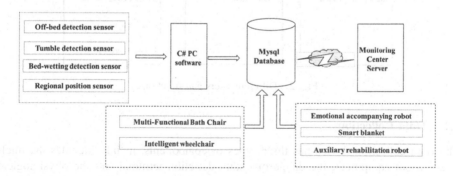

Fig. 1. Overall structure of the system

Figure 1 shows the overall structures of the system, The system uses the intelligent wheelchair, intelligent bath chair, emotional accompanying robot, rehabilitation robot, smart blanket, five kinds of old robot equipment, four kinds of elderly danger detection terminals to collect the use information of the elderly, record the use parameters of the elderly, and physiological parameters. For the dangerous state detection terminal, such a device requiring real-time performance, the protocol is first parsed by the C# host computer, and then written into the data storage center, so that the monitoring center records the data interaction.

3 System Architecture

The system is based b/s structure, the reason is that the nursing staff in the nursing home are often busy dealing with different affairs, adopting the b/s structure can facilitate the nursing staff, or the management personnel. even in different locations, they can remotely login the system to check the current status of the elderly, as long as he has reasonable permission. The system has the following functions: data collection, data storage, data interaction, data monitoring. The system is mainly for three kinds of users, and provides different functions according to different user requirements. The various modules and functions of the system described in Fig. 2 are provided:

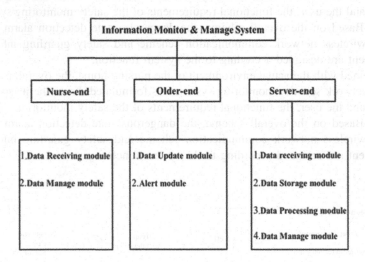

Fig. 2. Different users and functions

3.1 Data Collection

The data collection device has three types of components. mainly includes the intelligent robot equipment, the dangerous state detection terminal and the physiological parameter collection equipment.

The dangerous state detection terminal mainly includes three types of bed detection and detection terminals, a fall positioning detection terminal, and a toilet timeout detection terminal.

The intelligent robot equipment mainly includes: intelligent walking robot, multifunction bathing robot [8], bed-bed intelligent limb rehabilitation robot, and emotional accompanying robot. Combined with the robot body structure, the bed-based intelligent rehabilitation robot and the emotional accompanying robot adopt the wi-fi network to access the remote api, and read and write the data to the server-side database to realize the data acquisition (Fig. 3).

Pressure Sensor   Humidity Sensor   GPS Module   Infrared Sensor

Fig. 3. Sensors and module

3.2   Data Storage

Mysql is an associative database management system that stores data in separate tables instead of putting all the data in a large repository, which increases speed and flexibility. Mysql is one of the most popular relational database management system. Mysql is one of the best RDBMS (Relational Database Management System) applications in WEB applications.

We chose Mysql [9] database to store all data involved. The Mysql database is used to store data by analyzing the main data types of the monitoring system and the space required for the data. The basic structure of the database is shown in the Fig. 4.

The relationship between the table and the table is also displayed. The database center stores the basic information of the elderly, the caregiver, the equipment, the elderly family, and the bed. At the same time, according to the equipment and the elderly, the equipment and the bed are also set the relationship to facilitate data creation, query, modification, deletion and other operations.

Figure 4 depicts the table structure of the system and the mutual constraints between the tables. For example, the main entity table of the system includes an elderly person, a care worker, a bed, and a device table, wherein the relationship between the sensor device and the bed needs to be mutually constrained with the elderly or the bed of the elderly; for the elderly and the bed, a one-to-one constraint relationship needs to be established; For the old robot device, the care worker is required to help input the use information. Therefore, the device use record table is used to record the interaction information between the old person and the device.

Now, for alarm record, we chose this method to manage (Fig. 5). Firstly, establish an old person table to store the basic information of the elderly; secondly, establish a device table to record the basic information of the device (including the bedside terminal, the drop terminal, the bathroom timeout terminal); finally, establish the old device binding Relationship table, to solve the relationship between the elderly and the sensor worn; according to the relationship between the above table, the old man alarm information table is established to record the alarm information of the elderly, including the number, name, and type of the alarm Including bed detection, fall detection, urine and urine detection, the location of the alarm. The driving motors use maxon dc brush servo motor, encoder using hedl 5540, the number of 500 lines, two ab phase output.

According to the performance requirements of the motor, select mlds3620 dc servo motor drive, the dc power range of 12–48 V, the maximum continuous reading current of 20 A, power up to 960 W, can bus communication, with amplifier mode, torque mode, speed mode, position mode.

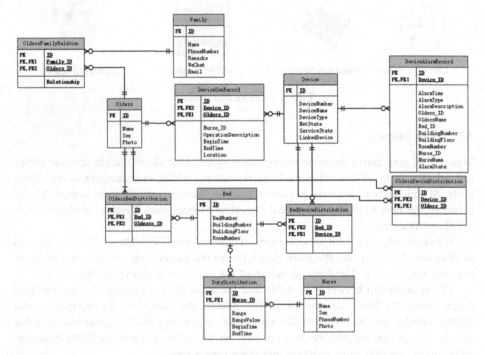

Fig. 4. Data storage structure

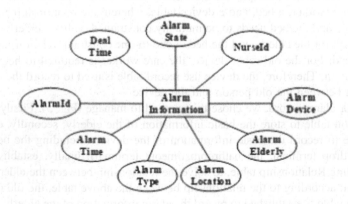

Fig. 5. E-R model for alarm information

3.3   Data Interaction

We adopt the b/s mode [10] web-based monitoring system design, we adopt the separation mode of front and back. For the front-end display interface, we mainly use html, css and JavaScript technology, for the back-end including business processing, the bottom layer. Data acquisition, we use the Java language to deal with, based on the spring boot framework, to achieve the web back-end business. In the information interaction, the main design of three modules, the nursing staff interaction module, the elderly family interaction module, the doctor interaction module.

The implementation of the monitoring system backend is based on the mvc [11] design pattern. mvc includes the model object: responsible for storing data and defining how to manipulate the data; view object: responsible for displaying and allowing the user to edit the Model object from the application, the view object is used to build the user interface, Interact with the user; Controller object: is the middleman between the Model object and the view object, responsible for passing data, listening to various events, managing the life cycle of other objects, and so on. The interaction process of the system is shown in the Fig. 6.

The part of the system that interacts with the nursing staff is the main part of the management function of the system. The system can help the nursing staff to record the living conditions of each elderly person in the nursing home every day, so that the nursing staff can take more comprehensive care. Different caregivers can have different management rights. For senior administrators, they have the functions of creating, deleting, and modifying the basic information of the elderly, general care workers, and equipment in the system, and establishing the relationship between the designated sensor terminals and the elderly. Comprehensive management of the elderly, nursing staff, equipment and beds in the nursing home; for the ordinary duty nurses, you can check the recent dangerous alarms of every old person, you can check the changes of the physiological parameters of all the elderly, and be able to check the elderly. We use statistical information such as higher frequency devices. For the nursing staff who are on duty, the nursing system can realize the care of the elderly who have a dangerous alarm. When the old man falls, the following warning will appear. The nursing staff can see the name, number and location of the fallen old man. Facilitate the timely disarming of caregivers.

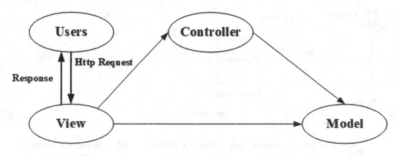

Fig. 6. MVC pattern

Elderly family display module: the family members of each elderly person can observe the basic physiological adoption information of the elderly by applying for the family's authority, and can check the monitoring status of the elderly in the nursing home every day according to the time. For example, we can see the elderly for nearly a week. The blood pressure situation, as well as the number of falls, so that family members can care about the lives of the elderly remotely.

Doctor display module: Because the elderly in nursing homes usually have chronic diseases, such as high blood pressure and high blood fat, these chronic diseases require long-term physical signs to better help doctors. Through the collection of the daily physiological parameters of the elderly in the monitoring system, when the doctor treats the elderly, he can directly retrieve the parameter record form of the elderly and combine his medical knowledge for treatment.

3.4   Data Monitoring

When a dangerous alarm occurs, the transmission danger detecting terminal communicates with the coordinator, and the coordinator communicates with the host computer software to transmit the position information of the elderly person and the name of the old person to the database of the data monitoring center.

Monitoring the data information of the dangerous detection equipment. Firstly, according to the actual environment of the nursing home, the Zigbee wireless network system is constructed. The system includes a coordinator, a wireless routing node, and an infinite terminal node. The network topology adopts a mesh topology and a network. After overlaying as shown below: Fig. 7.

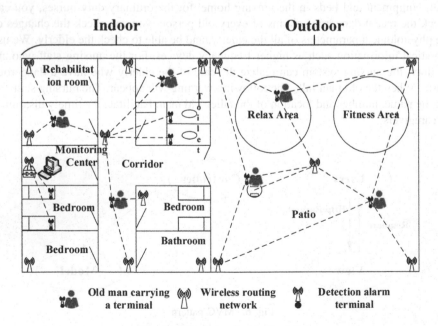

Fig. 7. Data transmission module

For the monitoring of physiological parameter information of the elderly, the intelligent sleep blanket accesses the data center database through the remote API, and stores the daily blood pressure, blood oxygen, respiration rate and other physiological parameter information of the elderly into the data center, and the long-term record will be obtained. The average value of the parameter information of the elderly, when the parameter information of the elderly exceeds the threshold, a security alert will appear in the personal information of the elderly, reminding the care worker to detect the physiological state of the elderly.

For the monitoring of the use information of the intelligent robot, through the realization of remote data access and the care worker input the basic information when the elderly uses the device, and the use record of the old man to the robot is finally stored in the data center.

4 Experiment and Result

The experiment was initially deployed and tested in Beijing Sijiqing Nursing Home. The test area is 1st floor of No.1 Building of the nursing home, 20 elderly rooms. As shown in the Fig. 8, From top to bottom is the integrated routing installation, indoor and outdoor route installation, alarm terminal placement. As you can see, the Figs. 9, 10 and 11 depicts the layout of the bathroom using timeout detection terminal, urine in bed detection terminal, and the fall detection terminal. When the sensor has a dangerous alarm, the alarm prompt message as shown in the Fig. 11 appears in the interface of the monitoring center to remind the care worker to urgently handle the problem.

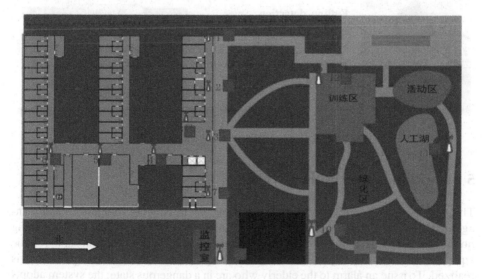

Fig. 8. Route distribution on map

Fig. 9. Route set up

Fig. 10. Bathroom use timeout terminal and off-bed detection terminal

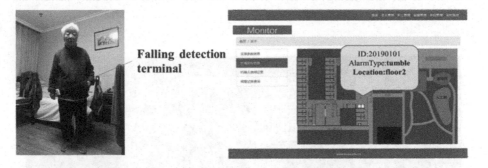

Fig. 11. Falling detection terminal and alarm display

5   Conclusion and Future Work

This paper proposes a highly integrated and intelligent network monitoring and management system, which has the management of the staff and equipment of the nursing home. At the same time, through the connection with various sensors and robotic equipment of the nursing home, the monitoring of the nursing home personnel is realized. To issue an alarm to the elderly who are in a dangerous state; the system adopts a hierarchical management method, which can realize different management authority for different personnel. Although the initial test of the system completes the functions of monitoring and management, it can improve the communication mode, speed up the data transmission, processing, and resolution, and provide better real-time performance.

With the application of smart medical care, machine learning, cloud computing and other technologies in HER records, the physiological parameters of the elderly collected by the system in the nursing home can be collected and stored in the health records of the elderly, making predictions for the health of the elderly, comprehensive Pay attention to the health of the elderly.

Acknowledgment. This research was supported by the National Key R&D Program of China (2017YFB1304105).

References

1. Malan, D., Fulford-Jones, T., Welsh, M., et al.: CodeBlue: an ad hoc sensor network infrastructure for emergency medical care. In: International Workshop on Wearable and Implantable Body Sensor Networks, May 2004
2. Trinugroho, Y.B.D., Rasta, K., Nguyen, T.H., et al.: A real-time web-based health monitoring system based on enterprise service bus. In: Proceedings of 2012 11th IADIS International Conference on WWW/Internet, pp. 165–172 (2012)
3. Zhu, X., Zhou, X., Chen, W., et al.: Estimation of sleep quality of residents in nursing homes using an internet-based automatic monitoring system. In: 2014 IEEE 11th International Conference on Ubiquitous Intelligence and Computing and 2014 IEEE 11th International Conference on Autonomic and Trusted Computing and 2014 IEEE 14th International Conference on Scalable Computing and Communications and Its Associated Workshops, pp. 659–665. IEEE (2014)
4. Shah, S.H., Iqbal, A., Shah, S.S.A.: Remote health monitoring through an integration of wireless sensor networks, mobile phones & cloud computing technologies. In: 2013 IEEE Global Humanitarian Technology Conference (GHTC), pp. 401–405. IEEE (2013)
5. Ansefine, K.E., Anggadjaja, E., Santoso, H.: Smart and wearable technology approach for elderly monitoring in nursing home. In: 2017 IEEE 3rd International Conference on Engineering Technologies and Social Sciences (ICETSS), pp. 1–6. IEEE (2017)
6. Liu, K., Jiang, J., Ding, X., et al.: Design and development of management information system for research project process based on front-end and back-end separation. In: 2017 International Conference on Computing Intelligence and Information System (CIIS), pp. 338–342. IEEE (2017)
7. Fook, V.F.S., Jayachandran, M., Jiliang, E.P., et al.: Fiber Bragg grating-based monitoring and alert system for care of residents in nursing homes. In: 2018 IEEE 4th World Forum on Internet of Things (WF-IoT), pp. 195–200. IEEE (2018)
8. Chen, D., Zeng, B., Sun, Z., et al.: An off-bed detection and bathroom accident monitor system for nursing home. In: 2016 International Conference on Advanced Robotics and Mechatronics (ICARM), pp. 53–58. IEEE (2016)
9. Widenius, M., Axmark, D., Arno, K.: MySQL Reference Manual: Documentation from the Source. O'Reilly Media Inc., Sebastopol (2002)
10. Yongcai, G., Zhu, B., Chao, G.: Design of the multifunctional remote data acquisition system based on B/S mode computer system & applications (2010)
11. Pop, D.P., Altar, A.: Designing an MVC model for rapid web application development. Proc. Eng. **69**, 1172–1179 (2014)

Region of Interest Growing Neural Gas for Real-Time Point Cloud Processing

Yuichiro Toda[(✉)], Xiang Li, Takayuki Matsuno,
and Mamoru Minami

Okayama University, Okayama, Japan
ytoda@okayama-u.ac.jp

Abstract. This paper proposes a real-time topological structure learning method based on concentrated/distributed sensing for a 2D/3D point cloud. First of all, we explain a modified Growing Neural Gas with Utility (GNG-U2) that can learn the topological structure of 3D space environment and color information simultaneously by using a weight vector. Next, we propose a Region Of Interest Growing Neural Gas (ROI-GNG) for realizing concentrated/distributed sensing in real-time. In ROI-GNG, the discount rates of the accumulated error and utility value are variable according to the situation. We show experimental results of the proposed method and discuss the effectiveness of the proposed method.

Keywords: Growing Neural Gas · Point cloud processing ·
Topological structure learning

1 Introduction

Recently, various types of robots have emerged in many fields as a progress of robot technologies. Especially, the expectation of disaster robots, which can be robustly utilized in a disaster area, is increasing for preventing the second disaster in the area [1]. It is important to extract the environmental information related to a movable area of the robot and a dangerous area such as rubble with the high possibility of collapse in order to act safely and quickly in the disaster area. In this paper, we focus on an environmental sensing technology using a 2D/3D point cloud for extracting the efficient and effective information in the disaster area. To realize the environmental sensing in the disaster area, an attention allocation for the target object is the one of the most important technologies because the robot should efficiently extract the detail object information for the target object and roughly monitor the other object for avoiding the collision of moving obstacles. Therefore, this paper proposes a Growing Neural Gas based real-time point processing method with the attention allocation function.

In our previous work, we proposed a framework for 3D point cloud processing [2]. Our proposed framework is based on Growing Neural Gas with Utility (GNG-U) because GNG-U can learn a topological structure of the 3D space environment and be applied to non-stationary data distribution. GNG-U proposed by Fritzke [3] is one of the competitive learning methods, and can dynamically change the topological

© Springer Nature Switzerland AG 2019
H. Yu et al. (Eds.): ICIRA 2019, LNAI 11742, pp. 82–91, 2019.
https://doi.org/10.1007/978-3-030-27535-8_8

structure based on the edge referring to the ignition frequency of the adjacent node according to the accumulated error. However, the standard GNG-U does not learn the topological structure of the 3D space environment and color information simultaneously. Therefore, we proposed the modified GNG-U (GNG-U2) [2], which uses the weight vector called as a relative importance for selecting the first and second winner nodes and the rule of node deletion is modified for adjusting the time series 3D point cloud quickly. However, GNG-U2 cannot realize the attention allocation function because the GNG based method learns the topological structure according to the data distribution appropriately. In this paper, we propose Region of Interest Growing Neural Gas (ROI-GNG) based on GNG-U2. ROI-GNG learns the dense topological structure for the target property and the sparse topological structure for the other properties by controlling the discount rate of the accumulated error. In addition, ROI-GNG adjusts the density of the total topological structure by controlling the discount rate of the utility value. By integrating these two updating rules of the discount rate, ROI-GNG can realize the attention allocation function for the topological learning method. Finally, we show an experimental result for verifying the effectiveness of our proposed method.

2 Modified Growing Neural Gas with Utility Value

We use a Growing Neural Gas (GNG) based algorithm for learning a topological structure of the point clouds. GNG proposed by Fritzke is one of the unsupervised learning methods [3]. Unsupervised learning is performed by using only data without any teaching signals. Self-organized map (SOM), neural gas (NG), growing cell structures (GCS), and GNG are well known as unsupervised learning methods [4–7]. Basically, these methods use the competitive learning. The number of nodes and the topological structure of the network in SOM are designed beforehand. In NG, the number of nodes is fixed beforehand, but the topological structure is updated according to the distribution of sample data. On the other hand, GCS and GNG can dynamically change the topological structure based on the adjacent relation (edge) referring to the ignition frequency of the adjacent node according to the error index. However, GCS does not delete nodes and edges, while GNG can delete nodes and edges based on the concept of ages. Furthermore, GCS must consist of k-dimensional simplexes whereby k is a positive integer chosen in advance. The initial configuration of each network is a k-dimensional simplex, e.g., a line is used for $k = 1$, a triangle for $k = 2$, and a tetrahedron for $k = 3$. GCS has applied to construct 3D surface models by triangulation based on 2-dimensional simplex. However, because the GCS does not delete nodes and edges, the number of nodes and edges is over increasing. Furthermore, GCS cannot divide the sample data into several segments. In addition, GNG cannot apply the non-stationary data distribution because GNG can only remove the nodes that are the nearest node of the first winner node in GNG. Therefore, we use modified GNG with Utility (GNG-U2) for learning the topological structure from 2D/3D space environment.

At first, we explain a modified GNG-U2 algorithm. The procedure and notation used in GNG-U are shown

h_i: The nth dimensional vector of a node
w: The nth dimensional weight vector
A: A set of nodes
c_{ij}: A set of edges between the ith and jth nodes
g_{ij}: Age of the edge between the ith and jth nodes

Step 0. Generate two units at random positions, w_1, w_2 in R^n where n is the dimension of input data. Initialize the connection set.

Step 1. Generate at random an input data v.

Step 2. Select the nearest unit (winner) s_1 and the second-nearest unit s_2 from the set of nodes by

$$s_1 = \arg \min_{i \in A} \| w * (v - h_i) \|$$
$$s_2 = \arg \min_{i \in A \setminus s_1} \| w * (v - h_i) \|, \tag{1}$$

where $*$ indicates elemental-wise product.

Step 3. If a connection between s_1 and s_2 does not yet exist, create the connection $(C_{s_1,s_2} = 1)$. Set the age of the connection between s_1 and s_2 at zero;

Step 4. Add the squared distance between the input data and the winner to a local error variable;

$$E_{s_1} \leftarrow E_{s_1} + \| w * (v - h_{s_1}) \|^2$$
$$U_{s_1} \leftarrow U_{s_1} + \| w * (v - h_{s_2}) \|^2 - \| w * (v - h_{s_1}) \|^2 \tag{2}$$

Step 5. Update the reference vectors of the winner and its direct topological neighbors by the learning rate η_1 and η_2 respectively, of the total distance to the input data.

$$h_{s_1} \leftarrow h_{s_1} + \eta_1 \cdot (v - h_{s_1})$$
$$h_j \leftarrow h_j + \eta_2 \cdot (v - h_j) \, if \quad c_{i,j} = 1 \tag{3}$$

Step 6. Increment the age of all edges emanating from s_1.

$$g_{s_1,j} \leftarrow g_{s_1,j} + 1 \, if \, c_{s_1,j} = 1 \tag{4}$$

Step 7. Remove edges with an age larger than amax. If this results in units having no more connecting edges, remove those units as well.

Step 8. If the number of input data generated so far is an integer multiple of a parameter κ, remove the node as follows.

i. Select the unit u with the maximal accumulated error and the uint l with the minimum utility value.

$$u = \arg \max_{i \in A} E_i$$
$$l = \arg \min_{i \in A} U_i \tag{5}$$

ii. Remove the unit from the topological structure if the following condition is satisfied.

$$E_u/U_l > k \tag{6}$$

Step 9. If the number of input data generated so far is an integer multiple of a parameter λ, insert a new unit as follows.

i. Select the unit u with the maximal accumulated error.

$$u = \arg \max_{i \in A} E_i \tag{7}$$

ii. Select the unit f with the maximal accumulated error among the neighbors of q.

iii. Add a new unit r to the network and interpolate its reference vector form q and f.

$$h_r = 0.5 \cdot (h_u + h_f) \tag{8}$$

iv. Insert edges connecting the new unit r with units q and f, and remove the original edge between q and f.

v. Decrease the error variables of q and f by a temporal discounting rate α.

$$\begin{aligned} E_u &\leftarrow E_u - \alpha E_u \\ E_f &\leftarrow E_f - \alpha E_f \end{aligned} \tag{9}$$

vi. Interpolate the local error variable of r from q and f.

$$E_r = 0.5 \cdot (E_u + E_f) \tag{10}$$

Step 10. Decrease the local error variables of all units by a temporal discounting rate β and χ.

$$\begin{aligned} E_i &\leftarrow E_i - \beta E_i \, (\forall i \in A) \\ U_i &\leftarrow U_i - \chi U_i \, (\forall i \in A) \end{aligned} \tag{11}$$

Step 11. Continue with step 2 if a stopping criterion (e.g., the number of nodes or some performance measure) is not yet fulfilled.

GNG based algorithm select the nearest unit (winner) s_1 and the second-nearest unit s_2 from the set of nodes and create the connection ($c_{s1, s2} = 1$) if a connection between s_1 and s_2 does not yet exist. In GNG-U, each node has the utility value U_i. The node with the minimum utility value is removed from the topological structure if the following condition is satisfied;

$$E_u/U_l > k \tag{12}$$

Generally, the standard GNG-U2 removes the node in the node insertion. In addition, our method removes the node if the number of input data generated so far is an integer multiple of a parameter k for controlling the number of nodes. Furthermore, our method uses the weight vector w called as a relative importance to learn the topological structure of the 2D/3D space environment. By using GNG-U2, the point cloud data distribution can be learned appropriately.

3 Region of Interest Growing Neural Gas

In this section, we propose Region of Interest Growing Neural Gas (ROI-GNG). ROI-GNG learns the dense topological structure for the target property and the sparse topological structure for the other properties. In addition, ROI-GNG adjusts the density of the total topological structure.

3.1 Node Density Adjustment Method for the Total Topological Structure

The ROI-GNG uses the discount rate χ of the utility value as a variable for adjusting the density of the total topological structure. The discount rate χ_i^t of the ith node at time step t is defined by the following equation,

$$\chi_i^t \leftarrow r^t \cdot \beta_i^t \tag{14}$$

where r^t is the scale parameter of the discount rate of the utility value for the discount rate of the accumulated error of the ith node at time step t. The node density of the total topological structure is adjusted by defining a criterion according to the task or situation. Specifically, r^t is reduced if the node density is increased, and r^t is increased if the node density is reduced. In this paper, the objective of the 2D/3D point processing is to realize the real-time processing. Therefore, the updating rule of scale rate r^t is calculated as follows,

$$\begin{aligned} r^t &\leftarrow r^t - \delta \quad \text{if } t^p \leq T^p \\ r^t &\leftarrow r^t + \delta \quad \text{otherwise} \end{aligned} \tag{13}$$

where T^p indicates the threshold value of the setting processing time and δ is the update width of the scale rate r^t. In this paper, δ is defined as the fixed value. In this way, ROI-GNG adjusts the node density of the total topological structure by controlling the discount rate of the utility value.

3.2 Node Density Adjustment Method for Target Objects

In this subsection, we explain the node density adjustment method for different properties. ROI-GNG learns the dense topological structure for the data distribution with the target properties and the sparse topological structure for the other data distribution simultaneously. As mentioned before, the node density of the total topological structure is adjusted by controlling the discount rate of the utility value. On the other hand, the discount rate of the accumulated error is used for realizing the node density adjustment for different properties. Specifically, we define the discount rate of the accumulated error as the variable β_i^t of the ith node at time step t. In addition, the discount rate β_i^t is updated as the follows,

$$\beta_i^t = \begin{cases} b_{high} & \text{if the } i\text{th node has objective feature} \\ b_{low} & \text{otherwise} \end{cases} \tag{14}$$

where b_{low} and b_{high} ($\geq b_{low}$) are the fixed values, and the values are determined empirically in this paper. By using this approach, ROI-GNG can learn the dense topological structure of the data distribution with the target properties and the sparse topological structure of the other data distribution.

4 Experimental Result

This section shows an experimental result for verifying the effectiveness of the proposed method in a 2D simulation environment. Figure 1 shows the 2D point cloud that is composed of red, green and blue rings. The total number of the point cloud is 10000, and the numbers of the red, green and blue rings are 4000, 4000 and 2000, respectively. In addition, the input vector of ROI-GNG is 2D position and color information composed of RGB value ($\mathbf{v} = (v_x, v_y, v_R, v_G, v_B)$), and the weight vector w of relative importance is $w = (1,1,0,0,0)$ for learning the topological structure of only 2D space.

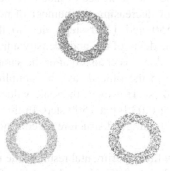

Fig. 1. Experimental dataset (Color figure online)

In this experiment, a target property is changed every 500 steps. The target property of the first 500 steps is the red ring in the point cloud, and the target property of the next 500 steps is the blue ring. The target property of the final 500 steps is red ring again. Table 1 shows the parameters of ROI-GNG in this experiment.

Table 1. Setting parameters

(a) ROI-GNG	
Learning rate η_1, η_2	0.05, 0.0006
Timing of node insertion λ	200
Maximum age g_{max}	88
Discount rate of accumulated error α	0.5
Threshold k	3
Desired sampling time T^p	0.03 [s]
Update range δ	0.01
Initial update rate r^0	1.00
Fixed discount rate b_{low}, b_{high}	0.00001, 0.005
(b) GNG-U2	
Learning rate η_1, η_2	0.05, 0.0006
Timing of node insertion λ	200
Maximum age g_{max}	88
Discount rate of accumulated error α, β	0.5, 0.005
Threshold k	3

Figure 2 shows a transition of the scale value r^t and the sampling time at each step for verifying the effectiveness of the node density adjustment of the total topological structure. In Fig. 2, the sampling time is increased and decreased around the setting time T^p (= 0.03 [s]) by controlling the scale value r^t. Specifically, the scale value r^t is increased if the sampling time is less than the threshold value T^p for increasing the number of nodes. On the other hand, the scale value r^t is increased if the sampling time is more than the value T^p for decreasing the number of nodes. Here, the sampling is largely decreased around 550 and 1150 steps, due to the transition of the target property. In addition, the time delay of the node density adjustment is occurred because the update rule of the scale value r^t is changed after the sampling time is more/less than the threshold value T^p. Due to the time delay, the sampling time between 1100 and 1500 steps is more than 0.04 [s]. However, the scale value r^t is headed for decreasing and the sampling time is near 0.03 [s] at 1500 step. In this way, ROI-GNG can adjust the node density of the total topological structure by controlling the discount rate of the utility value.

Next, Figs. 3 and 4 show the experimental result of the node density adjustment for the target property. Figure 3(a) and (b) show the result of our proposed method and GNG-U2, and Table 1(b) shows the parameters of GNG-U2. In our proposed method, the number of the target nodes is the most of any nodes without the target property in each 500 step. In addition, Fig. 4 shows examples of the learning result of the topological structure. In Fig. 4, the result of (a)–(f) is the same time step of (a)–(f) in Fig. 3 (a). From these results, our proposed method can learn the dense topological structure for the target property and the sparse topological structure for the other properties by controlling the discount rate of the accumulated error. On the other hand, GNG-U2 can learn the topological structure according to the data distribution of the 2D point cloud. This result indicates that GNG-U2 appropriately performs from the viewpoint of the

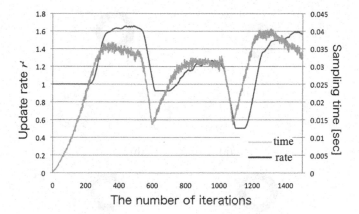

Fig. 2. Transitions of update rate and sampling time

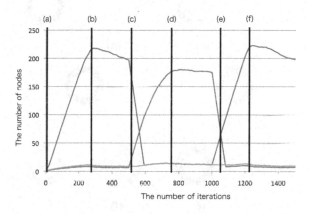

(a) Transition of the number of nodes (Proposed method)

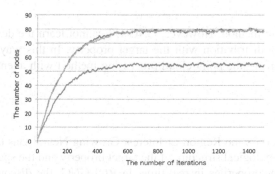

(b) Transition of the number of nodes (GNG-U2)

Fig. 3. Experimental results (Red, green and blue lines represents the number of red, green and blue nodes, respectively) (Color figure online)

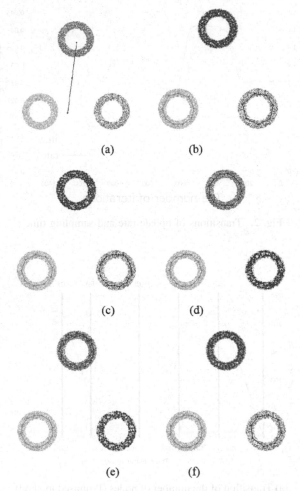

Fig. 4. An example of topological structure

unsupervised learning method. However, GNG-U2 cannot learn the dense topological structure for the data distribution with the target property. In this way, our proposed method realizes the real-time point cloud processing method with attention allocation.

5 Conclusion

In this paper, we propose the Region of Interest Growing Neural Gas (ROI-GNG) for learning the dense topological structure of the target property and the sparse topological structure of the other properties in real-time. In ROI-GNG, the discount rates of the utility value and accumulated error are updated for adjusting the node density according to the target property and sampling time. Next, we conducted an experiment in 2D simulation environment, and showed the effectiveness of our proposed method.

However, we did not apply our proposed method to a real sensing data such RGB-D camera. Therefore, we will apply our proposed method to 3D point cloud data, and verify the effectiveness of our proposed method.

References

1. Murphy, R.R., et al.: Search and rescue robotics. In: Siciliano, B., Khatib, O. (eds.) Springer Handbook of Robotics, pp. 1151–1173. Springer, Berlin (2008). https://doi.org/10.1007/978-3-540-30301-5_51
2. Toda, Y., Yu, H., Ju, Z., Takesue, N., Wada, K., Kubota, N.: Real-time 3D point cloud segmentation using growing neural gas with utility. In: The 9th International Conference on Human System Interaction, pp. 418–422 (2016)
3. Fritzke, B.: A self-organizing network that can follow non-stationary distributions. In: Gerstner, W., Germond, A., Hasler, M., Nicoud, J.-D. (eds.) ICANN 1997. LNCS, vol. 1327, pp. 613–618. Springer, Heidelberg (1997). https://doi.org/10.1007/BFb0020222
4. Fritzke, B.: A growing neural gas network learns topologies. Adv. Neural. Inf. Process. Syst. 7, 625–632 (1995)
5. Kohonen, T.: Self-Organizing Maps. Springer, Heidelberg (2000)
6. Martinetz, T.M., Schulten, K.J.: A "neural-gas"' network learns topologies. Artif. Neural Netw. 1, 397–402 (1991)
7. Fritzke, B.: Unsupervised clustering with growing cell structures. Neural Netw. 2, 531–536 (1991)

Detection of Divergence Point of the Optical Flow Vectors Considering to Gaze Point While Vehicle Cornering

Hiroyuki Masuta[✉], Yusuke Nagai, Yuta Kumano,
Tatsuo Motoyoshi, Kei Sawai, Takumi Tamamoto,
Ken'ichi Koyanagi, and Toru Oshima

Toyama Prefectural University, Kurokawa Imizu, Toyama 930-0956, Japan
masuta@pu-toyama.ac.jp

Abstract. This paper discusses on the relationship between a gaze direction and an optical flow and proposes a divergence point detection from optical flow vectors in a cornering behavior. Previously, we express optical flow radiates outward from the gaze center using the movie of the real vehicle. However, it is difficult to detect a divergence point corresponding with gaze position by applying vector analysis, because the acquired optical flow vectors considering with gaze position includes blank area and noise by matching error. Therefore, we propose the divergence point detection method based on particle swarm optimization. For verifying the proposed method, we perform the experiment using real driving movie. We discuss the effectivity and issue of the proposed method.

Keywords: Vehicle control · Spherical image · Optical flow · PSO

1 Introduction

Recently, self-driving cars are the center of attention in the world. Ordinary cars have advanced driving support systems. These cars are able to drive automatically in limited situations like highway [1, 2]. For example, adaptive cruise control (ACC) and advanced emergency braking system (AEBS) controls a car automatically without driving by a human. However, a human often has a feeling of strangeness with car motion by self-driving. It is important that a human does not have a feeling of strangeness for the car motion even if a self driving vehicle becomes popular.

Actually, ACC and AEBS are based on the human perception model to avoid having a feeling of strangeness. For example, the acceleration and deceleration control of ACC has applied Time to Collision (TTC) [3]. However, this index can only be applied to approaching the preceding vehicle. Therefore, a driver often feels strangeness while cornering. The research that linked ACC and driver behavior insists on the importance of to help the driver predict vehicle trajectory [4]. So, it is important to develop the human perception model like TCC on cornering. Our target is a development of the perceptual model based on human perception for realizing a vehicle cornering control that doesn't provide the feeling of strangeness.

© Springer Nature Switzerland AG 2019
H. Yu et al. (Eds.): ICIRA 2019, LNAI 11742, pp. 92–100, 2019.
https://doi.org/10.1007/978-3-030-27535-8_9

In the previous researches of human perception in driving, Miyoshi et al. showed that the gaze of a skilled driver follows the end of the curve compared with a beginner driver. And, they discussed that a gaze movement is important to control a vehicle [5]. Kishida et al. discussed the relationship between the optical flow and vision region while the vehicle is moving. They made an experiment to restrict a part of a vision region of the subject. As a result, the driver skill was improved and the workload was reduced [6]. The perception while vehicle moving is important not only the incident light information like optical flow but also the visual information which taken intentionally behavior. Okafuji et al. discussed the automatic steering control by using optical flow [7]. This study proposed focus of expansion (FOE) for vehicle control. FOE is the source point of the optical flow on the image. They showed that the FOE expresses the cornering quality. In addition, there are many researchers focus on optical flow [8–10]. According to the above discussions, we focus on the relationship between a gaze direction and an optical flow in a cornering behavior.

Previously, we have verified that the optical flow radiates outward from the gaze center by the simulation and the analysis using the movie of the real vehicle in the best vehicle motion in case of the best vehicle motion. A skilled driver can drive to put the divergence point of the optical flow vectors to the gaze point. In this paper, we propose the detection method of the divergence point of the optical flow vectors in the real image.

This paper is organized as follows. Section 2 explains our prototype Ultra-Compact Electric Vehicle. Section 3.1 explains the abstract of the relationship between optical flow and gaze point. Section 3.2 explains the proposed method using the spherical image. Section 4 shows the experimental results. Section 5 concludes this paper.

2 Prototype Ultra-Compact Electric Vehicle "TORiCLE"

2.1 TORiCLE

We are developing a prototype ultra-compact electric vehicle (UCEV), it is named "TOLiCLE". The standard of UCEV is made by The Ministry of Land, Infrastructure, Transport and Tourism, which is a single or two-seater vehicle, and equips with a motor having a rated power output of less than 8.0 kW [11]. Figure 1 shows TORiCLE that manufactured by TAKAYAMA CARS CO., LTD. TORiCLE is a two-seater EV for research usage. The size is about 1/4 of a full-size ordinary vehicle. TORiCLE is equipped with a drive motor of rated power of 4.5 [kW], a lithium battery for accessories and 6 lead-acid batteries for driving. We use MicroAutoBox made by dSPACE inc., for the control unit. TORiCLE can drive automatically by controlling the steering motor and the drive motor.

Fig. 1. The Prototype UCEV "TORiCLE"

2.2 Spherical Camera

A spherical camera is installed on the top of TORiCLE. We used a 6 M pixel CCD image sensor with Fisheye Lens as a spherical camera. The angle of view is 250°, and the maximum frame rate is 60 fps. The spherical camera projects the incoming light onto the specific plane according to the equidistance angle projection. The reason why applying the spherical camera is that it can take the entire curve by one image and the projected image is similar to the projected light on the human retina.

3 Perception in the Cornering

3.1 Optical Flow in the Cornering

We had performed the relationship between optical flow and gaze movement in the cornering by simulation and actual driving [12]. The optical flow was radiated outward from the gaze position when the gaze position is fixed on the destination position while cornering. Theoretically, the optical flow is radiated outward from the end position of a curve when a vehicle runs on the constant radius of curvature. Thus, a skilled driver can control vehicle motion that the divergence point of the optical flow vectors corresponds with the gaze position. However, a beginner driver cannot stabilize the vehicle motion, so the divergence position of the optical flow vectors doesn't correspond with the gaze position. It is expected to reduce the feeling of strangeness by the vehicle control can be divergence point matching to the gaze position. Moreover, a driver might be easy to predict the vehicle trajectory. Therefore, the divergence point should be detected from the optical flow vector considering with the gaze movement.

3.2 Divergence Position Detection

Figure 2 shows a snapshot of the optical flow. Figure 2(a) shows the experimental environment. The running trajectory is the circumference of 10 [m] radius. We put pylons for making a driving course and for calculating optical flow as landmarks. In order to clarify the gaze position, a red board is installed at the end of the corner. We instruct a driver to watch the red board. The vehicle speed is controlled 10 [km/h] constantly. Figure 2(b) shows a snapshot of the spherical camera in driving. We have applied Horn-Schunck algorithm to acquire optical flow vectors [13]. The position of the red board is corresponding to the gaze target position when image processing. Figure 2(c) shows acquired optical flow at a place. The direction of optical flows is shown by colors to improve visualization. The angle of vector is corresponding to the color expressed in the color bar. For example, red color means an optical flow directed to the right. In Fig. 2(c), almost all flows are directed to the right. Figure 2(d) shows optical flows considering with gaze movement (hereafter OF-G). OF-G is calculated by the subtraction the vector value of gaze movement from each optical flow. The gaze movement is calculated by the average of vectors around the red board area. As a result, it is observed that optical flows trend in the various directions from the red board. By using these optical flows, we want to detect the divergence point as the reaching point if the current vehicle motion will be continued.

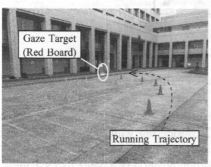

(a) Experimental Environment

(b) A Snapshot of the Spherical Camera

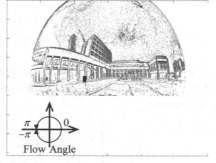

(c) Optical Flow without Gaze Movement

(d) Optical Flow with Gaze Movement

Fig. 2. A snap shot of optical flows (Color figure online)

3.3 Divergence Point Detection

Generally, divergence represents the outward of a vector field in the vector analysis. However, it is difficult to detect a divergence point by applying vector analysis, because the acquired OF-G includes blank area and noise by matching error. Therefore, we propose the divergence point detection method based on Particle Swarm Optimization (PSO).

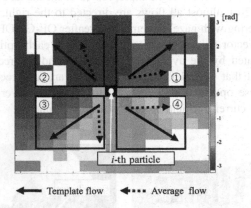

◄──── Template flow   ◄···· Average flow

Fig. 3. The template flow for the fitness function

PSO was developed by Kennedy and Eberhart in 1995, which was inspired by the behavior of bird flock [14]. We apply PSO considering with neighborhood particles [15, 16]. The first step of PSO is initialization that artificial particles are randomly placed. Each particle has four parameters: current position ($\mathbf{P}_i$), velocity ($\mathbf{V}_i$), these are represented as follows:

$$\begin{cases} \mathbf{P}_i \equiv (p_{i1}, \cdots, x_{in}, \cdots, x_{iN}) \\ \mathbf{V}_i \equiv (v_{i1}, \cdots, v_{in}, \cdots, v_{iN}) \end{cases} \tag{1}$$

where $i = 1, 2, \ldots, I$ is the number of particle and $n = 1, 2, \ldots, N$ is the number of variable. After initialization, the evaluation of each particle is calculated using the fitness function:

$$\begin{cases} F_m = \dfrac{\mathbf{F}_m^{temp} \cdot \mathbf{F}_m^{ave}}{\left\| \mathbf{F}_m^{temp} \right\| \left\| \mathbf{F}_m^{ave} \right\|} \\[2ex] T_{km} = -\left\| \dfrac{\mathbf{F}_k^{ave} \cdot \mathbf{F}_m^{ave}}{\left\| \mathbf{F}_k^{ave} \right\| \left\| \mathbf{F}_m^{ave} \right\|} \right\| \\[2ex] E_i = \sum_{j=1}^{4} F_j + (T_{14} + T_{23} + T_{12} + T_{34}) \end{cases} \tag{2}$$

where $\mathbf{F}_m^{temp}$ is the ideal flow vector hat radiates outward in the area with 0.7-by-0.7° neighborhood from the center of n-th particle position as shown in Fig. 3. The template makes 4 ideal flow by 4 divided areas in the neighborhood area. The ideal flow vector is directed outward from the i-th particle position. $\mathbf{F}_m^{ave}$ is the average of the flow vectors in each divided area. F_m is a similarity to radially outward which is calculated by cosine similarity in each divided area. m indicates the divided area corresponding to Fig. 3. Furthermore, the average flow vectors in the right and left divisions or top and bottom divisions are desired to be orthogonal direction, respectively. T_{nm} is calculated as the direction of flows between right and left division or top and bottom division. The evaluation value is a summation of F and T. If flow vectors in the neighborhood area at the i-th particle are similar to the ideal vector, the evaluation value has a large value. The best fitness value of all particles;

$$p^{gbest} = \arg \max_i \{E(\mathbf{P}_i)\} \tag{3}$$

Moreover, we apply the local best $\mathbf{P}_i^{lbest}$ that each particle has the best fitness value in its neighborhood.

$$\mathbf{P}_i^{lbest} \equiv \left(p_{i1}^{lbest}, \cdots, p_{in}^{lbest}, \cdots p_{iN}^{lbest}\right) \tag{4}$$

Next, v_i and p_i are updated to the following;

$$\begin{cases} v_{in}(t+1) = wv_{in}(t) + c_1 p_{in}^{cur} + c_2 \mathrm{rand}(\bullet)(p_{in}^{lbest} - p_{in}(t)) + c_3 \mathrm{Rand}(\bullet)(p^{gbest} - p_{in}(t)) \\ p_{in}(t+1) = p_{in}(t) + v_{in}(t+1) \end{cases} \tag{5}$$

where p_{in}^{cur} is the reverses flow vector of the i-th particle. The role of this term is the search to gradient direction. c_1, c_2 and c_3 are acceleration coefficient. $\mathrm{Rand}(\bullet)$ and rand $(\bullet)$ are randomly number from 0 to 1.0.

4 Experiment

This section verifies the proposed divergence detection method using real data by experiment. In this experiment, we use the real driving movie discussed in Sect. 3.2. As the setting of PSO, the number of particles is 150 and c_1, c_2 and c_3 are 6.0, 0.5 and 0.7, respectively.

Figure 4 shows the experimental result of each step of PSO. Black dots express the position of a particle that has the top 20% fitness value of all particles. As a first step, particles are distributed evenly across by the initialization process (see Fig. 4(a)). After, particles came closer step by step to around the red board (see Fig. 4(b)–(d)). After 40 steps, particles have converged on around the red board. Generally, the proposed method might have multiple divergence points as local minima according to PSO algorithm. However, this result is satisfied that particles converge only a point. Therefore, the acquired optical flow vectors have a trend outward from a specific point. And, the proposed divergence detection method can detect a divergence point, even if the acquired optical flow included blank area and noise.

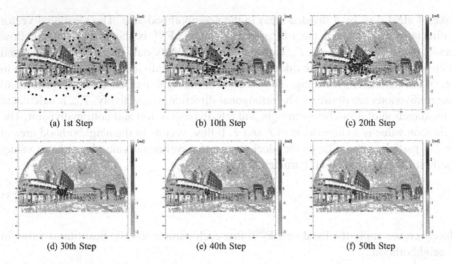

(a) 1st Step   (b) 10th Step   (c) 20th Step

(d) 30th Step   (e) 40th Step   (f) 50th Step

Fig. 4. Experimental result of PSO for detecting the divergence of optical flows (Color figure online)

On the other hand, the convergence point by PSO is a little bit different to the red board position. Figure 5 shows the expand figure that is expanded around the red board area of Fig. 4(f). The distance from the red board position and the center of a particle group has about 20° by solid angle. The supposable reasons are low accuracy of optical flow vectors and also the gaze movement vector. Moreover, it has a negative effect by vehicle vibration. Generally, a vision of human is divided into foveal vision and peripheral vision. The foveal area is about 10° from the gaze center. Therefore, we will improve the proposed method to realize the accuracy of the divergence point detection less 10°. Especially, we want to reduce noise and false detection in the optical flow calculation. After that, we will consider improving the proposed divergence point detection method.

Fig. 5. The expanded figure around the red board (Color figure online)

5 Conclusion

In this paper, we focus on the relationship between a gaze direction and an optical flow in a cornering behavior. Especially, we propose the detection method of the divergence point of the optical flow vectors to express the perception of cornering quality.

Our previous research expresses the optical flow radiates outward from the gaze center using the movie of the real vehicle. However, it is difficult to detect a divergence point by applying vector analysis, because the acquired OF-G includes blank area and noise by matching error. Therefore, we propose the divergence point detection method based on particle swarm optimization. For verifying the proposed method, we performed the experiment using real driving movie. For the result, the proposed divergence detection method could detect a divergence point, even if the acquired optical flow included blank area and noise. However, the convergence point by PSO was a little bit different to the red board position as the gaze position. The supposable reasons are low accuracy of optical flow vectors and also the gaze movement vector. We will improve the proposed method to realize the accuracy less than 10° according to a mechanism of human visual perception.

References

1. McCall, J.C., Trivedi, M.M.: Video-based on lane estimation and tracking for driver assistance: survey, system, and evaluation. IEEE Trans. Intell. Transp. Syst. 7(1), 20–37 (2006)
2. Fletcher, H., Petersson, L., Zelinsky, A.: Driver assistance systems based on vision in and out of vehicles. In: Proceedings of the IEEE Symposium on Intelligent Vehicles, pp. 322–327 (2003)
3. Van Der Horst, R., Hogema, J.: Time-to-collision and collision avoidance systems, pp. 129–143 (1993)
4. Moon, S., Yi, K.: Human driving data-based design of a vehicle adaptive cruise control algorithm. Veh. Syst. Dyn. 46(8), 661–690 (2008). International Journal of Vehicle Mechanics and Mobility
5. Nakayasu, H., Miyoshi, T., Kondo, N., Aoki, H., Patterson, P.: Analysis of driver perceptions and behavior when driving in an unfamiliar traffic regulation. J. Adv. Comput. Intell. Intell. Inf. 15(8), 1039–1048 (2011)
6. Kishida, E., Uenuma, K., Iwao, K., Matsuzaki, N.: A study on a device for controlling visual information to improve driver performance. SAE Technical paper 2009-01-0548. (2009) https://doi.org/10.4271/2009-01-0548
7. Okafuji, Y., Fukao, T., Inou, H.: Development of automatic steering system by modeling human behavior based on optical flow. J. Robot. Mechatron. 27(2), 136–145 (2015)
8. Giachetti, A., Campani, M., Torre, V.: The use of optical flow for road navigation. IEEE Trans. Robot. Autom. 14–1, 34–48 (1998)
9. Romuald, A., Gowdy, J., Mertz, C., Thorpe, C., Wang, C.C., Yata, T.: Perception for collision avoidance and autonomous driving. Mechatronics 13–10, 1149–1161 (2003)
10. Souhila, K., Karim, A.: Optical flow based robot obstacle avoidance. Int. J. Adv. Rob. Syst. 4–1, 13–16 (2007)
11. Ministry of Land: Infrastructure, Transport and Tourism: white paper on land, infrastructure, transport and tourism in Japan (2016)

12. Masuta, H., et al.: Spherical Optical flow in automatically controlled vehicle while cornering. In: Proceedings of the 2018 IEEE Symposium Series on Computational Intelligence (SSCI 2018), pp. 1614–1619 (2018)
13. Horn, B.K.P., Schunck, B.G.: Determining optical flow. Artif. Intell. **17**, 185–203 (1981)
14. Kennedy, J., Eberhart, R.C.: Particle swarm optimization. In Proceedings of the 1995 IEEE International Conference on Neural Networks, vol. 4, pp. 1942–1948 (1995)
15. Matsushita, H., Nishio, Y., Tse, C.K.: Network-structured particle swarm optimizer that considers neighborhood distances and behaviors. J. Signal Process. **18**(6), 291–302 (2014)
16. Lane, J., Engelbrecht, A., Gain, J.: Particle warm optimization with spatially meaningful neighbours. In: Proceedings of IEEE Swarm Intelligence Symposium, pp. 1–8 (2008)

Automatic Fiber Detection and Focus System from Image Frames

Wei Quan[⊠], Haibing Zhang[⊠], and Naoyuki Kubota[⊠]

Graduate School of System Design, Tokyo Metropolitan University,
6-6 Asahigaoka, Hino, Tokyo 191-0065, Japan
{quan-wei1,zhang-haibing}@ed.tmu.ac.jp, kubota@tmu.ac.jp

Abstract. With technology accelerating dramatically, human has become able to generate automated equipment for dealing with complex situations. At the same time, image processing has also been applied into lots of fields. This paper proposed a framework that providing an automatic fiber detection and focusing system, and the result shows that it performs a good accuracy and cost a low computation at the same time.

Keywords: Automation system · Image processing · Fiber detection

1 Introduction

With new technology accelerating dramatically, human has become able to generate automated equipment for dealing with complex situations. Automation usually implies that a system includes, or will include, equipment assumed to enhance man's capability to accomplish a required function [1,7].

Automation has been achieved by various solutions including mechanical, hydraulic, pneumatic, electrical, electronic devices and computers, and in combination in most of cases.

At the same time, image processing has been used in lots of fields such as bank surveillance and pedestrian tracking [3,4]. Image processing system which using static sensors has already been used in the area of static situation such as plaza mall, ATM, etc. [8,9]. It is also widely applied into automation system for industry.

In fiber manufacturing, it is necessary to connect several short fibers in order to create a longer fiber. In this case, the accuracy of connection would affect the quality of generated fiber because of that better connection lose less light due to reflection or misalignment of the fibers. However, this task is mainly depending on person's observation and operation currently. This would increase both cost of human resources and error rate. Therefore the introduction of automation system would be necessary and significant.

In this paper, we focus on solving this fiber connection problems by generating an image processing based fiber detection and focusing framework. The paper is organized as follows: Sect. 2 give a brief related work, and Sect. 3 explains the detail of proposed framework. Section 4 shows the experiment result and the last section give the conclusion and future extension of the proposed method.

© Springer Nature Switzerland AG 2019
H. Yu et al. (Eds.): ICIRA 2019, LNAI 11742, pp. 101–108, 2019.
https://doi.org/10.1007/978-3-030-27535-8_10

2   Related Work

The concept of automation system appeared in the around 50s of the previous century. The demand of automation system for industry kept rising while the development of industry. The ability of automation system has increasing dramatically since the development of technology for image processing.

In [5], the authors proposed an automation car license plate recognition system that solves the practical problem of car identification for real scenes. This system recognize license plate by capturing images, and it has already been used in all of country rules and different kinds of situations.

In [6], the authors utilized image processing system for kinematic analysis of human gait. They regarded it as a feature based multi-target tracking problem, and track the artificially induced features appearing in the image sequence due to the non-impeding contrast markers attached at different anatomical landmarks of the subject under analysis.

In this paper, we focus on image based fiber detection and focusing system from image frames.

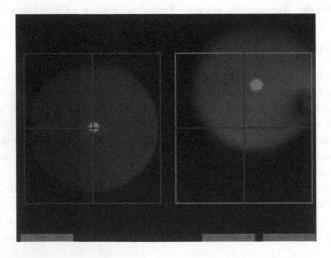

Fig. 1. Appearance of system screen. (Color figure online)

3   Framework Description

The appearance of image frames that we need to handle is shown in Fig. 1. Generally there are at most two fibers and they are located in any positions of the image. The rectangles with blue and red lines are the display of fiber movement control system, which shows the direction of fiber movement.

The aim of this system is to control the movement of fibers in order to make sure these two fibers are in the center of rectangles respectively, and also proper distances between fibers to cameras to make sure two fibers at the position with the highest intelligibility. Therefore it is necessary to evaluate the position and intelligibility of the fibers, and connect the two fibers by controlling their movement including focusing. The processing flow of framework is shown in Fig. 2.

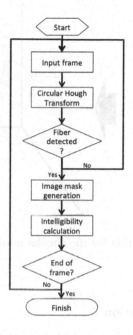

Fig. 2. Processing flow for the proposed method.

3.1 Circular Hough Transform for Fiber Localization

In most cases, the shape of cross section of a fiber is similar to a circle, therefore we utilize circular Hough transform for the first step of locating fibers in images. For each point, i.e. pixel in the image, (x, y) that constructing the edge of the circle, it follows like

$$(x - a)^2 + (y - b)^2 = r^2 \tag{1}$$

where a and b are the coordinates of center of circle, and r is the radius of circle. Then it is possible to transform it to

$$x = a + r * cos(\theta) \tag{2}$$

$$y = b + r * sin(\theta) \tag{3}$$

where θ are the parameters with a range of $[0, 2\pi]$. By this transformation, for each point (x, y), there will be a correspondent Conical space in the corresponding coordinate space. The point (a_0, b_0, c_0) that the cross of these cones would be the target circle. The illustration is shown in Fig. 3.

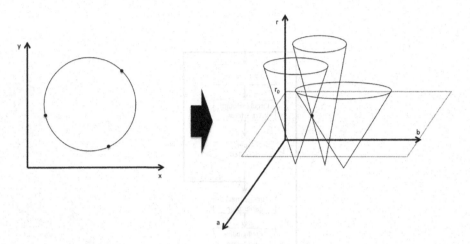

Fig. 3. Illustration for the circular hough transform.

3.2   Intelligibility Evaluation

The location of fibers in image provide information for controlling movement whereas the intelligibility provides the instructions for moving forward or moving backward. Because of the truth that the intelligibility of image is largely depending on the sharpness of edges, we first calculate the gradient on horizontal and vertical directions separately by Sobel operator:

$$S_x = \begin{bmatrix} -1 & 0 & 1 \\ -2 & 0 & 2 \\ -1 & 0 & 1 \end{bmatrix}, S_y = \begin{bmatrix} -1 & -2 & -1 \\ 0 & 0 & 0 \\ 1 & 2 & 1 \end{bmatrix} \tag{4}$$

Then we calculate the general gradient value for each pixel of image by

$$S(i,j) = \sqrt{S_x(x,y)^2 + S_y(x,y)^2} \tag{5}$$

On the other hand, it is obvious that their is also much noise such as light spot in the circle, and we also considering that there are several blue and red lines in the screen and would affect the evaluation, we introduce image mask for solving these issues. The mask image is a binary image, which means that the referent pixel in Sobel image would be calculated if $M(i,j) = 1$, and would be 0 otherwise. This mask just removes the unnecessary banner, and make the calculate circle only.

The intelligibility value of image would be calculated as:

$$I = \frac{\sum S(i,j) * M(i,j)}{N} \tag{6}$$

where $N = \sum M(i,j)$, which means the total number of non-zero pixels in image mask.

4 Low Pass Filter

The aim of this system gives the instruction for the movement of fibers, therefore it is necessary to provide a continuous and stable output for intelligibility in order to give the clear instruction for the fiber controlling. However, in real case, the output is always unstable because of the unpredictable noise. Based on this truth, we utilize low pass filter for converting signals in order to give more stable output.

Low pass filters exist in many different forms, including electronic circuits such as a hiss filter used in audio, anti-aliasing filters for conditioning signals prior to analog-to-digital conversion, digital filters for smoothing sets of data, acoustic barriers, blurring of images, and so on. In this paper, we applied it to smooth the continuous output of intelligibility of fibers.

Generally in discrete signal processing, low pass filter satisfies:

$$\hat{I(t)} = \alpha I(t) + (1 - \alpha)I(t - 1) \tag{7}$$

In order to make sure the graph is as smooth as we need, we extend it to

$$\hat{I(t)} = a_1 I(t) + a_2 I(t - 1) \ldots + a_k I(t - k + 1) \tag{8}$$

where $a_1 + a_2 + \ldots + a_k = 1$.

5 Experiment Result

In order to prove the performance of proposed framework, we applied it with videos for different cases. We take experiment for several steps. First we test the accuracy of circular detection. Figure 4 shows four typical situation: in the figure of upper left, there is only one fiber that can be detected, and there are two separated fibers, and the lower left shows the situation that only part of one fiber is shown in the screen, and lower right shows the situation with overlapping.

The result shows that fibers have been detected correctly with situation above. It need to be mentioned that only the situation that part of fiber overlapped or disappeared can be detected.

For the next step, we test the generation of mask image for each fiber, and examined the calculation of intelligibility, the performance is shown in Fig. 5.

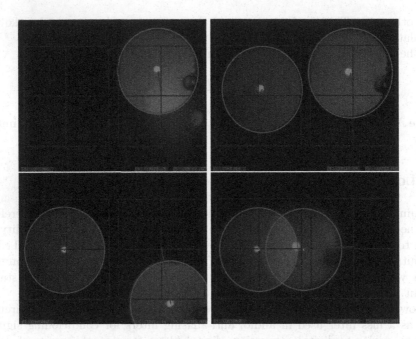

Fig. 4. Experiment result of fiber detection in several typical situation. (Color figure online)

Fig. 5. Experiment result of mask generation and Sobel operation

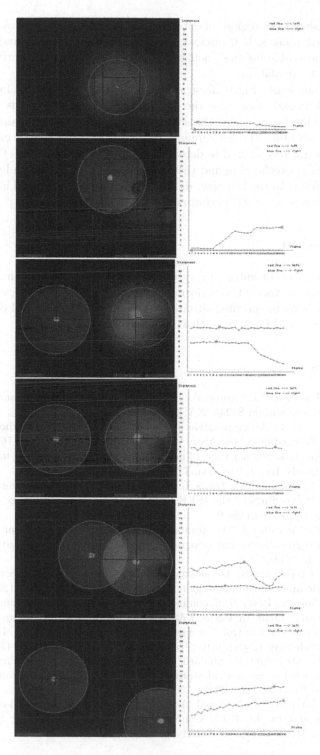

Fig. 6. Experiment result of intelligibility calculation.

The first row shows the regions of detected fibers, whereas second rows shows the generated mask images. It is obvious that the lines are removed and only edges of circles are available for the calculation. Third rows gives the performances of image gradient calculation.

Last but not least, Fig. 6 illustrates the result of continuous intelligibility. The first and second rows show the situation that one fiber tends to be clear, and third and forth rows show the situation that one keeps unchanged whereas another becomes blur. The performance of third row shows a little error because that the circle are too blurred to detect the edge. Fifth rows shows the situation that two fibers is overlapping and the intelligibility of left one is a little affected by right-side fiber. In the last row, right-side fiber partly appeared in the screen, but the result shows a good performance in this case.

6   Conclusion

This paper propose an automatic system for localizing and focusing the fibers. The experiment shows that it performs well under the low cost. However, it still has some problems in specified situations such as overlapping and occlusion. In the future, we would focus on such kind of issues.

References

1. Smith, D., Dieterly, D.L.: Automation literature: a brief review and analysis. NASA Technical Memorandum 81245, NASA:NASA (1980)
2. Yuen, H.K., et al.: A comparative study of Hough transform methods for circle finding. In: Proceedings of the Alvey Vision Conference, ALVEY, pp. 169–174 (1989)
3. Wang, J.: Analogue winner-take-all neural networks for determining maximum and minimum signals. Int. J. Electron. **77**(3), 355–367 (1994)
4. Haritaoglu, I., Harwood, D., Davis, L.: A real time system for detecting and tracking people. In: Proceedings of the IEEE Conference on Automatic Face and Gesture Recognition, pp. 15–64 (1999)
5. Conci, A., de Carvalho, J.E.R., Rauber, T.W.: A complete system for vehicle plate localization segmentation and recognition in real life scene. IEEE Lat. Am. Trans. **7**(5), 497–506 (2009)
6. Yeasin, M., Chaudhuri, S.: Development of an automated image processing system for kinematic analysis of human gait. Real-Time Imag. **6**(1), 55–67 (2000)
7. Abras, S., Ploix, S., Pesty, S., Jacomino, M.: A multi-agent home automation system for power management. In: Cetto, J.A., Ferrier, J.L., Costa dias Pereira, J., Filipe, J. (eds.) Informatics in Control Automation and Robotics. LNEE, vol. 15, pp. 59–68. Springer, Heidelberg (2008). https://doi.org/10.1007/978-3-540-79142-3_6
8. Foresti, G.L., Micheloni, C., Snidaro, L., et al.: Active video-based surveillance system: the low-level image and video processing techniques needed for implementation. IEEE Signal Process. Mag. **22**(2), 25–37 (2005)
9. Lim, S.N., Davis, L.S., Elgammal, A.: A scalable image-based multi-camera visual surveillance system. In: IEEE Conference on Advanced Video & Signal Based Surveillance. IEEE Computer Society (2003)

Lifelog Generation Based on Informationally Structured Space

Dalai Tang[1(✉)] and Naoyuki Kubota[2]

[1] College of Computer Information Management, Inner Mongolia University
of Finance and Economics, Inner Mongolia, China
tdl@imufe.edu.cn
[2] Graduate School of System Design, Tokyo Metropolitan University,
Tokyo, Japan
kubota@tmu.ac.jp

Abstract. As the problem of the increased number of elderly people and the
decreased number of children in Japan has arisen recently, the development of
robot partner and intelligent room for monitoring and measurement system has
become a main topic. On the other hand, the stability of both social rhythm and
biological rhythm is very important for extension of healthy life expectancy. It is
difficult for elderly people to understand the current stability of social rhythm
and biological rhythm in daily life. First of all, we have to generate detail lifelog.
We define lifelog composed of daily human behavior. In this paper, first, we
show different types of classification methods for human activity. We explain
our computation model for elderly care. Next, we introduce several human
behavior measurement methods for lifelog. And we show lifelog generation in
indoor, outdoor and by using robot partner. Finally, we discuss the effectiveness
of the proposed methods and future works.

Keywords: Lifelog · Informationally Structured Space ·
Human behavior estimation · Computation model

1 Introduction

Along with the increasing number of elderly people, one must note that the number of
those elderly people who are no longer able to look after themselves will also increase
proportionally. For instance, many of them will lose the ability to live independently
because of limited mobility, frailty or other physical or mental health problems [1, 2].
In Japan, the increasing number of elderly people who live alone or independently has
required a large forms of nursing care to support them. However, since the number of
caregivers is always limited, it is important to introduce another solution to tackle this
problem. One of the solutions is the introduction of the human-friendly robot partner
and intelligent room to support the elderly people in their daily life.

In the recent years, health care support system [3–5] based on application mainly
for disease management, health and wellness management, and aging independently
has developed rapidly (Fig. 1). This condition is also affected by the result of cooperation between companies on the integration of the digitalization of health and medical

© Springer Nature Switzerland AG 2019
H. Yu et al. (Eds.): ICIRA 2019, LNAI 11742, pp. 109–116, 2019.
https://doi.org/10.1007/978-3-030-27535-8_11

equipment. Now, we can acquire various information, starting from low dimensional measurement sensor data until high dimensional data to produce lifelog data. However, by recent technology, it is shown that we only can acquire data, but it is also not less important that the foundation system which connects the measurement system until support system foundation is also needed. In order to realize this, the fusion between robot technology, smart home, information technology and network technology is very important.

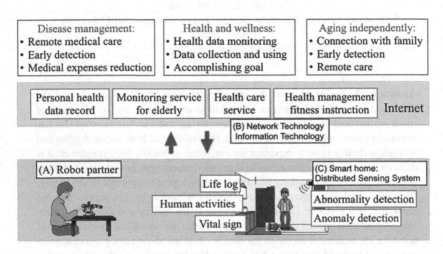

Fig. 1. Health care for elderly

Information and communication technology is one of the promising approaches to extend healthy life expectancy of elderly people. Steve Jobs explained that a Mac, in a short time, could serve as the Digital Hub that unites those disparate points in our digital life (2001). Based on the concept of Digital Hub, we proposed the concept of Life Hub that unites a person with physical and virtual information in addition to real world, e.g., people, communities, events, places, goods, environmental data, other robots, Internet information, and personal information (Fig. 2) [6, 7]. Based on Life Hub, people are able to interact with life environment by conversional interfaces [8]. Furthermore, the environment system can use Internet of Things (IoT) and Ambient Assisted Living (AAL) technologies to actively support people [9, 10]. A wireless sensor network system can measure the number of people, human motions and behaviors as well as environmental state surrounding people. Furthermore, robot partners can ask elderly people about their daily activities through verbal communication. However, we have to deal with huge size of measurement data gathered from different types of sensors simultaneously. Therefore, the environment surrounding people and robots should have a structured platform for gathering, storing, transforming, and providing information. Such an environment is called Informationally Structured Space (ISS) [11, 12].

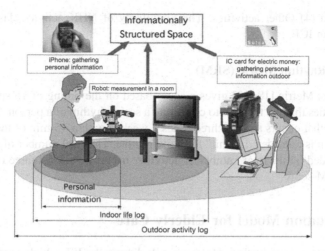

Fig. 2. The concept of Life Hub

2 Activity Classification for Lifelog

Various types of activity classification methods have been proposed until now [13]. Szalai conducted a multinational comparative time budget project in mid 1960s. The project used a two-digit coding system composed of 96 activity categories. In this section, we discuss human behaviors for lifelog. We select activity classification by NHK, because the granularity is much less than ICF.

2.1 International Classification of Functioning, Disability, and Health (ICF)

International Classification of Functioning, Disability, and Health is useful to evaluate human body functions, structures, and disability, while taking into account both environmental factors and personal factors. The advantage of ICF is in the hierarchical structure of coding [14, 15]. In ICF, a person's health and health-related states are given in an array of codes that encompass the two parts of the classification. Thus the maximum number of codes per person can be 34 at the one-digit level (8 body functions, 8 body structures, 9 performance and 9 capacity codes).

2.2 Activity Classification by NHK

NHK (Nippon Hoso Kyokai) has conducted Japanese Time Use Survey aimed at youths and adults aged 10 and older every five years since 1960 [16, 17]. Three-layers of categorization is used for the survey by NHK; classification, sub-classification, and minor classification. The classification is categorized to (1) Necessary activities (sleep, meals, personal chores etc.), (2) Obligatory activities (work, schoolwork, housework, commutation, etc.), (3) Free-time activities (leisure activities, conversation, mass media use, etc.), and (4) Other activities. The granularity of NHK activity classification is much less than ICF.

2.3   Social Rhythm Metric (SRM)

Social Rhythm Metric [18, 19] gives a score based on the timing of 15 specific and 2 built-in activities that are thought to constitute a social rhythm of a person. If the timing of an activity that occurs at least three times a week is within 45 min of the average or habitual time it is considered a "hit" for daily routine. The total number of hits of these activities divided by the total number of activities occurring at least three times a week gives the SRM-score.

3   Computation Model for Elderly Care

We explain ISS in introduction. Here, we will discuss the ISS which consists of three layers: (1) sensing layer, (2) feature extraction layer, and (3) monitoring layer (Fig. 3). In sensing layer, each sensor node measures human and environmental states while changing its sampling interval. (2) In feature extraction layer, human behavior estimation is conducted according to sensing data from the sensor node and robot. (3) In monitoring layer, spatiotemporal changing patterns are extracted from time-series of behaviors. This layer also generates individual daily life model and detects sensor failure as well as human anomaly life pattern. Additionally, the monitoring layer is able to control sampling interval of sensor node according to the change of the environmental condition.

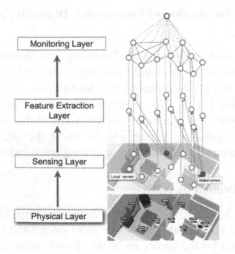

Fig. 3. Computation model for elderly care

4   Lifelog Generation

Base on computation model in session 3, we introduce several human behavior measurement method for lifelog. And we show lifelog generation in indoor, outdoor and by using robot partner.

4.1   Indoor Lifelog Generation by Distributed Sensing System

Many approaches have been proposed for human behavior modeling so far, for example Hidden Markov Model, Bayesian methods, Support Vector Machines and neural networks are widely applied [20–22]. However, they require supervised training data, they cannot handle the unknown states well. In my previous work, spiking neural network was applied to localize human, object and sensor device according to local and global sensor specification [12]. The important feature of spiking neural networks is the capability of temporal coding and resistance to noise [23]. In order to reduce the computational cost, a simple spike response model is used. Figure 4 shows simulation result for human behavior on iPad. Blue line and orange line are human tracks. Here, we use Kinect sensor to measure human position. Red circle defines the local measurement sensor position. When the local sensor is fired, we can use human position to localize the sensor position. we can also localize the sensor installed on the furniture and consumer electronics. Through this simulation, we can understand the spatial-temporal pattern of the human behavior [24, 26].

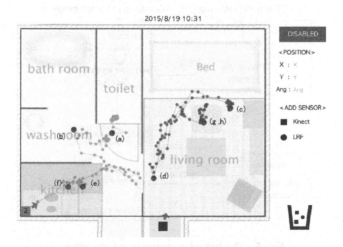

Fig. 4. Simulation result for human behavior

4.2   Outdoor Lifelog Generation by Smart Device

In outdoor measurement, different with indoor measurement, smart watch, smart band, and smart phone are used as sensor devices. However, one issue is the trade-off between energy consumption and measurement accuracy. In outdoor measurement, we also integrate two types of measurement; the global measurement (GPS) and local measurement (Accelerometer). This research estimates the smartphone state by consider the trade-off between energy consumption and measurement accuracy. Thus, we combine the global and local measurement to estimate human transport modes [25].

4.3   Lifelog Generation by Robot Partner

It is enable to measure the human behavior in both indoor and outdoor environments flexibly. However, it is difficult to estimate complex human activity by the proposed methods. We propose a method of complementarily using behavior information measured by the distributed sensing system and behavior information estimated by the robot partner in the feature extraction layer. The measurement components consist of device control, human activity estimation, and environment state estimation. Here, we propose to conduct the human activity estimation as a subcomponent. Figure 5 shows the behavior measurement algorithm for the fusion of distributed sensor system and robot partner system. In this algorithm there are some conditions that should be fulfilled such as unknown and sit on chair activity, then the robot partner will start to do active measurement. An example of scenario conversation (human sits on the chair) is show in Table 1. This example shows (Figs. 6 and 7) the conversation between robot partner and human, where the human actions were previously registered and the questions are made according to these. After the robot partner checked the human answer, the action is registered into the database.

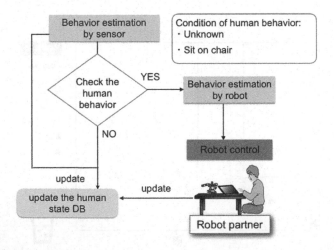

Fig. 5. The behavior measurement algorithm

Fig. 6. Snapshot of behavior estimation by robot partner

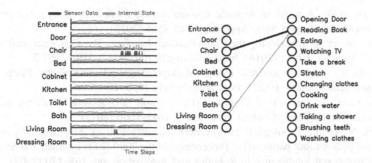

Fig. 7. An experimental result of behavior estimation by robot partner

Table 1. Conversation contents example for active measurement.

Robot partner:	(Question) What are you doing?
Human:	Reading book
Robot partner:	(Checking) Are you reading book?
Human:	Yes
Robot partner:	(Finished checking, DB registration) Understood

5 Conclusions

In this paper, we proposed a lifelog generation based on informationally structured space. First we showed different types of classification methods for human activity. We explained our computation model for elderly care. Next, we introduced several human behavior measurement method for lifelog. And we showed lifelog generation in indoor, outdoor and by using robot partner. As a future work, we intend to conduct experiments of the proposed method to elderly people.

References

1. Chernbumroong, S., et al.: Elderly activities recognition and classification for applications in assisted living. Expert Syst. Appl. **40**(5), 1662–1674 (2013)
2. Rueangsirarak, W., et al.: Fall-risk screening system framework for physiotherapy care of elderly. Expert Syst. Appl. **39**(10), 8859–8864 (2012)
3. Acampora, G., et al.: A survey on ambient intelligence in healthcare. Proc. IEEE **101**(12), 2470–2494 (2013)
4. Continua Health Alliance: Continua health alliance (2015). http://www.continua.jp/
5. Pantelopoulos, A., et al.: A survey on wearable sensor-based systems for health monitoring and prognosis. IEEE Trans. Syst. Man Cybern. Part C (Appl. Rev.) **10**(1), 1–12 (2010)
6. Tang, D., et al.: Informationally structured space for community-centric systems. In: Proceedings of the 2nd International Conference on Universal Village, UV 2014, Boston, USA (2014)

7. Tang, D., et al.: A novel multimodal communication framework using robot partner for aging population. Expert Syst. Appl. **42**, 4540–4555 (2015)
8. McTear, M., et al.: Introducing the Conversational Interface. The Conversational Interface, pp. 1–7. Springer, Cham (2016). https://doi.org/10.1007/978-3-319-32967-3
9. Georgieff, P.: Ambient assisted living. Marktpotenziale IT-unterstützter Pflege für ein selbstbestimmtes Altern, FAZIT Forschungsbericht **17**, 9–10 (2008)
10. Gubbi, J., et al.: Internet of Things (IoT): a vision, architectural elements, and future directions. Future Gener. Comput. Syst. **29**(7), 1645–1660 (2013)
11. Kubota, N., et al.: Topological environment reconstruction in informationally structured space for pocket robot partners. In: Proceedings of the 2009 IEEE International Symposium on Computational Intelligence in Robotics and Automation, pp. 165–170 (2009)
12. Kubota, N., et al.: Localization of human based on fuzzy spiking neural network in informationally structured space. In: Proceedings of the IEEE World Congress on Computational Intelligence, Spain, pp. 2209–2214 (2010)
13. Szalai, A., et al.: The Use of Time: Daily Activities of Urban and Suburban Populations in Twelve Countries. Mouton, The Hague (1972)
14. Gabriele, B., et al.: Outcome measures in older persons with acquired joint contractures: a systematic review and content analysis using the ICF (International Classification of Functioning, Disability and Health) as a reference. BMC Geriatr. **16**(1), 40 (2016)
15. Gabriele, B., et al.: Development of an International Classification of Functioning, Disability and Health (ICF)-based standard set to describe the impact of joint contractures on participation of older individuals in geriatric care settings. Arch. Gerontol. Geriatr. **61**(1), 61–66 (2015)
16. Kobayashi, T., et al.: National survey on schedule of a daily life in Japan. NHK Mon. Rep. Broadcast Res. 2–21 (2011)
17. Kobayashi, T., et al.: Sleeping time keeps decreasing, male housework time is increasing. From the 2010 NHK Japanese Time Use Survey (2010). https://www.nhk.or.jp/bunken/english/reports/pdf/report_110401.pdf
18. Alloy, L.B., et al.: Low social rhythm regularity predicts first onset of bipolar spectrum disorders among at-risk individuals with reward hypersensitivity. J. Abnorm. Psychol. **24**(4), 944–952 (2015)
19. Margraf, J., et al.: Social rhythm and mental health: a cross-cultural comparison. PloS one **11**(3), e0150312 (2016)
20. Candas, J.L.C., et al.: An automatic data mining method to detect abnormal human behavior using physical activity measurements. Pervasive Mob. Comput. **15**, 228–241 (2014)
21. Fang, H., He, L., Si, H., et al.: Human activity recognition based on feature selection in smart home using back-propagation algorithm. ISA Trans. **53**(5), 1629–1638 (2014)
22. Afsar, P., Cortez, P., Santos, H.: Automatic visual detection of human behavior: a review from 2000 to 2014. Expert Syst. Appl. **42**(20), 6935–6956 (2015)
23. Maass, W., Bishop, C.M.: Pulsed Neural Networks. MIT Press, Cambridge (1999)
24. Dalai, T., et al.: Social rhythm management support system based on informationally structured space. In: International Conference on Human System Interactions. IEEE (2016)
25. Dalai, T., János, B., Naoyuki, K.: Supervised learning based multi-modal perception for robot partners using smart phones. Acta Polytechnica Hungarica Journal of Applied Sciences **11**(8), 139–159 (2014)
26. Shuai, S., et al.: A fuzzy spiking neural network for behavior estimation by multiple environmental sensors. In: IEEE International Conference on Systems, Man, and Cybernetics, SMC 2018, Japan, TuAM-R05 (2018)

Continuum Mechanisms and Robots

A Soft Robotic Glove for Hand Rehabilitation Using Pneumatic Actuators with Variable Stiffness

Yiquan Guo[1,2] , Fengyu Xu[1,2(✉)] , Yurong Song[1,2] ,
Xudong Cao[1,2] , and Fanchang Meng[1,2]

[1] College of Automation and College of Artificial Intelligence,
Nanjing University of Posts and Telecommunications, Nanjing 210023, China
xufengyu598@163.com
[2] Jiangsu Engineering Lab for IOT Intelligent Robots (IOTRobot),
Nanjing 210023, China

Abstract. Traditional rigid robots exist many problems in rehabilitation training. Soft robotics is conducive to breaking the limitations of rigid robots. This paper presents a soft wearable device for the rehabilitation of hands, including soft pneumatic actuators that are embedded in the device for motion assistance. The key feature of this design is the stiffness of each actuator at different positions is different, which results in the bending posture of the actuator is more accordant with the bending figure of human hand. In addition, another key point is the use of a fabric sleeves allow actuators to gain greater bending force when pressurized, which gives the hand greater bending force. We verified the feasibility of actuator through simulation, the performance of soft actuator and the device also are evaluated through experiments. Finally, the results show that this device can finish some of the hand rehabilitation tasks.

Keywords: Rehabilitation training · Soft robot · Pneumatic actuator

1 Introduction

Traditional rehabilitation robots are mostly composed of rigid components such as linear brakes, rigid links and motors [1], such as iPAM [2], MIME [3, 4], MAHI EXO II [5]. They are bulky, heavy, uneasy to operate and uncomfortable to wear. The main body of soft rehabilitation robot is fabric gloves that exists widespread in our daily life, which makes the device in a high flexibility, a good adaptability and a high safety.

Harvard University Galloway [6] developed a soft robotic rehabilitation glove. Five soft fiber reinforced actuators are integrated in the back side of the glove, which can significantly limit radial expansion but requires a large driving force. A simple, easy-to-control soft robotic glove developed by the National University of Singapore Yap [1] research team. Researchers bonded the two plastic sheets together by mechanical pressing to form a gas-tight actuator. The design is simple and in a low cost, but the function is relatively simple, because it can only straighten the patient's contracted hand. This team developed a glove called MRC whose actuators have a corrugated

© Springer Nature Switzerland AG 2019
H. Yu et al. (Eds.): ICIRA 2019, LNAI 11742, pp. 119–129, 2019.
https://doi.org/10.1007/978-3-030-27535-8_12

outer layer, which enhances its bending ability [7], but its bending characteristic is different to hand bending characteristic. In addition, the team also designed a soft robotic glove with variable stiffness, which can adjust the stiffness of the actuator in different positions according to patients' hands [8], but uneven expansion of actuators exists in rehabilitation training. This team also developed a fully fabric glove that eliminates the need for a built-in air cavity. This device can bend and stretch hands but requires a strict fabrication process. Additionally, PneuNets actuators [10], fiber-reinforced actuators [11], fabric-enhanced actuators [12] and have been used for rehabilitation training. The results indicate that these actuators can actuate fingers. However, the curved motion profile of these actuators presents a circular configuration during actuation that does not conform to a normal human hand bending posture (Fig. 2).

This article presents a soft robotic glove for hand rehabilitation training. The main body of this device consists of a fabric glove and soft actuators. The key feature of the device is that a stiffness gradient method is used in each actuator their structural design, and it can also be customized according to the size of the human finger bones. Besides, the variable stiffness of actuators after pressurization can be achieved by the fabric sleeve, which helps patients to finish hand bending action and grasping task of some objects.

2 Soft Pneumatic Actuator

2.1 Design and Analysis of Soft Actuator

Design Principle of the Soft Actuator. In order to facilitate analysis, the cross-sectional (inner wall and air cavity) of actuator is selected. Before pressurization, the internal pressure as same as the external atmospheric pressure, and the pressure in air chamber in this state is indicated by P1. The strain restraining layer of soft actuator is represented by a line segment (Fig. 2). After pressurization, the air pressure (P2) satisfies the following relationship: P2 > P1. The inner wall of air chamber is squeezed at this time, because the material hardness of the l strain restraining layer (E2) is greater than the hardness of the silicone (E1). It can be satisfied as the following inequality: E2 > E1. strain restraining layer limits the elongation of bottom surface of actuator, which makes actuator bend [13]. The states of air cavity before and after pressurization are shown in Fig. 1 [14].

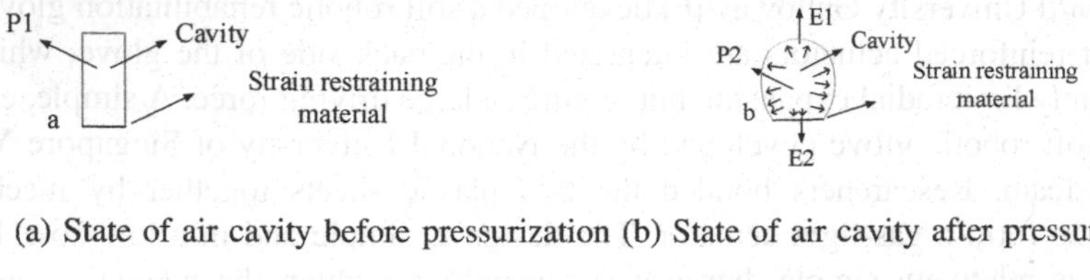

Fig. 1. (a) State of air cavity before pressurization (b) State of air cavity after pressurization

Modeling of Soft Actuator. The normal fingers except thumb are composed of three parts: Distal Phalange (DP), Middle Phalanx (MP) and Proximal Phalanx (PP). Specifically, the thumb consists of DP and PP. Figure 2 shows the posture of normal human fingers when bending. The black line in the figure depicts the curved trajectory of four fingers except thumb.

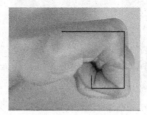

Fig. 2. The bending posture of fingers

The intended purpose of this design is to achieve the desired bending posture of the hand (Fig. 2). So, we propose a new type of soft actuator in which the region of higher stiffness corresponds to the segment of finger and the region of lower stiffness corresponds to finger joint. According to the length of different fingers, we have designed the specifications of the soft actuator reasonably, which not only ensures the fit of the driver and the finger, but also ensures the weight of device is not too high. The model of soft actuator is shown in Fig. 3 (It does not contain the strain restraining layer).

Fig. 3. (a) The top view of actuator (b) The bottom view of actuator

Simulation Analysis of Soft Actuator. For the feasibility of this design, the model shown in Fig. 3 was simulated using ABAQUS before fabrication. In the simulation, the properties of the silica material are set to hyperelasticity, and the elastomer with larger modulus of elasticity is used instead of the underlying limiting layer material [15].

Fig. 4. The simulation of actuator pressure deformation

The simulation results are shown in Fig. 4. The result shows that the actuator can produce large bending deformation under a small internal pressure (0.15 MPa), and its bending posture is similar to that of Fig. 2.

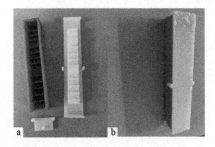

Fig. 5. (a) Mold before assembly (b) Mold after assembly

2.2   Design and Analysis of Soft Actuator

The fabrication of soft actuator mainly includes the following steps: 1. Establish model of actuator by SOLIDWORKS; 2. Use 3D printer to print mold; 3. Pour the prepared silicone into mold; 4. Package mold (Fig. 5); 5. Unmold after curing of silicone; 6. Do subsequent processing. Figure 6 gives a more intuitive description of the basic fabrication processes of the soft actuator. The index finger actuator produced is shown in Fig. 7.

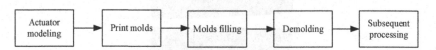

Fig. 6. The flow chart of soft actuator production

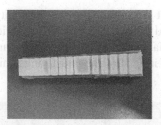

Fig. 7. Index finger actuator

Figure 8 shows the actuator bending gestures in different inflation levels. The results show that the bending gesture can achieve the result as shown in Fig. 4.

Fig. 8. Several postures of actuators

2.3   Characteristics of Actuator

Experiment of Actuator Bending Angle. In order to test the performance characteristics of soft actuator, related parameters are measured when inflated. The specific operation is following: Measure the variation of the bending angle of actuator under different inflation conditions. The experimental setup is shown in Fig. 9.

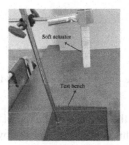

Fig. 9. The experimental setup

Since the end of actuator is a non-cavity solid structure, we clamp actuator tail through the experiment setup clamp to fix soft actuator and ensure that the actuator is vertically down. The amount of gas pumped into soft actuator is controlled by a syringe, and the end position are marked by the Tianyuan 3D scanner. The relative coordinates of the point are measured by the instrument, and then the bending angle of actuator can be calculated. For the convenience of analysis, we analyze the bending angle in a plan view. The calculation principle is shown in Fig. 10, where $\angle\theta$ is the bending angle. The angle can be expressed by the following formula:

$$\angle\theta = \arctan\frac{\Delta X}{\Delta Y} \qquad (1)$$

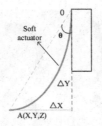

Fig. 10. The principle of calculating bending angle of actuator

Through the experiment we obtained the curve shown in Fig. 11, which depicts the relationship between the bending angles of actuator and the amount of inflation.

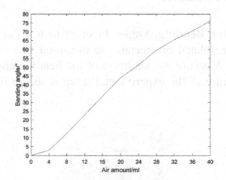

Fig. 11. The curve about bending angle and aeration amount

As can be seen from Fig. 11, the nonlinear change of bending angle of actuator with the increase of the aeration amount is more and more obvious. Because the nonlinearity of soft material and the soft actuator also needs to overcome a certain self-weight when bending. From the change in the slope of the curve, the conclusion of the influence of self-weigh is more and more obvious when the angle becomes bigger.

Tensile Experiment of Actuator. To further verify the tensile performance of soft actuator, we use the flexible telescopic sensor made by New Zealand flexible sensor manufacturer StretchSense to further verify the deformation of actuator. The change of actuator during the processes of inflation and deflation can be described by the increase and decrease of the capacitance: when inflating, the actuator expands, so the sensor stretches, and the capacitance gradually increases, and when deflating, the actuator contracts, so the sensor contracts, and the capacitance gradually decreases. Experimental data can be transferred to a computer via the StretchSense BLE APP for further data processing analysis. The device for actuator tensile experiment is shown in Fig. 12.

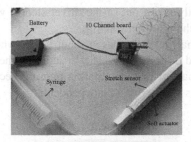

Fig. 12. The tensile experiment device of actuator

Try to ensure that the inflation rate is consistent during the inflation process and that the instantaneous inflation rate at each moment is considered consistent during the analysis. We process the data measured by the sensor through MATLAB (MathWorks Inc, USA) software to obtain the curve shown in Fig. 13. During this process, the sensor reached a maximum elongation of 7.72 mm when inflated with 30 ml of gas.

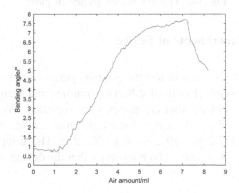

Fig. 13. The curve about elongation of actuator and the time

3   Soft Pneumatic Actuator

3.1   Design Method of Device

The main body of the device consists of a common fabric glove and five specially designed soft actuators (Fig. 14). Each of actuators were wrapped in fabric and sewn to the fabric gloves. Five actuators were connected to the splitter that is connected to the air pump through five tubes. Finally, ensuring that there is no air leak in our device is essential. Since the device is made of soft materials, which provides a soft, comfortable and healing environment for patients.

The sleeve of actuator serves three purposes: (1) To fix actuator (2) To prevent over-expansion of the actuator (3) To enhance bending force of actuator. Considering that there may be a situation that one of patient's hands can move normally, the actuator can be conveniently taken out of the driver sleeve, which increases the flexibility and specificity of rehabilitation training.

The weight of device that clear of tubes is about 120 g, which is much smaller than the typical standard of hand design 450 g [16]. In addition, the device does not impose additional weight on the patient in rehabilitation training because the control system and air source that controls the device is independent.

Fig. 14. The practicality picture of glove

3.2 Performance Experiments of Device

Grasping Experiment. In order to test the gripping performance of device, we carried out experiments on several objects of different volumes and weights by wearing the device. Weights of the objects that are grasped are recorded. We have captured five kinds of objects (Fig. 15(b–g)): paper, long can, tape, carton, cup, the masses are followed by: 64.9 g, 131.2 g, 139.2 g, 30 g, 322.2 g. The gripping performance is tested by grasping several objects, which indicates that the device can finish some basic grabbing tasks.

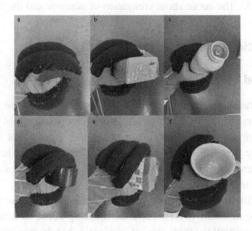

Fig. 15. (a) Glove that is pressurized (b) Grasp the paper (c) Grasp the long can (d) Grasp the tape (e) Grasp the carton (g) Grasp the cup

Tensile Experiment of Device. In order to test change in the stretch length of the index finger in device when grasping objects, we used the sensor that has been used to carry out the experiment. Figure 16 shows the state of the device before and after the glove is pressurized. When pressurizing, it is necessary to control the flow rate of the gas.

(a) Initial state of experiment   (b) Do experiment when pressurized

Fig. 16. Tensile experiment of device

During this process, the data fluctuates greatly, and the stretched length of the index finger changes with time as shown in Fig. 17. In this process, the maximum stretch length of the index finger is about 8.94 mm.

In order to test change in the stretch length of the index finger in device when grasping objects, we used the sensor that has been used in 2.3.1 to carry out the experiment. Figure 16 shows the state of the device before and after the glove is pressurized. When pressurizing, it is necessary to control the flow rate of the gas. During this process, the data fluctuates greatly, and the stretched length of the index finger changes with time as shown in Fig. 17. In this process, the maximum stretch length of the index finger is about 8.94 mm.

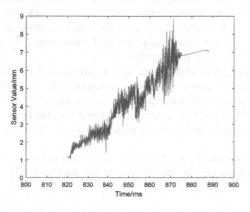

Fig. 17. The curve between elongation of device and time

4 Conclusion

In this paper, we present an easy-to-implement soft robotic glove that can help with rehabilitation of stroke patients. We adjust the pneumatic actuators with five soft fabric sleeves to limit undesired over-expansion, which allows the device to produce better bending and greater bending forces to help hand to grasp some objects. A rigid gradient structure is used in actuators that produces the desired bending posture when pressurized. Besides, the device can be tailored to the patient's hand. We have initially verified the feasibility of the device through experiments and we will optimize the structure of it and control system in our future work.

Acknowledgement. This research is supported by National Natural Science Foundation of China (51775284), Primary Research & Development Plan of Jiangsu Province (BE2018734), Joint Research Fund for Overseas Chinese, Hong Kong and Macao Young Scholars (61728302), and Postgraduate Research & Practice Innovation Program of Jiangsu Province (SJCX18_0299).

References

1. Yap, H.K., Lim, J.H., Goh, J.C.H., et al.: Design of a soft robotic glove for hand rehabilitation of stroke patients with clenched fist deformity using inflatable plastic actuators. J. Med. Devices **10**(4), 044504 (2016)
2. Kemna, S., Culmer, P.R., Jackson, A.E., et al.: Developing a user interface for the iPAM stroke rehabilitation system. In: IEEE International Conference on Rehabilitation Robotics, pp. 879–884. IEEE (2009)
3. Cai, Z., Tong, D., Meadmore, K.L., et al.: Design & control of a 3D stroke rehabilitation platform. In: IEEE International Conference on Rehabilitation Robotics (2011). 5975412
4. Lum, P.S., Burgar, C.G., Van der Loos, M.: MIME robotic device for upper-limb neurorehabilitation in subacute stroke subjects: a follow-up study. J. Rehabil. Res. Dev. **43** (5), 631 (2006)
5. Pehlivan, A.U., Celik, O., O'Malley, M.K.: Mechanical design of a distal arm exoskeleton for stroke and spinal cord injury rehabilitation. In: IEEE International Conference on Rehabilitation Robotics. IEEE (2011). 5975428
6. Polygerinos, P., Wang, Z., Galloway, K.C., et al.: Soft robotic glove for combined assistance and at-home rehabilitation. Robot. Auton. Syst. **73**(C), 135–143 (2015)
7. Yap, H.K., Lim, J.H., Nasrallah, F., et al.: MRC-glove: A fMRI compatible soft robotic glove for hand rehabilitation application. In: IEEE International Conference on Rehabilitation Robotics, pp. 735–740. IEEE (2015)
8. Yap, H.K., Lim, J.H., Nasrallah, F., et al.: A soft exoskeleton for hand assistive and rehabilitation application using pneumatic actuators with variable stiffness. In: IEEE International Conference on Robotics and Automation, pp. 4967–4972. IEEE (2015)
9. Yap, H.K., Khin, P.M., Koh, T.H., et al.: A fully fabric-based bidirectional soft robotic glove for assistance and rehabilitation of hand impaired patients. IEEE Robot. Autom. Lett. **PP** (99), 1 (2017)
10. Mosadegh, B., Polygerinos, P., Keplinger, C., et al.: Soft robotics: pneumatic networks for soft robotics that actuate rapidly. Adv. Funct. Mater. **24**(15), 2109 (2014)

11. Galloway, K.C., Polygerinos, P., Walsh, C.J., et al.: Mechanically programmable bend radius for fiber-reinforced soft actuators. In: International Conference on Advanced Robotics. IEEE (2014)
12. Yap, H.K., Lim, J.H., Nasrallah, F., et al.: Design and preliminary feasibility study of a soft robotic glove for hand function assistance in stroke survivors. Front. Neurosci. **11**, 547 (2017)
13. Yap, H.K., Ang, B.W., Lim, J.H., et al.: A fabric-regulated soft robotic glove with user intent detection using EMG and RFID for hand assistive application. In: IEEE International Conference on Robotics and Automation, pp. 3537–3542. IEEE (2016)
14. Yap, H.K., Lim, J.H., Nasrallah, F., et al.: Characterisation and evaluation of soft elastomeric actuators for hand assistive and rehabilitation applications. J. Med. Eng. Technol. **40**, 1–11 (2016)
15. Tong, M.: Design, Modeling and Fabrication of a Massage Neck Support Using Soft Robot Mechanis. The Ohio State University (2014)
16. Aubin, P.M., Sallum, H., Walsh, C., et al.: A pediatric robotic thumb exoskeleton for at-home rehabilitation: the Isolated Orthosis for Thumb Actuation (IOTA). In: Proceedings of IEEE International Conference on Rehabilitation Robotics, pp. 1–6 (2013)

Visual Servoing of Soft Robotic Arms by Binocular

Lizheng Feng, Xiaojiao Chen, and Zheng Wang$^{(\boxtimes)}$

Department of Mechanical Engineering, The University of Hong Kong,
Pokfulam, Hong Kong SAR, China
zheng.wang@ieee.org

Abstract. Soft robotic arms are complementing traditional rigid arms in many fields due to its multiple degrees of freedom, safety and adaptability to the environment. In recent years, soft robotic arms have become the focus in robotics research and gained increasing attention from scientists and engineers. Despite the rapid progress of its design and manufacturing processes in the past decade, an obstacle restricting the development of soft robotic arms remained unsolved. The suitable sensors for soft robotic arm have not appeared on the market and the integration of sensors into soft robotic arm has been difficult, since most sensors and actuator systems, such as those used in traditional robotic arms, are rigid sensors and rather simple. Therefore, finding a suitable soft robotic arm sensor has become an urgent issue in this field. In this paper, a simple and feasible method with a binocular camera is proposed to control the soft robotic arm. Binocular is employed to detect the spatial target position at first and then coordinates of target point will be transmitted to the soft robot to generate a control signal moving the soft robotic arm, and then the distance from target to the end effector will be measured in real time.

Keywords: Soft robotic arm · Visual servoing · Binocular disparity

1 Introduction

Soft robotic arms are safe, user-friendly and flexible in human-machine and machine-environment interaction [1], and therefore, they have a wide range of real-world applications and can revolutionize status quo with technological innovations [2]. For example, soft robotic arms can be applicable in the sorting of different shapes and fragile objects (fruits, vegetables, biological tissues etc.) [3], in medical and healthcare industry such as rehabilitation and auxiliary devices for stroke patients and assisted surgery [4, 5, 11]. Their physical adaptation to external environment empowers them with excellent capability to deal with uncertainty and disturbance [6, 7], allowing for low cost, safe and pleasurable human-robot interaction [8–10].

However, there is currently no suitable soft robotic arm sensor on the market and most of the soft robotic arms are still controlled by traditional sensors [12]. Although traditional rigid sensors have many applications on soft robotic arms, they are not

© Springer Nature Switzerland AG 2019
H. Yu et al. (Eds.): ICIRA 2019, LNAI 11742, pp. 130–143, 2019.
https://doi.org/10.1007/978-3-030-27535-8_13

always well-matched [13, 14]. Compared with traditional robotic arms, soft robotic arms have no so-called link and joint structure even do not need to drive with an electric motor [16]. In theory, the soft arm has multiple degrees of freedom, without an accurately characterized stiffness and damping [13]. Therefore, many mature sensors used in traditional robotic arms cannot be applied well in soft mechanical arms. These factors have greatly affected the control of the soft robotic arms [14]. To bridge the gap, a novel method to control the robotic arm with vision is employed. Visual control system automatically receives and processes images of real objects through optical and non-contact sensors to obtain the information required for robot motion [15, 18, 19].

Many current visual servoing robotic arms are not well solved in visual positioning problem. The main obstacle is the inability to apply the vision sensor alone to accurately obtain the depth of the target point [20]. For example, it is difficult to solve the depth problem with a monocular camera very accurately [27]. At present, the monocular measurement distance is very popular in machine learning model [28], and the data comes from statistics. Even if the correct rate is continuously improved under the supervised learning model, it is still only a regular information under big data, and there is no physical theory or geometric model to support it. The result analysis has uncontrollable factors. What's more, the monocular camera is fixed in focal length and cannot be zoomed as fast as the human eye, it cannot solve the problem of imaging at different distances accurately. The binocular camera is a good complement to this shortcoming. The binocular camera can cover different ranges of scenes by using two identical cameras, which solves the problem that the monocular camera cannot switch the focal length back and forth and can also solve the problem of recognizing the images sharply at different distances.

By using a binocular camera, depth measurement may also face many issues such as result accuracy, real-time trade-off [21], and difficulty in obtaining accurate corresponding disparity pixel values to the actual distance in a linear model [22–24]. Therefore, in this work, some simple and feasible methods are proposed to improve the measurement efficiency and accuracy of the binocular system, and at the same time, it is well combined with the soft robotic arm control.

There are two main tasks of the binocular camera in this proposed system:

First, measure the depth from the target point to the end effector by binocular disparity relatively, accurately and efficiently [25].

Second, employ the left camera of the binocular camera to establish the imaging geometry model. And the depth information is used to obtain the X, Y coordinates of the target point [26].

The novelty of this work:

① Proposes a simple method to improve the linear model of binocular disparity, making measurement results more accurate, and presents a strategy to improve the calculation speed of binocular disparity.

② Provides a new idea for the eye-in-hand model. Compared to the most eye-in-hand model by monocular, the binocular camera is used in this work to obtain accurate depth measurement in real time with a high positioning accuracy.

③ Matches the vision system with the soft robotic arm model to control the soft robotic arm moving to the target point.

2 Design

The soft robotic arm system is shown in Fig. 1. The vision system in this paper is a binocular camera with a variable baseline length from 4.2 cm to 17.0 cm, and the parameters of the binocular camera are listed in Table 1. It will be mounted on the end effector of the soft robot arm, moving with the end effector of the arm as the "hand-in-eye" model. And the details of binocular are shown in Fig. 2. Finally, the camera detects the depth of the target to the camera in real time and transmits it back to the base coordinate system and keeps end effector approaching the object to a predetermined distance.

The first part of this work is to use the binocular camera for depth measurement. At the beginning of the measurement, the camera is calibrated to remove the distortion, followed by the camera parameters and distortion coefficient. The intrinsic parameters will be combined with the depth information for the spatial position calculation. In this work, the camera is calibrated using the classic Zhang Zhengyou calibration method. A 50 mm * 50 mm, 10 * 6 calibration plate is chosen in this work. The binocular calibration phasing has special characteristics compared to the monocular calibration, and the calibration plate must appear in the left and right frames at the same time. Making the calibration plate appear in the entire view can effectively improve the accuracy of the calibration. A total of 30 pairs of image data to calibrate the binocular to get the camera parameters are conducted. Then the original frames are rectified with camera parameters and distortion coefficient. Next, the epipolar geometry is used to convert binocular into a standard format. Disparity calculation of two vertically aligned images is then conducted. There are currently three popular methods for calculating disparity: StereoBMState, StereoSGBMState, StereoGCState. The comparison of the three methods is as follows:

① Calculation speed: BM method > SGBM method > GC method.
② Disparity accuracy: BM method < SGBM method < GC method.

In this work, real-time and measurement accuracy are critical for the visual system, hence, average StereoSGBMState mode is used. Based on this algorithm, a scientific method will be employed to enhance the measurement results.

The spatial target point coordinate information is then transmitted back to the camera coordinate frame, after that from the camera coordinate frame to the end effector coordinate frame, and finally from the end effector coordinate frame to the robotic arm base coordinate frame.

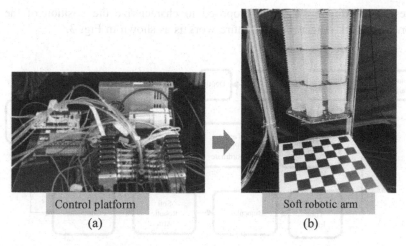

Fig. 1. (a) shows the control platform of the soft robotic arm system. (b) shows the soft robotic arm.

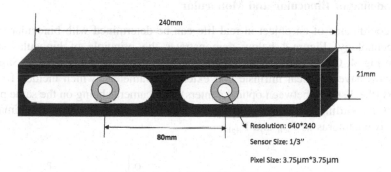

Fig. 2. Details of binocular

Table 1. Parameters of binocular

Image resolution	Baseline range	Sensor size	Pixel size	Image compression	Active array
640×320	42 mm–170 mm	$\frac{1}{3}''$	$3.75\,\mu m \times 3.75\,\mu m$	MJPG YUY2	MJPG (60FPS) YUY2 (10FPS)

3   Modeling

The soft robotic arm is different from the traditional rigid body arm, since its end-effector position is characterized by bending angle, rotation angle, and length. Therefore, in this paper, an algorithm transforming the software robot coordinate system into a Cartesian coordinate system is proposed to characterize the position of the end effector. The block diagram of the entire work is as shown in Fig. 3.

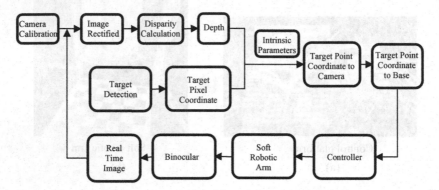

Fig. 3. Block diagram of visual servoing control by binocular vision

3.1 Modeling of Binocular and Monocular

The 3D coordinates of an object in real life can be determined with binocular stereo vision technology. Figure 4 below demonstrates the principle of binocular stereo vision. In Fig. 4, O_L and O_R are optical centers of the left and right cameras. Suppose two cameras have identical intrinsic and external parameters, which include f (focal length), B (the distance between optical centers), two cameras being on the same plane, and equal Y coordinates of their projection centers. The point P in space has imaging points in two cameras as P_{left} and P_{right}.

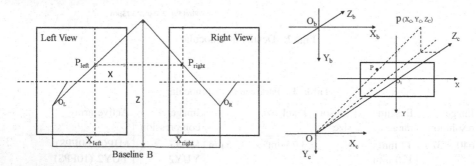

Fig. 4. The principle of binocular stereo vision   **Fig. 5.** Principle of camera projection

From trigonometry,

$$X_{left} = f\frac{x}{z} \tag{1}$$

$$X_{right} = f\frac{(x - B)}{z}$$ (2)

$$D = X_{left} - X_{right}$$ (3)

where X_{left}, X_{right} are the values of the target point in X direction of the left and right imaging planes, and x is the length of target point to the left camera in X direction. z is the depth from the target point to the binocular center. D is the disparity.

Solve (1), (2), (3) simultaneously to calculate depth as well. Consequently, it can be derived that:

$$z = \frac{Bf}{D}$$ (4)

During the imaging process of the camera, there exist 4 coordinate frames, which are pixel, image, camera and world coordinate systems. Figure 5 demonstrates the principle of camera imaging.

The relation between the pixel coordinate frame and the camera coordinate frame can be expressed with homogeneous matrices:

$$\begin{bmatrix} u \\ v \\ 1 \\ 1 \end{bmatrix} = \frac{1}{z_c} \begin{bmatrix} \frac{1}{d_x} & 0 & u_0 & 0 \\ 0 & \frac{1}{d_y} & v_0 & 0 \\ 0 & 0 & 1 & 0 \\ 0 & 0 & 0 & 1 \end{bmatrix} \begin{bmatrix} f & 0 & 0 & 0 \\ 0 & f & 0 & 0 \\ 0 & 0 & 1 & 0 \\ 0 & 0 & 0 & 1 \end{bmatrix} \begin{bmatrix} x_c \\ y_c \\ z_c \\ 1 \end{bmatrix}$$ (5)

where u, v represent the column and row numbers of the pixel in the image, u_0, v_0 represent pixel coordinate of the principle point, and d_x, d_y are the physical measurements of the unit pixel on the horizontal and vertical axes. Because depth will be considered in this issue, a 4×4 matrix format is used where x_c, y_c, z_c indicate the point in the camera coordinate frame, f represents the focal length of the camera. $\frac{f}{d_x}$, $\frac{f}{d_y}$ are abbreviated into f_x, f_y. Camera intrinsic parameters obtained from camera calibration can be shown below:

$$f_x = 2.3643976238380526 \times 10^2$$
$$u_0 = 1.5168679331906756 \times 10^2$$
$$f_y = 2.3486572411007802 \times 10^2$$
$$v_0 = 1.2106158962347398 \times 10^2$$

In this work, since the camera is mounted on the end effector, it is assumed that the camera coordinate frame and the robot end effector coordinate frame are the same.

3.2   Modeling of Soft Robotic Arm

The soft robotic arm studied in this paper is a light-weight backboneless soft robotic arm, consisting of 6 long elastic bellows installed circularly, and its end-effector position is characterized by bending angle α, rotation angle β, and length l. The geometry model of the soft arm is shown as follows in Fig. 6, and the frame transfer relation between the base and the end effector is shown in Fig. 7.

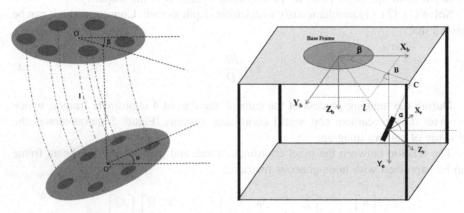

Fig. 6. Geometric model of the soft arm   **Fig. 7.** Frame transfer relation

The homogeneous transformation from base to end effector coordinate frame is shown as follows:

$$
{}^eT_b = \begin{bmatrix} c^2\beta(c\alpha - 1) + 1 & s\beta c\beta(c\alpha - 1) & c\beta s\alpha & -\frac{l}{\alpha}c\beta(c\alpha - 1) \\ c\beta s\beta(c\alpha - 1) & s^2\beta(c\alpha - 1) + 1 & s\beta s\alpha & -\frac{l}{\alpha}s\beta(c\alpha - 1) \\ -c\beta s\alpha & -s\beta s\alpha & c\alpha & \frac{l}{\alpha}s\alpha \\ 0 & 0 & 0 & 1 \end{bmatrix} \tag{6}
$$

Finally, (5) and (6) can be solved to obtain the result:

$$
\begin{bmatrix} u \\ v \\ 1 \\ 1 \end{bmatrix} = \frac{1}{Z(t)}\Omega_L {}^eT_b(t)\begin{bmatrix} x_b \\ y_b \\ z_b \\ 1 \end{bmatrix} \tag{7}
$$

in which Ω_L is the intrinsic parameter of the left camera.

Moreover, from calculation, it can be obtained that the target α, β, l are:

$$
\alpha = 2\arctan\left(\frac{\sqrt{x^2 + y^2}}{z}\right) \tag{8}
$$

$$\beta = \arctan\frac{y}{x} \tag{9}$$

$$l = \frac{\sqrt{x^2 + y^2 + z^2}}{\sin\left(\arctan\frac{\sqrt{x^2 + y^2}}{2}\right)} \cdot \arctan\frac{\sqrt{x^2 + y^2}}{z} \tag{10}$$

Plug the coordinates of the target point in the base coordinate frame into (8), (9), (10) and obtain the target soft robotic arm parameters α, β, l to control the arm close to the target point.

4   Improved Binocular Measurement Performance

4.1   Measurement Accuracy Optimization

Conversion of disparity pixel values to real distance. Since the soft robotic arm will combined with a gripper in the end and the length of gripper is 60 cm. The experiment is designed based on the actual range of 0–120 cm, with a gradient of 1 cm. And for each group, 10 sets of continuous pixel value output are recorded, which amounts to be a total of 1600 sets of data, as shown below in Fig. 8.

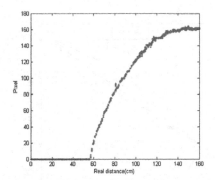
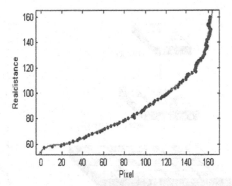

Fig. 8. Relationship between pixel and real distance

Fig. 9. Curving fitting result

Two regions are omitted in the disparity map during the experiment, including blind spot region when the distance is very close, and the undesirable low-resolution region when the distance is very large. As a result, a clear pattern between the pixel values and the real distances can be discovered. The data is then fitted with a high degree polynomial to obtain a more accurate fit curve, and the result is shown in Fig. 9. The curving fitting formula (11) is used to calculate the actual distance.

$$\text{Real Distance} = p_1x^7 + p_2x^6 + p_3x^5 + p_4x^4 + p_5x^3 + p_6x^2 + p_7x + p_8 \qquad (11)$$

where x is the value of pixel, and $p_1 = -4.847 \times 10^{-12}$, $p_2 = 2.856 \times 10^{-9}$, $p_3 = -5.756 \times 10^{-7}$, $p_4 = 2.668 \times 10^{-5}$, $p_5 = 0.006586$, $p_6 = -1.101$, $p_7 = 67.91$, $p_8 = -1532$.

4.2   Measurement Time Improvement

One challenge with binocular disparity is its overly long calculation time, which considerably restrains its application in real-time measurement. The algorithm of the binocular disparity map mainly calculates the difference of the corresponding points according to the matching of each pixel in the left and right images, hence, if a more accurate disparity map is to be obtained, a large amount of time will be consumed in the disparity calculation of left and right images. For example, during the initial experiment, the disparity calculation time for big-scale images was as long as 5 s, which certainly did not meet the time requirements for real-time measurements. To solve this problem, the proposed solution is to reduce the size of the target measurement area as shown in Fig. 10. The specific method is to take a square area of a certain size around the target point, and only perform disparity calculation on the pixels of this selected area. The relationship between the size of the region and the disparity calculation time by this method, and the relative error at each size is shown in Fig. 11.

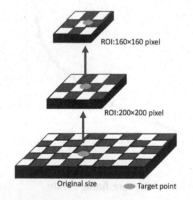

Fig. 10. Method of speeding up calculation time

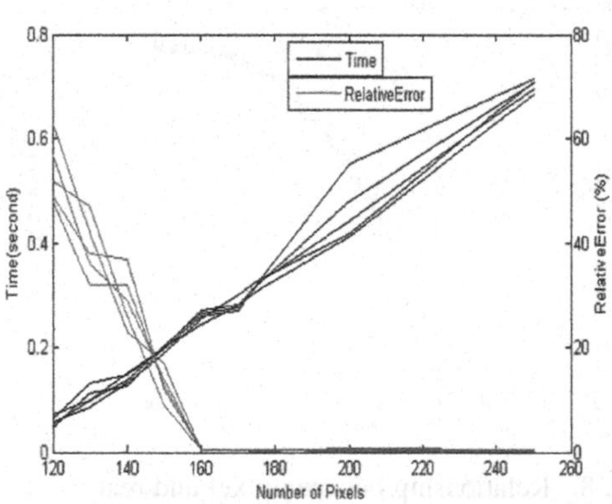

Fig. 11. Relation between time/error and region

From the relationship in Fig. 11, the calculation time is relatively short when the size of the region is 160×160 pixels with a high accuracy, for which the single running time of the vision system is about 0.2 s. Therefore, in the final calculation process, in order to maximize the real-time performance, a pixel area of 160×160 is selected.

4.3   Distance Measurement Error

According to the improvement method above, the distance measurement experiment was conducted. Experiments were conducted on the binocular measurement system, with a distance ranging from 57 cm to 120 cm. The measurement was recorded 10 times at each actual distance by two binocular disparity models which are linear and curve fitting. And the error of the experiment was calculated by the following expression

$$\text{relative error} = \frac{error}{real\,depth} \tag{12}$$

The error analysis chart is shown as follows in Fig. 12.

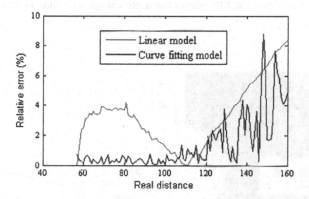

Fig. 12. Relative average error by real distance

Because the fitting model has a significantly higher measurement accuracy in the working area than the linear model. It can be seen from Fig. 12 that the binocular measurement system meets the required error in the working range well.

5   Experiment

5.1   Visual Servoing Experiment

Binocular is mounted on the center of the end effector and put the mark point at any position in the camera view. In experiment 1, the visual servoing control of robotic arm is set to the target point at a fixed distance. The initial distance is set to be 60 cm, then the robotic arm moves away from the target robotic arm, and finally, it comes back to 60 cm. The experiment 1 configuration is shown in Fig. 13. Experiment 2 is a real-time tracking of the target object. When the target moves in the view of the camera, the camera tracks the target and records the pixel coordinates. The experiment 2 configuration is shown in Fig. 14.

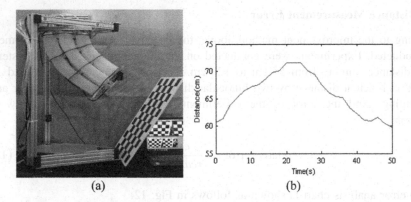

(a)   (b)

Fig. 13. (a) shows the visual servoing of the robot arm under bending condition to the fixed distance from the target point and (b) shows the depth change over time in experiment 1.

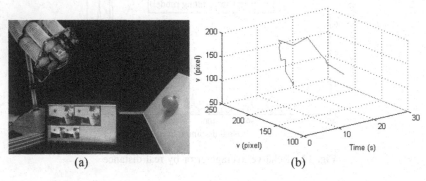

(a)   (b)

Fig. 14. (a) shows the real-time tracking of the target object. (b) shows the pixel coordinate change in the tracking task.

Based on the two experiments above, a third experiment to detect the object spatial position is operated. A control signal moving the soft robotic arm is generated so that the end of the arm points at the target and moves to a fixed distance from the target object. The experiment configuration is shown in Fig. 15. The target pixel coordinate in the image is tracked to the middle of the camera view. And the distance information is measured in real-time to reach the fixed distance in the task. The change of target pixel and distance are recorded and shown in Fig. 16.

Fig. 15. Experiment 3 configuration

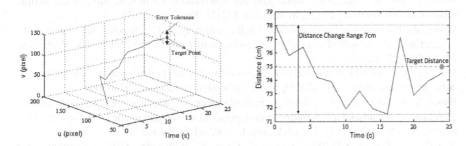

Fig. 16. The change of pixel coordinate and distance

6 Conclusion

In this work, the binocular vision system can rather accurately control the distance from the end effector to the target during the motion of the soft robotic arm so that the end-effector can perform the task within the acceptable error range.

This simple and feasible binocular servoing control method will provide new ideas and inspirations for solving the difficulties in soft robots controlling and sensing fields.

In the future, the aim is to achieve a more accurate estimation of the end position of the arm, enabling the motion control to be more precise, and to equip the soft robotic arms with better capabilities of fulfilling more tasks.

References

1. Zhou, J., Chen, X., Chang, U., Pan, J., Wang, W., Wang, Z.: Intuitive control of humanoid soft-robotic hand BCL-13. In: 2018 IEEE-RAS 18th International Conference on Humanoid Robots (Humanoids), pp. 314–319 (2018)
2. Chen, X., Hu, T., Song, C., Wang, Z.: Analytical solution to global dynamic balance control of the Acrobot. In: 2018 IEEE International Conference on Real-time Computing and Robotics, pp. 405–410 (2019)

3. Chen, X., Yi, J., Li, J., Zhou, J., Wang, Z.: Soft-actuator-based robotic joint for safe and forceful interaction with controllable impact response. IEEE Robot. Autom. Lett. **3**(4), 3505–3512 (2018)
4. Polygerinos, P., et al.: Modeling of soft fiber-reinforced bending actuators. IEEE Trans. Robot. **31**(3), 778–789 (2015)
5. Wang, Z., Peer, A., Buss, M.: Fast online impedance estimation for robot control. In: IEEE 2009 International Conference on Mechatronics, ICM 2009, pp. 1–6 (2009)
6. Yi, J., et al.: Customizable three-dimensional-printed origami soft robotic joint with effective behavior shaping for safe interactions. IEEE Trans. Robot. (2018, accepted)
7. Zhou, J., Chen, X., Li, J., Tian, Y., Wang, Z.: A soft robotic approach to robust and dexterous grasping. In: 2018 IEEE International Conference on Soft Robotics, RoboSoft 2018, no. 200, pp. 412–417 (2018)
8. Wang, Z., Peer, A., Buss, M.: An HMM approach to realistic haptic human-robot interaction. In: Proceedings - 3rd Joint EuroHaptics Conference and Symposium on Haptic Interfaces Virtual Environment Teleoperator Systems World Haptics 2009, pp. 374–379 (2009)
9. Wang, Z., Sun, Z., Phee, S.J.: Haptic feedback and control of a flexible surgical endoscopic robot. Comput. Methods Programs Biomed. **112**(2), 260–271 (2013)
10. Wang, Z., Polygerinos, P., Overvelde, J.T.B., Galloway, K.C., Bertoldi, K., Walsh, C.J.: Interaction forces of soft fiber reinforced bending actuators. IEEE/ASME Trans. Mechatron. **22**(2), 717–727 (2017)
11. Viry, L., et al.: Flexible three-axial force sensor for soft and highly sensitive artificial touch. Adv. Mater. **26**, 2659–2664 (2014). https://doi.org/10.1002/adma.201305064
12. Bauer, S., Bauer-Gogonea, S., Graz, I., Kaltenbrunner, M., Keplinger, C., Schwödiauer, R.: 25th anniversary article: a soft future: from robots and sensor skin to energy harvesters. Adv. Mater. **26**, 149–162 (2014). https://doi.org/10.1002/adma.201303349
13. Ilievski, F., Mazzeo, A.D., Shepherd, R.F., Chen, X., Whitesides, G.M.: Soft robotics for chemists. Angew. Chem. Int. Ed. **50**, 1890–1895 (2011). https://doi.org/10.1002/anie.201006464b
14. Espiau, B., Chaumette, F., Rives, P.: A new approach to visual servoing in robotics. IEEE Trans. Robot. Autom. **8**(3), 313–326 (1992)
15. Yi, J., Chen, X., Song, C., Wang, Z.: Fiber-reinforced origamic robotic actuator. Soft Robot. **5**(1), 81–92 (2017)
16. Wilson, W.J., Hulls, C.W., Bell, G.S.: Relative end-effector control using Cartesian position based visual servoing. IEEE Trans. Robot. Autom. **12**(5), 684–696 (1996)
17. Allen, P.K., Yoshimi, B., Timcenko, A.: Real-time visual servoing. In: Proceedings. 1991 IEEE International Conference on Robotics and Automation, Sacramento, CA, USA, vol. 1, pp. 851–856 (1991)
18. Jagersand, M., Fuentes, O., Nelson, R.: Experimental evaluation of uncalibrated visual servoing for precision manipulation. In: Proceedings of International Conference on Robotics and Automation, Albuquerque, NM, USA, vol. 4, pp. 2874–2880 (1997)
19. Vahrenkamp, N., Wieland, S., Azad, P., Gonzalez, D., Asfour, T., Dillmann, R.: Visual servoing for humanoid grasping and manipulation tasks. In: Humanoids 2008 - 8th IEEE-RAS International Conference on Humanoid Robots, Daejeon, pp. 406–412 (2008)
20. De Luca, A., Oriolo, G., Robuffo Giordano, P.: Feature depth observation for image-based visual servoing: theory and experiments. Int. J. Robot. Res. **27**(10), 1093–1116 (2008). https://doi.org/10.1177/0278364908096706
21. Malis, E.: Visual servoing invariant to changes in camera-intrinsic parameters. IEEE Trans. Robot. Autom. **20**(1), 72–81 (2004)

22. De Luca, A., Oriolo, G., Giordano, P.R.: On-line estimation of feature depth for image-based visual servoing schemes. In: Proceedings 2007 IEEE International Conference on Robotics and Automation, Roma, pp. 2823–2828 (2007)
23. Fujimoto, H.: Visual servoing of 6 DOF manipulator by multirate control with depth identification. In: 42nd IEEE International Conference on Decision and Control (IEEE Cat. No. 03CH37475), Maui, HI, vol. 5, pp. 5408–5413 (2003)
24. Zhang, Z.: A flexible new technique for camera calibration. IEEE Trans. Pattern Anal. Mach. Intell. 22(11), 1330–1334 (2000)
25. Zhang, Z.: Determining the epipolar geometry and its uncertainty: a review. Int. J. Comput. Vis. 27(2), 161–195 (1998)
26. Davison, A.: Real-time simultaneous localization and mapping with a single camera. In: Proceedings of International Conference Computer Vision, pp. 1403–1410, October 2003
27. Godard, C., Mac Aodha, O., Brostow, G.J.: Unsupervised monocular depth estimation with left-right consistency. In: The IEEE Conference on Computer Vision and Pattern Recognition (CVPR), pp. 270–279 (2017)
28. Kuznietsov, Y., Stuckler, J., Leibe, B.: Semi-supervised deep learning for monocular depth map prediction. In: The IEEE Conference on Computer Vision and Pattern Recognition (CVPR), pp. 6647–6655 (2017)

Design of a Teleoperated Rod-Driven Continuum Robot

Yue Liu[1], Shupeng Zhao[1], Chenghao Yang[1,2], Lisha Chen[2], and Rongjie Kang[1(✉)]

[1] Key Laboratory of Mechanism Theory and Equipment Design, Ministry of Education, School of Mechanical Engineering, Tianjin University, Tianjin 300072, China
rjkang@tju.edu.cn
[2] School of Mechanical Engineering, Tianjin Polytechnic University, Tianjin 300387, China

Abstract. Continuum robots have attracted increasing attention from robotic community due to their intrinsic compliance and high dexterity. However, the compliant body structures and multiple degrees of freedom (DOFs) make it difficult for operators to intuitively regulate the configuration of continuum robots. Therefore, this paper presents a rod-driven continuum robot with tele-operation device achieving master-slave control. The master articulated manipulator has the same number of joints as the slave continuum robot. The slave continuum robot is equipped with two continuum joints with elastic backbones. Each joint possesses two DOFs and is driven by three elastic rods. The configuration parameters of the master manipulator are acquired by embedded sensors and return to a host computer. After kinematics calculating, the control command is sent to the slave continuum robot, to reproduce the configuration of the master manipulator. Experimental results show that the robotic system can achieve good master-slave following performance.

Keywords: Continuum robot · Teleoperation · Kinematics

1 Introduction

Continuum robot is a new generation of bionic robot inspired by biological continuum structures such as, elephant trunks, lizard tongues and octopus tentacles [1]. Continuum robots possess flexible structures and hyper-redundant DOFs making them suitable for manipulation in narrow, complex and unconstructed environments.

Walker et al. have developed a large number of pneumatic continuum robots inspired by elephant trunks [2–4], which can achieve the motion of shortening and bending. Camarillo et al. designed a rod-driven continuum robot equipped with 6 DOFs, which has great application prospect in endoscopic therapy [5]. Simaan presented multi-module continuum robot using hyper-elastic NiTi alloy for the use of minimally invasive surgery [6, 7]. Similar design was used by Xu et al. to develop a single cavity mirror robot for minimally invasive surgery [8]. Kang et al. presented a

© Springer Nature Switzerland AG 2019
H. Yu et al. (Eds.): ICIRA 2019, LNAI 11742, pp. 144–154, 2019.
https://doi.org/10.1007/978-3-030-27535-8_14

continuum robot driven by pneumatic artificial muscles and utilized Kalman filter to estimate the Jacobian of the robot for path tracking [9, 10].

To complete a certain task, a continuum robot needs to be controlled by operators. However, it might be risky or even impossible for operators exposed directly in unconstructed and complex environments. Therefore, it is quite necessary to implement a teleoperation device into continuum robotic system. Master-slave interactive control have been used in rigid robotic systems for years [11]. Shin et al. developed a master-slave robotic system for needle indentation and insertion with force feedback. The master robot has 6-DOF and the slave robot was designed as a 1-DOF robot. The interaction force between the slave robot and tissue sample was measured from the force sensor and delivered to the control system through a USB-based DAQ board [12]. Franco et al. presented master-slave control system for teleoperated needle insertion under guidance by Magnetic Resonance Imaging (MRI) [13]. Hou et al. designed a master-slave system consisting of a hydraulic Stewart mechanism, which can be used for grinding complex curved surfaces while keeping the operator away from the harmful dust produced [14]. The above works provide inspirations for implementation of teleoperation control in continuum robots.

In this paper, a two-joint rod-driven continuum robot is proposed for highly compliant manipulation. In addition, an articulated teleoperation manipulator is designed to map its configuration to the continuum robotic arm. The kinematics of the continuum robotic arm is obtained based on the assumption of constant curvature in each module. The rest of this paper is organized as follows: Sect. 2 describes the mechanical design of the slave continuum robot and the master manipulator. Section 3 introduces the kinematic model for the presented robot. The experiment results are demonstrated in Sect. 4, and the conclusions are given in Sect. 5.

2 Prototype Design

The prototype of the master-slave robotic system is shown in Fig. 1, which is mainly composed of a master manipulator and a slave continuum robot. The slave continuum robot includes a gripper, a driving box and a two-joint continuum arm. Each joint, driven by three rods, has two DOFs, so that the whole arm has four DOFs.

2.1 The Continuum Arm

As shown in Fig. 2, each joint of the continuum arm is constructed by a backbone, three driving rods evenly distributed in a circle and eleven constraint disks. The backbone and rods are made of super elastic NiTi alloy to ensure the compliance and reliability of the arm. All the constraint disks are equally spaced on the backbone, and the rods are only fixed to the end disk of the corresponding joint but go through other disks allowing for relative sliding. The length of the backbone remains constant. By pushing or pulling the driving rods, the continuum joint will bend with different configuration, according to the displacements of the rod.

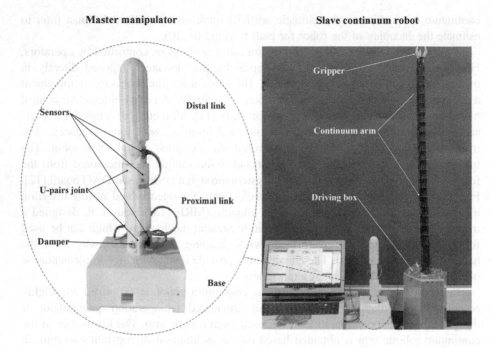

Fig. 1. Overall structure of the master-slave robotic system

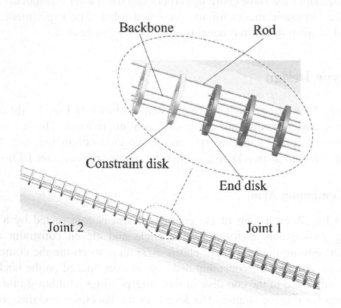

Fig. 2. Structure of the continuum arm.

2.2   The Driving Box

Regarding to the actuations of the continuum arm, six rods are arranged for two continuum joints. Therefore, six transmission units are equipped in the driving box. One end of the rod is anchored to the end disk, while another is attached to a corresponding transmission unit. The linear movement of a rod is achieved by the screw-rod sliding mechanism. Each transmission unit is composed of a group of screw, slider and rail, as shown in Fig. 3.

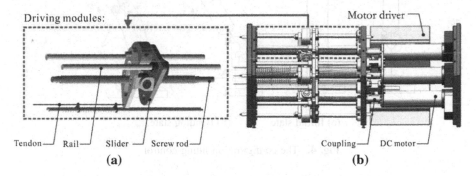

Fig. 3.   Driving box: (a) the transmission unit; (b) overview of the driving box.

2.3   The Master Manipulator

The design of the master-slave system adopts isomorphic absolute position control method. The master manipulator can be divided into three parts, including the base, the distal link and the proximal link. The proximal link corresponds to the first joint of the slave continuum arm while the distal link corresponds to the second joint of the slave continuum arm. Each link, connected by U-pairs has two DOFs of rotation relating to its own base coordinate system. Four sensors are installed in two U-pairs to measure the pitch and yaw angles, and the output analog signal is transformed to the digital signal in a Microprogrammed Control Unit (MCU) embedded in the base. The data is then sent to the PC through USB communication.

There are various control strategies according to different types of exchange information in master-slave control system. In this paper, we use the configuration-fitting control strategy for the master-slave system. As shown in Fig. 4 and Table 1, the yaw angle, δ, and the pitch angle, θ, of the master manipulator is equal to the rotation angle, δ', and the bending angle, θ', of the corresponding joint of the slave continuum robot. So the configuration of slave continuum robot can controlled by operating the master manipulator.

Solidworks is used in the design of the master manipulator for modeling and optimization. As shown in Fig. 4, in order to ensure that the configuration of master manipulator keep stable without external force, two damping couplings are assembled in two U-pairs. The selection of damper is determined according to the maximum torque of gravity under different configuration of the master manipulator. At the same time, in order to ensure that the master manipulator will not roll over, the location of the center is calculated so that it is always within the support range of the base.

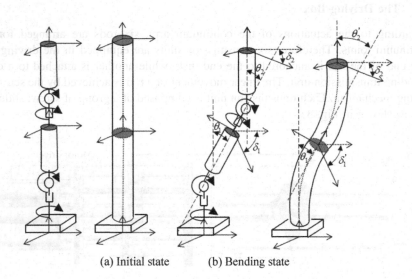

(a) Initial state   (b) Bending state

Fig. 4. The configuration-fitting control

Table 1. The configuration-fitting control

Configuration of the master manipulator	Configuration of the slave continuum robot
The pitch angle of the proximal link θ_1	The bending angle of the first joint θ_1'
The pitch angle of the distal link θ_2	The bending angle of the second joint θ_2'
The yaw angle of the proximal link δ_1	The rotation angle of the first joint δ_1'
The yaw angle of the distal link δ_2	The rotation angle of the second joint δ_2'

2.4   Control System

As shown in Fig. 5, the hardware of the control system consists of a PC, the master manipulator and various control objects. The control objects are directly connected to CAN bus include DC six brushed motors, step motor driver of the end effector and data acquisition card with multiple analog input and output. The data acquisition card is used to collect the driving force signal of the tension pressure sensor. The master manipulator communicates with PC through USB, and four angle sensors transmit the configuration parameters of the master manipulator to PC through MCU.

In the process of motion control of the master-slave robotic system, when users operate the master manipulator, the angle sensors send the configuration parameters, δ_i and θ_i, to the PC through the MCU. The PC receives several groups of configuration data using Microsoft Foundation Classes (MFC) message at a regular interval and stores them in memory temporarily. When system judges that the configuration parameters stop being updated, the system will stop storing the configuration parameters.

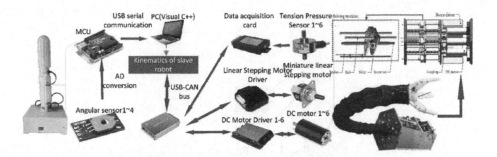

Fig. 5. Schematic diagram of the control system

The control system will activate the motion control of the slave continuum robot after obtaining the first groups of configuration parameters. Then the initial length of each driving rod is obtained to calculate the initial configuration of the slave continuum arm. The trajectory of desired motion is produced based on the difference value between the initial configuration and the first set of configuration parameters stored in the memory. The trajectory of the configuration mapping from the master manipulator to the slave continuum robot is established on the kinematic mappings and Jacobian matrix, which will be introduced in the following sections. After the first set of desired configurations is achieved, the program automatically takes the second set of configurations as the desired configurations, and then calculate the next trajectory. The processes are repeated until all configuration parameters obtained from the master manipulator are executed. When the operation is completed, the system will release the memory, and at the same time resets the initial configuration state of the continuum arm.

3 Kinematic Modeling

In this section, kinematics for the rod-driven slave continuum robot is introduced based on the constant curvature assumption.

3.1 Coordinates and Parameters Definition

The kinematic parameters of the continuum robot are defined, as illustrated in Fig. 6.

The global coordinate system O_0 (x_0, y_0, z_0) is established on the base of the whole arm. Two local coordinate systems O_i (x_i, y_i, z_i) $(i = 1, 2)$ is established on the end disk of each joint. Based on the assumption that each joint i is curved with constant curvature, the kinematic model can be divided into three spaces: the actuation space L, the configuration space Ψ and the workspace Q [5, 15]. The actuation space is defined as $L = [l_{11}, l_{12}, l_{13}, l_{21}, l_{22}, l_{32},]^T$, which describes the length of the driving rods. $l_{i,j}$ denotes the total length of the jth driving rod of the ith joint $(i = 1, 2; j = 1, 2, 3)$, as shown in Fig. 6. The configuration space is defined as $\Psi = [\theta_1, \delta_1, \theta_2, \delta_2]^T$, which describes the deformation of the continuum arm. θ_i describes the bending angle of the ith joint in the bending plane i, where the arc lies. δ_i describes the rotation angle of joint

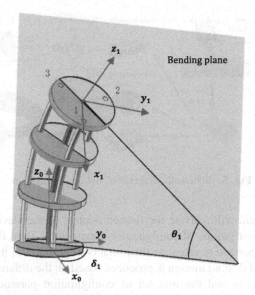

Fig. 6. Geometric description of continuum joint 1

i, that is the angle between the bending plane of joint i and the x_{i-1} axis of the $\{i-1\}$. The workspace is defined as $Q = [x\ y\ z]^T$, which represents the position of the end point.

The length of the backbone of each joint is L_i ($i = 1, 2$). $\alpha = 120°$ indicates the angle between the three driving rods evenly distributed for each joint. $\beta = 60°$ is the angle between the driving rods of joint 2 and joint 1. $R = 15$ mm represents the radius of the circumference of the evenly distributed driving rods.

3.2   Kinematic Mapping

The mapping relationship between the actuation space and the configuration space is derived on the basis of the geometric relationship between the driving rod and the backbone:

$$l_{i,j} = \sum_{g=1}^{i} [L_g - R\theta_g \cos(\delta_g + (j-1)\alpha + (i-1)\beta)] \tag{1}$$

Based on the geometric relationship of the coordinate system, the transformation matrix $_i^{i-1}T$ ($i = 1, 2$) of the coordinate system from $\{i-1\}$ to $\{i\}$ can be obtained as (2). Where, $\gamma = \beta - \delta_1 + \delta_2$

$$
{}_1^0T = Rot_z(\delta_1)Trans\left[\frac{L_1}{\theta_1}(1 - \cos \theta_1), 0, \frac{L_1}{\theta_1}\sin \theta_1\right]Rot_y(\theta_1)
$$

$$
{}_2^1T = Rot_z(\gamma)Trans\left[\frac{L_2}{\theta_2}(1 - \cos \theta_2), 0, \frac{L_2}{\theta_2}\sin \theta_2\right]Rot_y(\theta_2)
$$

(2)

$$
{}_2^0T = {}_1^0T \cdot {}_2^1T = \begin{bmatrix} R & P \\ 0 & 1 \end{bmatrix}
$$

(3)

In Eq. (3), ${}_2^0T$ represents the transformation matrix from frame {0} to frame {2}, where P is the multivariate function vector of $\theta_1 \delta_1 \theta_2 \delta_2$, which reflects the absolute coordinates of the end point. $P = [P_x \ P_y \ P_z]^T$ reflects the mapping relationship between the configuration space Ψ and the workspace Q.

3.3 Jacobian Matrix

In real task, the slave continuum robot is required not only to reach the position of the target, but also to provide certain speed for certain mission requirement. In addition, to achieve a smooth and safe motion, the moving speed of the slave continuum robot's configuration is necessary to be well controlled. The Jacobian reveals the relationship between the velocities in workspace, configuration space and actuation space.

Two velocity Jacobian matrixes $J_{\Psi L}$ and $J_{\Psi Q}$ are defined to describe the velocity mappings from the configuration space to the actuation space and the velocity mappings from the configuration space to the workspace.

The velocity mapping from the configuration space to the actuation space is expressed as Eq. (4):

$$
\dot{L} = J_{\Psi L}\dot{\Psi}
$$

(4)

By solving the derivative of L to Ψ in Eq. (1), the Jacobian matrix from the configuration space to the actuation space can be derived as:

$$
J_{\Psi L} = \begin{bmatrix} \frac{\partial L}{\partial \theta_1} & \frac{\partial L}{\partial \delta_1} & \frac{\partial L}{\partial \theta_2} & \frac{\partial L}{\partial \delta_2} \end{bmatrix}
$$

(5)

$$
\dot{L} = J_{\Psi L}\dot{\Psi} = \begin{bmatrix} J_1 & 0 \\ J_{21} & J_2 \end{bmatrix}\begin{bmatrix} \dot{\theta}_1 \\ \dot{\delta}_1 \\ \dot{\theta}_2 \\ \dot{\delta}_2 \end{bmatrix}
$$

(6)

The velocity mapping from the configuration space to the workspace is shown in Eq. (7):

$$
\dot{Q} = J_{\Psi Q} \cdot \dot{\Psi}
$$

(7)

According to Eq. (3), the partial derivative of P to each element of Ψ make up the Jacobian matrix from configuration space to the workspace as Eq. (8):

$$J_{\Psi Q} = \begin{bmatrix} \frac{\partial P}{\partial \theta_1} & \frac{\partial P}{\partial \delta_1} & \frac{\partial P}{\partial \theta_2} & \frac{\partial P}{\partial \delta_2} \end{bmatrix} \tag{8}$$

Consulting the linear equation theory (Boullion and Odell 2010), The inverse kinematics can be written as Eq. (9) [16]:

$$\dot{\Psi} = J_{\Psi Q}^+ \dot{Q} + (I - J_{\Psi Q} J_{\Psi Q}^+) w \tag{9}$$

where $J_{\Psi Q}^+$ is the generalized inverse matrix of $J_{\Psi Q}$, $(I - J_{\Psi Q} J_{\Psi Q}^+) w$ is the projection of w on the null space of $J_{\Psi Q}^+$, which is an additional item caused by the redundant degree of freedom of the continuum arm, making the continuum arm can reach a same point in several poses. If $w = 0$, a minimal norm solution of $\dot{\Psi}$ can be obtained [16].

By using Eqs. (4) and (9), the velocity mapping relationship between the workspace and the actuation space is derived as Eq. (10), considering the minimal norm solution of the configuration velocity.

$$\dot{L} = J_{\Psi L} J_{\Psi Q}^+ \cdot \dot{Q} \tag{10}$$

4 Control Experiment

In this section, experiments are carried out to validate the performance of the master-slave system. The master manipulator produces a large amount of configurations for the slave continuum robot to follow, as shown in Fig. 7.

Fig. 7. Record of experimental process

The bending angle of each joint is tested following a cosine curve from π/2 to π/6 and the rotation angle of each joint is tested following sine curve from −π to π, as shown in Fig. 8. We can read the length of all the six driving rods in real time. Then making use of the mapping relationship between the actuation space and the configuration space, the actual configurations angle of each joint can be derived. By comparing the configuration angles of master manipulator and the slave continuum robot, we can evaluate the precision of the teleoperation.

We can tell from the experiment results that there is some tiny deviation. The maximum error of master-slave following is less than 1°, so we can ignore the influence of the error in practical task. Therefore, the master-slave teleoperation device of the continuum robot can precisely and intuitively control the configuration of the continuum robot.

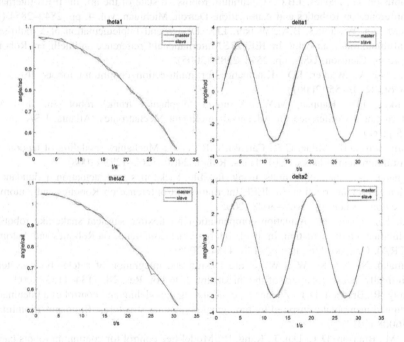

Fig. 8. Experiment result of configuration angle

5 Conclusion

In this paper, a teleoperated rod-driven continuum prototype is presented, containing a master manipulator and a slave continuum robot. The slave continuum robot is composed of a gripper, a driving box and a continuum arm. The continuum arm is constructed with an elastic backbone and three elastic driving rods, which provide the continuum arm with high flexibility. To achieve a good kinematic control of the continuum robot, the kinematic model is obtained based on the mapping relationships of actuation space, configuration space and workspace.

The master articulated manipulator having the same DOFs with the slave continuum arm is well designed. The slave continuum robot is controlled to reproduce the configuration of the master manipulator. The teleoperation device is helpful to enhance the intuitive feelings of remote operating. The experiments indicate the robot have a good master-slave tracking performance.

Acknowledgments. This work was supported by the National Natural Science Foundation of China (Grant No. 51875393, No. 51605329, No. 51535008), and the Tianjin Municipal Science and Technology Department Program (Grant No. 17JCQNJC03600).

References

1. Robinson, G., Davies, J.B.C.: Continuum robots - a state of the art. In: IEEE International Conference on Robotics and Automation, Detroit, Michigan, vol. 4, pp. 2849–2854 (1999)
2. McMahan, W., Jones, B.A., Walker, I.D.: Design and implementation of a multi-section continuum robot: air-octor. In: IEEE/RSJ International Conference on Intelligent Robots and Systems, Clemson, USA, pp. 2578–2585 (2005)
3. Jones, B.A., Walker, I.D.: Kinematics for multisection continuum robots. IEEE Trans. Robot. **22**, 43–55 (2006)
4. Walker, I.D., Hannan, M.W.: A novel 'elephant's trunk' robot. In: IEEE/ASME International Conference on Advanced Intelligent Mechatronics, Atlanta, USA, pp. 410–415 (1999)
5. Camarillo, D.B., Milne, C.F., Carlson, C.R., et al.: Mechanics modeling of tendon-driven continuum manipulators. IEEE Trans. Robot. **24**(6), 1262–1273 (2008)
6. Simaan, N.: Snake-like units using flexible backbones and actuation redundancy for enhanced miniaturization. In: IEEE International Conference on Robotics and Automation, Barcelona, Spain, pp. 3023–3028 (2005)
7. Xu, K., Simaan, N.: Actuation compensation for flexible surgical snake-like robots with redundant remote actuation. In: IEEE International Conference on Robotics and Automation (ICRA), Orlando, Florida, pp. 4148–4154 (2006)
8. Simaan, N., Xu, K., Wei, W., et al.: Design and integration of a telerobotic system for minimally invasive surgery of the throat. Int. J. Robot. Res. **28**, 1134–1153 (2009)
9. Kang, R., Branson, D.T., Zheng, T., et al.: Design, modeling and control of a pneumatically actuated manipulator inspired by biological continuum structures. Bioinspir. Biomim. **8**(3), 036008 (2013)
10. Li, M., Branson, D.T., Dai, J., Kang, R.: Model-free control for continuum robots based on an adaptive Kalman filter. IEEE/ASME Trans. Mechatron. **23**, 286–297 (2018)
11. Shao, Y., Jiang, Z.: Overview of master-slave teleoperation robot technology. Technol. Outlook **5**, 150 (2017)
12. Shin, J., Zhong, Y., Gu, C.: Master-slave robotic system for needle indentation and insertion. Comput. Assist. Surg. **22**, 100–105 (2017)
13. Franco, E., Ristic, M.: Adaptive control of a master-slave system for teleoperated needle insertion under MRI-guidance. In: Control & Automation. IEEE (2015)
14. Hou, J., Zhao, D.: Investigation of bilateral control for hydraulic stewart master-slave system. Inst. Mech. Eng. Part C: J. Mech. Eng. Sci. **229**(15), 2706–2718 (2015)
15. Xu, K., Simaan, N., et al.: An investigation of the intrinsic force sensing capabilities of continuum robots. IEEE Trans. Robot. **24**, 576–587 (2008)
16. Li, M., Kang, R., Geng, S., Guglielmino, E.: Design and control of a tendon-driven continuum robot. Trans. Inst. Meas. Control **40**, 3263–3272 (2017)

Aerodynamics of Soft Flapping Wings
of *Caudipteryx*

Yaser Saffar Talori⑩ and Jing-Shan Zhao(✉)⑩

Department of Mechanical Engineering, Tsinghua University, Beijing 100084,
People's Republic of China
jingshanzhao@mail.tsinghua.edu.cn

Abstract. This study explores the aerodynamic capacity of feathered forelimbs of *Caudipteryx*, the most basal non-volant maniraptoran dinosaur, with particular focus on flapping during terrestrial locomotion on a flat, horizontal substrate. In order to seek this subject, *Caudipteryx* and its wings have been modeled theoretically based on measuring the fossil data of *Caudipteryx* (IVPP V12344 and IVPP V12430). We divided the wings into various elements to enhance the analysis accuracy, and lift and thrust forces were estimated using a mathematical model and metabolic energy required to flap the forelimbs was estimated. Here we show that flapping feathered wings of flightless *Caudipteryx* would generate small amounts of aerodynamic forces based on our kinematic assumptions. Although the function of pennaceous feathers in oviraptorosaurs is uncertain and the feathers of dinosaur were believed not to originate for flight, theoretical analyses indicate that the feathered wings of *Caudipteryx*, could have produced small aerodynamic forces in rapid terrestrial locomotion. The winged Oviraptorosaurs utilized their feathered wings to produce aerodynamic forces in cursorial activities. Modeling of flapping while running showed similar limited aerodynamic force production.

Keywords: Soft flapping wings · Aerodynamics · Flight evolution ·
Caudipteryx

1 Introduction

Caudipteryx is the best known theropod from a small number of taxa in the Lower Cretaceous of northeast China that represent the most basal oviraptorosaurs and have pivotal, though frequently underappreciated, significance for understanding the origin of volancy (i.e. aerial locomotion, encompassing both powered flight and gliding) on the line to birds [1–15]. Recent phylogenetic analyses unanimously place oviraptorosaurs just outside the clade Paraves, encompassing birds, troodontids and dromaeosaurids [6]. Whereas volancy may be the ancestral condition for paravians, all known oviraptorosaurs were clearly terrestrial and non-volant despite resembling their paravian relatives in possessing sheets of pennaceous, bird-like feathers on the forelimbs and tail [16, 17]. Among dinosaurs endowed with such feather sheets, only oviraptorosaurs are widely agreed to be primitively flightless, raising the question of

© Springer Nature Switzerland AG 2019
H. Yu et al. (Eds.): ICIRA 2019, LNAI 11742, pp. 155–170, 2019.
https://doi.org/10.1007/978-3-030-27535-8_15

what function the feathered wings and tail served in these earthbound theropods [6, 18, 19]. The answer has large potential implications for the evolution of feathers and ultimately of volancy, because it is parsimonious to suppose that the function of the wings and tail in oviraptorosaurs is conserved from the unknown, presumably terrestrial and non-volant common ancestor of oviraptorosaurs and paravians. In other words, the role of the wings and tail in oviraptorosaurs may correspond to the function for which pennaceous feathers first evolved [20–25].

In the absence of volancy, proposed functions for the first pennaceous feathers include ornamentation, brooding behavior and some kind of role in terrestrial locomotion or maintaining balance [26–30]. Of these alternatives, the possibility that pennaceous feather surfaces could have been utilized to produce small aerodynamic forces in terrestrial locomotion is arguably the most amenable to test for finding the potential modern analogues of different kinds in wing-assisted incline running. WAIR was performed by chukar partridges and in the deployment of the wings by ostriches [4] in order to aid in maneuvers (a behavior exhibited by some juvenile birds today that involves using the wings to aid in running up slopes and clambering over obstacles). However, wing loading in basal oviraptorosaurs was likely too high for WAIR to have been feasible [13].

Our study focused on evaluating the potential aerodynamic function of the wings of *Caudipteryx* (see Fig. 1), a basal oviraptorosaur in which the skeleton and plumage are known from numerous specimens [31–35]. Two nominal species, *Caudipteryx dongi* and *Caudipteryx zoui*, have been described [16, 23, 29], but they differ only in a few osteological details [36–39]. Therefore, we centered our analysis on the wing of a generic *Caudipteryx*, incorporating information from multiple specimens (see Fig. 1). It is completely clear that the morphology of the shoulder girdle, joint, keeled sternum and flight muscles would not accommodate the necessary conditions for flapping flight and *Caudipteryx* could not fly. Hence, we used theoretical approaches to evaluate the possible utility of the wing for terrestrial locomotor behaviors, namely running while flapping. We carried out a theoretical analysis to investigate the aerodynamic forces that could have been produced by flapping the wings, in order to investigate the possibility that *Caudipteryx* might have used its wings to produce residual lift and thrust/drag in order to increase its motion performance.

We focused our analysis on a generic *Caudipteryx* with a body mass of 5 kg, an estimated value given that an empirical equation for estimating theropod body masses on the basis of femoral length [39] produces results ranging from 4.74 kg to 5.18 kg (mean value = 4.96 kg) for a total of five described specimens [16, 23, 29]. We also estimated the maximum running speed of *Caudipteryx* to be 8 m/s. This value was based on the skeletal hindlimb proportions of BPM 0001 and on adopting the assumptions [40, 41] with respect to the limb posture of small theropods and the range of Froude numbers (up to 17) they might have utilized in running.

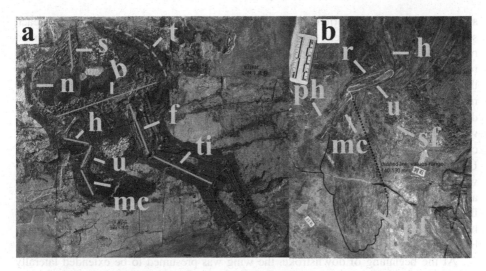

Fig. 1. Fossil of *Caudipteryx*. a, Skeleton of *Caudipteryx* IVPP V12430 and **b,** *Caudipteryx dongi* IVPP V 12344. The body mass is estimated about 5 kg for the holotype of *Caudipteryx zoui* (BPM 0001), based on a femur length of 149 mm (the average of the lengths of the left and right femora) [23, 27, 38, 39]. Abbreviations: **h,** humerus; **mc,** metacarpal; **pf,** primary feathers; **ph,** phalanx; **r,** radius; **sf,** secondary feathers; **u,** ulna; **t,** tail; **s,** skull; **n,** neck; **b,** body; **f,** femur; **ti,** tibia.

2 Materials and Methods

2.1 Theoretical Analysis of Aerodynamic Forces Produced by Flapping Wings of *Caudipteryx* During Terrestrial Running

The theoretical analyses are carried out as part of this study by considering the possible utility of the wings in locomotion behaviors: running while flapping. To this end, an aerodynamics model of *Caudipteryx* wings has been established. Flap-running was analyzed using calculations based on an unsteady aerodynamic model, whose elements are illustrated together with the assumed kinematic pattern of the wing in Fig. 2. The stretched length of the wing of *Caudipteryx* is 0.24 m measured from fossil, the area is 0.0179 m², the aspect ratio is 3.2 and the average chord is 0.0907 m (see Fig. 1). The model produced values of lift, thrust and power associated with flapping wings. The wing was assumed to have the same profile that was used as the basis for constructing the physical model. The wing was assumed to be depressed and elevated at an angular speed ω, rotating about a longitudinal axis passing through the head of the humerus. The surface of the wing was presumed to be twisted at a torsion angle of $\beta_0(°/m)$, representing the increase in angle of attack per unit distance towards the distal end of the wing. For the sake of easy analysis, the surface of the feathered wing was divided along its proximodistal axis into ten rectangular segments of equal width, with each segment having its own orientation. Anteroposterior length was averaged within each segment to calculate the length of the rectangle [42]. The orientation of each segment relative to the airstream was expressed by the angle of attack α' and pitch angle θ. Pitch represents the angle between the chord line of a given segment (i.e. the line connecting the leading and trailing edges of the segment's cross-section) and the vector U, representing the airflow incident on the surface of the entire wing. The angle α' was defined as the angle between the chord line of the wing and the relative velocity vector v, which represents the relative incident airflow as being applied at three fourths of chord point. The effect of v acting at the point in question is equivalent to the effect of U acting on the whole element. Because of interaction between the airflow and the wing surface, v was not necessarily identical to u, the vector representing the ambient airflow. Because *Caudipteryx* was presumed to be running horizontally, rather than flying, the incident airflow U was horizontal. The pitch angle θ was defined as the angle between u and the chord line of the segment, and could be equivalent to the angle between the chord line and the horizontal (see Fig. 2).

At the beginning of downstroke, the wing was presumed to be extended laterally from the body and elevated 22.5° above the horizontal. Flapping took place at a frequency f, resulting in an angular speed of $\omega = 2\pi f$ (in radians) for both the downstroke and the upstroke. The linear plunging velocity ($\dot{h}$) of each segment varied throughout the wingbeat cycle and also depended on the y value for the segment in question. At the beginning of downstroke, the base of the wing had a pitch angle of $\theta = 0°$, but the torsion angle caused more distal parts of the wing to assume a negative pitch based on the proximodistal distance y between the midline of each segment and the wing base. The entire wing pronates slightly during the downstroke and supinate slightly during the upstroke, such that θ decreased gradually throughout the first part of the downstroke, increased throughout the second part of the downstroke and the first part of the upstroke, and decreased throughout the second part of the upstroke. The rate of change in θ was given by $\delta\theta(y, t) = -\beta_0 y \sin(\omega t)$ where y is the distance between flapping axis and center of element (segment). We assume that the airflow over the wing of *Caudipteryx* would have remained attached to the wing surface (rather than separating, as in a stall) throughout the wingbeat cycle [43]. Circulation of the air about the wing during downstroke would have produced an upward lift force, the circulatory normal force (dN_c) acting at one fourth of chord on each segment. A separate upward inertial force acting at the mid-chord of each segment, termed the apparent mass effect (dN_a), would have resulted from downward acceleration of the wing. For a given segment, the sum of the two forces (dN) represents the total force acting upward and normal to the segment surface [44]:

$$dN = dN_c + dN_a \tag{1}$$

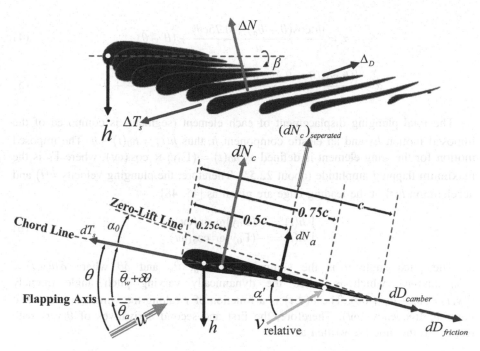

Fig. 2. An aerodynamic model and kinematics of flapping for each segment of the wing of *Caudipteryx*.

The element's circulatory normal force (see Fig. 2) is [45]

$$dN_v = \frac{\rho u v}{2} C_n(y) c \, dy \tag{2}$$

where ρ is the density of the airstream, v is the flow's relative velocity at the ¼ chord, C_n is $C_n(y) = 2\pi(\alpha' + \alpha_0 + \bar{\theta})$, $\bar{\theta} = \bar{\theta}_a + \bar{\theta}_w$ is the element's mean pitch angle, $\bar{\theta}_a$ is the angle between flapping axis and mean stream velocity (u), $\bar{\theta}_w$ is the mean angle between chord and flapping axis, α_0 is the angle of the zero lift line (the value is fixed for airfoil in each situation along the wing), α' is the flow's relative angle of attack at three quarters of chord point, it's given by

$$\alpha' = \frac{AR}{(2+AR)}[F'(k)\alpha + \frac{c}{2u}\frac{G'(k)}{k}\dot{\alpha}] - \frac{2(\alpha_0 + \bar{\theta})}{2+AR} \tag{3}$$

where AR is the wing aspect ratio of *Caudipteryx*, c is the wing element chord length, $k = \frac{c\omega}{2u}$ [46] is the reduced frequency, $F'(k) = 1 - \frac{c_1 k^2}{k^2 + c_2^2}$ and $G'(k) = -\frac{c_1 c_2 k}{k^2 + c_2^2}$ are simplified formulation of the modified Theodorsen function which were originally presented by Jones [47], $c_1 = \frac{0.5AR}{2.32+AR}$ and $c_2 = 0.181 + \frac{0.772}{AR}$. The equations of α and $\dot{\alpha}$ are given by [45, 48]

$$\alpha = \frac{[\dot{h}\cos(\theta - \bar{\theta}_a) + 0.75c\dot{\theta}]}{u} + (\theta - \bar{\theta}) \tag{4}$$

$$\dot{\alpha} = \frac{[(\ddot{h}\cos(\theta - \bar{\theta}_a) - \dot{h}\dot{\theta}\sin(\theta - \bar{\theta}_a) + 0.75c\ddot{\theta}]}{u} + \dot{\theta} \tag{5}$$

The total plunging displacement of each element (segment) is composed of the imposed motion h_0 and an elastic component $\tilde{h}$, thus $h(t) = h_0(t) + \tilde{h}$. The imposed motion for the wing element is defined as $h_0(t) = (\Gamma_0 y) \times \cos(\omega t)$, where Γ_0 is the maximum flapping amplitude (about 22.5°). Therefore, the plunging velocity $\dot{h}(t)$ and acceleration $\ddot{h}(t)$ at the leading edge are given as [45, 48]

$$\begin{cases} \dot{h}(t) = -(\Gamma_0 y)\omega \sin(\omega t) \\ \ddot{h}(t) = -(\Gamma_0 y)\omega^2 \cos(\omega t) \end{cases} \tag{6}$$

The pitch angle θ is the summation of $\bar{\theta}_a$, $\bar{\theta}_w$ and $\delta\theta$ where $\delta\theta(y,t) = -\beta_0 y \sin(\omega t)$, which is called the dynamically varying pitch angle (namely $\theta(y,t) = \bar{\theta}_a + \bar{\theta}_w + \delta\theta$). The $\theta(y,t)$ is a function of y (along the wing spanwise) and flapping frequency (ωt). Therefore, the first and second derivatives of $\theta(y,t)$ with respect to the time are written as

$$\begin{cases} \dot{\theta}(y,t) = -\beta_0 y\omega \cos(\omega t) \\ \ddot{\theta}(y,t) = \beta_0 y\omega^2 \sin(\omega t) \end{cases} \tag{7}$$

The downwash and the *Caudipteryx* wing motion relative to u are included to the flow velocity v mentioned in Eq. 2. Term of α' is composed along with the kinematic parameters as below [49]

$$v = \sqrt{\left\{ \left[u\cos\theta - \dot{h}\sin(\theta - \bar{\theta}_a) \right]^2 + \left[u(\alpha' + \bar{\theta}) - \frac{1}{2}c\dot{\theta} \right]^2 \right\}} \tag{8}$$

The apparent mass effect is

$$dN_a = \frac{\rho\pi c^2}{4}\dot{v}_2 dy \tag{9}$$

where $\dot{v}_2$ is the time rate of changing the mid-chord normal velocity component due to the *Caudipteryx* wing motion.

$$\dot{v}_2 = U\dot{\alpha} - \frac{1}{4}c\ddot{\theta} \tag{10}$$

The element's circulation distribution generates forces along the chord axis direction (see Fig. 2), hence the chordwise force due to the camber (dD_{camber}) and chordwise friction drag due to viscosity are given by [49, 50]

$$dD_{camber} = -2\pi\alpha_0(\alpha' + \bar{\theta})\frac{\rho uv}{2}cdy \tag{11}$$

$$dD_{friction} = (C_d)_f \frac{\rho v_x^2}{2}cdy \tag{12}$$

where $(C_d)_f = 0.89/(\log(\text{Re}_{chord}))^{2.58}$ is the friction drag coefficient [51] of the skin that is included of Reynolds number of local chord length and $v_x = u\cos\theta - \dot{h}\sin(\theta - \bar{\theta}_a)$ is the tangential flow speed to the element. For the two dimensional airfoil, Garrick expressed dT_s for the leading edge as below [52, 53]

$$dT_s = \eta_s 2\pi\left(\alpha' + \bar{\theta} - \frac{1}{4}\frac{c\dot{\theta}}{u}\right)^2 \frac{\rho uv}{2}cdy \tag{13}$$

where η_s is the efficiency term which illustrates that in reality because of having viscous effects, the efficiency of leading edge of most airfoils are less than 100%. Therefore, the total chordwise force along the chord axis is written by

$$dF_x = dT_s - dD_{camber} - dD_{friction} \tag{14}$$

Therefore, the equations of element's instantaneous lift and thrust are written as follows

$$dL = dN\cos\theta + dF_x\sin\theta$$
$$dT = dF_x\cos\theta - dN\sin\theta \tag{15}$$

where dL and dT are the instantaneous lift and thrust of the element, respectively. To integrate along the wingspan and to obtain whole wing's instantaneous lift and thrust, for wings, it is given by

$$L(t) = 2\int_0^l \cos\beta(t)dL$$

$$T(t) = 2\int_0^l dT \tag{16}$$

where l is the length of the *Caudipteryx* wingspan, $\beta(t) = \Gamma_0 \times \cos(\omega t)$ is the flapping angle which is a sinusoidal function of time. The average lift and thrust can be obtained via integrating Eq. 16 over the cycle ($\varphi = \omega t$).

$$\bar{L} = \frac{1}{2\pi} \int_0^{2\pi} L(\varphi) d\varphi$$

$$\bar{T} = \frac{1}{2\pi} \int_0^{2\pi} T(\varphi) d\varphi$$

(17)

where $\bar{L}$ and $\bar{T}$ are the means of the lift and thrust, individually. To calculate the required power against aerodynamic loads, from the attached flow is given by [49]

$$dP_{input} = dF_x \dot{h} \sin(\theta - \bar{\theta}_a) + dN \left[\dot{h} \cos(\theta - \bar{\theta}_a) + \frac{1}{4} c\dot{\theta} \right] + dN_a \left[\frac{1}{4} c\dot{\theta} \right] - dM_{ac}\dot{\theta}$$
$$- dM_a \dot{\theta}$$

(18)

where dM_{ac} is the element's pitching moment about its aerodynamic center and dM_a is composed of apparent camber and apparent inertia moments, which are given respectively as follows

$$\begin{cases} dM_{ac} = C_{mac} \frac{\rho uv}{2} c^2 dy \\ dM_a = -\left[\frac{1}{16} \rho \pi c^3 \ddot{\theta} u + \frac{1}{128} \rho \pi c^4 \ddot{\theta} \right] dy \end{cases}$$

(19)

where C_{mac} is the airfoil moment coefficient about its aerodynamic center. The instantaneous required aerodynamic power $P_{input}(t)$ for the whole wing is derived as follows

$$P_{input}(t) = 2 \int_0^l dP_{input}$$

(20)

Then the average input power in a cycle is found from

$$\bar{P}_{input} = \frac{1}{2\pi} \int_0^{2\pi} P_{input}(\varphi) d\varphi$$

(21)

The stiffness of the feathers of forelimbs are presumed to be much lower than that of modern birds as the aerodynamics was not the decisive function of the feather then, hence we assumed $\alpha_0 = 30°$ and $\beta_0 = 180°$ for a conservative estimation. The characteristics and parameters of the mathematical calculation in all situations are treated identically (see Fig. 3a). Lift and thrust were calculated for the whole wing (see Fig. 3b) during a full cycle (from 0 to 0.5 for downstroke; from 0.5 to 1 for upstroke) with forward velocity of near zero ($u = 0.05$ m/s). Other parameters were set to $\bar{\theta}_a = 0°$, $\bar{\theta}_w = 15°$, $\alpha_0 = 30°$, $\beta_0 = 180°$ and $\Gamma_0 = 22.5°$. Lift and thrust were also compared at flapping frequencies from 2 Hz to 10 Hz (see wing sections Fig. 3c) with no forward velocity.

In general cases, when *Caudipteryx* ran on the ground along a straight path at the velocity from 0 to 10 m/s and flapping frequency from 1 to 14 Hz, lift and thrust forces are acquired (see Fig. 4). The aerodynamic forces change when the flapping angle Γ_0 (see Fig. 5a and b) and pitch angle ($\bar{\theta}_a$ and $\bar{\theta}_w$) vary (see Fig. 5c and d). The required powers of flapping at different velocities and wing beats are captured and their changes have been analyzed (see Fig. 6).

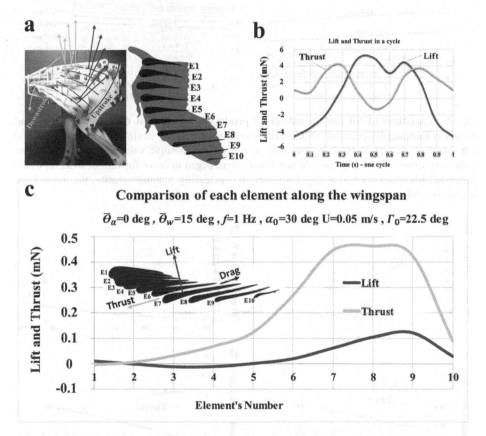

Fig. 3. **Aerodynamic forces of each element of the wing of *Caudipteryx*. a,** Schematic view of resultant forces per wing in one cycle. Each wing of *Caudipteryx* is divided into ten elements along the wing in order to better quantify the aerodynamic loads of each section (schematic of central 2d slice of each wing section is shown from E1 to E10). **b,** Variations of small values of lift and thrust of wings in a cycle with forward velocity of near zero ($u = 0.05$ m/s) when the frequency is one. Other parameters were set to $\bar{\theta}_a = 0°$, $\bar{\theta}_w = 15°$, $\alpha_0 = 30°$, $\beta_0 = 180°$ and $\Gamma_0 = 22.5°$. **c,** Comparison of each element along the wingspan by measuring lift and thrust. To compare any element along the *Caudipteryx* wingspan and capture the properties of each segment, the insignificant values of lift and thrust of ten elements for the given parameters were deduced supposing the wing beat was one in a cycle. Lift from element 4 to 9 and thrust from element 2 to 9 considering distance to the wing root are meaningful but the wing tip (element 10) has insignificant value.

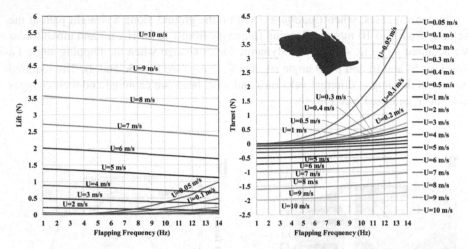

Fig. 4. Variations of lift and thrust forces produced by wings at different velocities and different flapping frequencies. While airflow or forward velocity is almost zero ($u = 0.05$ m/s) the average resultant force along the wing in a cycle has positive values for lift and positive values for thrust at any frequency. When *Caudipteryx* began to move forward or wind blew, the generated lift was increased at any frequency. By increasing running velocity, the thrust force decreased and changed to be a drag force.

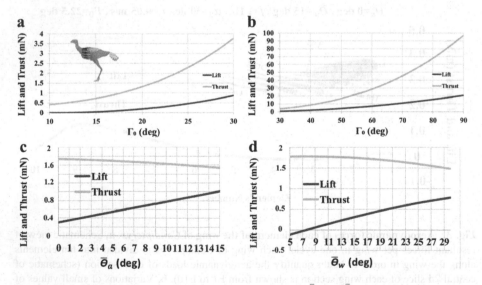

Fig. 5. Lift and thrust changes versus Γ_0 (flapping angle), $\bar{\theta}_a$ and $\bar{\theta}_w$. To analyze the effect of flapping angle, we suppose that the wing beat (flapping frequency) equals one, $\bar{\theta}_a$ is zero degree, $\bar{\theta}_w$ is 15°, α_0 is 30° and air speed is almost zero as an index. For lower flapping angle less than 22.5°, both lift and thrust are small but for larger angles, aerodynamic loads will be increased. Namely, the lift and thrust increase as the flapping angle of the wing increases. **a,** shows lift and thrust from 10 to 30° and **b,** shows lift and thrust from 30 to 90°. **c** and **d,** by increasing the angles of $\bar{\theta}_a$ and $\bar{\theta}_w$, when α_0 is 30°, Γ_0 is 22.5° and wing beat frequency is 1 Hz with the forward velocity of zero, the lift force increases and this is while the thrust force decreases slightly.

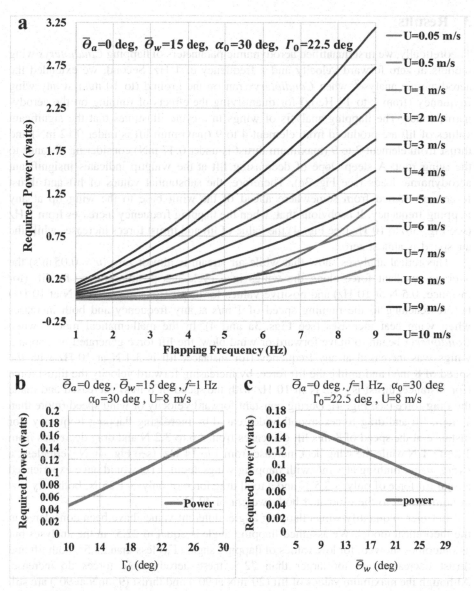

Fig. 6. a, Variations of required power in different velocities and different flapping frequencies of wings. By increasing the wing beat and wind velocity or the speed of *Caudipteryx*, the required metabolic power also increases. **b,** Variations of required power with flapping angle at the speed of 8 m/s while $\bar{\theta}_a = 0°$, $\bar{\theta}_w = 15°$, $\alpha_0 = 30°$ and $\beta_0 = 180°$ in a cycle. As flapping angle enhances, the required energy enhances. **c,** Variations of required power with the mean angle between chord and flapping axis at the speed of 8 m/s while $\bar{\theta}_a = 0°$, $\alpha_0 = 30°$, $\Gamma_0 = 22.5°$ and $\beta_0 = 180°$ in a cycle. The required power decreases as the mean angle between the chord and flapping axis increases.

3 Results

Theoretically, we first quantified aerodynamic parameters of flapping *Caudipteryx* wing models at zero forward velocity and a frequency of 1 Hz. Second, we extended the aerodynamic analyses when *Caudipteryx* ran on the ground (to 10 m/s) at any wing frequency (from 1 to 14 Hertz) for quantifying the effects of running on the aerodynamic loads. The flapping analysis of wings in a cycle illustrates that the significant values of lift are produced from element 4 to 9 (maximum lift is under 0.12 mN) and thrust from element 2 to 9 (maximum thrust is under 0.47 mN) considering distance to the wing root. A steep slope of decreasing lift at the wingtip indicates insignificant aerodynamic loads (see Fig. 3c). Therefore, the substantial values of lift and thrust forces are started from somewhere ahead of the wing base to the wing tip at any flapping frequency. It is obvious that, when the flapping frequency increases from 1 Hz (see Fig. 3b) to 10 Hz (see Fig. 4) the value of lift and thrust forces increases while the air speed is almost zero.

Theoretical analyses show that while air stream is almost zero ($u = 0.05$ m/s) the average resultant force along the wings in a cycle has positive values for lift (for instance, 0.5 N at 10 Hz) and positive values for thrust (for instance, 1.5 N at 10 Hz) before reaching to the running speed of 1 m/s at any frequency and both increases when wing beat increases (see Figs. 3a and 4). In the mathematical model, when *Caudipteryx* began to move forward or wind blew, the lift force generated by flapping wings was increased at any frequency (for instance, lift is 3.4 N at 10 Hz with the speed of 8 m/s) and unlike the lift force, by increasing forward velocity the thrust force (for instance, thrust is -1.2 N in 10 Hz with the speed of 8 m/s) decreased and made the drag force (see Fig. 4). During constant forward velocity or wind speed (more than 1 m/s), lift and drag forces smoothly decreased by increasing flapping frequency (for instance at the speed of 8 m/s lift decreases from 3.6 to 3.2 N and drag decreases from 1.25 to 1 N while the wing beat increase from 1 to 14 Hz) (see Fig. 4). Nevertheless, a *Caudipteryx* running at 8 m/s with flapping wings about 4 Hz would have experienced a total lift force of only ~ 3.5 N and a total drag force of only ~ 1.25 N, both very low in comparison to the estimated body weight of 49 N.

In order to quantify wings flapping angle, different values have been considered in the theoretical model. We assumed flapping angle is equal to $22.5°$ in the analyses but as outcomes showed, for low values of flapping angle (Γ_0) less than $22.5°$, both lift and thrust decreases and for larger than 22.5, these aerodynamic forces do increase. Although the maximum values of lift (20 mN at $90°$) and thrust (95 mN at $90°$) are still small for *Caudipteryx*, it shows the significant effects of flapping angle on aerodynamic loads. (see Fig. 5a and b). Theoretical model also shows by increasing the angle between flapping axis and mean stream velocity ($\bar{\theta}_a$) or mean angle between chord and flapping axis ($\bar{\theta}_w$), the lift force increases while the thrust force decreases slightly (see Fig. 5c and d).

Flapping would be metabolically costly for *Caudipteryx*. Therefore, theoretical model shows by increasing the wing beat frequency (from 1 to 9 Hz) and wind velocity (to 10 m/s) or the speed of *Caudipteryx*, the required metabolic power also increases (see Fig. 6a). In a similar situation, as flapping angle increases, the required energy in order to supply this angle ought to be increased (see Fig. 6b) but by increasing mean angle between chord and flapping axis $(\bar{\theta}_w)$, required power decreases and much lesser energy is needed (see Fig. 6c).

4 Discussion

The results of the theoretical analyses consistently demonstrate that the potential of the flapping wings of *Caudipteryx* in order to generate aerodynamic forces (lift and thrust/drag) in the context of terrestrial running was small. Nevertheless, the produced aerodynamic forces are considered relative to the estimated body weight of 49 N. In the case when *Caudipteryx* stood still (there was neither motion nor wind), the lift and thrust from flapping wings should be both positive. Hence, the significant outcome is that *Caudipteryx* could produce the lift force upward and the pushing force ahead during flapping wings (although the forces are small). However, this thrust force was neutralized and compensated by the strong legs. Nevertheless, theoretical analyses agree that the flapping wings of a running *Caudipteryx*, given the assumptions of the model, would not have been capable of generating substantial lift and drag.

Certainly, in order to have thrust force at any velocity, the descendants of *oviraptorosaurs* needed to develop their wing size and aspect ratio to the larger one for creating the positive thrust force along with the lift force. Also the accommodation of shoulder joints and flight muscles (non-volant flight structure) which are supposed to supply aerodynamic forces by the small wings were not assigned for flying or jumping up. Therefore, increasing aerodynamic properties of flapping wings of *Caudipteryx* by increasing flapping angle could suggest that the successive generations of *Caudipteryx* enhanced and optimized the accommodation of their shoulder joints to support larger flapping angle.

These results are consistent with the conclusion reached by other studies [3, 13] that *Caudipteryx* was clearly non-volant. *Caudipteryx* would have had to produce lift equivalent to a substantial percentage of its own body weight to jump using flapping. The outcomes of our research clearly demonstrate that this would not have been possible by flapping wings. Also, our analysis suggests that the wings of *Caudipteryx* would have had effects on its rapid cursorial performance even at lower flapping frequencies. However, this study does not address the possibility that aerodynamic loads generated by the flapping wings of *Caudipteryx* might have contributed to terrestrial maneuvers, as apparently occurs in modern ostriches [4], such as turning if the wings were fluctuated asymmetrically in some manner or symmetrically in braking.

Acknowledgement. The authors appreciate Prof. Dr. Corwin Sullivan from the Department of Biological Sciences, University of Alberta, Canada, Prof. Dr. Zhong-He Zhou and Prof. Dr. Min Wang from the Key Laboratory of Vertebrate Evolution and Human Origins, Institute of Vertebrate Paleontology and Paleoanthropology, Chinese Academy of Sciences, Beijing, 100044, P. R. China for their kind suggestions.

Author Contributions. Y.S.T. deduced formulas and prepared programs, simulations, tables and figures and wrote the first draft of the manuscript; J.-S.Z. supervised the project and provided the major suggestions in revision; All authors discussed the results and commented on the manuscript and contributed ideas to manuscript development and data analysis.

Funding. This project was supported by the National Natural Science Foundation of China under grant 51575291, the National Major Science and Technology Project of China under grant 2015ZX04002101, State Key Laboratory of Tribology, Tsinghua University, and the 221 program of Tsinghua University.

Competing Interests. The authors declare that they have no competing interests.

References

1. Ostrom, J.H.: Bird flight: how did it begin? Am. Sci. **67**, 46–56 (1979)
2. Foth, C., Tischlinger, H., Rauhut, O.W.M.: New specimen of *Archaeopteryx* provides insights into the evolution of pennaceous feathers. Nature **511**, 79–82 (2014)
3. Sullivan, C., Xu, X., O'Connor, J.K.: Complexities and novelties in the early evolution of avian flight, as seen in the Mesozoic Yanliao and Jehol Biotas of Northeast China. Palaeoworld **26**, 212–229 (2017)
4. Schaller, N.U.: Structural attributes contributing to locomotor performance in the ostrich. Ph.D. dissertation, University of Heidelberg, 129 p. (2008)
5. Forster, C.A., Sampson, S.D., Chiappe, L.M., Krause, D.W.: The theropod ancestry of birds: new evidence from the late cretaceous of madagascar. Science **279**, 1915–1919 (1998)
6. Garner, J.P., Taylor, G.K., Thomas, A.L.R.: On the origins of birds: the sequence of character acquisition in the evolution of avian flight. Proc. R. Soc. Lond. B **266**, 1259–1266 (1999)
7. Sereno, P.C.: The evolution of dinosaurs. Science **284**, 2137–2147 (1999)
8. Lewin, R.: How did vertebrates take to the air? Sci. New Ser. **221**, 38–39 (1983)
9. Gibbons, A.: New feathered fossil brings dinosaurs and birds closer. Sci. New Ser. **274**, 720–721 (1996)
10. Prum, R.O.: Dinosaurs take to the air. Nature **421**, 323–324 (2003)
11. Henderson, D.M.: Estimating the masses and centers of mass of extinct animals by 3-D mathematical slicing. Paleobiology **25**, 88–106 (1999)
12. Ji, S.A., Ji, Q., Padian, K.: Biostratigraphy of new pterosaurs from China. Nature **398**, 573–574 (1999)
13. Dececchi, T.A., Larsson, H.C.E., Habib, M.B.: The wings before the bird: an evaluation of flapping-based locomotory hypotheses in bird antecedents. PeerJ **4**, e2159 (2016)
14. Dyke, G.J., Norell, M.A.: *Caudipteryx* as a non avialan theropod rather than a flightless bird. Acta Palaeontol. Pol. **50**(1), 101–116 (2005)
15. Padian, K.: When is a bird not a bird? Nature **393**, 729–730 (1998)
16. Qiang, J., Currie, P.J., Norell, M.A., Shuan, J.: Two feathered dinosaurs from Northeastern China. Nature **393**, 753–761 (1998)
17. Swisher, C.C., Wang, Y.Q., Wang, X.L., Xu, X.: Cretaceous age for the feathered dinosaurs of Liaoning, China. Nature **400**, 58–61 (1999)
18. Xu, X., Wang, X.L., Wu, X.C.: A dromaeosaurid dinosaur with a filamentous integument from the Yixian formation of China. Nature **401**, 262–266 (1999)

19. Zhou, Z.: The origin and early evolution of birds: discoveries, disputes, and perspectives from fossil evidence. Naturwissenschaften **91**, 455–471 (2004)
20. Xu, X., et al.: Four-winged dinosaurs from China. Nature **421**, 335–340 (2003)
21. Xu, X., et al.: An integrative approach to understanding bird origins. Science **346**, 1253293 (2014)
22. Zhou, Z., Zhang, F.C.: Origin and early evolution of feathers: evidence from the early cretaceous of China. Acta Zoologica Sinica **52**(Suppl.), 125–128 (2006)
23. Zhou, Z.H., Wang, X.L.: A new species of *Caudipteryx* from the Yixian Formation of Liaoning, Northeast China. Vertebrata PalAsiatica **38**, 111–127 (2000)
24. Zhou, Z., Barrett, P.M., Hilton, J.: An exceptionally preserved lower cretaceous ecosystem. Nature **421**, 807–814 (2003)
25. Jones, T.D., Farlow, J.O., Ruben, J.A., Henderson, D.M., Hillenius, W.J.: Cursoriality in bipedal archosaurs. Nature **406**, 716–718 (2000)
26. Norell, M., Ji, Q., Gao, K., Yuan, C., Zhao, Y., Wang, L.: Modern feathers on a non-volant dinosaur. Nature **416**, 36–37 (2002)
27. Lee, M.S.Y., Cau, A., Naish, D., Dyke, G.J.: Sustained miniaturization and anatomical innovation in the dinosaurian ancestors of birds. Science **345**, 562–566 (2014)
28. Zhou, Z.: Evolutionary radiation of the jehol biota: chronological and ecological perspectives. Geol. J. **41**, 377–393 (2006)
29. Zhou, Z., Wang, X.L., Zhang, F.C., Xu, X.: Important features of *Caudipteryx* evidence from two nearly complete new specimens. Vertebr PalAsiat **38**, 241–254 (2000)
30. Norberg, U.M.: Vertebrate Flight in Zoophysiology (1989). ISBN 9783642838507
31. Henk, T.: The Simple Science of Flight (2009). ISBN 9780262513135
32. Bruderer, B., Boldt, A.: Flight characteristics of birds: I. Radar measurements of speeds. Ibis **143**, 178–204 (2001)
33. Baumel, J.J. (ed.): Handbook of Avian Anatomy. Nuttal Orn. Club, Cambridge (1993)
34. Shyy, W., et al.: Recent progress in flapping wing aerodynamics and aeroelasticity. Progress Aerosp. Sci. **46**, 284–327 (2010)
35. Woolley, J.D.: The functional morphology of the avian flight muscle M. Coracobrachialis posterior. J. Exp. Biol. **203**, 1767–1776 (2000)
36. Biewener, A.A.: Muscle function in avian flight: Achieving power and control. Philos. Trans. R. Soc. B **366**, 1496–1506 (2011)
37. Hutchinson, J.R., Allen, V.: The evolutionary continuum of limb function from early theropods to birds. Naturwissenschaften **96**(4), 423–448 (2009)
38. He, T., Wang, X.L., Zhou, Z.: A new genus and species of *Caudipteryx* dinosaur from the Lower Cretaceous Jiufotang Formation of Western Liaoning China. Vertebrata PalAsiatica **46**, 178–189 (2008)
39. Christiansen, P., Farina, R.A.: Mass prediction in theropod dinosaurs. Hist. Biol. **16**, 85–92 (2004)
40. Hutchinson, J.: Biomechanical modeling and sensitivity analysis of bipedal running ability I. Extant Taxa. J. Morphol. **262**, 421–440 (2004)
41. Hutchinson, J.: Biomechanical modeling and sensitivity analysis of bipedal running ability II. Extant Taxa. J. Morphol. **262**, 441–461 (2004)
42. Delaurier, J.D., Harris, J.M.: A study of mechanical flapping wing flight. Aeronaut. J. **97**, 277–286 (1993)
43. Kamakoti, R., et al.: A computational study for biological flapping wing flight. Trans. Aeronaut. Astronaut. Soc. Republic China **32**(4), 265–279 (2000)
44. Delaurier, J.D.: An ornithopter wing design. Can. Aeronaut. Space J. **40**, 10–18 (1994)
45. Delaurier, J.D.: An aerodynamic model for flapping wing flight. Aeronaut. J. **97**, 125–130 (1993)

46. Mueller, T.J., DeLaurier, J.D.: Aerodynamics of small vehicles. Annu. Rev. Fluid Mech. **35** (1), 89–111 (2003)
47. Jones, R.T.: The Unsteady Lift of a Wing of Finite Aspect Ratio. NACA Report 681 (1940)
48. Delaurier, J.D.: The development of an efficient ornithopter wing. Aeronaut. J. **97**, 153–162 (1993)
49. Delaurier, J.D., Larijani, R.F.: A nonlinear aeroelastic model for the study of flapping wing flight, chapter 18. In: The American Institute of Aeronautics and Astronautics (2001)
50. Delaurier, J.D.: Drag of wings with cambered airfoils and partial leading edge suction. J. Aircr. **20**, 882–886 (1983)
51. Hoerner, S.F.: Fluid dynamic drag. Brick Town, NJ 2, 1–16 (1965)
52. Garrick, I.E.: Propulsion of a Flapping and Oscillating Aerofoil. NACA Report 567 (1936)
53. Hoerner, S.F.: Pressure drag, fluid dynamic drag. Brick Town, NJ, 3–16 (1965)

A Finite Element Model and Performance Analysis of a Hybrid Continuum Robot

Dian Zhuang, Xinrui Wang[✉], Cijing Sun, and Rongjie Kang

Key Laboratory of Mechanism Theory and Equipment Design of the Ministry
of Education, International Centre for Advanced Mechanisms and Robotics,
Tianjin University, Tianjin 300354, China
{wangxr,rjkang}@tju.edu.cn

Abstract. The intrinsic compliance and flexibility make continuum robots more competent to work in unstructured environments as compared to conventional rigid robots, but at the expense of stiffness and positional precision. To handle this problem, this paper builds a static finite element model of such hybrid continuum robot to describe the individual structure of pneumatic muscles and rods in one actuator and identify the performance of each actuation method. The model agreed with the experimental results with an error less than 10 mm (4.76% of its initial length). Moreover, the simulated and experimental results validated the different performances of two different actuation methods.

Keywords: Continuum robot · Finite element model · Hybrid actuation · Variable stiffness

1 Introduction

Traditional rigid robots consist of discrete joints as well as rigid links and are widely employed in industrial production. However, when it comes to performing tasks in unstructured environment, these rigid robots are incompetent due to their limited flexibility and compliance. To extend robots' working environment, researchers, inspired by continuum structures in nature, such as elephant trunks, lizard tongues, and octopus tentacles [1], are paying more and more attention to continuum robots. This kind of robots have structural compliance, making them have promising potential to operate in unstructured, irregular and highly constrained environment, including minimally invasive surgery (MIS) [2] and rescue operations in collapsed buildings [3]. In conclusion, continuum robots with have attracted more and more attention as they are more suitable for operations requiring for high flexibility and compliance.

Since the concept of continuum robot was put forward by Robinson and Davies [4], various actuators have been proposed to realize the movement of continuum robots. The thermal shape memory alloys (SMAs) actuators [5, 6] are easy to control and can generate large contractile stress, but their temperature control characteristic slows down their motion frequency and cycle time. The electro-active polymers (EAPs) [7] have the advantages of relatively high efficiency and light weight. However, extremely high voltage is often required and their output force and displacement are usually limited. Fluid-driven actuators are also widely used in continuum robots. These fluid-driven

© Springer Nature Switzerland AG 2019
H. Yu et al. (Eds.): ICIRA 2019, LNAI 11742, pp. 171–182, 2019.
https://doi.org/10.1007/978-3-030-27535-8_16

actuators, either pneumatically [8] or hydraulically [9], can achieve large deformation, displacement and strength. Nevertheless, because of the leakage phenomenon and the compressibility of fluid, it is difficult for these kinds of actuators to realize high positioning accuracy. Cable-driven continuum robots [10], have high resolution when transmitting contracting movement, but low stiffness when taking compressive and lateral forces. The elastic Ni-Ti rods [11] improve the overall stiffness of the robot, however, at the cost of lower compliance in comparison with cable-driven robot. Through above analysis, it is found that every actuating method has its advantages and disadvantages, which means that it is difficult to balance the performance on workspace, precision, strengths, stiffness as well as compliance.

To deal with this problem, some researchers tried to change the stiffness of robots, making them maintain compliant and flexible when navigating through complicated environment and become stiff and accurate when manipulating targets. Brown et al. [12] delineated a universal stiffness-variable robotic gripper based on the jamming of granular material. Li et al. [13] proposed the principle of passive particle jamming, making the vacuum power not necessary. And the variable stiffness of continuum robot was also achieved by Shiva et al. [14] utilizing inherently antagonistic actuation scheme. Apart from that, smart materials have been applied to realize variable stiffness as well. Taniguchi et al. [15] produced two types of soft magnetic materials and developed new soft actuators with magnetic intelligent fluids, of which phase change can lead to stiffness change. Finally, another effective method to achieve comprehensive performance of continuum robots is hybrid actuation. Kang et al. [16] arranged additional steel cables inside pneumatic muscles. The pneumatic muscles are designed to realize preliminary positioning, while the embedded cables are responsible for fine adjustment of position. Although this hybrid continuum robot is able to improve positioning accuracy and, at the same time, maintain large displacement capability, considering the fact that cables cannot bear compressive and lateral forces, the stiffness and the precision it improves is actually limited. Similar hybrid actuation method is used in this paper. The pneumatic muscles are kept to achieve large-scale flexible movement while elastic rods, whose stiffness is higher in the axial and lateral directions compared with cables, are used to realize high positioning accuracy. Such type of hybrid actuation method is promising to achieve comprehensive performance, such as high flexibility, large workspace, high positioning precision and large strengths, into one continuum robot.

The working principles as well as actuation and control methods of continuum robots are quite different from conventional rigid robots, which means that the existing kinematics, statics and dynamics models built based on rigid bodies are no longer applicable for continuum robots. To investigate the motion and control of such robots, quantities of researchers have been trying to build the mathematical models of continuum robots. Jones and Walker [17] presented the kinematic models of continuum robots based on the assumption of piece constant curvature (PCC), which are widely recognized by related researchers. Xu and Simaan [18] used elliptic integrals to derive an analytic formulation for kinematics and statics of continuum robots. Renda et al. [19] established a dynamic model according to discrete Cosserat beam theory. Kang et al. [20] developed a dynamic model for a multi-segmented pneumatic continuum robot based on the Newton-Euler equation. They also presented a static model for a hybrid continuum robot using an improved Kirchhoff rod theory [21]. All in all, these models considered the continuum actuator as one body structure. However, the actuators of hybrid continuum robot mentioned in [21] include both pneumatic artificial muscles and elastic rods, which are actually two structures arranged in parallel. To handle this problem, this paper builds astatic finite element model of such hybrid continuum robot to describe the individual structure of pneumatic muscles and rods in one actuator and identify the performances of each actuation method.

This paper is organized as follows. Firstly, the prototype is briefly introduced in Sect. 2. Subsequently, the static finite element model is represented in Sect. 3. And the model is validated in Sect. 4. Finally, conclusions are drawn in Sect. 5.

2 Prototype

The prototype of hybrid continuum robot is presented in this section. As shown in Fig. 1, the prototype consists of a continuum arm and a driving unit.

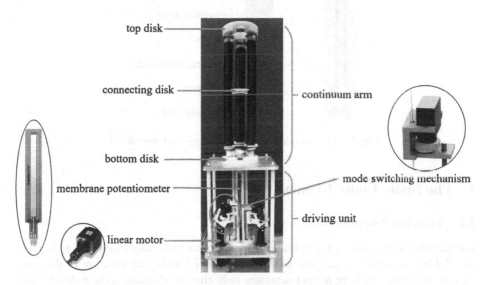

Fig. 1. The overall structure of the prototype

The continuum arm is composed of three parallel hybrid actuators and three disks, whose function is to keep the hybrid actuators together and parallel to each other. The hybrid actuators are elastic rods embedded artificial pneumatic muscles (eREMs), whose structure is shown in Fig. 2. The eREM consists of an elastic rod, a nylon braided mesh, a rubber tube, a top connector, a bottom connector and five blocks. The function of the top connector is to fix the elastic rod with the top of the pneumatic muscle using aluminum collet and hot melt adhesive. The bottom connector, connecting the airway, pneumatic muscle and elastic rod, is hollow to allow the elastic rod to pass through. And a rubber seal is placed to prevent air leaking. Equally distributed along the elastic rod, the five blocks are used to make sure the elastic rod will always be coaxial with the central axis of the pneumatic muscle.

Moreover, the driving unit below the continuum arm includes linear motors, sensing system and mode switching mechanisms. The detailed design of the continuum robot can be found in our previous work [21].

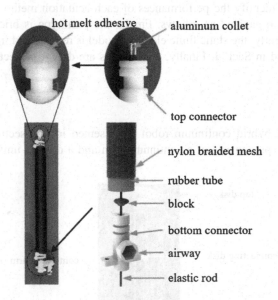

Fig. 2. The overview and exploded view of the eREM

3 The Static Finite Element Model

3.1 Structure Simplification

The simplified structure of the hybrid continuum robot is demonstrated in Fig. 3. Three parallel hybrid actuators and one top disk is kept. To make the structure of the robot easy to simulate, the kept hybrid actuators only consist of elastic rods, nylon braided meshes and rubber tubes in the finite element model. Besides, the elastic rods made of Ni-Ti alloy are fixed to the top of the pneumatic muscles while going through and sliding along the bottom of the pneumatic muscles. And the bottom of three pneumatic muscles is fixed.

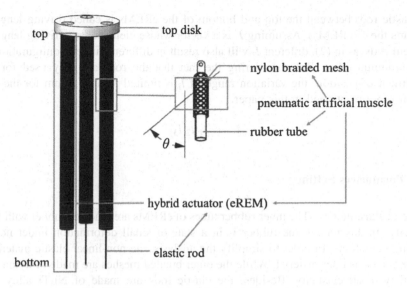

top

top disk

nylon braided mesh

pneumatic artificial muscle

rubber tube

θ

hybrid actuator (eREM)

elastic rod

bottom

Fig. 3. The basic structure of the hybrid continuum robot

3.2   Working Principle

Large-Scale Flexible Movement for Preliminary Positioning. The large-scale flexible movement is achieved pneumatically and the elastic rods act in a passive mode. The excellent performance, including large output force, high speed, big stroke and flexibility, of pneumatic actuators are fully utilized for large-scale movement. As shown in Fig. 3, the elasticity of the inner rubber tube is large while the elasticity of the outer braided meshes, which are made of nylon, is extremely small. With the initial angle θ between the nylon fiber and the eREM axis greater than $54°44'$, the outer nylon braided meshes can limit the radial expansion of the eREMs, making the eREMs elongated in the axial direction when inflated. Since there are three parallel eREMs, when eREMs are elongated with different pressures, P_i (i means the ith eREMs), the robot will bend. Moreover, the robot will elongate along its axis if all three eREMs are pressurized in the same degree at the same time ($P_1 = P_2 = P_3$). Besides, twisting will not happen and is not considered for the ideal robot model. Assuming P is a vector whose elements are pressures of different eREMs, as in (1), different P will result in different curved configurations of the continuum robot.

$$P = [P_1 \; P_2 \; P_3] \tag{1}$$

Fine Adjustment of Position. After the preliminary positioning is realized and the end of the continuum arm has arrived near the target working point, the elastic rods work in an active mode and drive the robot to achieve fine adjustment of position with high positioning accuracy. With the bottom of three eREMs fixed, the robot will also bend when the elastic rods are pushed or pulled with different displacement. The length of the elastic rods between the top and bottom of the eREMs is called driving length, l_i (i means the ith eREMs). Assuming L is a vector whose elements are driving length of different rods, as in (2), different L will also result in different curved configurations of the continuum robot. But considering the fact that the rods are only used for fine adjustment of position, the variation range of l_i is limited to only 5 mm for the continuum robot mentioned in this paper.

$$L = [l_1 \; l_2 \; l_3]$$ (2)

3.3   Parameters Setting

Material Parameters. The inner rubber tubes of eREMs are made of rubber with large elasticity. In this model, the rubber is in a state of small deformation under normal working conditions. In order to simplify the analysis, the non-linear elastic material is approximated as liner material. While the outer braided meshes are made of nylon with extremely small elasticity. Besides, the elastic rods are made of Ni-Ti alloy. The material of the top disk, which can be fabricated by 3D printer, is UV Curable Resin. Therefore, the common parameters of these materials, shown in Table 1, are set in the finite element model.

Table 1. Material parameters

	Density (kg/m^3)	Poisson ratio	Elastic modulus (Pa)
Rubber tubes	1.2×10^3	0.49	1.5×10^6
Braided meshes	1.4×10^3	0.28	3.3×10^9
Elastic rods	6.5×10^3	0.30	1.6×10^{11}
Disk	1.2×10^3	0.39	2.3×10^9

Geometric Parameters. The geometric parameters of the rubber tubes, braided meshes, elastic rods and disk are demonstrated in Table 2.

Table 2. Geometric parameters

	Items	Value
Rubber tubes	Outer diameter (mm)	13
	Thickness (mm)	1.5
	Initial length (mm)	200
Braided meshes	The initial angle between the nylon fiber and the eREM axis	60
Elastic rods	Diameter (mm)	1
	Length (mm)	260
Disk	Diameter (mm)	66
	Thickness (mm)	10
	The distribution diameter of eREMs on the disk (mm)	46

3.4   Modeling and Analysis Method

The static finite element model is built in the commercial software Abaqus 6.14. Three processes are simulated in the finite element model. Firstly, the large-scale flexible movement are simulated with different pressure combinations set in the eREMs. Secondly, the same pressure combinations of large-scale flexible movement are kept and at the same time elastic rods are driven, to simulate the process of the fine adjustment after preliminary positioning. Thirdly, an external force is applied to the end of the robot arm to learn the different influence on the configurations of the robot actuated pneumatically or by the elastic rods. Besides, the gravity and frictions are all considered in the model. The braided meshes limits the radical expansion of rubber tubes, so that rubber tubes will not expand like the inflated balloon but extend along the radical.

To record the configurations of the continuum arm, an absolute coordinate system, defined as reference coordinate system, is built as shown in Fig. 4. Six sampling points along the continuum arm are set in the model so that their coordinates can be obtained. Besides the mechanical properties of the model, such as stress and strain, can also be acquired in Abaqus.

Figure 5(a) is the analysis result of large-scale flexible movement with the vector P set as [100 kPa, 50 kPa, 50 kPa] while Fig. 5(b) is the analysis result of fine adjustment with the vector L set as [262 mm, 260 mm, 260 mm] and vector P same as that in Fig. 5(a). The simulated results of Fig. 5(a) and (b) are similar and difficult to

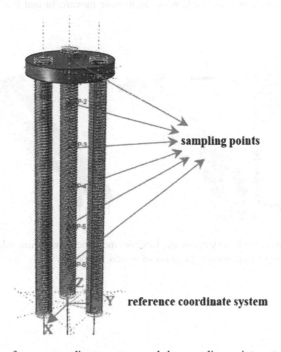

Fig. 4. The reference coordinate system and the sampling points set in the model

distinguish by the naked eyes, since the fine adjustment actuated by the rods is with 5 mm. Moreover, Figs. 6 and 7 are analysis results of the continuum robots when an external force $F = 1.5$ N is applied to the end of the robot under the circumstances when the elastic rods are in passive and active modes. A qualitative conclusion can be made that the hybrid actuation is beneficial to the repeatability of the robot. This because the structure stiffness of the robot improves in the locked mode.

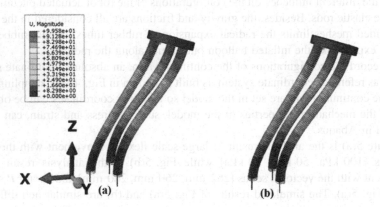

Fig. 5. The analysis result of large-scale flexible movement and fine adjustment

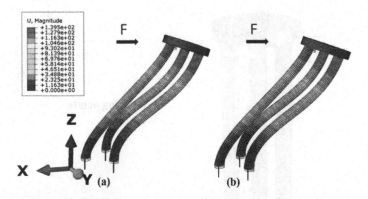

Fig. 6. The analysis result of large-scale flexible movement and fine adjustment when an external force pointing the negative direction of x axis is applied

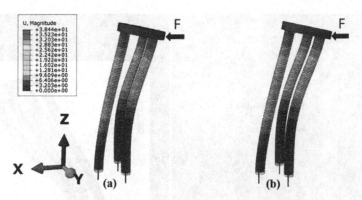

Fig. 7. The analysis result of large-scale flexible movement and fine adjustment when an external force pointing the positive direction of x axis is applied

4 Model Validation

In order to verify the accuracy and reliability of the finite element model, multiple sets of simulated configurations and experimental configurations of above prototype under the same driving conditions were compared.

4.1 Experimental Setup

To get the configurations of the prototype, it is necessary to measure the coordinates of sampling points in Fig. 4, so an electromagnetic sensing system was built. The electromagnetic sensing system (3D Guidance tranSTAR, manufactured by *Ascension Technology Corporation*), whose measurement error is within 0.5 mm, consists of a magnetic field emitter, an electronic converter and an electromagnetic sensor. The prototype was placed in the magnetic field emitted by the magnetic field emitter. With the aid of the electromagnetic position sensor, the coordinates of the sampling points in the magnetic field coordinate system whose origin is built on the magnetic field emitter could be accurately measured. Then a coordinate transformation from the magnetic field coordinate system to the reference coordinate system shown in Fig. 4 was implemented, for the convenience of comparing the simulated configurations with the experimental configurations of the prototype. The experimental setup and corresponding simulated results are shown in Fig. 8.

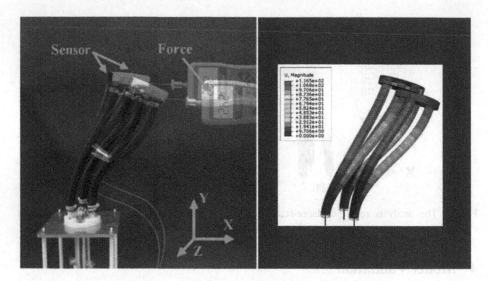

Fig. 8. Experimental setup and corresponding simulated results

4.2 Result Comparison of Simulation and Experiment

The model was validated in totally three cases.

Case (a). The continuum robot in case (a) is in the large-scale movement mode and the P is set as [200 kPa, 50 kPa, 50 kPa]. The comparing result is shown in Fig. 9(a).

Case (b). The continuum robot in case (b) is also in the large-scale movement mode and the P is also set as [200 kPa, 50 kPa, 50 kPa]. Besides, a 1 N external force pointing to the positive direction of x-axis is then applied to the top disk of the robot. The comparing result is shown in Fig. 9(b).

Case (c). The continuum robot in case (c) firstly move in the large-scale movement mode (the P is also set as [200 kPa, 50 kPa, 50 kPa]) and then the system is switched to the fine adjustment mode. Besides, a 1 N external force in the same direction as in case (b) is also applied to the top disk of the robot. The comparing result is shown in Fig. 9(c).

Due to the ideal finite element model is based on simplified structure and ignores the effect of twisting and torsion, there must be deviations of the sampling points coordinates between the simulated configurations and the experimental configurations. But the errors are within 10 mm (4.76% of the initial length of the actuator), which means that the finite element model built in this paper can predict the configurations of the hybrid continuum robots accurately.

Moreover, according to the comparing results in Fig. 8, it can be seen that the stiffness of the continuum robot in case (c) is higher than that in case (b) because the elastic rods in case (c) are in active mode. These results prove that the performance and function of each actuation method should be identified respectively. Many uncertainties remain such as friction, leakage, hysteresis and measurement errors.

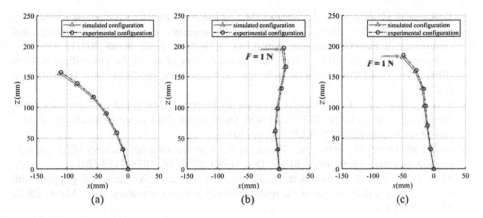

Fig. 9. The comparing results of case (a), (b) and (c)

5 Conclusion

Considering the fact that various actuation methods all have their advantages and disadvantages, it is important, but difficult, to achieve the comprehensive performance of continuum robots. The robot prototype discussed in this paper, which could either be driven pneumatically or by elastic rods, took advantage of a hybrid actuation method to deal with the performance problem. As the actuators of the robot contain two different structures, a dynamic finite element model was built to predict the configurations of the continuum robot. The proposed finite element model could identify the two structures of the actuators independently, rather than regarding them as one single structure, used in most existing models. The comparison between the simulated and experimental results verified the reliability of the finite element model and the necessity to model the two actuating structures separately.

Finally, the division of the mesh, can also have an impact on the stiffness and performance of the robot. Future work will investigate the exact influence of meshing of parts. The hybrid actuation indeed improved the positioning precision, but at the expense of light weight of the whole system. It can be optimized continuously in the future.

Acknowledgment. This research was supported by National Key R&D Program of China (Grant No. 2018YFB1304600) and Natural Science Foundation of China (Grant 51875393 and 51721003). We thank Chenghao Yang and Yue Liu for helpful suggestions and device supports in building the finite element model.

References

1. Li, M., Kang, R., Branson, D.T., Dai, J.S.: Model-free control for continuum robots based on an adaptive Kalman filter. IEEE/ASME Trans. Mechatron. **23**(1), 286–297 (2018)
2. Burgner-Kahrs, J., Rucker, D.C., Choset, H.: Continuum robots for medical applications: asurvey. IEEE Trans. Robot. **31**(6), 1261–1280 (2015)

3. Tsukagoshi, H., Kitagawa, A., Segawa, M.: Active hose: an artificial elephant's nose with maneuverability for rescue operation. In: Proceedings of 2001 IEEE International Conference on Robotics and Automation, pp. 2454–2459. IEEE, Seoul (2001)
4. Robinson, G., Davies, J.B.C.: Continuum robots - a state of the art. In: Proceedings of 1999 IEEE International Conference on Robotics and Automation, pp. 2849–2854. IEEE, Detroit (1999)
5. Yuk, H., Shin, J.H., Jo, S.: Design and control of thermal SMA based small crawling robot mimicking C. elegans. In: 2010 IEEE/RSJ International Conference on Intelligent Robots and Systems, pp. 407–412. IEEE, Taipei (2010)
6. Jani, J.M., Leary, M., Subic, A., Gibson, M.A.: A review of shape memory alloy research, applications and opportunities. Mater. Des. (1980–2015) 56, 1078–1113 (2014)
7. Shintake, J., Rosset, S., Schubert, B., Floreano, D., Shea, H.: Versatile soft grippers with intrinsic electroadhesion based on multifunctional polymer actuators. Adv. Mater. 28(2), 231–238 (2015)
8. Walker, I.D., et al.: Continuum robot arms inspired by cephalopods. In: Unmanned Ground Vehicle Technology VII. SPIE (2005)
9. Yuk, H., Lin, S., Ma, C., Takaffoli, M., Fang, N.X., Zhao, X.: Hydraulic hydrogel actuators and robots optically and sonically camouflaged in water. Nat. Commun. 8, 14230 (2017)
10. Calisti, M., et al.: An octopus-bioinspired solution to movement and manipulation for soft robots. Bioinspiration Biomim. 6(3), 036002 (2011)
11. Xu, K., Simaan, N.: Actuation compensation for flexible surgical snake-like robots with redundant remote actuation. In: Proceedings 2006 IEEE International Conference on Robotics and Automation. IEEE (2006)
12. Brown, E., et al.: Universal robotic gripper based on the jamming of granular material. Proc. Natl. Acad. Sci. 107(44), 18809–18814 (2010)
13. Li, Y., Chen, Y., Yang, Y., Wei, Y.: Passive particle jamming and its stiffening of soft robotic grippers. IEEE Trans. Robot. 33(2), 446–455 (2017)
14. Shiva, A., et al.: Tendon-based stiffening for a pneumatically actuated soft manipulator. IEEE Robot. Autom. Lett. 1(2), 632–637 (2016)
15. Taniguchi, H., Miyake, M., Suzumori, K.: Development of new soft actuator using magnetic intelligent fluids for flexible walking robot. In: International Conference on Control Automation and Systems, pp. 1797–1801. IEEE, Gyeonggi-do (2010)
16. Kang, R., Guo, Y., Chen, L., Branson III, D.T., Dai, J.S.: Design of a pneumatic muscle based continuum robot with embedded tendons. IEEE/ASME Trans. Mechatron. 22(2), 751–761 (2017)
17. Jones, B.A., Walker, I.D.: Kinematics for multisection continuum robots. IEEE Trans. Robot. 22(1), 43–55 (2006)
18. Xu, K., Simaan, N.: Analytic formulation for kinematics, statics, and shape restoration of multibackbone continuum robots via elliptic integrals. J. Mech. Robot. 2(1), 011006 (2010)
19. Renda, F., Cacucciolo, V., Dias, J., Seneviratne, L.: Discrete Cosserat approach for soft robot dynamics: a new piece-wise constant strain model with torsion and shears. In: 2016 IEEE/RSJ International Conference on Intelligent Robots and Systems, pp. 5495–5502. IEEE, Daejeon (2016)
20. Kang, R., Branson, D.T., Zheng, T., Guglielmino, E., Caldwell, D.G.: Design, modeling and control of a pneumatically actuated manipulator inspired by biological continuum structures. Bioinspiration Biomim. 8(3), 036008 (2013)
21. Sun, C., Chen, L., Liu, J., Dai, J.S., Kang, R.: A hybrid continuum robot based on pneumatic muscles with embedded elastic rods. In: Proc. Inst. Mech. Eng. Part C J. Mech. Eng. Sci. (2019). https://doi.org/10.1177/0954406218822013

Design and Experiment of a Foldable Pneumatic Soft Manipulator

Xiang Zhang[1,2(✉)], Zhuoqun Liu[2], Hongwei Liu[1], Lu Cao[1],
Xiaoqian Chen[1], and Yiyong Huang[1]

[1] National Innovation Institute of Defense Technology,
Academy of Military Sciences, Beijing, China
zxstudy@hotmail.com, liuhw05@163.com
[2] College of Aerospace Science and Technology,
National University of Defense Technology, Changsha, China

Abstract. The purpose of this paper is to present a design of a foldable pneumatic soft manipulator. The soft manipulator is made up of three foldable pneumatic soft modules, which are stacked in series. The foldable pneumatic soft module is composed with a pneumatic actuator and an inflatable beam. The function of the pneumatic actuator is to make the directional movement, while the inflatable beam is the section with foldability. In order to get the performance of this kind of design, one of the soft modules is developed. Moreover, the pulling force of the pneumatic actuator, the bending stiffness of the inflatable beam and the pointing movement of the soft module are tested in the experiment. The concept of the foldability and extension of the soft manipulator is also validated.

Keywords: Soft manipulator · Foldable · Pneumatic · Design · Experiment · On-orbit service

1 Introduction

Soft manipulator is a special type of soft robot, which has already been a hot topic in robot research. The traditional robot is always made of rigid components, which are actuated by the motors. The actuation of the soft manipulator is completely different. It has none motor and is driven by the pressured gas, the cable, the voltage and so on [1]. According to different actuation type, the researchers have presented kinds of novel ideas in the design of the soft manipulator. In the gas-driven mode, Sanan et al. [2–4] address a design of soft manipulator just like human's arm totally by using a number of soft inflatable bags. Walker and Neppalli et al. [5, 6] designed and developed the OctArm to simulate the motion of elephant's trunk. Ishibashi et al. [7] proposed a soft robotics arm for human assistant robots by using pneumatic system. In the cable-driven mode, Voisembert et al. [8–10] presented a design of a long range robotic arm based on an inflatable structure. The joints are driven by the cables. Wang et al. [11, 12] presented a design of soft manipulator, which is made of silicone and driven by the ropes. Thakkar et al. [13] presented a novel cable-driven robotic platform for human surgery. In the voltage-driven mode, He et al. [14] conceived a fiber-reinforced torsional

© Springer Nature Switzerland AG 2019
H. Yu et al. (Eds.): ICIRA 2019, LNAI 11742, pp. 183–192, 2019.
https://doi.org/10.1007/978-3-030-27535-8_17

dielectric elastomer (DE) actuator by embedding one family of helical fibers into a DE tube. Nguyen et al. [15] presented a development of a printable hexapod walking robot driven by the multiple-degrees-of-freedom (multi-DOF) soft actuators based on dielectric elastomer. Takashima et al. [16, 17] applied the SMP sheet to a curved type pneumatic artificial muscle and evaluated the dynamic motion of the resulting actuator. In addition, Kim et al. [18] proposed a foldable arm by implementing a simple stiffening mechanism that used an origami principle of perpendicular folding. Rafsanjani et al. [19] enhanced the crawling capability of a soft actuator by using harnessing kirigami principles. Currently, these three driving modes are the most widely studied. There are also researchers just focusing on the design and experiment of the inflated beams [20, 21], in order to get its performance.

In this paper, a foldable pneumatic soft manipulator as well as its experiment system is designed and developed. In Sect. 2, the design schematic of the foldable pneumatic soft manipulator as well as its one module is described. In Sect. 3, the component experiment of the soft manipulator is conducted. The pulling force of the pneumatic actuator and the bending stiffness of the inflatable beam are tested. The foldability and the pointing movement of the pneumatic soft module are played. Finally, the conclusions are given.

2   Design of a Foldable Pneumatic Soft Manipulator

The soft manipulator is made up of three foldable pneumatic soft modules. Before inflating, the soft manipulator is in a compact state, which saves the storage space. After inflating, the soft manipulator is in a stretching state, which extends its reaching scope. The design schematic of the foldable pneumatic soft manipulator is shown in Fig. 1.

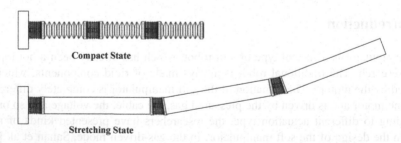

Fig. 1. Design schematic of the foldable pneumatic soft manipulator.

The foldable pneumatic soft module is the basis component of the soft manipulator. Three pneumatic soft modules stack in series to be the pneumatic soft manipulator. The foldable pneumatic soft module is composed with a pneumatic actuator and an inflatable beam, shown in Fig. 2. The pneumatic actuator is made up of three inflatable bellows, which are connected by a series of rigid plates. The three bellows distribute symmetrically as an equilateral triangle. The bellows extend when the pressured gas is inputted. The pneumatic actuator bends when the three bellows are inputted with different gas pressure. The inflatable beam is composed by two levels, the internal level and the external level. The internal level is made by the soft silicone rubber while the external level is made by nylon fabric. The internal level is for sealing. The external level is for shape constraint. The inflatable beam can transfer between contraction state and stretching state when the gas is evacuated or inputted.

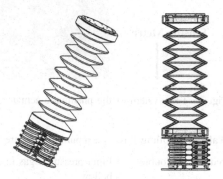

Fig. 2. Design schematic of the foldable pneumatic soft module.

3   Component Experiment of the Soft Manipulator

According to the design of the soft manipulator, it is known that its performance is determined by two basic components: the pneumatic actuator and the inflatable beam. Therefore, the experiment systems of these two components are designed and developed.

3.1   Pulling Force of the Pneumatic Actuator

The pneumatic actuator is made up of three inflatable bellows, which are connected and fixed by a series of thin rigid plates. The bellows will elongate in response to the pressured gas. The movement and constraints between the bellows and the thin rigid plates lead to the constrained orientation of the pneumatic actuator. Due to the fact that the pneumatic actuator is to provide the directional actuation force for the soft manipulator, the pulling force under different gas pressure is its key performance. Thus, the experiment to reveal the relationship between the pulling force and the inputting pressure is designed and developed, shown in Fig. 3.

In Fig. 3, the pneumatic actuator is suspended. The pressured gas is inputted from the top side. The tension meter is connected with the bottom of the actuator using steel rope. Thus, the pulling force of the pneumatic actuator can be measured by the tension meter when the pressured gas is inputted into the relative bellow. The bending actuation of the pneumatic actuator has two patterns: actuation by inputting pressured gas in double bellows and actuation by inputting pressured gas in single bellow. The pulling forces versus the inputting pressures in these two patterns are recorded in the following Table 1.

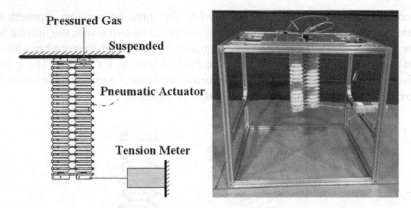

Fig. 3. Test system of the pneumatic actuator.

Table 1. Pulling force vs. inputting pressure.

Input pressured gas in double bellows		Input pressured gas in single bellow	
Gas pressure/bar	Pulling force/N	Gas pressure/bar	Pulling force/N
0.20	5.10	0.20	6.00
0.25	6.20	0.25	6.80
0.30	7.10	0.30	7.70
0.31	7.20	0.35	8.50
0.40	8.90	0.40	9.30
0.45	10.00	0.45	10.10
0.50	11.10	0.50	10.90

In Table 1, it is seen that the gas pressure changes from 0.2 bar to 0.5 bar, the pulling force of the double bellows pattern is from 5.1 N to 11.1 N, while the pulling force of the single bellow pattern is from 6 N to 10.9 N. The fitting results of the pulling force versus inputting pressure are shown in Fig. 4.

From the distribution of the test data shown in Fig. 4, it can be seen that the pulling force versus the gas pressure is almost linear. Therefore, the linear polynomial fitting equation is adopted. The fitting result in the double bellows pattern is:

$$F_{pulling} = 19.6117 \cdot P_{gas} + 1.1908 \tag{1}$$

The fitting result in the single bellow pattern is:

$$F_{pulling} = 16.0268 \cdot P_{gas} + 2.9536 \tag{2}$$

From Eqs. (1) and (2), it is known that the gradient of the fitting line in the double bellows pattern is 19.6117, a little higher than the gradient of the fitting line in the single bellow pattern (16.0268). In the condition that the pulling force in these two

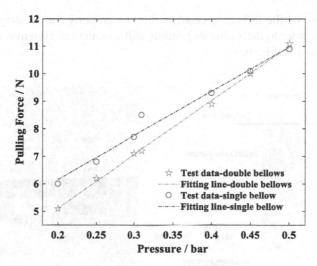

Fig. 4. Fitting results of the pulling force vs. inputting pressure.

patterns is equal, the gas pressure is about 0.492 bar. It means that the double-bellows actuation is stronger than the single-bellow actuation when the gas pressure is more than 0.492 bar.

3.2 Bending Stiffness of the Inflatable Beam

The inflatable beam is made up of two layers: the internal layer and the external layer. The internal layer is a silicone soft bellow for sealing function. It is casted by injecting the liquid silicone into a special designed mold. The external layer is a cylindrical tube made of nylon fabric. It is used to strengthen the stiffness of the inflatable beam by deformation constraint. Before the beam is inflated, the two layers shrink to a compact state. After the beam is inflated, the internal layer expands until the external layer reaches to its space limit. The foldability of the inflatable beam is shown in Fig. 5.

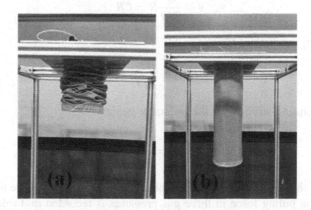

Fig. 5. Foldability of the inflatable beam: (a) Compact state, (b) Stretching state.

The stiffness of the inflatable beam is the key property for its usage in the soft manipulator. In order to determine its bending stiffness, the test system is designed and developed, shown in Fig. 6.

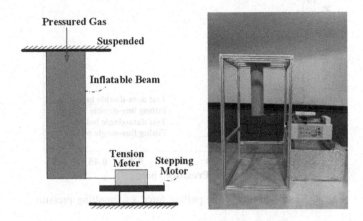

Fig. 6. Test system of the inflatable beam.

In Fig. 6, the inflatable beam is suspended. The pressured gas is inputted from its top side. The tension meter is mounted on the stepping motor and its displacement can be recorded by the stepping motor. The tension meter is connected with the bottom of the inflatable beam. Thus, the pulling force can be recorded by the tension meter and the deflection of the inflatable beam can be recorded by the stepping motor. The range of the tension meter is 500 N and the accuracy is 0.1 N. The range of the stepping motor is 150 mm.

Assumed that the pulling force is R, the length of the inflatable beam (stretching state) is L, the bending stiffness is EI, the deflection is v. The inflatable beam can be similar to the cantilever beam before its structure yield. Thus,

$$v = \frac{L^3}{3EI} R = CR \qquad (3)$$

where, the fitting coefficient C is

$$C = \frac{L^3}{3EI} \qquad (4)$$

Then the bending stiffness of the inflatable beam is

$$EI = \frac{L^3}{3C} \qquad (5)$$

It is known that the length of the inflatable beam L = 550 mm. The test data of the deflection versus puling force in three gas pressures is recorded in Table 2.

Table 2. Deflection vs. pulling force.

0.2 bar		0.42 bar		0.61 bar	
Force/N	Deflection/mm	Force/N	Deflection/mm	Force/N	Deflection/mm
4.1	9.0	7.6	8.5	7.8	8.5
7.9	19.5	13.0	15.0	14.4	16.5
10.9	32.0	18.3	23.0	20.3	24.5
12.7	40.0	22.4	31.0	25.6	32.5
14.4	48.0	25.7	38.5	30.3	40.0
16.0	56.0	28.8	45.5	34.3	48.0
17.6	64.0	31.4	53.0	37.9	55.0

The fitting results of the deflection versus the pulling force in these three conditions are shown in Fig. 7.

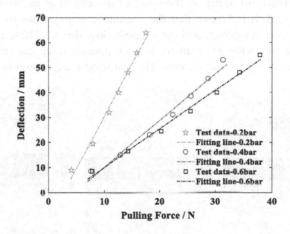

Fig. 7. Fitting results of the deflection vs. pulling force.

From the distribution of the test data shown in Fig. 7, it can be seen that the deflection versus the pulling force is almost linear. Therefore, the linear polynomial fitting equation is adopted. The fitting coefficient C relative to the three cases is 4.139 (0.2 bar), 1.866 (0.4 bar), 1.5413 (0.6 bar). Thus, the bending stiffness of the inflatable beam in these three gas pressure is 0.0134 N m^2 (0.2 bar), 0.0297 N m^2 (0.4 bar), 0.036 N m^2 (0.6 bar).

3.3 Pointing Test of the Foldable Pneumatic Soft Module

The foldable pneumatic soft module is assembled with the pneumatic actuator and the inflatable beam, shown in Fig. 8. The pneumatic control system is based on Festo Motion Terminal VTEM. It can be seen that the soft module can transfer between the compact state and the stretching state.

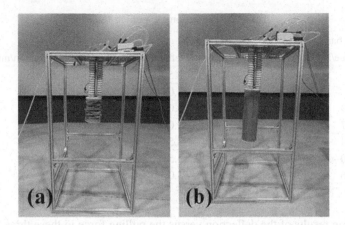

Fig. 8. The assemble of the foldable pneumatic soft module: (a) compact state, (b) stretching state.

Based on the platform in Fig. 8, the pointing movement of the foldable pneumatic soft module is tested. It is known that the pneumatic actuator has two actuation patterns: the double-bellows-driven and the single-bellow-driven. These two patterns are both tested in the following experiment. In each pattern, three gas pressures that are 0.5 bar, 0.8 bar, and 1.2 bar are chosen. The test results are shown in Fig. 9.

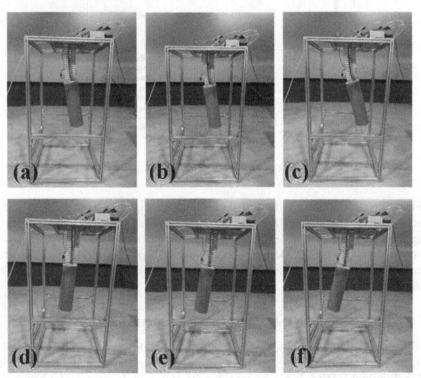

Fig. 9. Pointing test in different conditions: (a) 0.5 bar in double bellows, (b) 0.8 bar in double bellows, (c) 1.2 bar in double bellows, (d) 0.5 bar in single bellow, (e) 0.8 bar in single bellow, (f) 1.2 bar in single bellow.

In Fig. 9(a)–(c), it is seen that the left two bellows (double-bellows-driven) are elongated as the pressured gas inputting. The soft module bends to the right side and its bending amplitude increases with the increasing of the gas pressure. In Fig. 9(d)–(f), it is seen that the right one bellow (single-bellow-driven) is elongated as the pressured gas inputting. The soft module bends to the left side and its bending amplitude also increases with the increasing of the gas pressure. From all above, it can be known that the soft module can point to different orientations under different actuation patterns.

4 Conclusions

In this paper, a foldable pneumatic soft manipulator was designed. It is assembled by three soft modules. In order to validate its foldability and the movement ability, one soft module was developed in this investigation. The pneumatic soft module is composed by a pneumatic actuator and an inflatable beam. The pulling force of the pneumatic actuator determines the movement ability of the soft manipulator; the bending stiffness of the inflatable beam determines the stability of the soft manipulator. According to the test results, the bending stiffness of the inflatable beam increases with the increasing of the inputting gas pressure, and it can satisfy the requirement of the pneumatic actuator by inputting enough gas pressure. The pulling force of the pneumatic actuator is stronger in the double-bellows pattern when the gas pressure increases to a certain level. From the pointing test of the foldable pneumatic soft module, it is known that the pneumatic actuator can take the inflatable beam to move in different directions. When the specific inflating pattern is loaded into the soft module, it can make the movement accordingly. In the next, the whole soft manipulator stacked by several soft modules will be developed. Its deployment and operation test will be carried on the air-bearing platform with multi-degree of freedom.

Acknowledgments. The authors gratefully acknowledge the fundings by the Postdoctoral Science Foundation and the Natural Science Foundation of China, under Grants No. 11702320, 11725211 and 61690213.

References

1. Webster III, R.J., Jones, B.A.: Design and kinematic modeling of constant curvature continuum robots: a review. Int. J. Robot. Res. **29**, 1661–1683 (2010)
2. Sanan, S.: Soft inflatable robots for safe physical human interaction. Carnegie Mellon University (2013)
3. Sanan, S., Lynn, P.S., Griffith, S.T.: Pneumatic torsional actuators for inflatable robots. J. Mech. Robot. **6**, 031003 (2014)
4. Sanan, S., Ornstein, M.H., Atkeson, C.G.: Physical human interaction for an inflatable manipulator. In: 2011 Annual International Conference of the IEEE Engineering in Medicine and Biology Society, EMBC, pp. 7401–7404. IEEE (2011)
5. Rahn, C., Walker, I.: Design and experimental testing of the OctArm soft robot manipulator. In: ProcSpie, vol. 6230 (2006)

6. Neppalli, S., Jones, B., Mcmahan, W., Chitrakaran, V.: OctArm - a soft robotic manipulator. In: IEEE/RSJ International Conference on Intelligent Robots and Systems, p. 2569 (2007)
7. Ishibashi, A., Yokota, S., Matsumoto, A., Chugo, D., Hashimoto, H.: Inflatable arm with rigidity for safe robots - 1st report: proposal of joint structure. In: IEEE International Conference on Industrial Technology (2017)
8. Voisembert, S., Mechbal, N., Riwan, A., Aoussat, A.: Design of a novel long-range inflatable robotic arm: manufacturing and numerical evaluation of the joints and actuation. J. Mech. Robot. **5**, 045001 (2013)
9. Voisembert, S., Riwan, A., Mechbal, N.: Numerical evaluation of a new robotic manipulator based on inflatable joints. In: IEEE International Conference on Automation Science and Engineering, pp. 544–549 (2012)
10. Voisembert, S., Mechbal, N., Riwan, A., Barraco, A.: A novel inflatable tendon driven manipulator with constant volume. In: ASME 2011 International Design Engineering Technical Conferences and Computers and Information in Engineering Conference, pp. 1233–1242 (2011)
11. Deng, T., Wang, H., Chen, W., Wang, X., Pfeifer, R.: Development of a new cable-driven soft robot for cardiac ablation. In: Proceeding of the IEEE International Conference on Robotics and Biomimetics (ROBIO), Shenzhen, China, pp. 728–733 (2013)
12. Wang, H., Zhang, R., Chen, W., Liang, X., Pfeifer, R.: Shape detection algorithm for soft manipulator based on fiber bragg gratings. IEEE/ASME Trans. Mechatron. **21**, 2977–2982 (2016)
13. Thakkar, S., et al.: A novel, new robotic platform for natural orifice distal pancreatectomy. Surg. Innov. **22**, 274–282 (2015)
14. He, L., Lou, J., Du, J., Wu, H.: Voltage-driven nonuniform axisymmetric torsion of a tubular dielectric elastomer actuator reinforced with one family of inextensible fibers. Eur. J. Mech.-A/Solids **71**, 386–393 (2018)
15. Nguyen, C.T., Phung, H., Nguyen, T., Jung, H., Choi, H.: Multiple-degrees-of-freedom dielectric elastomer actuators for soft printable hexapod robot. Sens. Actuators A: Phys. **267**, 505–516 (2017)
16. Takashima, K., Sugitani, K., Morimoto, N., Sakaguchi, S., Noritsugu, T., Mukai, T.: Pneumatic artificial rubber muscle using shape-memory polymer sheet with embedded electrical heating wire. Smart Mater. Struct. **23**, 10 (2014)
17. Takashima, K., Noritsugu, T., Rossiter, J., Guo, S., Mukai, T.: Curved type pneumatic artificial rubber muscle using shape-memory polymer. J. Robot. Mechatron. **24**, 8 (2012)
18. Kim, S.-J., Lee, D.-Y., Jung, G.-P., Cho, K.-J.: An origami-inspired, self-locking robotic arm that can be folded flat. Sci. Robot. **3**, eaar2915 (2018)
19. Rafsanjani, A., Zhang, Y., Liu, B., Rubinstein, S.M., Bertoldi, K.: Kirigami skins make a simple soft actuator crawl. Sci. Robot. **3**, eaar7555 (2018)
20. Veldman, S.L.: Design and Analysis Methodologies for Inflated Beams, p. 467. Delft University Press, Delft (2005)
21. Inman, D., Main, J.A., Lhernould, M.: Vibration testing and finite element analysis of an inflatable structure. AIAA J. **41**, 1556–1563 (2003)

Unmanned Underwater Vehicles

Underwater Image Target Detection with Cascade Classifier and Image Preprocessing Method

Lingcai Zeng[1], Bing Sun[1(✉)], Wei Zhang[2], and Daqi Zhu[1]

[1] Shanghai Maritime University,
1550 Haigang Avenue, Shanghai 201306, China
hmsunbing@163.com
[2] Shanghai Dianji University, 1350 Ganlan Road, Shanghai 201306, China

Abstract. Underwater image target detection is an important part of exploring the ocean. This paper adopts cascade classifier and image preprocessing method. Firstly, it selects candidate regions on a given picture, then extracts feature from them and finally uses the trained classifier to detect. It focuses on the self-defined training of the cascade classifier, and trains the cascade classifier by collecting a large number of underwater target images. Secondly, it uses some of image preprocessing to make the detection effect more accurate. Finally, the simulation results show that it can achieve the target detection of underwater image by using the method of self-defined cascade classifier and image preprocessing.

Keywords: Target detection · Cascade classifier · Image preprocessing

1 Introduction

At present, there are two ways to obtain underwater information: underwater sonar technology and underwater optical imaging technology. Underwater optical imaging technology has the advantages of intuitive detection target and high imaging resolution, which is more suitable for target detection in short distances. However, the underwater environment is complex and diverse, making it difficult to obtain information. Images obtained from underwater generally have these problems: (1) image unclear due to unstable light source or shadows on the object itself in the water; (2) some impurities in the water may cause the imaging background not to be single. (3) the underwater image is a two-dimensional projection of the three-dimensional scene, so there will be spatial geometric distortion in the image. The research on underwater image target detection technology is to solve these problems. Traditional target detection methods include: Haar feature and Adaboost algorithm [1], Hog feature and SVM algorithm [2] and DPM algorithm [3]. This paper use cascade categorizer and image preprocessing to

This project is supported by the National Natural Science Foundation of China (61873161, U1706224).

H. Yu et al. (Eds.): ICIRA 2019, LNAI 11742, pp. 195–205, 2019.
https://doi.org/10.1007/978-3-030-27535-8_18

achieve underwater target detection. Through simulation experiment, it can be verified that the proposed method can obtain a better underwater target detection result.

2   Introduction and Training of Cascade Classifier

2.1   Overview of Cascade Classifier

A cascade classifier consists of different stages, each stage is a collection of weak classifiers. A weak classifier is a simple classifier called a decision tree. Each stage is trained by using techniques called boosting. Boosting provides the ability to train highly accurate classifiers by weighted averaging of weak classifier decisions (Fig. 1).

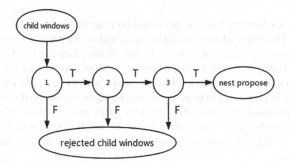

Fig. 1. Target detection process for cascade classifier

2.2   Working Principle of Cascade Classifier

Boosting. Boosting is a machine learning integration meta-method that is mainly used to reduce bias. It is also a variation in supervised learning, and a series of machine learning algorithms. The classifier can be converted into strong classifier. It is a method to improve the precision of weak classification algorithms by constructing a series of prediction functions and then combining them into prediction functions in a certain way.

Adaboost (Adaptive Boosting). Adaboost is one of the many algorithms in Boosting algorithm family, which is an adaptive algorithm. It aim at Boosting algorithm used in the training sample is randomly selected, and the combination of weak classifier make adjustment through the average distribution of the two problems.

The specific algorithm flow is as follows [4]:

Given: $(x_1, y_1), \ldots, (x_m, y_m)$ where $x_i \in X, y_i \in Y = \{-1, +1\}$

$$D_1 = (w_{11}, w_{12}, \ldots, w_{1i}, \ldots, w_{1N}), \quad w_{1i} = \frac{1}{N}, \quad 1, 2 \ldots N$$

for $t = 1, \ldots, T$

1. Train weak classifier using weights D_t.
2. Get the basic classifier:

$$G_m(x) : X \rightarrow \{-1, +1\} \tag{1}$$

3. Calculate the classification error rate of $G_m(x)$ on the training data set:

$$e_m = P(G_m(x_i) \neq y_i) = \sum_{i=1}^{N} w_{mi} I(G_m(x_i) \neq y_i) \tag{2}$$

4. Calculate the coefficient of $G_m(x)$, α_m indicates the importance of $G_m(x)$ in the final classifier:

$$\alpha_m = \frac{1}{2} \log \frac{1 - e_m}{e_m} \tag{3}$$

5. Update the weight distribution of the training data set for the next iteration:

$$D_{m+1} = \left(w_{m+1,1}, w_{m+1,2}, \ldots, w_{m+1,i}, \ldots, w_{m+1,N}\right) \tag{4}$$

$$w_{m+1,i} = \frac{w_{mi}}{Z_m} exp(-\alpha_m y_i G_m(x_i)), \quad i = 1, 2, \ldots, N \tag{5}$$

where Z_m is the normalization factor, making D_{m+1} is a probability distribution:

$$Z_m = \sum_{i=1}^{N} w_{mi} exp(-\alpha_m y_i G_m(x_i)) \tag{6}$$

6. Combine each weak classifier:

$$f(x) = \sum_{m=1}^{M} \alpha_m G_m(x) \tag{7}$$

Get the final classifier:

$$G(x) = sign(f(x)) = sign\left(\sum_{m=1}^{M} \alpha_m G_m(x)\right) \tag{8}$$

Gentle AdaBoost. In fact, the AdaBoost algorithm also has categories such as Discrete AdaBoost, Real AdaBoost, Logit AdaBoost and Gentle AdaBoost [5].

Through experiments and data review, this paper chooses Gentle AdaBoost algorithm as the final algorithm. The specific algorithm flow is as follows [6]:

1. Start with weights $w_i = 1/N$, $i = 1, 2, \ldots, N$, $F(x) = 0$
2. Repeat for $m = 1, 2, \ldots, M$:

(a) Fit the regression function $f_m(x)$ according to the least squares weighted by w_i for y_i to x_i

(b) Update $F(x) \leftarrow F(x) + f_m(x)$

(c) Update $w_i \leftarrow w_i exp(-y_i f_m(x_i))$ and renormalize

3. Output the classifier

$$sign[F(x)] = sign\left[\sum_{m=1}^{M} f_m(x)\right] \qquad (9)$$

Feature Extraction. MATLAB platform supports three feature types: Haar, LBP (local binary patterns) [7], HOG (histograms of oriented gradients). Among them, Haar and LBP features are often used for face recognition because they are suitable for representing fine textures. HOG features are often used to detect objects such as people and cars. They can be used to capture the overall shape of the object, so this paper use HOG for feature extraction.

The HOG feature is a directional gradient histogram feature, which is constructed by calculating and statistic the gradient direction histogram of the local region of the image.

2.3 Training of Cascade Classifier

The training of the cascade classifier requires a set of positive samples (including the image of the target) and a set of negative images (images that do not contain the target), and the region of interest needs to be designated as a positive sample in the frontal sample. Negative samples are automatically generated from the negative images provided. It is also necessary to set acceptable detector accuracy, number of stages, feature type and some other functional parameters. Figure 2 shows the training process of the cascade classifier.

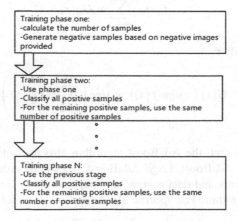

Fig. 2. Training process of the cascade classifier

3   Preprocessing of Underwater Image

3.1   Target Detection of Underwater Images Without Preprocessing

When the underwater image is detected, no processing is initially performed on the image. The final detect results are not very ideal. The experimental results are shown in the following Fig. 3:

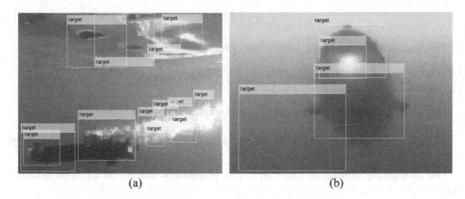

(a)   (b)

Fig. 3. The detect result of two underwater images without pretreatment.

3.2   Image Gray Processing

There are many methods for image gray processing: component method, maximum method, average method and weighted average method [8]. In this paper, weighted average method is chosen according to the importance and other indicators (the human eye is most sensitive to green and the sensitivity to blue is the lowest), and the three color components of red, green and blue are weighted and averaged by different weights. The result as shown in Fig. 4, the specific formula is as follows:

$$Gray(i,j) = 0.2989 \times R(i,j) + 0.5870 \times G(i,j) + 0.1140 \times B(i,j) \qquad (10)$$

(a)   (b)

Fig. 4. (a) Represents the original image (b) Representation of grayscale images (Color figure online)

3.3   Histogram Equalization

Process Analysis of Histogram Equalization [9]. Set r and s is the gray level of the original image and the gray level of the image after the histogram equalization, and normalize r and s for discussion:$0 \leq r, \ s \leq 1$.

For a given image, the normalized gray level distribution in the range of $0 \leq r \leq 1$. Transform any r value in the interval $[0, 1]$ as follows [10]:

$$s = T(r) \tag{11}$$

The transformation should satisfy the conditions:

(1) For $0 \leq r \leq 1$, there is $0 \leq s \leq 1$.
(2) Within the interval of $0 \leq r \leq 1$.

The inverse transformation from s to r is expressed by:

$$r = T^{-1}(s) \tag{12}$$

The probability density of r is $P_r(r)$. The probability density of s can be obtained from

$$P_s(s) = \left(P_r(r) \frac{dr}{ds} \right) \Big|_{r = T^{-1}(s)} \tag{13}$$

Assume that the transformation function is:

$$s = T(r) = \int_0^r P_r(\omega) d\omega \tag{14}$$

where w is the integral variable, and $\int_0^r P_r(\omega) d\omega$ is the cumulative distribution function of r.

Derivation of r in the formula

$$\frac{ds}{dr} = \frac{dT(r)}{dr} = P_r(r) \tag{15}$$

Substitute the result into the previous formula:

$$P_s(s) = \left[P_r(r) \frac{dr}{ds} \right]_{r=T^{-1}(s)} = \left[P_r(r) \frac{1}{ds/dr} \right]_{r=T^{-1}(s)} = \left[P_r(r) \frac{1}{P_r(r)} \right] = 1 \tag{16}$$

It can be seen that the probability density of the transformed variable s in its domain is evenly distributed.

Image Histogram Equalization Result. See (Fig. 5).

3.4   Gray Linear Transformation

(a)   (b)   (c)

Fig. 5. (a) original image (b) grayscale image (c) histogram equalized image

Gray Linear Transformation Principle. Set the original image $f(x, y)$ gray scale range is $[a, b]$, and hope that the transformed image $g(x, y)$ gray scale range is extended to $[c, d]$ (Fig. 6), then the gray scale linear transformation can be expressed as [11]:

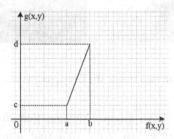

Fig. 6. Function diagram of gray linear transformation

$$g(x,y) = \frac{d-c}{b-a}[f(x,y) - a] + c \qquad (17)$$

Gray Piecewise Linear Transformation [12]. The gray piecewise linear transformation is to stretch the gray value of part or different range, so as to enhance the gray range of interest in the image and relatively weaken the gray range of interest. Its mathematical expression and corresponding function image (Fig. 7) as follows:

$$g(x,y) = \begin{cases} \frac{c}{a}f(x,y), & 0 \le f(x,y) \le a \\ \frac{d-c}{b-a}[f(x,y) - a] + c, & a \le f(x,y) \le b \\ \frac{L-1-d}{L-1-b}[f(x,y) - b] + d, & b \le f(x,y) \le L-1 \end{cases} \qquad (18)$$

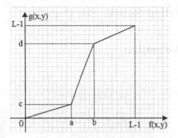

Fig. 7. Function image of gray piecewise linear transformation

Gray Piecewise Linear Transformation Effect. In this paper, the local stretch is used to stretch the gray scale in $[0.1, 0.5]$ to $[0, 1]$ (Fig. 8).

$$(a) \qquad\qquad\qquad\qquad (b)$$

Fig. 8. (a) Histogram equalized image (b) Gray piecewise linear transformed image

It can be seen from the above group of images that after this gradation transformation, it can be clearly seen that some irrelevant information contained in the background of the image has disappeared, such as bubbles, ripples and some impurities in the water, which makes the subsequent target detection more accurate.

3.5 Median Filtering

Principle of Median Filtering. The median filtering implementation method [13] is to use a smoothing window to arrange pixels in the window according to the size of the pixel values to generate a set of two-dimensional data sequences that are monotonically increasing or monotonically decreasing. The formula is as follows:

$$g(x, y) = med\{f(x - k, y - l), (k.l \in w)\} \tag{19}$$

where $f(x, y)$ is the original image, $g(x, y)$ is the processed image, w is a sliding window, and its size is usually 3 * 3, 5 * 5, 7 * 7, and 9 * 9.

Median Filtering Effect. In this paper, the different size of the sliding window, 3 * 3, 5 * 5, 7 * 7 and 9 * 9 is simulated, so that the best window size can be selected in the experiment. And the filtered original image is an image after the gray piecewise linear transformation (Fig. 9).

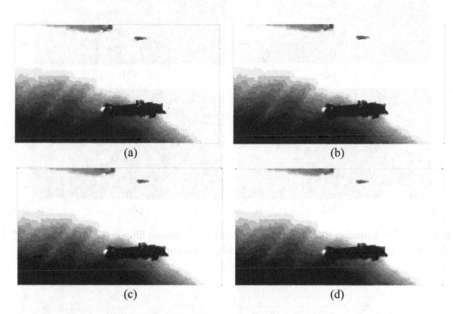

(a)   (b)

(c)   (d)

Fig. 9. (a) 3 * 3 window median filtered image (b) 5 * 5 window median filtered image (c) 7 * 7 window median filtered image (d) 9 * 9 window median filtered image

From the above group of images, it is found that after the median filtering of the images through different window sizes, the obtained image cannot be clearly distinguished in the naked eye, but the computer can detect differences that are invisible to the naked eye, and these subtle differences can affect the subsequent detection, so the window size should be selected in the subsequent target detection experiment.

4 Simulation Experiment

In this experiment, total use of 248 positive images and 85 negative images. The false alarm rate is set to 0.1, the number of stages is 5, and the detection target is the whole of the underwater machine. Observing by changing the size of the sliding window in the median filtering, and finally comparing the size of the sliding window that can make the detection effect better. The experimental results are as shown in Fig. 10.

By observing and comparing the above images, it can be concluded that the sliding window size in the median filtering has a certain influence on the final target detection result. In the above image, except for the detection effect map of the 5 * 5 window, the difference between the other three images is not very obvious, and further experiments are needed for comparison (Fig. 11).

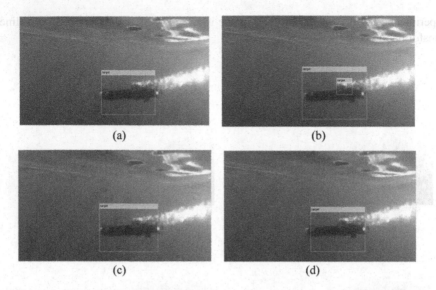

(a)   (b)

(c)   (d)

Fig. 10. (a) 3 * 3 median filter detection result (b) 5 * 5 median filter detection result (c) 7 * 7 median filter detection result (d) 9 * 9 median filter detection result

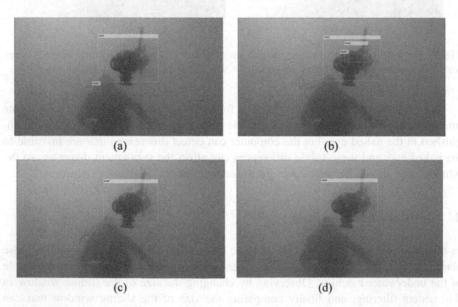

(a)   (b)

(c)   (d)

Fig. 11. (a) 3 * 3 median filter detection result (b) 5 * 5 median filter detection result (c) 7 * 7 median filter detection result (d) 9 * 9 median filter detection result

In the experiment, which are more than two images used for detection, through the observation and comparison of multiple underwater images, for the samples used in this experiment, the median filtering of the 7 * 7 window is performed in the four window sizes of the median filtering. The effect is relatively good, there will be no false detection, and the markup boxes will not overlap.

5 Conclusion

In this paper, the method of cascade classifier and image preprocessing is used to achieve the target detection of underwater image successfully. In the experiment, we set different size filter windows and obtain the best detection effect by comparison, but there is still room for improvement in accuracy.

References

1. Viola, P., Jones, M.: Rapid object detection using a boosted cascade of simple features. In: CVPR 2001, pp. 511–518 (2001)
2. Dalal, N., Triggs, B.: Histograms of oriented gradients for human detection. In: CVPR 2005, pp. 1063–6919 (2005)
3. Felzenszwalb, P.F., Girshick, R.B., McAllester, D., et al.: Object detection with discriminatively trained part-based models. IEEE Trans. Pattern Anal. Mach. Intell. **32**(9), 1627–1645 (2010)
4. Freund, Y., Schapire, R.E.: A short introduction to boosting. J. Jpn. Soc. Artif. Intell. **14**(5), 771–780 (1999)
5. Li, X., Wang, L., Sung, E.: AdaBoost with SVM-based component classifiers. Eng. Appl. Artif. Intell. **21**(5), 785–795 (2008)
6. Zhang, L., Chu, R., Xiang, S., Liao, S., Li, S.Z.: Face detection based on multi-Block LBP representation. In: Lee, S.-W., Li, S.Z. (eds.) ICB 2007. LNCS, vol. 4642, pp. 11–18. Springer, Heidelberg (2007). https://doi.org/10.1007/978-3-540-74549-5_2
7. Tran, C.K., Lee, T.F., Chang, L., et al.: Face description with local binary patterns and local ternary patterns: improving face recognition performance using similarity feature-based selection and classification algorithm. In: International Symposium on Computer, pp. 520–524 (2014)
8. Zhou, J., Peng, F.: A method of selective image graying. Comput. Eng. **32**(20), 198–200 (2006)
9. Yelmanova, E., Romanyshyn, Y.: Histogram-based method for image contrast enhancement. In: Experience of Designing & Application of Cad Systems in Microelectronics, pp. 165–169 (2017)
10. Gonzalez, R.C., Woods, R.E.: Digital Image Processing. Publishing House of Electronics Industry (2007)
11. Ye, Y., Sun, Q., Shi, L., et al.: A adaptive dual-platform deep space infrared image enhancement algorithm based on linear gray scale transformation. In: Chinese Control Conference, pp. 7434–7438 (2014)
12. Yamasaki, I., Ohshima, T., Hasegawa, M., et al.: Segmentation of gray-scale images using piecewise linear approximation. Syst. Comput. Jpn. **27**(1), 69–76 (1996)
13. Tafti, A.D., Mirsadeghi, E.: A novel adaptive Recursive Median Filter in image noise reduction based on using the entropy. In: IEEE International Conference on Control System, pp. 520–523 (2013)

Autopilot System of Remotely Operated Vehicle Based on Ardupilot

Zongtong Luo[1], Xianbo Xiang[1,2(✉)], and Qin Zhang[3]

[1] School of Naval Architecture and Ocean Engineering,
Huazhong University of Science and Technology,
Wuhan 430074, People's Republic of China
xbxiang@hust.edu.cn
[2] Shenzhen Huazhong University of Science and Technology Research Institute,
Shenzhen 518057, China
[3] State Key Laboratory of Digital Manufacturing Equipment and Technology,
Huazhong University of Science and Technology, Wuhan 430074, China

Abstract. This paper firstly present the autopilot architecture of a remotely operated vehicle (ROV), and then introduces the hardware of the underwater ROV. Secondly, it focuses on the autopilot software design of the ROV. Finally, experiments in water are carried out to validate the autopilot functions. The main work of this paper is the re-design and implementation of the proposed autopilot system based on Ardupilot. To maintain the integrity of the original functions of Ardupilot, some new functions are added to design a new flight mode. At the same time, in order to ensure that the original ground control station 'QGroundControl' can run simultaneously with the PC control software, modifications of Ardupilot motor library and message parsing methods are formulated. Further more, through the PC control software, it is possible to send control commands such as depth hold and attitude hold to the ROV while the relevant data can be recorded for analysis of control performance.

Keywords: Unmanned underwater vehicle · Ardupilot

1 Introduction

The ocean is an important resources source, and its position in military strategy and social economy is very important. As resource development gradually shifts from land to ocean, underwater vehicles are playing an increasingly important role. Underwater vehicles are used for underwater applications such as underwater observation, surveying, salvage, etc., including Remotely Operated Vehicles (ROVs) and Autonomous Underwater Vehicles (AUVs). In the process of exploring the ocean, the depth of human diving is limited, and it is impossible to directly complete the task of detecting deep-sea resources. Underwater vehicles are capable and reliable, and can replace humans to accomplish underwater operations and survey missions [1–4].

© Springer Nature Switzerland AG 2019
H. Yu et al. (Eds.): ICIRA 2019, LNAI 11742, pp. 206–217, 2019.
https://doi.org/10.1007/978-3-030-27535-8_19

After the structural design of the ROV, control system design is also a challenging and complex task to achieve the underwater motion capabilities. These control architectures might be characterized by the following attributes: real-time, multitasking, concurrency, and distributed over communication networks [5]. In [6], the control architecture of a scientific ROV was presented. In [7] and [8], two software architecture of AUVs were described.

Ardupilot is an open source autopilot software that is widely used in Unmanned Aerial Vehicles (UAVs) [9,10]. After years of development, Ardupilot currently includes a variety of sensor drivers and cutting edge attitude sensor data fusion algorithm. The idea of this work is to make full use of the technology accumulation in the field of drones, and to design a control system for underwater vehicles based on Ardupilot, which makes it more convenience with the needs of scientific research and general applications.

This paper is organized as follows. In Sect. 2, the description of the Autopilot's software and hardware are presented. Section 3 introduces the hardware of the ROV, and Sect. 4 introduces the pilot software design. In Sect. 5, some tests are conducted and experimental results show the pilot function. Section 6 contains the conclusion and future work of this paper.

2   Autopilot of Underwater Vehicle

In this section, the software and hardware of autopilot are introduced respectively. The software of autopilot is called Ardupilot, and the harware is Pixhawk.

2.1   Ardupilot Software

Ardupilot is an advanced, full-featured, reliable open source autopilot software. As an open source autopilot software, Ardupilot can be used not only on fixed-wing aircraft, multi-rotor aircraft and helicopters, but also on unmanned surface vehicles and unmanned underwater vehicles. Since Ardupilot has advanced data logging and analysis tools and reliable simulation tools, in the meantime it's always at the cutting edge of technology development because open source, Ardupilot is being widely used by a large number of companies, research institutes and individual enthusiasts [11].

The software architecture of Ardupilot is shown in Fig. 1. Take the Pixhawk platform as an example. The bottom layer is the ChibiOS real-time operating system. The flight control software is a software that is sensitive to real-time performance. It requires the operating system to provide accurate and predictable timing and timer functions. As a small real-time operating system, ChibiOS can meet the real-time requirements of flight control codes. It is small enough that consume less resources on the system and it is powerful enough. Ardupilot builds the base layer of the flight control code based on the real-time operating system. The base layer includes a hardware abstraction layer, sensor driver software, and a general software library for flight control code. The hardware abstraction layer encapsulates the interface functions provided by the operating

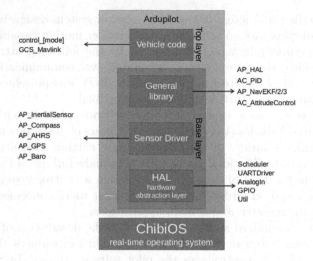

Fig. 1. Ardupilot architecture

system. Since Ardupilot's goal is to build a common autopilot suite, supporting different hardware and software platforms is necessary.

At present, Ardupilot supports two operating systems: Linux system running on various types of SoC development boards with strong performance, and a real-time operating system ChibiOS running on a single-chip microcomputer. In order to reduce the repetitive work of the upper layer code for different platforms, a hardware abstraction layer is required to unify the upper layer code to call the underlying platform interface. The hardware abstraction layer provides a unified implementation of peripheral devices driver such as UART, I2C, SPI, analog inputs, GPIO. Based on the hardware abstraction layer, some sensors are adapted to form a unified sensor driver. In addition, the base layer provides some higher-level general-purpose software libraries such as EKF, PID, and attitude controllers. Finally, the logic of the vehicle is implemented on the basis of the base layer [12]. Ardupilot has derived a number of versions for different vehicles, such as ArduPlane for fixed-wing drones, ArduCopter for multi-rotor drones, ArduRover for unmanned ground vehicles and ArduSub for unmanned underwater vehicles.

2.2 Pixhawk Hardware

Pixhawk is the hardware part of open source project PX4. PX4 is a software and hardware open source project (BSD License) to provide a low-cost, high-performance, high-end autopilot for academic, hobby, and industrial groups. The project originated from the PIXHawk project of the Computer Vision and Geometry Laboratory, the Autonomous Systems Laboratory and the Automation Control Laboratory at the Federal Institute of Technology in Zurich [13].

Fig. 2. Pixhawk

Pixhawk 1 was further modified based on the FMUv2 project. Pixhawk is shown in Fig. 2. FMUv2 consists of two parts: PX4FMU and PX4IO. PX4FMU is the core control part of the autopilot. PX4FMU is mainly responsible for the execution of algorithms such as attitude calculation while PX4IO is mainly responsible for the management of peripheral devices of the autopilot [14]. The FMU project has now iterated to FMUv5, although FMUv2 is somewhat outdated compared to FMUv5's latest design, but FMUv2 based autopilot is still very popular because FMUv2's performance is still sufficient for regular applications.

3   Hardware of the Vehicle

The hardware of the vehicle is introduced in this section. The hybrid ROV designed in the Lab of Advanced Robotic Marine Systems (ARMs), Huazhong University of Science and Technology (HUST), is shown in Fig. 3.

Fig. 3. Hybrid ROV designed in the Lab of ARMs, HUST

There are a total of eight thrusters, four vertical thrusters provide vertical thrust to assist the underwater vehicle to perform the up and down movements, and four horizontal thrusters provide the horizontal thrust to assist the underwater vehicle to perform the front, rear, left and right translational motion of the horizontal plane and Rotational motion about the z-axis. Since the designed vehicle is a remotely operated vehicle, tether winch is needed for communication as well as joystick for manually operation.

As shown in Fig. 4, the core controller of the underwater vehicle includes three parts, a PC on the shore ground station and a Raspberry Pi and autopilot in the vehicle cabin. The PC is used to run the ground station software and the PC control software.

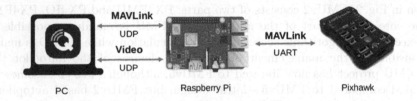

Fig. 4. Controller of the hybrid ROV

The Raspberry Pi is used for the forwarding of MAVLink messages and the transmission of video streams. The autopilot is the motion control core of the underwater vehicle. The hardware block diagram of the hybrid ROV is shown in Fig. 5.

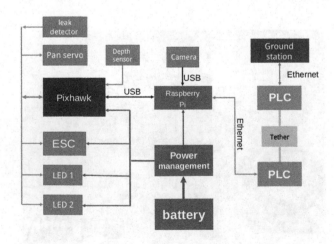

Fig. 5. Hardware architecture of the hybrid ROV

4   Software of the ROV

This section details the software of the vehicle. Firstly, introduce the architecture of the software. Then communication protocol, PC control software and autopilot software are introduced respective.

4.1   Software Architecture

As shown in Fig. 6, the software of the underwater vehicle mainly consists of three parts. The first part is the software running on the ground station PC. The main function of this part is to monitor and control the underwater vehicle. The second part is the software running on the Raspberry Pi in the underwater vehicle cabin. This part of the software is mainly responsible for forwarding MAVLink communication data and transmitting video stream. The third part is the Ardupilot running on the autopilot. Ardupilot is the core of the underwater vehicle motion control. It responsible for attitude estimate and control of the underwater vehicle. Ardupilot collects information of sensors such as inertial sensors and electronic compasses in real time, and integrates multiple sensor data by EKF algorithm. Ardupilot receives commands from ground station PC via the MAVLink communication protocol and performs corresponding attitude and motion control based on the commands.

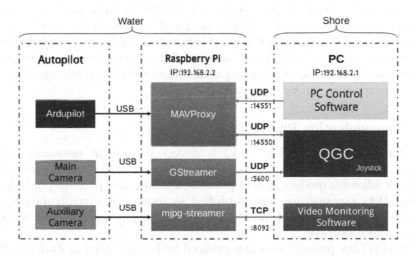

Fig. 6. Software architecture of the hybrid ROV

The Raspberry Pi is a single-board general-purpose computer running Linux. In this system, the Raspberry Pi is used as the companion computer of the autopilot. Its main function is to forward MAVLink communication messages and transmit the video stream. There are three softwares related to this control system running in the Raspberry Pi, namely MAVProxy, GStreamer, and mjpg-streamer. MAVProxy converts the MAVLink channel that transmits data in the form of serial communication to the form of Ethernet UDP communication. In order to allow the self-developed PC control software to run in parallel with the original ground station software QGroundControl (QGC), configure the MAVProxy to monitor the two ports 14550 and 14551 respectively. QGC uses the 14550 port to communicate with the autopilot. The self-developed PC control software uses the 14551 port to communicate with the autopilot. GStreamer and mjpg-streamer are software for transmitting video streams. GStreamer is software for transmitting video stream of main camera to QGroundControl use UDP protocol. Mjpg-streamer is a software for transmitting video in mjpg format. The transmission method is to establish an HTTP server, and the client can access the server to see the video stream. Compared to GStreamer, the quality of the video it transmits is low but it consumes less CPU.

There are three softwares running on the ground station PC, namely QGC ground station software, video monitoring software and PC control software. The QGroundControl ground station software is the ground station software officially supported by Ardupilot [15]. In this system, its function is to monitor the state of the underwater vehicle, observe the video stream of the main camera, and recapture the control of the PC control software in an emergency and perform emergency manual control. The video surveillance software is used to observe and save the video stream of the auxiliary camera. Since QGroundControl can only be manually operated by the joystick, it is not possible to specify the specific depth and attitude of the underwater vehicle. In order to realize a series of intelligent operations such as depth hold and attitude hold, the PC control software was developed. The PC control software can work simultaneously with QGroundControl. The PC control software also has the function of recording data such as the attitude and heading of the vehicle. With the relevant data, the control performance can be evaluated.

4.2   Communication Protocol

MAVLink (Micro Air Vehicle Link) is a very lightweight messaging protocol for communicating with drones (and between onboard drone components). MAVLink follows a modern hybrid publish-subscribe and point-to-point design pattern: Data streams are sent/published as topics while configuration subprotocols such as the mission protocol or parameter protocol are point-to-point with retransmission [16].

The MAVLink protocol was first released by Lorenz Meier in Zurich in 2009 [17]. Due to its lightweight, expandable and easy-to-use advantages, MAVLink is widely used in communication between ground station systems and unmanned small equipment. It is suitable for rotor or fixed-wing drones, unmanned vehicles and others small intelligent vehicle.

The MAVLink v2 frame contains the frame header, the frame tail, the payload data, the checksum, and an optional signature. As shown in Fig. 7, the frame header consists of the frame header flag, data length, incompatible flag, compatibility flag, data frame sequence number, system ID, component ID, and message ID. the frame tail consists of the CRC checksum and optional signature. The number of bytes of data in the frame ranges from 0 to 255. A minimum data frame that carry 0 byte data has 12 bytes, and a largest data frame containing a signature has 281 bytes [18,19].

| STX | LEN | INC FLAGS | CMP FLAGS | SEQ | SYS ID | COMP ID | MSG ID (3 bytes) | PAYLOAD (0 - 255 bytes) | CHECKSUM (2 bytes) | SIGNATURE (13 bytes) |

Fig. 7. MAVLink v2 frame

The messages in the MAVLink protocol are defined by XML files. Each XML file defines a set of messages that are supported by a particular system, each of which is referred to as a "dialect." A collection of messages supported by most ground station software and autopilots is defined in "common.xml". Ardupilot's "dialect" is defined in the "ardupilotmega.xml" file. MAVLink's toolchain "compiles" messages defined in XML files into files in supported languages. The languages supported include C/C++, Python, C#, Obj-C, Java, JS, Lua, etc. In this system C language version is used. The C language version of the MAVLink implementation is a set of pure header files that can be used in systems with extremely limited RAM and flash capacity due to their high optimization [20].

4.3 PC Control Software

As shown in Fig. 8(a), the PC control software is divided into seven modules: api, io, msg, sqlite, log, ini and thread according to different functions. The api module defines common functions that can be used externally by the library. The io module includes UDP and serial communication. The msg module contains the parsing function of the MAVLink message, and the sqlite module save the vehicle data to sqlite database. The log module can print the log information to the command line form and/or save it to a text file. The ini module can save some library configuration parameters to the ini file, the thread module includes continuous operations. The program flow chart of the host computer control software sending depth hold and attitude hold messages is shown in Fig. 8(b).

4.4 Autopilot Software

Ardupilot contains several different flight modes and always operates in exactly one flight mode at any given time. In ArduSub, there are mainly five modes: manual, stabilize, althold, poshold, surface. ArduSub always boots in manual mode. In manual mode, the vehicle receives manual control commands from the ground station. In stabilize mode, the vehicle can automatically recover the change in the attitude of the vehicle due to external torque. In the althold mode, the vehicle can perform the deep hold operation in addition to automatically recovering the change in the altitude of the vehicle due to external torque. The

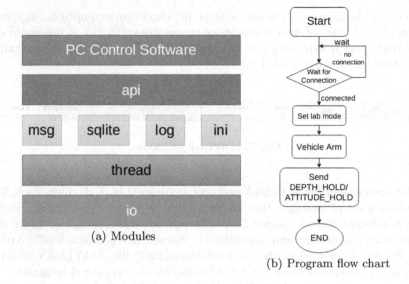

(a) Modules

(b) Program flow chart

Fig. 8. PC control software

surface mode is an emergency mode. In this mode, the vehicle cannot complete the dive action.

It is necessary to create a new lab mode to implement some custom functions in order to isolate the modifications from the existing motion controller. In order to allow the upper computer to implement individual control of the motor the original motor control part has been modified. The modifications makes it easy to specified pwm value of each motor in lab mode.

5 Experiments

In order to verify the communication function of the PC control software, the software communication test was carried out in the laboratory environment. The test scenario is shown in Fig. 9(a). The underwater vehicle autopilot and Raspberry Pi are connected to PC via USB cable. The Raspberry Pi is directly connected to the PC via Ethernet. First, QGroundControl is used to confirm that the system can work normally. Then the host computer control software is run. The printout of the control software is shown in Fig. 9(b), the data can follow the movement of the underwater vehicle. Prove that the communication function works properly.

After the laboratory communication test is completed, the pool test was carried out in water. The pool tests are manual control of the vehicle to perform translational movement and diving movement through PC control software. Figure 10 shows the pool test in water. The pilot test results show that the control system can achieve the expected manual control functions.

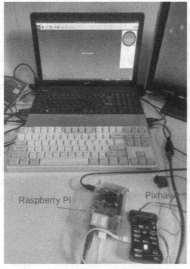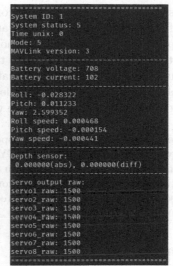

(a) Test scenario   (b) PC control software output

Fig. 9. Test in the lab

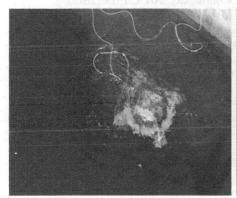

(a) ROV in the water   (b) Pilot test of the diving ROV

Fig. 10. Test in the pool

6   Conclusion

This paper firstly introduces the autopilot of the ROV, which includes the software Ardupilot and the hardware Pixhawk. And then, the software architecture of Ardupilot is briefly analyzed. The Pixhawk part gives a brief description of performance and composition of Pixhawk, and then the hardware part of the underwater vehicle is introduced. This is followed by the overall software architecture, and the MAVLink communication protocol and the MAVLink message frame was briefly presented. The PC control software part mainly consists of the module of the software and the program flow chart is explained. The autopilot software part mainly introduces the modifications of Ardupilot. Finally, in order to verify the functions of the system, the laboratory test and the test in water carried out. The test results show that the proposed control system can meet the actual needs of the ROV. Extended closed loop control of the ROV based on the proposed software architecture will be tested in future.

Acknowledgment. This work was supported in part by the Shenzhen Science and Technology Plan Project under Grant JCYJ20170413113305468, in part by the National Key Research and Development Program of China (Grant 2017YFB1302302), in part by the National Natural Science Foundation of China under Grant 51579111 and in part by the Research Fund from Science and Technology on Underwater Vehicle Technology under Grant SXJQR2017KFJJ06.

References

1. Zhang, F., Marani, G., Smith, R.N., Choi, H.T.: Future trends in marine robotics [TC spotlight]. IEEE Robot. Autom. Mag. **22**(1), 14–122 (2015)
2. Zhang, Q., Zhang, J., Chemori, A., Xiang, X.: Virtual submerged floating operational system for robotic manipulation. Complexity **2018**, 1–18 (2018)
3. Phamduy, P., Vazquez, M.A., Kim, C., Mwaffo, V., Rizzo, A., Porfiri, M.: Design and characterization of a miniature free-swimming robotic fish based on multimaterial 3D printing. Int. J. Intell. Robot. Appl. **1**(2), 209–223 (2017)
4. Yu, C., Xiang, X., Lapierre, L., Zhang, Q.: Robust magnetic tracking of subsea cable by auv in the presence of sensor noise and ocean currents. IEEE J. Ocean. Eng. **43**(2), 311–322 (2018)
5. De Assis, F.H., Takase, F.K., Maruyama, N., Miyagi, P.E.: Developing an ROV software control architecture: a formal specification approach. In: IECON 2012– 38th Annual Conference on IEEE Industrial Electronics Society, pp. 3107–3112, October 2012
6. Cadiou, J.F., Coudray, S., Leon, P., Perrier, M.: Control architecture of a new deep scientific ROV: VICTOR 6000. In: IEEE Oceanic Engineering Society, OCEANS 1998, Conference Proceedings (Cat. No.98CH36259), vol. 1, pp. 492–497, September 1998
7. Ganesan, K., Smith, S.M., White, K., Flanigan, T.: A pragmatic software architecture for UUVs. In: Proceedings of Symposium on Autonomous Underwater Vehicle Technology, pp. 209–215, June 1996
8. Jalving, B., Kristensen, J., Størkersen, N.: Program philosophy and software architecture for the HUGIN seabed surveying UUV. IFAC Proc. Vol. **31**(30), 211–216 (1998)
9. Bin, H., Justice, A.: The design of an unmanned aerial vehicle based on the ArduPilot. Indian J. Sci. Technol. **2**(4), 12–15 (2009)
10. Hadi, G.S., Varianto, R., Trilaksono, B., Budiyono, A.: Autonomous UAV system development for payload dropping mission. J. Instrum. Autom. Syst. **1**(2), 72–77 (2014)
11. ArduPilot: About. http://ardupilot.org/about
12. He, B., Justice, A.: The design of an unmanned aerial vehicle based on the ArduPilot. Indian J. Sci. Technol. **2**, 12–15 (2009)

13. Home Page - Pixhawk. http://pixhawk.org/
14. Feng, L., Fangchao, Q.: Research on the hardware structure characteristics and EKF filtering algorithm of the autopilot PIXHAWK. In: 2016 Sixth International Conference on Instrumentation Measurement, Computer, Communication and Control (IMCCC), pp. 228–231, July 2016
15. Zurich, E.: QGroundcontrol: ground control station for small air land water autonomous unmanned systems. http://qgroundcontrol.com/
16. Introduction · MAVLink Developer Guide. https://mavlink.io/en/
17. Meier, L., Camacho, J., Godbolt, B., Goppert, J., Heng, L., Lizarraga, M., et al.: MAVlink: micro air vehicle communication protocol (2009)
18. Atoev, S., Kwon, K., Lee, S., Moon, K.: Data analysis of the MAVLink communication protocol. In: 2017 International Conference on Information Science and Communications Technologies (ICISCT), pp. 1–3, November 2017
19. Serialization · MAVLink Developer Guide. http://mavlink.io/en/guide/serialization
20. Dietrich, T., Andryeyev, O., Zimmermann, A., Mitschele-Thiel, A.: Towards a unified decentralized swarm management and maintenance coordination based on MAVLink. In: 2016 International Conference on Autonomous Robot Systems and Competitions (ICARSC), pp. 124–129, May 2016

Optimized SOM Algorithm to Solve Problem of Invalid Task Allocation

Yun Qu, Daqi Zhu[✉], and Mingzhi Chen

Shanghai Engineering Research Center of Intelligent Maritime
Search & Rescue and Underwater Vehicles, Shanghai Maritime University,
Haigang Avenue 1550, Shanghai 201306, China
zdq367@aliyun.com

Abstract. Because the factually turning radius of the Autonomous Underwater Vehicle (AUV) will affect the task allocation of multi-AUV system, the optimized SOM algorithm is proposed in this paper. The aim of the optimized SOM algorithm is giving the reasonable allocated scheme for corresponding tasks. Due to the existence of the invalid task allocation, there are two problems in the traditional self-organizing map (SOM) algorithm. One problem is wasting more time for calculating the winning neuron. Another is causing more energy consumption because the farther AUV is allocated to the corresponding target. The optimized algorithm is proposed to solve the problem of the invalid task allocation. In order to demonstrate the effectiveness of the proposed algorithm, this paper gives simulation results.

Keywords: Turning radius · Autonomous Underwater Vehicle (AUV) · Optimized SOM

1 Introduction

With the rapidly developing of the synergetic technology, the multi-robot system is a hot topic in the research [1–4]. The multi-robot system, which has the highly intelligence and efficiency, offers more solutions than single system. The problem of the task allocation is one of the hot topics in the multi-AUV system. Task allocation of multi-AUV [5–7] system refers to reasonable allocation the AUV to the destination. Tsiogkas [7] carries out different task allocation strategies under communication constraints. These methods include a greedy allocation method, a k-Means method and the linear programming formulation. The market algorithm [8] is used in task allocation. The framework of the market is inspired by the daily economic events occurring around us aiming to assign resources dynamically. Although these algorithms are better to solve the problem of the task allocation, these method will recalculate the all results of the task allocation when the new target is inputted to the method.

This project is supported by the National Natural Science Foundation of China (51575336, 91748117) the Creative Activity Plan for Science and Technology Commission of Shanghai (16550720200, 18JC1413000, 18DZ1206305).

H. Yu et al. (Eds.): ICIRA 2019, LNAI 11742, pp. 218–224, 2019.
https://doi.org/10.1007/978-3-030-27535-8_20

The SOM neural network was proposed by Kohonen [9]. The SOM neural network is a non-supervision learning method. The aim of SOM neural network is classifying neurons in the input layer and classified results are outputted in the output layer. Because the task allocation is similar with the SOM neural network, the SOM algorithm applied to the task allocation of the multi-AUV system. After using the method to the multi-AUV system, targets are automatically assigned to the corresponding AUV. Zhu et al. [10, 11] puts forward the SOM to solve the problem of task allocation in the multi-AUV system. The method solves the problem of unknown number of Autonomous Underwater.

Vehicles (AUVs) and targets. The method allows the AUV, which has the shortest Euclidean distance between the AUV and the target, to arrive the corresponding target. Because the AUV actually has the turning radius and the initial orientation, the SOM algorithm may led to the invalid task allocation in multi-AUV system. So as to solve the problem of the invalid task allocation, the optimized SOM algorithm is proposed in this paper. The optimized SOM algorithm not only saves time for calculating the winning neuron, but also selects the AUV with the shorter practically navigation distance than in the traditional SOM algorithm to access the target.

The remainder of this paper is organized as follows: Sect. 2 introduces the task allocation problem of the multi-AUV system. The optimized SOM algorithm is proposed in Sect. 3. The conducted experiments and analyses their results in Sect. 4. The last part summarizes the conclusion.

2 Problem Description

The problem of task allocation in multi-AUV system is how to select the reasonably AUV for the corresponding target. A diagram of targets and AUVs is illustrated in Fig. 1. The red dots are represents AUVs and the green dots are represents targets. AUVs have different initial azimuths and turning radius in the workspace. The energy consumption of the AUV is actually navigation distance from its initial position to the target location. So as to reduce the energy consumption, the algorithm selects the winning neuron, which has the shortest navigation distance, to access the target. The invalid task allocation refers to a case where the AUV, which is nearby the target, cannot be allocated to the corresponding target because of AUV's turning radius. For example, it is assumed that the turning radius of the AUV is 2 m and the initial azimuths is shown in Fig. 1. Because the selection of the winning neuron depends on the Euclidean distance between the AUV and the target, the winning neuron is R1. R1 is an invalid task allocation for T1 because the AUV, which has the turning radius and the initial azimuths, cannot access to the target. The method continually calculates the winning neuron until energy of the AUV has been running out of and it wastes time in calculating the winning neuron. Then the method will calculate the new winning neuron and the farther AUV is allocated to the target. The method causes more energy consumption of multi-AUV system.

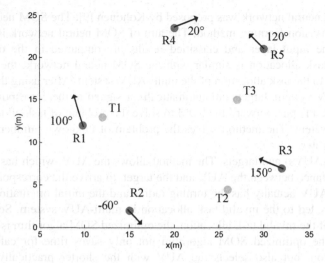

Fig. 1. The problem of task allocation in multi-AUV system (Color figure online)

2.1 Optimized SOM Algorithm

The SOM algorithm structure is illustrated in Fig. 2. The first layer is the input layer and represents the location of targets. The second layer is the output layer and represents the location of AUVs. The weight is used to connect the neuron of the input layer with neuron of the output layer. The weight represents the Euclidean distance between the AUV and the target. The output layer compares and analyzes input patterns to find the rules and classify them.

Because the selection of the winning neuron in the traditional algorithm depends on the Euclidean distance, it exists the problem of invalid task allocation. In order to solve it, the optimized SOM algorithm is proposed through the valid judgment of the winning neuron and changing the selection of the winning neuron. The optimized SOM algorithm flow chart is introduced in Fig. 3. First, some parameters are initialized such as the learning rate, turning radius, running speed and so on. Second, the coordinates of targets are inputted in the input layer. $X = (x_1, x_2, \ldots, x_K)$ represents the neuron in input layer. K is the number of targets, x_K represents the coordinates of the K_{th} target in the Cartesian coordinate system. The coordinates of AUVs are initialized in the output layer. $W_{KN} = (W_{11}, \ldots, W_{1N}, \ldots, W_{21}, \ldots, W_{2N}, W_{K1}, \ldots, W_{KN})$ represents coordinates of targets in output layer. N is the number of AUVs, and W_{KN} represents the weight of the N_{th} neuron (AUV) from the K_{th} group. $Angle = (\theta_1, \theta_2, \ldots, \theta_N)$ represents initial angles of AUVs and θ_N represents initial angle of the N_{th} AUV. The invalid neuron refers the AUV, which is nearby to the target, cannot be allocated to the target because of the turning radius and initial azimuth of the AUV. Due to the initial azimuth and turning radius of the AUV, there is the invalid neuron (AUV) in the output layer although the invalid neuron (AUV) is nearby to the target. In order to select the AUV with the shortest navigation distance as the winning neuron, the algorithm will compare the navigation distance between all AUVs and the target. So, the invalid neuron (AUV) need to become the valid neuron (AUV). Solution of the invalid neuron

(AUV) is illustrated in Fig. 4. The green dot represents the AUV and the blue dot represents the target. θ is the initial angle of the AUV and P represents the intersection of the black dotted line and the red dotted line. O_2 is the center of the circle drawn by a black dotted line and O_3 is the center of the circle drawn by a red dotted line. d is the distance between the target and O_1. k_1 is the slope of the AUV and it defined as follows:

$$k_1 = \tan(\beta) \tag{1}$$

where β represents the angle between the x-axis and the line which connects the target and the AUV. k_2 is the slope of the line which connects the O_1 with the AUV and defined as:

$$k_2 = -1/k_1 \, (k_1 \neq 0) \tag{2}$$

where O_1 represents the center of the circle drawn by a red solid line. x_{o1} represents the abscissa of the O_1 and is defined as follows:

$$x_{o1} = x_r - R/\sqrt{1 + k_2^2} \tag{3}$$

where x_r represents the abscissa of the AUV and R is the turning radius of the AUV. y_{o1} represents the ordinate of the O_1 and is defined as:

$$y_{o1} = k_2 x_{o1} + y_r - k_2 x_r \tag{4}$$

where y_r represents the ordinate of the AUV. x_{o3} represents the abscissa of the O_3 and is defined as follows:

$$x_{o3} = x_r + R/\sqrt{1 + k_2^2} \tag{5}$$

y_{o3} represents the ordinate of the O_3 and is defined as:

$$y_{o3} = k_2 x_{o3} + y_r - k_2 x_r \tag{6}$$

d, which represents the distance between the O_1 and the AUV, is given by:

$$d = \min(\sqrt{(x_T - x_{o1})^2 + (y_T - y_{o1})^2}, \sqrt{(x_T - x_{o3})^2 + (y_T - y_{o3})^2}) \tag{7}$$

where x_T represents the abscissa of the target and y_T represents the ordinate of the target. Then the algorithm judges the validity of the AUV. When d is more than R, the corresponding AUV is a valid neuron, the AUV navigates along the red solid line until the AUV arrives at the target. When d is less than R, the corresponding AUV is an invalid neuron. In order to make the invalid neuron (AUV) become the valid neuron (AUV), the AUV navigates along the red dotted line in Fig. 4 until d is more than R. Then the AUV navigates along the black solid line until the AUV arrives at the target.

The selection of the winning neuron depends on actually navigation distance of AUVs. The neighborhood function is defined as follows:

$$f(d_m, g) = \begin{cases} e^{-d_m^2/g^2(t)}, & d_m < \lambda \\ 0, & others \end{cases} \tag{8}$$

Radius λ represents the center of the winning neuron and the neighbor neurons are nearby the winning neuron. $d_m = |N_m - N_j|$ represents the Euclidean distance between the m_{th} AUV and the winner. The function $g^2(t)$ is calculated as follows:

$$g^2(t) = (1 - \partial)^t g_o \tag{9}$$

The fixed learning rate is ∂ and $\partial < 1$. The update rule of the AUV is calculated as follows:

$$R(t+1) = \begin{cases} T, & D \leq D_{min} \\ R(t) + \partial \times f(d_m, g) \times (T - R(t)), & D > D_{min} \end{cases} \tag{10}$$

D represents the Euclidean distance between the target and the AUV. D_{min} represents a maximum navigation distance of the AUV during one iteration. When D is less than D_{min}, the weight is replaced by the coordinate of corresponding target. When D is more than D_{min}, the weight's adjustment depends on the learning speed ∂, neighborhood function $f(d_m, g)$ and the location of the winner and neighbors (Fig. 5).

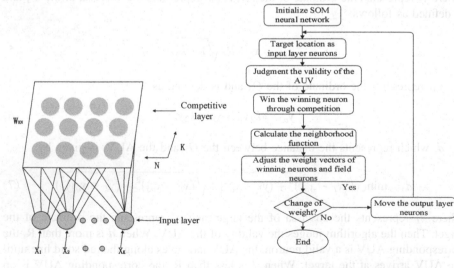

Fig. 2. SOM neural network structure   Fig. 3. SOM algorithm flow chart

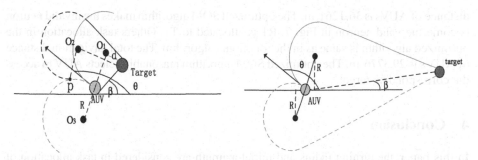

Fig. 4. Solution of invalid task allocation   **Fig. 5.** Initial moment steering problem

3 Simulation Study

The simulation experiments and analysis show in two-dimensional (2D) workspace. There are five AUVs and three targets in Figs. 6 and 7. The running speed of the AUV is 0.349 m/s and the turning radius is 2 m. The maximum turning angle of the AUV is 10° during one iteration. The initial angle of AUVs are illustrated in Figs. 6 and 7. The blue line represents navigation distance between the AUV and the target in the traditional SOM algorithm and the red line represents navigation distance of the invalid neuron (AUV) in Fig. 6. The black line represents the navigation distance between the AUV and the target in optimized SOM algorithm and the red line represents the navigation distance when the invalid neuron becomes the valid neuron in Fig. 7.

Because the selection of the winning neuron depends on the Euclidean distance between AUVs and the target, R1 is the invalid neuron when the algorithm selects the winning neuron for T1. R1 continually moves along the red solid line in Fig. 6 until the energy of the AUV runs out of. It wastes more time for calculating the winning neuron. Then R2 is allocated to T1, which causes more energy consumption. The total navigation

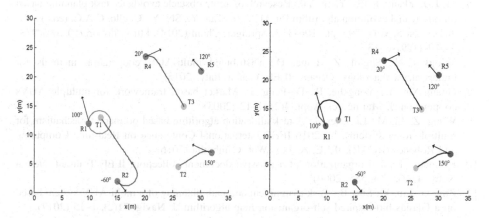

Fig. 6. Task allocation in traditional SOM method (Color figure online)   **Fig. 7.** Task allocation in optimized SOM method (Color figure online)

distance of AUVs is 36.1261 m. The optimized SOM algorithm makes the invalid neuron become the valid neuron in Fig. 7. R1 is allocated to T1. Others task allocation in the optimized algorithm is same as in the traditional algorithm. The total navigation distance of AUVs is 29.3776 m. The optimized SOM algorithm reasonably selects AUV to access the corresponding target.

4 Conclusion

In this paper, the turning radius and initial azimuth are considered in task allocation of the multi-AUV system and proposed the optimized SOM algorithm. The optimized SOM algorithm solves the problem of the invalid neuron. On the one hand, it saves the time for calculating the winning neuron. On the other hand, it reasonably allocates the AUV, which has the shortest navigation distance, to the target. The optimized SOM algorithm can be extended to more complex case, such as three-dimensional plane.

References

1. Xiang, C., Sun, H., Jan, G.E.: Multi-AUV cooperative target search and tracking in unknown underwater environment. Ocean Eng. **150**, 1–11 (2018)
2. Hert, S., Tiwari, S., Lumelsky, V.: A terrain-covering algorithm for an AUV. Auton. Robot **3**(2), 91–119 (1996)
3. Yang, Q., Hao, S.U., Tang, G., et al.: Robust optimal sliding MODE Control for AUV system with uncertainties. Inf. Control **47**(2), 176–183 (2018)
4. Liu, Y., Zhu, D.: Task assignment and path planning of AUV system based on Glasius bio-inspired self-organizing map neural network algorithm. Syst. Simul. Technol. **13**(3), 230–240 (2017)
5. Juan, L.I., Kun-Yu, Z.: University H E.: Heterogeneous Multi-AUV Cooperative Task Allocation Based on Improved Contract Net Algorithm. J. Unmanned Undersea Syst. **25**(5), 418–423 (2017)
6. Li, J.-J., Zhang, R.-B., Yang, Yu.: Research on route obstacle avoidance task planning based on differential evolution algorithm for AUV. In: Tan, Y., Shi, Y., Coello, C.A.C. (eds.) ICSI 2014. LNCS, vol. 8795, pp. 106–113. Springer, Cham (2014). https://doi.org/10.1007/978-3-319-11897-0_13
7. Tsiogkas, N., Saigol, Z., Lane, D.: Distributed multi-AUV cooperation methods for underwater archaeology. Oceans. IEEE, Genoa, Italy (2015)
8. Guang-Xin, Y., Yong-Jie, P., Da-Peng, J.: Market based framework for multiple AUVs cooperation. J. Marine Sci. Appl. **4**(2), 7–12 (2005)
9. Wang, Z., Li, M., Li, J., et al.: A task allocation algorithm based on market mechanism for multiple robot systems. In: 2016 IEEE International Conference on Real-time Computing and Robotics (RCAR). IEEE, Angkor Wat, Cambodia (2016)
10. Kohonen, T.: Self-organization of a massive document collection. IEEE Transact. Neural Netw. **11**(3), 574–585 (2000)
11. Zhu, D., Liu, Y., Sun, B.: Task assignment and path planning of a multi-AUV system based on a Glasius bio-inspired self-organising map algorithm. J. Navig. **71**(2), 1–15 (2017)

Multiple Underwater Target Search Path Planning Based on GBNN

Tingting Zhu, Daqi Zhu, and Mingzhong Yan[✉]

Shanghai Engineering Research Center of Intelligent Maritime
Search & Rescue and Underwater Vehicles, Shanghai Maritime University,
Haigang Avenue 1550, Shanghai 201306, China
zdq367@aliyun.com, mzyan@shmtu.edu.cn

Abstract. For the underwater target search problem of Autonomous Underwater Vehicle (AUV), this paper proposes a search path planning method for multiple underwater targets based on GBNN. Firstly, the underwater two-dimensional environment discrete grid map is constructed. Secondly, the corresponding two-dimensional GBNN model is constructed according to the grid map. Finally, the GBNN model is used to adaptively suppress the obstacle and adaptively attract the target search area. AUV can search and detect underwater targets in close proximity according to the activity output values of neural network neurons. The simulation results show that AUV can avoid obstacles autonomously and search and detect underwater targets.

Keywords: Autonomous underwater robot · GBNN · Underwater target search

1 Introduction

The vast ocean is rich in biological, mineral and marine resources. The development of marine resources is of great positive significance, and the exploration of the ocean will become the future development trend surely [1]. The research and development trends of Autonomous Underwater Vehicles (AUV) will become better and better, as an important tool for marine development. With the continuous development and utilization of marine resources, the application of AUV is more and more extensive and it plays an indispensable role in anti-submarine, surveillance and patrol [2, 3].

Path planning technology is one of the key technologies for AUV to accomplish tasks safely and efficiently [4]. The path of AUV planning is often closely related to its mission and the most common path planning is two. One is the path from the starting point to the target location. This kind of path planning is often used in the recovery of AUV, which already had quite a lot of mature research results. The other is complete coverage search and detection for the target area that needs to be searched. This technique often requires AUV to perform complete coverage path planning for local areas and is mostly used in AUV underwater target detection and search. There have been some related research results on underwater target search and detection. The paper [5] proposes a collaborative region search algorithm based on predictive control ideas, studies the effects of various communication restrictions on regional search function and improves the function of regional search. The paper [6] proposes a decentralized

© Springer Nature Switzerland AG 2019
H. Yu et al. (Eds.): ICIRA 2019, LNAI 11742, pp. 225–232, 2019.
https://doi.org/10.1007/978-3-030-27535-8_21

control algorithm for bacterial heuristic search targets and improves computational efficiency. The paper [7, 8] proposes an adaptive algorithm to complete monitoring tasks through path planning of robots in an unknown environment. The basic idea of this method is to perform adaptive adjustments to complete monitoring tasks. However, there is a strong dependence on the information acquired within the line of sight in the re-path planning. However, these methods still lack flexible path planning methods and are not able to comprehensively search for targets, and the adaptability is poor.

In response to this problem, this paper proposes an improved biological heuristic algorithm, GBNN (Glasius Bio-inspired Neural Network, GBNN) algorithm, which uses the difference equation to calculate the activity value in the neural network, which has the advantages of no learning and self-adaptation and improves the speed of the algorithm. For the unknown underwater environment, the GBNN algorithm can make the AUV perform the path planning of the target search according to the real-time update value of the neurons of the neural network, and the adaptability is strong.

This article is divided into 4 sections. The first section introduces the background and research significance of this paper; the second section introduces the principle of GBNN neural network based on the established discrete grid map; the third section shows the path of AUV to multiple underwater targets in MATLAB simulation environment Search and testing; the fourth section summarizes the full text.

2   GBNN Principle

GBNN is a discrete-time Hopfiled neural network. The corresponding two-dimensional neural network model is shown in Fig. 1. Each circle represents a neuron, and each neuron has a straight line or a diagonal connection on its neighboring neurons. Take the central neuron i as an example, and it is connected with the surrounding eight neurons. The activity values of neurons can be transferred to each other through these connection relationships [9, 10].

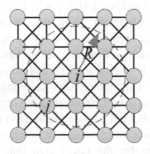

Fig. 1. Two-dimensional neural network model

2.1 GBNN Principle

In a two-dimensional neural network, the activity value of a neuron can be expressed by the formula (1):

$$y_j(t+1) = g\left(\sum_{0<|ij|\leq\sqrt{3}} W_{ij}[y_i(t)]^+ + I_i \right) \tag{1}$$

$$g(x) = \begin{cases} -1, & x<0 \\ \alpha x, & 0\leq x<1, \ \alpha>0 \\ 1, & x\geq 1 \end{cases} \tag{2}$$

Equation (2) represents the transfer function in the expression of the neuron activity value $g(x)$; $y_j(t+1)$ represents the activity value of the neuron j at $t+1$, and $y_i(t)$ is the activity value of the neuron j connected to the neuron i at t. $[y_i(t)]^+ = max[y_i(t), 0]$ indicates that only the positive activity values in the neurons can propagate outward through the connections between the neurons, thereby affecting the magnitude of the activity values of the surrounding neurons, but the negative activity values do not have this property. W_{ij} represents the connection weight coefficient of neuron i and j, and the expression is as shown in Eq. (3):

$$W_{ij} = \begin{cases} e^{-\beta|i-j|^2}, & i \text{ is connected to } j \\ 0, & i \text{ is not connected to } j \end{cases} \tag{3}$$

where, β is a constant, $|i-j|$ represents the Euclidean distance between neurons i and j. In a two-dimensional neural network, the neurons connected to neuron j can only have a maximum of 8, so the value of $|ij|$ is 0 to $\sqrt{2}$. The external stimulus term $\sum_{0<|ij|<\sqrt{3}} W_{ij}[y_i(t)]^+$ represents the sum of the external excitations of the individual neurons connected to the neuron j, which has global transitivity and is dependent on the connection between the neurons. I_i is the external input of the neuron i, and $I_i>0$ indicates the input of the excitation signal, $I_i<0$ indicates the input of the suppression signal.

2.2 Two-Dimensional Grid Map Model Based on GBNN

In the corresponding two-dimensional grid map, each grid represents each state in the map. These grids represent occupied space, which may be the target area or the obstacle area, or free space. In the two-dimensional mountain grid map shown in Fig. 2(a), the white grid represents free space, and the black grid represents occupied space. Thereby, a neural network corresponding to the grid map can be established, so that each neuron in the neural network can be associated with each grid in the map one by one, that is, the black neurons correspond to the occupied space in the grid map and white neurons correspond to free space. For example, the neurons i in Fig. 2(b) correspond to the grid i in Fig. 2(a).

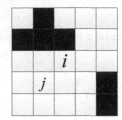   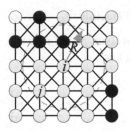

(a) Discretized two-dimensional grid map   (b) Corresponding two-dimensional neural network

Fig. 2. Correspondence between two-dimensional underwater environment and neural network

In a two-dimensional discrete grid map, the external input I_i of the neuron i is redefined as:

$$I_i = \begin{cases} +E, & \text{neurons corresponding to the task area} \\ -E, & \text{neurons corresponding to the occupied area} \\ 0, & \text{neurons corresponding to the other area} \end{cases} \quad (4)$$

Among them, the value of E is much larger than 1 and the range of $\sum_{0<|ij|<\sqrt{3}} W_{ij}[y_i(t)]^+$ is between 0 and 1. When the AUV performs a task, for the task area, the signal of the neuron comes from the external input signal of $+E$ and $\sum_{0<|ij|<\sqrt{3}} W_{ij}[y_i(t)]^+$, and the active output value of the neuron maintains the peak value $+1$, attracting the AUV to perform the covering task; For the obstacle area or target area, the position corresponding to the neural network introduces an external suppression signal of $-E$; the other areas in the map are free spaces, I_i is defined as 0, meaning that these areas hasn't external signal input. The activity value of neurons is only derived from the external excitation term, that is, only the activity value of the connection relationship between the neurons is received, so the activity value of the neuron is smaller.

2.3 Path Selection Strategy

When the AUV performs a task, AUV select a suitable adjacent grid as the next choice according to the activity value of the neuron. The AUV determines the next navigation position according to the path selection strategy [11]. The path selection strategy is expressed by Eq. (5):

$$Path = \{P_n | x_{P_n} = \max\{x_i + cy_i, i = 1, 2, \ldots, m\},$$
$$P_p = P_c, P_c = P_n\} \quad (5)$$

P_c is the current position of the AUV, P_n is the next position of the AUV, P_p is the position of the previous step of the AUV, c is the normal number; x_{P_n} is the activity value of the neuron i; m represents the number of neurons connected to i; y_i is direction parameter, Its expression is:

$$y_i = 1 - \frac{\Delta \varphi_i}{\pi} \tag{6}$$

$$\Delta \varphi_i = |\varphi_i - \varphi_c| = \left| a \tan 2(y_{P_i} - y_{P_c}, x_{P_i} - x_{P_c}) - a \tan 2\left(y_{P_c} - y_{P_p}, x_{P_c} - x_{P_p}\right) \right| \tag{7}$$

$\left(x_{P_p}, y_{P_p}\right)$ indicates the position of the AUV previous step; $\left(x_{P_c}, y_{P_c}\right)$ indicates the current position of the AUV; $\left(x_{P_i}, y_{P_i}\right)$ indicates the coordinates of the next possible position of the AUV. According to the formula and the heading of the AUV, it can be drawn $\Delta \varphi_i \in [0, \pi]$, $y_i \in [0, 1]$. When the AUV sails from the current position to the next position, the AUV selects the grid corresponding to the largest neuron from the adjacent neurons as the next position according to the path selection strategy of Eq. (5), In the long run, until the AUV completes the search task for all underwater targets.

3 Simulation Experiment and Analysis

3.1 Task Description

As shown in Fig. 3, in the task of performing underwater target search, the AUV starts from a prescribed starting point, first sails to the starting point of the task that needs to be searched, and then detects the underwater target, and returns to the end of the AUV after the task is completed. Because AUVs generally operate in large-scale working environments such as lakes and oceans, their size is negligible compared to the entire working environment. In order to simplify the model, we regard the AUV as an object with a certain mass regardless of its size, that is a particle. At the same time, the direction of the AUV is regarded as an instantaneous change, ignoring its steering process. The parameters in GBNN are set to: $\alpha = 0.7, \beta = 3, E = 50, c = 0.5$, where, α represents the coefficient of the transfer function $g(x)$, β is the weight value, E is the external stimulus of the neuron, and c is the direction coefficient of the path selection strategy.

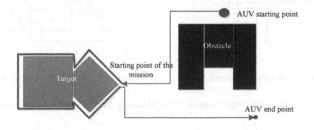

Fig. 3. Schematic diagram of underwater target search

3.2 Multiple Underwater Target Search Path Planning for Obstacle-Free Objects

The underwater environment set in this paper is a 15 × 15 two-dimensional grid map. As shown in Fig. 4(a), the AUV starts from the starting point (2, 2) and the end point is set to (15, 2). The target information in the environment is known. As shown in Fig. 4(a), under the attraction of the activity value of the neuron corresponding to the task area, the AUV goes to the task start point of the target 1, and performs the underwater target 1 search for tasks. As shown in Fig. 4(b), the AUV completes the search task for the underwater target 1. At this time, AUV is driven to the target 2 for excitation under the excitation of the positive activity value of the target 2. The AUV plans a path to the starting point of target 2 according to the size of the GBNN neurons activity value. As shown in Fig. 4(c), the AUV completes the search task for the target 2. At this time, the AUV returns to the end point (15, 2), as shown in Fig. 4(d).

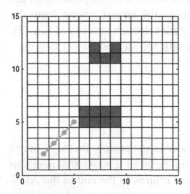

(a) AUV sails from the starting point to starting point of target 1 mission

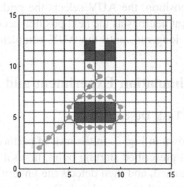

(b) AUV goes to the starting point of the target 2 mission

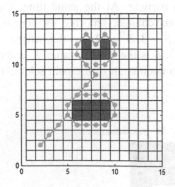

(c) AUV completes the target 2 search task

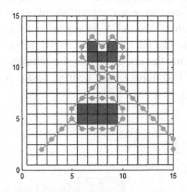

(d) AUV returns to the end point (15, 1)

Fig. 4. Underwater multi-target search path planning for AUV in obstacle-free situations

3.3   Multiple Underwater Target Search Path Planning with Obstacles

The underwater environment set in this paper is a 15×15 two-dimensional grid map. Set the AUV to start from the starting point (2, 2) and set the return point to (15, 2). As shown in Fig. 5(a), the AUV starts from the starting point (2, 2). Because of the blocking of static obstacles, the AUV cannot walk through (3, 3) and (4, 4), as shown in Fig. 4(a). As shown in Fig. 5(a), AUV receives the external input signal from the neurons corresponding to the obstacle area, then bypasses the static obstacle and selects the grid with the largest peripheral activity value according to formula (5) as the next choice. As shown in Fig. 5(b), the AUV completes the search task for the underwater target 1, and the obstacle 2 moves the current position to block the advancement of the

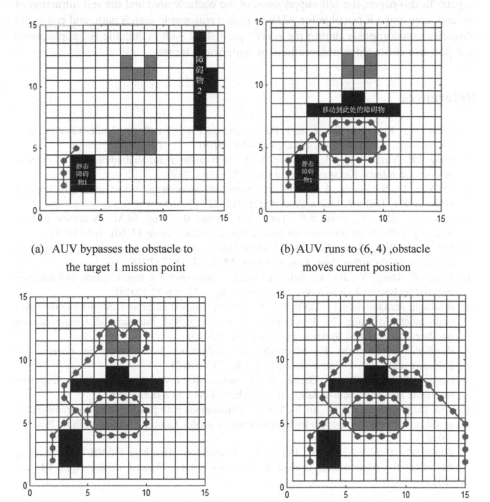

(a) AUV bypasses the obstacle to
the target 1 mission point

(b) AUV runs to (6, 4) ,obstacle
moves current position

(c) AUV completes the search for target 2

(d) AUV returns to the end (15,2)

Fig. 5. AUV search path planning for multiple underwater targets with obstacles

AUV. At this time, the AUV senses the input of the suppression signal of the area corresponding to the obstacle, and automatically avoids the dynamic obstacles and re-plans a path to the task point of the target 2. As shown in Fig. 5(c), the AUV completes the detection of the underwater target 2. When the AUV searches through all under-water targets, the AUV plans a path to the end point, as shown in Fig. 5(d).

4 Conclusion

In this paper, an improved bio-heuristic neural network algorithm–GBNN algorithm is proposed and applied to the problem of searching for the coverage path of underwater targets. In this paper, the self-suppression of the obstacle area and the self-attraction of the task area make it possible for AUV to plan a reasonable search path, and can avoid obstacles autonomously during the search path. This path is suitable for applications that perform close-range observations of underwater targets.

References

1. Yang, Y.: Research Status and Future Prospect of Intelligent Underwater Vehicle Technology . Electron. Prod. (04), 24–25+55 (2019)
2. Song, J.H., Yun, Y., Luo, L.B., Wang, X.M.: Application of artificial intelligence in the field of deep sea robots. Electronic World (06), 185–186 (2019)
3. Li, Y.P., Li, S., Zhang, A.Q.: Research status of autonomous/remote control underwater vehicles. Sci. Technol. Innov. Prod. **8**(02), 217–222 (2016)
4. Huang, S., Shu, Y., Tang, S.F., Tong, Z.Y., Song, B., Tong, M.M.: A review of path planning methods for autonomous mobile robots. Softw. Guide **17**(10), 1–5 (2018)
5. Fu, X.W., Wei, G.W., Gao, X.G.: Multi-UAV collaborative area search in uncertain environment algorithm. Syst. Eng. Electron. **38**(4), 821–827 (2016)
6. Yang, B., Ding, Y., Jin, Y.: Self-organized swarm robot for target search and trapping inspired by bacterial chemotaxis. Rob. Auton. Syst. **72**, 83–92 (2015)
7. Renzagli, A., Doitsidis, L., Martinelli, A.: Cognitive-based adaptive control for cooperative multi-robot Coverage. In: Proceedings of the IEEE/RSJ International Conference on Intelligent Robots and Systems, pp. 3314–3320 (2010)
8. Renzagli, A., Doitsidis, L., Martinelli, A.: Multi-robot three-dimensional coverage of unknown areas. Int. J. Robot. Res. **31**(6), 738–752 (2012)
9. Glasius, R., Komoda, A., Gielen, S.: A biologically inspired neural net for trajectory formation and obstacle avoidance. Biol. Cybern. **6**(84), 511–520 (1996)
10. Zhu, D.Q., Sun, B., Li, L.: An AUV's 3-D autonomous path planning and secure obstacles avoidance algorithm based on biological heuristic model. Control Decisions **30**(5), 798–806 (2015)
11. Zhu, D.Q., Liu, Y., Sun, B., Liu, Q.Y.: Autonomous Heuristic GBNN Path Planning Algorithm for Autonomous Underwater Vehicles [J/OL]. Control Theory Appl. **04**, 1–9 (2019)

Path Planning for Swarm AUV Visiting Communication Node

Chao Geng[1,2,3(✉)], Guannan Li[1,2,4], and Hongli Xu[1,2]

[1] The State Key Laboratory of Robotics, Shenyang Institute of Automation,
China Academy of Science (CAS), Shenyang 110016, China
{gengchao,liguannan,xhl}@sia.cn
[2] Institutes for Robotics and Intelligent Manufacturing,
China Academy of Science (CAS), Shenyang 110016, China
[3] School of Information Science and Engineering,
Northeastern University, Shenyang 110819, China
[4] University of Chinese Academy of Sciences, Beijing 100049, China

Abstract. This paper proposes a method for path planning of an underwater robot swarm. The method is based on biological inspired neural network to plan path between robots and communication nodes. The robot swarm is used to search wild sea area. To solve the long distance communication problem, we deploy some communication nodes ahead, forming a communication network under the water. The robots visit the nodes to communicate. With this method, robots can also avoid obstacles in real time. Firstly, put the landscape into grid map. Then build biologically inspired neural network based on the grid map. The node attracts the robots and the obstacles reject the robots through neural activity. At last, robots plan their path by the activity with a steepest gradient descent rule. Simulation result shows the method may lose in local optimum, so we improve the method to avoid repetitive path. The results show that the improvement effective for path planning.

Keywords: Path planning · AUV swarm · Biological inspired neural network

1 Introduction

AUV (Autonomous Underwater Vehicle) is the key to organize the ocean robot system [1]. Individual AUV technology has developed for many years, it has a relatively ripe application. And we aim to use swarm intelligent technology on AUV. We use swarm AUV for searching targets in a wild sea area. And the problem of communication under the water for long distance is developing.

Development of underwater wireless communication technology has major breakthrough. Wireless electromagnetic wave, underwater acoustic and optical communication grow more mature but can't afford long distance. The communication of gravitational wave, neutrino and underwater quantum are developing now. They are on

This work is supported by National Defense Science and Technology Innovation Special Zone Project "x AUV Long-Term Resident Technology" (No. 18-H863-00-TS-002-034-01).

H. Yu et al. (Eds.): ICIRA 2019, LNAI 11742, pp. 233–239, 2019.
https://doi.org/10.1007/978-3-030-27535-8_22

experimental stage [2]. The area we are going to search may be range of 100 km * 100 km. So we use communication nodes for building communication network. In this way, the nodes should be set up under the water ahead. Each node can use acoustic equipment to communicate with AUV.

The nodes network has been developing for many years. Company and academy use the node robots to detect earthquake under the ocean. Like Autonomous Robotics Limited company and Geospace Technologies company [3].

In this paper, we mainly talk about the method of planning path. The path is the shortest way to connect the robot and node. The current method of path planning is artificial potential field method [4], genetic algorithm [5], neural network and so on. The biological inspired neural network method has developed late. It can used under unknown environment and has a low complexity [6–8]. According to the sea chart, we can drop the big and obvious obstacle into the grid map, but the moving obstacle and mini one are unknown. Our method can plan path and avoidance collision in real time. But there is a shortcoming about the method, when the path is long, robot may lose in local. So we improve the method and the simulation show the work has some effective.

The rest of this paper is organized as follows. The biological inspiration model is presented in Sect. 2. The algorithm improvement and the individual robot simulation are given in Sect. 3. In Sect. 4, we make the algorithm and simulation experiment on swarm robot. At last, several properties are conclude in Sect. 5.

2   Model of Biological Inspiration Neural Network

A biological neural system using electrical circuit elements was first proposed by Hodgkin and Huxley. By this primitive model, the biological inspiration model [9] is obtained as

$$\frac{dx_i}{dt} = -Ax_i + (B - x_i)S_i^e - (D + x_i)S_i^i \tag{1}$$

where x_i is the neural activity of the ith neuron in the neural network. A, B and D are nonnegative constants the passive decay rate, the upper and lower activity bounds. S_i^e and S_i^i are the excitatory and inhibitory inputs to the neuron.

Now the landscape is put into grid map. And the biological inspiration neural network is been build based on the grid map. The neural in the network and the position of the grid map are corresponding. Figure 1 shows the neuron cell in 2D environment. There are eight grids around the neuron, the robot may choose one of the eight as its next step. The most activity cell is the best way. According to Eq. 1, the output of i th neuron activity can be given by next Equation [10]:

$$\frac{dx_i}{dt} = -Ax_i + (B - x_i)\left([I_i]^+ + \sum_{j=1}^{k} w_{ij}[x_j]^+\right) - (D + x_i)[I_i]^- \tag{2}$$

Where x_i is the ith neural activity, x_j is the neighbor neural activity. k is the number of neural connections of the ith neuron to its neighbor neurons. I_i is the external input of ith neuron. If I_i greater than zero, it expressed as positive signal. And the one less than zero expressed as negative signal. $[I_i]^+ = \max\{I_i, 0\}$ $[I_i]^- = \min\{I_i, 0\}$. A, B and D are positive constant. $-A$ expresses the activity attenuation rate of x_i. B and D give the boundaries of x_i. w_{ij} is the connection weight between i and j.

And $w_{ij} = f(|q_i - q_j|)$, the $|q_i - q_j|$ represents the Euclidean distance between vectors q_i and q_j. The equation of $f(a)$ is as follow

$$f(a) = \begin{cases} \mu/a, & 0 \le a < r \\ 0, & a \ge 0 \end{cases} \tag{3}$$

μ and r are positive constants. The connection between two neural has no direction.

From Eq. (2), the input contains $[I_i]^+$ and $\sum_{j=1}^{k} w_{ij}[x_j]^+$. That means one of the input comes from outside and the other from the connected neural. If $I_i \le 0$, then there is only $\sum_{j=1}^{k} w_{ij}[x_j]^+$ stand as input. The negative signal all come from outside.

Therefore, the positive signal can transmit between neural in the global grid map, and negative can transmit just in the local grid map.

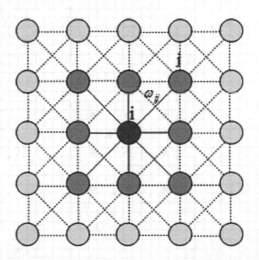

Fig. 1. 2-D biologically inspired neural network with two-layer neighbors.

3 Development of Path Planning

The original grid map contains all zero. According to the sea chart, the obstacle can fill into the grid map. And we also set up the nodes into the map. Each of the nodes has an exact position. We draw the position on the grid map. Then the initialized grid map is already done. When the AUV needs to communicate with node, the positions of AUV and the node are settled. From the algorithm in the Sect. 2, we can calculate the activity and choose the path connecting AUV and node. Let the robot always choose the maximum of the activity.

Firstly, we verify the algorithm into single robot path planning. The algorithm can work well under the distance below ten grids. When the distance increase, the path may lose into local optimum. The result also related with the position of obstacle. To solve this problem, we improve the method.

One improved method is let the robot never repeat walking the same grid. When the maximum activity neural is not only one. The robot can choose random from the grid matrix. After simulation, only with this improvement can't plan the shortest way. So the other improvement is calculate the distance between next step and the original position. The robot should never choose the distance less than current distance. Under the improvement the path planning can improve two time long than before.

The method can also provide a real time obstacle avoidance. The path may contain 10 or 20 grids, but the robot just take one step by the planning path. When the robot move to the next grid, the path will plan again till the robot reach the node. In this way, if a moving obstacle appears in the grid beside of the robot, the robot can calculate in real time.

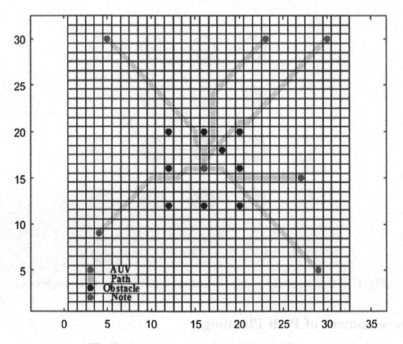

Fig. 2. One robot visit one node in six times.

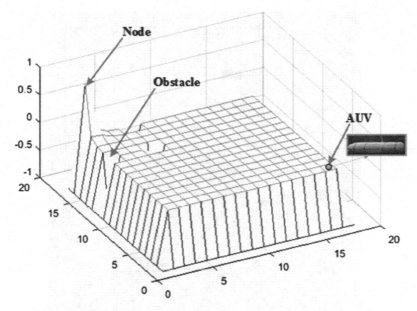

Fig. 3. The neural network based on the grid map of one visiting path.

Figure 2 shows the single robot visiting the node for six times. The green spots represent the original position of the robot. The black spots show the obstacle location. The red spot is the node. And the blue lines are the paths we get. From the figure, we can see the robot can avoid the obstacles and walk to the node in a shortest way. Figure 3 can tell the relationship between neural network and grids map. The top is the node and bottom are the obstacles. The robot start from the right corner.

4 Simulation for Swarm AUV

In this section, we put the method into swarm robot and widely grids map. The simulation is made on Matlab. We set up the grids map with 110 * 110 square. The distance between nodes are 30 grids. The control parameters are as follow: A = 10, B = 1, D = −1, μ = 0.5, r is the distance of eight neighbors. This paper assume the robot and node are only point. We overlook the kinematical equation of robot. To verify the method, the robot is set to step of next grid.

The simulation organized the swarm by 5 and 10 robots. Figures 4 and 5 show the results. The red point is node. The black point is obstacle. The line is the path that AUV walk to the node. The line has some colors. Each color represent one same AUV. Because the AUV can voyage around the whole map. The position of the time to visit the node is counted by itself. We set some rectangle obstacles. The other obstacles are just points. They are set random on the map.

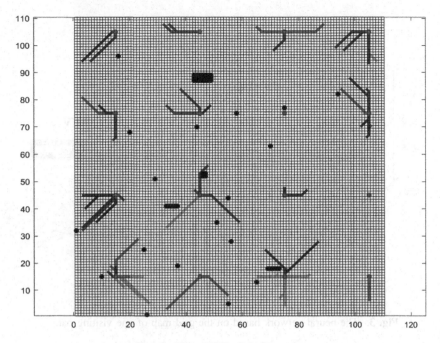

Fig. 4. Five AUVs visit the nodes.

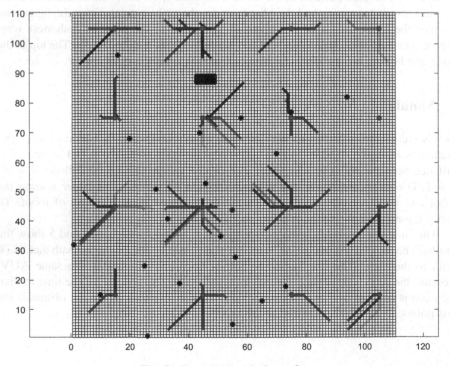

Fig. 5. Ten AUVs visit the nodes.

5   Conclusion

This paper propose a method to plan path for AUV. Then AUV can visit the communication nodes in a shortest way. That is to make AUV and the communication network get together. At the time of visiting, the method set a real time obstacle collision for AUV. The simulations show the result match anticipate well. Though, we have some improvement. Two or three methods should contrast with our method. Build a small ground robot to verify the method. Then put the method into real AUV for test. Thanks for predecessors working on this algorithms.

References

1. Feng, X., Li, Y., Xu, H.: The next generation of unmanned marine vehicles dedicated to the 50 anniversary of the human world record diving 10912 m. Robot **33**(1), 113–118 (2011)
2. Wang, Y., Zhou, M., Song, Z.: Development of underwater wireless communication technologyle. Commun. Technol. **47**(6), 589–594 (2014)
3. Geospace Technologies, Houston, TX, USA. www.geospace.com
4. Zhang, X., Memg, Q., Gao, Y., Yang, S., Zhang, J., Qi, Y.: Optimal path planning in complex environments based on optimization of artificial potential. Robot **25**(6), 531–535 (2003)
5. Chen, G., Shen, L.: Genetic path planning algorithm for complex environment path planning. Robot **23**(1), 40–44 (2003)
6. Cao, X., Sun, C.: Cooperative target search of multi-robot in grid map. Control Theory Appl. **35**(3), 273–282 (2018)
7. Zhu, D., Sun, B., Li, L.: Algorithm for AUV's 3-D path planning and safe obstacle avoidance based on biological inspired model. Control Decis. **30**(5), 798–806 (2015)
8. Fan, L., Wang, Q., Sun, F.: Simulation research and improvement on biologically inspired neural network path planning. J. Beijing Jiaotong Univ. **30**(2), 84–88 (2006)
9. Yang, S.X., Meng, M.: An efficient neural network method for real-time motion planning with safety consideration. Robot. Auton. Syst. **32**, 115–128 (2000)
10. Luo, C., Yang, S.X.: A bioinspried neural network for real-time concurrent map building and complete coverage robot navigation in unknown environments. IEEE Trans. Neural Netw. **19**(7), 1279–1298 (2008)

A Dynamic Tracking Control for the 4500 m-Human Occupied Vehicle

Wenyang Gan[1], Daqi Zhu[1(✉)], and Zhen Hu[2]

[1] Shanghai Engineering Research Center of Intelligent Maritime
Search & Rescue and Underwater Vehicles, Shanghai Maritime University,
Haigang Avenue 1550, Shanghai 201306, China
zdq367@aliyun.com
[2] Underwater Engineering Institute, China Ship Scientific Research Center,
Wuxi 214082, China
7000m@vip.sina.com

Abstract. In this paper, a model predictive adaptive control strategy is proposed for the two-dimensional plane trajectory tracking with the constant ocean current of the 4500 m-Human Occupied Vehicle (HOV). The control strategy consists of a quantum-behaved particle swarm model predictive kinematics controller (QPSO-MPC) and an adaptive dynamics controller. In the kinematics control, the relative reference velocity vector under the influence of ocean current is obtained by combining the ocean current velocity vector with the reference velocity vector. The position error is inputted to the QPSO-MPC controller to obtain the virtual relative expected velocity, which completes position tracking. In the dynamics control, the virtual relative expected velocity and the actual velocity is taken as the input. The thrust of each degree of freedom (DOF) is obtained by using the adaptive controller, which means the velocity tracking is completed. Then, from 4500 m-HOV thruster arrangement, the thrust is assigned to each thruster. Compared with the traditional adaptive control strategy, the simulation results illustrate that the proposed model predictive adaptive control strategy can achieve the tracking control without large velocity jump and driver saturation phenomenon under the ocean current disturbance.

Keywords: Human Occupied Vehicle · Ocean current · Tracking control ·
Adaptive control · Model predictive control

1 Introduction

Underwater vehicles [1] are important tools to explore marine resources. It has been developed rapidly under the study of researchers from all over the world. There are also many manufacturers producing related parts and developing a number of commercial

---

This project is supported by the National Natural Science Foundation of China (51575336, 91748117); the Creative Activity Plan for Science and Technology Commission of Shanghai (16550720200, 18JC1413000, 18DZ1206305).

H. Yu et al. (Eds.): ICIRA 2019, LNAI 11742, pp. 240–249, 2019.
https://doi.org/10.1007/978-3-030-27535-8_23

underwater vehicles. With the exploration and development of the ocean, the underwater vehicles have more and more influence in the ocean field, such as submarine pipeline detection and maintenance [2], underwater target observation [3], sea search and rescue [4], and so on. In recent years, the most famous application of underwater vehicles is using the "Bluefin-21" autonomous unmanned vehicle (AUV) to search for the black box signal of Malaysia Airlines MH370 [5].

As the basis of various activities for underwater vehicles, tracking control has got the attention and research of many scholars. Some control methods have been systematized. At present, the main tracking control methods are: PID control [6], fuzzy control [1], neural network control [7], sliding mode control [8], backstepping control [9] and so on. These control methods have their own advantages and shortcomings, a single control method can't meet the increasing control accuracy and demand. The hybrid control strategy of several intelligent control methods is more common, which can compensate each other. For example, in Literature [10], a stable adaptive fuzzy inference system is embedded in sliding mode control, which makes the control method robust to parameter uncertainty and disturbance in AUV control process. In Literature [11], the combination of adaptive control and fuzzy control is used to compensate the influence of actuator saturation, which ensures the stability of tracking system under the condition of actuator saturation. In Literature [12], the adaptive neural network control is used to deal with the uncertainties and disturbances in the control process of AUV system.

In this paper, the model predictive control [13] combined with adaptive control is used to design a tracking control system for 4500 m-HOV in the ocean current environment. The virtual relative expected velocity is obtained from the kinematic controller design by the position difference, in which the reference system is the relative reference system of the ocean current. The speed constraint is added in the optimization process, so that the sudden change of velocity will not occurred because of the ocean current in the course of HOV sailing. The velocity difference is used to design the dynamic controller for adaptive control, and the thrust control law under the influence of ocean current is obtained. Compared with the traditional adaptive control which gets the thrust control law directly from the position difference, the proposed algorithm has the advantages of double negative feedback, velocity constraint and so on, which makes it stable and meet the requirements of tracking control in the case of the ocean current.

This paper is arranged as follows: In Sect. 2, the kinematics and dynamics of 4500 m-HOV is introduced. In Sect. 3, the tracking control strategy including a QPSO-MPC kinematic controller and an adaptive dynamic controller is presented. In Sect. 4, the thruster arrangement of 4500 m-HOV and the simulation results tracked by QPSO-MPC-adaptive compared with the traditional adaptive control method are shown with the relevant comparisons and analyses. In Sect. 5, concluding remarks are summarized.

2   The Kinematics and Dynamics of 4500 m-HOV

4500 m-HOV is another significative deep sea equipment after "Jiaolong" 7000 m-HOV in China, and its design depth in the sea is 4500 m. Because 4500 m basically covers the depth of exploitation of resources in China's main sea areas and international sea areas. Figure 1 is the appearance of 4500 m-HOV. The length, width, height, weight in air and maximum speed of the 4500 m-HOV are listed in Table 1.

Fig. 1. 4500 m-HOV

Table 1. The basic parameters of 4500 m-HOV

Name	Unit	Value
Length	m	9.3
Width	m	3
Height	m	4
Weight in air	ton	20
Maximal speed	kn	2.5 (1.287 m/s)

The kinematic simultaneous dynamic equations of 4500 m-HOV are shown below [14]:

$$(M_{RB} + M_A)\dot{v} + (C_{RB}(v) + C_A(v))v + D(v)v + (g\eta) = B\tau \tag{1}$$

$$\dot{\eta} = J(\eta)v \tag{2}$$

3   The Tracking Control Strategy

The tracking control strategy proposed in this paper is composed of a QPSO-MPC kinematics controller and an adaptive dynamics controller.

3.1 The Kinematic Controller in the Influence of the Ocean Current

Given the fact that HOV is manned, roll and pitch in 6 degrees of freedom (6DOF) should not occur in order to ensure the safety of operators. And the tracking control on the two-dimensional plane is studied in this paper. So the tracking control of 3DOF: surge, sway and yaw is given in the below.

The reference trajectory and its velocity are given as $\eta_d = [x_d \quad y_d \quad \psi_d]^T$ and $v_d = [u_d \quad v_d \quad r_d]^T$. In the underwater environment with the ocean current, the reference velocity of the kinematics controller is changed. How to take the ocean current information into account in the reference system is given as follows. The ocean current can be expressed as: $v_E = [u_x \quad u_y]^T$ in the inertial coordinate system. In this paper, the influence of the constant current to the tracking control is studied. The ocean current in the body-fixed coordinate system can be expressed as: $u_u = u_x \cos\psi + u_y \sin\psi, v_v = -u_x \sin\psi + u_y \cos\psi$. The relative reference velocity is: $u_d' = u_d - u_u, v_d' = v_d - v_v, r_d' = r_d$.

The kinematics controller to make HOV track reference system which given as $\eta_d = [x_d \quad y_d \quad \psi_d]^T$ and $v_d' = [u_d' \quad v_d' \quad r_d']^T$ is designed below. According to the linear MPC method, the kinematic Eq. (2) is become the following form by Taylor series expansion. Then the linear error model of HOV is got:

$$
\begin{aligned}
\dot{\tilde{\eta}} = \dot{\eta} - \dot{\eta}_d &= J(\eta_d)v_d' + \left.\frac{\partial J(\eta)v}{\partial \eta}\right|_{\substack{\eta = \eta_d \\ v = v_d'}} (\eta - \eta_d) + \left.\frac{\partial J(\eta)v}{\partial v}\right|_{\substack{\eta = \eta_d \\ v = v_d'}} \left(v - v_d'\right) - J(\eta_d)v_d' \\
&= \begin{bmatrix} 0 & 0 & -u_d \sin\psi_d - v_d \cos\psi_d \\ 0 & 0 & u_d \cos\psi_d - v_d \sin\psi_d \\ 0 & 0 & 0 \end{bmatrix} \begin{bmatrix} x & x_d \\ y - y_d \\ \psi - \psi_d \end{bmatrix} + \begin{bmatrix} \cos\psi_d & -\sin\psi_d & 0 \\ \sin\psi_d & \cos\psi_d & 0 \\ 0 & 0 & 1 \end{bmatrix} \begin{bmatrix} u - u_d' \\ v - v_d' \\ r - r_d' \end{bmatrix}
\end{aligned}
\tag{3}
$$

The above equation is needed to be discretized to be used in the MPC controller [14]:

$$
\tilde{\eta}(k+1) = a_{k,t}\tilde{\eta}(k) + b_{k,t}\tilde{v}(k)
\tag{4}
$$

T is the sampling time.

In the rolling optimization, the predictive output in the predictive domain (N_p) is represented as: $y(t) = \Lambda_t \eta(t|t) + \Phi_t V_c(t)$, the form of Λ_t, Φ_t can be found in our previous work Literature [14]. $\eta(t|t)$ is known.

The control vector $V_c(t)$ in the control domain (N_c) can be obtained by setting the suitable objective function. The form of the objective function is given as:

$$
F(k) = \sum_{i=1}^{N_p} \|\eta(k+i|t) - \eta_d(k+i|t)\|_Q^2 + \sum_{i=1}^{N_c-1} \|V_c(k+i|t)\|_R^2
\tag{5}
$$

where Q and R are the weight matrixes. The objective function shows the decreasing the position error. In the process of the rolling optimization, the constraint on speed is added.

Control constraint is presented as $V_{min}(t+k) \leq V_c(t+k) \leq V_{max}(t+k), k = 0, 1, \cdots N_c - 1$.

Solving the objective function can be transformed into solving the following QPSO problem:

$$\min_{\Delta v(t)} V_c(t) H_t V_c(t)^T + f_t V_c(t)^T \tag{6}$$

The form of H_t, f_t can be found in our previous work Literature [14]. When the QPSO optimization process is completed, the solution $\Delta V_t^* = \begin{bmatrix} \Delta v_t^* & \cdots & \Delta v_{t+N_c-1}^* \end{bmatrix}^T$ is returned to the kinematics controller. So the relative expected virtual speed is $v_c(t) = \Delta v_t^* + v_d'(t)$.

3.2 The Dynamic Controller with the Ocean Current

The virtual speed error is defined as follows is given as $e_c = v_c - v_r$, v_r is the real velocity of HOV. The sliding mode surface obtained by the virtual speed error is given as follows:

$$s = \dot{e}_c + 2\Lambda e_c + \Lambda^2 \int e_c \tag{7}$$

The adaptive dynamic control law is built based on the speed error as follows:

$$\tau = \Phi(\dot{v}_r, v_r, v, \eta)\hat{\theta}_1 - K_d s \tag{8}$$

Here the adaptive law of parameter $\hat{\theta}_1$ (assuming that $\dot{\theta}_1 = 0$):

$$\dot{\hat{\theta}}_1 = -\Gamma \Phi^T(\dot{v}_r, v_r, v, \eta)s \tag{9}$$

4   Experimental Results

In this section, the thrusts arrangement of 4500 m-HOV is given. The experimental result of two-dimensional straight line case obtained by the proposed control algorithm is given in the following.

4.1   Thruster Arrangement of 4500 m-HOV

Figure 2 shows the thrusters layout on horizontal plane of 4500 m-HOV. It is equipped with three thrusters, each marked as $T^i, i \in [1, 3]$.

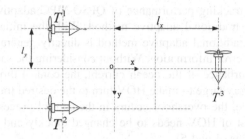

Fig. 2. Thruster arrangement on horizontal plane

The relationship between the thrust of each DOF and that of the thruster is as follows:

$$\tau = B \cdot T \tag{10}$$

where B is thruster arrangement matrix. According to the thrusters' arrangement of 4500 m-HOV, the thruster arrangement matrix B can be got as follows:

$$B = \begin{bmatrix} 1 & 1 & 0 \\ 0 & 0 & 1 \\ l_y & l_y & l_x \end{bmatrix} \tag{11}$$

where l_x, l_y are constant distances between thrusters of 4500 m-HOV (shown in Fig. 2).

4.2 The 2D Straight-Line Tracking with the Ocean Current

The Simulation Without Considering Thrust Constraint
Here, the thrust of HOV is assumed to be unconstrained. The thrust calculated by two methods can be offered by the thrusters. The comparison of tracking effect between two algorithms and the analysis are given. The reference trajectory is $x_d(t) = 0.15 * t$, $y_d(t) = 0.15 * t$, $\psi_d = \pi/4$. The actual start position is $[0\ 5\ \pi/2]$. It is assumed that there is a current $v_E = \begin{bmatrix} u_x\, u_y \end{bmatrix}^T = \begin{bmatrix} 0.2 & 0.2 \end{bmatrix}^T$ in the inertial coordinate system.

The straight line tracking results with the ocean current influence is shown in Fig. 3. Figure 4 displays the thrust curve on each thruster during the tracking process. According to the information queried, the maximum thrust provided by each thruster of HOV is about 880 N. So in Fig. 4, two black dashed lines near 1000 N and −1000 N represent these maximum thrusts, which are 880 N and −880 N, respectively. Figure 6 shows the absolute value of maximal T^1, T^2 and T^3 controlled by two methods, respectively.

From Fig. 3, the tracking performance of QPSO-MPC adaptive method is clearly better to that of the traditional adaptive method. With the initial position error, the control law for the traditional adaptive method is directly generated according to the position and attitude error information. Without considering the saturation factor of the thruster and the disturbance of the ocean current, the control thrust of the traditional adaptive method is very large to make HOV turn to the desired trajectory quickly. Due to the excessive force, the overshoot occurs in the control process. Overshoot means that the control thrust of HOV needs to be changed quickly and generated largely to adjust its attitude (Figs. 4 and 5).

The tracking performance of QPSO-MPC adaptive method is relatively smooth and it is not going to produce such large thrust due to the constraints on speed, take the ocean current disturbance into control law design, the dual feedback mechanism. The purpose of stable tracking is achieved after one smooth convergence from the initial position error. The control performance of QPSO-MPC adaptive method is superior to the traditional adaptive method under the disturbance of the ocean current. And the thrusts calculated by QPSO-MPC adaptive method are evidently smaller than the traditional adaptive method and can be guaranteed in the range. QPSO-MPC adaptive method can satisfy the hardware constraints on the premise of accurate tracking with the ocean current disturbance.

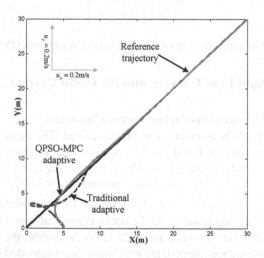

Fig. 3. Straight line tracking in the ocean current environment

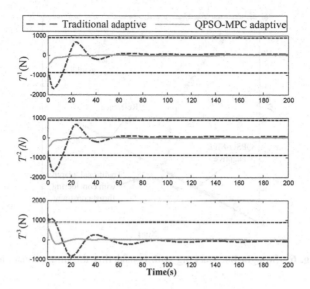

Fig. 4. Straight line tracking control thrust

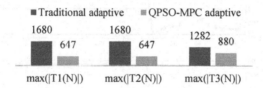

Fig. 5. The absolute value of maximal thrust

The Simulation with Considering Thrust Constraint

In the previous chapter, the tracking control without considering thrust constraints is given, which is not in line with the actual situation. The thrust provided by the thruster is limited, so the thrust constraint is added to the dynamic control in this chapter. The obtained thrust is not directly fed back to the HOV, but is confined to the specified range and then fed back to the HOV, so that the tracking control effect under the thrust constraint can be obtained.

All simulation conditions are the same as the last chapter. Figure 6 indicates straight-line tracking results of two methods under consideration of thrust constraint. Figure 7 shows the thrusts after being constrained. It can be seen that the thrusts of both two methods are controlled in the specified range [−880 N 880 N]. In this case, take a review on the tracking effect of two algorithms in Fig. 6, it is obvious that the tracking effect of QPSO-MPC adaptive method is better. The tracking performance of the traditional adaptive method is obviously worse than that of QPSO-MPC adaptive method, and it can't keep up with the known trajectory even in the whole process, so it can be said that its tracking is a failure.

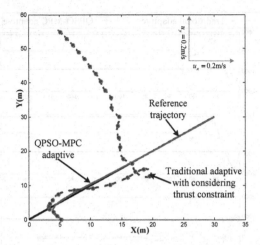

Fig. 6. Straight line tracking with considering the thrust constraint

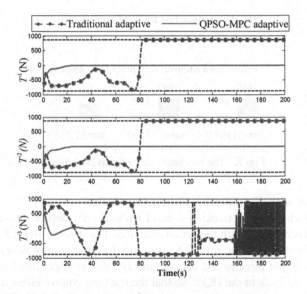

Fig. 7. Straight line tracking control thrusts with the thrust constraint

5 Conclusion

In this paper, the 2D trajectory tracking control under the ocean current condition of 4500 m-HOV is studied. A model predictive adaptive control method is proposed. The method consists of a position tracker (i.e. kinematics controller) and a velocity tracker (i.e. dynamics controller). The ocean current information is brought into the kinematics controller design, and the velocity constraint is added to the kinematics controller to ensure that the driver saturation problem will not occur in the dynamics controller.

Compared with the traditional adaptive control, the proposed model predictive adaptive control can achieve a stable and efficient tracking effect without jitter due to its speed constraint and the double negative feedback control loop with considering the ocean current.

References

1. Xiang, X., Yu, C., Lapierre, L., et al.: Survey on fuzzy-logic-based guidance and control of marine surface vehicles and underwater vehicles. Int. J. Fuzzy Syst. **20**(2), 572–586 (2018)
2. Zhang, S.G., Xiao, X., Sun, D.C.: Research on maneuverability and simulation of underwater vehicles for pipeline detection and maintenance. China Ocean Eng. **20**(1), 147–154 (2006)
3. Guo, J.: Optimal measurement strategies for target tracking by a biomimetic underwater vehicle. Ocean Eng. **35**(5–6), 473–483 (2008)
4. Murphy, A., Landamore, M., Birmingham, R.: The role of autonomous underwater vehicles for marine search and rescue operations. Underw. Technol. Int. J. Soc. Underw. **27**(4), 195–205 (2008)
5. Lehardy, P.K., Moore, C.: Deep ocean search for Malaysia airlines flight 370. In: Oceans, pp. 1–4, IEEE, St. John's (2015)
6. Kuo, C.L., Tsui, C.K., Pai, N.S., et al.: A PID controller for the underwater robot station-keeping. In: 2016 IEEE 14th International Conference on Industrial Informatics (INDIN), pp. 1242–1246, IEEE, Poitiers (2016)
7. Shojaei, K.: Three-dimensional neural network tracking control of a moving target by underactuated autonomous underwater vehicles. Neural Comput. Appl. **1**, 1–13 (2017)
8. Tanakitkorn, K., Wilson, P.A., Turnock, S.R., et al.: Sliding mode heading control of an overactuated, hover-capable autonomous underwater vehicle with experimental verification. J. Field Robot. **35**(3), 396–415 (2017)
9. Liu, S., Liu, Y., Ning, W.: Nonlinear disturbance observer-based backstepping finite-time sliding mode tracking control of underwater vehicles with system uncertainties and external disturbances. Nonlinear Dyn. **88**(1), 465–476 (2017)
10. Lakhekar, G.V., Saundarmal, V.D.: Novel adaptive fuzzy sliding mode controller for depth control of an underwater vehicles. In: 2013 IEEE International Conference on Fuzzy Systems (FUZZ-IEEE), pp. 1–7. IEEE, Hyderabad (2013)
11. Yu, C., Xiang, X., Qin, Z., et al.: Adaptive fuzzy trajectory tracking control of an under-actuated autonomous underwater vehicle subject to actuator saturation. Int. J. Fuzzy Syst. **20**(1), 1–11 (2017)
12. He, W., Chen, Y., Yin, Z.: Adaptive neural network control of an uncertain robot with full-state constraints. IEEE Trans. Cybern. **46**(3), 620–629 (2017)
13. Zhang, W., Yu, C., Teng, Y., et al.: Research on UUV path tracking control based on model predictive control. Chin. J. Sci. Instrum. **38**(11), 2659–2666 (2017)
14. Gan, W., Zhu, D., Ji, D.: QPSO-model predictive control-based approach to dynamic trajectory tracking control for unmanned underwater vehicles. Ocean Eng. **158**, 208–220 (2018)

Development of a Full Ocean Depth Hydraulic Manipulator System

Yanzhuang Chen[1,2,3], Qifeng Zhang[1,2(✉)], Xisheng Feng[1,2],
Liangqing Huo[1,2], Qiyan Tian[1,2], Linsen Du[1,2], Yunfei Bai[1,2,3],
and Cong Wang[1,2,3]

[1] State Key Laboratory of Robotics, Shenyang Institute of Automation,
Chinese Academy of Sciences, Shenyang 110016, China
zqf@sia.cn
[2] Institutes for Robotics and Intelligent Manufacturing,
Chinese Academy of Sciences, Shenyang 110169, China
[3] University of Chinese Academy of Sciences, Beijing 100049, China

Abstract. This paper presents the development of a full ocean depth master-slave hydraulic manipulator system for marine engineering and research in the harsh hadal environment. Three basic modules of the slave arm including a linear cylinder, a single-vane swing cylinder, and a new wrist joint are designed. The electronic system and software are developed then. Laboratory experiments on the single-vane swing cylinder and the new wrist joint were carried out to verify the performance of new joints. Additionally, a 11000 m pressure experiment is conducted, and the results demonstrate that the full ocean depth hydraulic manipulator system works well in the 11000 m environment.

Keywords: Full ocean depth hydraulic manipulator ·
Single-vane swing cylinder · 11000 m pressure experiment

1 Introduction

The hadal zone accounts for 45% of the total ocean depth range, and it is one of the frontiers in marine science. Exploration of the hadal zone requires advanced engineering technology in marine [1]. Hence, a variety of marine equipment including unmanned underwater vehicles (UUVs), landers and In-situ instruments are developed [2–4]. As a typical operation tool, underwater manipulator plays an irreplaceable role in marine scientific research and resource development. Usually, human occupied vehicles (HOVs) and remotely operated vehicles (ROVs) are equipped with two manipulators, one simple, powerful grabber to hold the vehicle near the structure or wreck, while the other manipulator performs the actual task. And in some cases, underwater manipulators are equipped on autonomous underwater vehicles (AUVs) [5].

Underwater hydraulic manipulators are used in subsea Intervention, Repair, and Maintenance (IRM) operations in offshore industries, including oil and gas, marine construction, marine science, naval defence, and Marine Renewable Energy (MRE) [6]. As they are being used in a wide range of applications, underwater hydraulic manipulators are designed for different purposes and can work at any ocean depth with the

H. Yu et al. (Eds.): ICIRA 2019, LNAI 11742, pp. 250–263, 2019.
https://doi.org/10.1007/978-3-030-27535-8_24

pressure compensator balancing the tank pressure with the ambient pressure [7]. Typically, most underwater manipulators are rated between 3000 and 6500 m of sea water (msw), whereas there are some hydraulic manipulators which can perform tasks in depths up to 7000 msw, such as Titan4, the most widely used hydraulic manipulator produced by Schilling Robotics and a prototype manipulator developed by Shenyang Institute of Automation [8, 9]. However, there are still challenges existing in the hadal scientific expedition equipment, especially the hydraulic manipulator. The high hydrostatic pressure (about 115 MPa in 11000 m depth) in the hadal environment will make the kinematic viscosity of the oil significantly increase, which will affect the performance of the manipulator [10, 11]. It is difficult to maintain similar dynamic and tracking performance in different working conditions for an underwater hydraulic manipulator [12].

There are some systems designed for full ocean depth (11000 msw), one such manipulator for Mariana Trench exploration mission was designed by Woods Hole Oceanographic Institute and Kraft Robotics [13]. Others include "40500(R)" produced by Hydro-Lek, "Magnum 7", a product of ISE Ltd. and, "The ARM" and "MK-37" developed by the Western Space and Marine, Inc. [5]. However, a complete article encapsulating the design and key technical issues of a full ocean depth underwater hydraulic manipulator system cannot be found in any literature.

In this paper, we developed the first full ocean depth master-slave hydraulic manipulator system in China. First, we design hydraulic actuators that can work at full ocean depth including a linear cylinder, a single-vane swing cylinder, and a new wrist-gripper module. Then, the electronic system and software are developed respectively. Finally, laboratory and pressure experiments are conducted to validate the system.

The remainder of the paper is organized as follows: Sect. 2 describes mechanical, electronic and software design features of the underwater hydraulic manipulator. Section 3 focuses on experiments scenarios and presents the results. Finally, Sect. 4 holds the conclusions and future work.

2 Design of the Full Ocean Depth Hydraulic Manipulator System

2.1 System Overview

The system is mainly comprised of a surface control box (including a surface controller and a master arm), a power supply box, a valve pack, a slave arm, a pressure compensator, and a hydraulic power unit. The system composition is shown in Fig. 1. The system can be divided into two parts: the underwater part and the surface part. The surface control box and the power supply box belong to the surface part, while the underwater part consists of the valve pack, the slave arm, the pressure compensator, and the hydraulic power unit. The slave arm is controlled by the master arm, commands are sent to hydraulic control valve pack which contains a slave controller and seven servo valve blocks. Then, the slave controller drives the motion of the slave arm and returns the real-time work state of the slave arm.

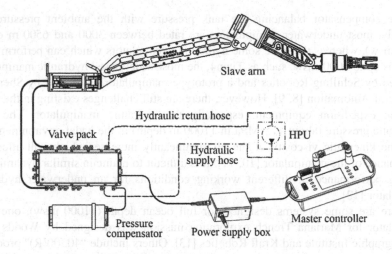

Fig. 1. The whole configuration of the underwater manipulator.

The underwater manipulator is designed with six degrees of freedoms (DOFs) for achieving arbitrary position and orientation of the end-effector in the workspace. The slave arm includes a stationary base, a shoulder joint, a main arm, an elbow joint, a forearm, a wrist joint, and a gripper. Six true DOFs motion plus one actuator for gripper make up seven functions. The main performance specification of the slave arm is shown in Table 1.

Table 1. Performance specification of the slave arm.

Item	Value
Depth rating	11000 m
Working pressure	21 MPa
Weight in air	73 kg
Weight in water	50 kg
Lift at full extension	65 kg
Maximum reach	1890 mm
Elbow torque	320 Nm
Wrist torque	160 Nm
Gripper opening	140 mm

The distribution and the range of motion of each joint in the full ocean depth 7-function hydraulic manipulator are shown in Fig. 2. The whole manipulator system consists of seven sets of hydraulic actuators, including linear cylinder, rotary actuator, cycloid motor, etc., which are coordinated with each other. In the course of the operation, the joints control is completed by a plurality of servo valves, thereby realising the spatial positioning in a multi-degree of freedom space and flexible operation.

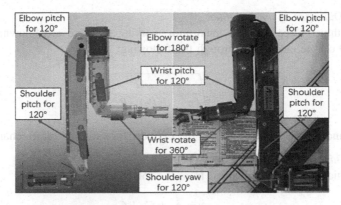

Fig. 2. The distribution of joints in the manipulator.

2.2   Mechanical Design

A. Design for Linear Cylinders

The first, second, third and fifth joints of the slave arm are driven by linear cylinders, and the linear cylinder consists of a cylinder block, a piston, an end cap, a sensor, a pipe joint. The linear cylinders drive the relevant joints of the master-slave hydraulic manipulator rotation, and the joints rotation angle can be measured directly or converted by measuring the position of the linear cylinder piston. The sensors are integrated into the cylinder to provide stability and ensure correct feedback information.

All joints of the slave arm bear the maximum force and torque when the slave ram is fully extended, and the linear cylinder of the second joint bears the maximum external load including the weight of the whole slave arm and clamping load. If the linear cylinder of the second joint meets the requirements, other linear cylinders can also meet the requirements.

The main parameters of the hydraulic cylinder include cylinder inner diameter D, piston rod diameter d, cylinder stroke S, wall thickness δ, etc. The equation of moment is as follow:

$$Fb = 1.1 \sum M_i \tag{1}$$

where F is the thrust force supplied by cylinder, b is the moment arm of the thrust force, $\sum M_i$ is the total moment of each joint, and a margin of 10% was taken into account.

(1) *Diameter of the Piston Rod*
Since the linear cylinder needs to bear a high load, the diameter of the piston rod is designed according to the strength requirement:

$$d \geq \sqrt{\frac{4F}{\pi\sigma}} \tag{2}$$

where σ is the allowable material stress of the rod.

(2) Inner Diameter of the Cylinder
Since the thrust force and the maximum working pressure are known, the inner diameter D can be calculated through the following:

$$D = \sqrt{\frac{4F}{(\pi - d^2 P_2)/(P_1 - P_2)}} \tag{3}$$

where P_1 and P_2 are the pressures in the cylinder forward and return chamber.

(3) Wall Thickness
The wall thickness can be obtained from the following:

$$\delta = \delta_0 + C_1 + C_2 \tag{4}$$

$$\delta_0 \geq \frac{D}{2}\sqrt{\frac{\sigma - 0.4P_{max}}{\sigma - 1.3P_{max}} - 1} \tag{5}$$

where δ_0 is the minimum strength required of the material, C_1 is the tolerance of outer diameter of the cylinder, C_2 is the corrosion allowance, P_{max} is the maximum working pressure.

(4) Stroke of the Cylinder
The stroke S of the linear cylinder is mainly determined according to the structure and motion requirements of the slave arm.

The load of the cylinder mainly includes the environmental pressure 115 MPa and the working pressure 25 MPa. To reduce the overall weight of the slave arm and protect the cylinder from corrosion, we choose 6061-T6 aluminum as the material. Considering the maximum load and the motion range of each joint, we can obtain the parameters of the linear cylinder as shown in Table 2.

Table 2. Performance specification of the slave arm.

Item	Value
Diameter of the piston rod	25 mm
Inner diameter of the cylinder	45 mm
Wall thickness	6 mm
Stroke of the cylinder for first and fifth joints	70 mm
Stroke of the cylinder for second and third joints	95 mm

B. Design for Elbow Joint

The rotary actuator is a compact module that realises the joints rotation of the slave arm. Connecting the front and rear oil passages of the joint and passing the sensor line without increasing the external pipeline are difficult in this study. A single-vane swing cylinder is designed to ensure elbow movement in the hadal environment. To facilitate the overall arrangement of the sensor line and the oil pipe, the centre axis of the single-vane swing cylinder is hollow, and multiple oil channels are designed between the motion pairs. Considering the thickness of the oil channels and the overall size of the elbow joint, we design the structure parameters as shown in Fig. 3(a) and (b) shows the diagram and of the single-vane swing cylinder.

Main parameters	Value
Length of the vane B	80mm
Internal diameter of the cylinder R_1	52mm
External diameter of the spindle R_2	32.5mm

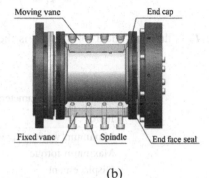

(a)   (b)

Fig. 3. (a) The structure parameters of the single-vane swing cylinder (b) The diagram of the internal structure of the single-vane swing cylinder.

The output torque will change when the working condition of the single-vane swing cylinder changes, and it is necessary to calculate the geometric displacement, theoretical output torque and other essential parameters of the single vane swing cylinder.

(1) *Displacement*
Assuming that the hydraulic oil is an ideal liquid and the axial and radial clearance leakage of the motor is excluded, the theoretical displacement of the single-vane swing cylinder is as follows:

$$V = \frac{1}{2\pi} \pi \cdot \left(R_1^2 - R_2^2\right) \cdot B \tag{6}$$

where V is the displacement of the single-vane swing cylinder, B is the length of the vane, R_1 is the internal diameter of the cylinder, R_2 is the external diameter of the cylinder.

(2) *Flow and Speed*
If the angle of the moving vane is $d\varphi$ during the time dt, the instantaneous flow is as follow:

$$q = V\frac{d\varphi}{dt} = V\omega \tag{7}$$

$$\omega = \frac{q}{B\left(R_1^2 - R_2^2\right)} \tag{8}$$

where q is the instantaneous flow, ω is the angular velocity.

(3) *Theoretical Torque*

The leakage and friction resistance of the single-vane swing cylinder are ignored, and the theoretical torque is as follow:

$$T_t = \int_{R_1}^{R_2} B \cdot \Delta P \cdot r \mathrm{d}r \tag{9}$$

where T_r is the theoretical torque, ΔP is the pressure difference on both sides of the vane.

Table 3. Performance parameters of the single-vane cylinder.

Item	Value
Maximum working pressure	21 MPa
Maximum torque	790.92 Nm
Displacement	0.038 L/rad

According to the structure parameters designed above, the performance parameters of the single-vane swing cylinder can be obtained through Eqs. (6–9). Table 3 shows the performance parameters of the single-vane swing cylinder.

The brush and diaphragm of the rotary potentiometer are respectively fixed on the relatively rotating front end cover and the oil distribution shaft to detect the rotation angle information. The single-vane swing cylinder adopts the contact friction between the flexible body and rigid body, which overcomes the damage of servo valve under heavy load.

C. Design for Wrist-gripper Module

The wrist-gripper module integrates the cycloid motor, and the linear cylinder can realise 360° rotation of the wrist and open or close the gripper. We reform the cycloid motor and design the linear cylinder used to drive the movement of the gripper and connected with the wrist joint to realise the compact design of the wrist-gripper module. To meet the design output torque index of 160 Nm, we choose appropriate parameters of the cycloid motor as shown in Fig. 4(a). A cycloid motor adopting split gearmotor is used in a hydraulic manipulator which can perform tasks at a depth of 7000 m [9]. While, problems such as high starting pressure, inconsistency between positive and negative directions, low output torque and narrow speed range determine that it cannot be used in the hadal environment.

To improve the performance of the wrist joint to operate normally in depths up to 11,000 msw, we optimised the structure of the wrist joint and adopted the integral gearmotor cycloidal motor, the schematic diagram of the wrist-gripper module is shown in Fig. 4(b).

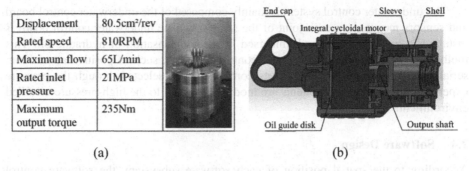

Displacement	80.5cm²/rev
Rated speed	810RPM
Maximum flow	65L/min
Rated inlet pressure	21MPa
Maximum output torque	235Nm

(a)   (b)

Fig. 4. (a) The parameters of the cycloid motor (b) The schematic diagram of the full ocean depth wrist-gripper module

2.3   Electronic Design

The control system of the full ocean depth hydraulic manipulator is based on the ARM microprocessor, and it can realise the real-time online control of the slave arm and the expansion of related functions. Electronic system consists of a surface part and an underwater part, the architecture diagram of the electronic system is shown in Fig. 5.

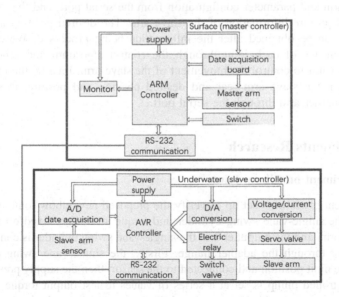

Fig. 5. The architecture diagram of the electronic system.

The surface control system consists of two parts: a surface control box and a surface power box. The surface control box is composed of a core processor, data acquisition card, LCD monitor and transfer expansion board, etc., and can realise man-machine interaction and signal processing. The surface power box is an auxiliary device from which the power supply is supplied to the whole control system.

The underwater control system is mainly composed of the underwater control board and sensors mounted on each joint of the slave arm. The underwater control board is installed in the valve pack and immersed in the compensation of hydraulic oil. This motherboard integrates all underwater control functions, such as position acquisition, serial port communication, etc. All its components are selected through the pressure experiment, and some components are modified to adapt to the high-pressure oil-filled environment.

2.4 Software Design

According to the spatial position of each software subsystem, the software control system can be divided into two parts: surface part (software of master arm) and underwater part (software of slave arm). Firstly, the software of master arm collects and processes the angle information of each joint of the master arm and the state of each button on the control panel, and then set some related parameters. After that the state information of the master arm and commends are sent to the software of slave arm through the serial port, at the same time, the software of master arm receives the real position information and the desired position information, etc. from the slave arm feedback.

The software of slave arm firstly receives the position and posture information of the master arm and parameter configuration from the serial port, and then acquire the position and posture information of the slave arm. The desired position and posture information can be obtained after the information being processed. We can get the control commands of each joint through the control algorithm and send it to the hydraulic actuator to control the movement of the slave arm. Finally, the information, obtained from the slave arm real and desired position and posture, is sent to the software of master arm through the serial port.

3 Experiments Research

3.1 Experiment on Elbow Joint

An experiment platform is set up to verify the proposed new elbow joint as shown in Fig. 6(a). The single-vane swing cylinder and torque sensor are fixed on the experimental platform, and the output end of the single-vane swing cylinder is connected to a torque sensor through the adapter flange. Firstly, the single-vane swing cylinder is rotated to the limit position and connected to the sensor, then the supply pressure of the pressure-controlled pump is set at a series of values to test output torque value. The relationship between working pressure and the output torque is obtained as shown in Fig. 6(b).

The results show that the maximum output torque of the new elbow joint can reach 400 Nm, however when the working pressure continues to rise, the leakage increases, resulting in a decrease in output torque. Many factors are affecting the output torque and internal leakage of the oscillating cylinder, including seal material, the pre-compression amount of the sealing ring, the matching gap between the vane and the

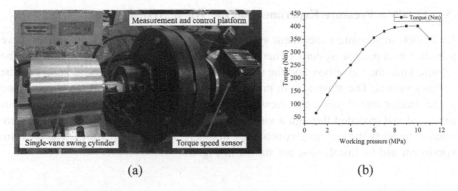

(a)   (b)

Fig. 6. (a) The platform of the experiment. (b) The relationship between working pressure and output torque

cylinder body, the vane angle, and the hydraulic oil viscosity, etc. In the future, relevant studies will be carried out on various aspects of the performance of the single-vane swing cylinder.

3.2 Experiment on Wrist-Gripper Module

To test the performance of the wrist joint, we carried out an experiment as shown in Fig. 7. The results of the experiment show that compared with the original wrist joint used on the 7000 m hydraulic manipulator, the dynamic and static performance of the new wrist joint is improved, the internal leakage and starting pressure are reduced, the output torque and the range of speed are increased. The results of the experiment are shown in Table 4.

Table 4. The comparison between conventional and new wrist joint

Item	Wrist joint used in 7000 m	Wrist joint for 11000 m
Starting pressure	5 MPa	0.5 MPa
Forward and backward speed	Clockwise fast Anti-clockwise slowly	Same
Torque output	≤ 100 Nm	≤ 230 Nm
Range of speed	10–20 rpm	4–45 rpm

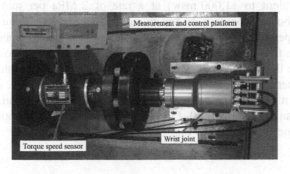

Fig. 7. The performance test of wrist joint

3.3   11,000 m Pressure Experiment on the Whole System

The 11,000 m pressure experiment system consists of a full ocean depth master-slave hydraulic manipulator system (where the surface control box is placed outside the pressure tank, the valve box and the slave arm are placed in the pressure tank) and the auxiliary system. The slave arm in pressure tank could move in small range controlled by the master arm outside the pressure tank. The whole experimental process was monitored and recorded through a video. Besides, the angle signals of each joint were obtained to verify the response consistency in different ambient pressures. The pressure experiment and its installation are shown in Fig. 8.

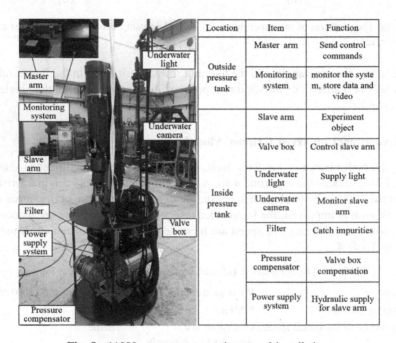

Location	Item	Function
Outside pressure tank	Master arm	Send control commands
	Monitoring system	monitor the system, store data and video
Inside pressure tank	Slave arm	Experiment object
	Valve box	Control slave arm
	Underwater light	Supply light
	Underwater camera	Monitor slave arm
	Filter	Catch impurities
	Pressure compensator	Valve box compensation
	Power supply system	Hydraulic supply for slave arm

Fig. 8. 11000 m pressure experiment and installation.

In the experiment, the pressure in the pressure tank was gradually pressurised to 115 MPa (equivalent to 11,000 msw) at a rate of 2 MPa per minute. During the pressure tank boosting process, a functional test is performed for every 10 MPa increase. The operator observes the monitoring system and operates the left-right movement of the first joint, the up-down movement of the second joint, the up-down movement of the third joint, and the left-right movement of the fourth joint, fifth joint up-down movement, sixth joint clockwise-counterclockwise rotation, seventh function opening-closing movement to verify the comprehensive function and performance of the slave arm at any ocean depth (0–115 MPa). The master arm operating and the slave arm monitor scenes are shown as Fig. 9.

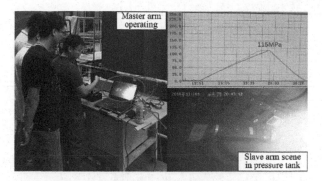

Fig. 9. The master arm operating and the slave arm monitor scenes.

The results of 11000 m pressure experiment shown in Figs. 10 and 11 demonstrate that (1) there is no structural and functional damage from the slave arm and the valve box (including the servo valves and the slave arm controller), at any ocean depth (0–115 MPa). (2) the 6-DOF movement joints and gripper of the salve arm work well.

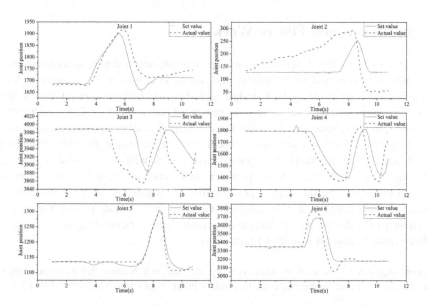

Fig. 10. The results of the experiment under the pressure of 10 MPa.

It can be seen from the results shown in Figs. 10 and 11 that the fourth, fifth, sixth joints have good response consistency and tracking ability with a large range of movement. However, the dynamic response of the first, second, third joints is not so well because the joints can only perform a small range of movement with the limited space in the pressure tank. The control algorithm which is used now needs to be improved.

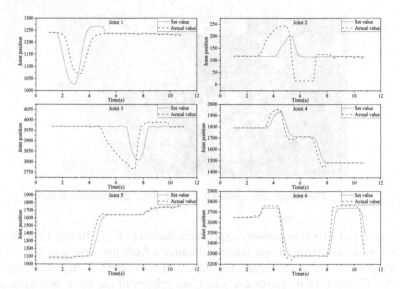

Fig. 11. The results of the experiment under the pressure of 115 MPa.

4 Conclusions and Future Work

This paper presents the development of the first full ocean depth underwater manipulator which is powered by hydraulic and works in a master-slave mode in China. A detailed description of system design including mechanical subsystem, electronic subsystem, and software subsystem is presented subsequently. The results of the experiment in the laboratory show that there is a significant performance improvement of the new elbow joint and wrist joint. The 11,000 m pressure experiment verified that the full ocean depth hydraulic manipulator could work well in the hadal environment.

Future work with the new manipulator will move in several related directions. Research on improving the sealing performance of single-vane swing cylinder will be conducted. Additionally, a new control algorithm which can realise the response consistency of hydraulic manipulator at any ocean depth is being designed. Testing it in offshore trials is also an essential future work.

Acknowledgment. This work is supported by the National Natural Science Foundation of China (51705514) and by the National Key R&D Program of China (2016YFC0300401).

References

1. Jamieson, A.: The Hadal Zone: Life in the Deepest Oceans, 2nd edn. Cambridge University Press, Cambridge (2015)
2. Zereik, E., Bibuli, M., Miskovic, N., Ridao, P., Pascoal, A.: Challenges and future trends in marine robotics. Annu. Rev. Control **46**, 350–368 (2018)

3. Hardy, K., Bulman, T., Cameron, J., Pausch, S., Herbst, L.: Hadal landers: the DEEPSEA CHALLENGE ocean trench free vehicles. In: 2013 Oceans - San Diego. IEEE Press, San Diego (2013)
4. Phillips, B.T., Gruber, D.F., Vasan, G., Roman, C.N., Pieribone, V.A., Sparks, J.S.: Observations of in situ deep-sea marine bioluminescence with a high-speed, high-resolution sCMOS camera. Deep-Sea Res. Part I-Oceanogr. Res. Pap. **111**, 102–109 (2016)
5. Sivcev, S., Coleman, J., Omerdic, E., Dooly, G., Toal, D.: Underwater manipulators: a review. Ocean Eng. **163**, 431–450 (2018)
6. Sivcev, S., Rossi, M., Coleman, J., Omerdic, E., Dooly, G., Toal, D.: Collision detection for underwater ROV manipulator systems. Sensors (Basel) **18**(4), 1117 (2018)
7. Wang, F., Chen, Y.: Dynamic characteristics of pressure compensator in underwater hydraulic system. IEEE-ASME Trans. Mechatron. **19**(2), 777–787 (2014)
8. Dana, R.Y., Hagen, S., David, M.D.: Design and performance evaluation of an actively compliant underwater manipulator for full-ocean depth. J. Robot. Syst. **8**, 371–392 (1991)
9. Zhang, Q.F., et al.: 7000M pressure experiment of a deep-sea hydraulic manipulator system. In: 2014 Oceans - St. John's. IEEE Press, St. John's (2014)
10. Gold, P.W., Schmidt, A., Dicke, H., Loos, J., Assmann, C.: Viscosity–pressure–temperature behaviour of mineral and synthetic oils. Lubr. Sci. **18**(1), 51–79 (2006)
11. Kim, J.-H., et al.: Experimental study on compressibility modulus of pressure compensation oil for underwater vehicle. Ocean Polar Res. **37**(1), 73–80 (2015)
12. Mattila, J., Koivumaki, J., Caldwell, D.G., Semini, C.: A survey on control of hydraulic robotic manipulators with projection to future trends. IEEE-ASME Trans. Mechatron. **22**(2), 669–680 (2017)
13. Bowen, A.D., et al.: The Nereus hybrid underwater robotic vehicle for global ocean science operations to 11,000 m depth. In: Oceans 2008, Quebec, pp. 1–10. IEEE Press (2008)

Thruster Fault Identification for Autonomous Underwater Vehicle Based on Time-Domain Energy and Time-Frequency Entropy of Fusion Signal

Baoji Yin[1,2,3(✉)], Xi Lin[1,3], Wenxian Tang[1,3], and Zhikun Jin[1,3]

[1] School of Mechanical Engineering, Jiangsu University of Science
and Technology, Zhenjiang 212003, China
yinbaoji@just.edu.cn
[2] Science and Technology on Underwater Vehicle Technology,
Harbin Engineering University, Harbin 150001, China
[3] Jiangsu Provincial Key Laboratory of Advanced Manufacture and Process
for Marine Mechanical Equipment, Jiangsu University of Science
and Technology, Zhenjiang 212003, China

Abstract. In order to deal with the problem of low classification accuracy in thruster fault identification based on single fault feature, a fault identification algorithm based on time-domain energy and time-frequency entropy of fusion signal is proposed. Firstly, the fault singular signals from two single aspects, such as surge speed and control voltage, are fused into a fusion signal to reflect fault information more comprehensively. Then, the peak region energy feature of the fusion signal is extracted in time domain, and the entropy feature of the fusion signal is extracted in time-frequency domain, so as to obtain the multi-domain fault features. Finally, based on support vector data description algorithm, a multi-classifier is established, and the relative distance between fault sample and each hypersphere in the multi-classifier is calculated. The fault severity corresponding to the fault sample is determined by the minimum relative distance. The experimental results of an experimental prototype in a pool show that the classification accuracy of the proposed method is 95.2%. In comparison to the classification models corresponding to the surge speed and control voltage, the classification accuracy is increased by 5.2% and 22.8% respectively.

Keywords: Autonomous underwater vehicle · Thruster fault ·
Fault identification · Fusion signal · Time-domain energy ·
Time-frequency entropy

1 Introduction

Autonomous underwater vehicles (AUVs) play an important role in ocean missions, such as searching, rescuing, mapping, observation of underwater structure, and so on [1, 2]. To complete the missions, AUV needs good propulsion performance [3]. Thrusters are one of the key parts for AUV propulsion system [4]. However, the strong

© Springer Nature Switzerland AG 2019
H. Yu et al. (Eds.): ICIRA 2019, LNAI 11742, pp. 264–275, 2019.
https://doi.org/10.1007/978-3-030-27535-8_25

working intensity might induce faults on the thrusters [5]. Common fault modes of thruster are blade damage, blade winding, dome blockage, etc. Because the actual thrust is less than the theoretical thrust when the above-mentioned faults occur, the above-mentioned faults are generally generalized as thrust loss faults [6]. Thruster fault directly decreases the whole propulsion performance of AUVs. The modern controllers are designed to be capable of dealing with the unanticipated thruster faults [7]. They use fault-tolerant control technology to make the AUV continue to fulfil the task [8]. The fault-tolerant control technology, especially active fault-tolerant control technology, needs the real-time knowledge of fault severity [9]. Fault identification is a common way to get the faulty severity [10, 11]. Therefore the research on thruster fault identification is of great significance to ensure that AUV completes its assigned tasks [12].

Among thruster fault identification techniques, classification model-based methods are widely used. They extract fault feature firstly. And then they use the fault feature to train classifier and take the classifier to identify fault severity [13, 14]. In terms of fault feature extraction, the wavelet coefficient modulus maximum method extracts fault feature from surge speed signal [15]. The wavelet coefficient fusion method and the fractal feature method get fault feature from surge speed signal and control voltage signal [16, 17]. These methods all extract fault features from different single signals respectively. The extracted fault feature can only reflect fault information from one single aspect. In terms of classifier building, the support vector data description algorithm (SVDD) can construct several separating hyperspheres by treating fault samples of each severity as target sample respectively, and then integrates multiple one-classifiers to a multi-classifier [18]. This modeling strategy is suitable for multi-classes classification.

In this paper, a thruster fault identification method based on time-domain energy and time-frequency entropy of fusion signal is presented. It fuses the surge speed and control voltage signals firstly. And then it extracts peak region energy and time-frequency entropy features from the fusion signal. Finally, fault samples constructed by the extracted fault features are classified based on SVDD and the thruster fault severities are gotten. The effectiveness of the proposed method is verified by an experimental prototype navigating in a pool.

2 Fault Diagnosis System

2.1 The Overall Structure of the Fault Diagnosis System

The overall structure of the fault diagnosis system used in this article mainly consists of three steps, as illustrated in Fig. 1. Step one, AUV surge speed signal and the changing rate of thruster control voltage are fused based on evidence theory. Step two, the peak region energy and time-frequency entropy are extracted from the fusion signal. Step three, the fault severity is identified based on SVDD.

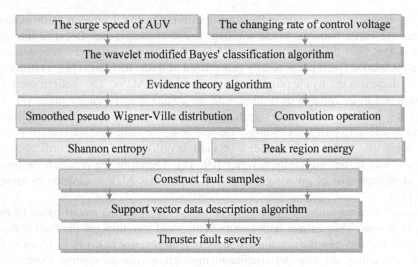

Fig. 1. The schematic diagram of the fault diagnosis system.

2.2 Signal Fusion

Since that the surge speed signal and control voltage signal only reflect the fault information from a single aspect, the two signals are fused to obtain more comprehensive fault information. The fusion process is described as follows:

(1) A time window is used to intercept the surge speed signal of the underwater vehicle and the changing rate signal of thruster control voltage.

(2) The obtained data are decomposed by wavelet and the wavelet approximate components are extracted. Then the components are operated by modified Bayes' classification algorithm and the results $d_{sA}(n)$ are obtained.

(3) That the thruster fault occurs at the nth time step is defined as a focal element B_n. All the B_n forms a fault evidence recognition framework $\Theta = \{B_n\}$. Formula 1 is used to calculate the basic probability assignment function $m(B_n)$. The $m(B_n)$ is instantiated to $m_U(B_n)$ and $m_C(B_n)$, which represent the basic probability assignment functions corresponding to surge speed and control voltage respectively. The $m_U(B_n)$ and $m_C(B_n)$ are put into Formulas 2–3 for fusion. The fusion result $m_F(B_n)$ is obtained.

$$m(B_n) = \frac{d_{SA}(n)}{\sum\limits_{i=1}^{N_5} d_{SA}(i)} \tag{1}$$

$$m_F(B_n) = \frac{1}{K_5} \sum_{B_i \cap B_j = B_n} m_U(B_i) m_C(B_j) \tag{2}$$

$$K_5 = \sum_{B_i \cap B_j = \emptyset} m_U(B_i) m_C(B_j) \tag{3}$$

Where $d_{SA}(n)$ is the result calculated by the wavelet modified Bayes' classification algorithm, $m_F(B_n)$ is the basic probability assignment function of the fault evidence corresponding to the fusion signal.

2.3   Fault Feature Extraction

In this paper, the peak region energy and time-frequency entropy are extracted from the fusion signal.

The process of peak region energy extraction is described as follows. Convolution of the basic probability assignment function $m_F(B_n)$ corresponding to the fusion signal is performed by equation $m_{conv}(n) = m_F(B_n) * m_F(B_n)$. Find all of the minimum points in the $m_{conv}(n)$. The sum of the data between the two adjacent minimum points is regarded as one peak region energy. The maximum peak region energy in the $m_{conv}(n)$ is defined as the time-domain energy feature (given the symbol F_{TE}) of the fusion signal.

The process of time-frequency entropy extraction is presented as follows. The smoothed pseudo Wigner-Ville distribution algorithm is adopted to obtain the energy distribution $SPWVD(n, m)$ of the signal $m_F(B_n)$ in time-frequency domain, as shown in Formula 4 [19]. The Shannon entropy F_{TFH} of the $SPWVD(n, m)$ is calculated by Formulas 5–6 [20]. The F_{TFH} are taken as the time-frequency entropy feature of the fusion signal.

$$SPWVD(n, m) = 2 \sum_{k=-(L-1)}^{L-1} h(k) \sum_{l=-(M-1)}^{M-1} g(l) z(n+l+k) z * (n+l-k) e^{\frac{-j2\pi km}{N}} \tag{4}$$

$$p(n, m) = |SPWVD(n, m)| \Big/ \sum \sum |SPWVD(n, m)| \tag{5}$$

$$F_{TFH} = -\sum \sum p(n, m) \log_2 p(n, m) \tag{6}$$

Where $h(k_1)$ and $g(l_1)$ are smoothing window functions in time direction and frequency direction, respectively. $z(n)$ is the analytic signal of the fusion signal, $z * (n)$ conjugates with $z(n)$.

2.4   Fault Identification

In this paper, one-classifiers corresponding to each fault severity are trained firstly. And then multiple one-classifiers are integrated together to constitute a multi-classifier. Finally, the multi-classifier is used to classify the new fault sample and get the fault severity. The detailed process is as follows.

(1) Establish a one-classifier

For a certain thruster fault severity, the fault sample $x = [F_{TE} \quad F_{TFH}]^T$ is composed of the time-domain energy feature F_{TE} and the time-frequency entropy feature F_{TFH} of the fusion signal. Multiple fault samples can construct a fault sample set, given the symbol $X = \{x_i\}$. In the fault sample set $X = \{x_i\}$, 50% fault samples are randomly selected as training samples, given the symbol $X_{Tr} = \{x_{Tri}\}$. The remaining 50% fault samples are used as test samples, given the symbol $X_{Te} = \{x_{Tei}\}$. The training sample set $X_{Tr} = \{x_{Tri}\}$ is substituted into Formula 7 for optimization calculation and the global optimal solution $\alpha = \{\alpha_i\}$ is obtained, where, most $\alpha_i = 0$, a few $\alpha_i > 0$, and the training sample x_{Tri} corresponding to the non-zero α_i is the support vector, represented by x_{svi}. The hypersphere radius R is calculated through Formula 8.

$$\max L(\alpha) = \sum_{i=1}^{N_6} \alpha_i K(x_{Tri}, x_{Tri}) - \sum_{i=1, j=1}^{N_6} \alpha_i \alpha_j K(x_{Tri}, x_{Trj}) \tag{7}$$

$$R^2 = K(x_{svi}, x_{svi}) - 2\sum_{i=1}^{N_6} \alpha_i K(x_{svi}, x_{Tri}) + \sum_{i=1, j=1}^{N_6} \alpha_i \alpha_j K(x_{Tri}, x_{Trj}) \tag{8}$$

Where, the condition constraint is $\sum_{i=1}^{N_6} \alpha_i = 1$, $0 \leq \alpha_i \leq C$, C is the penalty coefficient, the kernel function $K(x_i, x_j) = \exp\left(-\|x_i - x_j\|^2 / \sigma^2\right)$.

The training sample set $X_{Tr} = \{x_{Tri}\}$, the global optimal solution $\alpha = \{\alpha_i\}$, the support vector x_{svi}, and the hypersphere radius R together describe the one-classifier corresponding to this certain fault severity.

(2) Establish multi-classifier and identify fault severity

Get the dynamic signal data of underwater vehicle when the thruster fault severity is λ_k, where the k describes different fault levels. Following the instructions in Step (1), multiple one-classifiers ^kS can be established. The ^kS are described by training sample set $^kX_{Tr} = \{^kx_{Tri}\}$, global optimal solution $^k\alpha = \{^k\alpha_i\}$, support vector $^kx_{svi}$, and hypersphere radius ^kR. All of the ^kS together construct the multi-classifier.

In the fault identification, according to Formula 9, the generalized distance ^kD between the new sample x_{new} and multiple one-classifiers ^kS are calculated.

$$^kD^2 = K(x_{new}, x_{new}) - 2\sum_{i=1}^{N_6} {}^k\alpha_i K(x_{new}, {}^kx_{Tri}) + \sum_{i=1, j=1}^{N_6} {}^k\alpha_i {}^k\alpha_j K({}^kx_{Tri}, {}^kx_{Trj}) \tag{9}$$

Formula $^k\varepsilon = {}^kD/{}^kR$ is used to calculate the relative distance $^k\varepsilon$ between the new sample x_{new} and multiple one-classifiers ^kS. The fault severity corresponding to the minimum relative distance is the identification result.

3   Experimental Results and Discussion

3.1   Experimental Data

In order to verify the method proposed in this paper, experimental data should be obtained firstly and then analyzed. In this paper, the experimental data is gotten by making an experimental prototype of underwater vehicle navigate in a pool. The underwater vehicle starts from the static state, and then the underwater vehicle speed and thruster control voltage gradually increase. From the 101st time step, the underwater vehicle starts to run at a steady speed of 0.3 m/s. From the 250th time step to the end of the experiment, the thruster has a fault of thrust loss, where the thrust lost percent is 0%, 10%, 20%, 30%, and 40%, respectively. Here, the thrust loss fault is simulated by the software method, which is decreasing the control voltage actually loaded to driver of the thruster [17]. The surge speed of underwater vehicle and the changing rate of thruster control voltage are collected at a sampling frequency of 5 Hz. By observing the experimental data, it is found that the experimental data from step 100 to step 500 contains fault information. So these data are selected and shown in Figs. 2 and 3, respectively.

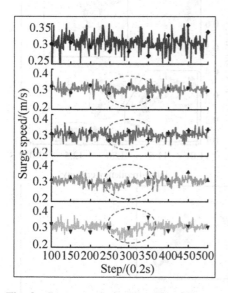 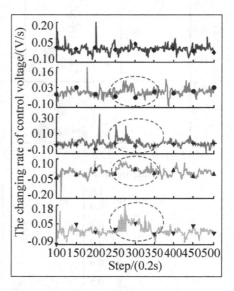

Fig. 2. Surge speed signals under different fault severities.

Fig. 3. The changing rate of control voltage under different fault severities.

As shown in the ellipse marker in Figs. 2 and 3, from step 250 to step 350, the surge speed signals form a singular signal which firstly decrease and then rise, and the changing rate signals of control voltage form a singular signal which firstly rise and then fall. These singular signals contain abundant fault information. So this paper extracts fault features from these singular signals.

3.2 Fault Feature Extraction Experiments

In order to make a comparative analysis of the fault sample distributions, fault features are extracted from the surge speed signal, the changing rate signal of control voltage, and the fusion signal, respectively. A time window of length $L_1 = 300$ is used to cut out surge speed data from step 101 to step 400. The time-domain energy and time-frequency entropy features extracted from the signals construct a fault sample. Move the time window to the right for 100 time steps. For each time step, a group of fault samples is obtained. A total of 500 fault samples are obtained for different fault severities. The distribution of fault samples is shown in Fig. 4(a). The same process is used to make fault samples corresponding to control signal and fusion signal, respectively. The results are shown in Fig. 4(b) and (c) respectively.

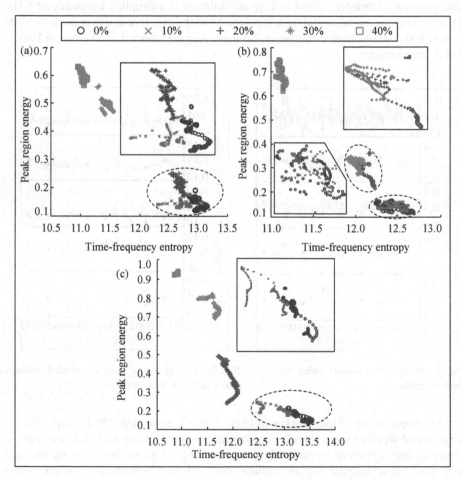

Fig. 4. The distribution of fault samples corresponding to different signals: (a) speed signal; (b) control signal; (c) fusion signal.

Figures 4(a), (b), and (c) are analyzed comparatively. In the distribution corresponding to speed signal, as shown in Fig. 4(a), corresponding to fault severities 30% and 40%, the overall distance of centers of classes is big. Corresponding to fault severities 0%, 10%, and 20%, the overall distance of centers of classes is small. In the distribution corresponding to control signal, as shown in Fig. 4(b), the fault samples with a fault severity of 10% are close to the fault samples with a fault severity of 0%, and the fault samples with a fault severity of 30% are close to the fault samples with a fault severity of 20% as well. In the distribution corresponding to fusion signal, as shown in Fig. 4(c), the fault samples with a fault severity of 10% slightly overlap with the fault samples with a fault severity of 0%, but the fault samples of the other three categories are far from each other. By comparing the fault sample distributions in the above three graphs, it can be seen that for the fault samples obtained from the fusion signal, the overall distance of centers of classes is relative big, and the dispersion of fault samples in each class is relative small. This will facilitate fault identification.

3.3 Fault Identification Experiments

In this paper, five one-classifiers are built for each fault severity. And then the five one-classifiers together constitute a multi-classifier.

One-Classifier Experiment
To build one-classifiers corresponding to each fault severity and then test the performance of the one-classifiers. The fault samples are divided. For the fault samples shown in Fig. 4, 50% fault samples are randomly selected as training samples, and the remaining 50% fault samples are taken as test samples. For a certain fault severity, the corresponding training samples are used to establish the one-classifier, and all of the test samples are used to test the performance of the one-classifier. The fault sample partitioning results are shown in Table 1. The receiver operating characteristic (ROC) [21] curve of each one-classifier is shown in Fig. 5.

Table 1. Fault sample construction in experiment.

One-classifiers	0%	10%	20%	30%	40%
Training sample	50	50	50	50	50
Test sample	50	50	50	50	50

According to Fig. 5, the performance of one-classifiers for fusion signal are higher than or equal to the one for speed signal and control signal, except the fault severity being 0% case, in which case, the performance of the one-classifier for fusion signal is slightly lower than the one for speed signal.

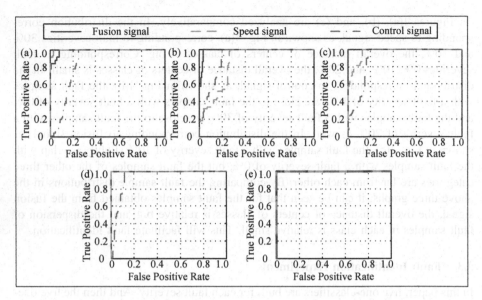

Fig. 5. The ROC curve of one classifier corresponding to each fault severity: (a) 0%; (b) 10%; (c) 20%; (d) 30%; (e) 40%.

To quantitatively describe the performance of one-classifiers, the areas under the curves (AUCs) [21] of different one-classifiers are calculated. The results are shown in Table 2.

Table 2. The AUCs of one-classifiers corresponding to different signals.

One-classifiers	0%	10%	20%	30%	40%
Fusion signal	0.9891	0.9894	1	1	1
Speed signal	0.9977	0.8481	0.9691	1	1
Control signal	0.8472	0.9013	0.897	0.9415	1

According to Table 2, the observation from Table 2 is consistent with the conclusion from Fig. 5.

The above experimental results show that the overall performance of one-classifiers for fusion signal is higher than the one for speed signal and control signal.

Multi-classifier Experiment

Make the five one-classifiers construct one multi-classifier. Calculate the relative distance between the test sample with a fault severity of 0% and each one-classifier. The one-classifier corresponding to the smallest relative distance is taken as the type which the test sample belongs to. In the same way, test samples corresponding to fault severities 10%, 20%, 30%, and 40% are classified. The results are shown in Fig. 6.

The number of samples classified correctly is summarized in Table 3. With the total number of samples classified correctly divided by the total number of test samples, the result is the classification accuracy of the multi-classifier.

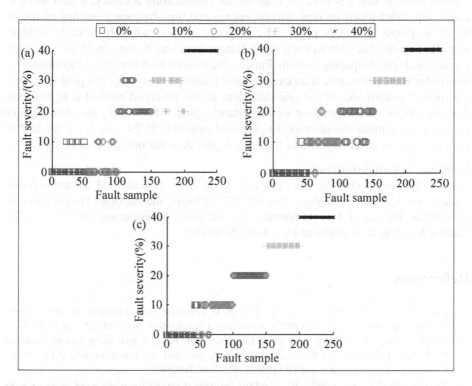

Fig. 6. The relative distance between test samples and each one-classifier for different signals: (a) speed signal; (b) control signal; (c) fusion signal.

As shown in Table 3, the classification accuracy is 95.2% for the fusion signal, whereas it is 90.0% for speed signal and 72.4% for control signal. The results indicate that the classification accuracy for the fusion signal is 5.2% higher than the one for speed signal and is 22.8% higher than the one for control signal.

Table 3. The number of test samples classified correctly corresponding to different signals.

Fault severity	0%	10%	20%	30%	40%	Total	Accuracy
Test sample	50	50	50	50	50	250	——
Fusion signal	45	43	50	50	50	238	0.952
Speed signal	48	42	35	50	50	225	0.900
Control signal	42	11	39	39	50	181	0.724

4 Conclusion

On identifying thruster fault severity for an AUV based on single fault feature, the classification accuracy is low. To improve the classification accuracy, a fault identification algorithm based on time-domain energy and time-frequency entropy of fusion signal is proposed in this paper. The proposed method not only fuses two single singular signals, but also extracts fault feature from the fusion signal in both time domain and time-frequency domain. Finally, the thruster fault severity is identified by a multi-classifier. The results of an experimental prototype navigating in a pool show that the overall performance of the one-classifiers for the proposed method is higher than that for single speed signal or single control signal. Meanwhile, the classification accuracy of the multi-classifier for the proposed method is 95.2%, which is 5.2% higher than the one for speed signal and is 22.8% higher than the one for control signal.

Funding Acknowledgement
The work is supported by the Research Fund from Science and Technology on Underwater Vehicle Technology (No. 6142215180306), and the Open Project Funding of Jiangsu Provincial Key Laboratory of Advanced Manufacture and Process for Marine Mechanical Equipment (No. JSKL2018006).

References

1. Zhu, D., Tian, C., Sun, B., et al.: Complete coverage path planning of autonomous underwater vehicle based on GBNN algorithm. J. Intell. Rob. Syst. **94**, 237–249 (2019)
2. Yu, C., Xiang, X., Wilson, P.A., et al: Guidance-error-based robust fuzzy adaptive control for bottom following of a flight-style AUV with saturated actuator dynamics. IEEE Trans. Cybern. (2019) https://doi.org/10.1109/TCYB.2018.2890582
3. Pugi, L., Pagliai, M., Allotta, B.: A robust propulsion layout for underwater vehicles with enhanced manoeuvrability and reliability features. Proc. Inst. Mech. Eng. Part M-J. Eng. Marit. Environ. **232**(3), 358–376 (2018)
4. He, J., Li, Y., Li, Y., et al.: Fault diagnosis in autonomous underwater vehicle propeller in the transition stage based on GP-RPF. Int. J. Adv. Rob. Syst. **15**(6), 1–9 (2018)
5. Liu, F., Demin, X., Jin, Yu., et al.: Fault isolation of thrusters under redundancy in frame-structure unmanned underwater vehicles. Int. J. Adv. Rob. Syst. **15**(2), 1–11 (2018)
6. Dos Santos, C.H.F., Cardozo, D.I.K., Reginatto, R., et al.: Bank of controllers and virtual thrusters for fault-tolerant control of autonomous underwater vehicles. Ocean Eng. **121**, 210–223 (2016)
7. Qiao, L., Zhang, W.: Double-loop integral terminal sliding mode tracking control for UUVs with adaptive dynamic compensation of uncertainties and disturbances. IEEE J. Oceanic Eng. **44**(1), 29–53 (2019)
8. Liu, X., Zhang, M., Yao, F.: Adaptive fault tolerant control and thruster fault reconstruction for autonomous underwater vehicle. Ocean Eng. **155**, 10–23 (2018)
9. Liu, L., Wei, Yu., Zhen, Yu.: Active fault-tolerant control design for a submarine semi-physical simulation system. Int. J. Control Autom. Syst. **16**(5), 2363–2372 (2018)
10. Lei, Y., Jia, F., Kong, D., et al.: Opportunities and challenges of machinery intelligent fault diagnosis in big data era. J. Mech. Eng. **54**(5), 94–104 (2018)

11. Yin, B., Yao, F., Wang, Y., et al.: Fault degree identification method for thruster of autonomous underwater vehicle using homomorphic membership function and low frequency trend prediction. Proc. Inst. Mech. Eng. Part C-J. Mech. Eng. Sci. **233**(4), 1426–1440 (2019)
12. He, J., Li, Y., Jiang, Y., et al.: Propeller fault diagnosis based on a rank particle filter for autonomous underwater vehicles. Brodogradnja **69**(2), 147–164 (2018)
13. Abed, W., Sharma, S., Sutton, R., et al.: An unmanned marine vehicle thruster fault diagnosis scheme based on OFNDA. J. Marine Eng. Technol. **16**(1), 37–44 (2017)
14. Yao, F., Wang, F., Zhang, M.: Weak thruster fault detection for autonomous underwater vehicle based on artificial immune and signal pre-processing. Adv. Mech. Eng. **10**(2), 1–13 (2018)
15. Wang, J., Wu, G., Wan, L.: Sensor fault diagnosis for underwater robots. In: Proceedings of the 7th World Congress on Intelligent Control and Automation, Chongqing, pp. 254–259 (2008)
16. Zhang, M., Juan, W., Wang, Y.: A method of multi-sensor simultaneous fault detection for autonomous underwater vehicle. Robot **32**, 298–305 (2010)
17. Liu, W., Wang, Y., Yin, B., et al.: Thruster fault identification based on fractal feature and multi-resolution wavelet decomposition for autonomous underwater vehicle. Proc. Inst. Mech. Eng. Part C-J. Mech. Eng. Sci. **231**(13), 2528–2539 (2017)
18. Li, Y., Liu, S., Zhu, P., et al.: Extraction of visual texture features of seabed sediments using an SVDD approach. Ocean Eng. **142**, 501–506 (2017)
19. Wu, J., Chen, X., Ma, Z.: A signal decomposition method for ultrasonic guided wave generated from debonding combining smoothed pseudo Wigner-Ville distribution and Vold–Kalman filter order tracking. Shock Vib. 1–13 (2017). https://doi.org/10.1155/2017/7283450
20. Zhao, H., Yao, R., Ling, X., et al.: Study on a novel fault damage degree identification method using high-order differential mathematical morphology gradient spectrum entropy. Entropy **20**(9), 1–18 (2018)
21. Zheng, S.: Smoothly approximated support vector domain description. Pattern Recogn. **49**, 55–64 (2016)

Design and Implementation of Monitoring System for Deep Sea Ore Sampling Machine

Donglei Dong[1], Xianbo Xiang[1,2(✉)], Jinrong Zheng[3], and Qin Zhang[4]

[1] School of Naval Architecture and Ocean Engineering,
Huazhong University of Science and Technology,
Wuhan 430074, People's Republic of China
xbxiang@hust.edu.cn

[2] Shenzhen Huazhong University of Science and Technology Research Institute,
Shenzhen 518057, China

[3] Institute of Deep-Sea Science and Engineering, Chinese Academy of Sciences,
Sanya 572000, People's Republic of China

[4] State Key Laboratory of Digital Manufacturing Equipment and Technology,
Huazhong University of Science and Technology, Wuhan 430074, China

Abstract. Deep sea sampling machine is an important tool for deep sea mining of cobalt crusts, in order to accomplish the sampling mission of mineral resources undersea. According to the design requirements of a deep sea ore sampling machine, this paper introduces the whole architecture of this sampling machine, analyzes its function and presents the software development of a surface monitoring system by using Visual Studio and database tools. In order to address the problem of heterogeneous communication nodes and remote real-time communications with multiple equipments, the hybrid communication technology by adopting the serial Modbus and Ethernet Modbus network in parallel is firstly proposed to accommodate heterogeneous communications with multi-node accesses. Secondly, the dual channel Ethernet communication technology is adopted, which improves the real-time performances of the whole monitoring system under complicated communication situations. Finally, the effectiveness of the monitoring system for deep sea ore sampling machine is verified by the simulation test and the hardware in loop test, which provides a reference to the development of other similar marine monitoring system.

Keywords: Deep sea sampling machine · Monitoring system ·
Hybrid communication · Dual channel communication

1 Introduction

With the consumption of resources on land, countries around the world have paid attentions to vast oceanic resources by developing intelligent marine equipments [1–3]. The ocean is rich in biological resources, oil and gas resources and

© Springer Nature Switzerland AG 2019
H. Yu et al. (Eds.): ICIRA 2019, LNAI 11742, pp. 276–288, 2019.
https://doi.org/10.1007/978-3-030-27535-8_26

mineral resources, such as mineral cobalt crusts and fierce crusts [4]. These deep sea ores contain valuable fierce, copper, nickel, cobalt, front, silver, gold, etc. These rare metal elements, which are widely used in machinery manufacturing, construction, steel, aerospace, chemical, electronic battery and military industries, are likely to become important strategic resources [5]. The reserves of such ores of cobalt-rich crusts on the ocean floor at present are as high as one trillion tons, containing hundreds of millions of tons of cobalt, much higher than the reserves of land [6, 7].

In order to make these resources beneficial to human beings, marine science and technology experts and professional technicians are urgently needed for legal research and exploration and development. In the context of the development of a new era of maritime powers, it is necessary to seize the trend of the times, increase investment in research and development of deep-sea equipment, master its core technologies, and develop deep-sea robots with independent intellectual property rights. The deep sea cobalt-rich crust sampler equipment is a typical representative of deep-sea robot equipment. At present, China does not have deep sea cobalt-rich crust sampling technology. In order to actively explore, a research institute of the Chinese Academy of Sciences took the lead in undertaking the research and development of the sampling machine. The development of the cobalt crust sampler is a preliminary exploration and technical accumulation of the exploitation and utilization of deep-sea mineral resources in the late period. It has unraveled the research road for marine scientific research, and has made the country's gradual transition from a maritime country to a maritime power country with important historical significance.

Fig. 1. Deep sea sampling machine

In Fig. 1, it shows a typical deep sea mining vehicle. Since the whole work of deep sea ore sampling machine is quite heavy, this article briefly introduces the overall overview of the sampling machine first, and then focuses on the software design and implementation of the monitoring system. Finally, the developed monitoring system for deep sea ore sampling machine is verified by the simulation test and the hardware in loop test.

2   Deep Sea Sampling Machine Test Device Architecture

The Sampling machine body can be divided into two parts: a water surface control system and an underwater control system. The upper part of the water surface is the core, and the underwater part is centered on the PC104 computer. The system architecture of the entire test device is shown in Fig. 2.

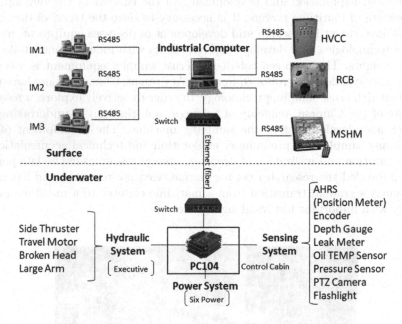

Fig. 2. Architecture of the deep sea sampling machine

2.1   Surface Control System

As shown in the water surface of the test device system structure diagram, the industrial computer with the PC software is mainly used as the core, and the industrial computer is connected with six serial devices and one network port device. The network transmission medium is optical fiber to meet the communication requirements of 4500 m underwater, six serial ports are connected with High Voltage Control Cabinet (HVCC), Remote Control Box (RCB) (PTZ camera control and sampling vehicle joystick), Mother Ship Heading Meter (MSHM), three BENDER Insulation Monitor (IM) modules. Through the Remote Control Box, the Sampling Machine can be controlled to travel, and the underwater four-way pan/tilt camera works, including rotating the pan/tilt, adjusting the aperture and focal length, etc. to obtain Machine video with different directions and different distances. The communication data of all equipments on the water surface are connected to the host computer. After receiving, calculating and processing, a part of the data is directly displayed on the upper computer interface, and some of the other control signals along with the host computer are connected to the lower computer through the Ethernet. The data received by the lower computer is sent to the database storage so that it can be taken out at any time when needed. In addition to the equipment connected to the industrial computer, the water surface also has a hard disk recorder and a display, so that the underwater camera mounted on the Sampling Machine can transmit the video information back to the water surface in real time.

2.2 Underwater Control System

Also shown in the underwater portion of Fig. 2, the PC 104 computer housed in the control cabin is the core. The signal on the water part is transmitted to the lower computer through the fiber optic cable, which manages the three underwater systems, the power distribution system, the hydraulic system and the sensing system. The power distribution system consists of six power boards, which supply power to all parts of the equipment. The hydraulic system is mainly composed of side thrusters, travel motors, and broken head. The sensing system is mainly composed of AHRS, encoder, PTZ camera, lighting and various sensors. These auxiliary components provide a guarantee for the safe and efficient operation of the Underwater Sampling Machine.

3 Design and Implementation of Monitoring System

3.1 Software Development Environment

The Sampling Machine PC software is designed and developed by Visual Studio 2013 dialog-based MFC, running on Windows 7 64-bit operating system, and the database is MySQL database management system [8].

By creating an MFC project [9], the PC software sets up the connection with different devices, mainly based on the MFC main window, and then coordinates the processing data by creating multiple threads. In addition, the label control is used to manage different contents by paging, Real-time curve display and data communication using Active X controls such as TeeChart [10] and MSComm, and uses the OpenGL [11] application programming interface to realize the drawing of multiple virtual instruments on the interface of the monitoring system, so that the data interaction is clearer and more intuitive. Data storage plays an important role in the monitoring system. All devices in the water surface must interact with the host computer software. The MySQL database is used to store some important parameters of the interactive PC software into the database, which can be retrieved at any time. Viewing the data also creates conditions for multiple remote access and control that will be done later.

3.2 Monitoring System Function

The monitoring system mainly plays the two functions of monitoring and controlling the Underwater Sampling Machine. Surveillance is the display and alarm of multiple parameters of the Sampling Machine body and multiple equipments on the water. The control is controlled by the software interface on the Sampling Machine body and its ancillary equipment, and on the other hand, by the control box of the vehicle joystick and the PTZ camera to handles it. The Underwater Sampling Machine can walk on the seabed, and the distribution characteristics of the cobalt-rich crust ore body are detected by means of underwater cameras, booms and broken heads, and then sampled and collected for further analysis.

The host computer interface is mainly composed of a main window and four subwindows. The main window is mainly used to set the communication settings of the connected devices. For example, the network communication can set the IP address and port number, and the serial communication can set the serial port number, baud rate and other parameters. And display some basic parameters of the system and display the total status alarm. Once there is a dangerous situation such as water leakage or high temperature, an audible light alarm will be issued. At this time, you can switch to the specific sub-window to view the detailed alarm situation. The interface of the host computer main window is shown in Fig. 3.

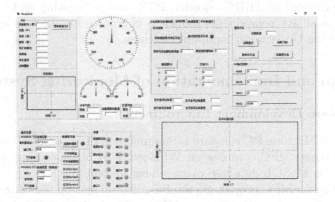

Fig. 3. Software interface of the surface monitoring system

The sub-window 1 is mainly a power-on control of the Subsea Sampling Machine auxiliary device and a status display of a plurality of device parameters. It can turn off and off underwater cameras, lights and various sensors. It can also display the water leakage status of underwater devices such as control cabin, fuel tank and power distribution box, the temperature status of each part, and the current of six underwater power boards. Voltage and insulation values, phase voltage line voltage and relay status of the power distribution cabinet, and insulation of the 3000 V high voltage cable detected by the BENDER module. This sub-window monitors the status of multiple devices on the water and underwater. Once an abnormality occurs in a device, it can be discovered and processed in time.

Sub-window 2 is primarily motion control of the sampler actuator. Here, the hydraulic supply of the side thruster and the crawler wheel travel motor can be switched, so that the Sampling Machine can be placed in the direction of retraction and the walking during operation, By input the PID parameter to achieve precise control. It is also possible to remotely control the boom, the broken head and the collecting pump. And real-time display and curve plotting of some of the operating parameters, these parameters are very important. The control process is fed back in time to achieve the best control effect.

The sub-window 3 is mainly used for storing and managing data. By connecting with the MySQL database, some important data is stored in the database, and any desired data can be extracted from the database by time period and displayed or saved to the text in a curved form. This facilitates the data analysis work that may be needed later, and also provides support for multi-machine remote access and control.

The sub-window 4 is called the developer debug page, and the administrator password is entered to enter the debugger. Here, each module of the underwater surface can be debugged individually, and the communication of a single module can be set and the most original data received can be displayed to detect which modules have problems in which links, and corresponding solutions are adopted according to the debugging results.

3.3 Mixed Communication

The shipboard industrial computer on the water is connected with multiple equipments. The design depth of the Subsea Sampling Machine is 4,500 m. Because of its long communication distance and reliable communication, it adopts standard Modbus/TCP communication protocol with various advantages such as real-time performance [12,13]. The High-Voltage Control Cabinet on the water uses the serial port based Modubus/RTU communication protocol, and the Mother Ship Heading Instrument, Remote Control Box and three BENDER modules all adopt pure serial communication protocol.

The overall data interaction framework of the host computer is shown in Fig. 4. Modbus/TCP and Modbus/RTU are implemented by request response. The receiving and sending threads are created separately. The data format is hexadecimal and the communication period is 100 ms. The Remote Control Box is also the request response mode. The Mother Ship Heading Meter and the BENDER are automatic transmission mode. The data type of the Mother Ship Heading Meter is string, $T = 500$ ms, the BENDER data type is hexadecimal, $T = 500$ ms.

The Modbus protocol includes ASCII, RTU, TCP, Modbus/ASCII and Modbus/RTU for serial communication, RS232 or RS485 communication, and Modbus/TCP for Ethernet network communication. The Modbus/RTU mode uses a 16 bit CRC check, while the Modbus/TCP mode has no additional checksums because the TCP protocol is already a reliable connection-oriented protocol.

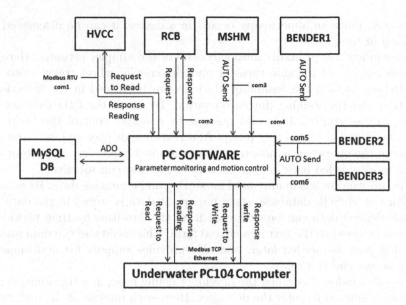

Fig. 4. Data communication diagram

The monitoring system and the underwater PC104 computer adopt the Modbus/TCP communication protocol, and the water High Voltage Control Cabinet adopts the Modbus/RTU communication protocol.

3.3.1   Modbus/TCP Communication

Modbus/TCP communication has multiple function codes. In the communication between the monitoring system and the lower computer, two function codes are mainly used, one is to read the input register (function code is 0x04), and the other is to write multiple registers (function code is 0x10). Tables 1 and 2 are the request format and response format of the data read by the monitoring system. The format of the written data is similar.

Table 1. Modbus/TCP read input register (host request)

Message header	Function code	Starting address	Number of registers
00 2F 00 00 00 06 01	04	00	00 5A

Table 2. Modbus/TCP read input register (PC104 response)

Message header	Function code	Number of data bytes	Read data (90 total)
00 2F 00 00 00 B7 01	04	B4	00 01......

The value in the upper computer read/write register has been defined in the lower computer, a total of 184 registers, 90 read input registers, 94 write multiple holding registers, the data in each register represents a different meaning.

In the realization of communication, in order to improve programming efficiency and reliability, directly call modbus.dll dynamic link library [14]. Use the modbus_new_tcp core function to create the connection, use the core code modbus_read_input_registers function and the modbus_write_registers function to read the input register and write multiple holding registers, respectively.

3.3.2   Modbus/RTU Communication

Modbus/RTU communication is similar to Modbus/TCP communication. The biggest difference is that Modbus/RTU is used for serial communication and has a two-byte CRC check at the end of the data frame to ensure reliable serial communication. The beginning of the data frame uses an address code that occupies 1 byte instead of the message header, but the address code also has a function code. The monitoring system uses the 0x03 function code to read 21 register data in the High Voltage Control Cabinet. Each register also defines different meanings. The data frame format is shown in Tables 3 and 4.

Table 3. Modbus/RTU data frame format (request)

Slave address	Function code	Starting address	Number of registers	CRC check
04	03	00 00	00 15	84 50

Table 4. Modbus/TCP read input register (response)

Slave address	Function code	Number of data bytes	Read data (21 total)	CRC check
04	03	2A	00 01......	F8 8A

3.3.3   Serial Communication

The host computer is connected with six serial communication devices, in addition to Modbus/RTU communication, there are five common serial communication. The Mother Ship Heading Meter sends string data, and other devices send hexadecimal data. The data frame format of the Mother Ship Heading Meter: $HEHDT, 201.72, T19CRLF, of which 201.72 indicates the heading of the mother ship.

Ordinary serial communication uses the MSComm control in the software implementation. By registering the control and then dragging it into the MFC dialog box, to achieve simultaneous communication with five serial devices, you can add five MSComm controls to bind different variables. In the process of receiving and transmitting, it monitors and responds to some events and errors through different port numbers and baud rates, and uses event drivers to handle the interaction of serial ports. When the request command is required, it can be set in the timer or thread. When the five-way serial port communicates at the same time, the corresponding OnComm event and CommEvent attribute will capture and check the communication event and the error value to complete the corresponding information interaction. When a communication event or error occurs, the OnComm event is fired and the value of the CommEvent property is changed.

3.4   Dual Channel Real-Time Communication

The host computer monitoring software communicates with the lower computer using Modbus/TCP communication protocol, and uses fiber optic Ethernet to transmit data and control signals. When using the Modbus/TCP communication protocol for network communication, it is no longer necessary to create additional sockets, etc., and only need to create a communication connection to communicate, because the socket and other related contents have been encapsulated in the communication protocol.

As described above, only a single connection communication is created. When the read and write speeds are not fast, the communication is normally stable, but when the speed is increased to 500 ms, occasionally an error occurs within a few tens of minutes to disconnect the connection. Such an error obviously does not satisfy the high real-time requirements of the test device. In order to solve this problem, we try to create another connection, and the previous connection forms a two-channel communication.

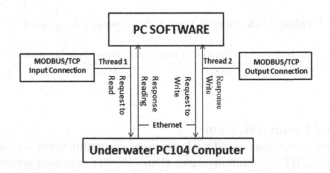

Fig. 5. Modbus/TCP dual channels for real-time communications

As shown in Fig. 5, one channel is dedicated to receiving data, and the other channel is dedicated to writing data. The two are independent of each other. No interference, greatly improving the data reading and writing rate, meeting the requirements of high real-time. In the experiment and test section, we verified the advantages of this design.

4   Experimental Test

4.1   Simulation Test

In the simulation test, it conducts a feasibility test based on the designed monitoring system software, by using Modbus Slave debugging assistant and serial port assistant to work with virtual serial port for the hybrid communication verification. First, open Modbus Slave assistant and configure the relevant parameters of Modbus TCP and Modbus RTU communication ID and function code respectively, and then open five serial port assistants to simulate five waters. The device is set with different parameters, and the monitoring system software is turned on and communicates with them.

In the communication test with the lower computer, multiple tests are performed using single channel and dual channel respectively. After continuously increasing the communication speed, a large difference can be obtained. The test results are shown in Table 5 below. The results show that even if the speed of the two-channel communication is up to 15 ms, The communication can still be stable without dropping, and the single channel will have an error at 500 ms, which verifies the stability and reliability of the monitoring system using twochannel communication.

Table 5. Stability of single and dual channels at different speeds.

Period (ms)	Single channel stable communication time	Dual channel stable communication time
1500	Stable	Stable
1000	Stable	Stable
500	About 30 min	Stable
300	About 20 min	Stable
200	About 5 min	Stable
100	About 2 min	Stable
50	0 min	Stable
15	0 min	Stable

When testing the whole system software, the value in the defined register in the Modbus Slave assistant and the corresponding data in the serial port assistant are changed. The monitoring system can display the corresponding data in real time through the calculation. A plurality of parameters are defined in the register and are associated with each other. A change of a certain data changes the associated multiple data states on the interface, and if the set threshold is crossed, an audible light alarm is issued. The simulation test interface is shown in Fig. 6.

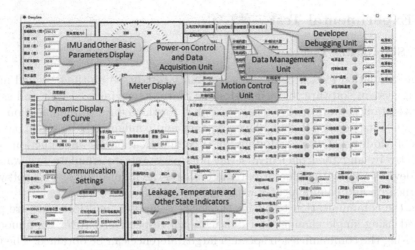

Fig. 6. Modus slave and serial port test

4.2 Hardware in Loop Test

Hardware in loop test of the monitoring system is conducted by connecting the underwater machine and multiple devices above the water. First, test the power supply system multiple power boards, then test the auxiliary system such as lights, underwater cameras, and then start the test of actuators such as the large arm and travel motor of the sampling machine. In Fig. 7, it shows the hardware in loop system being tested one by one.

Fig. 7. Hardware in loop test system

Simulation and hardware in loop test results verify the effectiveness of the surface monitoring system, which will be validated in the sea test in future.

5 Conclusion

This paper mainly presents the software development of monitoring system for the deep sea sampling machine. Firstly, the design background of the monitoring system is put forward. Secondly, the system architecture of the whole test device is introduced. And then, the design and implementation of the surface monitoring system are introduced. Finally, the key technology is verified to show the effectiveness of the monitoring system through simulation test and hardware in loop test. This research on the deep sea cobalt crust sampling machine is a preliminary exploration and technical implementation for the utilization of deep-sea mineral resources in nearly future. The surface monitoring system is a key part of the undersea sampling machine and plays an important role in the field applications. The successful development of the monitoring system is beneficial for the undersea sampling machine, and it also provides a good reference for the development of other similar marine monitoring system.

Acknowledgments. This work was supported in part by the Shenzhen Science and Technology Plan Project under Grant JCYJ20170418311305468, in part by the National Natural Science Foundation of China under Grant 51579111, in part by the National Key Research and Development Program of China (Grant 2017YFB1302302) and in part by the Research Fund from Science and Technology on Underwater Vehicle Technology under Grant SXJQR2017KFJJ06.

References

1. Yu, C., Xiang, X., Lapierre, L., Zhang, Q.: Robust magnetic tracking of subsea cable by AUV in the presence of sensor noise and ocean currents. IEEE J. Oceanic Eng. **43**(2), 311–322 (2018)
2. Phamduy, P., Vazquez, M.A., Kim, C., Mwaffo, V., Rizzo, A., Porfiri, M.: Design and characterization of a miniature free-swimming robotic fish based on multi-material 3D printing. Int. J. Intell. Robot. Appl. **1**(2), 209–223 (2017)
3. Zhang, Q., Zhang, J., Chemori, A., Xiang, X.: Virtual submerged floating operational system for robotic manipulation. Complexity **2018**, 1–18 (2018)
4. Dubiński, J.: Sustainable development of mining mineral resources. J. Sustain. Min. **12**(1), 1–6 (2013)
5. Liu, Z., Xu, W., Yang, D.: Study on strategic environmental assessment in exploitation of mineral resources. Sci. Geogr. Sin. **26**(6), 235 (2006)
6. Shun, L.Z., Liang, X.W., M.Y.D.: Study on strategic environmental assessment in exploitation of mineral resources. J. Earth Sci. **11**(2), 54–57 (2000)
7. Wu, G., Zhou, H., Chen, H.: Progress in the research of cobalt-rich crusts. Geol. J. China Univ. **7**(4), 379–389 (2001)
8. Blansit, B.D.: The basics of relational databases using MySQL. J. Electron. Resour. Med. Libr. **3**(3), 135–148 (2006)
9. Tan, D., Li, G., Meng, D., Xiao, X.: Design of remote power plant monitoring system based on LabVIEW and VC++ software. Sens. Transducers **21**(5), 66 (2013)
10. Song, Y.L., Shi, X.P., et al.: The application of TeeChart control in natural gas development. In: Proceedings of 2011 International Conference on Electronic & Mechanical Engineering and Information Technology, vol. 8, pp. 4368–4370. IEEE (2011)

11. Shreiner, D., Sellers, G., Kessenich, J., Licea-Kane, B.: OpenGL Programming Guide: The Official Guide to Learning OpenGL, Version 4.3. Addison-Wesley, Boston (2013)
12. Liu, Y., Ma, C., Lv, H.: Development of automatic downloads system for slub yarn parameters based on MODBUS/TCP. In: Qi, E., Shen, J., Dou, R. (eds.) The 19th International Conference on Industrial Engineering and Engineering Management, pp. 1343–1349. Springer, Heidelberg (2013). https://doi.org/10.1007/978-3-642-38442-4_141
13. Kobayashi, T.H., Batista, A.B., Medeiros, J.P.S., Filho, J.M.F., Brito, A.M., Pires, P.S.M.: Analysis of malicious traffic in Modbus/TCP communications. In: Setola, R., Geretshuber, S. (eds.) CRITIS 2008. LNCS, vol. 5508, pp. 200–210. Springer, Heidelberg (2009). https://doi.org/10.1007/978-3-642-03552-4_18
14. Wang, P.B., Chen, F.Y.: Embedded control system with SCADA Modbus network for monitoring heat treating furnace. In: Advanced Materials Research, vol. 1006, pp. 909–912. Trans Tech Publications (2014)

An Automated Launch and Recovery System for USVs Based on the Pneumatic Ejection Mechanism

Shuanghua Zheng, Yang Yang, Yan Peng, Jianxiang Cui$^{(\boxtimes)}$, Junjie Chen, Xingang Jiang, and Yonghui Feng

Shanghai University, Shanghai 200444, China
cuijianxiang@shu.edu.cn

Abstract. Unmanned surface vehicles (USVs) have been widely used in the fields of marine scientific research and submarine exploration. However, the launch and recovery of these vehicles are considerably affected by sea waves, thereby making their operation complicated and dangerous; this is a challenging problem that restricts the successful operation of USVs. This study involved the development of an automated launch and recovery system (L&RS) for a USV. The proposed L&RS is composed of a catapult mechanism, stabilized platform mechanism and docking mechanism. To improve the success rate of the launch and recovery of a USV, the aiming angle of air projectile was calculated, and its validity was verified by simulation. From the results obtained considering a field application, it was confirmed that the developed L&RS could safely and efficiently recover a USV to its mother ship in an actual environment.

Keywords: Unmanned surface vehicle (USV) ·
Launch and recovery system (L&RS) ·
Aiming angle · Pneumatic ejection

1 Introduction

In recent years, with the constant attention paid to the development of marine resources, the technology of unmanned surface vehicles (USVs) has developed rapidly. Compared with common manned surface boats, the USV has the advantages of shallow draft, flexible task loading, wide activity area and low cost of use. It can independently complete tasks such as information collection, inshore island mapping, submarine survey, target search and satellite communication.

Many countries have performed research on USV technology, in which the United States and Israel have attained the most advancements in the research and application of USVs. As early as in 2002, the United States developed the "Spartan Scout" USV with airborne warning capability [1]. In 2009, Furfaro et al. designed the "Nereus" USV, a two-body unmanned boat for river and coastal observation [2]. Israel developed the "Protector" USV for maritime operations

© Springer Nature Switzerland AG 2019
H. Yu et al. (Eds.): ICIRA 2019, LNAI 11742, pp. 289–300, 2019.
https://doi.org/10.1007/978-3-030-27535-8_27

in 2003; this USV is a rigid inflatable vessel with stealth protection and high mobility, and it can be used for anti-terrorism, surveillance, reconnaissance, and electronic warfare [3]. In addition, the "Sentry" USV [4] of Britain, "Inspector" USV [5] of France, "Piraya" USV [6] of Sweden, "UMV-O" USV of Japan, and "Venus" USV of Singapore have also been successfully applied to the fields of environmental monitoring, coastal patrol, marine exploration, etc.

The "Unmanned Systems Integrated Roadmap FY 2013–2038" [7] lists seven key technologies for future USV applications, in which the launch and recovery technology is the key to the successful operation of the USV. The challenges are attributed to the safety and operability of the recovering operation, autonomy and efficiency of the L&RS, and the potential conflicts between the USV and mother ship platform interfaces. To solve these challenges, researchers and engineers have developed L&RSs that can be divided into two types: stern ramp type and davit type. The first type is composed of a set of winches and slideway system. Kern et al. designed a low drag ramp with a plurality of driven wet-traction members, which could be utilized for the launch and recovery of both surface and underwater vehicles [8]. Crane et al. developed a movable endwall mounted on the stern of the ship that could slide the unmanned underwater vehicles (UUV) down. The launch and recovery device included a telescopic arm for capturing and recovering the UUV from the water [9]. In contrast, davit L&RSs are more widely used. The davits are generally installed on one side of the mother ship deck, which can lower or lift the USV. The RHP L&RS developed by the German company Global Davit GmbH has a low center of gravity and high safety performance, and thus, it can safely realize the launch and recovery operation of working boats weighing from $1000-3500\,\mathrm{kg}$ [10]. The davit L&RS designed by British Caley-ocean Systems is equipped with a safe and simple control system that can be applied for boats less than 3.5 tons; it has been used in Japanese fishing patrol boats.

This paper presents an automated L&RS for USVs, based on the pneumatic ejection mechanism, and calculates the aiming angle of air projectile. The paper is organized as follows. Section 2 describes the concept and mechanism of the developed system. The calculation method of aiming angle is given in Sect. 3. The performance test simulation and the field application in the East China Sea are described in Sect. 4. The conclusions and plans for future studies are presented in Sect. 5.

2   Launch and Recovery System (L&RS)

To improve the efficiency and safety, this study developed an automated L&RS for USVs. The L&RS can work in a marine environment with various and uncertain waves and realize autonomous separation and docking of the USV and the mother ship without the presence of an operator in the USV.

2.1   Mechanism

As shown in Fig. 1(a), the developed system is composed of the following sub-systems.

   i. Catapult mechanism: The catapult mechanism has double-canister launchers and projectiles (Fig. 1(b)). If one projectile fails, the other one is activated to improve the success rate. The two ends of the air projectile are connected with a guide rope and an air valve. The air valve is fixed at the rear of the canister launcher, and the other end is connected with an air pump. The air projectile is inflated through the air valve. When the DC motor at the rear of the canister launcher activates the buckle, the air projectile is separated from the air valve and propelled by the stored high-pressure gas.
  ii. Stabilized platform mechanism: The catapult mechanism is mounted on a 2-DOF stabilized platform that can realize pitching and rotation motion (Fig. 1(c)). The initial pitching angle of the launching canister to the horizontal plane is 60°. The launching direction can be adjusted through the stabilized platform, and the range of the azimuth joint and the elevation joint are from −90° to 90° and from 30° to 90°, respectively.
 iii. Docking mechanism: The docking mechanism is used to connect the USV with the davit on the mother ship (Fig. 1(d)), and it consists of a conical dock entrance, a contact switch and a locking mechanism. The conical dock entrance and the conical butt joint form a mother−child envelope, which facilitates the positioning of the conical butt joint. The contact switch is attached at the bottom of the docking mechanism to determine the docking state. The locking mechanism is driven by two linear actuators to realize the releasing or locking of the conical butt joint.

2.2   Control System

The structure of the control system is shown in Fig. 2. The system is protected by a waterproof case and contains an on-board computer and a controller based on STM 32. The on-board computer is used to receive the information measured by the USV sensors and the mother ship sensors. Based on the distance information of the USV from the mother ship and the attitude information of the USV, the computer calculates the desired joint angles of the stabilized platform and transmits them to the controller, and subsequently, the controller drives the stabilized platform to aim the mother ship and launch the air projectile. Once the conical butt joint enters the conical dock entrance, and the contact switch transmits the signal to the on-board computer, it controls the linear actuators to lock the conical butt joint.

2.3   Operation Process

When the mother ship arrives at the mission area, the hoisting boom lifts the USV from the mother ship and lowers it to the sea surface. Then, the locking

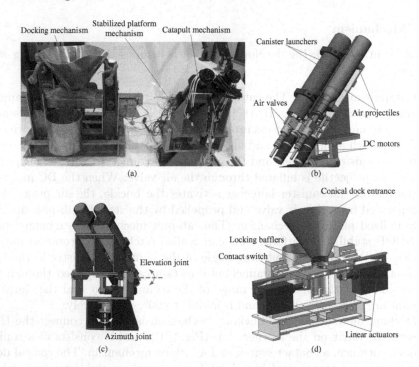

Fig. 1. Schematic of an automated launch and recovery system (L&RS): (a) prototype, (b) catapult mechanism, (c) stabilized platform mechanism, (d) docking mechanism.

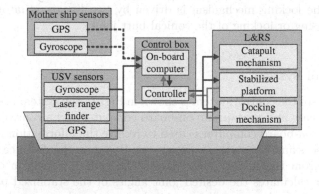

Fig. 2. Control system.

mechanism is unlocked, and the conical butt joint is separated from the docking mechanism. After the mission is completed, the USV is required to be recovered from the sea surface to the mother ship. During this period, the USV needs to overcome the influence of the sea waves and realizes its connection and fixation to the conical butt joint in an unattended state. This process is shown in Fig. 3.

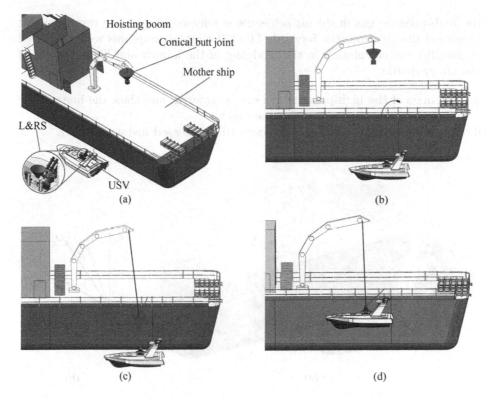

Fig. 3. Operation process of recovering USV: (a) homing and aiming phase, (b) launching phase, (c) docking phase, (d) lifting phase.

i. Homing and aiming phase: The USV navigates to the vicinity of the mother ship, and the control box controls the stabilized platform to compensate the rocking motion of the USV so that the canister launchers are aimed at the target point (Fig. 3(a));

ii. Launching phase: The launching switch is activated, and the air projectile drives the guide rope to launch and drop onto the mother ship; next, the crew on the mother ship recovers the air projectile and passes the guide rope through the hole of the conical butt joint (Fig. 3(b));

iii. Docking phase: The butt joint is slowly slid along the guide rope into the docking mechanism of the USV (Fig. 3(c));

iv. Lifting phase: When the contact switch of the docking mechanism feeds back a signal of good docking status, the locking mechanism locks the conical butt joint, and the hoisting boom lifts the USV onto the mother ship (Fig. 3(d)).

3   Aiming Angle

In this section, the aiming angle of the air projectile is discussed to realize recovery the USV. Once the air projectile is separated from the inflation valve, the high-pressure gas in the air projectile is released to generate reverse thrust to propel the air projectile forward. The following assumptions were employed to simplify the calculation in the modeling of the launch and flight process of the air projectile.

i. The mass of the high-pressure gas can be ignored, and thus, the mass of the air projectile is constant during the flight.
ii. The high-pressure gas in the air projectile is released instantaneously.

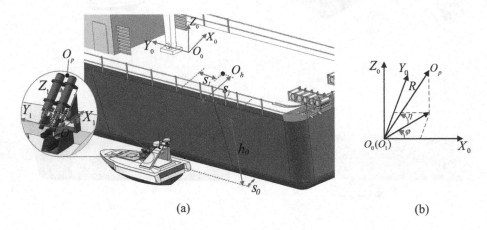

(a)   (b)

Fig. 4. Coordinate systems: (a) overview, (b) aiming angle in the MS-coordinate system.

Based on the distance and orientation between the USV and the mother ship, an appropriate aiming angle is required to ensure that the air projectile drops onto the mother ship. The coordinate systems are established, as shown in Fig. 4(a). $O_0X_0Y_0Z_0$ is the mother ship (MS) coordinate system, where the O_0Y_0 axis points to the bow; the O_0Z_0 axis is perpendicular to the sea level, opposite to the direction of gravity, and the direction of the O_0X_0 axis is determined by the right-hand rule. The port of the canister launcher O_p and the target landing point of the air projectile O_h in the MS-coordinate system are defined as (x_p^0, y_p^0, z_p^0) and (x_h^0, y_h^0, z_h^0), respectively. The distance between the base of the stabilized platform and the port side of the mother ship is s_0; the distance between the stabilized platform and the target landing point along the direction of the O_0Y_0 axis is s_1; the height of the mother ship relative to the USV is h_0; and the distance between the target landing point and the mother ship board is s_j.

To improve the success rate, the center position of the mother ship rear deck is selected as the target landing point of the air projectile. Thus, the relationship between the position of the target landing point and the launch port in the MS-coordinate system satisfy (1).

$$\begin{cases} x_h^0 - x_p^0 = s_0 + s_j \\ y_h^0 - y_p^0 = \text{sgn}(y_h^0 - y_p^0) \cdot s_1 \\ z_h^0 - z_p^0 = h_0 \end{cases} \tag{1}$$

As shown in Fig. 4(b), the azimuth angle φ and the elevation angle η of the stabilized platform in the MS-coordinate system are defined as the angle between the projection of the canister launcher in the horizontal plane and the O_0X_0 axis and the angle between the canister launcher and the horizontal plane, respectively. Thus, φ can be calculated from (2).

$$\varphi = \arctan \frac{y_h^0 - y_p^0}{x_h^0 - x_p^0} = \arctan \frac{\text{sgn}(y_h^0 - y_p^0) \cdot s_1}{s_0 + s_j} \tag{2}$$

During the flight, since the speed of the air projectile is not too high, it is assumed that the resistance is proportional to the first order of the speed. Therefore, the resistance D can be obtained from (3).

$$D = bv \tag{3}$$

where b is the damping coefficient and v is the speed of the air projectile. According to [11], the trajectory of the air projectile is

$$\begin{cases} l_s = \frac{m}{b} v_0 \cos \eta (1 - e^{-\frac{b}{m}t}) \\ l_h = \frac{m^2}{b^2} (\frac{b}{m} v_0 \sin \eta + g)(1 - e^{-\frac{b}{m}t}) - \frac{m}{b} gt \end{cases} \tag{4}$$

where l_s and l_h are, respectively, the horizontal and vertical displacements of the air projectile; m, v_0 and t are the mass, initial velocity and flight time of the air projectile, respectively. According to (4), (5) can be obtained [12,13].

$$l_h = \left(\frac{gm}{v_0 b \cos \eta} + \tan \eta \right) l_s + \frac{m^2 g}{b^2} \ln \left(1 - \frac{b l_s}{v_0 m \cos \eta} \right) \tag{5}$$

According to [14], (5) can be solved analytically, and the result can be written as the Lambert $W(x)$ function in closed form. Thus, the elevation angle of the air projectile can be obtained as

$$\eta = \arcsin \left[\frac{cW(\frac{c^2-1}{e} e^{\frac{b^2 l_h}{m^2 g}})}{c^2 - 1 - W(\frac{c^2-1}{e} e^{\frac{b l_h}{m^2 g}})} \right] \tag{6}$$

where $c = \frac{bv_0}{mg}$. The Lambert function is a many-valued complex function as (7).

$$W(x)e^{W(x)} = x \tag{7}$$

where x is a complex number. The detailed relationship between x and the Lambert $W(x)$ function can be found in [12].

Therefore, it can be confirmed that the elevation angle η depends on the position of the target landing point, the initial velocity v_0 of the air projectile, and the damping coefficient b. As shown in Fig. 4(a), the horizontal displacement l_s and the vertical displacement l_h of the air projectile when it falls to the target landing point are

$$
\begin{cases}
l_s = \sqrt{(s_0 + s_j)^2 + (-s_1)^2} \\
l_h = h_0
\end{cases}
\tag{8}
$$

Thus, when aiming at the target landing point, the elevation angle η of the air projectile can be obtained from (9).

$$
\eta = \arcsin\left[\frac{cW(\frac{c^2-1}{e}e^{\frac{b^2 h_0}{m^2 g}})}{c^2 - 1 - W(\frac{c^2-1}{e}e^{\frac{b^2 h_0}{m^2 g}})}\right]
\tag{9}
$$

Therefore, the aiming angle of the air projectile in the MS-coordinate system (Fig. 4(b)) can be obtained from (2) and (9) from the measured distance between the stabilized platform and the target landing point in the three-axis direction.

4   Field Experiment

4.1   Aiming Experiment

The experiments were first preformed to test the error of the aiming angle calculated in Sect. 3. The parameters are listed in Table. 1. When the elevation angles are $30°$, $45°$, $60°$ and $75°$ respectively, the flight trajectories of the air projectile are shown in the red curves in the Fig. 5. It can be confirmed that the height and the distance of the actual experiments were smaller than those of the predict results, and the error increased with the increase of the elevation angles. It is attributed to the influence from the guide rope, the lateral wind, etc.

Table 1. Simulation parameters

Parameters	Value
Air projectile mass m	$2.13\,\mathrm{kg}$
Initial velocity v_0	$19.60\,\mathrm{m/s}$
Damping coefficient b	$5.88\mathrm{e}{-}02$
Acceleration of gravity g	$9.82\,\mathrm{m/s^2}$

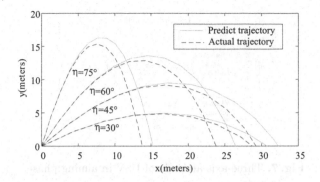

Fig. 5. Predict and actual trajectories of air projectile.

4.2 Launch and Recovery Experiment

In a certain sea area, we carried out field experiments on the L&RS. After the preparations were completed, the USV was launched at 10:00 am. It successfully completed the investigation of seawater pollution, determined the location of the sunken ship, and sampled the seawater from the accident waters. Later, the USV returned to the vicinity of the mother ship at 1:00 pm to prepare for recovery.

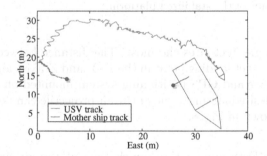

Fig. 6. Track of USV and mother ship in homing phase.

Homing Phase. Figure 6 shows the trajectory of the mother ship and the USV within the homing phase. The mother ship was stopped, and its position continuously changed due to the influence of sea waves. Guided the navigation system, the USV finally stopped approximately 3 m away from the port side of the mother ship with the same heading.

Aiming Phase. After the propeller was stalled, the USV switched to the aiming phase. The attitude of the USV under the disturbance of the sea wave is shown in Fig. 7. It can be seen that the change in the attitude of the USV is irregular,

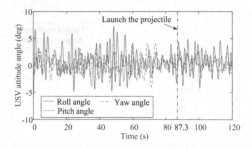

Fig. 7. Three-axis attitude of USV in aiming phase.

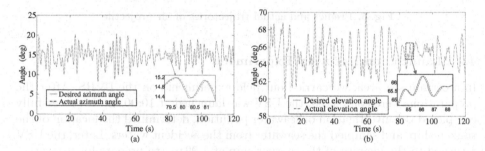

Fig. 8. Actual rotation angle and desired rotation angle of (a) the azimuth joint, and (b) the elevation joint of the stabilized platform.

and the rolling angle fluctuates the most. The distance between the stabilized platform and the target landing point in the X, Y and Z-axis can be measured by the laser rangefinder and GPS positioning system mounted on the USV. Based on the data, the desired aiming angle of the air projectile can be calculated from (2) and (9), as shown in Fig. 8.

Launch Phase. Determining the launch time of the air projectile requires the consideration of various factors such as the three-axis attitude of the USV, movement state of the stabilized platform, and aiming angle of the air projectile. In the experiment, the change in the attitude of the USV due to the sea waves is rapid and irregular (Fig. 7), which may cause the projectile to deviate from the desired trajectory and fall into the water, thereby leading to failure of the recovery process. In this experiment, We chose to fire air projectile when the three-axis attitude deviation of the USV approaches zero. The air projectile was launched at 87.3 s, and the air projectile landed accurately on the deck of mother ship.

Docking and Lifting Phase. After the air projectile landed on the deck, the crew untied the guide rope from the air projectile and passed the guide rope through the conical butt joint; next, they operated the hoisting boom to drop

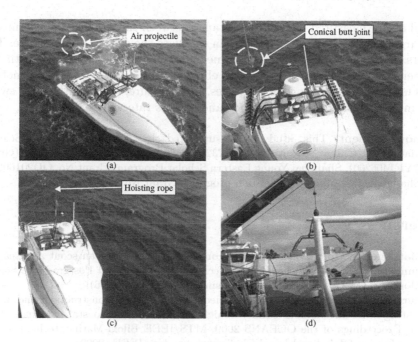

Fig. 9. Launch and recovery process in field application.

the conical butt joint along the guide rope (Figs. 9(b)(c)). When the contact sensor detected that the conical butt joint had entered the conical dock entrance, the locking mechanism was activated to lock the conical butt joint. Then, the hoisting rope on the hoisting boom was retracted, and the USV was lifted and placed on the mother ship deck (Fig. 9(d)).

4.3   Discussion

The process of recovering USV took approximately 5 min from the homing phase to the launch phase and 24 min for the docking and lifting phases. A total of eight operators participated in the launch and recovery operation, including a crane operator, a commander, and other people responsible for pulling the USV in both directions of the head and stern through ropes during the lifting process to reduce the sway of the USV. In this field experiment, the air projectile was successfully launched onto the deck of the mother ship. During the recovery process, there was no crew onboard the USV, which greatly reduced the danger of the launch and recovery operation.

5   Conclusion

This study involved the development of a L&RS for the USVs. It is composed of the catapult mechanism, stabilized platform mechanism and docking mechanism.

Based on the measured data of the distance between the stabilized platform and the target landing point, the system can calculate the desired aiming angle. The results of the field experiment confirmed that the developed L&RS with the compensation strategy can safely and efficiently recover USVs to their mother ships under the interference of sea waves. In the future, reducing the USV swing and improving the recovery efficiency and success rate will be considered.

Acknowledgment. This study was supported by National Natural Science Foundation of China (Grant No. 61773254), Shanghai Sailing Program (Grant No.17YF1406200), Shanghai Young Eastern Scholar Program (Grant No. QD2016029), and Shanghai civil-military integration program (Grant No. JMRH-2018-1043).

References

1. Matthew, R.: Operational manning considerations for spartan scout and sea fox unmanned surface vehicles (USV). Technical report, Naval Postgraduate School Monterey CA Graduate School of Business and Public (2006)
2. Furfaro, T.C., Dusek, J.E., von Ellenrieder, K.D.: Design, construction, and initial testing of an autonomous surface vehicle for riverine and coastal reconnaissance. In: Proceedings of the OCEANS 2009, MTS/IEEE Biloxi-Marine Technology for Our Future: Global and Local Challenges, pp. 1–6. IEEE (2009)
3. Breivik, M., Hovstein, V.E., Fossen, T.I.: Straight-line target tracking for unmanned surface vehicles. Model. Ident. Control **29**(4), 131–149 (2008)
4. Liu, Z., Zhang, Y., Yu, X., Yuan, C.: Unmanned surface vehicles: an overview of developments and challenges. Annu. Rev. Control **41**, 71–93 (2016)
5. Yang, W.R., Chen, C.Y., Hsu, C.M., Tseng, C.J., Yang, W.C.: Multifunctional inshore survey platform with unmanned surface vehicles. Int. J. Autom. Smart Technol. **1**(2), 19–25 (2011)
6. Sonnenburg, C.R., Woolsey, C.A.: Modeling, identification, and control of an unmanned surface vehicle. J. Field Robot. **30**(3), 371–398 (2013)
7. DoD, U.: Unmanned Systems Integrated Roadmap: Fy2013-2038. Diane Publishing, Washington, DC (2013)
8. Kern, F.R.: Launch and recovery devices for water vehicles and methods of use. US Patent 7,581,507, September 2009
9. Crane, J.W., Portmann, H.: Launch and recovery system for unmanned underwater vehicles. US Patent 6,779,475, August 2004
10. Bergmann, H.D.: Device for a watercraft for picking up and launching boats. US Patent 7,815,394, October 2010
11. Morales, D.A.: Exact expressions for the range and the optimal angle of a projectile with linear drag. Can. J. Phys. **83**(1), 67–83 (2011)
12. Hu, H., Zhao, Y., Guo, Y.J.: Analysis of linear resisted projectile motion using the Lambert W function. Acta Mech. **223**(2), 441–447 (2012)
13. Packel, E.W., Yuen, D.S.: Projectile motion with resistance and the Lambert W function. College Math. J. **35**(5), 337–350 (2004)
14. Warburton, R.D., Wang, J.: Analysis of asymptotic projectile motion with air resistance using the Lambert W function. Am. J. Phys. **72**(11), 1404–1407 (2004)

Intelligent Robots for Environment Detection or Fine Manipulation

The UAV Path Planning Method Based on Lidar

Lanxiang Zheng, Ping Zhang$^{(\boxtimes)}$, Jia Tan, and Mingxuan Chen

School of Computer Science and Engineering, South China University of Technology,
Guangzhou 510006, Guangdong, China
pzhang@scut.edu.cn

Abstract. This paper designs a path planning algorithm based on a two-dimensional lidar. The algorithm is divided into two steps: static global path planning and dynamic local path planning. Static global path planning relies on the risk index map established by the known environment. In addition, a multi-objective optimization heuristic function is constructed to obtain the optimal path. Dynamic local path planning is enabled when UAV encounter obstacles. To overcome the limitations that lidar can only obtain partial obstacle information (the shape and size cannot be obtained), local target points are introduced into the dynamic path planning algorithm. In order to avoid obstacles and return to the planned path quickly, a multi-objective optimization problem based on energy consumption is constructed. Experimental results show that the path planning method can effectively complete the UAV path planning task. And UAV quickly return to the original path after avoiding obstacles.

Keywords: UAV · Static global path planning ·
Dynamic local path planning · Lidar · Risk index map · Avoidance

1 Introduction

In the last decade, Unmanned Aerial Vehicles (UAVs) [1] received an increasing attention from academia. UAV is an autonomous, semi-autonomous or remote-controlled unmanned aerial vehicle with light weight, small size, high maneuverability, good concealment and adaptability. UAVs can perform dangerous, difficult-to-operate air applications and reduce costs [2]. It has been widely used in search and rescue [3], aerial mapping [4], target tracking [5], autonomous flight formation [6] and collaborative search [7]. Moreover, path planning is one of the most important guarantees for the success of these applications.

Path planning is the process of determining a collision-free pathway between a UAVs current position and its destination. There are many algorithms for path planning and have good performance. The potential field method [8], vector field

This project is supported by the Guangdong Provincial Science and Technology Project (2017B010116001).

© Springer Nature Switzerland AG 2019
H. Yu et al. (Eds.): ICIRA 2019, LNAI 11742, pp. 303–314, 2019.
https://doi.org/10.1007/978-3-030-27535-8_28

histogram method [9] and Voronoi diagram method [10] are typical geometric methods, which use the geometric information of obstacles in the map as the input of the algorithm to obtain the path. The graph search approach aims to find the shortest path between two vertices in a certain graph, where the A* algorithm is known to be effective at finding the shortest path to a target destination while avoiding obstacles [11]. In addition, there are speed space methods that consider the shape, kinematics and dynamics constraints of the vehicle, such as the curvature velocity method [12] and the dynamic window method [13]. Although these algorithms can provide path for UAV, they more dependent on GPS information and never consider the detection range of sensors carried on the UAV.

The environmental awareness sensors carried on UAV can be divided into three categories, the vision sensor system [14], the ultrasound system [15], and the lidar system [16]. The visual sensor system has strict requirements for the light so it is unsuitable for all-weather flight systems. The cost of the ultrasound system is low, but the ultrasonic wave emitted to the obstacle is sensitive to the surface of the obstacle, which resulting in the obstacle information mixed with much noise. The lidar system has the characteristics of long detection range, high measurement accuracy, high angular resolution, good directionality, and adaptability to the environment. Therefore, We use lidar as the environmental awareness system for UAV.

The remainder of the paper is organized as follows. The UAV position uncertainty model and motion model are defined in Sect. 2. In Sect. 3, the static global path planning algorithm based on risk index map is introduced. Section 4 introduces the local target point selection strategy and dynamic path planning algorithm. The simulation results of the path planning algorithm are presented in Sect. 5. Finally Sect. 6 concludes the present study.

2   System Model

Path planning can be divided into static global path planning and dynamic local path planning [17]. Static global path planning plans a feasible path before UAV takes off. Dynamic local path planning works when encountering obstacles, to avoid obstacles. In order to plan a optimal path, we construct the following system model.

2.1   Position Uncertainty Model

UAVs generally use GPS as a global positioning system. GPS positioning accuracy is lower in civil field, which has a horizontal accuracy of 5 to 10 m with 95% confidence [18]. To better estimate the position, we use a simple two-dimensional Gaussian model [19]. Probability is used to estimate the location of the UAV, and the UAV position probability function p can be expressed as

$$p(x_g, y_g, \sigma_x, \sigma_y) = \frac{1}{2\pi\sigma_x\sigma_y}e^{-\left(\frac{(x-x_g)^2}{2\sigma_x^2} + \frac{(y-y_g)^2}{2\sigma_y^2}\right)} \tag{1}$$

Where σ_x and σ_y are the standard deviations, (x_g, y_g) is the coordinate of the position obtained by the GPS, and $p(x_g, y_g)$ is the probability of the UAV at position (x, y). Figure 1(a) shows the location distribution of the UAV. The darker the color in the Fig. 1(a), the greater the probability that the UAV will be in that position.

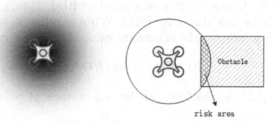

(a) Position uncertainty (b) UAV collision obstacle
model model

Fig. 1. Probability model (Color figure online)

The distribution of the UAV position satisfies the PauTa criterion, that is, the probability of p in interval $(\mu - \sigma, \mu + \sigma)$ is 0.6827, the probability in interval $(\mu - 2\sigma, \mu + 2\sigma)$ is 0.9545, and the probability in $(\mu - 3\sigma, \mu + 3\sigma)$ is 0.9973. Since the probability in $(\mu - 3\sigma, \mu + 3\sigma)$ is almost close to 1, so we ignores the position of UAV is out of $(\mu - 3\sigma, \mu + 3\sigma)$.

When a UAV is flying, it may collide due to GPS error, as shown in Fig. 1(b) where the obstacle is represented by gray areas, and the red area represents the risk area. So given an uncertain (x_g, y_g), the risk of collision can be denoted by

$$P_r(x_g, y_g) = \int_{\psi \in \Psi} p(x_g, y_g, \sigma_x, \sigma_y) d\psi \tag{2}$$

Where Ψ represents the risk area shown in Fig. 1(b).

3 Static Global Path Planning

The static path planning mainly relies on the known distribution of obstacles, and provides a feasible path before the UAV starts the task.

3.1 Risk Index Map Construction

The path planning algorithm in this paper relies on the Risk Index map (RIM). The RIM is made up of risk index for each point in the map, and reflecting the level of risk at that point. The point near the obstacle has a high risk index and the far ones have low risk index. Priority is given to points with lower risk index when planning a path.

Therefore, we construct a RIM with the start and target points, and initialize the risk index of each point to zero. Based on Formula 2, we define the RIM as

$$RIM(s) = \frac{10^{P_r(x,y)}}{10} \tag{3}$$

Where $s(x,y)$ is the coordinates of a point in RIM, $P_r(x,y)$ is the probability of collision can be calculated by Eq. 2. When a point is affected by multiple obstacles, its risk index is the maximum value of each risk index at that point:

$$RIM(s) = \max\{RIM(s_i)\} \tag{4}$$

Where $RIM(s_i)$ is the risk index of the i-th obstacle at point s.

3.2 Multi-objective Path Planning

In order to get a practical path, a multi-objective path planning (MOPP) problem is formulated. In this paper we mainly consider the following constraints:

(1) Safety constraint. The UAV's own global positioning system and the inertial measurement unit have errors, so that the UAV cannot obtain its own certain motion state and the specific information of the obstacle during flight, which may increase the risk of collisions.

(2) UAV motion characteristics constraints. The direction and speed of UAV should be dynamically changed depending on the environment. Cruises of constant speed are established in most cases, but the speed should be slowed down when moving around the obstacles.

(3) Flight time constraints. Flight time is one of the important constraints in path planning, and limited by flight speed, flight path, etc. The shorter the path is, the less time would be spent. Therefore, we need to find the optimal path as short as possible.

According to the Heuristic function in A* algorithm, and considering the above three constraints, our optimization strategy and heuristic function are defined as follows:

(1) Dynamic speed adjustment. The UAV's speed is dynamically adjusted, maintaining high-speed motion without obstacles, and slowing down near obstacles. Assume that the normal speed of UAV is V, the speed after adjustment is V', and the conversion between V and V' at position s is as follows:

$$V'(s) = \begin{cases} \frac{V(s)}{\alpha RIM(s) + (1-\alpha)} & RIM(s) \neq 0 \\ V(s) & RIM(s) = 0 \end{cases} \tag{5}$$

(2) Heuristic function. The heuristic function estimate the cost by calculating the distance between the current position point and the target point. To better estimate the cost, the speed constraint is added to the heuristic function, and the improved heuristic function $h(x)$ is defined as follows:

$$h(x) = distance(x, STOP)/V' \tag{6}$$

Where the $distance()$ function calculates the distance between two points, and $STOP$ represents the target point. We use $g(x)$ to represent the cost from the starting point $START$ to current position, then it can be defined as

$$g(x) = distance(START, x) \tag{7}$$

And the heuristic function is defined as

$$f(x) = g(x) + h(x) \tag{8}$$

Integrating the previous chapters, we get static global path planning algorithm as shown in Algorithm 1.

Algorithm 1. Static global path planning

Input: RIM—Risk Index Map; START—start point; STOP—goal point; α—weighted factor; pos—position of UAV; V—speed of UAV

Output: PATH = set containing feasible path; VELOCITY = set of velocity for each path point in RIM

1: GMAP = set containing all point in RIM
2: COST = cost set of position in RIM
3: NEARBY = set containing 8 neighbors of pos
4: pos = START
5: update NEARBY
6: **while** pos != STOP **do**
7:     **for** point in NEARBY **do**
8:         V' calculated by Formula. 5
9:         VELOCITY[point] = V'
10:        COST[point] = distance(point, STOP)/V'
11:    **end for**
12:    next = smallest cost point in NEARBY
13:    PATH += next
14:    pos = next
15:    GMAP -= NEARBY
16:    update NEARBY
17:    **if** next == STOP **then**
18:        return PATH and VELOCITY
19:    **end if**
20: **end while**
21: return find path fail

---

4   Dynamic Local Path Planning

Static path planning relies on offline maps. Offline maps differ from the actual environment in some details, so there may be risk areas on the planned path. Therefore, the path needs to be dynamically planned when the risk is discovered.

In this paper, a 2D lidar is used as an environmental awareness system for UAVs. It returns obstacle information includes angle and distance information of the obstacle relative to the lidar start position. Let α_i be the angle of ith data, and ρ_i be the distance.

4.1   Update RIM

While the UAV is flying according to the planned path, the lidar is detecting obstacles around it. The UAV updates the RIM when it encounters an obstacle that does not match the known environmental map. Before updating RIM, we need to convert the data from the lidar coordinate system to the global coordinate system, and the conversion formula is as follows

$$\begin{cases} x_{ig} = \lfloor (x_c + \rho_i \sin \alpha_i \cos \theta)/l_g \rfloor \\ y_{ig} = \lfloor (y_c + \rho_i cos\alpha_i \sin \theta)/l_g \rfloor \end{cases} \tag{9}$$

After the conversion, we calculate the new RIM using Eq. 3, and update RIM according to Eq. 4.

4.2   Local Target Point Dynamic Selection

Lidar can obtain information about obstacles close to the lidar side (such as distance and angle), but it is difficult to obtain all the characteristic information (such as size, shape, material, etc.). Most sensors have such limitations like lidars, but most research on path planning ignores this. As shown in Fig. 2, the four obstacles in the figure are lines (angles different) in the obstacle information returned by lidar, but actually have different shapes. Simply expanding the obstacles into circular or rectangle based on limited local information, which is difficult to apply to various obstacles and affecting the accuracy of dynamic path planning.

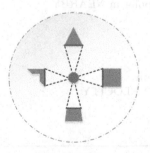

Fig. 2. Schematic diagram of lidar detection obstacles

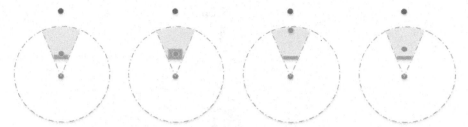

(a) The local target (b) The local target (c) The local target (d) A suitable local
point is close to ob- point in the obstacle point away from ob- target point
stacle   stacle

Fig. 3. Local target point selection (Color figure online)

Therefore, when encountering obstacles that affect the UAV along the
planned path, we need to perform dynamic path planning. First, we should
select a point from the planned path as the local target point of the dynamic
local path planning, and current position of UAV is the starting point. In order
to return to the original path as soon as possible, the first point after the path
occluded by the obstacle is selected as the local target point, and then determine whether it meets the judgment condition. The location of the local target
point may be as shown in the four cases in Fig. 3. The blue dot represents the
location of the UAV, orange represents the selected local target point, the red
dot represents the final target point, the dark gray square represents the obstacle, and the light gray represents the unknown area blocked by the obstacle.
In Fig. 3(a), the local target point is close to the obstacle and can be reached,
but it will affect the safety of UAV. In Fig. 3(b), the local target point is within
the obstacle and is unreachable. In Fig. 3(c), the local target is too far away to
return to the static global path as soon as possible. The target point selection in
Fig. 3(d) is appropriate. In order to select a more appropriate local target point,
the following conditions need to be satisfied:

(1) Local target point is safe and reachable. The local target point is outside the
influence of the obstacle, and can be reached. That is, we can use SIM to replace
the cost of risk at the local target point.

$$\cos t_r(s) = \sum_{i \in O} SIM(t_i) \tag{10}$$

Where O represents the set of obstacles, t is the local target point, and $SIM(t_i)$
represents the risk index at the point t with ith obstacle.

(2) Minimal cost. For missions that need to cruise along a given path, the longer
the UAV is flying along the planned path, the better the mission will be. In this
paper, the penalty cost for flying deviate from the planned path is constructed,
as show in Fig. 4. The optimization goal can be defined here as

$$cost_c = \mu \times distance(P, GOAL) + distance(COAL, STOP) \tag{11}$$

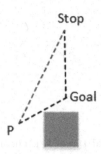

Fig. 4. Return to the original path

According to Eqs. 10 and 11, we can get the final optimization goal is

$$cost = \kappa \cos_r + \tau \cos_c \qquad (12)$$

Where $\mu(\mu > 1)$ is penalty factor for flying deviate from the planned path, κ and τ are adjustment parameters. Then, the point selected from the planned path, and which minimizes the Formula 12 is the appropriate local target point. At last, we show the dynamic local path planning algorithm in Algorithm 2 and the integral path planning algorithm 3.

Algorithm 2. Dynamic local path planning

Input: RIM,COST,GMAP—was constructed in Algorithm 1; PATH—planned path;
    STOP—goal point; pos—position of UAV;
Output: PATH—path after replanned
 1: **if** encounter obstacles **then**
 2:    **for** point in PATH **do**
 3:        find the minimum cost point using Equation. 12
 4:    **end for**
 5:    GOAL = minimum cost point
 6:    delete the point between pos and GOAL
 7:    NEARBY = set containing 8 neighbors of pos
 8:    **while** pos != GOAL **do**
 9:        update the RIM and COST
10:        next = smallest cost point in NEARBY
11:        add next to PATH behind pos and in front of GOAL
12:        pos = next
13:        GMAP -= NEARBY
14:        update NEARBY
15:        **if** next == GOAL **then**
16:            return PATH
17:        **end if**
18:    **end while**
19: **end if**

Algorithm 3. Path planning algorithm

Input: STOP—goal point; MAP–known environmental map
Output: PATH—set containing feasible path;
  1: RIM = construct RIM using Equation. 3 and 4 based on MAP
  2: PATH = plan path using Algorithm. 1
  3: **while** encounter obstacles **do** dynamic plan and update PATH using Algorithm. 2
  4:    **if** find STOP **then**
  5:       return success.
  6:    **end if**
  7: **end while**

---

5 Simulation

5.1 Simulation in MATLAB

In order to verify the feasibility of the algorithm, we simulated the algorithm on MATLAB and Gazebo. The algorithm is simulated in MATLAB under Windows system. The main hardware parameters of the computer are Intel(R) Core i7-670 CPU @ 3.40 GHz and 8.00 GB memory, the operating system is Windows 10 64-bit home Chinese version, and the MATLAB version is 2018a.

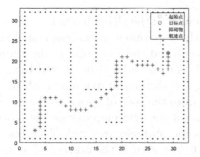 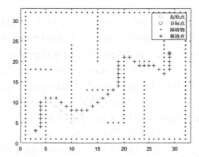

(a) The result of static global planning   (b) The result of static global planning and dynamic local planning

Fig. 5. The result of path planning algorithm (Color figure online)

In the 35×35 map, we randomly set up obstacles as known maps, setting the range that the UAV can detect is 5. We use the static global path planing algorithm to plan a path show in Fig. 5(a). The green circle represents the starting point, the red circle represents the target point, the black point is the obstacle, and the blue point is the path obtained by using the global static path planning.

During the flight, we added some new obstacles in the map. The UAV uses the dynamic path planning algorithm to re-plan the path when it detects obstacles affecting flight. The re-plan path is shown in Fig. 5(b). The pink point is an

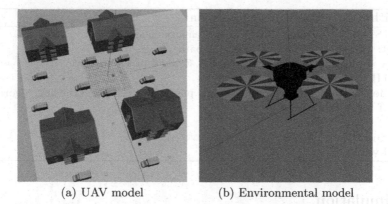

(a) UAV model   (b) Environmental model

Fig. 6. Models in Gazebo (Color figure online)

obstacle that does not exist in the known environmental map, and the light blue point is the path replanned by the dynamic path planning algorithm. Through Fig. 5(b), we can find that the UAV quickly returns to the original path after replanning, and reaches the final target point.

5.2 Simulation in GAZEBO

To further verify the algorithm, we further simulated the algorithm in the Gazebo under the same system. Figure 6(a) shows the experimental environment built in Gazebo, the blue point is the starting point and the red point is the target point. The UAV model is shown in Fig. 6(b), and the lidar is in the red box.

Under the action of static path planning algorithm and dynamic path planning algorithm, the UAV successfully moves from the starting point to the target point. Figure 7(b) shows the real-time update of the grid map during the movement. In the Fig. 7(c), the dark gray area is the obstacle area, the black line is the path that the UAV moves, and the light gray area is the obstacle-free area or the unknown area.

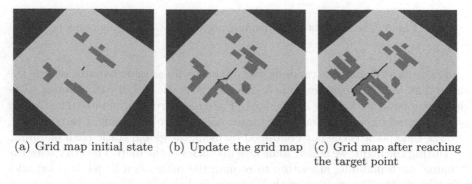

(a) Grid map initial state   (b) Update the grid map   (c) Grid map after reaching
                                                             the target point

Fig. 7. The update of grid map

6   Conclusion

In this paper, two-dimensional lidar is used to sense obstacles in the environment, and the static global path planning algorithm and dynamic local path planning algorithm on the UAV are realized. The feasibility and practicability of the algorithm are fully proved by simulation in MATLAB and GAZEBO.

Through the analysis of the uncertainty of UAV's position, the uncertainty is converted into the collision probability with the obstacle, and the RIM is constructed. Rely on RIM and change the speed to ensure the safety of the UAV. The avoidance of unknown structural feature obstacles is realized by dynamically selecting the target point, and quickly return to the original path by computing the minimum cost.

This paper fully considers the uncertainty of UAV's position and the incompleteness of the sensor. The path planning algorithm solves the problem of the difference between the known map and the actual environment during the flight, and can better avoid obstacles. The research results in the paper have a good effect on path planning and obstacle avoidance.

References

1. Saripalli, S., Montgomery, J.F., Sukhatme, G.S.: Visually guided landing of an unmanned aerial vehicle. IEEE Trans. Robot. Autom. **19**(3), 371–380 (2003). https://doi.org/10.1109/TRA.2003.810239
2. Sinopoli, B., Micheli, M., Donato, G., Koo, T.J.: Vision based navigation for an unmanned aerial vehicle. In: IEEE International Conference on Robotics and Automation, pp. 1757–1764, May 2001. https://doi.org/10.1109/ROBOT.2001.932864
3. Zhao, W., Meng, Q., Chung, P.W.H.: A heuristic distributed task allocation method for multivehicle multitask problems and its application to search and rescue scenario. IEEE Trans. Cybern. **46**(4), 902–915 (2016). https://doi.org/10.1109/TCYB.2015.2418052
4. Ni, W., et al.: Mapping three-dimensional structures of forest canopy using UAV stereo imagery: evaluating impacts of forward overlaps and image resolutions with LiDAR data as reference. IEEE J. Sel. Top. Appl. Earth Obs. Remote Sens. **11**(10), 3578–3589 (2018). https://doi.org/10.1109/JSTARS.2018.2867945
5. Zengin, U., Dogan, A.: Real-time target tracking for autonomous UAVs in adversarial environments: a gradient search algorithm. IEEE Trans. Robot. **23**(2), 294–307 (2007). https://doi.org/10.1109/TRO.2006.889490
6. Liao, F., Teo, R., Wang, J.L., Dong, X., Lin, F., Peng, K.: Distributed formation and reconfiguration control of VTOL UAVs. IEEE Trans. Control Syst. Technol. **25**(1), 270–277 (2016). https://doi.org/10.1109/TCST.2016.2547952
7. Bertuccelli, L.F., Cummings, M.L.: Operator choice modeling for collaborative UAV visual search tasks. IEEE Trans. Syst. Man Cybern. **42**(5), 1088–1099 (2012). https://doi.org/10.1109/TSMCA.2012.2189875
8. Lifen, L., Ruoxin, S., Shuandao, L., Jiang, W.: Path planning for UAVS based on improved artificial potential field method through changing the repulsive potential function. In: Guidance, Navigation and Control Conference, pp. 2011–2015, August 2016. https://doi.org/10.1109/CGNCC.2016.7829099

9. Yim, W.J., Park, J.B.: Analysis of mobile robot navigation using vector field histogram according to the number of sectors, the robot speed and the width of the path. In: International Conference on Control, pp. 1037–1040, October 2014. https://doi.org/10.1109/ICCAS.2014.6987943

10. Takahashi, O., Schilling, R.: Motion planning in a plane using generalized Voronoi diagrams. IEEE Trans. Robot. Autom. **5**(2), 143–150 (1989). https://doi.org/10.1109/70.88035

11. Rabin, S.: A* speed optimizations and A* aesthetic optimizations. In: Deloura, M. (ed.) Game Programming Gems, pp. 264–287. Charles Rive Media (2000)

12. Jayasinghe, J.A.S., Athauda, A.M.B.G.D.A.: Smooth trajectory generation algorithm for an unmanned aerial vehicle (UAV) under dynamic constraints: using a quadratic Bezier curve for collision avoidance. In: 2016 Manufacturing & Industrial Engineering Symposium (MIES), October 2016. https://doi.org/10.1109/MIES.2016.7780258

13. Fox, D., Burgard, W., Thrun, S.: The dynamic window approach to collision avoidance. IEEE Robot. Autom. Mag., pp. 23–33. (1997). https://doi.org/10.1109/100.580977

14. Dolgov, D., Thrun, S., Montemerlo, M., Diebel, J.: Path planning for autonomous vehicles in unknown semi-structured environments. Int. J. Robot. Res. **29**(5), 485–501 (2010). https://doi.org/10.1177/0278364909359210

15. Chen, B., Cai, Z., Xiao, Z., Yu, J., Liu, L.: Real-time detection of dynamic obstacle using laser radar. In: 2008 The 9th International Conference for Young Computer Scientists, pp. 1728–1732, November 2008. https://doi.org/10.1109/ICYCS.2008.357

16. Odelga, M., Stegagno, P., Bülthoff, H.H.: Obstacle detection, tracking and avoidance for a teleoperated UAV. In: IEEE International Conference on Robotics and Automation, pp. 2984–2990, May 2016. https://doi.org/10.1109/ICRA.2016.7487464

17. Yin, C., Xiao, Z., Cao, X., Xi, X., Yang, P., Wu, D.: Offline and online search: UAV multi-objective path planning under dynamic urban environment. IEEE Internet Things J. **5**(2), 546–558 (2017). https://doi.org/10.1109/JIOT.2017.2717078

18. Mcdonald, K.D.: The modernization of GPS: plans, new capabilities and the future relationship to Galileo. Positioning **1**(1), 1–17 (2002). https://doi.org/10.5081/jgps.1.1.1

19. Rathbun, D., Kragelund, S., Pongpunwattana, A., Capozzi, B.: An evolution based path planning algorithm for autonomous motion of a UAV through uncertain environments. In: Digital Avionics Systems Conference, pp. 8.D.2-1–8.D.2-12, October 2002. https://doi.org/10.1109/DASC.2002.1052946

CSLAM and GPS Based Navigation for Multi-UAV Cooperative Transportation System

Hang Yu[1,2], Fan Zhang[1,2(✉)], and Panfeng Huang[1,2(✉)]

[1] Research Center for Intelligent Robotics, School of Astronautics,
Northwestern Polytechnical University, Xian 710072, Shaanxi, China
yuhang@mail.nwpu.edu.cn, {fzhang,pfhuang}@nwpu.edu.cn
[2] National Key Laboratory of Aerospace Flight Dynamics,
Northwestern Polytechnical University, Xian 710072, Shaanxi, China

Abstract. Multi-UAV cooperative technology is developing vigorously due to its convenience and expandability. In the future, more and more military or civilian transport tasks will be accomplished by multi-UAV. At present, the biggest problem of long-distance transportation is that GPS signal is not available throughout the whole journal. In this paper, we propose a complete navigation scheme for the multi-UAV cooperative transportation system in the two cases with or without GPS signal, which is designed based on visual simultaneous localization and mapping (SLAM) and GPS. If the multi-UAV cooperative system is in the GPS-denied environment, the system will make real-time positioning and mapping through collaborative SLAM (CSLAM). In this case, the relative position between the UAVs, and their absolute positions as well are available under the proposed scheme. On the contrary, if the multi-UAV cooperative transportation system can detect the GPS signal, GPS will provide a high accuracy correction of the CSLAM, and finally output more precise information compared to CSLAM only. Moreover, the navigation scheme can switch automatically according to the presence or absence of GPS signal in the process of task without human intervention. Different data sets are used for experiments, including multi-UAV CSLAM, and the fusion of CSLAM and GPS. The experiment results show the efficiency and accuracy of the proposed navigation scheme.

Keywords: Multi-UAV · CSLAM · GPS · Stereo vision · Navigation · Map fusion

1 Introduction

Multi-robot cooperative operation technologies are developing in recent years. No matter it is a ground mobile robot, an aerial UAV, or even a space robot, the cooperative operation ability based on multi-robot is much stronger than that of a single robot. To such a system, multi-robot cooperative navigation is still a big problem. Both the positions of each robot in the environment and the relative positions of the robots with high precision are necessary for navigation, specifically for the long-distance cooperative operation. However, to our best knowledge, there is no complete

© Springer Nature Switzerland AG 2019
H. Yu et al. (Eds.): ICIRA 2019, LNAI 11742, pp. 315–326, 2019.
https://doi.org/10.1007/978-3-030-27535-8_29

multi-robot cooperative navigation scheme for outdoor use, especially in GPS-uncertainly environment.

At present, GPS is the main method to get navigation information for outdoor multi-robot cooperative operation. However, in some remote areas with complex environment, due to the lack of GPS signal, many UAVs will lose their navigation ability. Moreover, UAV formation flying requires accurate relative position of UAV, which cannot be achieved by GPS alone. Real-time kinematic (RTK) has a very high outdoor positioning accuracy, and its accuracy can reach centimeter level. However, RTK is extremely expensive and requires a ground station, so RTK cannot work well outside its signal range. The development of visual SLAM solves the problem of autonomous navigation of robots in the GPS-Denied environment, and each robot only needs a USB camera with low cost. However, to solve the navigation problem of multi-UAV cooperative operation, it is not feasible to use traditional SLAM, because the traditional SLAM can't obtain the relative position and attitude information between UAVs. CSLAM is designed to allocate the computational load to different machines. Each client has its own location and mapping function. The server is responsible for map fusion and global optimization. If CSLAM is used to obtain the navigation information of the multi-robot cooperative operation system, we cannot only obtain the relative positions of the robots but also their positions in the environment. However, the process of CSLAM is an open loop, so the navigation error will increase with time.

Many scholars have published articles on autonomous navigation of multi-robot cooperative operation. In [1], an advanced vision-aided flocking system for UAV is proposed. The system can measure the relative motion of UAV under different illumination conditions by using two kinds of vision sensors, i.e. day and thermal camera. But the UAVs communicate with each other only in relative positions, without maps. [2] designed a navigation system based on GPS and low cost Inertial Navigation System (INS). This system is used to provide position, velocity and attitude (PVA) information for navigating UAV. The authors use optical flow as an additional observation in data fusion to enhance the estimation of PVA. In [3], a map merging algorithm based on virtual robot motion is proposed for multi-robot SLAM. The spatial skeleton of grid map is constructed by thinning algorithm, and the mobile robot is simulated on a map. If the localization is successful, the relative posture assumption between the two maps can be easily calculated. In [4], the authors propose a knowledge sharing mechanism for multiple robots in which one robot can inform other robots about the changes in map, like path blockage, or new static obstacles, encountered at specific areas of the map. This symbiotic information sharing allows the robots to update remote areas of the map without having to explicitly navigate those areas, and plan efficient paths. A novel method for the localization and navigation of multiple mobile robots is proposed in [5]. The method uses coded light superimposed onto a visual image and projected onto the robots. Robots localize their position by receiving and decoding the projected light, and follow a target using the coded velocity vector field. The entire system only requires a projector to navigation the robot swarm; thus, it can be used on any projection area.

There are also some researches work on map fusion. In [6], a cooperative positioning and mapping system based on ground mobile robots and UAVs is proposed. In [7], Piasco considered cooperative stereo-vision as a mean of localization for a fleet of micro-air vehicles (MAV) equipped with monocular cameras, inertial measurement units and sonar sensors. In this paper, a sensor fusion scheme based on extended Kalman filter (EKF) is designed to estimate the position and direction of all vehicles through these distributed measurements. A framework for cooperative localization and mapping with multiple MAVs in unknown environments is presented in [8]. The framework has realized the independent creation of maps by each MAV and the map fusion in the ground central server. After testing, the framework can realize real-time positioning and mapping of up to three MAVs. A real-time approach to stitch large-scale aerial images incrementally is presented in [9]. A monocular SLAM system is used to estimate camera position and attitude, and meanwhile 3D point cloud map is generated. But the method presented in this paper is mainly used for high-altitude large-scale 2D image mosaic, not for multi-UAV navigation. How to fuse the maps observed from different UAVs has become the focus of CSLAM research. Some literatures, such as [10] and [11], proposed the method of map fusion by matching the images observed by different UAVs. In [10], the authors introduce a software framework for real-time multi-robot collaborative SLAM. The framework aggregates local pose graphs obtained from its multiple robots into a global pose graph, which it then feeds back to the robots to increase their mapping and localization effectiveness. In [11], a cooperative monocular-based SLAM approach for multi-UAV systems that can operate in GPS-denied environments is presented. The main contribution of the work is to show that, using visual information obtained from monocular cameras mounted onboard aerial vehicles flying in formation, the observability properties of the whole system are improved.

Although there are many theories and methods have been proposed on multi-robot cooperative navigation, some works are still blank. This paper innovatively studies the navigation system of multi-UAV cooperative transportation system in unknown environment, with or without GPS signal. Both CSLAM and GPS are used to solve the problem of multi-UAV cooperative navigation. When the Multi-UAV cooperative transportation system is in unknown environment, each UAV platform will sent all the information to the central server, the server will fuse the map and send the latest map information to each UAV platform. The UAV platforms can not only acquire the information of relative environment, but also share the position and attitude information of other UAV platforms. This paper also innovatively integrates the final output information of CSLAM with GPS information, which not only improves the accuracy of state estimation of multi-UAV cooperative transportation system, but also ensures that the state information can be obtained in the environment with or without GPS signal.

2 Navigation Scheme

2.1 Multi-UAV Cooperative Transportation System

A multi-UAV cooperative transportation system is introduced in Fig. 1, which consists of UAV platforms, flexible net and ground station. Each UAV platform includes UAV, control panel and binocular camera. Flexible net is used to place objects to be carried. Ground Station is mainly used for ground monitoring.

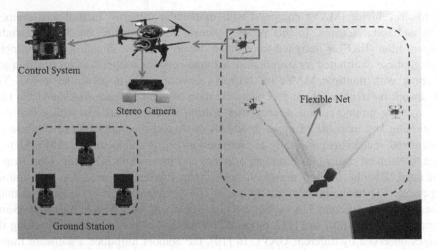

Fig. 1. The multi-UAV cooperative transportation system. The green box on the left represents the ground side, and the green box on the right represents the sky side. The UAV is equipped with a stereo camera and a control system. (Color figure online)

As shown in Fig. 1, there is a large flexible net which is used to carry objects between UAVs. The objects are placed on a flexible net, and we control the UAV to fly in a certain formation. This method has the following advantages: 1. It can transport large and irregular objects; 2. The transportation system is theoretically not limited by the weight of the objects being carried; 3. Several small UAVs cost much less than a heavy-duty UAV; 4. UAVs can avoid different types of obstacles by changing their formation.

As shown in Fig. 2, each UAV platform is equivalent to a client, which can independently locate and map. One of the UAV platforms is also a server, which collects all the information from each UAV, and carries out map fusion and global optimization. Each client independently executes three threads: tracking, local mapping, and communication; the server executes three threads: communication, loop closer and map fusion. The dotted line in Fig. 2 shows that if GPS and IMU signals can be received, the odometer information calculated by GPS and IMU can be fused with the visual odometer information obtained by CSLAM.

2.2 Process of Clients

Tracking thread is used to detect and track ORB (Oriented FAST and Rotated BRIEF) feature points. PnP (Perspective-n-Point) algorithm is used to calculate the pose of each frame of the camera and the three-dimensional coordinates of the map points. Finally, key frames (KFs) and map points (MPs) are saved. Local Mapping thread receives the KFs and MPs from the tracking thread and optimizes them locally. Then the optimized KFs and MPs are fed back to the tracking thread. The communication thread translates the local map created by the client into a custom Robot Operating System (ROS) message, and then publishes the message for the server to receive.

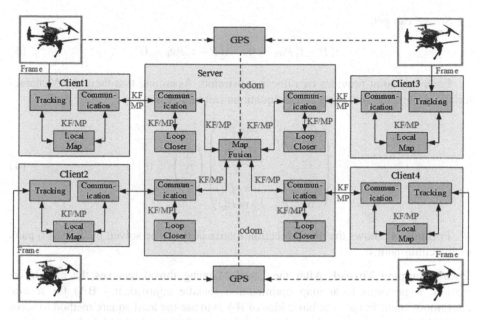

Fig. 2. System framework diagram. The figure shows the process of merging four clients to build a map. Each client independently executes three threads: tracking, local mapping, and communication. The server executes three threads: communication, loop closer and map fusion.

Tracking Thread. The Monocular SLAM is difficult to obtain real scale information, so the binocular stereo camera is chosen. Binocular stereo camera calculates the three-dimensional coordinates of key points by disparity image. The pose between frames is calculated by PnP algorithm. Consider a space point P whose homogeneous coordinates are $(X, Y, Z, 1)$. In image I_1, point P is projected to point x(expressed in homogeneous coordinates of normalized plane). At this time, the pose R and t of the camera are unknown. The augmented matrix $[R|t] \in \mathbb{R}^{3 \times 4}$ is defined, which contains rotation and position information. The expansion form is formulated as:

$$s \begin{pmatrix} u_1 \\ v_1 \\ 1 \end{pmatrix} = \begin{pmatrix} t_1 & t_2 & t_3 & t_4 \\ t_5 & t_6 & t_7 & t_8 \\ t_9 & t_{10} & t_{11} & t_{12} \end{pmatrix} \begin{pmatrix} X \\ Y \\ Z \\ 1 \end{pmatrix} \quad (1)$$

The s can be eliminated, and two constraints are given as:

$$u_1 = \frac{t_1 X + t_2 Y + t_3 Z + t_4}{t_9 X + t_{10} Y + t_{11} Z + t_{12}}, \quad v_1 = \frac{t_5 X + t_6 Y + t_7 Z + t_8}{t_9 X + t_{10} Y + t_{11} Z + t_{12}} \quad (2)$$

So we can get:

$$t_1^T P - t_3^T P u_1 = 0, \quad t_2^T P - t_3^T P v_1 = 0 \tag{3}$$

Each key point provides two linear constraints. Assuming that there are N characteristic points, the following linear equations can be listed:

$$\begin{pmatrix} P_1^T & 0 & -u_1 P_1^T \\ 0 & P_1^T & -v_1 P_1^T \\ \vdots & \vdots & \vdots \\ P_N^T & 0 & -u_N P_N^T \\ 0 & P_N^T & -v_N P_N^T \end{pmatrix} \begin{pmatrix} t_1 \\ t_2 \\ t_3 \end{pmatrix} = 0 \tag{4}$$

Formula (4) shows that the projection matrix $[R|t]$ can be solved by at least 6 pairs of matching points.

Local Mapping Thread. After the Local Mapping thread receives the map information, it performs local map optimization (bundle adjustment - BA) for several continuous multi-frame. The basic idea of BA is to use the least square method to solve the optimal projection matrix and map point coordinates which minimize the observation error. The Lie algebra ξ is used to represent the pose of the camera, p to represent the three-dimensional coordinates of the map points, and $z \triangleq [u_s, v_s]^T$ to represent the observation data. According to the idea of least square method, we can get the observation error:

$$e = z - h(\xi, p) \tag{5}$$

Local Mapping threads optimize continuous multi-frame optimization, so the observations from other times should be also taken into account. Let z_{ij} be the data generated by observing map point p_j at pose ξ_i, then the overall cost function is:

$$\frac{1}{2} \sum_{i=1}^{m} \sum_{j=1}^{n} \|e_{ij}\|^2 = \frac{1}{2} \sum_{i=1}^{m} \sum_{j=1}^{n} \|z_{ij} - h(\xi_i, p_j)\|^2 \tag{6}$$

According to the idea of non-linear optimization, we should constantly look for incremental Δx to find the optimal solution of the objective function. We define independent variables as all variables to be optimized:

$$x = [\xi_1, \ldots, \xi_m, p_1, \ldots p_n]^T \tag{7}$$

When an increment to the independent variable is be given, the objective function is reformulated as:

$$\frac{1}{2}\|f(x+\Delta x)\|^2 \approx \frac{1}{2}\sum_{i=1}^{m}\sum_{j=1}^{n}\|e_{ij}+F_{ij}\Delta\xi_i+E_{ij}\Delta p_j\|^2 \tag{8}$$

where Δx is the increment of the whole independent variable; F_{ij} denotes the partial derivative of the whole cost function to the camera attitude in the current state; E_{ij} defines the partial derivative of the function to the three-dimensional coordinates of the map points. The specific deduction methods of F_{ij} and E_{ij} will not be further elaborated.

Communication Thread. Communication thread is used to process information exchange between client and server. ROS infrastructure was been used to make communication easier. The basic information of KFs and MPs is packed and distributed, and a buffer is set up to ensure that all information can be received by the server.

The communication between the server and the client is bidirectional. Because the server performs the task of map fusion and global optimization, the map information on the server is more accurate than that on the client. The updated information on the client include the pose of the KFs, the coordinates of the MPs, and the observation relationship between the KFs and the MPs.

2.3   Process of Server

Loop Closer Thread. The Loop closer thread is used to check whether the camera has passed through the previous place. According to the observation relationship, we can select the closed-loop candidate KFs of the current KF. Then, each closed-loop candidate frame is scored by the bag of word (BOW), and the KF with the highest score and enough matching map points is selected as the closed-loop KF. After selecting the closed-loop KF, the Sim3 (Similarity transformation group) between the closed-loop KF and the current KF is calculated. Finally, the global BA is executed according to the results of Sim3, and the map is optimized.

Map Fusion Thread. Map fusion thread is similar to loop closer thread. Loop closer thread associates and optimizes KFs and MPs come from a single client, but map fusion thread needs to associate KFs from different clients. The thread uses BOW to detect whether each client's KFs pass through the same place. Take the map of one client as the parent-map and the map of other clients as the sub-map. Find out the Fusion KFs of sub-maps and calculate the Sim3 between Fusion KFs. Then the sub-maps are optimized according to the results of sim3. Finally, a global BA is executed for both parent-map and sub-maps.

2.4   Fusion of CSLAM and GPS

If the GPS signal can be received, the result of GPS and CSLM will be fused to get the final navigation information.

It is assumed that two observations have been obtained: GPS and CLAM. GPS can get real-time position (x_g, y_g, z_g) (GPS signal can provide the accuracy σ of this position at that time), which has no accumulated error, and the accuracy is low. CSLAM can get the position (x_c, y_c, z_c) and the corresponding attitude quaternion (w, a, b, c) all the time, which has accumulated error and high accuracy in a short time. In order to get a better fusion result, we adopt this strategy: the initial position of observation is provided by GPS, and CSLAM observation provide the displacement and attitude change from i to j. The absolute displacement and the absolute rotation attitude obtained by CSLAM are not trusted. We only trust the short-term change from i to j, and use this change as the observation value of the whole cost function to solve the problem.

Nonlinear optimization toolbox Ceres is used to calculate the fusion of CSLAM and GPS. Two residual terms are set to correspond to the position signals of GPS and the pose changes estimated by CSLAM in a short time from i to j.

3   Experimental Results

In order to verify the feasibility of the proposed algorithm, two groups of experiments were designed to verify it. The EuRoC data set which contains binocular camera information and IMU data was used in the first experiment. The main purpose of this experiment is to verify the cooperative positioning and mapping ability of multi-UAV transportation system under pure vision. The KITTI data set which also provides binocular camera information in the second experiment. In addition, this data set also contains GPS information. Therefore, this experiment mainly verifies the fusion algorithm of CSLAM and GPS. Four computers were used in the first group of experiments. An ALIENWARE notebook with a Core i7-8750U @ 2.60 GHz × 12 and 16 GB RAM was used as the server and three NVIDIA JETSON TX2 computers were used as the clients. Only two computers were used in the second experiment. Similarly, the server uses ALIENWARE notebook and the client uses NVIDIA JETSON TX2 computer.

3.1   Collaborative SLAM Without GPS

Three sets of UAV flight data from the EuRoC were downloaded. At the beginning, the map information received by the server is the origin of the Earth coordinate system at each client's initial position. Therefore, as shown in the left of Fig. 3, each client starts at the same point before the server detects the fusion. With the increase of KFs in the map, UAVs from different clients will see the same scene, and then the server will detect the fusion conditions. The fused map is based on Client1, and the Sim3 between other Clients and Client1 were calculated. Than the server corrects the overall map and feeding the latest map information back to each Client.

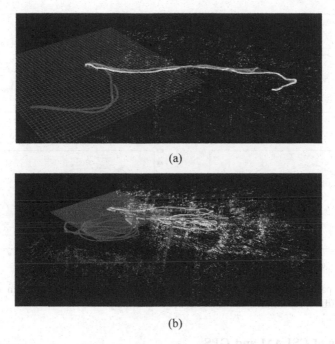

(a)

(b)

Fig. 3. Multi-UAV cooperative positioning and mapping experiment. (a) shows the beginning stage of fusion mapping. (b) shows the final map.

The final map of the multi-UAV fusion is shown in the right of Fig. 3. The map contains the pose of all KFs in the overall environment of each client and the coordinates of MPs that each client can observe. With this information, we can not only locate the multi-UAV transportation system in the environment, but also acquire the relative position and orientation of UAVs. At the same time, it can also be masked by the established map.

In order to make the experimental results more intuitive, the location data of KFs in the map is exported, and the three clients' path maps are drew as Fig. 4 respectively. As shown in Fig. 4(a)–(c), the path of each UAV is quite complex. The clients pass through the same place many times during flight, and at this time the loop closer thread will optimize the whole loop according to the Sim3 between the current KF and the closed-loop KF. Figure 4(d) shows the path diagrams of three clients in the same coordinate system. Finally, when all maps are established, the server will execute a global BA to correlate and optimize maps from various clients.

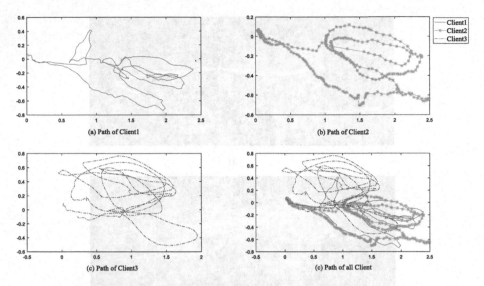

Fig. 4. KFs path map. (a), (b) and (c) represent the UAV path maps from three clients, respectively, (d) represent their locations in the overall map.

3.2 Fusion of CSLAM and GPS

We use a large number of KITTI data sets to test the feasibility of CSLAM and GPS fusion algorithm. Because of the large volume of KITTI dataset, if multi-clients were used for integration mapping, the configuration of server should meet a high requirement. Due to the limited conditions, we only validate the fusion of a client and GPS.

We chose a set of outdoor data sets. The data set is consists of the scenes taken by binocular cameras traveling back and forth on the same road, the GPS information and IMU information. The position information acquired by GPS has no accumulative error, but its accuracy is low. The odometer calculated by SLAM has accumulated errors and high accuracy in a short time. In order to get a better result, the initial position is provided by GPS, and the displacement and attitude change of CSLAM in a short time are used.

As shown in Fig. 5(a), the results of CSLAM and GPS fusion are close to the real situation (the same road travels back and forth). But in Fig. 5(b), we plotted the KFs path obtained by CSLAM only. CSLAM has a large error in turning, and this error accumulates over time. The results of loop optimization of CSLAM after detecting closed-loop KF were also shown in Fig. 5(c). It is obvious to find that loop detection can effectively reduce the drift of CSLAM. But in the real scenario of multi-UAV cooperative transportation, using loop closer to correct the drift of odometer is not entirely reliable. So if GPS information is involved in the fusion, the success rate of mission execution can be greatly improved.

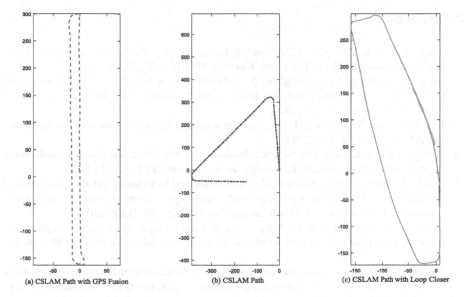

Fig. 5. Paths under three different modes. (a) Represents the KFs path of CSLAM and GPS fusion output. (b) Represents the KFs path obtained by running only CSLAM. (c) Represents the key frame path after only running CSLAM but executing Loop Closer. The above three paths are obtained under the same data set.

4 Conclusion

Aiming at the multi-UAV cooperative transportation system, a complete set of scheme is proposed. This paper mainly studied the navigation scheme of CSLAM and the fusion of CSLAM and GPS for the proposed multi-UAV cooperative transportation system. In order to solve the problem of multi-UAV cooperative navigation in the GPS-denied environment, a multi-robot collaborative SLAM algorithm is proposed. The algorithm is composed of a server and several clients. Through ROS communication, the independent mapping of the client can be fused on the server. The algorithm can ensure that the UAV can acquire both absolute coordinates of relative environment and relative coordinates of UAV during cooperative flight. The CSLAM/GPS fusion algorithm mainly solves the drift problem of odometer information obtained only by CSLAM, and can improve navigation accuracy.

This paper uses EuRoC data set and KITTI data set to verify the CSLAM algorithm and CSLAM/GPS fusion algorithm respectively. For the GPS-Denied environment, the map fusion algorithm was successfully implemented using three clients and one server. For the GPS signal environment, we validate the effectiveness and necessity of CSLAM/GPS fusion algorithm in outdoor scenes.

However, there are still some progress can be achieved in future: 1. CSLAM requires a high level of server configuration and is difficult to adapt to larger scenarios; 2. The results of CSLAM algorithm are prone to drift (especially when the camera turns); 3. The accuracy of scale information calculated by binocular camera is not high. This work might be improved in future work.

References

1. Tang, Y.Z., Hu, Y.C., Cui, J.Q.: Vision-aided multi-UAV autonomous flocking in GPS-denied environment. IEEE Trans. Ind. Electron. **66**, 616–626 (2019)
2. Ding, W.D., Wang, J.L., Almagbile, A.: Adaptive filter design for UAV navigation with GPS/INS/optic flow integration. In: International Conference on Electrical and Control Engineering, pp. 4623–4626 (2010)
3. Liu, Y.L., Fan, X.P., Zhang, H.: A fast map merging algorithm in the field of multirobot SLAM. Sci. World J. 1–8 (2013)
4. Abhijeet, R., Ankit, R., Yukinori, K., Takanori, E.: Symbiotic navigation in multi-robot systems with remote obstacle knowledge sharing. Sensors **17**(7), 1–17 (2017)
5. Hiraki, T., Fukushima, S., Naemura, T.: Projection-based localization and navigation method for multiple mobile robots with pixel-level visible light communication. In: IEEE/SICE International Symposium on System Integration, pp. 862–868. IEEE (2017)
6. Vidal-Calleja, T.A., Berger, C., Solà, J.: Large scale multiple robot visual mapping with heterogeneous landmarks in semi-structured terrain. Robot. Auton. Syst. (RAS) **59**, 654–674 (2011)
7. Piasco, N., Marzat, J., Sanfourche, M.: Collaborative localization and formation flying using distributed stereo-vision. In: International Conference on Robotics and Automation (ICRA), pp. 1202–1207. IEEE (2016)
8. Forster, C., Lynen, S., Kneip, L.: Collaborative monocular SLAM with multiple micro aerial vehicles. In: 2013 IEEE/RSJ International Conference on Intelligent Robots and Systems. IEEE (2013)
9. Bu, S.H., Zhao, Y., Wan, G.: Map2DFusion: real-time incremental UAV image mosaicing based on monocular SLAM. In: 2016 IEEE/RSJ International Conference on Intelligent Robots and Systems (IROS). IEEE (2016)
10. Deutsch, I., Liu, M., Siegwart, R.: A framework for multi-robot pose graph SLAM. In: IEEE International Conference on Real-Time Computing & Robotics. IEEE (2016)
11. Trujillo, J.-C., Munguia, R., Guerra, E.: Cooperative monocular-based SLAM for multi-UAV systems in GPS-denied environments. Sensors **18**(5), 1–24 (2018)

A New Concept of UAV Recovering System

Jun Jiang, Houde Liu$^{(\boxtimes)}$, Bo Yuan, Xueqian Wang, and Bin Liang

Graduate School at Shenzhen, Tsinghua University,
Shenzhen 518055, People's Republic of China
{jiang.jun,liu.hd}@sz.tsinghua.edu.cn

Abstract. This paper introduces a new concept of recovering UAVs to their carrier using manipulator, aiming to better use the carrier's carrying capability. The state-of-the-art of recycling UAVs are stated in the first place, the advantages and the setbacks of the current available recycling systems are introduced, and the reason for the setbacks are further analyzed before this new concept is introduced. To accomplish the basic recovering task, a minimum system configuration that can explain the idea is introduced and the model of the system is built based on several important assumptions. To further explain how the system works, a simulation based on the above configuration is given. The simulation result indicates that the system can fulfill the task of recovering the UAV, and the result also verified the efficiency of the new system, which implies its potential usefulness in the future application.

Keywords: Multi-copter · Manipulator · UAV recovering

1 Introduction

The multi-copter has been a hot topic in scientific research field and also in commercial field for more than a decade. Its indomitable vitality originates from its irreplaceable advantages, which includes but not limited to: agile, light, portable, simple structure, small noise, cheap, foldable, reliable, small vibration, maintenance friendly, and etc. But the disadvantages of this aircraft are also obvious and lethal: short duration, low capacity, unstable, small operation range, which hinder the multi-copter from being applied in more broad and important fields. And among these shortcomings, the short duration and small operation range are the 'Achilles' heels'. A nature way of solving this problem is to combine the multi-copter with a kind of long-range-oriented vehicle to form a new almighty system. And many attempts have been made to build such systems.

A group of researchers focus on developing robust control algorithm for precise landing on the traditional moving platforms. Literature [1] developed a joint decentralized controller for the landing of a quadrotor on skid-steered UGV, the instability problem due to time delay was solved by introducing a RFDE method. Literature [2] designed a control structure by combing estimation module, trajectory module, and tracking module together for fast and precise landing of the quadrotor. The proposed controller proves to be efficient in leading the quadrotor onto the platform. Tang [3] designed a longitudinal-constant-velocity guiding method for docking a quadrotor, the

© Springer Nature Switzerland AG 2019
H. Yu et al. (Eds.): ICIRA 2019, LNAI 11742, pp. 327–338, 2019.
https://doi.org/10.1007/978-3-030-27535-8_30

inner-loop controller is designed to aligns the quadrotor to the carrier's direction, and an augmented estimator is developed for wind rejection. A good amount of work has been done for the navigating the quadrotor to the target. In paper [4], visual servoing method is applied to control the quadrotor towards the moving target, and the variables needed by the controller is reduced to a limited margin. Paper [5] innovatively used a smartphone as the omnidirectional vision acquisition and combined this information with the dynamic model in order to estimate the states of the moving platform. Paper [6] developed non-linear model predictive method to land the quadrotor onto a inclined platform. The proposed system imitates the landing situation on the ship deck. In paper [7], a CPU/GPU based real-time system for relative pose estimation is designed, the system works at a rate of 30 fps, which is sufficient for landing. Paper [8] considered the uncertainties in the land proceeding and used L_1 adaptive loop to enhance the tracking velocity commands. Paper [9] integrated the information of laser and vision to localize the moving platform, and estimate the pose of the deck using a downward facing monocular camera.

The focus of current solution of recovering a quadrotor is to enhance the landing precision of the multi-copter on a deck built for recovering. As the aforementioned literatures covers, the key points of recovering the quadrotor lies in precise localization and the precise position estimation either in absolute or in relative form. The weak points of these methods are: (1), Due to the under-actuated feature, the quadrotor cannot land precisely on the expected point when suffering from constant horizontal disturbance; (2), Traditional precise localization systems are too heavy for the small-sized quadrotors, and low precise sensors are not qualified for precise localization; (3), The decks for recovering quadrotor occupies too much space, and therefore the space utilization is low; (4), The recovered quadrotor cannot be further manipulated after landing onto a deck.

To overcome the weaknesses mentioned above, this paper introduces a new concept of recovering multi-copter system. By replacing the deck with a manipulator, the new system can recover the multi-copter in several more efficient ways. The paper evolves in this way: The following paragraph describes the composition and configuration of the system. Section 3 builds the model of the combined system. A simulation in Sect. 4 was conducted to show the feasibility of the new concept system.

2 System Configuration and Modeling

2.1 System Configuration

The configuration of the system is depicted by Fig. 1. There are four main components in this system: The carrier, the manipulator, the launched aircraft, and the ground station. The carrier in the system usually refers to the aircrafts that are has the complementary characters vs. the launched aircraft. In this paper, the carrier (labeled by 1) is a fixed-wing aircraft, manned or unmanned, and the launched aircraft (labeled by 3) is a multi-copter. The manipulator (labeled by 2) is a 3DOF arm which is able to compensate the residual position error between the fixed-wing aircraft and the multi-copter, leaving the remained 3DOF to be tackled by a specially designed connector, which is not the focus of this paper. To schedule the tasks and monitoring the whole unmanned system, a ground control station (labeled by 4) is included in the system. During the launch operation, the multi-copter manages to stabilize itself despite the uncertain initial states, which is not this paper's focus. During the recovering procedure, the multi-copter first formats with the fixed-wing aircraft, using onboard localization equipment, mainly the compound GPS-based navigation system. Due to the low precision of the GPS, the capture maneuver is not to be executed, this formation stage is considered to be coarse formation. A further more precise formation has to be done. As they come close to each other, the manipulator and the multi-copter locate each other through vision-base measurement, and the wireless communication devices transmit the states that cannot be observed. When permitted, the capture maneuver is executed.

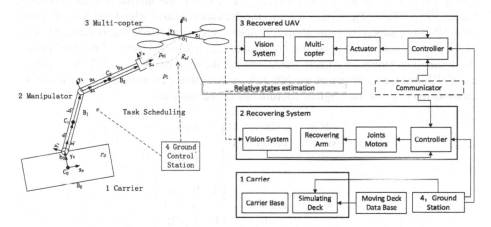

Fig. 1. The concept composes of 4 components: The carrier, the manipulator, the UAV, and the ground control station. The whole system is configured as the right part of the figure shows.

By replacing the deck with a manipulator and space-saving storage device, much space for recovering is saved compared with traditional-landing way. And due to the foldable advantages of the multicopter, much more launched multi-copters are able to be recovered, and therefore, more powerful system is developed. Residue position compensation is the key point of the system and the rest of the paper will focus on explaining it.

2.2 Modeling of the System

To simplify the explanation of the concept, and to make the following modeling and simulation work reasonable, the following assumptions are made:

(1) The manipulator together with its carrier moves at a constant velocity.
(2) All parts of the system are considered as rigid body.
(3) The quadrotor is symmetry, and the joint coincidence with the CoM (Centre of Mass)

(4) The two pats are allowed to get all necessary information from each other.
(5) The carrier is much bigger than the manipulator, so the interaction is neglected.
(6) The weight of the quadrotor is within the capability of the manipulator.
(7) The wind has effect on the quadrotor, but has no effect on the manipulator
(8) The end effector of the manipulator manages to grasp the quadrotor only if the distance between the CoM of the quadrotor and the end effector is smaller than a given value, despite of the other states of the quadrotor.

Figure 2 shows the coordinate frames of the system. Global coordinate frame is set at the bottom of the first link. For link i: m_i stands for the mass, $^0v_{iC}$ stands for the speed of the CoM, l_i stands for its length, r_{iCOM} stands for the vector from the origin to the CoM, q_i stands for the angle, ω_i stand for the angle velocity wrt. ith coordinate frame, $_0\omega_{iC}$ stands for the angle velocity wrt. the global coordinate frame, τ_i stands or the torque exerted on the joint, $^{iC}I_i = \text{diag}(I_{i11}, I_{i22}, I_{i33})$ is the inertial wrt. ith coordinate frame, $^0T_{iS}$, $^{iS}T_{iC}$, $^{iS}T_{iE}$, $^{iS}o_{iC}$, $^{iS}o_{iE}$ are the transition matrix where the S, E, C in the subscripes and superscripts are short for 'Start', 'End', and 'CoM'; o_q is the CoM of the Multi-copter, and o_q-$x_qy_qz_q$ is the coordinate attached to it. Both of the two models share the same global coordinate frame, but use different conventions. The manipulator use ENU, and the multi-copter use NED. According to the coordinate frames above, the rotation matrixes of the original coordinates of the links are:

$$^0R_{1S} = \begin{bmatrix} \cos q_1 & -\sin q_1 & 0 \\ \sin q_1 & \cos q_1 & 0 \\ 0 & 0 & 1 \end{bmatrix} = \begin{bmatrix} cq_1 & -sq_1 & 0 \\ sq_1 & cq_1 & 0 \\ 0 & 0 & 1 \end{bmatrix} \tag{1}$$

$$^1R_{1post} = Rx(90) = \begin{bmatrix} 1 & 0 & 0 \\ 0 & 0 & -1 \\ 0 & 1 & 0 \end{bmatrix} \tag{2}$$

$$^{1post}R_{2S} = Rz(q_2) = \begin{bmatrix} cq_2 & -sq_2 & 0 \\ sq_2 & cq_2 & 0 \\ 0 & 0 & 1 \end{bmatrix} \tag{3}$$

$$^{2E}R_{3S} = \begin{bmatrix} cq_3 & -sq_3 & 0 \\ sq_3 & cq_3 & 0 \\ 0 & 0 & 1 \end{bmatrix} \tag{4}$$

Where, the q_i represents the joint angle i, c and s are short for cosine and sine. According to the Lagrange method, the torque exerted on joint i can be computed as,

$$u_i = \frac{d}{dt}\frac{\partial L}{\partial \dot{q}_i} - \frac{\partial L}{\partial q_i} \tag{5}$$

Where $L = T - U$, and T is the kinetic energy and U is the potential energy of the manipulator. And according to König's theorem,

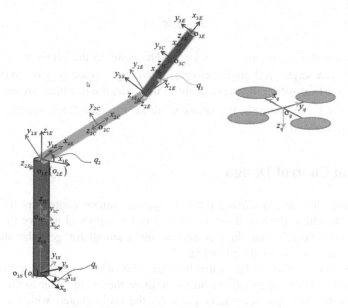

Fig. 2. The coordinate frames of the system.

$$T = \frac{1}{2} \sum m v_{iC}^T v_{iC} + \frac{1}{2} \sum \omega_i^T I_i \omega_i \qquad (6)$$

$$U = \sum m_i g h_i \qquad (7)$$

Considering the transition relationship between the links depicted by (1)–(4), the model is constructed as the following standard form.

$$\tau = M(q)\ddot{q} + C(q,\dot{q}) + G(q) \qquad (8)$$

The matrices of M, C, G are too big to be presented here, please see Appendix 1 for detail. The controlled plant is depicted in the third line in Fig. 3.

For the multi-copter, typical Newton-Euler method is used to develop the model, and to simplify the explanation, the quadrotor is considered as rigid body.

$$\begin{bmatrix} m_q I_{3\times3} & 0 \\ 0 & I_{3\times3} \end{bmatrix} \begin{bmatrix} \dot{V} \\ \dot{\omega}_q \end{bmatrix} + \begin{bmatrix} \dot{\omega}_q \times m_q V \\ \omega_q \times m_q \omega_q \end{bmatrix} = \begin{bmatrix} F \\ u_\tau \end{bmatrix} \qquad (9)$$

Where, the ω_i stand for the angle velocity of the quadrotor, m_q stands for the weight, the right subtitle is short for quadrotor, $I_{3\times3}$ is the inertial of the body, V is the linear velocity, F is the total thrust and u_τ is the inner loop torque. The concise form of the quadrotor dynamic is showed as the following equation, and the detail can be seen in Appendix 1.

$$\dot{x} = f(x, u) \tag{10}$$

Where, $x = \begin{bmatrix} \phi\ \theta\ \psi\ \omega_p\ \omega_q\ \omega_r\ x\ y\ z\ \dot{x}\ \dot{y}\ \dot{z} \end{bmatrix}^T$. The items in the vector x are roll angle, pitch angle, yaw angle, roll angle velocity, pitch angle velocity, yaw angle velocity, position in x axis, position in y axis, position in z axis, the rest three are the velocities. $u = \begin{bmatrix} F\ \tau_x\ \tau_y\ \tau_z \end{bmatrix}^T$, the items in the vector u are the resultant force, and the torques on the x_q, y_q, z_q body axis.

3   System Control Design

As this paper aims at introducing the new system, simple controllers for each sub-system are designed. Both of the two controllers are supposed to have the full information of each other's, and in this design, the manipulator gets the states of the multicopter and uses it for the planning.

The mission is accomplished when the end point of the manipulator coincide with the CoM of the multi-copter, so our aim is to drive the manipulator to the position of the multi-copter. We first set a rally point for the multi-copter, which is within the manipulator's working space. The manipulator gets the multi-copter's position and velocity, and plans its movement.

For the control of the arm manipulator, a simple PD + gravity compensation algorithm is applied. In Fig. 3, x_d is the state of the multi-copter, and is used for planning. The inverse kinetic of the manipulator is easily got, and can be seen in Appendix 3.

The PD + gravity compensation controller is given in the second line in Fig. 3 and is rewritten as (11), the input of the desired joint angles are from the inverse kinetic of the manipulator, which is based on the multi-copter's current states.

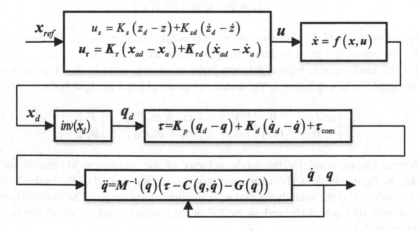

Fig. 3. The control structure of the manipulator.

$$\tau = K_p(q_d - q) + K_d(\omega_d - \omega) + \tau_{com} \tag{11}$$

Where, τ_{com} is the gravity compensation torque, and $q_d = [q_{1d}\ q_{2d}\ q_{3d}]^T$ is for the desired angle of the joints. And $\omega_d = [\omega_{1d}\ \omega_{2d}\ \omega_{3d}]^T$ stands for the desired angle velocities of the joints. The gravity compensation item is the function of q_i, l_i, and m_i, and can be easily calculated as (12):

$$\tau_{com} = \begin{bmatrix} 0 \\ \frac{l_3}{2}m_3g\cos(q_2 + q_3) + \frac{l_2}{2}m_2g\cos q_2 + m_3gl_2\cos q_2 \\ \frac{l_3}{2}m_3g\cos(q_2 + q_3) \end{bmatrix} \tag{12}$$

For the multi-copter, a cascade structure controller is designed. And for the outer loop control:

$$u_z = K_z(z_d - z) + K_{zd}(\dot{z}_d - \dot{z}) \tag{13a}$$

$$F = m(g - u_z)/\cos\phi\cos\theta \tag{13b}$$

As the multi-copter works at the equilibrium, design two temporary states for horizontal movement as in (14b) and (14c), and are calculated by (14a),

$$u_{xy} = [u_{xd}\ u_{yd}]^T = K_{xy}(x_{xyd} - x_{xy}) + K_{xyd}(\dot{x}_{xyd} - \dot{x}_{xy}) \tag{14a}$$

$$u_{xd} = \cos\phi\sin\theta\cos\psi + \sin\phi\sin\psi \tag{14b}$$

$$u_{yd} = \cos\phi\sin\theta\sin\psi - \sin\phi\cos\psi \tag{14c}$$

The desired angles are given as (15a) and (15b), and the inner loop control algorithm is given as (15c), the desired yaw is constantly zero and not to be shown here:

$$\phi_d = a\sin(\sin\psi u_{xd} - \cos\psi u_{yd}) \tag{15a}$$

$$\theta_d = a\sin((\cos\psi u_{xd} + \sin\psi u_{yd})/\cos\phi_d) \tag{15b}$$

$$u_\tau = K_\tau(x_{ad} - x_a) + K_{\tau d}(\dot{x}_{ad} - \dot{x}_a) \tag{15c}$$

4 Recovering Simulation

4.1 Simulation Condition Set

The initial states of the angles of the manipulator are: $[0\ 0\ 0]^T$. The desired tip position of the manipulator keeps with the CoM of the quadrotor in real time.

For the manipulator, a PD + gravity compensation controller is designed.

Link1: cylinder: radius: 0.03 m, length: 0.5 m, density: 2700 kg/m^3.
Link2: cuboid: 0.05*0.05*0.5 m density: 2700 kg/m^3.
Link3: cuboid: 0.05 * 0.05 * 0.5 m density: 2700 kg/m^3.

$$K_{arm} = \begin{bmatrix} 20 & 6 & 0 & 0 & 0 & 0 \\ 0 & 0 & 40 & 15 & 0 & 0 \\ 0 & 0 & 0 & 0 & 20 & 6 \end{bmatrix}$$

The parameters of the quadrotor are: m = 1.64, l = 0.4 m; I_{xx} = 0.044 kg m^2, I_{yy} = 0.044 kg m^2, I_{zz} = 0.088 kg m^2, J_r = 90*10^{-6}; For the simulation, the initial states of the quadrotor is set to be a little off its equilibrium, which are, angle: [0.5 0.5 0]^T, angle velocity: [0 0 0]^T, position: [2.657 2 3]^T, velocity: [0 0 0]^T. The desired position: [0.5 0.5 0.5]^T, and the desired velocity: [0 0 0]^T. In this scenario, the yaw angle is insignificant, and is constantly set to zero (Fig. 4).

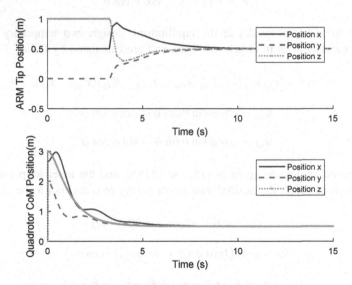

Fig. 4. The positions vs. time of the system components.

The control matrixes are as follows:

$$K_z = [3.1623 \quad 4.0404]$$

$$K_{xy} = \begin{bmatrix} 0.25 & 0.4195 & 0 & 0 \\ 0 & 0 & 0.25 & 0.4195 \end{bmatrix}$$

$$K_\tau = \begin{bmatrix} 12.2474 & 4.5911 & 0 & 0 & 0 & 0 \\ 0 & 0 & 12.2474 & 4.5911 & 0 & 0 \\ 0 & 0 & 0 & 0 & 37.4166 & 14.3731 \end{bmatrix}$$

The quadrotor enters the manipulator's scope at about 3rd second, and triggers the actuation of the manipulator, then the quadrotor settles at about 8th second. And the manipulator carries on pursuing the CoM of the quadrotor, and the tip of it finally reaches the CoM of the quadrotor at about 10th second (Fig. 5).

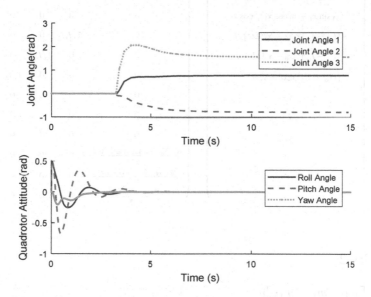

Fig. 5. Angles in the system.

This figure shows the angles vs. time of the quadrotor and the manipulator. The quadrotor settles at about 5th second. As the manipulator has a limited scope, the joints start at about 3rd second when the quadrotor enters its scope, and as the tip of the manipulator reaches the multi-copter's CoM, the joints' angles of the manipulator converge.

5 Conclusion

A new concept of recovering a UAV to its carrier is proposed, and the system is explained by illustrating the composition of the system and the operating mechanism. To give an intuitive impression of the system, the model of the system is built and a simulation was conducted. The result shows that, the system is able to recover the UAV, and the combination of the system implies its potential practicality. The proposed concept can be further used in more dynamic scenarios, such as air-based systems, and become more useful in more application fields.

Acknowledgments. This work was partially supported by the National Natural Science Foundation of China (No. U1813216 and No. 61803221), the Science and Technology Research Foundation of Shenzhen (JCYJ20160301100921349 and JCYJ20170817152701660).

Appendix 1

$$
\begin{pmatrix} \dot{x}_1 \\ \dot{x}_2 \\ \dot{x}_3 \\ \dot{x}_4 \\ \dot{x}_5 \\ \dot{x}_6 \\ \dot{x}_7 \\ \dot{x}_8 \\ \dot{x}_9 \\ \dot{x}_{10} \\ \dot{x}_{11} \\ \dot{x}_{12} \end{pmatrix}
=
\begin{pmatrix} x_4 + x_5 \sin x_1 \tan x_2 + x_6 \cos x_1 \tan x_2 \\ x_5 \cos x_1 - x_6 \sin x_1 \\ (x_5 \sin x_1 + x_6 \cos x_1)/\cos x_2 \\ ((I_{yy} - I_{zz})x_5 x_6 - x_5 \Omega Jr)/I_{xx} \\ ((I_{zz} - I_{xx})x_4 x_6 + x_4 \Omega Jr)/I_{yy} \\ ((I_{xx} - I_{yy})x_4 x_5 - \Omega Jr)/I_{zz} \\ x_{10} \\ x_{11} \\ x_{12} \\ 0 \\ 0 \\ g \end{pmatrix}
+
\begin{pmatrix} 0 & 0 & 0 & 0 \\ 0 & 0 & 0 & 0 \\ 0 & 0 & 0 & 0 \\ 0 & 1/I_{xx} & 0 & 0 \\ 0 & 0 & 1/I_{yy} & 0 \\ 0 & 0 & 0 & 1/I_{zz} \\ 0 & 0 & 0 & 0 \\ 0 & 0 & 0 & 0 \\ 0 & 0 & 0 & 0 \\ \frac{\cos x_1 \sin x_2 \cos x_3 + \sin x_1 \sin x_3}{m} & 0 & 0 & 0 \\ \frac{\cos x_1 \sin x_2 \sin x_3 - \sin x_1 \cos x_3}{m} & 0 & 0 & 0 \\ -\frac{\cos x_1 \cos x_2}{m} & 0 & 0 & 0 \end{pmatrix}
\begin{pmatrix} F \\ \tau_{1q} \\ \tau_{2q} \\ \tau_{3q} \end{pmatrix}
$$

Appendix 2

$$
M = \begin{bmatrix} m_{11} & m_{12} & m_{13} \\ m_{21} & m_{22} & m_{23} \\ m_{31} & m_{32} & m_{33} \end{bmatrix}
$$

$$
\begin{aligned}
m_{11} = {} & \frac{I_{2xx} + I_{3xx} + I_{2yy}}{2} + I_{3yy} + I_{1zz} - \frac{(I_{3xx} + I_{3yy} + m_3 r_{3com}^2)\cos(2q_2 + 2q_3)}{2} \\
& + \frac{l_2^2 m_3 + m_2 r_{2com}^2 + m_3 r_{3com}^2}{2} + \frac{(I_{2yy} - I_{2xx} + l_2^2 m_3 + m_2 r_{2com}^2)\cos 2q_2}{2} \\
& + l_2 m_3 r_{3com}\cos q_3 + l_2 m_3 r_{3com}\cos(2q_2 + q_3)
\end{aligned}
$$

$$m_{12} = 0$$

$$m_{13} = 0$$

$$m_{22} = m_3 l_2^2 + 2m_3\cos q_3 l_2 r_{3com} + m_2 r_{2com}^2 + m_3 r_{3com}^2 + I_{2zz} + I_{3zz}$$

$$m_{23} = m_{32} = m_3 r_{3com}^2 + l_2 m_3 \cos q_3 r_{3com} + I_{3zz}$$

$$m_{33} = m_3 r_{3com}^2 + I_{3zz}$$

$C(q, \dot{q}) =$

$$
\begin{bmatrix}
\begin{aligned}
&-\dot{q}_1\big((I_{2yy}\dot{q}_2 - I_{2xx}\dot{q}_2 + l_2^2 m_3\dot{q}_2 + m_2\dot{q}_2 r_{2com}^2)\sin 2q_2 \\
&+ (I_{3yy}\dot{q}_3 + I_{3yy}\dot{q}_2 - I_{3xx}\dot{q}_3 - I_{3xx}\dot{q}_2 + m_3\dot{q}_2 r_{3com}^2 + m_3\dot{q}_3 r_{3com}^2)\sin(2q_2 + 2q_3) \\
&+ (2l_2 m_3\dot{q}_2 r_{3com} + l_2 m_3\dot{q}_2 r_{3com})\sin(2q_2 + q_3) + l_2 m_3\dot{q}_3 r_{3com}\sin q_3\big) \\[6pt]
&((I_{2yy}\dot{q}_1^2 - I_{2xx}\dot{q}_1^2)\sin 2q_2)/2 - ((I_{3xx}\dot{q}_1^2 + I_{3yy}\dot{q}_1^2)\sin(2q_2 + 2q_3))/2 \\
&+ ((l_2^2 m_3\dot{q}_1^2 + m_2\dot{q}_1^2 r_{2com}^2)\sin 2q_2)/2 + (m_3\dot{q}_1^2 r_{3com}^2\sin(2q_2 + 2q_3))/2 \\
&- l_2 m_3\dot{q}_3^2 r_{3com}\sin q_3 + l_2 m_3\dot{q}_1^2 r_{3com}\sin(2q_2 + q_3) - 2l_2 m_3\dot{q}_2\dot{q}_3 r_{3com}\sin q_3 \\[6pt]
&(I_{3yy}\dot{q}_1^2\sin(2q_2 + 2q_3))/2 - (I_{3xx}\dot{q}_1^2\sin(2q_2 + 2q_3))/2 \\
&+ (m_3\dot{q}_1^2 r_{3com}^2\sin(2q_2 + 2q_3))/2 + (l_2 m_3\dot{q}_1^2 r_{3com}\sin q_3)/2 \\
&+ l_2 m_3\dot{q}_2^2 r_{3com}\sin q_3 + (l_2 m_3\dot{q}_1^2 r_{3com}\sin(2q_2 + q_3))/2
\end{aligned}
\end{bmatrix}
$$

$G(q) =$

$$
\begin{bmatrix}
0 \\
-m_3 g(r_{3com}(\cos q_2\cos q_3 - \sin q_2\sin q_3) + l_2\cos q_2) - m_2 g r_{2com}\cos q_2 \\
-m_3 g r_{3com}(\cos q_2\cos q_3 - \sin q_2\sin q_3)
\end{bmatrix}
$$

Appendix 3

$$q_1 = a\tan 2(x_y, x_x)$$

$$q_3 = \pm\left(\pi - a\cos\left(\frac{(x_z - l_1)^2 + x_x^2 + x_y^2 - l_2^2 - l_3^2}{2l_2 l_3}\right)\right)$$

$$q_2 = a\tan 2\left(x_z - l_1, \sqrt{x_x^2 + x_y^2}\right) - a\tan 2(l_2 + l_3\cos q_3, l_3\sin q_3)$$

References

1. Daly, J.M., Yan, M., Waslander, S.L.: Coordinated landing of a quadrotor on a skid-steered ground vehicle in the presence of time delays. Auton. Robots 38(2), 179–191 (2015)
2. Botao, H., Lu, L., Mishra, S.: Fast, safe and precise landing of a quadrotor on an oscillating platform. In: 2015 American Control Conference (ACC), pp. 3836–3841 (2015)
3. Tang, Z., et al.: Homing on a moving dock for a quadrotor vehicle. In: 2015 IEEE Region 10 Conference, TENCON 2015, pp. 1–6 (2015)
4. Zheng, D., Wang, H., Chen, W.: Image-based visual tracking of a moving target for a quadrotor. In: 2017 11th Asian Control Conference (ASCC), pp. 198–203 (2017)

5. Kim, J., et al.: Outdoor autonomous landing on a moving platform for quadrotors using an omnidirectional camera. In: 2014 International Conference on Unmanned Aircraft Systems (ICUAS), pp. 1243–1252 (2014)
6. Vlantis, P., et al.: Quadrotor landing on an inclined platform of a moving ground vehicle. In: 2015 IEEE International Conference on Robotics and Automation (ICRA), pp. 2202–2207 (2015)
7. Benini, A., Rutherford, M.J., Valavanis, K.P.: Experimental evaluation of a real-time GPU-based pose estimation system for autonomous landing of rotary wings UAVs. Control Theory Technol. 16(2), 145–159 (2018)
8. Jung, Y., Cho, S., Shim, D.H.: A trajectory-tracking controller design using L1 adaptive control for multi-rotor UAVs. In: 2015 International Conference on Unmanned Aircraft Systems (ICUAS), pp. 132–138 (2015)
9. Chen, X., et al.: System integration of a vision-guided UAV for autonomous landing on moving platform. In: IEEE International Conference on Control and Automation, pp. 761–766 (2016)

Design and Integration
of a Reconfiguration Robot

Jun Jiang, Houde Liu$^{(\boxtimes)}$, Bo Yuan, Lunfei Liang, and Bin Liang

Graduate School at Shenzhen, Tsinghua University,
Shenzhen 518055, People's Republic of China
{jiang.jun,liu.hd}@sz.tsinghua.edu.cn

Abstract. Based on the kinematic topology of bionic robot and robot motion planning modeling, this paper designs the mechanical structure of highly integrated robotic joint module, the fast self-reconfigurable module, the drive control software, and the hardware for the system. Through the experimental verification and simulation data analysis, the robot joint module and the fast self-reconfiguration module designed in this paper meet the performance requirement of the reconfigurable intelligent robot. Finally, the prototype verification of the reconfigurable intelligent robot is realized in this paper.

Keywords: Reconfigurable robot · Joint module · Reconfiguration module

1 Introduction

In the early 1990s, researchers proposed a recombination system based on chain structure [1] and dot matrix format [2], on which the future development trend of modular robots were based. Subsequently, self-reconfigurable robots have been greatly developed in countries around the world, and Japan and the United States have developed most rapidly in this regard. Some universities and research institutions [3–8] in the United States and Japan have conducted extensive and in-depth research on reconstruction techniques, deformation strategies, motion planning, control algorithms, architecture, and collaborative control of reconstructed robots. The reconstruction method of the robot also evolved from the initial static reconfigurable method to the dynamic self-reconfiguration method, and established a variety of model experiment systems. This research has made great progress both in technology and in performance.

In addition, the controller and the driver are embedded in the joint module with the internal wiring, that is used to obtain a modular joint module with light weight, large load-to-weight ratio, and low power consumption. As the core component of the robot, the modular joint module uses a quick connection mechanism for easy maintenance and robot configuration changes.

Therefore, this paper studies the design of the joint module that constitutes the necessary components of the robot, the quickly carried out the self-reconstruction module between the joint modules, and the corresponding drive controller that can realize the motion control of the joint module. Through the corresponding gait simulation analysis and research, this paper completed the design and integration of reconfigurable intelligent robots.

© Springer Nature Switzerland AG 2019
H. Yu et al. (Eds.): ICIRA 2019, LNAI 11742, pp. 339–350, 2019.
https://doi.org/10.1007/978-3-030-27535-8_31

2 Reconfigurable Intelligent Robot Overall Design

The overall system of the reconfigurable intelligent robot mainly includes the robot joint module, the fast self-reconfiguration module, the drive controller, and the central control system. The main functions of these four parts are as follows.

The robot joint module is mainly used to construct the robot body shape, and configure the appropriate motion freedom to facilitate the robot to walk or fine manipulation. The rapid self-reconfiguration module is mainly used to realize the reconfigurable transformation mode of the robot, and to realize more possible manipulation of the robot by expanding the degree of freedom of the robot arm. The drive controller is mainly used to realize the motion control of the robot joint module and rapid self-reconfiguration module, and communicate with the robot central controller. The robot central controller mainly realizes robot motion planning, motion pattern and motion mode, and controls the robot intelligent reconfigurable according to the requirements.

3 Design of Important Parts of Reconfigurable Robot

3.1 Reconfigurable Intelligent Robot Topology

According to different bionic objects, the bionic quadruped robot can be generally divided into mammalian robots [9], reptile robots [10] and insect animal robots [11], as shown in Fig. 1. The quadruped reptile and insect animal robots have lower center of gravity and higher stability. However, these two types of robots require large joint torque to bear their own weight and therefore have poor load capacity. But, the legs of the quadruped mammal are basically under the torso, which has a strong load capacity, can load heavier cargo and can move forward at a faster speed, and the stability control stability is also higher. In view of the advantages of quadruped mammalian robots in terms of weight and flexibility, this paper will focus on the study of reconfigurable intelligent robots in the form of quadruped mammals.

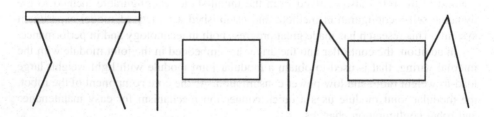

(a) Bionic quadruped mammalian   (b) Bionic quadruped reptile robots   (c) Bionic quadruped insect animal robot

Fig. 1. Bionic quadruped robot topology.

The reconfigurable intelligent robot three-dimensional model designed in this paper is shown in Fig. 2. The robot adopts a symmetrical regular quadrilateral arrangement. Each leg is evenly distributed around the body and has three rotational degrees of freedom. The foot end has a passive cushioning mechanism and a six-dimensional force sensor used to measure the change of the foot end force during the walking of the quadruped robot.

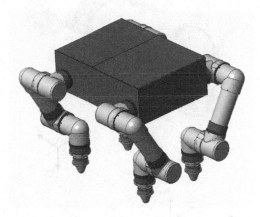

Fig. 2. The three-dimensional model of the reconfigurable robot

3.2 Reconfigurable Intelligent Robot Kinematics Modeling

At present, the methods of kinematics modeling of quadruped robots include D-H method [12], Lie algebra method [13] and spiral theory [14]. Among them, the D-H method is a more common method, which can solve the forward kinematics problem of a series mechanism with arbitrary degrees of freedom. In view of the fact that the reconfigurable intelligent robot has only three degrees of freedom in one leg, it is suitable to establish the kinematic equation of the robot by D-H method. In addition, since the four legs of the reconfigurable intelligent robot are identical in structure, it is only required to solve the kinematic equation of one leg. As shown in Fig. 3, it is a three-dimensional model diagram of one leg and a corresponding coordinate system.

The one-legged D-H kinematics model was established according to the Craig method [15]. The D-H parameters are shown in Table 1.

Table 1. D-H parameters of one-leg.

Joint j	$\alpha_{j-1}/(°)$	$a_{j-1}/(mm)$	$d_j/(mm)$	$\theta_j/(°)$
1	0	0	87	$\theta_1^{(i)} - 90$
2	−90	0	107	$\theta_2^{(i)}$
3	0	260.3	−107	$\theta_3^{(i)}$

In Table 1, α, a, and d is the torsion angle, length, and offset distance of joint connecting rod, respectively, and θ is the joint angle.

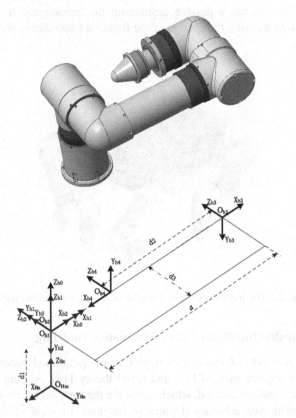

Fig. 3. Three-dimensional model diagram of one leg and a corresponding coordinate system

Based on one-legged kinematic D-H parameters of the quadruped robot, this paper establishes the positive kinematics model on it. The transformation matrix of the quadruped robot joint established by the D-H parameter method is as shown in the formula (1).

$$^{j-1}_{j}T = \begin{bmatrix} \cos\theta_j & \cos\theta_j - \sin\theta_j & 0 & a_{j-1} \\ \sin\theta_j\cos\theta_{j-1} & \cos\theta_j\cos\alpha_{j-1} & -\sin\alpha_{j-1} & -\sin\alpha_{j-1}d_j \\ \sin\theta_j\sin\alpha_{j-1} & \cos\theta_j\sin\alpha_{j-1} & \cos\alpha_{j-1} & \cos\alpha_{j-1}d_j \\ 0 & 0 & 0 & 1 \end{bmatrix} \quad (1)$$

In formula (1), $^{j-1}_{j}T$ represents the coordinate transformation matrix from joint $j - 1$ to joint j. By substituting the D-H parameters of each joint in Table 1 into formula (1), the transformation matrix of each joint can be obtained.

3.3   Design of Reconfigurable Intelligent Robot Joint Module

This paper presents a highly integrated modular joint design. The joint adopts the hollow wire routing mode, the driving mechanism is a DC brushless motor [16], and the harmonic reducer [17] is used as the transmission mechanism to increase the output torque and has a strong load capacity. The joint has a wealth of sensor resources with greater precision, and has better environmental adaptability. In addition, a motion control driver is integrated inside the joint, and the overall structural composition of the joint is shown in Fig. 4.

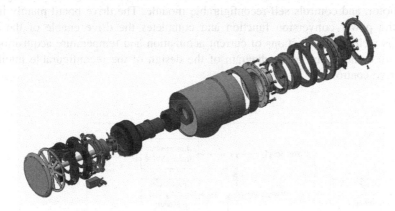

Fig. 4. The design drawing of reconfigurable intelligent robot joint module

3.4   Design of Fast Self-reconfigurable Module

The fast self-reconfigurable module interface adopts permanent magnet connection technology [18], and realizes power-off locking and power-on disconnection. So, this paper adopts plug and socket design, as shown in Fig. 5. Both the plug and the socket are designed with a large tolerance cone angle structure to facilitate connection and separation of the interface. The mating section of the plug and socket is designed with a spline-like structure for transmitting torque. The outer surface of the plug and the inner surface of the socket are provided with elastic electrical connecting sheets. When the plug is inserted into the socket, the elastic electrical connecting sheet is deformed to generate sufficient contact stress and contact area to form a reliable electrical connection. The plug and the socket are connected to the joint module through the connecting flange.

Fig. 5. The plug and socket of the fast self-reconfigurable module

3.5   Drive Controller Hardware Design of the Joint

In this paper, the drive controller is designed for joint module and self-reconfiguration module of the reconfigurable intelligent robot. The main functions of the drive controller include emergency brake enable, self-reconfiguration mechanism control and joint motor drive.

The drive controller system solution consists of two parts: the control board and the drive board. The control board adopts a processor [19] with an ARM core as the main control unit, executes the control commands from the host computer, collects the data information of various sensors, realizes the drive control and emergency braking of the servo motor, and controls self-reconfigurable module. The drive board mainly implements the power conversion function and completes the drive enable of the servo motor, as well as the functions of current acquisition and temperature acquisition.

Figure 6 shows the block diagram of the design of the reconfigurable intelligent robot drive controller.

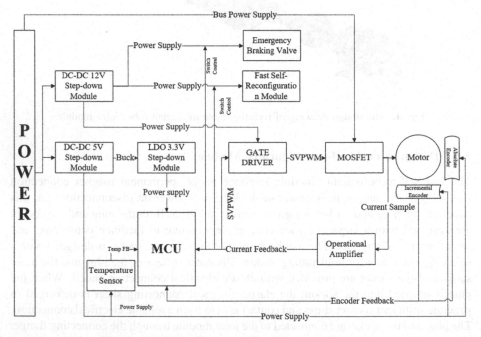

Fig. 6. The block diagram of the drive controller design

3.6   Drive Controller Software Design of the Joint

In this paper, a software system is designed for the hardware system of the robot joint module and the fast self-reconfiguration module, and ensures them can work safely and efficiently. After the entire software solution is powered on, the initialization operation is completed. Under normal circumstances, it is completely controlled by the upper computer, and the operation command can be executed only after receiving the instruction of the upper computer. The flow chart of the entire system is shown in Fig. 7.

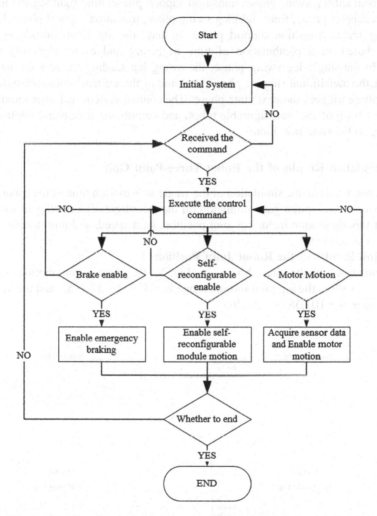

Fig. 7. The flow chart of the drive controller software design of the joint

4 Simulation and Verification

This paper studies the motion planning of the reconfigurable intelligent robot and uses the robot three-point gait method [20] to verify the performance of the reconfigurable intelligent robot. The three-point gait is a slow, static steady motion gait, suitable for motion in complex terrain environments, such as stairs, ruins, and other terrains with large undulating obstacles. In the face of this environment, the robot can swing at most one leg at any time, and at least three legs are supported simultaneously. So there is always a support domain during the movement, so that the quadruped robot can maintain static stability.

According to the gait characteristics, one gait cycle can be divided into eight state phases: front left leg swing phase, transition support phase, hind right leg swing phase, transition support phase, front right leg swing phase, transition support phase, hind left leg swing phase, transition support phase. In here, the algorithm introduces a state machine based on a combination of time triggering and event triggering for gait control. In the single-leg swing phase, the swing leg landing triggers the next state phase; in the transitional support phase, the time of the currently planned transitional support phase triggers the next state phase. The control system real-time monitors the state of each leg of the reconfigurable robot, and outputs the state phase control signal according to the state transition.

4.1   Simulation Results of the Robot Three-Point Gait

In this paper, the dynamic simulation of the single-step motion time of the robot is 0.8 s by performing three-point gait simulation on the reconfiguration intelligent robot. The output of this simulation including joint position, joint speed, and joint torque, and the results are as follows.

Simulation Results of the Robot Joint Position
The simulation results are shown in Fig. 8, the root joint motion range is $-16.331 \sim 15.896°$, the hip joint motion range is $-20.324 \sim 57.215°$, and the knee joint motion range is $-101.387 \sim -24.263°$.

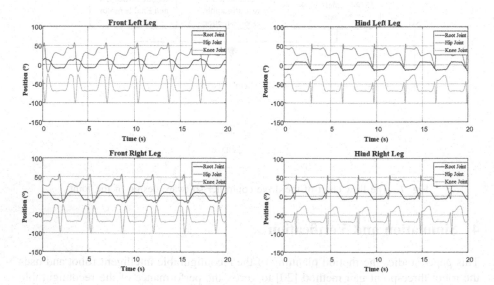

Fig. 8. The position curve of the robot joint

Simulation Results of the Robot Joint Speed

The simulation results are shown in Fig. 9, the maximum speed of the root joint, the hip joint, and the knee joint is 40.551°/s, 312.924°/s, and 412.605°/s, respectively.

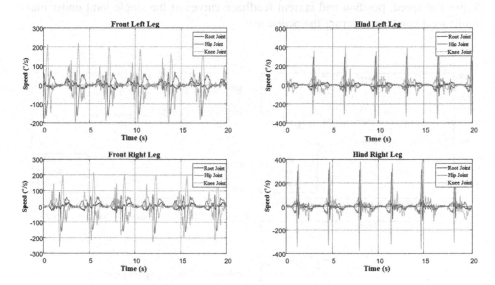

Fig. 9. The speed curve of the robot joint

Simulation Results of the Robot Joint Torque

The simulation results are shown in Fig. 10, the maximum torque of the root joint, the hip joint, and the knee joint are 28.947 Nm, 31.211 Nm, and 39.327 Nm, respectively.

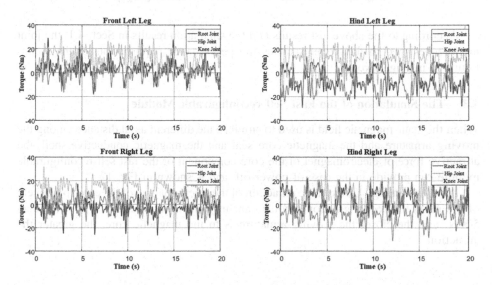

Fig. 10. The torque curve of the robot joint

4.2   The Test Results of the Joint of the Reconfigurable Intelligent Robot

The joint module designed in this paper can realize single-circle 360° position detection, maximum 3850 RPM speed operation, and 49 NM torque output. Figure 11 shows the speed, position and current feedback curves of the single joint under maximum load conditions during the actual test.

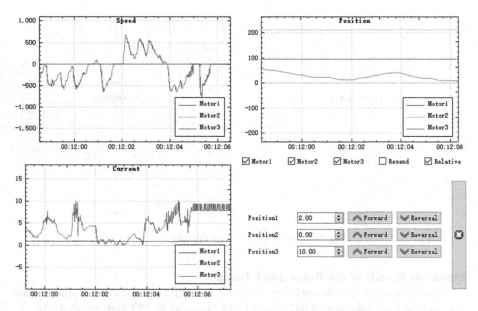

Fig. 11. The motion feedback curves of the single joint

According to the above test results and the simulation results in Sect. 4.1, the joint module designed in this paper satisfies the performance requirements of the reconfigurable intelligent robot.

4.3   The Simulation of the Fast Self-reconfigurable Module

When the static magnetic field is used to simulate the different axial distance among the moving armature and the magnetic core seat and the magnetic conductive shell, the attractive force of electromagnet of the core component of the fast self-reconfigurable module can provide in the case of power-off, and is shown in Fig. 12.

As shown in Fig. 12, the static attraction of the electromagnet of the core component of the rapid self-reconfiguration module can fully meet the requirement of more than 500N, and the closer the moving armature is to the magnetic core, the greater the attraction.

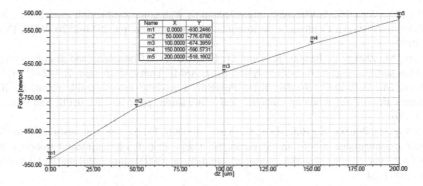

Fig. 12. The curve of electromagnet attractive force with spacing

5 Conclusions

This paper designed and implemented a reconfigurable intelligent robot. First, the topology of the reconfigurable intelligent robot is determined by the topology analysis of the bionic robot. After the kinematics modeling of the reconfigurable intelligent robot, the performance parameters of the robot joint module are obtained. In addition, through the reconfigurable intelligent robot gait planning simulation to confirm the range of motion of the joints of the robot, the speed of motion, and the maximum torque of motion. On this basis, the paper completed the software and hardware scheme design and rapid self-reconfiguration module design of the robot joint module. Finally, the experimental results show that the design indicators meet the performance requirements of reconfigurable intelligent robots.

Acknowledgments. This work was partially supported by the National Natural Science Foundation of China (No. U1813216 and No. 61803221), the Science and Technology Research Foundation of Shenzhen (JCYJ20160301100921349 and JCYJ20170817152701660). The author is thankful to several brilliant engineers, including: Xingzhang Wu, Guanyu Wang (HIT), Ruiping Zhao, Xun Ran, and Shuanglong Li, Jing Xiao for providing support and necessary facilities.

References

1. Will, P., Castano, A., Shen, W.-M.: Robot modularity for self-reconfiguration. In: Proceedings of SPIE Sensor Fusion and Decentralized Control in Robotic Systems II, vol. 3839, pp. 236–245 (1999)
2. Suh, J.W., Homans, S.B., Yim, M.: Telecubes: mechanical design of a module for a self-reconfigurable robotics. In: International Conference on Robotics and Automation, pp. 4095–4101. IEEE, Washington DC (2002)
3. Kotay, K., Rus, D., Vona, M., McGray, C.: The self-reconfiguring robotic molecule: design and control algorithms. In: Algorithmic Foundations of Robotics (1998)
4. Murata, S., Kurokawa, H., Yoshida, E., Tomita, K., Kokaji, S.: A 3-D self-reconfigurable structure. In: 1998 IEEE International Conference on Robotics and Automation, pp. 432–439. IEEE, Leuven (1998)

5. Rus, D., Vona, M.: Self-reconfiguration planning with compressible unit modules. In: 1999 IEEE International Conference on Robotics and Automation, pp. 2513–2520. IEEE, Detroit (1999)

6. Yim, M., Zhang, Y., Roufas, K., Duff, D., Eldershaw, C.: Connecting and disconnecting for chain self-reconfiguration with PolyBot. IEEE/ASME Trans. Mechatron. 7, 442–451 (2000)

7. Yim, M., Duff, D.G., Roufas, K.D.: PolyBot: a modular reconfigurable robot. In: IEEE International Conference on Robotics and Automation, pp. 514–520. IEEE, San Francisco (2000)

8. Zhang, Y., Roufas, K., Eldershaw, C., Yim, M., Duff, D.: Sensor computations in modular self reconfigurable robots. In: Siciliano, B., Dario, P. (eds.) Experimental Robotics VIII. STAR, vol. 5, pp. 276–286. Springer, Heidelberg (2003). https://doi.org/10.1007/3-540-36268-1_24

9. Guan, X., Zheng, H., Zhang, X.: Biologically inspired quadruped robot biosbot: modeling, simulation and experiment. In: 2nd International Conference on Autonomous Robots and Agents, pp. 261–266. IEEE, Palmerston North (2004)

10. Hayashi, I., Iwatsuki, N., Iwashina, S.: The running characteristics of a screw-principle microrobot in a small bent pipe. In: Sixth International Symposium on Micro Machine and Human Science, pp. 225–228. IEEE, Nagoya (1995)

11. Arikawa, K., Hirose, S.: Development of quadruped walking robot TITAN-VIII. In: IEEE/RSJ International Conference on Intelligent Robots and Systems, pp. 208–214. IEEE, Osaka (1996)

12. Denavit, J., Hartenberg, R.: A kinematic notation for lower-pair mechanisms based on matrices. Trans. ASME J. Appl. Mech. 23, 215–221 (1955)

13. Park, F.C., Kim, M.W.: Lie theory, Riemannian geometry, and the dynamics of coupled rigid bodies. Zeitschrift fur angewandte Mathematik und Physik ZAMP 51(5), 820–834 (2001)

14. Mladenova, C.D.: Group-theoretical methods in manipulator kinematics and symbolic computations. J. Intell. Syst. 8(1), 21–34 (1993)

15. Craig, J.J.: Inroduction to Robotics, 3rd edn. China Machine Press, Beijing (2005)

16. The Kollmorgen Torquer Brushless Motor Series direct drive frameless motor. https://www.kollmorgen.com/en-us/products/motors/direct-drive/tbm-series/

17. The Leaderdriver LHSG-I Series harmonic reducer. http://www.leaderdrive.om/product.-hp?id=21

18. Li, J., Tan, Q., Zhang, Y., Zhang, K.: Study on the calculation of magnetic force based on the equivalent magnetic charge method. In: 2012 International Conference on Applied Physics and Industrial Engineering, Physics Procedia, pp. 190–197 (2012)

19. STMicroelectroincs, STM32F103 devices use the Cortex-M3 core, with a maximum CPU speed of 72 Mhz. https://www.st.com/en/microcontrollers-microprocessorsstm32f103.html

20. Hirose, S., Yoneda, K., Tsukagoshi, H.: TITAN VII: quadruped walking and manipulating robot on a steep slope. In: IEEE International Conference on Robotics and Automation, pp. 494–500. IEEE, Albuquerque (1997)

The Longitudinal Stability of FWMAVs Considering the Oscillation of Body in Forward Flight

Dong Xue[1,2]($\boxtimes$), Bifeng Song[2], Wenping Song[2], Wenqing Yang[2], and Wenfu Xu[1]

[1] Harbin Institute of Technology, Shenzhen, China
xuedong@hit.edu.cn
[2] Northwestern Polytechnical University, Xi'an, China

Abstract. FWMAVs (Flapping Wing Micro Air Vehicles) turn to be a flexible multibody system when the inertia and flexibility of flapping wing are considered. The flight dynamic stability considering the oscillation of body in forward flight are still an open question. In this study, based on a method coupled CFD (Computational fluid dynamics), CSD (Computational structural dynamics) and equations of longitudinal motion for FWMAVs, the periodic derivatives of forces and moment during whole flapping course can be computed. The dynamic stability is analysed by Floquet method specially for the cyclic-motion equilibrium. Results show that the FWMAV in forward flight is stable and character of eigenvalue is similar to that of fixed-wing vehicles. However, the effect of pitch rate damping is different from its role played for the fixed wing vehicle. As the pitch rate damping increases, the system turns to be unstable. These results can inform designs of FWMAV from the perspective of dynamic stability.

Keywords: Flapping wing · Computational fluid dynamics (CFD) ·
Computational structural dynamics (CSD) · Multibody dynamics ·
Flight stability

1 Introduction

FWMAVs have aroused intense focus by virtue of distinctive advantages including high aerodynamics efficiency at low Reynolds numbers [1], extensive flight ability (forward and hovering flight) [2], gust resistance [3]. Despite many kinds of FWMAVs have been developed, such as Hummingbird [4], RoboBee [5], DelFlys [6] and Chinese "Dove" [7], there is a long way to be widely utilized in civil or military fields for there still have many challenges that hinder the development of FWMAVs.

These challenges include aerodynamics modelling, optimization of wing structure, dynamic analysis, control design and MEMS (micro electro-mechanical systems) manufacturing. As the size of FWMAVs increases from insect-size to bird-size, the wing to body ratio increases (>5%) and the flapping frequency decreases [8], and periodic movement of flapping wing brings about more obvious body oscillation, which will in turn influences the flapping movement of flexible wing. It turns to be a

© Springer Nature Switzerland AG 2019
H. Yu et al. (Eds.): ICIRA 2019, LNAI 11742, pp. 351–361, 2019.
https://doi.org/10.1007/978-3-030-27535-8_32

multibody, nonlinear time-periodic (NLTP) system. The tight coupling between aerodynamic, flexible wing structure and body dynamics becomes the one of principal challenge to understand dynamic characters and develop a successful bird-inspired FWMAVs.

For the FWMAVs with relative high wing-to-body mass ratio and low flapping frequency, the interaction between the wing and body motion cannot be neglected. There are two methods have been proposed to investigate the dynamic stability of such NLTP system: One method is a direct time integration of the multibody dynamics equations coupling with the aerodynamic and structural simulations [9, 10]. The other method is to linearize the NLTP system leads to a linear time periodic (LTP) system whose stability analysis could be checked via Floquet theory. The Floquet stability analysis can give the natural modes of motion of the perturbation and general stability property of the periodic motion. Here we take the second method to analyse the dynamic stability of FWMAVs.

The article is structured as follows: the research subject "Dove" FWMAVs is first presented and continues with its geometric and structural parameters. Then CFD, CSD and the coupling method CFD/CSD/MBD is briefly described. The longitudinal stability of FWMAVs considering effect of oscillation of body in forward flight will be presented successively in the last section.

2   Methods

2.1   "Dove" FWMAV

This study considers a bird-like FWMAV: "Dove" [7], which has two wings, a vertical and a horizontal tail (as shown in Fig. 1). Its cruise speed and take-off weight are 8 m/s–10 m/s and 170 g–230 g respectively depends on the need of flight task. It has the ability to operate fully autonomously, fly lasts twenty minutes and transmit live stabilized colour video to a ground station over 4 km away.

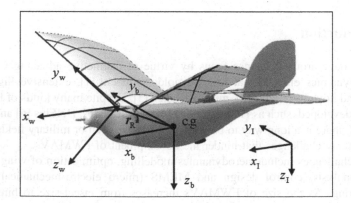

Fig. 1. "Dove" FWMAV and its reference frame

2.2   Reference Frame and Geometry of "Dove" FWMAV

In order to determine the motion of the body in the inertial coordinate system and the position of the flexible flapping wing, three coordinate systems need to be defined (as shown in Fig. 1): the I-coordinate system represents the inertial coordinate system and is used to describe the global coordinate. The b-coordinate system represents the body coordinate system whose origin coincides with the centre of gravity of the "DOVE". The positive direction of the x_b-axis points to the head and parallels to the axis of the drive motor. The positive direction of the y_b-axis points to the right side of the aircraft body, perpendicular to the vertical symmetry of the body. The definition of the z_b-axis follows the right-hand rule. The w-coordinate system is the coordinate system of the right flapping wing, and its origin is located at the root of the right rocker arm of the flapping mechanism. Due to the setting angle of the flapping wing is zero, the positive direction of x_w is parallel to x_b-axis, and the positive direction of y_w is parallel the front beam and points to the outer segment. The definition of the z_w-axis follows the right-hand rule. The distance between origin of the b-coordinate system and the origin of the w-coordinate system is expressed by the radius vector r_R.

The flapping wing of the "DOVE" has only one degree of freedom: rotating around x_b-axis. The kinematic model of flapping amplitude is given by equation

$$\varphi = 33° \cos(2\pi ft) \tag{1}$$

where f represents flapping frequency.

The flapping wing of "Dove" has a quarter-circle platform, and its geometrical parameter is shown in the Fig. 2.

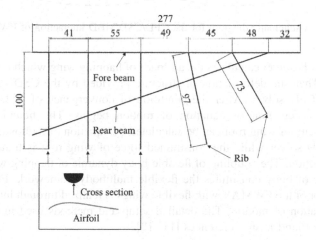

Fig. 2. Geometry of flapping wing (mm)

The longitudinal equilibrium of moment is trimmed by the horizontal tail. The geometrical parameter of horizontal tail is presented in the Fig. 3.

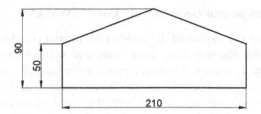

Fig. 3. The geometrical parameter of horizontal tail

2.3 CFD/CSD/MBD

The "DOVE" FWMAV should be treated as a multibody system especially for relatively low flapping frequency and high wing-to-body mass ratio. And the direct solution to a multibody dynamic usually depends on explicit expression of air loads while aerodynamic force calculated by CFD cannot be obtained directly. Here we present a loosed coupled method to decompose flexible multibody system to three single body system: one body and two flexible flapping wings. Through interaction of the boundary constrained condition between body and flapping wings, the solution of multibody dynamic can be iterated to convergence and obtained (Fig. 4).

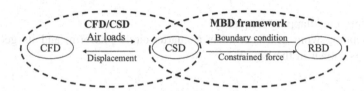

Fig. 4. A schematic diagram for the CFD/CSD/MBD interaction of FWMAVs

First the CFD solver calculates the air loads of flapping wing which is transferred to CSD solver. Then the deformation of structure provided by the CSD solver is transferred to the CFD solver. After the condition of convergence of CSD and CFD is achieved, the calculation of equation of motion begins. The boundary condition including velocity of wing root can be calculated by equation of motion of body and is offered to CSD solver while the constrained force of wing root is transferred to the equation of motion. The coupling of flexible body dynamic of flapping wing and rigid body dynamic of body constitutes the flexible multibody framework. Finally, A free flight simulator of the FWMAV with flexible wings is realized through integrated CFD, CSD and equation of motion. The detailed setup and methods used in the CFD and CSD could be found in the references [11, 12].

2.4 Equation of Motion in Longitudinal Direction

The longitudinal motion is only considered in the present paper, the vehicle has three freedom: horizontal displacement x_b and vertical displacement z_b and pitch angle θ. The Newton–Euler-based equations of body are simplified to

$$\frac{\mathrm{d}u(t)}{\mathrm{d}t} = \frac{1}{m}X(t) - g\,\sin\theta - q(t)w(t)$$
$$\frac{\mathrm{d}w(t)}{\mathrm{d}t} = \frac{1}{m}Z(t) + g\,\cos\theta + q(t)u(t)$$
$$I_{yy}\frac{\mathrm{d}q(t)}{\mathrm{d}t} = M(t)$$
$$\frac{\mathrm{d}\theta(t)}{\mathrm{d}t} = q(t)$$

(2)

where θ represents the pitch angle between the horizontal plane and the x_b-axis. The u, w represent x_b and z_b component of velocity respectively. And q represents the y_b component of angular velocity. X and Z are the resultant forces from wing roots along x_b and z_b axes respectively and M represents the resultant moment from wing roots around the y_b-axes. I_{yy} represents the pitching moment of inertia about y_b-axis.

In order to analyse the longitudinal dynamic stability of "DOVE" FWMAV in forward flight, the equation of disturbance motion can be derived as follows.

According to Sect. 2.4, the equilibrium can be obtained and the motion of body of vehicle is cyclic. Set $u_0(t)$, $w_0(t)$, $q_0(t)$, $\theta_0(t)$ as the periodic solution of trimmed forward flight of "DOVE". They satisfy equation:

$$\frac{\mathrm{d}u_0(t)}{\mathrm{d}t} = \frac{1}{m}X_0(t) - g\,\sin\theta_0(t) - q_0(t)w_0(t)$$
$$\frac{\mathrm{d}w_0(t)}{\mathrm{d}t} = \frac{1}{m}Z_0(t) - g\,\cos\theta_0(t) - q_0(t)u_0(t)$$
$$I_{yy}\frac{\mathrm{d}q_0(t)}{\mathrm{d}t} = M_0(t)$$
$$\frac{\mathrm{d}\theta_0(t)}{\mathrm{d}t} = q_0(t)$$

(3)

where

$$u(t) = u_0(t) + \delta u(t)$$
$$w(t) = w_0(t) + \delta w(t)$$
$$q(t) = q_0(t) + \delta q(t)$$
$$\theta(t) = \theta_0(t) + \delta\theta(t)$$

(4)

$$X(t) = X_0(t) + \delta X(t)$$
$$Z(t) = Z_0(t) + \delta Z(t)$$
$$M(t) = M_0(t) + \delta M(t)$$

(5)

Substituting Eqs. (4) and (5) into Eq. (3), and neglecting the second and higher order terms give

$$\frac{\mathrm{d}\delta u(t)}{\mathrm{d}t} = \frac{1}{m}\delta X(t) - g\delta\theta(t)\cos\theta_0(t)$$
$$-q_0(t)\delta w(t) - w_0(t)\delta q(t)$$
$$\frac{\mathrm{d}\delta w(t)}{\mathrm{d}t} = \frac{1}{m}\delta Z(t) - g\delta\theta(t)\sin\theta_0(t)$$
$$+q_0(t)\delta u(t) + u_0(t)\delta q(t)$$
$$I_{yy}\frac{\mathrm{d}\delta q(t)}{\mathrm{d}t} = \delta M(t)$$

(6)

The disturbance values of the resultant forces and moment can be expressed as an infinite series according to Taylor's theorem and neglecting the second and higher order terms.

$$
\begin{aligned}
\delta X(t) &= \frac{\partial X(t)}{\partial u}\delta u(t) + \frac{\partial X(t)}{\partial w}\delta w(t) + \frac{\partial X(t)}{\partial q}\delta q(t) \\
\delta Z(t) &= \frac{\partial Z(t)}{\partial u}\delta u(t) + \frac{\partial Z(t)}{\partial w}\delta w(t) + \frac{\partial Z(t)}{\partial q}\delta q(t) \\
\delta M(t) &= \frac{\partial M(t)}{\partial u}\delta u(t) + \frac{\partial M(t)}{\partial w}\delta w(t) + \frac{\partial M(t)}{\partial q}\delta q(t)
\end{aligned}
\tag{7}
$$

The partial derivatives with respect to u are respectively defined as

$$
\begin{aligned}
\frac{\partial X(t)}{\partial u} &= \lim_{\Delta u \to 0}\frac{\Delta X(t)}{\Delta u} \approx \frac{\Delta X(t)}{\Delta u} \\
\frac{\partial Z(t)}{\partial u} &= \lim_{\Delta u \to 0}\frac{\Delta Z(t)}{\Delta u} \approx \frac{\Delta Z(t)}{\Delta u} \\
\frac{\partial M(t)}{\partial u} &= \lim_{\Delta u \to 0}\frac{\Delta M(t)}{\Delta u} \approx \frac{\Delta M(t)}{\Delta u}
\end{aligned}
\tag{8}
$$

Substituting Eqs. (7) and (8) into Eq. (6) gives

$$
\begin{bmatrix} \delta \dot{u} \\ \delta \dot{w} \\ \delta \dot{q} \\ \delta \dot{\theta} \end{bmatrix} = \mathbf{A}(t) \begin{bmatrix} \delta u \\ \delta w \\ \delta q \\ \delta \theta \end{bmatrix}
\tag{9}
$$

where $\dot{u} = \frac{\mathrm{d}u}{\mathrm{d}t}, \dot{w} = \frac{\mathrm{d}w}{\mathrm{d}t}, \dot{q} = \frac{\mathrm{d}q}{\mathrm{d}t}, \dot{\theta} = \frac{\mathrm{d}\theta}{\mathrm{d}t}$, $\mathbf{A}(t)$ is called as system matrix.

$$
\mathbf{A}(t) = \begin{bmatrix}
\frac{X_u(t)}{m} & \frac{X_w(t)}{m} - q_0(t) & \frac{X_q(t)}{m} - w_0(t) & -g\cos\theta_0(t) \\
\frac{Z_u(t)}{m} + q_0(t) & \frac{Z_w}{m} & \frac{Z_q(t)}{m} + u_0(t) & -g\sin\theta_0(t) \\
\frac{M_u(t)}{I_{yy}} & \frac{M_w(t)}{I_{yy}} & \frac{M_q(t)}{I_{yy}} & 0 \\
0 & 0 & 1 & 0
\end{bmatrix}
\tag{10}
$$

where $X_u = \partial X(t)/\partial u$, $X_w = \partial X(t)/\partial w$, $X_q = \partial X(t)/\partial q$, $Z_u = \partial Z(t)/\partial u$, $Z_w = \partial Z(t)/\partial w$, $Z_q = \partial Z(t)/\partial q$, $M_u = \partial M(t)/\partial u$, $M_w = \partial M(t)/\partial w$, $M_q = \partial M^{wing}(t)/\partial q + M^{tail}(t)/\partial q$.

According to the method used by Taylor et al. [13], here we take same method to obtain X_w, Y_w, Z_w. Hence, the w-derivatives are simply

$$
\begin{aligned}
X_w &= \frac{\partial X}{\partial w} \approx u_e^{-1}\frac{\partial X}{\partial \alpha} \\
Z_w &= \frac{\partial Z}{\partial w} \approx u_e^{-1}\frac{\partial Z}{\partial \alpha} \\
M_w &= \frac{\partial M}{\partial w} \approx u_e^{-1}\frac{\partial M}{\partial \alpha}
\end{aligned}
\tag{11}
$$

Since neglecting the rate derivatives does not in general lead to a loss of stability in aircraft [13], here the X_q, Y_q, Z_q^{wing} are ignored during the dynamic analysis. But the pitch damping provided by horizontal tail is important and cannot be neglected, and can be obtained approximately by the equations

$$\partial M^{\text{tail}}(t)/\partial q$$
$$= \frac{\partial (L^{\text{tail}}(t) * l_{\text{tail-wing}})}{\partial (w_{\text{tail}}/l_{\text{tail-wing}})}$$
$$= \frac{\partial L^{\text{tail}}(t) l^2_{\text{tail-wing}}}{\partial w_{\text{tail}}} \tag{12}$$
$$\approx u_e^{-1} l^2_{\text{tail-wing}} \frac{\partial L^{\text{tail}}}{\partial \alpha}$$

where $l_{\text{tail-wing}}$ represents the distance between aerodynamic centre of flapping wing and horizontal tail.

3 Results

3.1 Resultant Force and Moment Derivatives

The equilibrium condition for dynamic stability analysis is presented in the Table 1.

Table 1. Equilibrium condition for dynamic stability analysis

Parameter	Value
Total mass: m_e/g	210
Cruise speed: U_e/m s^{-1}	9
Angle of attack: α_e/deg	12
Flapping frequency: f_e/Hz	9
Setting angle of horizontal tail: δ_e/deg	4.0

After the equilibrium flight conditions have been achieved, aerodynamic forces X, Z in the - x_b and - z_b direction respectively and moment M around the y_b direction of horizontal tail can be obtained while disturbing the δ_e, which are presented in the Fig. 5. According to the Eq. (12), pitch rate damping M_q can be calculated after the $\frac{\partial L^{\text{tail}}}{\partial \alpha}$ obtained from the Fig. 5.

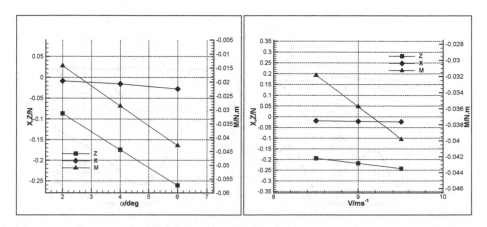

Fig. 5. X, Z and M of horizontal tail

Resultant forces and moment of flapping wing for α-series are plotted in Fig. 6, resultant forces and moment on the flapping wing for u-series are plotted in Fig. 7.

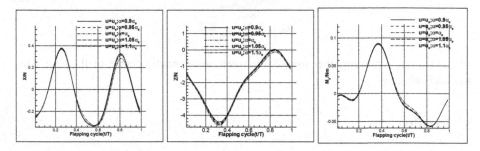

Fig. 6. Resultant force X, Z and M while α varies from the equilibrium value α_e

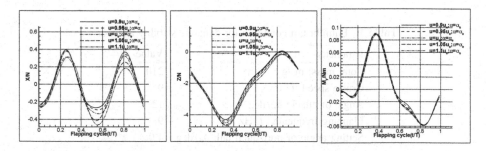

Fig. 7. Resultant force X, Z and M while varies from the equilibrium value u_e

According to the Figs. 6 and 7, the time course of derivatives can be calculated and shown in the Figs. 8 and 9. It is known to us that the derivatives are periodic functions for cyclic motion as shown in the following figures.

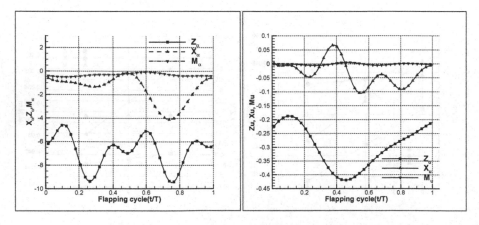

Fig. 8. Periodic derivatives of X, Z and M with respect to α and u (symbol spacing = 2)

3.2   Floquet Method to Analyse Stability of Linear Periodic Coefficient Systems

Equation (9) can be solved to obtain the characters of flight stability of the periodic kinematic of FWMAVs. If the perturbations δu, δw, δq die out as time increases, the periodic solution or the equilibrium of flight is stable, otherwise it is unstable. The stability analysis for such a periodic system can be via Floquet theory [14, 15].

The stability of the periodic solution can be achieved according to Table 2.

Table 2. Zero solution stability criterion for motion equation

Floquet multiplier	Floquet index	Characteristic of system
$\max (|\rho_i|) > 1$	$\max (\mathrm{Re}(\lambda_i)) > 0$	Unstable
$\max (|\rho_i|) < 1$	$\max (\mathrm{Re}(\lambda_i)) < 0$	Stable
$\max (|\rho_i|) = 1$	$\max (\mathrm{Re}(\lambda_i)) = 0$	Critical

According to the above method, two stable oscillatory motion is obtained as shown in the Table 3. And it consists a long period stable mode ($T_{\mathrm{long}} = 5.51$ s) and a short period stable mode ($T_{\mathrm{short}} = 0.64$ s). $\lambda = n \pm i\omega$ represents a damped oscillatory mode which has period $T = 2\pi/\omega$. Since there are two pairs of complex eigenvalues with a negative real part, representing the system is stable.

Table 3. Eigenvalues of "Dove" FWMAV

$\lambda_{1,2}$	$\lambda_{3,4}$
$-0.0050 \pm 1.140i$	$-10.075 \pm 9.835i$

What's more, the damping character of the oscillation mode can be demonstrated by the halve time in magnitude, where

$$t_{\mathrm{half}} = \frac{\ln 2}{|n|} \tag{13}$$

According to the Eq. (13), the time to halve magnitude is 138 s and 0.068 s for long period mode and short period mode, respectively. Since the flapping frequency is 9 Hz (the wing-flapping period is 0.11 s), thus the perturbation of the short period oscillation will be half in less half of wing-beat for the short period mode. While the perturbation of the oscillation will be half in 1242 wing-beats for the long period mode for lack of damping effects.

It is noticeable that such flight stability is very similar to that of fixed-wing aircraft whose longitudinal equations of motion also have two pairs of complex conjugate roots, the short period motion and a much longer period known as phugoid mode. The long period mode is an interchange between potential and kinetic energy, which leads to a steady rise and fall in altitude. Normally, it is accompanied by slight changes in pitch while the angle of attack remains constant during the ups and downs.

3.3   The Influence of Pitch Rate Damping M_q

Pitch rate damping M_q provides a nose-down damping moment when the body experience a nose-up pitch rate and vice versa. In order to study the effect of pitch rate damping M_q on the eigenvalue of system, here gives the root locus plots by decreasing pitch rate damping M_q from zero to -0.03. It can be seen from the Fig. 9 that the eigenvalue representing short period mode decreases along the negative x-direction when the pitch rate damping M_q decreases. However, the absolute value of image part of eigenvalue representing long period mode decreasing and its real part turns to be positive from negative, which means the system turns to be unstable. Above results shows the dynamic character of FWMAV in forward flight is very sensitive to the pitch rate damping M_q. And pitch rate damping provided by horizontal tail plays a contrary role in the dynamic stability of FWMAVs in forward flight compared with fixed wing vehicle.

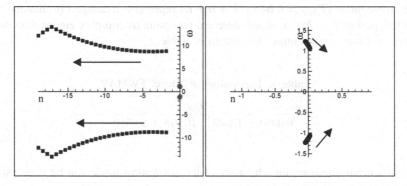

Fig. 9. Root locus plots by decreasing pitch rate derivative M_q from 0 to -0.03(left), partial enlargement of eigenvalues of long period mode(right)

4   Conclusion

Based on the CFD/CSD/MBD method, the flight of FWMAVs can be simulated while the oscillation of body is considered. According to the computational results, two stable oscillatory motion is obtained and it consists a long period stable mode ($T_{long} = 5.51$ s) and a short period stable mode ($T_{short} = 0.64$ s). Since there are two pairs of complex eigenvalues with a negative real part, representing the system is stable. The character of eigenvalues is similar to that of fixed-wing vehicles.

However, the effect of pitch rate damping is different from its role played for the fixed wing vehicle. As the pitch rate damping increases, the system turns to be unstable. These results can inform designs of FWMAVs.

Acknowledgements. This study was supported by the National Key Research and Development Program of China under Grant 2017YFB1300102, National Natural Science Foundation of China, Grants No. 11572255.

References

1. Bayiz, Y.E., Ghanaatpishe, M., Fathy, H., et al.: Hovering efficiency comparison of rotary and flapping flight for a rigid and rectangular wings via dimensionless multi-objective optimization. Bioinspir. Biomim. **13**(4), 046002 (2018)
2. Shyy, W., et al.: Recent progress in flapping wing aerodynamics and aeroelasticity. Prog. Aerosp. Sci. **46**(7), 284–327 (2010)
3. Fisher, A., Ravi, S., Watkins, S., et al.: The gust-mitigating potential of flapping wings. Bioinspir. Biomim. **11**(4), 046010 (2016)
4. Keennon, M., Klingebiel, K., Won, H.: Development of the nano hummingbird: a tailless flapping wing micro air vehicle. In: 50th AIAA Aerospace Sciences Meeting Including the New Horizons Forum and Aerospace Exposition, Nashville, Tennessee (2012)
5. Ma, K., Chirarattananon, P., Fuller, S., Wood, R.: Controlled flight of a biologically inspired. Insect-Scale Robot. Sci. **340**(6132), 603–607 (2013)
6. de Croon, G., de Clercq, K., Ruijsink, R., Remes, B., deWagter, C.: Design, aerodynamics, and vision-based control of the DelFly. Int. J. Micro Air Veh. **1**(2), 71–97 (2009)
7. Yang, W., Wang, L., Song, B.: Dove: a biomimetic flapping-wing micro air vehicle. Int. J. Micro Air Veh. **10**(1), 70–84 (2017)
8. Shyy, W., Kang, C.K., Chirarattananon, P.: Aerodynamics, sensing and control of insect-scale flapping-wing flight. Proc. Math. Phys. Eng. Sci. **472**(2186), 20150712 (2016)
9. Wu, J.H., Zhang, Y.L., Sun, M.: Hovering of model insects: simulation by coupling equations of motion with Navier-Stokes equations. J. Exp. Biol. **212**(20), 3313–3329 (2009)
10. Kim, J.K., Han, J.H.: A multibody approach for 6-DOF flight dynamics and stability analysis of the hawkmoth manduca sexta. Bioinspir. Biomim. **9**(1), 016011 (2014)
11. Yang, W., Song, B., Wang, L., Chen, L.: Dynamic fluid-structure coupling method of flexible flapping wing for MAV. J. Aerosp. Eng. **28**(6), 04015006 (2015)
12. Xue, D., Song, B.F., Song, W.P., et al.: Effect of wing flexibility on flight dynamics stability of flapping wing MAVs in forward flight. Int. J. Micro Air Veh. **8**(3), 170–180 (2016)
13. Taylor, G.K., Thomas, A.L.R.: Dynamic flight stability in the desert locust *Schistocerca gregaria*. J. Exp. Biol. **206**, 2803–2829 (2003)
14. Rugh, W.J.: Linear System Theory. Prentice-Hall, Inc., Upper Saddle River (1996)
15. Yakubovich, V.A., Starzhinskii, V.M.: Linear Differential Equations with Periodic Coefficients. Wiley, New York (1975)

Design and Control of a Small Intelligent Camera Stabilizer for a Flapping-Wing Robotic Bird

Xu Liang, Erzhen Pan, Hui Xu, Juntao Liu, Yuanpeng Wang,
Xiaokun Hu, and Wenfu Xu[✉]

School of Mechanical Engineering and Automation,
Harbin Institute of Technology, Shenzhen 518055, China
wfxu@hit.edu.cn

Abstract. A Flapping-wing robotic bird is an aircraft that mimics the structure and flight of a bird. It flies by fluttering the wings and uses the tail to adjust the attitude of the fuselage in real time. Such type of flight poses a challenge for visual surveillance, because the position of its center of mass and the attitude of the body are very difficult to maintain stable and supply ideal conditions for the camera on it. In this paper, we develop a small intelligent camera stabilizer for a flapping-wing robotic bird. It is designed by considering the flight characteristics and the constrains on size, power and mass. It is composed of mechanical subsystem, sensing subsystem and an embedded controller. The main mechanism has 3-DOF, including 1-DOF for telescopic structure and 2-DOF for attitude adjustment. The sensing subsystem uses MPU6050 as attitude sensor and uses attitude quaternion to calculate Euler angle of both robotic bird and camera. The embedded controller is based on STM32F4 microchip and the Keil Uvision5 platform. Finally, the camera stabilizer is fabricated by integrating the subsystems. It only has 52 g in mass. Furthermore, it is tested and experimented. The results show that it has good stabilizing effect.

Keywords: Camera stabilizer · HIT-Hawk · Robotic bird · Ornithopter · Flapping wing

1 Introduction

With advances in technology, unmanned aerial vehicles as a simple and easy to operate aircraft, has been rapidly developed. Currently the development of mature UAVs are mainly two types of rotorcraft and fixed wing aircraft, already widely used in military and civilian fields. Flapping wing aircraft is an unconventional aircraft, flying through imitating the birds, with high energy efficiency, noise and other advantages over conventional aircraft at low speeds. Due to the complex air flow field of the flapping-wing flight, there are many factors affect the flight efficiency of the flapping wing aircraft, so its development difficulty is greater than that of the traditional aircraft. Many domestic and foreign research institutions in the field of flapping-wing aircraft is still in the development stage.

© Springer Nature Switzerland AG 2019
H. Yu et al. (Eds.): ICIRA 2019, LNAI 11742, pp. 362–375, 2019.
https://doi.org/10.1007/978-3-030-27535-8_33

The visual surveillance function is of great significance to the flapping-wing aircraft, which can make the flapping-wing aircraft carry out the flight at a longer distance, and can obtain the information of the airspace and the ground from the first perspective for environmental monitoring. Because of its shape and flight mode, it has high concealment and can be effectively used for military reconnaissance.

During the flight, the fuselage of flapping-wing aircraft will have attitude changes during each flapping period. Therefore, its posture and center of mass will change frequently. In order to capture a stable picture, it is necessary to use the stabilizer for the camera. At present, the existing camera stabilizer is mostly used for the rotorcraft aerial photography system or the handheld photography system. Its weight, response speed and structure are difficult to meet the requirements of the flapping-wing aircraft. Therefore, it is necessary to study camera stabilizer for flapping-wing aircraft.

2 Mechanical Design

2.1 Flapping-Wing Robotic Bird HIT-Hawk

Although the flapping-wing aircraft are flying in the manner of fluttering wings, the parameters such as fuselage size, flight performance, flutter frequency, and load capacity of different flapping-wing aircraft are quite different. In this paper, we take the HIT-Hawk developed by Harbin Institute of Technology (SZ) as the carrier to make the research of the camera stabilizer. The HIT-Hawk is shown in Fig. 1.

Fig. 1. HIT-hawk

HIT-Hawk is a kind of flapping-wing robotic bird that simulates large-sized bird flight. It has three degrees of freedom. The wings provide the necessary lift and thrust for flying. The tail has two degrees of freedom, pitch and roll, and controls the lift and turn of aircraft. The parameters of the HIT-Hawk are shown in Table 1:

Table 1. Parameters of the HIT-Hawk

Parameters	Value
Total mass	510 g
Wingspan	2.3 m
Flapping frequency	3–7 Hz
Load	<100 g
Battery	3S Lipo 11.1 V 800 mAh
Flight endurance	15 min

2.2 Mechanical Design of Camera Stabilizer

According to the parameters of the HIT-Hawk, combined with the flight characteristics of the flapping-wing aircraft, the mechanical design of the camera stabilizer must meet the following conditions:

1. The range of motion is large. During the process of flapping-wing flight, the flight attitude is adjusted in real time according to the flight conditions. The attitude changes frequently and the range of change is large. Therefore, the camera stabilizer needs a large motion compensation range.
2. Compact and lightweight. The load of HIT-Hawk is less than 100 g, and the space for installing the camera stabilizer in the fuselage is limited, so the camera needs to be compact and light in weight.
3. Camera protection. The HIT-Hawk often take off by throwing and landed by gliding. During the landing process, the fuselage will have direct contact with the ground and with a certain degree of impact. Therefore, the camera can neither hinder the throwing take off, but also protect the camera when landing.

According to the above requirements for the camera stabilizer, we designed the mechanical structure. The three-dimensional model is shown in Fig. 2. The mechanical structure of the camera stabilizer mainly includes two parts: the attitude adjustment structure and the telescopic structure. The attitude adjustment structure are composed of two outer rotor brushless DC motors, IMU attitude sensors, a camera and some connecting units.

The rotorcraft camera stabilizer often uses three servo motors to adjust the attitude of the camera from yaw, roll, and pitch directions to eliminate the camera's attitude deviation. Considering that the flapping-wing aircraft cannot hover or pan in all directions like a rotorcraft, and the load capacity is far lower than rotorcraft, the attitude adjustment structure of FAV only compensates the attitude deviation in roll direction and pitch direction. The yaw axis direction is consistent with the fuselage. On the one hand, it can reduce the overall weight of the camera stabilizer, and on the other hand, it can be helpful for the first-person view control.

The telescopic structure of the camera stabilizer is mainly used for the protection of camera. When taking off, landing and some unexpected situations happen, the camera can be taken back to the lower part of the fuselage. On the one hand, it does not hinder the take off, and on the other hand, it protects the camera when landing. When the

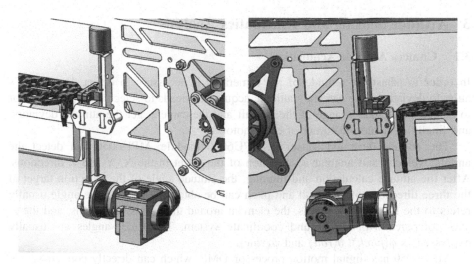

Fig. 2. 3D model of the camera stabilizer

robotic bird is flying smoothly, the camera can be extended to obtain a wider field of view, and the effect display is shown in Fig. 3. The telescopic uses the structure of the micro stepping motor and the screw slide rail to complete the telescopic function. The structure has the advantages of light weight and high integration, and can effectively utilize the limited installation space.

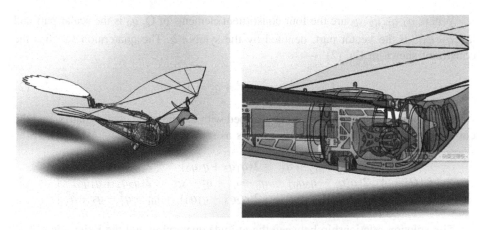

Fig. 3. Camera shooting status (left), camera retracted status (right)

3   Attitude Sensing and Kinematics Analysis

3.1   Camera Attitude Acquisition

In order to adjust the attitude of the camera, it is necessary to detect the camera's attitude deviation. The camera's attitude acquisition needs to select appropriate sensor to detect the attitude change of the aircraft and the camera, get the attitude deviation and finally calculate the corner of each motor.

The attitude detection sensor is MPU6050 module. MPU6050 can detect the angular velocity and angular acceleration of the target in the X, Y and Z directions. After the attitude calculation and filtering, the attitude angle of the detection target in the three directions of yaw, roll and pitch can be obtained. The attitude angle usually refers to the Euler angle, that is, the element around the x-axis, the y-axis, and the z-axis compared with the ground coordinate system. The Euler angles are usually expressed as $\varphi(pitch)$, $\theta(roll)$ and $\psi(yaw)$.

MPU6050 has digital motion processor DMP, which can directly convert sensor raw data, i.e. triaxial angular velocity and angular acceleration, into attitude quaternion. The attitude quaternion Q is a generalization of complex numbers and consists of four elements, as defined by Eq. (1).

$$Q = q_0 + q_1 i + q_2 j + q_3 k = q_0 + q = \begin{bmatrix} q_0 \\ q \end{bmatrix} = \begin{bmatrix} q_0 \\ q_1 \\ q_2 \\ q_3 \end{bmatrix} \tag{1}$$

Where q_0, q_1, q_2, q_3 are the four constituent elements of Q, q_0 is the scalar part and $[q_1, q_2, q_3]^T$ is the vector part, denoted by the symbol q. The quaternion satisfies the constraint shown in Eq. (2)

$$q_0^2 + q_1^2 + q_2^2 + q_3^2 = 1 \tag{2}$$

The attitude quaternion can be transformed with the direction cosine matrix, and the corresponding transformation relationship is as shown in Eq. (3).

$$C(Q) = \begin{bmatrix} q_0^2 + q_1^2 - q_2^2 - q_3^2 & 2(q_1 q_2 + q_3 q_0) & 2(q_1 q_3 - q_2 q_0) \\ 2(q_1 q_2 - q_3 q_0) & q_0^2 - q_1^2 + q_2^2 - q_3^2 & 2(q_2 q_3 + q_1 q_0) \\ 2(q_1 q_3 + q_2 q_0) & 2(q_2 q_3 - q_1 q_0) & q_0^2 - q_1^2 - q_2^2 + q_3^2 \end{bmatrix} \tag{3}$$

The solution relationship between the attitude quaternion and the Euler angle is as shown in Eq. (4). By placing the MPU6050 on the camera, combined with the conversion relationship between the attitude quaternion and the Euler angle, the Euler angle of the camera and the FAV can be acquired.

$$\begin{bmatrix} \psi \\ \theta \\ \varphi \end{bmatrix} = \begin{bmatrix} a\tan 2(2(q_0q_1 + q_2q_3), 1 - 2(q_1^2 + q_2^2)) \\ \arcsin(2(q_0q_2 - q_1q_3)) \\ a\tan 2(2(q_0q_3 + q_1q_2), 1 - 2(q_2^2 + q_3^2)) \end{bmatrix} \tag{4}$$

3.2 Kinematics Analysis

The camera stabilizer consists of two rotating joints that compensate the camera in the roll and pitch directions. The coordinate system of the camera stabilizer includes body coordinate system S_1, pitch axis coordinate system S_2, and roll axis coordinate system S_3. The angles α and β represent the joint angles of the rolling direction and the pitch direction, as shown in Fig. 4.

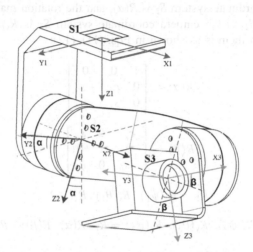

Fig. 4. Coordinate system of camera stabilizer

Let the rotation matrix of each coordinate system relative to the earth coordinate system rotate around the x-axis, y-axis, and the z-axis represented by R_φ, R_θ, and R_ψ, as shown in Eqs. (5)–(7).

$$R_x(\varphi) = \begin{bmatrix} 1 & 0 & 0 \\ 0 & c_\varphi & -s_\varphi \\ 0 & s_\varphi & c_\varphi \end{bmatrix} \tag{5}$$

$$R_y(\theta) = \begin{bmatrix} c_\theta & 0 & s_\theta \\ 0 & 1 & 0 \\ -s_\theta & 0 & c_\theta \end{bmatrix} \tag{6}$$

$$R_z(\psi) = \begin{bmatrix} c_\psi & -s_\psi & 0 \\ s_\psi & c_\psi & 0 \\ 0 & 0 & 1 \end{bmatrix} \tag{7}$$

$$R = R_z(\psi) \cdot R_y(\theta) \cdot R_x(\varphi) = \begin{bmatrix} c_\theta c_\psi & c_\psi s_\varphi s_\theta - c_\varphi s_\psi & s_\varphi s_\psi + c_\varphi c_\psi s_\theta \\ c_\theta s_\psi & c_\varphi c_\psi + s_\varphi s_\theta s_\psi & c_\varphi s_\theta s_\psi - c_\psi s_\varphi \\ -s_\theta & c_\theta s_\varphi & c_\varphi c_\theta \end{bmatrix} \tag{8}$$

With Euler angles, the rotation matrix from the ground coordinate system to the body coordinate system S_1 and the camera coordinate system S_3 can be obtained by Eq. (8). Let the rotation matrix from the ground coordinate system to the body coordinate system S_1 is R_1, the rotation matrix from the ground coordinate system to the camera coordinate system S_3 is R_3, The rotation matrix from body coordinate system S_1 to the pitch axis coordinate system S_2 is $R(\alpha)$, and the rotation matrix of the roll axis coordinate system S_2 to the camera coordinate system S_3 is $R(\beta)$. The conversion relationship between them is as shown in Eqs. (11)–(12):

$$R(\alpha) = \begin{bmatrix} 1 & 0 & 0 \\ 0 & c_\alpha & -s_\alpha \\ 0 & s_\alpha & c_\alpha \end{bmatrix} \tag{9}$$

$$R(\beta) = \begin{bmatrix} c_\beta & 0 & s_\beta \\ 0 & 1 & 0 \\ -s_\beta & 0 & c_\beta \end{bmatrix} \tag{10}$$

$$R_1 = R_z(\psi_1) \cdot R_y(\theta_1) \cdot R_x(\varphi_1) \tag{11}$$

$$R_3 = R_z(\psi_3) \cdot R_y(\theta_3) \cdot R_x(\varphi_3) = R_1 \cdot R(\alpha) \cdot R(\beta) = R_1 \cdot Rt \tag{12}$$

Let the rotation matrix from the body coordinate system S_1 to the roll axis coordinate system S_3 is R_t, then R_t can be obtained by the Eq. (13), and the values of the two joint angles α and β can be obtained by the Eq. (14).

$$R_t = R1^T \cdot R3 = R(\alpha) \cdot R(\beta) = \begin{bmatrix} \cos\beta & 0 & \sin\beta \\ \sin\beta \cdot \sin\alpha & \cos\alpha & -\cos\beta \cdot \sin\alpha \\ -\cos\alpha \cdot \sin\beta & \sin\alpha & \cos\beta \cdot \cos\alpha \end{bmatrix} \tag{13}$$

$$\begin{cases} \beta = a\tan 2(R_t(1,3), R_t(1,1)) \\ \alpha = a\tan 2(R_t(3,2), R_t(2,2)) \end{cases} \tag{14}$$

Since the camera stabilizer adjusts the attitude of the camera only in roll and pitch directions, in yaw direction, the camera and the fuselage are consistent, so the existence of the solution needs to be considered when setting the camera target attitude. Let the yaw angle of fuselage ψ_1 and yaw angle of camera ψ_3 be the same as the restriction, the following conditions must be satisfied, as shown in Eq. (15).

$$a\tan 2(R_1(2,1), R_1(1,1)) = a\tan 2(R_3(2,1), R_3(1,1)) \tag{15}$$

We can get the result as shown in Eq. (16).

$$\begin{cases} \varphi_3 = 0 \\ |\theta_3 + \beta| < 90° \end{cases} \tag{16}$$

That is, during the process of stabilization, when the target posture angle of the camera in pitch direction is 0°, and the absolute value of the target roll angle of camera is less than 90°, the attitude of camera can remain stable.

4   Camera Stabilizer Control

4.1   Attitude Control Strategy

The camera stabilizer is based on the STM32F407 microcontroller and the Keil Uvision5 platform. The system is divided into three parts: attitude acquisition, data processing and motor drive. The attitude acquisition part is used to detect the attitude of the camera and the aircraft fuselage, and transmitting the information to the microcontroller through the IIC interface for data solving and processing. The controller calculates the processed signal to obtain the relative attitude of the camera and the aircraft fuselage, then calculates the target angle of each joint of the camera stabilizer. The motor drive part converts the target rotation angle of the camera stabilizer motor into PWM wave signals, then modulates, amplifies and transmits it to the brushless motor to change the attitude of the camera by adjusting the motor rotation angle and keep the camera in the target position.

As can be seen from Sect. 3.2, the camera's pitch axis target attitude angle is 0°, and the roll axis's target attitude angle adjustment range is ±90°. The roll angle of the camera is determined by the remote control signal. The knob of the remote control controls the PWM pulse width of the corresponding channel to the aircraft receiver. Through this signal, the camera's ideal roll angle can be determined. We set the camera's ideal roll angle range as $0 \sim -90°$.

4.2   Motor Servoing Control

Due to the limited load capacity of the Robotic bird, it is necessary to minimize the weight and volume of the camera stabilizer. Therefore, brushless DC motors without position sensor are selected as driving components. The motors are driven by SPWM method, and the position control of the motor is performed by using the MPU6050 as position sensor. In this way, the weight and the wires of the camera stabilizer can be effectively reduced. In addition, the SPWM control method can make the motors rotate smoothly at a low speed, which is very suitable for the camera stabilizer.

The SPWM method uses PWM wave whose pulse width changes according to the sinusoid to control the on and off of the MOS tube, thereby controlling the input voltage of the motor, and the phase difference of each 2 phases that input to the motor is 1/3 period. The forward or reverse rotation of the motor is controlled by direction of the sinusoid. The rotation speed is determined by the change rate of the sinusoidal voltage.

The relationship between the motor rotation period and the system interruption period is as shown in Eq. (17):

$$T = \frac{360°}{\omega_b(°/s)} = t_{sys}(s) \cdot T_{\sin} \cdot p \tag{17}$$

In this equation, T is the time required for the motor to rotate one revolution, ω_b is the minimum speed of the motor, t_{sys} is the period of the system interrupt function, $T_{\sin}$ is the period of the sine wave, and p is the pole pair of the motor. When the minimum motor speed is set to be ω_b, the motor rotates one cycle when the system interrupt function runs $T \cdot p$ times. According to the target motor speed calculated by the PID, the speed of the motor varies with the adjustment of the sine wave. Let the change of the motor phase voltage in each interrupt period be ΔV, then the relationship between the change and the rotation speed is as shown in Eq. (18):

$$\Delta V = A\left(\sin\omega\left(t + \frac{\omega_a}{\omega_b} + \varphi \right) + 1 \right) \tag{18}$$

In this equation, A represents the amplitude of the sine wave, which is related to the reference voltage of the PWM wave. ω represents the angular velocity of the sine wave, whose value is $\frac{2\pi}{T_{\sin}}$. ω_a is the target speed after PID calculation, its unit is degree/second. φ is the initial phase of each motor phase.

In order to verify the above algorithm, the motor SPWM control is simulated by Matlab. The motor model with 4 pole pairs is selected. The period of system interrupt function is set to be 5 ms and motor minimum speed is set to be 5°/s. The motor control model is built by using the Simulink toolbox, as shown in Fig. 5. In the simulation, the target rotation speed input by the step signal is set to be 30°/s, and the three-phase sinusoidal control signal is calculated and obtained, as shown in Fig. 6.

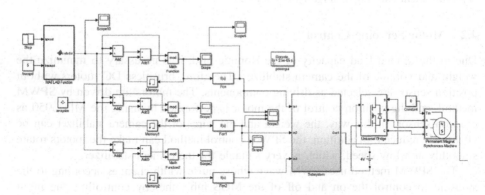

Fig. 5. Simulation of motor PWM control

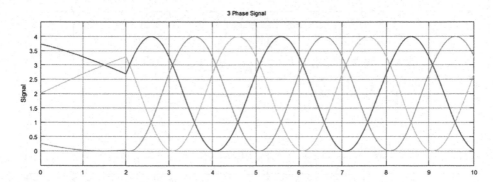

Fig. 6. Three-phase sinusoidal signal

The three-phase sinusoidal signal are modulated with high-frequency sawtooth wave and convert into high-frequency PWM waves of different pulse widths, and the signal is converted into the on-off information of the MOS tube through the three-phase full-bridge rectifier module, and finally output to the motor model. The motor phase current can be obtained as shown in Fig. 7. The three-phase current of the motor changes with the input signal as a PWM wave with a sinusoidal variation. The motor speed is shown in Fig. 8. It can be seen that when the input signal changes, the motor speed responses and gradually approaches the target speed, the motor speed is slightly smaller than the target speed, because the rotor of the brushless DC motor rotates following the stator magnetic field, so its speed lags behind the magnetic field speed. When the input voltage of the motor changes, the speed will also produce a small jump, which tends to be stable after the shock.

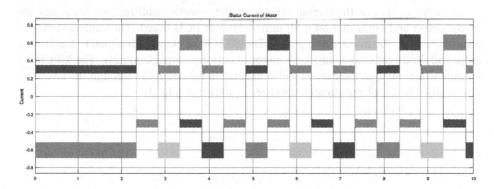

Fig. 7. Phase current of the motor

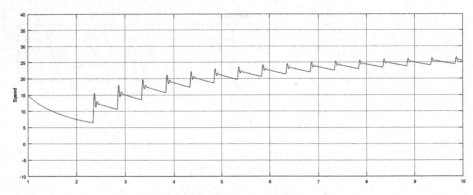

Fig. 8. Motor speed curve

5   Prototype and Experiment

5.1   Camera Stabilizer Prototype

In order to verify the control method designed above, we selected suitable hardware to make the camera stabilizer prototype, and did the experiment.

The prototype uses two small-sized brushless DC motors to change the camera attitude, and uses a small stepping motor with a diameter of 10 mm to make the lifting slide control camera telescopic. The slide rails are equipped with PTFE and aluminum alloy axes, which can reduce the overall weight of the prototype. The camera stabilizer prototype is shown in Fig. 9. The mounting frame is the fuselage of HIT-Hawk, made by carbon fiber. It can be seen that the occupied space of camera stabilizer is relatively small. The overall weight of the prototype is only 52 g.

In order to reduce the overall weight of the camera stabilizer, we integrates the motor driver and controller on a 50 mm × 50 mm PCB board. The camera stabilizer uses drv8313 as the motor driving chip. The STM32F4 chip sends signal to the driving chip, and the driver chip controls the motor to perform correspondingly. The MPU6050 module is mounted on the camera and connected to the controller through IIC interface. The control board of the camera stabilizer is shown in Fig. 10.

Fig. 9. Camera stabilizer prototype, retracted state (left), extended state (right)

Fig. 10. Control board, front (left), back (right)

5.2 Experiments

Since the camera stabilizer does not have the data storage function, it is difficult to perform outdoor data collection experiments, the indoor experiment is temporarily used. The MPU6050 sensors are installed on both HIT-Hawk fuselage and the camera, the attitude data of the two MPU6050 are separately collected through the serial port. By simulating the flapping fight attitude change and comparing the attitude angle of the fuselage and the camera, we can see the stabilizing effect of the camera stabilizer. The experimental comparison results are shown in Figs. 11 and 12.

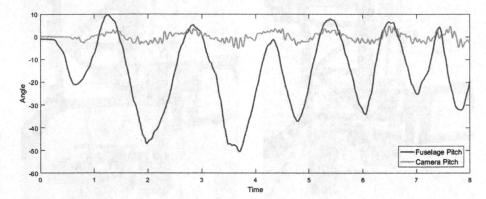

Fig. 11. Pitch angle comparison of fuselage and camera

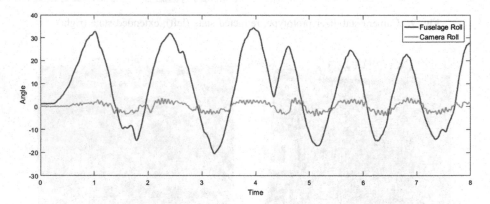

Fig. 12. Roll angle comparison of fuselage and camera

It can be seen that the camera will have a corresponding attitude change trend when the aircraft fuselage has a large pitch and roll change, but in comparison, the camera attitude change is much smaller than the fuselage. The stabilizer can effectively compensate the attitude deviation to keeps the camera stable, and the larger the fuselage attitude changes, the more obvious the compensation effect.

6 Conclusions

In this paper, we developed a small but intelligent camera stabilizer for a large-wing robotic bird. The mechanical structure, sensing subsystem and embedded controller were all designed by considering the flight characteristics and various constraints. The stabilizer can supply stable conditions for visual surveillance through the camera on it. In the future, the performance of the stabilizer will be further improved based on a large number of flight tests. The coordinated sensing and control of the robot body and the stabilizer will also be studied.

Acknowledgement. This work was supported by the National Natural Science Foundation of China (Grant No. U1613227), and Guangdong Special Support Program (Grant No. 2017TX04X 0071) and Individual Maker Project of Shenzhen Maker Special Fund (AK24405057).

References

1. Rajesh, R.J., Kavitha, P.: Camera gimbal stabilization using conventional PID controller and evolutionary algorithms. In: International Conference on Computer, Communication and Control (IC4), pp. 1–6. IEEE (2015)
2. Pan, E., Chen, L., Zhang, B., Xu, W.: A kind of large-sized flapping wing robotic bird: design and experiments. In: Huang, Y., Wu, H., Liu, H., Yin, Z. (eds.) ICIRA 2017. LNCS (LNAI), vol. 10464, pp. 538–550. Springer, Cham (2017). https://doi.org/10.1007/978-3-319-65298-6_49
3. Xiang-Hua, B., Yue-Jin, Z.: Model and simulation of permanent magnet brushless DC motor and control system based on SIMULINK. Electrical Drive Automation (2005)
4. Cunxue, J., Hongxin, C., Kaiwu, Y.: Design of a remote-controlled stepless motor-driven camera platform based on single chip microprocessor. Mach. Tool Hydraul. 35 (2011)
5. Zhu, D., Qiu, X., Xing, C.: Disturbance compensation for gun control system of tank based on LADRC. In: International Conference on Electrical & Control Engineering, pp. 2198–2201. IEEE (2011)
6. Ping, Y.E., Sun, H.X., Jia, Q.X., et al.: Application of magnetic encoder in phase commutation control of BLDCM. Instrum. Tech. Sens. 1 (2007)
7. Chu, J.U., Moon, I.H., Choi, G.W., et al.: Design of BLDC motor controller for electric power wheelchair. In: International Conference on Mechatronics, p. 92-7e. IEEE (2004)

Movement-Mode-Switching Mechanism for a Hybrid Wheel/Legged Mobile Robot

Xiaolin Guo, Yufeng Su, and Han Yuan[✉]

School of Mechanical Engineering and Automation,
Harbin Institute of Technology Shenzhen, Shenzhen 518055, China
{guoxiaolin,suyufeng}@stu.hit.edu.cn,
yuanhan@hit.edu.cn

Abstract. This paper introduces a movement-mode-switching mechanism for a hybrid wheel/legged mobile robot. With the switching mechanism, two movement modes are achieved independently sharing the same actuator, thus fewer actuators are used in the robots. A clutch is designed to accomplish the movement-mode-switching process. The trapezoid tooth meshing as a tolerance design is used, which not only leads to better engagement, but also increases the transmission accuracy. The drawing back and recovery of the shape memory alloy conduces to the reciprocation of the clutch, which transfers motion towards wheels and legs from the bevel gears, respectively. Then, motion and force simulation of the switching process is made with Adams. The results are used to check the material of the clutch and ensure the feasibility of the switching mechanism. Finally, a practical application is introduced using the switching mechanism, showing an adaptive capacity of the system to most wheel/legged robots.

Keywords: Movement-mode-switching mechanism · Tolerance design · Shape memory alloy

1 Introduction

Modern robots are mostly developed from three basic types, i.e. legged robots, wheeled robots and crawler robots, to conquer new difficulties. For example, to locomote rapidly in even terrain and steadily on uneven landform, so-called hybrid wheel/legged robots are designed [1–3]. The legs for uneven terrain and wheels for even landform. More novel and practical wheel/legged mobile robots [4] are designed and manufactured to update existing functions or solve brand new problems.

The morphing mobile robot with six-legged and spherical movement [5] designed by Wenfu, has a good combination of rolling and walking, and can switch movement modes properly to accommodate different situations. The robot changes the rapid movement method from walking with legs to rolling with its own sphere body. The movement-mode-switching is realized by mechanism design and the absence of wheels greatly decreases the volume of the robot. The six-legged and spherical movement robot has good locomotion ability, deformation ability and rolling ability with tactful mechanism design, sensors and embedded control system.

© Springer Nature Switzerland AG 2019
H. Yu et al. (Eds.): ICIRA 2019, LNAI 11742, pp. 376–385, 2019.
https://doi.org/10.1007/978-3-030-27535-8_34

Some other kinds of wheel/legged robot are designed to meet the need of the coexistence of walking and rolling. The Transleg [6] performs as a quadruped robot in the legged mode and a four-wheel vehicle in the wheeled mode. Two actuators are used to drive the wheel/legged mechanism. The wheels are placed on the knees and the shanks lift until the wheels have full contact with the ground. After that, the shanks are fixed at the specific position. The Transleg provides a good idea that the wheels can be fixed on the knees of the legs to save total volume. However, some problems are flawing the design, such as the simultaneous movement of the legs and the wheels or redundant actuators used for locomotion and switching.

Although the available wheel/legged robots are able to complete their missions, there are still a lot to be optimized. First of all, different actuators are arranged to control the wheels and the legs. Consequently, the whole robot consists of a chunk of actuators to realize the given motion. Not talking about the cost of the high-precision motors, the superfluous actuators greatly increase the total weight of the robot. Besides, the excessive actuators lead to a great decrease of actuator utilization: when one set of actuators is working, the other sets are powered off. Moreover, most wheel/legged robots are setting the wheels on the ends of the legs, resulting in a corpulent bulk and sometimes unsteady during switching process. So, in the hybrid wheel/legged robot, a clutch component is designed to switch the motion from the legs to the wheels and vice versa, which gives rise to cutting down the total number of the motors. In addition, the wheels are placed in the parallel direction of knees. This design helps reduce the overall size: bigger wheels do not contribute to a larger volume in vertical direction. A separation motion of legs and wheels also works out slipping problem during switching.

The remainder of the paper is organized as follows. Demand analysis covers the technical requirements of our design. Mechanical design section covers the basic design of our leg-wheel system, the specific design for each component, and the function implement. Simulation is made to verify the feasibility of the system. The material of the clutch and the switching process are checked with the result from simulation with Adams. The application section gives a practical prototype using the switching system, which shows a good adaptive capacity of the system to most wheel/legged robots. The strengths of the system are then concluded. Finally, the conclusion summarizes the whole paper and provides some information for further development.

2 Demand Analysis

To control the hybrid wheel/legged robot, the following technical requirements are to be satisfied:

(1) Independent movement. The movements of wheels and legs have to be independent. For example, when the robot is walking with legs, the wheels do not rotate.
(2) Automatic mode-switching. The mode-switching process is accomplished automatically.
(3) Insurance of the basic function. The design has to guarantee the rotation of the legs and the wheels are able to move forward and backward.

3 Mechanism Design

3.1 Overall Mechanism Design

In order to meet these requirements, two detached axes (see Fig. 1) are designed to decouple the rolling mode and walking mode. Meanwhile, a clutch is designed to accomplish the mode-switching process.

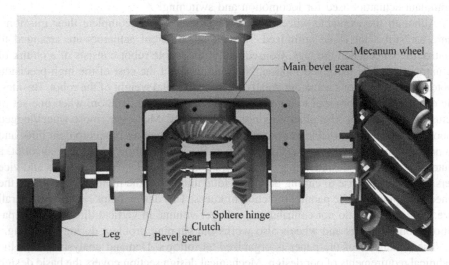

Fig. 1. Overall mechanism design (Mecanum wheel is designed by Abdullah Ahmed from GRABCAD).

4 Specific Design for Each Component

Shape Memory Alloy. The current length of the memory alloy is related to the temperature of the alloy and its total length [7]. When the current is switched on, the heat production follows the Joule's law. As the temperature reaches the memory point, the spring begins to shrink to its memory length. When the current is switched off, the heat would be taken away through conduction, convection and radiation. The spring tends to return to its original length under the help of the return spring placed on the opposite side [8].

The combination of shape memory alloy and return spring is considered because of the simple structure and small working space. In order to guarantee the enough length, the spring shape memory alloy is designed. One end of the shape memory alloy is connected with the center of the clutch and the other end with the bottom of the hole. The natural length is the distance between the clutch inner end face and the bottom of the hole when the clutch meshes with the bevel gear assembled on the leg axis.

The shape memory alloy spring is 0.5 mm in diameter and 200 mm wire length. The return spring has a working stroke of 6 mm, maximum force 15 N. The wire for the heating process of the shape memory alloy is placed in the grooves in the main axis, the sphere hinge and the clutch.

Axis Design. One end of the axis (see Fig. 3) connects with the leg by screw thread, whereas the other end is cogging shape, which is used to mesh with the clutch. Meanwhile, the clutch can reciprocate along the axis on the cogging. In addition, a hole (see Fig. 2) is designed in the axial direction which is connected with the wheel (hereinafter referred to as wheel axis) to settle the shape memory alloy and another hole (see Fig. 2) is designed in the axis which is connected with the leg (hereinafter referred to as leg axis) to settle the return spring. The natural length of the return spring is the distance between the end face of the leg axis and the bottom of the hole in the leg axis.

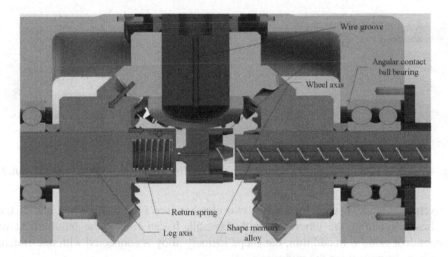

Fig. 2. Cutaway (Color figure online)

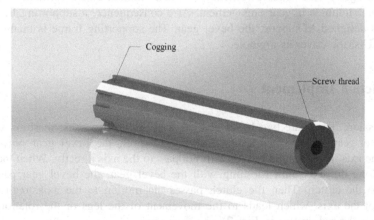

Fig. 3. Leg axis

Modified Bevel Gear. A trapezoid structure like cogging is designed on the end face of the bevel gear to mesh with the clutch.

Clutch Design. One clutch has two meshing structures (see Fig. 1). One part meshes with the bevel gear. It has some trapezoidal gear teeth whose gradient are the same as the trapezoid structure on the bevel gear, which is called the tolerance design. The tolerance design makes sure the clutch can mesh smoothly without idle stroke which decreases the motion accuracy. Meanwhile, there is a gap (see Fig. 4(a)) between the gear of clutch and the cogging of bevel gear, which can lower the requirement of machining accuracy. The other part (see Fig. 4(b)) meshes with the cogging of the axis, synchronizing rotation. Moreover, the clutch is able to move along the axis, ensuring the feasibility of mode-switching.

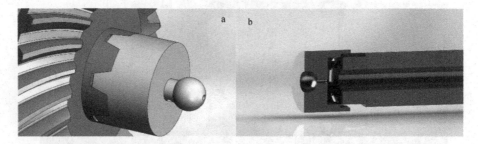

Fig. 4. (a) The bevel gear meshes with the clutch. (b) The wheel axis meshes with the clutch.

A sphere hinge is used to connect two clutches (see Fig. 4(a)). When one of the clutches is rotating, the other one will stay still. It can satisfy the requirement of independent motion. In addition, the shape memory alloy is connected with one clutch, providing the power for the reciprocation.

Supporting Frame of the Bevel Gear. Two axes are cantilevers forced by the gravity of the bevel gear, which causes vertical minor deformation. This deformation may give rise to some troubles in gear engagement. As a consequence, a supporting frame (see Fig. 5) is designed to support the bevel gear. The supporting frame is manufactured with the U-shape cover as a whole.

5   Function Implement

Transmission. There are two bevel gears assembled on two axes, meshing with the main bevel gear which provides the power. However, the bevel gear only rotates around the axis. It means the motion will not pass to the axis directly. When the clutch moves along the axis until meshing with the bevel gear, the bevel gear passes the motion to the clutch. Then the clutch passes the motion to the axis, realizing the rotation of the axis, which leads to the movement of the legs or the rotation of the wheels (see the red arrows in Fig. 2).

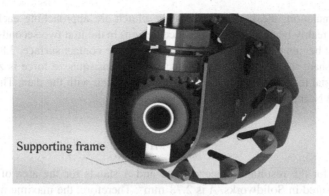

Fig. 5. Supporting frame

Switching. Assuming the clutch meshes with the bevel gear assembled on the leg axis initially. When the main bevel gear begins to rotate, the motion passes to the leg axis, realizing the movement of the legs.

After receiving the signal of switching to rolling mode, the current for the shape memory alloy is switched on. Then the shape memory alloy will shrink after heated up, drawing back the clutch to mesh with the bevel gear assembled on the wheel axis and the return spring is stretched. Therefore, the motion passes to the wheel axis, realizing the rotation of the wheel.

After receiving the signal of switching to walking mode, the current of the shape memory alloy is switched off. The shape memory alloy restores to the original length. Meanwhile, the return spring pulls the clutch to mesh with the bevel gear assembled on the leg axis.

6 Modeling and Simulation

6.1 Clutch Material Checking

The movement is simulated in Adams and the resultant squeeze force between the bevel gear and the clutch is shown in Fig. 6.

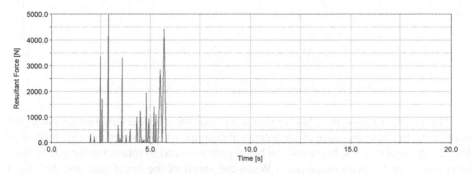

Fig. 6. The resultant force versus time in Adams simulation.

In the simulation, the bevel gear and the clutch are approaching each other (not happening in reality because of the tolerance design) in the first two seconds. After that, the bevel gear begins to rotate and force appears on the contact surface. 3.8 s later, two components share the common speed thus the resultant squeeze force is zero.

The material feasibility of the clutch is to be checked with the data. The maximum force is 5000 N and the maximum shear stress.

$$\tau = \frac{F}{A} \tag{1}$$

F stands for the resultant squeeze force and A stands for the area of the contact surface. Measured in Solidworks, A is 2.78 mm^2. Therefore, the maximum shear stress is 2.7 MPa, which is much smaller than shear strength of the aluminum alloy [9]. In short, the clutch works well using the aluminum alloy.

6.2   Switching Process Analysis

According to the experiment of the shape memory alloy, the force supplied by the 200-millimeter-spring is 15.3 N by shrinking 6 mm (see Table 1).

Table 1. Ni-Ti shape memory alloy experiment data (φ 0.5 mm*200 mm)

Force [N]	Shrink length [mm]	Voltage [V]	Current [A]	Shrink time [s]
15.3	6	1.4	1	18

The resistance in axial direction is simulated in Adams, which is resultant friction shown in Fig. 7.

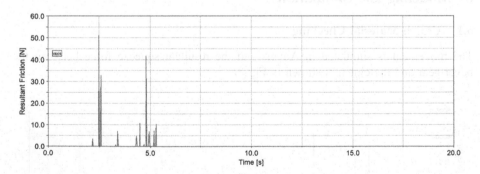

Fig. 7. The resultant friction versus time in Adams simulation.

The bevel gear and the clutch mesh with each other in the first two seconds (not happening in reality because of the tolerance design), which causes the zero friction in Fig. 7. In the next 3.8 s, however, the bevel gear is forced to rotate and there is friction force between the two components. When the speed of the bevel gear and the clutch come to a same value, the friction drops to zero, which means that even tiny force in axial direction would drag the clutch to the prospective location. As a result, as long as the force provided by the return spring is smaller than the force by the shape memory alloy, the clutch would be able to reach the prospective location.

7 Application Case

The movement modes switching mechanism can be used in all kinds of wheel/legged robots. The following figures give an example of the application of the mechanism.

Figure 8 shows the robot in walking mode. The robot can locomote steadily with legs on uneven landform. After receiving the signal to switch modes, the robot squats down until the wheels which are placed on the knees have full contact with the ground. Then the shanks lift (see Fig. 9). In the meanwhile, the current for the shape memory alloy is switched on. The shape memory alloy will shrink after heated up, drawing back the clutch to mesh with the bevel gear. Then the wheels roll and the mode-switching function is realized. After that, the robot locomote rapidly with wheels in even terrain.

Fig. 8. The robot in walking mode

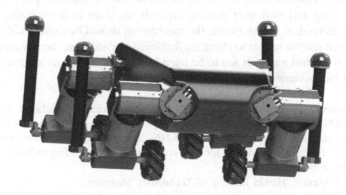

Fig. 9. The robot in rolling mode

8 Discussion

The hybrid wheel/legged robot has widely developed for its flexible locomotion capability. However, most hybrid robots use double motors to motivate the legs and wheels. In this paper, a mechanism for wheel/legged movement modes is designed, which can accomplish the locomotion modes switching without extra actuators. When the robot is walking with legs, the wheels stop and vice versa. Limited actuators are used, which not only saves energy cost, but increases the utilization coefficient of actuator. The only actuator drives the leg and the wheel controlled by the main processor, which makes the actuator turning whatever the mode of the robot is working at.

The robot is able to switch its movement mode automatically when the operator gives the orders for example pushing a button. Instead of designing a complicated transmission mechanism, the shape memory alloy and spring system, fixing on opposite sides of the axes, is used in the robot. This system subtly solves the problem of designing and installing a mechanism in such a small space. With no need of manual control, the switching system automatically changes the movement mode.

Tolerance design is introduced in the hybrid wheel/legged robot. Instead of using rectangle teeth, a trapezoidal structure is designed to engage the clutch and the bevel gear. The structure solves the problem when the tooth on the clutch and the cogging of the bevel gear do not accurately align.

9 Conclusion

In this paper, a movement-mode-switching mechanism for hybrid wheel/legged mobile robots is designed. Fewer actuators, tolerance design and the introduction of shape memory alloy contribute to the advantages of the mechanism. With the switching mechanism, the two movement modes are completed independently sharing the same actuator. A clutch is designed to accomplish the movement modes switching process. The trapezoid tooth as a tolerance design is used, which not only leads to better engagement, but also increases the transmission accuracy. The drawing back and recovery of the shape memory alloy conduces to the reciprocation of the clutch, which transfers motion towards wheels and legs from the bevel gears, respectively. Clutch material checking and switching process analysis are done to demonstrate the feasibility of the mechanism. In the future, the mechanism should be used in different kinds of wheel/legged mobile robots to check its feasibility. In addition, the advanced sensing and intelligent control methods are to be used in the mechanism to achieve the ability of switching its movement modes.

Acknowledgement. This work was supported by the Natural Science Foundation of Guangdong Province [grant No. 2018A030313247]; and the Science and Technology Innovation Committee of Shenzhen [grant No. JCYJ20170811155308246]. In addition, the authors would like to acknowledge the following individuals for their contributions by providing technical insight and guidance to the authors.

Wenfu Xu, Professor. Harbin Institute of Technology Shenzhen

Peng Kang, PhD candidate. Harbin Institute of Technology Shenzhen

Xin Wang, Master. Harbin Institute of Technology Shenzhen
Guo Yang, Master candidate. Harbin Institute of Technology Shenzhen
Yihong Li, Bachelor candidate. Harbin Institute of Technology Shenzhen
ZhongHua Hu, PhD candidate. Harbin Institute of Technology Shenzhen

References

1. Max, S., Tobias, R.: Hybrid driving-stepping locomotion with the wheeled-legged robot Momaro. 2016 IEEE International Conference on Robotics and Automation (ICRA). LNCS, pp. 5589–5595. IEEE, Stockholm (2016)
2. Xu, L., Haitao, Z.: Design and experiments of a novel hydraulic wheel-legged robot (WLR). 2016 IEEE International Conference on Robotics and Automation (ICRA). LNCS, pp. 3292–3297. IEEE, Stockholm (2016)
3. Yongming, W., Xiaoliu, Y.: Force model and its simulation analysis of wheel-legged lunar rover. 2010 Second International Conference on Information Technology and Computer Science. LNCS, pp. 122–125. IEEE, Kiev (2010)
4. Peng, K., Guisen, G.: A small morphing leg-wheel hybrid quadruped robot. In: 2018 IEEE International Conference on Information and Automation (ICIA), LNCS. IEEE, Wuyi Mountain (2018)
5. Wenfu, X., Shunyao, W.: A morphing mobile robot with six-legged and spherical movement modes. In: 2018 IEEE International Conference on Information and Automation (ICIA), LNCS. IEEE, Wuyi Mountain (2018)
6. Zhong, W., Guangming, S.: Transleg: A wire-driven leg-wheel robot with a compliant spine. 2016 IEEE International Conference on Information and Automation (ICIA). LNCS, pp. 7–12. IEEE, Ningbo (2016)
7. Duerig, T.W., Melton, K.N., Stöckel, D.: Engineering Aspects of Shape Memory Alloys, 1st edn. Butterworth-Heinemann, London (1990)
8. Jani, J.M.: A review of shape memory alloy research, applications and opportunities. Mater. Des. 56, 1078–1113 (2014)
9. Ziv, I.: The shear strength of alumina/aluminum alloy interfaces. Scripta Mater. 40(11), 1243–1248 (1999)

Two Experimental Methods to Test
the Aerodynamic Performance of HITHawk

Erzhen Pan, Hui Xu, Juntao Liu, Xu Liang, Yuanpeng Wang,
Xiaokun Hu, and Wenfu Xu[(⊠)]

School of Mechanical Engineering and Automation,
Harbin Institute of Technology (SZ), Shenzhen 518055, China
wfxu@hit.edu.cn

Abstract. This paper introduces two experimental platforms for testing the
aerodynamic forces of our HITHawk. These two platforms are frequently used
during the iterative designing and testing process of our prototypes. The first one
is a fixed six-dimensional load cell platform, which is used to measure the
aerodynamic performance of HITHawk when flapping in the absence of relative
airflow. The other one is then a rotary stand, which is equipped with force and
speed transducers, to measure the aerodynamic performance of HITHawk when
flapping with relative airflow. The functions and purposes of the two platforms
are not the same and they are not perfect indeed, but the combination of the two
can comprehensively evaluate the quality of each flapping wing aerial vehicle
(FAV) prototype, mainly about the designing of wing structures and flapping
parameters. The testing results would be utilized to provide guidance for the
design of the new models of our FAV prototype and the design of the corresponding controlling system. After the design and fabrication of the test platforms, we tested the performance of a HITHawk prototype we designed, and the
test results can meet the requirements, which proves the feasibility of the two
solutions.

Keywords: HITHawk · Flapping wing aerial vehicle · FAV · Bionic bird ·
Ornithopter · Robotic bird · Experiment and test

1 Introduction

With the gradual development of materials technology, battery and energy technology,
machine processing technology and the control theory and methods, people have
achieved more and more fruit in the field of flapping wing aerial vehicle (FAV) research. The many plentiful in-depth research findings and successful fabrication of
Delfly [1], Robotic Hummingbird [2–4], Robobee [5], Roboraven [6] and Smartbird [7]
etc. marks that people have gained insights into the physics of flapping flight. Due to
the advantages of the high flight efficiency in the low-speed flight field, FAV has
become a new hot research field.

According to the objective animal it imitates, FAVs can be divided into insect-like
flapping-wing aircraft, bat-like flapping-wing aircraft, and bird-like flapping-wing
aircraft. Different types of flapping wing aircraft usually utilize different kinds of

© Springer Nature Switzerland AG 2019
H. Yu et al. (Eds.): ICIRA 2019, LNAI 11742, pp. 386–398, 2019.
https://doi.org/10.1007/978-3-030-27535-8_35

flapping flight mechanisms. For small-sized flapping-wing aircrafts, they mostly have excellent maneuverability due to its extremely high flapping frequency. However, they are also characterized by small body mass and small load capacity, short flight endurance and mileage. Relatively speaking, large bird-like FAV usually outperforms than their small counterparts. Large bird-like FAVs, in other words, the HITHawk, usually have long cruising range, strong load capacity, and the ability to gliding and soaring.

Mostly, small sized FAVs, or flapping micro aerial vehicles (FMAV), are usually tested in wind tunnel [8] or in a certain confined space which is monitored by motion capture system or high speed video [9], or by using custom-made load cell platform and so on. However, for bird-like FAVs, there are little options to choose when testing, except from the conventional expensive wind tunnel solutions. So, in this paper, we introduced two easy and convenient testing methods when FAV prototypes have been made.

2 Requirements for Designing Force Measuring Platforms for HITHawk

The key to successful outdoor flight of a HITHawk is that the prototype itself could produce sufficient lift and thrust when it flaps. And besides, the three-axial moments generated by the aerodynamic force relative to the prototype's center of gravity also needs to be maintained in the appropriate range of values, the amplitude of which is decided by its structural features.

During the process of designing and improving, in order to accurately measure the aerodynamic forces and aerodynamic moments generated by the HITHawk during flapping, the most ideal experimental solution should be to design a specialized six-dimensional force measuring platform and put it into the wind tunnel environment, which is filled with stable airflow of constant speed. In this way, it can simultaneously obtain the aerodynamics produced by the protype. However, since the size of the HITHawk we are developing now is kind of large, the wingspan of which are mostly between 1.2 m–2.5 m, so frequently wind tunnel experiments with large enough cavity would result in high cost and time-consuming in this project. For this reason, we designed the following two experimental platforms that can effectively measure the flapping performance of the prototype, and have also introduced their calculation and analysis methods, as well as a complete experiment to verify its functional feasibility.

3 Fixed Measuring Platform Based on a 6-Axis Force Sensor

In the absence of relative airflow, the various forces and moments produced by the prototype wings during flapping can also illustrate the characteristics of the prototype. The flight performance of the prototype is directly determined by the aerodynamic lift, thrust and aerodynamic moments relative to the center of gravity. The rationality of the design of the prototype wings and the flapping law then determines the formation and generation of these forces. When it is impossible to carry out the flapping experiment in the wind tunnel, we installed the prototype on a fixed experimental platform with 6-axis force sensor and let the HITHawk flaps at different frequencies and different angles of attack (AOA), and we obtain the force and torque values measured during the wing flapping. By comparing the values with parameters used in outdoor free flight, it is possible to preliminarily estimate whether the designed prototype wing structure and the corresponding flapping law are suitable for real outdoor flight.

Although this method is not quite precise and rigorous, it's quite easy and it can also save us a lot of time and cost for our prototype development process.

3.1   Structure of the Fixed Measuring Platform

The base of the measuring platform is a six-axis force sensor mounted on the mounting table, which is connected to the bird body by a specially designed clamping tool. There are holes for mounting the HITHawk and the different mounting holes on the tool corresponds to the different installation angles of the fuselage of the HITHawk. For the setup, the five installation angles are 0°, 5°, 10°, 15° and 20° separately, which corresponds to the same angle of attack of the prototype. When the prototype flaps its wings at different frequencies and different angles of attack, the six-axis force sensor would measure the aerodynamic forces generated by the wings and the aerodynamic moments experienced by the fuselage under the condition of no relative airflow.

The structural schematic of the measuring platform is shown in the following Fig. 1.

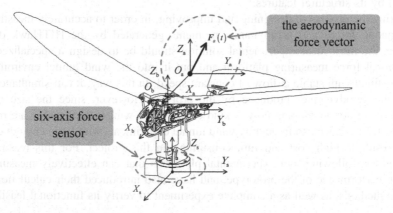

Fig. 1. Fixed aerodynamics measurement platform based on a six-axis force sensor

3.2   Principles of Force Conversion

Firstly, a coordinate system for describing the various forces and moments and positional relationship between different variables need to be established.

The sensor frame $S_s - O_sX_sY_sZ_s$ of the six-axis force sensor itself is set according to the instructions of the product manual. The body frame of the HITHawk is $S_b - O_bX_bY_bZ_b$, where the origin of the coordinate system is the center of gravity of the prototype. In addition, according to the characteristics of the flapping movement of the wings, we know that the magnitude and direction of the aerodynamic force vector generated by the wings during a flapping cycle are constantly changing. Assume that the working point of the aerodynamic force at certain moment of time t is as shown in Fig. 1 as O_a, and the aerodynamic force vector is as shown in the figure as $F_a(t)$. In order to define the aerodynamic force actually produced by flapping motion at any time, the aerodynamic coordinate system $S_a - O_a X_a Y_a Z_a$ is established with the aerodynamic center as the origin at each moment.

The three coordinate axes x, y and z of the body coordinate system and the aerodynamic coordinate system are kept in the same direction with the sensor coordinates.

Aerodynamics Action Point Position

The aerodynamic force measured by the fixed measuring platform is the force generated by the prototype when there is no relative airflow. The measured aerodynamic torque is the aerodynamic moments caused by the aerodynamic force relative to the origin of the sensor coordinate system. Since there is an offset between the center of gravity of the prototype and the origin of the sensor coordinate system, the measured torque value needs to be properly converted to get the aerodynamic torque.

The position of the aerodynamic force action point $O_a(x_{sa}, y_{sa}, z_{sa})$ can be calculated based on the measured force components F_{sx}, F_{sy} and F_{sz} along the three axes of the 6-axis force sensor and the torque components M_{sx}, M_{sy} and M_{sz} around the three axes of the sensor:

$$\begin{cases} M_{sx} = F_{sz} \cdot y_{sa} - F_{sy} \cdot z_{sa} \\ M_{sy} = F_{sx} \cdot z_{sa} - F_{sz} \cdot x_{sa} \\ M_{sz} = F_{sy} \cdot x_{sa} - F_{sx} \cdot y_{sa} \end{cases} \tag{1}$$

Where x_{sa}, y_{sa} and z_{sa} are the coordinates values of the action point of the aerodynamic force in the sensor frame, which are variables need to be confirmed.

Convert it into the matrix form we can get the following equation:

$$\begin{bmatrix} M_{sx} \\ M_{sy} \\ M_{sz} \end{bmatrix} = \begin{bmatrix} 0 & F_{sz} & -F_{sy} \\ -F_{sz} & 0 & F_{sx} \\ F_{sy} & -F_{sx} & 0 \end{bmatrix} \begin{bmatrix} x_{sa} \\ y_{sa} \\ z_{sa} \end{bmatrix} \tag{2}$$

Since the rank of the right coefficient matrix in the above algebraic equation is 2 and the rank of the augmented matrix is 3, this equation has no solution. In the actual calculation process, we use the pseudo-inverse method to solve the position of the aerodynamic action point.

Aerodynamic Forces and Aerodynamic Moments Experienced by the HITHawk

Through the three-dimensional model of the HITHawk created in SolidWorks, its center of gravity of the body can be directly obtained after assembly in the software. And then we can get the position of this center of gravity in the sensor frame according to the positional relationship determined by the mounting setup, which is denoted as $O_b(x_{sb}, y_{sb}, z_{sb})$.

After that, we can get the triaxial force (F_{bx}, F_{by}, F_{bz}) received in the body coordinate system and the three-axis moment (M_{bx}, M_{by}, M_{bz}) relative to the origin of the body coordinate system when the HITHawk flaps. The triaxial force along the body coordinate system (F_{bx}, F_{by}, F_{bz}) and the force measured in the sensor coordinate system (F_{sx}, F_{sy}, F_{sz}) are the same both in amplitude and direction. And the three-axis moments received in the body coordinate system can be obtained according to the following formula.

$$\begin{bmatrix} M_{bx} \\ M_{by} \\ M_{bz} \end{bmatrix} = \begin{bmatrix} 0 & F_{bz} & -F_{by} \\ -F_{bz} & 0 & F_{bx} \\ F_{by} & -F_{bx} & 0 \end{bmatrix} \begin{bmatrix} x_a - x_{sb} \\ y_a - y_{sb} \\ z_a - z_{sb} \end{bmatrix} \tag{3}$$

At this point, both the aerodynamic force components along the three-axis of the body coordinate system and the aerodynamic moment components around the three-axis of the body coordinate system can be obtained.

3.3   Experimental Process and Experimental Analysis

The parameters of the cloth wing prototype HITHawk used in this experiment are shown in Table 1 below. The prototype is an improved version based on the prototype and the corresponding avionics [10, 11] we developed earlier. In the outdoor free flight experiments, we use a remote control to control its flight and the throttle amount is between 35% and 40%, corresponding to the flapping frequency range from 4.4 Hz to 4.9 Hz. Between this flapping frequency range, sufficient lift and thrust can be generated to achieve flight and manoeuvre.

Table 1. Parameters of the HITHawk for testing

Wing span	1200 mm
Wing chord	265 mm
Total mass (battery included)	462 g
Flapping frequency	2–6.4 Hz
Battery	3S LiPo 800 mAh
Flight endurance	8 min

The installation of HITHawk in the experiment is shown in Fig. 2. The HITHawk are fixed on the six-axial force sensor measurement platform in turn, with 0°, 5°, 10°, 15° and 20° installation angles. And then flaps from low frequency to the highest.

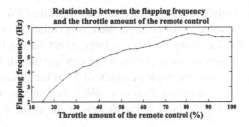

Fig. 2. Installation of HITHawk on the platform

Fig. 3. Relationship between the flapping frequency and the throttle amount of the RC

During the experiment, the relationship between the percentage of the throttle amount of the remote control and the flapping frequency of the HITHawk is shown in Fig. 3. When the remote control throttle amount increases from 15% to 100%, the resulting HITHawk flapping frequency ranges from 2 Hz to 6.4 Hz correspondingly.

By gradually changing the flapping frequency of the wing, the triaxial force and the triaxial moment measured by the sensor at different flapping frequencies can be obtained, and then the lift and thrust force and the aerodynamic torque actually acted on the center of gravity of the HITHawk prototype can be obtained by using the force conversion formula (3) introduced above.

The following Figs. 4, 5, 6, 7, 8 and 9 showed the results of aerodynamic forces and aerodynamic moments generated by the sample at different flapping frequencies and different angles of attack.

Analysis of Lift and Thrust Results

According to the above experimental results, we can see that in the case of a certain angle of attack, as the throttle of the remote controller increases within a certain range, the generated lift and thrust will increase accordingly. When the throttle rod reaches above 80% of the full scale, the thrust and lift no longer increase. This phenomenon is caused by the structural characteristics of the prototype wing, and this feature guided us to not hope to increase the lift and thrust by relying on increasing the flapping frequency to a rather high value during the outdoor flight tests. In addition, when the amount of throttle is constant, the effect of increasing the angle of attack on the thrust is relatively small, and the amplitude of the increase in lift as the angle of attack increases is more pronounced. These two conclusions told us that when the thrust is sufficient, we should rely on adjusting the pitching moment of the body to change the height of the HITHawk, instead of by adjusting the flapping frequency only.

Relationship Between Lift and Different Combinations of Flapping Frequency and AOA

The weight of the prototype used in this test is 480 g. In the outdoor free flight test, the prototype only needs 35%–40% of the throttle amount, and the flight angle of attack only needs about 5°. In the test process on this fixed force measurement platform, when the throttle rudder amount is 81% and the angle of attack is 20°, the average thrust can reach 5.475 N, but the average lift force is only 2.126 N. And if the HITHawk wants to stay aloft, the lift generated during the flapping should be at least 4.5276 N, which is the weight of the prototype. The measured lift value tends to be smaller than the free flight value is just because there is no relative airflow during the test, and the magnitude of the incoming flow has a large effect on the lift. Based on the characteristics of this force measurement platform, we can use the lift generated by the throttle rudder amount of 40% and the angle of attack of 5° as the reference, which is 0.3754 N. As long as the lift value is greater than this value, the combinations of flapping frequency and angle of attack can be used to the design of the control system.

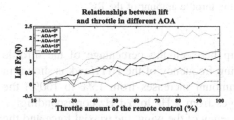

Fig. 4. Relationships between lift and throttle in different AOA

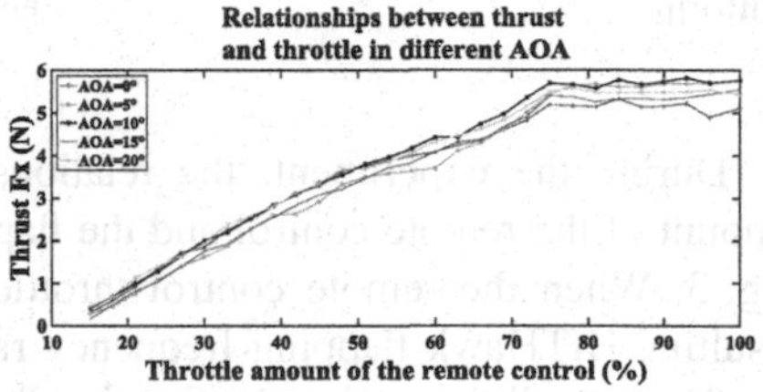

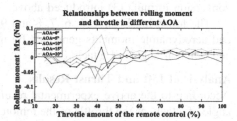

Fig. 5. Relationships between thrust and throttle in different AOA

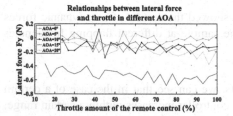

Fig. 6. Relationships between lateral force and throttle in different AOA

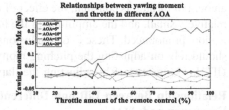

Fig. 7. Relationships between rolling moment and throttle in different AOA

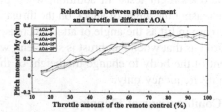

Fig. 8. Relationships between pitch moment and throttle in different AOA

Fig. 9. Relationships between yawing moment and throttle in different AOA

4 Rotary Measuring Platform with Induced Relative Airflow

In order to make the measurement of the aerodynamic force more closer to the aerodynamic force actually generated when the HITHawk is flying freely outside, the influence of relative airflow should be considered in the experiment. The most ideal experimental environment is still in wind tunnel that with uniform airflow and controllable wind speed. However, for our HITHawk of wingspan ranges from 1200 mm to 2000 mm, to do experiment in a large enough wind tunnel for one time is very dear. So, in order to save costs and make it more convenient to do tests for our frequently and rapidly prototype improvement work, we have developed the rotating measuring platform shown in the Fig. 10 below with reference to the lift and thrust measurement scheme used in the Smartbird design process [12, 13]. The measuring platform can be used to measure the lift and thrust during the wing flapping motion and to tell whether the prototype could make a fly in the outdoor environment.

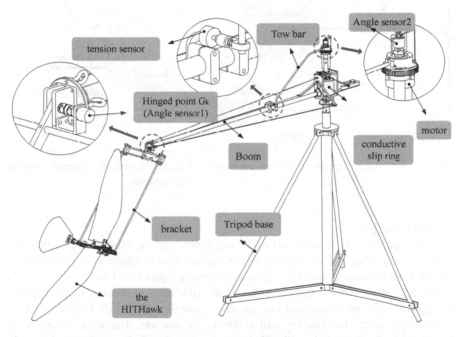

Fig. 10. Structural diagram of the rotary measuring platform

4.1 Structure of the Rotary Measuring Platform

The structure of the rotary measuring platform mainly comprises two parts, a fixed tripod base and a rotating mechanism.

The rotating mechanism includes a motor and a transmission mechanism on the top ot the tripod, a tow bar, a boom and a bird support. There is one angle sensor mounted between the bracket and the boom for measuring the angle between the bracket and the boom, and another angle sensor mounted at the top of the rotating mechanism to measure the angular position of the boom relative to the base of the tripod. A tension sensor is mounted between the tow bar and the boom to measure the force applied by the tow bar when the motor starts to work and to drag the boom. The motor and the wires of each sensor are connected by a conductive slip ring that is attached to the base of the tripod.

4.2   Principles to Measure the Lift and Thrust

The measurement and calculation principles of the lift and thrust of the HITHawk when flapping on the rotary measuring platform are discussed in detail below. The schematic diagram of the lift measurement process is shown in Fig. 11. And the schematic diagram of the thrust measurement is shown in Fig. 12.

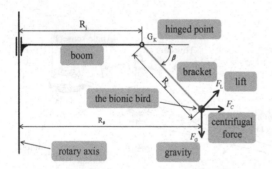

Fig. 11. Schematic diagram of lift measurement

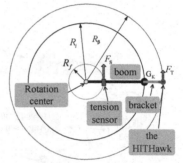

Fig. 12. Schematic diagram of thrust measurement

Working Principle

Firstly, the speed of the motor is set to the maximum, and the bird's wings do not flap initially. At this time, the output end of the transmission mechanism is pulled by the boom and the maximum angular velocity of the rotary part is 3.4 rad/s. Since the the distance from the central symmetry plane of the HITHawk to the axis of the tripod is about 2.05 m, the circumferential line speed is approximately 7 m/s. Under the action of centrifugal force, the bracket will rotate to the outside. The angle between the bracket and the horizontal plane β will change compared with the static state. When the rotation is stable, the angle β should remain constant. And then, the 12-bits ADC module on the STM32F407 is used to sample at a sampling frequency of 200 Hz, and the values θ_1, θ_2 of the two angle sensors and the value of the tension sensor F_P are recorded.

Then gradually increase the throttle of the remote control, the wings and then flap at a certain frequency. The lift generated by the wings would cause the brackets connecting the boom and the HITHawk to leave the original position. The movable part behind the hinge point G_k would under the joint action of centrifugal force F_C, aerodynamic lift F_L and the overall weight F_G of the HITHawk and the bracket. These forces would together raise the bracket to a new equilibrium position, and the measurement will be performed again after the throttle maintains at a certain value for 10 s and when the flight is stable. Repeat the above procedure to obtain measurements under different throttles and different angles of attack.

According to the schematic diagram of the measurement methods of lift, the lift is calculated by the principle of torque balance at the hinge point G_k.

From the torque balance relationship, the following formula can be obtained:

$$M_{G_K} = F_G \cdot R_a \cdot \cos(\beta) - F_C \cdot R_a \cdot \sin(\beta) - F_L \cdot R_a = 0 \qquad (4)$$

Where M_{G_K} is the sum of the torques at the hinge point G_k, F_G is the gravity of the HITHawk, F_C is the centrifugal force exerted on the HITHawk, R_a is the length of the cantilever bracket, and F_L is the lift of the prototype.

By introducing the expressions of centrifugal force and gravity into the above equation, we can get:

$$F_L = m \cdot \cos(\beta) \cdot \left[g - R_\beta \cdot w^2 \cdot \tan(\beta) \right] \qquad (5)$$

Where m is the mass of the prototype and the connecting part of the bracket w is the angular velocity of rotation of the boom around the fixed triangular bracket R_β, which is the length of the centrifugal force arm.

In this measurement, the mass of the prototype and the bracket connection part m is 0.5 kg, the length of the bracket R_a is 0.755 m, and the length of the boom R_i is 1.585 m.

To calculate the thrust, we compare the value of the tension sensor F_P and F_{P0}, which represent force sensor values when the HITHawk is flapping and when the HITHawk is kept still respectively, while the motor speed are kept the same. The force arm of the tension sensor is fixed at R_p.

Theoretically speaking, the HITHawk could generate certain amount of thrust when flapping on the platform. Since the thrust direction is consistent with the rotary direction of the platform, the force measured by the tension sensor will thus be reduced. The thrust can be calculated according to the following formula:

$$F_T = \frac{(F_{P0} - F_P)R_p}{R_\beta} \qquad (6)$$

The force sensor arm R_p of the tension sensor has a length of 0.33 m. So R_β can get by this formula:

$$R_\beta = R_i + R_a \cos(\beta) \qquad (7)$$

5 Experiment

Experimental Process

The installation of the HITHawk and the experimental process of this platform is shown as follows (Fig. 13).

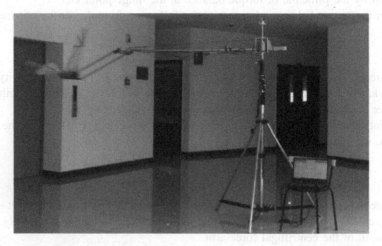

Fig. 13. Indoor lift and thrust measurement on the rotating measuring platform

When testing, we installed the HITHawk prototype on the rotating test platform. The platform works as described in the above section. After obtaining the data, the graphs of analysis were plotted in the following Figs. 14 and 15.

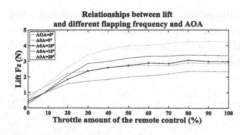

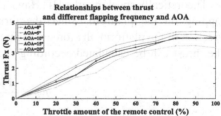

Fig. 14. Relationships between lift and different flapping frequency and AOA

Fig. 15. Relationships between thrust and different flapping frequency and AOA

Experimental Results Analysis

Analysis of the experimental results:

1. It can be seen from the analysis results shown in the above two figures that the lift and thrust amplitude measured here by the rotary measuring platform are significantly higher than those tested on the fixed measuring platform.
2. However, the measured lift amplitude is still relatively smaller than the actual value of the HITHawk prototype when freely flying outdoors. The main reason is that the measuring platform has frictional resistance and dynamic load when working. For the moment, we didn't pay too much attention to these factors, but they do matter.
3. Same as the testing process on the fixed measuring platform, we take the status of throttle amount of 40% and angle of attack of 5° as reference, of which the measured lift is 3.6754 N and thrust is 2.7862 N respectively, the combination of flapping frequency and AOA can be used to control the flight of the HITHawk and as the source data to be programmed in the autopilot onboard in outdoor flight as long as the lift and thrust larger than these two values.
4. It can be seen from the test results that when the flapping frequency increases, the lift and thrust both show an increasing trend, but when the throttle amount reaches above 80%, the lift does not increase any more, and the thrust will decrease. This is consistent with the results measured in the fixed measurement platform.
5. The lift reaches the maximum at AOA of about 5° and the smallest at AOA of about 0°. This is very consistent with the characteristics of the thin wingless wing we use. The generation of lift need certain AOA, but also the AOA shouldn't be too large, or the efficiency would decrease dramatically.

6 Conclusion

There exists a large gap between the test results obtained by the two measuring methods here and the real absolute lift and thrust force values generated when our HITHawk freely flaps outdoors, but anyway the tests here can offer us the trend of aerodynamic force generated by different parameters combined with the prototype. By summarizing the trend and compare them with the results of outdoor actual flight experiments data could make us get a knowledge of the potential performance of the prototype in advance before it get tested outdoor. Besides, the experimental data we get from these two testing platforms could also be used to the designing of the autopilot and control system onboard, since they showed us what kind of combinations of flapping frequency and AOA would be efficient in changing the status of the prototype.

Still, there also exists quite a lot of shortcomings in these two platforms. Such as low accuracy, too much noise for the collected data, limited consideration for the structural friction and vibration. Especially for the rotary measuring platform, all these factors would have a very bad impact. In the coming research stage, we would improve the test stands performance, make it more versatile and the testing results more precise.

Acknowledgement. This work was supported by the National Natural Science Foundation of China (Grant No. U1613227) and Guangdong Special Support Program (Grant No.2017TX04X0071), and is also funded by the Individual Maker Project of Shenzhen Maker Special Fund (AK24405057).

References

1. Karásek, M., Muijres, F.T., De Wagter, C., Remes, B.D., de Croon, G.C.: A tailless aerial robotic flapper reveals that flies use torque coupling in rapid banked turns. Science **361** (6407), 1089–1094 (2018)
2. Zhang, J., Fei, F., Tu, Z., Deng, X.: Design optimization and system integration of robotic hummingbird. In: 2017 IEEE International Conference on Robotics and Automation (ICRA), pp. 5422–5428. IEEE (2017)
3. Coleman, D., Benedict, M., Hrishikeshavan, V., Chopra, I.: Design, development and flight-testing of a robotic hummingbird. In: AHS 71st Annual Forum, pp. 5–7 (2015)
4. Keennon, M., Klingebiel, K., Won, H.: Development of the nano hummingbird: a tailless flapping wing micro air vehicle. In: 50th AIAA Aerospace Sciences Meeting Including the New Horizons Forum and Aerospace exposition, pp. 588 (2012)
5. Wood, R.: RoboBees project. Harvard University (2015)
6. Gerdes, J., et al.: Robo Raven: a flapping-wing air vehicle with highly compliant and independently controlled wings. Soft Robot. **1**(4), 275–288 (2014)
7. Smartbird homepage. https://www.festo.com/group/en/cms/10238.htm
8. Kim, D.K., Han, J.H., Kwon, K.J.: Wind tunnel tests for a flapping wing model with a changeable camber using macro-fiber composite actuators. Smart Mater. Struct. **18**(2), 024008 (2009)
9. Graule, M.A., et al.: Perching and takeoff of a robotic insect on overhangs using switchable electrostatic adhesion. Science **352**(6288), 978–982 (2016)
10. Pan, E., Chen, L., Zhang, B., Xu, W.: A kind of large-sized flapping wing robotic bird: design and experiments. In: Huang, Y., Wu, H., Liu, H., Yin, Z. (eds.) ICIRA 2017. LNCS (LNAI), vol. 10464, pp. 538–550. Springer, Cham (2017). https://doi.org/10.1007/978-3-319-65298-6_49
11. Pan, E., Liu, J., Chen, L., Xu, W.: The Embedded on-board controller and ground monitoring system of a flapping-wing aerial vehicle. In: 2018 IEEE International Conference on Real-time Computing and Robotics (RCAR), pp. 72–77. IEEE(2018)
12. Send, W., Fischer, M., Jebens, K., Mugrauer, R., Nagarathinam, A., Scharstein, F.: Artificial hinged-wing bird with active torsion and partially linear kinematics. In: Proceeding of 28th Congress of the International Council of the Aeronautical Sciences (2012)
13. Send, W., Scharstein, F., GbR, A.N.: Thrust measurement for flapping-flight components. In: 27th ICAS Congress, pp. 19–24. Nice, France (2010)

Tension Optimization of a Cable-Driven Coupling Manipulator Based on Robot Dynamics with Cable Elasticity

Yanan Li[1], Ying Li[2], Deshan Meng[3], Yu Liu[1($\boxtimes$)], Xueqian Wang[3], and Bin Liang[4]

[1] Harbin Institute of Technology, Harbin 150000, China
liuyunum@163.com
[2] Yingkou Vocational and Technical College, 115000 Yingkou, China
[3] Tsinghua University, Graduate School at Shenzhen, Shenzhen 518055, China
[4] National Laboratory for Information Science and Technology, Tsinghua University, Beijing 100084, China

Abstract. This paper presents a method for tension optimization of a 3-DOF planar cable-driven coupling manipulator based on robot dynamics which contains cable elasticity. The robot is driven by two independent actuated cables, the cables are modeled as axial linear springs. The key point is to minimize cable tension in case of breakage, at the same time always keeping a positive value to avoid slack behavior. By using Pseudo spectral algorithm and considering robot dynamics equation as constraint, cable tension is optimized in force and cable length control mode respectively. The simulation results show effectiveness of the optimization algorithm.

Keywords: Tension optimization · Cable-driven · Elasticity · Dynamics

1 Introduction

Cable-driven robots own the advantages of slender body, large workspace, as well as innate compliance, thus have been widely applied in snake-arm robot [1], robot hand [2], continuum and soft robot [3].

There are two modes to control a cable-driven robot. One is force control mode with force sensors as feedback, directly control the tension on the rope. The other is cable length control mode, cable is regarded as a axial linear spring, the tension is controlled indirectly by adjusting cable length. Either way, it's the cable tension that ultimately drives the robot. However, cable tension is limited by self strength properties, mainly material and radius, as well as strength of end fixation. Besides, cable slack is a common problem for cable-driven robots, cable elasticity affects the precision of end-effector. All of those, to a certain extent, have limited the use of cable-driven robots.

© Springer Nature Switzerland AG 2019
H. Yu et al. (Eds.): ICIRA 2019, LNAI 11742, pp. 399–411, 2019.
https://doi.org/10.1007/978-3-030-27535-8_36

Thus tension optimization is essential for cable-driven robots. First, it is helpful for choosing suitable cable and guiding the mechanism design. Second, by reducing the maximum tension of the cable, the possibility of breakage decreases. Third, prevent slack behavior during the motion. Four, reduce rope loss caused by friction between cable and routine. In [4], a generalized methodology for designing optimized cable routines is developed for a given robot and desired task with minimal cable tensions. Since the cable-driven robot is always redundant actuated, cable tension solution is not unique. The adjustable tension solution for each pose is obtained using a modified gradient projection method in [5], the proposed method is generic and can be applied to cable-driven robots with any number of redundant actuation. In [6], a novel linear-program formulation is presented for rapid computation of optimally safe tension distributions.

Cable tension varies by adjusting cable length. However, trajectory planning for cable-driven robot in previous studies have always been done from the perspective of kinematics instead of dynamics and not consider the effect of cable elasticity. However, cable elasticity plays an important role in robot dynamics. On one hand, the characteristics of light weight and low inertia by relocating the heavy motors and gear box to the base frame show possibility of highly dynamics, on the other hand, cable elasticity destabilizes the manipulator, affects the accuracy of end-effector and limits its application, which contrary to the original intention of design. Thus cable elasticity should be considered to fully explore the potential of cable-driven robots. A method for estimating cable length in an under-actuated, hyper-redundant, snake-like manipulator is presented [7]. A physics-based model incorporating cable friction is developed and its predictions are compared with experimental data in [8]. Cable pretension was estimated indirectly by estimating stiffness parameter of cables in [9]. The dynamic modulus of cable elasticity is experimentally identified through dynamic mechanical analysis in [10].

The purpose of this paper is to optimize cable tension to a predetermined location. Cable elasticity increases the complexity of robot dynamics. We establish the robot's dynamics equation involving the elasticity of the cable and use pseudo spectral algorithm to optimize cable tension, which regards robot dynamics equation as constraint. Furthermore, minimum tension is set as boundary condition to avoid cable slack.

The paper is organized as follows: Sect. 2 introduces the robot model and basic kinematic. In Sect. 3, dynamics equation of cable-driven robot is presented, cable elasticity is considered to calculate cable tension. In Sect. 4, Pseudo-spectral algorithm is used to optimize cable tension, robot dynamics equation is taken as constraint. Section 5 shows the result of tension optimization with cable tension and length as control input respectively. Section 6 concludes the summary and future work.

2   Robot Model and Kinematics

Figure 1 is a 3-DOF planar cable-driven coupling robot. The robot can be divided into three parts: rigid body, active actuated cables, coupling cables. The meaning of each part is:

Rigid body: the robot has three rotational joints and links and rotates in the plane.

Active actuated cables: two independent cables actuate the robot actively. There are some holes in the disk at each end of link, the cable goes through the holes and attaches to end link by a knot. Once there is tension on the rope, it will exert force on the link at the hole and drive the link to move.

Coupling cables: coupling ropes are a special mechanism design that guarantees all joints to rotate the same angle. Once angle difference occurs, coupling cables work to ensure equal curvature bending, as shown in Fig. 1(b).

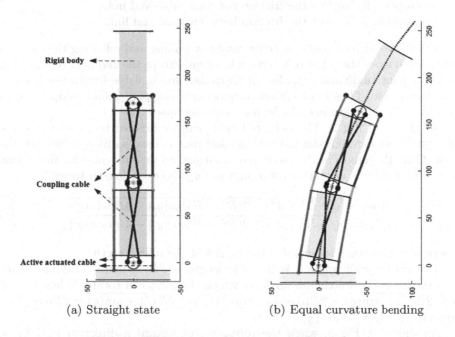

(a) Straight state   (b) Equal curvature bending

Fig. 1. 3-DOF planar cable-driven coupling robot

To calculate cable-driven robot's dynamics, here are some simplifications and assumptions before modelling:

Assumption 1: There is a point contact between cable and hole.
Assumption 2: Neglect the cable mass, since it is small compared to links.
Assumption 3: Cable deformation is linear and modeled as axial linear spring.
Assumption 4: Cable can only carry loads in tension but not in compression.
Assumption 5: Neglect the influence of gravity, robot moves in the plane.

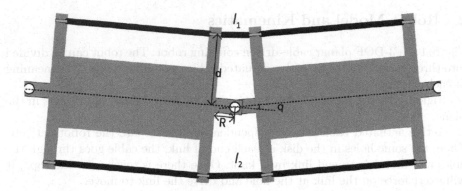

Fig. 2. Actuation cable

Assumption 6: Neglect the friction between cable and hole.
Assumption 7: Neglect the friction between joint and link.

Since cable-driven robots actuate joints by pulling and releasing the cable. If we wand to move the robot to a certain location, except the mapping relationship between joint angle and end-effector Cartesian space, cable length needs to be calculated first. Thus cable-driven robots have mapping relationship between cable length, joint angle, end-effector Cartesian space.

As shown in Fig. 2, The actuated cable can be divided into two parts, the first part goes through the link, the second part connects different links at the joint. Only the length of the latter part changes. So we only consider the second part, when there is a relative rotation angle q_i, the cable length varies.

$$l_1(q_i) = \sqrt{2(R^2 + d^2) + 2(R^2 - d^2)cos(q_i) - 4Rdsin(q_i)}$$
$$l_2(q_i) = \sqrt{2(R^2 + d^2) + 2(R^2 - d^2)cos(q_i) + 4Rdsin(q_i)} \tag{1}$$

where R is curvature radius, d is the height of the rolling teeth.

The initial joint angle q is 0, cable length is $2R$. When $q = 2atan(R/d)$, $l_1 = 0$, this is the maximum angle at which the joint can rotate. When $R = d$, $l_1 = 2R\sqrt{1 - sin(q)} = 2R(cos(\frac{q}{2}) - sin(\frac{q}{2}))$, $l_2 = 2R\sqrt{1 + sin(q)} = 2R(cos(\frac{q}{2}) + sin(\frac{q}{2}))$, $l_2 - l_1 = 4Rsin(\frac{q}{2})$.

As shown in Fig. 3, when the robot moves toward a direction initially in the straight state, the pull length is always larger than release length, which means the link cannot be driven by only one motor with this joint design. So two independently actuated cable is the power of joint.

$$l_1 = \sum_{i=1}^{N} l_1(q_i)$$
$$l_2 = \sum_{i=1}^{N} l_2(q_i) \tag{2}$$

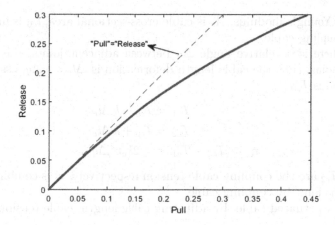

Fig. 3. Relative cable length: pull and release

3   Dynamics Equation

In Sect. 2, the robot is divided into three parts, we first analysis the coupling cable part. As shown in Fig. 4, two cables connect the adjacent joints, four dark dots represent the internal tangents points between cables and pulleys. Assuming that joint 1 is actuated by motor directly without considering active actuated cable. When joint 1 rotates clockwise, cable tension T_{c1} decreases, tension T_{c2} increases, the difference will produce a combined torque on the joint 2, the tension of the two cables are equal until joint 2 rotates the same angle and so on with joint 3.

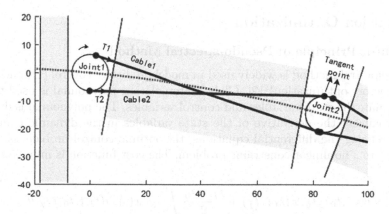

Fig. 4. Coupling cable

The elasticity coefficient of coupling cable can be defined as:

$$k_c = \frac{E_c A_c}{l_{c0}} \tag{3}$$

where E_c is Young's modulus, A_c is cable cross-sectional area, l_{c0} is initial cable length of coupling cable.

When there is a relative angle Δq between adjacent joints, r is the cable wrapping radius, then the cable length deformation is $\Delta l_c = r\Delta q$, assuming the cable preload is T_{c0}.

$$T_{c1} = T_{c0} - k\Delta l_c \tag{4}$$

$$T_{c2} = T_{c0} + k\Delta l_c \tag{5}$$

$$\tau_c = (T_{c2} - T_{c1})\, r = 2k_c r^2 \Delta q \tag{6}$$

where T_{c1}, T_{c2} are the coupling cable tension respectively, τ_c is combined torque acting on the joint by coupling cable.

For active actuated cable, by adjusting cable length, cable tension varies.

$$\Delta l_a^{\cdot} = l(q) - l_{a0} - l_m \tag{7}$$

$$T = \frac{E_a A_a}{l(q)} \Delta l_a \tag{8}$$

$$\tau = H(q)T \tag{9}$$

Where $l(q)$ is the current moment cable length calculated by the current moment joint angle q, l_{a0} is initial cable length, l_m is motor driven length, Δl_a is the total amount of rope deformation. T is cable tension, $H(q)$ is the mapping relationship between cable tension and joint torque, τ is the joint torque.

Combine with Rigid body dynamics, the robot dynamics equation is:

$$M(q)\ddot{q} + c(q,\dot{q})\dot{q} + \tau_c = \tau \tag{10}$$

Where $M(q)$ is generalized mass matrix. $c(q,\dot{q})\dot{q}$ is centrifugal and Coriolis items.

4 Tension Optimization

4.1 Basic Principle of Pseudo-spectral Method

Pseudo-spectral method is widely used in model predictive control [11] and reentry trajectory optimization [12]. Global interpolation polynomial is used the to approximate the state variables and control variables. The polynomial is derived to approximate the derivative of the state variables in the dynamic equation. By discretizing the differential equations, the optimal control problem is transformed into a nonlinear constraint problem. The cost function is minimized:

$$J = \Phi\left(x\left(t_0\right), t_0, x\left(t_f\right), t_f\right) + \frac{t_f - t_0}{2} \int_{t_0}^{t_f} g\left(x(t), u(t), t; t_0, t_f\right) dt \tag{11}$$

Subject to the dynamic constraint, boundary conditions, inequality path constraints:

$$\dot{x}(t) = f\left(x(t), u(t), t; t_0, t_f\right)$$
$$\phi_{\min} \le \phi\left(x\left(t_0\right), t_0, x\left(t_f\right), t_f\right) \le \phi_{\max} \tag{12}$$
$$C_{\min} \le C\left(x(t), u(t), t\right) \le C_{\max}$$

4.2 Design of Optimization

Case 1: Force Control Mode
In force control mode, we directly control the cable tension, the system control input is cable tension, as shown in Eq. 11, the objection function has two parts, Φ is state variables at the boundary time, g is a integral items in the whole process. We only consider the second part with maximum tension, and minimize the objective function:

$$g = max(u) \tag{13}$$

State and control variables:

$$\begin{aligned}
q &= [q_1 \quad q_2 \quad q_3] \\
x &= [q \quad \dot{q}] \\
u &= [T_1 \quad T_2]
\end{aligned} \tag{14}$$

Dynamics constraint:

$$\begin{aligned}
\dot{x} &= [\dot{q} \quad M^{-1}(\tau - \tau_c - c(q,\dot{q})\dot{q})] \\
\tau &= H(q)u
\end{aligned} \tag{15}$$

Case 2: Cable Length Control Mode
Cable length is system control input in cable length control mode, it is usually measured by motor encoder, spring pot or calculated by joint angle.
State and control variables:

$$\begin{aligned}
q &= [q_1 \quad q_2 \quad q_3] \\
x &= [q \quad \dot{q}] \\
u &- [l_1 \quad l_2]
\end{aligned} \tag{16}$$

Dynamics constraint:

$$\begin{aligned}
\dot{x} &= [\dot{q} \quad M^{-1}(\tau - \tau_c - c(q,\dot{q})\dot{q})] \\
\tau &= H(q)T \\
T &= \frac{E_a A_a}{l(q)}(l(q) - l_{a0} - u)
\end{aligned} \tag{17}$$

Inequality path constraints:

$$T_{\min} \leq T \leq T_{\max} \tag{18}$$

5 Results

Robot Parameters
The robot parameters are shown in Table 1:

Table 1. Robot parameters

Link			Coupling cable		Active actuated cable	
Mass (g)	Center (mm)	Inertia (g.mm^2)	E (Pa)	Radius (mm)	E (Pa)	Radius (mm)
90	[0 0 33.7]	[65.73 62.05 19.08]	2.1e9	0.3	2.06e11	0.4

Point-to-Point Trajectory Planning
The cable-driven robot is actuated by adjusting cable length or tension rather than using motor directly. In tension control mode, firstly, the planned joint angle is interpolated, then the required joint torque is calculated according to the inverse dynamics of rigid links, finally the corresponding rope tension is solved by the mapping relationship between the rope tension and joint torque. In cable length control mode, the planned joint angle is interpolated, the cable length is solved according to the mapping relationship between the cable length and joint angle.

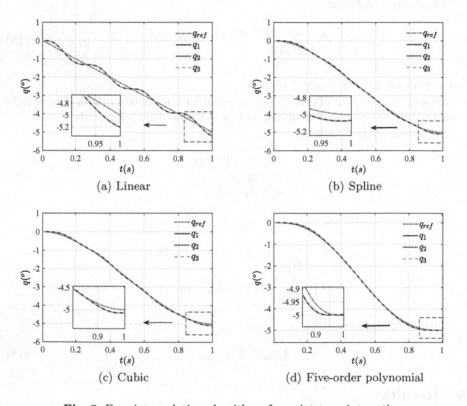

(a) Linear

(b) Spline

(c) Cubic

(d) Five-order polynomial

Fig. 5. Four interpolation algorithms for point-to-point motion

Four conventional interpolation algorithms, linear interpolation, spline interpolation, cubic polynomial interpolation, fifth-order polynomial interpolation, are applied to the robot for point-to-point motion. The initial joint angle is $q_{t0} = [0\ 0\ 0]$, the final angle is $q_{tf} = [-5°\ -5°\ -5°]$, the termination time is $t_f = 1\,\mathrm{s}$, cable preload is $T_{preload} = 0.05\,\mathrm{N}$, the robot is in cable length control mode. As shown in Fig. 5(a), the three joint angles are basically the same which shows good effect of coupling cable. However, there is a obvious difference between the reference angle and dynamics calculated joint angles. At the end moment, $q_{linear} = [-5.2010°\ -5.1985°\ -5.1972°]$, the difference is mainly due to the cable elasticity. Figure 5(b–d) are the results of other three interpolation algorithms, the joint angle respectively in termination are: $q_{spline} = [-5.0693°\ -5.0683°\ -5.0678°]$, $q_{cubic} = [-5.0693°\ -5.0683°\ -5.0678°]$, $q_{five} = [-4.9980°\ -4.9981°\ -4.9981°]$.

The cable can only pull in tension but can not push, thus cable-driven robot can perform tasks only if all cable tensions are non-negative. The common practice is to give a preload on the cable in initial state. Figure 6 is the cable tensions during the motion with different initial preload. The data shows interpolation algorithm cannot ensure positive cable tension, by increasing cable preload, cable slack phenomenon can be alleviated while at the cost of increasing maximum tension.

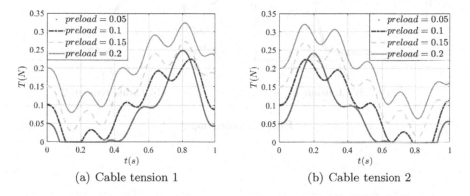

(a) Cable tension 1   (b) Cable tension 2

Fig. 6. Cable tension with different initial preload

Tension Optimization

Case 1: Force control mode
System control input u is cable tension, to avoid cable slack, u_{min} is set with value 0.05 to avoid slack.

$$x(t_0) = zeros(1, 6)$$
$$x(t_f) = [-5 * ones(1, 3) \quad zeros(1, 3)]$$
$$x_{min} = [-6 * ones(1, 3) \quad -10 * ones(1, 3)]$$
$$x_{max} = [6 * ones(1, 3) \quad 10 * ones(1, 3)] \tag{19}$$
$$u_{min} = [0.05 \quad 0.05]$$
$$u_{max} = [0.22 \quad 0.22]$$
$$u(t_0)_{guess} = [0.05 \quad 0.05]$$
$$u(t_f)_{guess} = [0.05 \quad 0.05]$$

Figure 7 is the optimized tensions, the maximum tension is 0.22 N, the minimum tension is 0.05 N. The joint angle and joint angle velocity are shown in Fig. 8, and both meet the joint limits, the calculated joint angle is smooth intuitively reach the desired position.

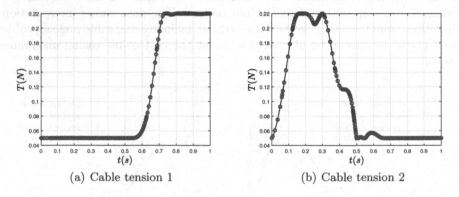

(a) Cable tension 1   (b) Cable tension 2

Fig. 7. Control input

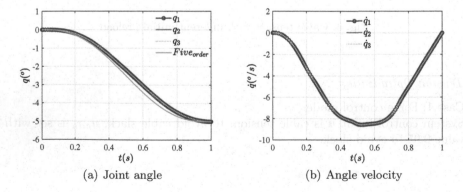

(a) Joint angle   (b) Angle velocity

Fig. 8. State varibles

Case 2: Cable Length Control Mode

In cable length control mode, cable length as system input which can be directly controlled, tension is decided by deformation of cable and calculated with system dynamics. The cable length corresponding to the joint angle at the end time is [5.4503 − 5.5417] mm, which firstly calculated by mapping relationship of kinematic. Cable tension is limited by inequality path constraints: with a minimum value [0.05 0.05] N, maximum value [0.3 0.3] N.

$$
\begin{aligned}
x(t_0) &= zeros(1,6) \\
x(t_f) &= [-5 * ones(1,3) \quad zeros(1,3)] \\
x_{min} &= [-6 * ones(1,3) \quad -12 * ones(1,3)] \\
x_{max} &= [6 * ones(1,3) \quad 12 * ones(1,3)] \\
u_{min} &= [0 \quad -7.2] \\
u_{max} &= [7.2 \quad 0] \\
u(t_0)_{guess} &= [0 \quad 0] \\
u(t_f)_{guess} &= [5.4503 \quad -5.5417] \\
C_{min} &= [0.05 \quad 0.05] \\
C_{max} &= [0.3 \quad 0.3]
\end{aligned}
\tag{20}
$$

Figure 9 is the optimized cable length, at the end time with a value [5.4458 − 5.5416], there is a difference compared with the value calculated by kinematics. However, that's because the cable elasticity is taken into account, the joint angle at the end time is accurate [5° 5° 5°], the angle velocity at the end time is accurate [0 0 0], as shown in Fig. 11. Cable tension is shown in Fig. 10 and meet the path constraint.

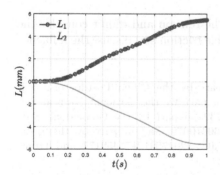

Fig. 9. Control input: cable length

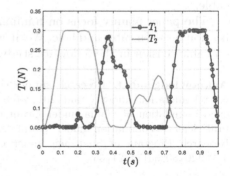

Fig. 10. Path constraint: cable tension

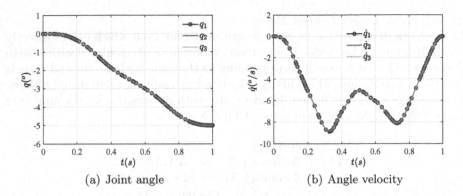

(a) Joint angle   (b) Angle velocity

Fig. 11. State variables

6   Conclusions and Future Work

This paper presents a method for tension optimization of a 3-DOF planar cable-driven coupling manipulator based on robot dynamics which contains cable elasticity. Since cable elasticity affects the precision of end-effector and increases the complexity of robot dynamics. Regular interpolation algorithm cannot ensure positive cable tension, by increasing cable preload, cable slack phenomenon can be alleviated while at the cost of increasing maximum tension. The pseudo spectral algorithm optimizes the cable tension with the constraint of robot dynamics equation. With the optimized cable tension or length as control input, the end-effector has higher position accuracy duo to considering the elasticity of the cable.

The paper mainly focus on minimizing the tension and didn't consider the friction between cable and hole. We'll add cable friction and discuss the influence on cable tension in the follow-up study.

Acknowledgement. Research supported in part by the China Postdoctoral Science Foundation under Grant 2018M631473, in part by the National Natural Science Foundation of China under Grant 61673239, in part by the Guangdong Natural Science Foundation under Grant 2018A030310679, and in part by the Basic Research Program of Shenzhen under Grant JCYJ20170412171459177 and Grant JCYJ20180306174321766.

References

1. Buckingham, R., Graham, A.: Nuclear snake-arm robots. Ind. Robot Int. J. **39**(1), 6–11 (2012)
2. Palli, G., Borghesan, G., Melchiorri, C.: Modeling, identification, and control of tendon-based actuation systems. IEEE Transact. Robot. **28**(2), 277–290 (2012)
3. Yip, M.C., Camarillo, D.B.: Model-less feedback control of continuum manipulators in constrained environments. IEEE Transact. Robot. **30**(4), 880–889 (2014)

4. Bryson, J.T., Jin, X., Agrawal, S.K.: Optimal design of cable-driven manipulators using particle swarm optimization. J. Mech. Robot. **8**(4), 041003 (2016)
5. Lim, W.B., Yeo, S.H., Yang, G.: Optimization of tension distribution for cable-driven manipulators using tension-level index. IEEE/ASME Transact. Mechatron. **19**(2), 676–683 (2014)
6. Borgstrom, P.H., Jordan, B.L., Sukhatme, G.S., Batalin, M.A., Kaiser, W.J.: Rapid computation of optimally safe tension distributions for parallel cable-driven robots. IEEE Transact. Robot. **25**(6), 1271–1281 (2009)
7. Segreti, S.M., Kutzer, M.D.M., Murphy, R.J., Armand, M.: Cable length estimation for a compliant surgical manipulator. In: 2012 IEEE International Conference on Robotics and Automation, pages 701–708. IEEE (2012)
8. Moses, M.S., Murphy, R.J., Kutzer, M.D.M., Armand, M.: Modeling cable and guide channel interaction in a high-strength cable-driven continuum manipulator. IEEE/ASME Transact. Mechatron. **20**(6), 2876–2889 (2015)
9. Haghighipanah, M., Miyasaka, M., Hannaford, B.: Utilizing elasticity of cable-driven surgical robot to estimate cable tension and external force. IEEE Robot. Autom. Lett. **2**(3), 1593–1600 (2017)
10. Baklouti, S., Courteille, E., Caro, S., Dkhil, M.: Dynamic and oscillatory motions of cable-driven parallel robots based on a nonlinear cable tension model. J. Mech. Robot. **9**(6), 061014 (2017)
11. Yang, L., Zhou, H., Chen, W.: Application of linear gauss pseudospectral method in model predictive control. Acta Astronaut. **96**, 175–187 (2014)
12. Zhao, J., Zhou, R., Jin, X.: Reentry trajectory optimization based on a multistage pseudospectral method. Sci. World J. **2014**, 1–13 (2014)

Parallel Robotics

Structure Design and Kinematic Analysis of a Partially-Decoupled 3T1R Parallel Manipulator

Ke Xu[1], Haitao Liu[1(⊠)], Huiping Shen[2], and Tingli Yang[2]

[1] Key Laboratory of Mechanism Theory and Equipment Design,
Ministry of Education, Tianjin University, Tianjin 300350, China
liuht@tju.edu.cn
[2] School of Mechanical Engineering, Changzhou University,
Changzhou 213016, China

Abstract. A partially-decoupled three-translation and one-rotation (3T1R) parallel manipulator is proposed and analyzed in this paper. The new mechanism features with a symmetric layout and simple kinematic structure for generation of 3T1R motion in pick-and-place operations. The kinematics of this mechanism, including forward and inverse position problems, are analyzed. The closed-form solution of direct kinematics is obtained and verified by inverse kinematics. Moreover, the partially-decoupled performance can be found through the forward kinematics. The proposed mechanism is mainly composed of revolute joints and presents better performance. Hence, more potential applications of this manipulator can be expected.

Keywords: 3T1R · Parallel mechanism · Structure design · Kinematic analysis

1 Introduction

The parallel manipulators (PMs) with three translations and one rotation (3T1R), also known as Schönflies-motion parallel robots, have a great potential of various applications in the manufacturing industry. Many 3T1R robots have been proposed and developed. Examples include H4 [1], I4 [2], I4R [3], Par4 [4], Heli4 [5]. These robots have similar architectures but with different designs of the moving platform. A parallel Schönflies-motion robot admitting a rectangular workspace, which allows to utilize the shop-floor space efficiently for flexible pick-and-place applications, was recently proposed by Wu et al. [6]. Many other 3T1R robots constructed adopting quite different kinematic structures are available in literature. Zhao, Huang et al. [7] proposed a 4-URU-type 3T1R parallel robot. Jin and Yang [8] proposed a family of 3T1R parallel mechanisms based on single-open-chain structures. Kong et al. [9] synthesized a group of PMs with the same sub-chains based on screw theory. Huang et al. [10] developed a 3T1R-type high-speed parallel manipulator called as Cross-IV. Liu et al. [11] developed a X4 parallel robot prototype with one moving platform.

It is noted that the above stated 3T1R parallel mechanisms all have higher coupling degree, and are not input-output motion decoupled, which lead to their forward

© Springer Nature Switzerland AG 2019
H. Yu et al. (Eds.): ICIRA 2019, LNAI 11742, pp. 415–424, 2019.
https://doi.org/10.1007/978-3-030-27535-8_37

kinematics and dynamics analysis, motion control and trajectory planning are more complex. Partially or fully decoupled parallel manipulators are desirable. There are already some parallel mechanisms with partial motion decoupling or complete decoupling properties proposed, for example, mechanisms of decoupled two-rotation DOF [12], one-translation and two-rotation DOF [13], three-translation [14], etc. Examples include also a XYZ parallel elasticity mechanism [15], a partially decoupled 3-PPR robot with U-shape base [16]. In spite of the above proposed partially decoupled parallel mechanisms, very few 3T1R PMs with motion decoupling are reported. The SCARA parallel robot of FlexPicker [17] has partial motion decoupling, which is based on the Delta mechanism, attached with a RUPU kinematic chain, in order to achieve the rotation around the normal of the moving platform.

In this paper, a novel partially-decoupled 3T1R parallel manipulator is proposed. The kinematics analysis of this 3T1R PM is also the subject of this paper. The paper is organized as follows: Sect. 2 illustrates this 3T1R PM of 2-(RPa‖3R)3R with type synthesis method based on POC equations [18]. In Sect. 3, the closed-form equations are established and the direct kinematics of this mechanism is solved. The reported work is concluded in Sect. 4.

2   Structure Design of a 2-(RPa‖3R)3R Manipulator

The 3T1R parallel manipulator proposed here is shown in Fig. 1. The base platform 0 is connected to the moving platform 1 by left and right two identical hybrid chains. Each hybrid chain contains a sub-parallel mechanism (sub-PM) and a 3R serial kinematic chain. The manipulator is symmetrical about the plane $x-y = 0$. The intersecting line of the plane and the base is the line t-t.

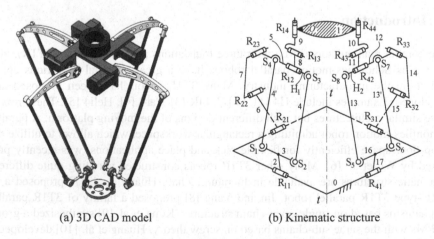

(a) 3D CAD model   (b) Kinematic structure

Fig. 1. 3D CAD model and kinematic structure of 3T1R robot

With reference to the symmetric plane, the left hybrid chain composed of links 2, 3, 4, 4′, 5, 6, 7, 8 and 9, as shown in Fig. 1(b), is selected to illustrate the structure of manipulator. The CAD design of the hybrid chain is shown in Fig. 2(a). The shorter link 3 of a parallelogram composed of four spherical pairs (S_1, S_2, S_3 and S_4) is connected by actuated arm 2, to the base 0 by a revolute joint R_{11}, which is denoted as RPa. The extended part of the opposite link 5 of the parallelogram is connected in parallel to a sub-chain composed of two links 6 and 7 and three parallel revolute joints (3R, i.e., $R_{21} \| R_{22} \| R_{23}$). The connection line of the two spherical joints S_3 and S_4 is collinear with the axis of the rotation joints R_{12} but perpendicular to the axis of the revolute joint R_{23}. Thus, a sub-parallel mechanism (sub-PM) is generated, as shown in Fig. 2(b), and denoted as RPa$\|$3R.

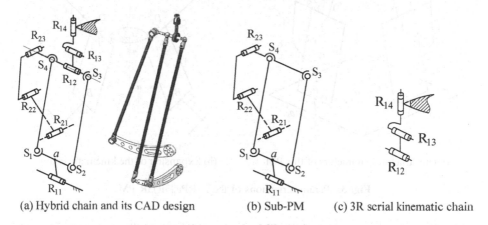

(a) Hybrid chain and its CAD design   (b) Sub-PM   (c) 3R serial kinematic chain

Fig. 2. Kinematic structures of chains

This sub-PM is then further connected with a 3R serial kinematic chain composed of two links 8 and 9 and 3R serial kinematic chain, i.e., $R_{12} \| R_{13} \perp R_{14}$, as shown in Fig. 2(c), which leads to a hybrid chain. Since the PM has two identical hybrid chains, the whole manipulator is recorded as 2-(RPa$\|$3R)3R. The four rotation joints R_{11}, R_{21}, R_{31} and R_{41} on the base platform 0 are active and mutually perpendicular to each other, which means $R_{11} \perp R_{41}$, $R_{11} \perp R_{21}$ and $R_{41} \perp R_{31}$. Two rotation joints R_{14} and R_{44} on the moving platform are all parallel to the normal of the moving platform 1, i.e., $R_{14} \| R_{44}$. Here, the symbols $\|$ and $\perp$ stand respectively for being parallel and vertical, the same hereinafter.

3   Kinematic Analysis

3.1   Establishment of the Coordinate System and Parameterization

Without losing of generality, let the base platform 0 be a square. The four actuated joints R_{11}, R_{21}, R_{31} and R_{41} are located on the midpoint of its each side, i.e., A_1, A_2, A_3, A_4, as shown in Fig. 3. Furthermore, the frame coordinate system $o\text{-}xyz$ is established on the base platform 0. The origin is located at the geometric center, point o, of the base platform 0. The axes x and y are collinear with and vertical to the connection line A_1A_3, respectively. On the moving platform 1, the moving coordinate system p-uvw is established at point p that is the midpoint of the connection line between the points F_1 and F_2. u axis is perpendicular to the line F_1F_2, while v axis coincides with this line F_1F_2. Both z and w axes are determined by the right-hand Cartesian coordinate rule, as shown in Fig. 3(a). For ease of understanding, the 2-(RPa||3R)3R PM is redrawn as stretched to a planar view, as shown in Fig. 3(b).

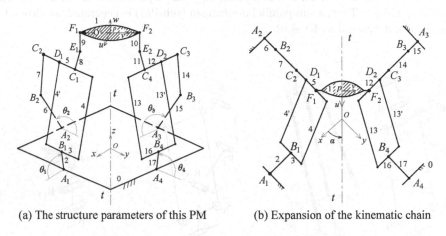

(a) The structure parameters of this PM   (b) Expansion of the kinematic chain

Fig. 3. Parameterizations of the 2-(RPa||3R)3R PM

The structure parameters of the PM are denoted in the following way. The side length of the square base platform 0 is noted by $2l_1$, and the length of the moving platform 1, i.e., $F_1F_2 = 2l_2$. For other link lengths, we have

$$A_1B_1 = A_2B_2 = A_3B_3 = A_4B_4 = l_3(l_3 \neq l_1), B_1C_1 = B_2C_2 = B_3C_3 = B_4C_4 = l_4$$
$$D_1C_1 = C_2D_1 = C_3D_2 = C_4D_2 = l_5, C_1E_1 = C_4E_2 = F_1E_1 = F_2E_2 = l_6$$

The four input angles are defined as θ_1, θ_2, θ_3 and θ_4 for the four active joints, as shown in Fig. 3(a). The moving platform position is defined by the coordinates of point p as (x, y, z), and its orientation by angle α, the angle from the forward direction of u-axis to x-axis or from the forward direction of v-axis to y-axis, as shown in Fig. 3(b).

3.2   Solution to Forward Position Problem

In the forward position analysis, we need to obtain output parameters, i.e., the coordinates of point p of the moving platform, defined by (x, y, z), and the orientation angle α, as a function of the known input angles θ_1, θ_2, θ_3 and θ_4.

Solve Coordinates of Points C_1 and C_4. The coordinates of four points A_1, A_2, A_3 and A_4 on the base platform 1 are $(l_1,0,0)$, $(0,-l_1,0)$, $(-l_1,0,0)$ and $(0,l_1,0)$, respectively. The coordinates of each end point of the four actuated arms 2, 6, 15 and 17, i.e., points B_1, B_2, B_3 and B_4, are easily calculated as respectively, $(l_1 + l_3\cos\theta_1, 0, l_3\sin\theta_1)$,

$(0, -l_1 + l_3\cos\theta_2, l_3\sin\theta_2)$, $(-l_1 + l_3\cos\theta_3, 0, l_3\sin\theta_3)$ and $(0, l_1 + l_3\cos\theta_4, l_3\sin\theta_4)$. As stated in Sect. 2.2.1, the output links 5 and 12 of the left and right sub-PMs can only produce a motion in the plane o-yz and o-xz respectively. That is, $x_{C1} = 0$ and $y_{C4} = 0$. Hence, the coordinates of points C_2 and C_3 are found as $(0, y_{C1} - 2l_5, z_{C1})$ and $(x_{C4} - 2l_5, 0, z_{C4})$ respectively. The link length constraints defined by $B_1C_1 = B_2C_2 = B_3C_3 = B_4C_4 = l_4$ imply that

$$\begin{cases} x_{B_1}^2 + y_{C_1}^2 + (z_{B_1} - z_{C_1})^2 = l_4^2 \\ (y_{B_2} - y_{C_1} + 2l_5)^2 + (z_{B_2} - z_{C_1})^2 = l_4^2 \end{cases} \quad (1)$$

$$\begin{cases} x_{C_4}^2 + y_{B_4}^2 + (z_{B_4} - z_{C_4})^2 = l_4^2 \\ (x_{B_3} - x_{C_4} + 2l_5)^2 + (z_{B_3} - z_{C_4})^2 = l_4^2 \end{cases} \quad (2)$$

Equation (1) leads to

$$a_1 y_{C_1} + b_1 z_{C_1} = c_1 \quad (3)$$

here, $a_1 = 2(y_{B2} + 2l_5)$, $b_1 = 2(z_{B2} - z_{B1})$, $c_1 = (y_{B2} + 2l_5)^2 + z_{B2}^2 - x_{B1}^2 - z_{B1}^2$.   If $a_1 = 0$ and $b_1 = 0$, then $c_1 = -x_{B1}^2 = 0$. However, due to $l_3 \neq l_1$, i.e., $x_{B1} \neq 0$, a_1 and b_1 are not zero at the same time. Hence, we have two cases as follows

$$\begin{cases} z_{C_1} = \frac{c_1}{b_1}, y_{C_1} = \pm\sqrt{l_4^2 - (z_{B_1} - z_{C_1})^2 - x_{B_1}^2} & \text{if } a_1 = 0 \\ z_{C_1} = \frac{e_1 \pm \sqrt{e_1^2 - 4d_1 f_1}}{2d_1}, y_{C_1} = \frac{c_1 - b_1 z_{C_1}}{a_1} & \text{if } a_1 \neq 0 \end{cases} \quad (4)$$

here, $d_1 = a_1^2 + b_1^2$, $e_1 = 2(b_1 c_1 + z_{B1} a_1^2)$, $f_1 = a_1^2(x_{B1}^2 + z_{B1}^2 - l_4^2) + c_1^2$.   Similarly, Eq. (2) leads to $a_2 x_{C4} + b_2 z_{C4} = c_2$ and coordinates of point C_4 can be obtained.

Solve Coordinates of Point p and Orientation α. Once the coordinates of points C_1 and C_4 are obtained, the upper parts of each hybrid chain, i.e., links 8, 9 and 10, 11, and the moving platform 1 can be treated as a special single loop chain 6R mechanism, as shown in Fig. 4(a). A planar view is shown in Fig. 4(b).

As shown in Fig. 4(a), let δ be the angle between vector C_1E_1 and x-axis. We assume two planes m and n pass through the points C_1, E_1 and F_1, and the points C_4, E_2 and F_2, respectively, as shown in Fig. 4(b). Thus, motions of two groups of points (C_1, E_1, F_1) and (C_4, E_2, F_2) always keep in the planes m and n, respectively. Then, we get

$$y_{E_1} = y_{C_1}, x_{E_2} = x_{C_4} \quad (5)$$

Hence the coordinates of points E_1 and E_2 are calculated. The constraint equation is expressed as $y_{E_2}^2 + (z_{C4} - z_{E2})^2 = l_6^2$. It is obtained, due to $z_{E1} = z_{E2}$ and $y_{C4} = 0$, by

$$y_{E_2} = \pm\sqrt{l_6^2 - (z_{C_4} - z_{C_1} - l_6\sin\delta)^2} \quad (6)$$

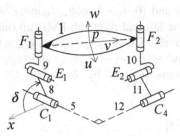

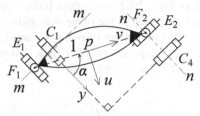

(a) Single loop space 6R mechanism   (b) Plan view of single loop 6R mechanism

Fig. 4. Upper part of the robot

From Fig. 3(b), it is known that $F_1F_2 = E_1E_2 = 2l_2$, and hence we establish another constraint equation as

$$(x_{C_4} - l_6\cos\delta)^2 + (y_{E_2} - y_{C_1})^2 = 4l_2^2 \tag{7}$$

Let $u = \tan \delta/2$. By expanding Eq. (7), we obtain a high-order polynomial equation with only one variable u as following

$$f(u) = \sum_{i=0}^{8} g_i u^i \tag{8}$$

$$g_0 = 16l_2^4 - 16l_2^2l_6^2 + 4l_6^4 + 8l_2^2t^2 - 4l_6^2t^2 + t^4 + x_{C_4}(16l_2^2l_6 - 8l_6^3 + 4l_6t^2 - 8l_2^2x_{C_4}$$
$$+ 8l_6^2x_{C_4} - 2t^2x_{C_4} - 4l_6x_{C_4}^2 + x_{C_4}^3) - y_{C_1}^2(8l_2^2 - 2t^2 + 4l_6x_{C_4} - 2x_{C_4}^2 - y_{C_1}^2),$$

$$g_1 = 8l_6t(2l_6^2 - 4l_2^2l_6 - 2l_6t^2 - 2l_6x_{C_4} + l_6x_{C_4}^2 - l_6y_{C_1}^2),$$

$$g_2 = 4(16l_2^4 - 4l_6^4 + 8l_2^2t^2 + 4l_6^2t^2 + t^4) + 4x_{C_4}(8l_2^2l_6 + 4l_6^3 + 2l_6t^2 - 8l_2^2x_{C_4} - 2t^2x_{C_4}$$
$$- 2l_6x_{C_4}^2 + x_{C_4}^3) + 4y_{C_1}^2(2t^2 - 8l_2^2 - 2l_6x_{C_4} + 2x_{C_4}^2 + y_{C_1}^2),$$

$$g_3 = 8l_6t(3x_{C_4}^2 - 12l_2^2 - 2l_6^2 - 2l_6x_{C_4} - 3y_{C_1}^2 - 3t^2),$$

$$g_4 = 96l_2^4 + 32l_2^2l_6^2 + 24l_6^4 + 48l_2^2t^2 + 40l_6^2t^2 + 6t^4 - 2x_{C_4}^2(24l_2^2 - 8l_6^2 + 6t^2 + 3x_{C_4}^2)$$
$$+ 6y_{C_1}^2(2t^2 + 6x_{C_4}^2 - 8l_2^2 + y_{C_1}^2),$$

$$g_5 = 8l_6t(2l_6x_{C_4} - 12l_2^2 - 2l_6^2 + 3x_{C_4}^2 - 3t^2 - 3y_{C_1}^2),$$

$$g_6 = 64l_2^4 - 16l_6^4 + 32l_2^2t^2 + 16l_6^2t^2 + 4t^4 - 4x_{C_4}(8l_2^2l_6 + 4l_6^3 + 4l_6t^2 + 8l_2^2x_{C_4}$$
$$+ 2t^2x_{C_4} + 2l_6x_{C_4}^2 + x_{C_4}^3) + 4y_{C_1}^2(2t^2 - 8l_2^2 + 2l_6x_{C_4} + 2x_{C_4}^2 + y_{C_1}^2),$$

$$g_7 = 8l_6t(2l_6^2 - 4l_2^2 + 2l_6x_{C_4} + x_{C_4}^2 - y_{C_1}^2 - t^2),$$

$$g_8 = 4(4l_2^4 - 4l_2^2l_6^2 + l_6^4 + 2l_2^2t^2 - l_6^2t^2)^2 + t^4 + x_{C_4}(8l_6^3 - 16l_2^2l_6 - 4l_6t^2 - 8l_2^2x_{C_4}$$
$$+ 8l_6^2x_{C_4} - 2t^2x_{C_4} + 4l_6x_{C_4}^2 + x_{C_4}^3) + y_{C_1}^2(4l_6x_{C_4} + 2t^2 - 8l_2^2 + 2x_{C_4}^2 + y_{C_1}^2),$$

$$t = z_{C_4} - z_{C_1}.$$

Real roots of the equation yield the corresponding angle δ, then y_{E2} (with two values) by Eq. (6). By putting y_{E2} values into Eq. (7), we obtain the real value of y_{E2} or y_{C4}. Finally, the coordinates (x, y, z) of point p on the moving platform 1 and rotation angle α can be easily obtained. The equations show that the translation motion of point F_1 on the moving platform 1, along y axis, is determined only by the two joints R_{11} and R_{21} (i.e., θ_1 and θ_2), and the translation motion of point F_2 on the moving platform 1, along x axis, only by the two joints R_{31} and R_{41} (i.e., θ_3 and θ_4), while the translation along z axis and orientation angle α are determined by four input angles θ_1, θ_2, θ_3 and θ_4. In this light, we say the PM has partial motion decoupling property.

3.3 Inverse Position Solution

The purpose of the inverse position solutions is to obtain the input angles θ_1, θ_2, θ_3 and θ_4 as a function of the known output variables, i.e., the coordinates of point p of the moving platform 1, defined by (x, y, z), and the orientation angle of the end-effector α. In the moving coordinate system p-uvw, the coordinates of points E_1 and E_2 are $(0, -l_2, -l_6)$ and $(0, l_2, -l_6)$ respectively. Since the coordinates of points B_1, B_2, B_3 and B_4 are known in the forward position problems afore-mentioned, we may establish the four constraint equations below according to the link length constraints and inverse kinematics can be obtained

$$\theta_i = 2\arctan\frac{2l_3 z_i \pm \sqrt{4z_i^2 l_3^2 - h_i t_i}}{h_i}, (i = 1, 2, 3, 4), \tag{9}$$

$$z_1 = z_{C_1}, \; z_2 = z_{C_2}, \; z_3 = z_{C_3}, \; z_4 = z_{C_4}$$

$$h_1 = l_1^2 - 2l_1 l_3 + l_3^2 - l_4^2 + y_{C_1}^2 + z_{C_1}^2$$

$$t_1 = l_1^2 + 2l_1 l_3 + l_3^2 - l_4^2 + y_{C_1}^2 + z_{C_1}^2$$

$$h_2 = l_1^2 + 2l_1 l_3 + l_3^2 - l_4^2 + 2l_1 y_{C_2} + 2l_3 y_{C_2} + y_{C_2}^2 + z_{C_2}^2$$

$$t_2 = l_1^2 - 2l_1 l_3 + l_3^2 - l_4^2 + 2l_1 y_{C_2} - 2l_3 y_{C_2} + y_{C_2}^2 + z_{C_2}^2$$

$$h_3 = l_1^2 - l_4^2 + 2l_1 l_3 + l_3^2 + 2l_1 x_{C_3} + 2l_3 x_{C_3} + x_{C_3}^2 + z_{C_3}^2$$

$$t_3 = l_1^2 - l_4^2 - 2l_1 l_3 + l_3^2 + 2l_1 x_{C_3} - 2l_3 x_{C_3} + x_{C_3}^2 + z_{C_3}^2$$

$$h_4 = l_1^2 + l_3^2 - 2l_1 l_3 - l_4^2 + x_{C_4}^2 + z_{C_4}^2$$

$$t_4 = l_1^2 + l_3^2 + 2l_1 l_3 - l_4^2 + x_{C_4}^2 + z_{C_4}^2$$

It is easy to find that when the coordinates of the point p and orientation angle of the moving platform 1 are known, the input angles θ_1, θ_2, θ_3 and θ_4 have two sets of solutions, and the points C_1 and C_4 have two sets of the coordinate solutions. Hence the number of the inverse solutions is 64(4 × 16), which leads to the PM has totally 64 configurations.

3.4 Verification of Forward and Inverse Kinematics

The structure parameters are $l_1 = 300$ mm, $l_2 = 70$ mm, $l_3 = 350$ mm, $l_4 = 800$ mm, $l_5 = 100$ mm and $l_6 = 50$ mm, respectively. The four input angles θ_1, θ_2, θ_3 and θ_4 take the values of 58.6839°, 150.8342°, 144.9223° and 61.2457°, respectively. Considering the actual configuration of the PM, we take $z_{C1}>0$ and $z_{C4}>0$, according to Eqs. (1)–(4), the coordinates of points C_1 and C_4 are obtained, which are (0, −134.5310, 923.2359) and (−99.1480, 0, 947.7786), respectively. We substitute these values into Eq. (8) and obtain

$$f(u) = 10^8 \times (3.75252 - 1.33078u + 4.45452u^2$$
$$-7.90246u^3 + 8.28859u^4 - 9.84914u^5$$
$$+ 2.29185u^6 - 3.27747u^7 - 1.29474u^8) = 0$$

The real roots of above equation are found as: $u_1 = -3.71915$, $u_2 = 0.867349$. The forward solutions are obtained and shown in Table 1.

Table 1. Forward position solutions

No	x /mm	y /mm	z /mm	α /°
1	−71.2029	−70.3510	948.1609	23.5291
2	−46.0400	−88.9291	1022.7338	49.3485

Substituting this group of the forward solutions into the inverse solutions Eq. (9), and considering that $z_{E1}>z_{C1}$, $z_{E2}>z_{C4}$, the sets of inverse solutions are reduced to 16, one of which is just one of the given inputs, i.e., $\theta_1 = 58.684°$, $\theta_2 = 150.8342°$, $\theta_3 = 144.9223°$ and $\theta_4 = 61.2457°$. The values are consistent with the four known input angles, which verifies the forward and inverse solutions.

4 Conclusion

A novel parallel manipulator 2-(RPa‖3R)3R generating three-translation and one-rotation output is proposed. In this work, the kinematics analysis of the new PM was conducted. The close-form forward solutions of the PM are obtained and verified by inverse kinematics. In addition, the PM features motion decoupling which can be found through kinematics.

The contributions of this work are the development of the new 3T1R parallel manipulator 2-(RPa‖3R)3R and establishment of its kinematics. The proposed manipulator is symmetric in structure and mainly composed of revolute joints. The new design will lead to less material use and lightweight, and consequentially, a reduced manufacturing cost. Hence, more potential applications can be expected.

References

1. Pierrot, F., Company, O.: H4: A New Family of 4-DOF Parallel Robots. In: 1999 IEEE/ASME International Conference on Advanced Intelligent Mechatronics, Atlanta, USA, pp. 508–513 (1999)
2. Krut, S., Company, O., Benoit, M., et al.: I4: a new parallel mechanism for scara motions. 2008 IEEE Int. Conf. Robot. Autom. 2(2), 1875–1880 (2008)
3. Krut, S., Nabat, V., Company, O., et al.: A high-speed parallel robot for scara motions. 2004 IEEE International Conference on Robotics and Automation, New Orleans, USA, pp. 4109–4115 (2004)
4. Nabat, V., de la O Rodriguez M., Company, O., et al.: Par4: very high speed parallel robot for pick-and-place. In: IEEE/RSJ International Conference on Intelligent Robots and Systems, IEEE Xplore, Edmonton, Canada, pp. 553–558(2005)
5. Lüdinghausen, M.V., Miura, M., Würzler, N.: Heli4: a parallel robot for scara motions with a very compact traveling plate and a symmetrical design. In: The 2006 IEEE/RSJ International Conference on Intelligent Robots and Systems (IROS), Beijing, China, pp. 1656–1661 (2006)
6. Wu, G., Bai, S., Hjørnet, P.: Architecture optimization of a parallel Schönflies-motion robot for pick-and-place applications in a predefined workspace. Mech. Mach. Theory 09(5), 148–165 (2016)
7. Zhao, T.S., Huang, Z.: Theory and application of selecting actuating components of spatial parallel mechanisms. Chin. J. Mech. Eng. 36(10), 81–85 (2000)
8. Yang, T., Jin, Q., Liu, A., et al.: Structure synthesis of 4-dof (3-translation and 1-rotation) parallel robot mechanisms based on the units of single-opened- -chain. In: Proceedings of the ASME 2001 Design Engineering Technical Conference and Computers and Information in Engineering Conference, No. DETC2001/DAC-21152 (2001)
9. Kong, X., Gosselin, C.M.: Type synthesis of 3T1R 4-DOF parallel manipulators based on screw theory. Robot. Autom. IEEE Transact. 20(2), 181–190 (2004)
10. Huang, T., Zhao, X., Mei, J., et al.: A parallel mechanism with three translations and one rotation, China, ZL201220007884.X (2012)
11. Liu, X., Xie, F.: A kind of four degrees of freedom of moving platform parallel mechanism with SCARA exercise, China, 201210435375.1 (2012)
12. Hou, Y., Lu, W., Zeng, Q., et al.: Motion decoupling two rotational degrees of freedom parallel mechanism, China, 201010617042 (2010)
13. Jin, Q., Yang, T.: Synthesis and analysis of a group of 3-degree-offreedom partially decoupled parallel manipulators. J. Mech. Des. 126, 301–306 (2004)
14. Kong, X., Gosselin, C.M.: A class of 3-DOF translational parallel manipulators with linear input–output equations. In: Proceedings of the Workshop on Fundamental Issues and Future Research Directions for Parallel Mechanisms and Manipulators, Quebec City, Quebec, Canada, pp. 25–32 (2002)
15. Awtar, S., Ustick, J., Sen, S.: An XYZ parallel-kinematic flexure mechanism with geometrically decoupled degrees of freedom. ASME Int. Des. Eng. Tech. Conf. Comput. Inf. Eng. Conf. 5(1), 119–126 (2011)

16. Bai, S., Caro, S.: Design and analysis of a 3-PPR planar robot with U-shape base. In: International Conference on Advanced Robotics, Munich, Germany (2009)
17. Liao, B.: A large workspace parallel manipulator for high-speed pick-and-place applications. Harbin Institute of Technology (2012)
18. Yang, T., Liu, A., Shen, H., et al.: Topology Design of Robot Mechanisms. Springer, Singapore (2018). https://doi.org/10.1007/978-981-10-5532-4

A New Four-Limb Parallel Schönflies Motion Generator with End-effector Full-Circle Rotation via Planetary Gear Train

Guanglei Wu[1]([✉]), Zirong Lin[1], Huiping Shen[2], Wenkang Zhao[1], and Sida Zhang[1]

[1] School of Mechanical Engineering, Dalian University of Technology, Dalian 116024, China
gwu@dlut.edu.cn
[2] School of Mechanical Engineering, Changzhou University, Changzhou, China
shp65@126.com

Abstract. This paper introduces a new four-limb parallel Schönflies motion generator for the pick-and-place application, whose end-effector adopts a planetary gear train as the amplification mechanism to realize the full-circle rotation. The preliminary kinematic analysis and workspace/dexterity evaluation are carried out to depict the workspace quality and dexterous working envelope. The performance comparison with different geometric parameters show the influence of the variables to the robot performance.

Keywords: Schönflies motion generator · Parallel robot · Pick-and-place application · Planetary gear train

1 Introduction

The parallel Schönflies motion generators (SMGs), which can produce three independent translations and one rotation around a fixed axis of rotation, have been widely used in material handling for pick-and-place (PnP) applications, thanks to their advantages of high speed and lightweight structure. Up to date, a number of parallel SMGs have been presented. Most of the parallel SMGs inherit the architecture of the H4 [13] robot, created by the Pierrot's group from LIRMM, with four identical limbs and an articulated traveling plate [5]. Later on, the same research group developed the I4 [9], the symmetrical Par4 [12] and the Heli4 robots [6]. The latter two counterparts both have been commercialized as the Adept Quattro robot [1] and the Veloce robot [2], respectively. Other four-limb parallel SMGs with different mobile platforms [3,8,11,14–17] are also noticeable for their high performance.

Parallel SMGs with end-effectors of large orientation are preferable in the PnP operations, for which the amplification mechanisms, such as pulley-belt

© Springer Nature Switzerland AG 2019
H. Yu et al. (Eds.): ICIRA 2019, LNAI 11742, pp. 425–435, 2019.
https://doi.org/10.1007/978-3-030-27535-8_38

mechanism [12], rack-pinion mechanism [9], gears and screw mechanism [2], are usually required to enhance the rotational capability. The SMGs with the previous amplification mechanisms have been patented, therefore, new parallel SMG architecture needs to be developed for the industrial applications. Compared to the isostatic two-limb robot counterparts [4,7,10], the parallel SMGs with four limbs behaves hyperstatic. Sequentially, robot end-effector with full-circle rotation will be an advantage in the PnP application.

In this paper, a new parallel SMG with full-circle rotation is introduced, of which the planetary gear train (PGT) is adopted to construct the mobile platform. The mobilities of the proposed robot is verified with the displacement group. The kinematics of the robot is studied, and the workspace and dexterity are analyzed with different sets of geometric parameters to show the influence of the variables to the performance.

2   Manipulator Architecture

The conceptual design of the new four-limb robot is shown in Fig. 1. As depicted in Fig. 1(a), each limb is composed of a proximal link and a distal arm (parallelogram, a.k.a '$\varPi$ joint') connected to the base and mobile platforms. The arrangement positions of the four proximal limbs on the base frame is located at the vertices of a rectangle to avoid the singularities when the robot is in some symmetric configurations.

The mobile platform is consisted of a constant-orientation sub-platform as the gear ring and a rotational sub-platform as the carrier in the PGT. Both sub-platforms connect a pair of opposite limbs, where the rotational one has two additional revolute pairs at the connecting positions rather than the remaining limbs. The end-effector orientation is amplified by the PGT, which can be simplified as a revolute pair, as shown in Fig. 1(b). The orientation of the rotational sub-platform is hence can be computed from the required end-effector orientation and speed ratio of the PGT, where the speed ratio is calculated as

$$i_{eH} = \frac{\omega_e}{\omega_H} = 1 + \frac{z_r}{z_e} \tag{1}$$

where ω_e and ω_H stand for the speeds of the end-effector speed and the rotational sub-platform, and z_r and z_e are the number of the tooth of the gear ring and the output sun gear, respectively. One example is $i_{eH} = 8$ with $z_r = 140$ and $z_e = 20$ to realize the end-effector full-circle rotation with the sub-platform rotation 45°.

3   Displacement Group and Mobility Analysis

The mobilities of the new SMG presented is derived by the Group Theory. The robot is composed of two $RR\varPi RR$ and two $RR\varPi R$ typed limbs as shown in Fig. 2 and has a symmetry plane Oxz or Oyz. The kinematic bond $\mathcal{L}_i$ of the ith limb, $i = 2, 4$, is the product of the following four bonds:

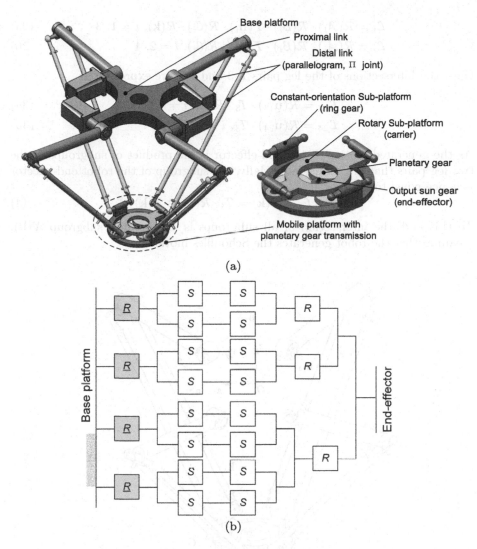

(a)

(b)

Fig. 1. The design concept of the new SMG: (a) CAD model; (b) joint-and-loop graph.

- The rotation subgroup $\mathcal{R}(\mathcal{A}_i)$ passing through A_i and parallel to $\mathbf{u}_{24}$.
- The rotation subgroup $\mathcal{R}(\mathcal{B}_i)$ passing through B_i and parallel to $\mathcal{A}_i$.
- The translation subgroup $\mathcal{T}(\mathbf{n}_i)$ corresponding to the parallelogram lying in a plane normal to $\mathbf{n}_i$.
- The rotation subgroup $\mathcal{R}(\mathcal{C}_i)$ passing through C_i and parallel to $\mathcal{B}_i$.

and one more rotation subgroup $\mathcal{R}(\mathbf{k})$ passing through C_i exist in the first and third limbs, where $\mathbf{k}$ is the unit vector of z-axis. Thus, the kinematic bonds of the ith limb is

$$\mathcal{L}_i = \mathcal{R}(\mathcal{A}_i) \cdot \mathcal{R}(\mathcal{B}_i) \cdot \mathcal{T}(\mathbf{n}_i) \cdot \mathcal{R}(\mathcal{C}_i) \cdot \mathcal{R}(\mathbf{k}), \, i = 1, 3 \qquad (2a)$$

$$\mathcal{L}_i = \mathcal{R}(\mathcal{A}_i) \cdot \mathcal{R}(\mathcal{B}_i) \cdot \mathcal{T}(\mathbf{n}_i) \cdot \mathcal{R}(\mathcal{C}_i), \, i = 2, 4 \qquad (2b)$$

thus, the intersections of the leg pairs 1–3 and 2–4 are expressed as

$$\mathcal{L}_{13} = \mathcal{R}(\mathbf{u}_{13}) \cdot \mathcal{T}_3 \cdot \mathcal{R}(\mathbf{k}), \, i = 1, 3 \qquad (3a)$$

$$\mathcal{L}_{24} = \mathcal{R}(\mathbf{u}_{24}) \cdot \mathcal{T}_3, \, i = 2, 4 \qquad (3b)$$

As the generated motion at the end-effector is the product of subgroups of the two leg pairs that are connected serially, the subgroup of the robot end-effector is hence equal to

$$\mathcal{L}_{13} \cap \mathcal{L}_{24} \cdot \mathcal{R}(\mathbf{k}) = \mathcal{T}_3 \cdot \mathcal{R}(\mathbf{k}) \equiv \mathcal{X}(\mathbf{k}) \qquad (4)$$

To this end, the intersection of all subgroups is a Schönflies subgroup $\mathcal{X}(\mathbf{k})$, meaning that the robot generates the Schönflies motion.

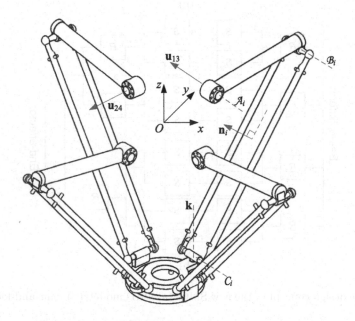

Fig. 2. The joints of the ith limb with rotation input.

4   Position Analysis and Jacobians of the Robot

The reference coordinate frame $\mathcal{F}_b$ is built with the origin located at the geometric center of the base platform, of which x-axis is parallel to the segment A_2A_1 (A_3A_4) and the z-axis is normal to the plane $A_1A_2A_3A_4$ pointing upward. The moving coordinate frame $\mathcal{F}_p$ is attached to the rotational sub-platform with the origin located at the geometric center, and its X-axis is parallel to segment

C_3C_1. In the ith limb, the axis of rotation of the ith actuated joint is parallel to unit vector $\mathbf{u}_i$, and unit vectors $\mathbf{v}_i$ and $\mathbf{w}_i$ are parallel to segments A_iB_i and B_iC_i, respectively (Fig. 3).

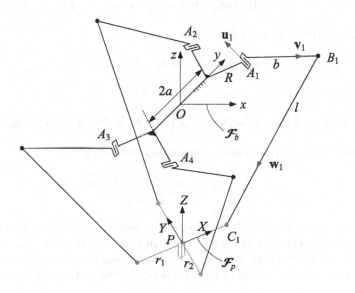

Fig. 3. The parameterization of the robot structure.

Let $\mathbf{i}$, $\mathbf{j}$, and $\mathbf{k}$ denote the unit vectors along x-, y-, and z-axis, respectively, the Cartesian coordinates of the ith actuated joint in the frame $\mathcal{F}_b$ is denoted as

$$\mathbf{a}_i = R\mathbf{e}_i + a\mathbf{j}, \ i = 1, 2; \ \mathbf{a}_i - R\mathbf{e}_i - a\mathbf{j}, \ i = 3, 4 \tag{5}$$

where $\mathbf{e}_i = \begin{bmatrix} \cos\eta_i \ \sin\eta_i \ 0 \end{bmatrix}^T$, $\eta_i = (2i-1)\pi/4$, $i = 1, 2, 3, 4$. The corresponding axis of rotation of the ith actuated joint is described by

$$\mathbf{u}_i = \begin{bmatrix} -\sin\eta_i \ \cos\eta_i \ 0 \end{bmatrix}^T \tag{6}$$

The Cartesian coordinates of point B_i in the frame $\mathcal{F}_b$ is derived as

$$\mathbf{b}_i = b\mathbf{v}_i + \mathbf{a}_i; \ \mathbf{v}_i = \mathbf{R}_z(\eta_i)\mathbf{R}_y(\theta_i)\mathbf{i} \tag{7}$$

Let the end-effector pose be denoted by $\mathbf{x} = \begin{bmatrix} \mathbf{p}^T \ \phi \end{bmatrix}^T$, $\mathbf{p} = \begin{bmatrix} x \ y \ z \end{bmatrix}^T$, the Cartesian coordinates of point C_i in frame $\mathcal{F}_b$ is expressed as

$$\mathbf{c}_i = \mathbf{Q}\mathbf{c}'_i + \mathbf{p}, \ i = 1, 3; \ \mathbf{c}_i = \mathbf{c}'_i + \mathbf{p}, \ i = 2, 4 \tag{8}$$

where $\mathbf{Q} = \mathbf{R}_z(\phi)$ is the rotation matrix of the end-effector and $\mathbf{c}'_i$ is the position vector of C_i in the frame $\mathcal{F}_p$:

$$\mathbf{c}'_1 = -\mathbf{c}'_3 = r_1\mathbf{i}, \ \mathbf{c}'_2 = -\mathbf{c}'_4 = r_1\mathbf{j}, \tag{9}$$

4.1   Inverse Geometric Problem

The inverse geometry is solved from the following kinematic constraints:

$$(\mathbf{c}_i - \mathbf{b}_i)^T (\mathbf{c}_i - \mathbf{b}_i) = l^2, \quad i = 1, ..., 4 \tag{10}$$

which can be written in the following expression:

$$I_i \sin\theta_i + J_i \cos\theta_i + K_i = 0 \tag{11}$$

with

$$I_i = -2b(\mathbf{c}_i - \mathbf{a}_i)^T \mathbf{k}, \ J_i = 2b(\mathbf{c}_i - \mathbf{a}_i)^T \mathbf{e}_i, \ K_i = l^2 - b^2 - \|\mathbf{c}_i - \mathbf{a}_i\|^2 \tag{12}$$

Consequently, the inverse geometry problem is solved as

$$\theta_i = 2\tan^{-1} \frac{-I_i \pm \sqrt{I_i^2 + J_i^2 - K_i^2}}{K_i - J_i} \tag{13}$$

For a given pose of the robot end-effector, each limb can have two postures, which are characterized by the sign "$-/+$" in Eq. (13). It means that the robot can have up to 16 working modes, i.e., 16 solutions to the inverse kinematics problem. Here, the "+" mode of each limb is selected as the working mode.

4.2   Kinematic Jacobian Matrix

Let $\mathbf{w}_i = (\mathbf{c}_i - \mathbf{b}_i)/l$, differentiating the four Eq. (10) with respect to time yields

$$\mathbf{A}\dot{\mathbf{x}} = \mathbf{B}\dot{\boldsymbol{\theta}} \tag{14}$$

with

$$\mathbf{A} = \begin{bmatrix} \mathbf{w}_1^T & r_1 \mathbf{w}_1^T \mathbf{s}_1 \\ \mathbf{w}_2^T & 0 \\ \mathbf{w}_3^T & r_1 \mathbf{w}_3^T \mathbf{s}_3 \\ \mathbf{w}_4^T & 0 \end{bmatrix}, \ \dot{\mathbf{x}} = \begin{bmatrix} \dot{x} \\ \dot{y} \\ \dot{z} \\ \dot{\phi} \end{bmatrix} \ ; \ \mathbf{s}_i = \mathbf{Q}\mathbf{R}_z(\eta_i)\mathbf{j}, \ i = 1, 3 \tag{15a}$$

$$\mathbf{B} = \begin{bmatrix} h_1 & & & \\ & h_2 & & \\ & & h_3 & \\ & & & h_4 \end{bmatrix}, \ \dot{\boldsymbol{\theta}} = \begin{bmatrix} \dot{\theta}_1 \\ \dot{\theta}_2 \\ \dot{\theta}_3 \\ \dot{\theta}_4 \end{bmatrix} \ ; \ h_i = b\mathbf{w}_i^T(\mathbf{u}_i \times \mathbf{v}_i) \tag{15b}$$

where $\mathbf{A}$ and $\mathbf{B}$ are the forward and inverse Jacobian matrices, respectively. The kinematic Jacobian matrix is hence obtained as

$$\mathbf{J} = \mathbf{A}^{-1}\mathbf{B} \tag{16}$$

5   Workspace and Dexterity Analysis

The workspace (WS) is one of the most important performance for the robot, which can be found through the geometrical approach reported in [3]. Here, the CAD software Solidworks is adopted to visualize the workspace. With different

Table 1. Geometric parameters of the robot with different designs.

Design ID	a [mm]	R (mm)	b (mm)	l (mm)	r_1 (mm)	r_2 (mm)
ID-1	50	140	245	500	80	80
ID-2	80	140	245	500	80	80
ID-3	50	140	245	500	90	80

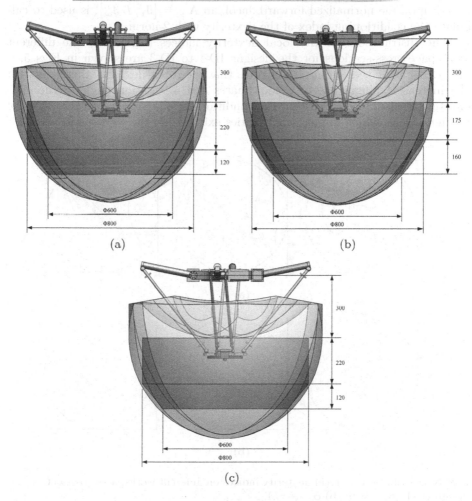

(a)   (b)

(c)

Fig. 4. The workspace of the SMG with different geometric parameters: (a) ID-1; (b) ID-2; (c) ID-3.

geometric parameters listed in Table 1, the reachable and regular WS is displayed Fig. 4. It is found that design ID-2 has the smallest workspace volume, meaning that larger parameters a will decrease the workspace size.

Dexterity is another utmost important concern, which is usually evaluated by the condition number of the kinematic Jacobian matrix. Since the elements in the forward Jacobian matrix $\mathbf{A}$ of the robot are not homogeneous due to the mixed end-effector mobilities, the following characteristic length is introduced for the normalization:

$$L = \sqrt{\frac{3\mathbf{J}_\omega^T\mathbf{J}_\omega}{\mathrm{tr}(\mathbf{J}_v^T\mathbf{J}_v)}} \tag{17}$$

where $\mathbf{J}_v$ is the entry of the first three columns and $\mathbf{J}_\omega$ is the last one in $\mathbf{A}$, respectively. Sequentially, the normalized kinematic Jacobian matrix $\mathbf{J}_N = \mathbf{A}_N^{-1}\mathbf{B}$, based upon the normalized forward Jacobian $\mathbf{A}_N = \begin{bmatrix} \mathbf{J}_v/L\ \mathbf{J}_\omega \end{bmatrix}$, is used to calculate the conditioning index of the dexterity with 2-norm.

The distributions of the local dexterity indices (LCI) over the different workspace cross-sections for the designs ID-1 to ID-3 are shown in Figs. 5, 6 and 7. It can be seen from these figures that the robot dexterity increases with the increasing magnitude of z coordinates and orientation angle of the end-effector. It should be noted that the conditioning index is close to zero in some configurations, which implies singularities exist within the workspace.

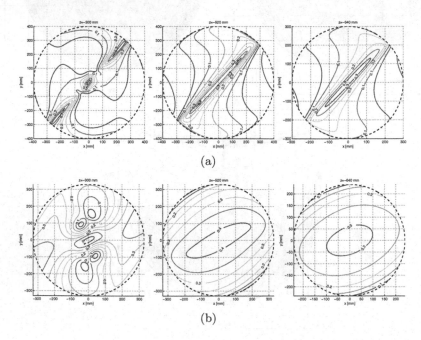

(a)

(b)

Fig. 5. Distributions of local dexterity indices on different workspace cross-sections for design ID-1: (a) $\phi = 0$; (b) $\phi = -\pi/4$.

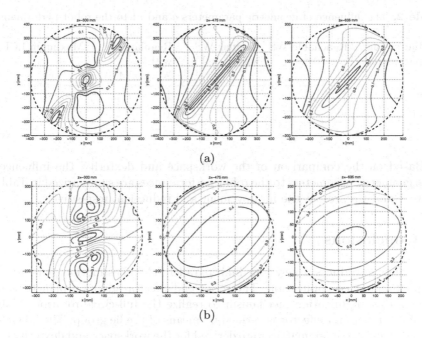

(a)

(b)

Fig. 6. Distributions of local dexterity indices on different workspace cross-sections for design ID-2: (a) $\phi = 0$; (b) $\phi = -\pi/4$.

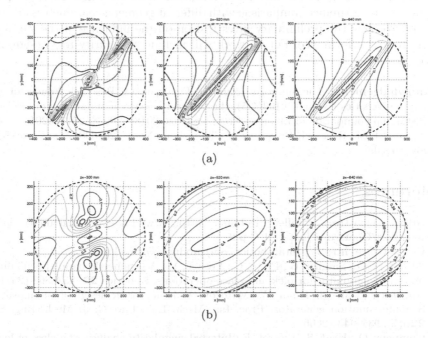

(a)

(b)

Fig. 7. Distributions of local dexterity indices on different workspace cross-sections for design ID-3: (a) $\phi = 0$; (b) $\phi = -\pi/4$.

Table 2. The influence of geometric parameters a and $r1$ to the robot performances.

Increasing parameters	Reachable WS	Regular WS with $\phi = 0$	Regular WS with $\phi = -\pi/4$	Maximum LCI
a	↓	↓	↓	↑
r_1	-	-	↓	↓

Based on the comparison of the workspace and dexterity, the influence of some geometric parameters to the robot performances are summarized in Table 2, where ↑ and ↓ represent the improvement and reduction, respectively.

6 Conclusions

This paper introduces a new four-limb parallel Schönflies motion generator for the pick-and-place application. The robot end-effector adopts a planetary gear train as the amplification mechanism to realize the full-circle rotation. Mobilities of the robot end-effector is verified by means of the lie group. The kinematic geometry and Jacobian matrices are derived for the workspace and dexterity evaluation. Workspace size and shape are visualized by a geometric approach, and the isocontours of the local dexterity distributions show the dexterous workspace region. The performance comparison with different geometric parameters are carried out to show the preliminary investigation on the influence of the variables to the robot performance. Future work will include singularity-free design and robot prototyping.

Acknowledgement. The supports from the Fundamental Research Funds for the Central Universities (No. DUT19JC25), the Natural Science Foundation and the Doctoral Start up Foundation of Liaoning Province (Nos. 20180520028, 20170520134), and the Applied Basic Research Programs of Changzhou (No. CJ20180017) are gratefully acknowledged.

References

1. Adept Quattro Parallel Robots. http://www1.adept.com/main/ke/data/Archived/Quattro/sQuattro_UG.pdf
2. Penta Veloce. http://pentarobotics.com/products/#brochure
3. Altuzarra, O., Şandru, B., Pinto, C., Petuya, V.: A symmetric parallel Schönflies-motion manipulator for pick-and-place operations. Robotica **29**, 853–862 (2011)
4. Angeles, J., Caro, S., Khan, W., Morozov, A.: Kinetostatic design of an innovative Schönflies-motion generator. Proc. Ins. Mech. Eng. Part C: J. Mech. Eng. Sci. **220**(7), 935–943 (2006)
5. Company, O., Krut, S., Pierrot, F.: Internal singularity analysis of a class of lower mobility parallel manipulators with articulated traveling plate. IEEE Trans. Robot. **22**(1), 1–11 (2006)

6. Corbel, D., Gouttefarde, M., Company, O., Pierrot, F.: Actuation redundancy as a way to improve the acceleration capabilities of 3T and 3T1R pick-and-place parallel manipulators. ASME J. Mech. Robot. **2**(4), 041002 (2010)
7. Harada, T., Angeles, J.: Kinematics and singularity analysis of a CRRHHRRC parallel Schönflies motion generator. CSME Trans. **38**(2), 173–183 (2014)
8. Kim, S.M., Kim, W., Yi, B.J.: Kinematic analysis and optimal design of a 3T1R type parallel mechanism. In: IEEE International Conference on Robotics and Automation, pp. 2199–2204 (2009)
9. Krut, S., Benoit, M., Ota, H., Pierrot, F.: I4: a new parallel mechanism for SCARA motions. In: IEEE International Conference on Robotics and Automation, vol. 2, pp. 1875–1880. IEEE (2003)
10. Lee, P.C., Lee, J.J.: Singularity and workspace analysis of three isoconstrained parallel manipulators with schoenflies motion. Front. Mech. Eng. **7**(2), 163–187 (2012)
11. Liu, S., Huang, T., Mei, J., Zhao, X., Wang, P., Chetwynd, D.G.: Optimal design of a 4-DOF SCARA type parallel robot using dynamic performance indices and angular constraints. ASME J. Mech. Robot. **4**(3), 031005 (2012)
12. Nabat, V., de la O Rodriguez, M., Company, O., Krut, S., Pierrot, F.: Par4: very high speed parallel robot for pick-and-place. In: IEEE/RSJ International Conference on Intelligent Robots and Systems, pp. 553–558. IEEE (2005)
13. Pierrot, F., Company, O.: H4: a new family of 4-DOF parallel robots. In: IEEE/ASME International Conference on Advanced Intelligent Mechatronics, pp. 508–513. IEEE (1999)
14. Wu, G.: Kinematic analysis and optimal design of a wall-mounted four-limb parallel Schönflies-motion robot for pick-and-place operations. J. Intell. Robot. Syst. **85**(3), 663–677 (2017)
15. Wu, G., Bai, S., Caro, S.: A transmission quality index for a class of four-limb parallel schönflies motion generators. ASME J. Mech. Robot. **10**(5), 051014 (2018)
16. Wu, G., Bai, S., Hjørnet, P.: Architecture optimization of a parallel Schönflies-motion robot for pick-and-place applications in a predefined workspace. Mech. Mach. Theory **106**, 148–165 (2016)
17. Xie, F., Liu, X.: Design and development of a high-speed and high-rotation robot with four identical arms and a single platform. ASME J. Mech. Robot. **7**(4), 041015 (2015)

Design and Kinematic Analysis on a Novel Serial-Parallel Hybrid Leg for Quadruped Robot

Jianzhuang Zhao[1,2], Kai Liu[1,2], Fei Zhao[1,2]([✉]), and Zheng Sun[1,2]

[1] Shaanxi Key Laboratory of Intelligent Robots, Xi'an Jiaotong University,
Xi'an 710094, Shaanxi, People's Republic of China
ztzhao@xjtu.edu.cn
[2] School of Mechanical Engineering, Xi'an Jiaotong University,
Xi'an 710094, Shaanxi, People's Republic of China

Abstract. Aiming to improve the performances and reduce the manufacturing cost of the current legs for quadruped robots, this paper presents a novel 3 DOF serial-parallel hybrid leg. We design a prototype 3D model and give the analytical expressions of inverse and forward kinematics. End-effector workspace is computed using the numerical forward kinematics. The analysis and calculations show that this hybrid leg with simple structure combines the advantages of both serial and parallel mechanisms: high stiffness, high bearing capacity, low structural inertia and large workspace. This research has great significance to a series of further studies on dynamic analysis, mechanism optimal and system control of this novel hybrid leg.

Keywords: Quadruped robot · Serial-parallel hybrid leg ·
Kinematic analysis · Co-simulation

1 Introduction and Related Works

Quadruped robot is an essential part of robotics and has become a research hotspot in the past decade (Ananthanarayanan et al. 2012), since this kind of robots can complete a lot of difficult works in dangerous and complex environments instead of human, such as disaster relief, minesweeping, environmental detection etc. (Gehring et al. 2016). One of the most important components of quadruped robot is the leg which determines the motion performance (Seok et al. 2015).

Most structures of legs for current quadruped robot are serial such as BigDog (Ding et al. 2015) from Boston Dynamic company. HyQ robot (Semini et al. 2011) was developed by Italy and Shandong University designed Scalf robot (Chai et al. 2014). These serial structures have large workspace, but the stiffness and bearing capacity are low. On the other hand, walking robot with parallel leg was raised by Rong et al. (2012). WL-15, WL-16RIV (Sugahara et al. 2005)

© Springer Nature Switzerland AG 2019
H. Yu et al. (Eds.): ICIRA 2019, LNAI 11742, pp. 436–447, 2019.
https://doi.org/10.1007/978-3-030-27535-8_39

was proposed by Waseda University and Minitaur (Kenneally et al. 2016) was designed by University of Pennsylvania. These parallel structure legs with complex structure and small workspace have high stiffness, high bearing capacity, high stability and low weight-load ratio. In order to combine the advantages of the two structures, Xinghua et al. summarized the characteristics of these legs' configurations of current quadruped robots, and proposed three different hybrid leg structures (Xianbao and Chenkun 2013). Gao et al. proposed a new 4-DOF hybrid leg and solved the kinematics problems (Gao et al. 2015). These hybrid legs showed the expected performance and achieved good effects in practical applications. While, some of these hybrid legs used complex spatial structures which are difficult to manufacture and the costs are high.

To overcome the limitations of serial and parallel structures, and reduce manufacturing costs of current serial-parallel hybrid legs, we propose a novel and simplified serial-parallel hybrid leg, which is composed of two planar mechanisms in this paper. The paper is organized as follows. The mechanical design of the hybrid leg is introduced firstly. Section 3 analyze the degrees-of-freedom (DOF) of this novel structure and design a prototype. In Sect. 4, we report the details of this hybrid leg kinematics. Workspace analysis and verification results are presented in Sect. 5. Our conclusions and future work are discussed in Sect. 6.

2   Overview of Mechanical Design

The schematic diagram of the proposed serial-parallel leg is shown in Fig. 1, including the frame 1, the links 2A, 2B, 3A, 3B, 4A and 4B, the rotating shafts 5, the thigh link 6, the hip joint 7, the thigh 8 and the calf 9. The geometrical parameters of (N)A and (N)B are same.

This serial-parallel mechanism is composed of one parallel part and one serial part. The overall spatial mechanism can be disassembled into two planar mechanisms to simplify the kinematic analysis. And the following sections are based on this method. The parallel portion is horizontally connected the frame 1 by the links 2A, 2B. And the links 2A, 2B are fixed with frame 1. The serial section is vertical. The two portions are connected through the thigh link 6, and all the motion pairs in the entire mechanism are rotating pairs.

3   Analysis of DOF and Prototype Design

The separated two parts are shown in Fig. 2. Firstly, for the serial portion, the open-loop four-link mechanism consists of the frame 1, the hip joint 7, the thigh 8 and the calf 9. The frame 1 is fixed with no DOF, and the remaining three members are free. Connected by three rotating pairs, this structure has no virtual constraints and local DOF. Above all, the DOF of the serial portion can be written by Kutzbach-Grübler(KG) formula as follows:

$$f_1 = 3n - (2p_l + p_h) = 3 \times 3 - (2 \times 3) = 3 \tag{1}$$

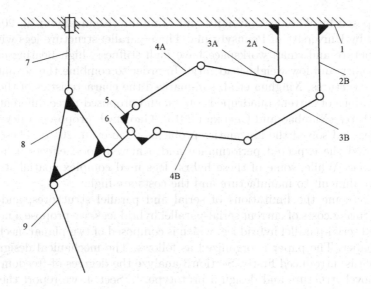

Fig. 1. Schematic diagram of whole structure.

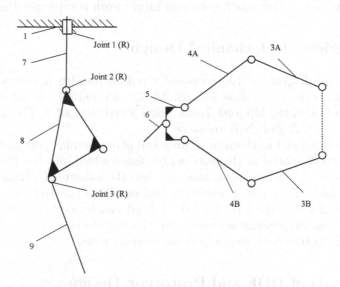

Fig. 2. Separated serial and parallel parts.

where f_1 is the DOF of serial part, n is the number of links, p_l is the number of lower pair and p_h is the number of higher pair. Then, for the DOF of the parallel portion, this portion can be simplified as a plane-symmetric six-link mechanism with external constraint. The rotating shafts 5 is indirectly connected to the frame 1 through the thigh link 6 and the serial part. It is externally constrained, losing one DOF. Therefore, the DOF of the parallel portion is:

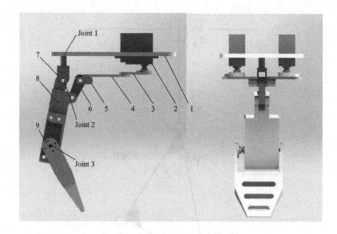

Fig. 3. 3D model of the novel parallel-serial hybrid leg.

$$f_2 = 3n - (2p_l + p_h) = 3 \times 4 + 2 - (2 \times 6) = 2 \qquad (2)$$

where f_2 is the DOF of parallel part.

For the whole structure, it should be note that the hip joint 7 and the thigh 8 are driven by the parallel portion through the thigh link 6. They are not independent components. Only the rotation of the knee between the thigh 8 and the calf 9 is independent in serial portion. So, there are 3 DOF for the entire parallel-serial leg, 2 DOF in the parallel portion, and 1 DOF in the serial part, respectively.

From the above analysis, we design the links 3A, 3B driven by two servo motors and another motor is used for the thigh 8 at the joint 3 to drive the calf 9. The 3D model designed by Solidworks is shown in Fig. 3 where 2, 3 and 4 represent the links 2(A, B), 3(A, B) and 4(A, B). And, the three joints of the serial part is also marked in Fig. 3.

It can be easily found that there are two servo motors fixed in the frame 1 compared with the traditional 3-DOF serial leg in which only one motor is fixed in the base. Moreover, three chains from the end of the calf 9 to the frame 1 can be found in this hybrid leg. Therefore, this novel hybrid leg has the advantages of high stiffness, high bearing capacity and low weight-load ratio. At the same time, this design reduces the inertia when the robot lifts the leg, which improves the efficiency and the flexibility of this leg. Last but not least, all components of this hybrid leg can be easily made, and the cost is lower.

4 Kinematic Analysis

4.1 Modified D-H Model

The kinematic model is critical for solving the inverse and forward kinematics. We define the positive axes direction as counterclockwise rotation. The schematic of the frames of serial part is shown in Fig. 4.

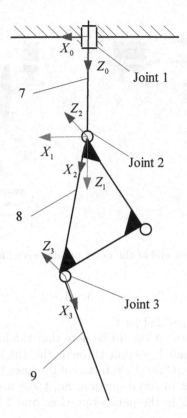

Fig. 4. Frames of serial part.

Based on this model and given the range of the joint angles, the following modified D-H parameters of the serial part were determined in Table 1.

Table 1. Modified D-H parameters of serial part.

i	a_{i-1}	α_{i-1}	d_i	θ_i	Range of θ_i
1	0	0°	d_1	θ_1	$[-40°, 40°]$
2	0	$-90°$	0	θ_2	$[-140°, -75°]$
3	a_2	0°	0	θ_3	$[-90°, 90°]$

For the modified D-H parameters, the general homogeneous transformation matrix $_i^{i-1}T$ can be written as:

$$
_i^{i-1}T = \begin{bmatrix} c\theta_i & -s\theta_i & 0 & 0 \\ s\theta_i c\alpha_{i-1} & c\theta_i c\alpha_{i-1} & -s\alpha_{i-1} & -d_i s\theta_i \\ s\theta_i s\alpha_{i-1} & c\theta_i s\alpha_{i-1} & -s\alpha_{i-1} & d_i c\alpha_{i-1} \\ 0 & 0 & 0 & 1 \end{bmatrix} \tag{3}
$$

where $c\theta_i = cos\theta_i$, $s\theta_i = sin\theta_i$, $c\alpha_{i-1} = cos\alpha_{i-1}$, $s\alpha_{i-1} = sin\alpha_{i-1}$.

Bring the parameters from Table 1 into formula 3, the ^0_1T, ^1_2T, ^2_3T can be obtained. Since the axes of joint 2 and joint 3 are parallel, ^1_3T calculated first using $^1_3T = ^1_2T^2_3T$. Finally, by $^0_3T = ^0_1T^1_3T$, the complete transformation matrix ^0_3T can be got.

$$^0_3T = ^0_1T^1_3T = \begin{bmatrix} c_1c_{23} & -c_1s_{23} & -s_1 & a_2s_{23} \\ s\theta_ic\alpha_{i-1} & c\theta_ic\alpha_{i-1} & -s\alpha_{i-1} & -d_is\theta_i \\ s\theta_is\alpha_{i-1} & c\theta_is\alpha_{i-1} & -s\alpha_{i-1} & d_ic\alpha_{i-1} \\ 0 & 0 & 0 & 1 \end{bmatrix} \tag{4}$$

where $c_1 = cos\theta_1$, $s_1 = sin\theta_1$, $c_{23} = cos(\theta_2 + \theta_3)$, $s_{23} = sin(\theta_2 + \theta_3)$.

4.2 Inverse Kinematics

The inverse kinematics computation of this hybrid leg includes the following two steps:

(a) Inverse solution of workspace to joint space.
(b) Inverse solution of joint space to driving space.

Inverse Solution of Workspace to Joint Space. The equation of motion for the serial part can be written as:

$$^0_3T = \begin{bmatrix} n_x & o_x & a_x & p_x \\ n_y & o_y & a_y & p_y \\ n_z & o_z & a_z & p_z \\ 0 & 0 & 0 & 1 \end{bmatrix} = ^0_1T(\theta_1)^1_2T(\theta_1)^2_3T(\theta_3) \tag{5}$$

The idea of the inverse solution of the workspace to the joint space is that we know the configuration of the end effector (foot ending) to find the joint angles θ_1, θ_2, θ_3. Multiplying $^0_1T^{-1}(\theta_1)$ on the left of the two sides of Eq. 5, we can get the Eq. 6. The elements (2, 4) of the two matrixes are equal and the equation $-s_1p_x + c_1p_y = 0$ can be obtained. So, the expression of θ_1 is: $\theta_1 = arctan(p_y/p_x)$.

$$\begin{bmatrix} c_1 & s_1 & 0 & 0 \\ -s_1 & c_1 & 0 & 0 \\ 0 & 0 & 1 & -d_1 \\ 0 & 0 & 0 & 1 \end{bmatrix} \begin{bmatrix} n_x & o_x & a_x & p_x \\ n_y & o_y & a_y & p_y \\ n_z & o_z & a_z & p_z \\ 0 & 0 & 0 & 1 \end{bmatrix} = ^1_2T(\theta_2)^2_3T(\theta_3) = ^1_3T(\theta_2, \theta_3) \tag{6}$$

Then, make the elements (1, 4) and (3, 4) of the two matrixes are equal, the expression of θ_2 can be written as:

$$\begin{cases} p_xc_1 + p_ys_1 = a_2c_2 \\ p_z - d_1 = -a_2s_2 \end{cases} \rightarrow \theta_2 = arctan[(d_1 - p_z)/(p_xc_1 + p_ys_1)] \tag{7}$$

Next, multiplying $^1_2T^{-1}(\theta_2)$ on the left of the two sides of Eq. 6. The elements (1, 1) and (2, 1) of the two matrixes are equal. We can get the following equation: $\theta_3 = arctan[-(n_xc_1s_2 + n_ys_1s_2 + n_zc_2)/(n_xc_1c_2 + n_ys_1c_2 - n_zs_2)]$.

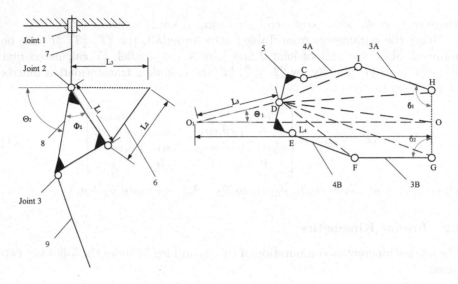

Fig. 5. Sketch of inverse kinematics.

Finally, the inverse kinematic solution from the workspace to joint space is shown in Eq. 8.

$$\begin{cases} \theta_1 = arctan(p_y/p_x) \\ \theta_2 = arctan[(d_1 - p_z)/(p_x c_1 + p_y s_1)] \\ \theta_3 = arctan[-(n_x c_1 s_2 + n_y s_1 s_2 + n_z c_2)/(n_x c_1 c_2 + n_y s_1 c_2 - n_z s_2)] \end{cases} \quad (8)$$

Inverse Solution of Joint Space to Driving Space. In this step, geometric constraints are used to find the relationship between the joint angles θ_1, θ_2 and the driving angles β_1, β_2. Because the range of θ_1 is symmetrical, we can only focus on half of it.

The inverse solution structure sketch of the two parts is shown is shown in Fig. 5. The motion of serial part in the vertical plane is analyzed firstly. In Fig. 5, assuming L_1, ϕ_1 and L_2 are known of the $\triangle(L_1 L_2 L_3)$, the length of L_3 can be solved by the cosine theorem which is:

$$L_3 = L_1 cos(\theta_2 - \phi_1) + \sqrt{[2L_1 cos(\theta_2 - \phi_1)]^2 - 4[(L_1)^2 - (L_2)^2]}/2 \quad (9)$$

In order to make the following calculations of parallel part concise, we named the links and angles as follows: $CD = DE = L_5$, $CI = EF = L_6$, $IH = FG = L_7$, $HO = OG = L_8$, $DO = L_9, DH = L_{10}$, $DI = L_{11}$, $DG = L_{12}$, $DF = L_{13}$; $\angle O_1 OD = \phi_2$, $\angle OHD = \phi_3$, $\angle HDI = \phi_4$, $\angle CDI = \phi_5$, $\angle DHI = \phi_6$, $\angle FDG = \phi_7$, $\angle EDF = \phi_8$, $\angle DGO = \phi_9$, $\angle DGF = \phi_{10}$.

In $\triangle O_1OD$, L_9 can be known by cosine theorem and ϕ_2 can be known by sine theorem which can be written as:

$$\begin{cases} L_9 = \sqrt{(L_3)^2 + (L_4)^2 - 2L_3L_4cos\theta_1} \\ \phi_2 = arcsin(L_3sin\theta_1/L_9) \end{cases} \tag{10}$$

Then, the $\angle O_1DO$ and $\angle DOH$ can be written as:

$$\begin{cases} \angle O_1DO = \pi - \theta_1 - \phi_2 \\ \angle DOH = \pi/2 - \phi_2 \end{cases} \tag{11}$$

After that, ϕ_3 can be found in $\triangle HOD$ using the same method in $\triangle O_1OD$ which is:

$$\phi_3 = arcsin[L_9sin(\pi/2 - \phi_2)/L_{10}] \tag{12}$$

At the same time, $\angle ODH$ and $\angle CDI$ can be written as:

$$\begin{cases} \angle ODH = \pi/2 + \phi_2 - \phi_3 \\ \angle CDI = \phi_5 = \theta_1 + \phi_3 - \phi_4 \end{cases} \tag{13}$$

Next, regard L_{11} as an unknown parameter, ϕ_4 and L_{11} can be known using the cosine theorem in $\angle CID$ and $\angle HID$ which can be written as:

$$\begin{cases} \phi_5 = \theta_1 + \phi_3 - \phi_4 \\ L_{11} = L_{10}cos\phi_4 - \sqrt{(2L_{10}cos\phi_4)^2 - 4[(L_{10})^2 - (L_7)^2]}/2 \ \rightarrow \phi_4 \rightarrow L_{11} \\ L_{11} = L_5cos\phi_5 - \sqrt{(2L_5cos\phi_5)^2 - 4[(L_5)^2 - (L_6)^2]}/2 \end{cases} \tag{14}$$

So, ϕ_6 can be known by:

$$\phi_6 = arcsin(L_{11}sin\phi_4/L_7) \tag{15}$$

Because the parallel part is symmetrical, ϕ_9 and ϕ_{10} can be obtained by same process, which can be written as:

$$\phi_9 = arcsin[L_9sin(\pi/2 + \phi_2)/L_{12}]; \phi_{10} = arcsin(L_{13}sin\phi_7/L_7) \tag{16}$$

Finally, the expressions of β_1, β_2 can be written as:

$$\begin{cases} \beta_1 = \phi_3 + \phi_6 = arcsin[L_9sin(\pi/2 - \phi_2)/L_{10}] + arcsin(L_{11}sin\phi_4/L_7) \\ \beta_2 = \phi_9 + \phi_{10} = arcsin[L_9sin(\pi/2 + \phi_2)/L_{12}] + arcsin(L_{13}sin\phi_7/L_7) \end{cases} \tag{17}$$

What needs to be explained here is that the Eq. 17 gives the relationship between joint angles (θ_1, θ_2) and the driving angles (β_1, β_2). Therefore, in the forward kinematics part, we only focus on the serial part.

4.3   Forward Kinematics

The forward kinematic problem is that the joint angles are already given to find the expression of the end of this hybrid leg in frame 0. In this paper, we regard the central point P which is at the end of calf 9 as the end of this leg. So, θ_1, θ_2, θ_3 is known and the expression of point P in frame 3 is $P_3 = (x_3, y_3, z_3)$.

Above all, it is easy to solve the forward kinematic problem using homogeneous transformation matrix ${}^0_3T$, which can be written as:

$$P_0 = \begin{bmatrix} x_0 \\ y_0 \\ z_0 \\ 1 \end{bmatrix} = {}^0_3T P_3 = \begin{bmatrix} c_1 c_{23} & -c_1 s_{23} & -s_1 & a_2 s_{23} \\ s\theta_i c\alpha_{i-1} & c\theta_i c\alpha_{i-1} & -s\alpha_{i-1} & -d_i s\theta_i \\ s\theta_i s\alpha_{i-1} & c\theta_i s\alpha_{i-1} & -s\alpha_{i-1} & d_i c\alpha_{i-1} \\ 0 & 0 & 0 & 1 \end{bmatrix} \begin{bmatrix} x_3 \\ y_3 \\ z_3 \\ 1 \end{bmatrix} \tag{18}$$

where $P_0 = (x_0, y_0, z_0)$ is the position of point P in frame 0. When the joint angle is given, the P_0 can be uniquely determined.

5   Workspace Analysis and Verification

5.1   Workspace Analysis

The workspace of the mechanism refers to the position that the end effector or reference point of the mechanism can reach. It is an important indicator to measure the performance of the robot. For this structure, we chose point P as the reference point. And the geometric parameters of the 3D model designed before were given in Table 2. a_3 is the length of the calf 9.

Table 2. The geometric parameters of serial part.

Name	d_1	a_2	a_3
Length/(mm)	35	81.27	90

Bring the joint angles into the forward kinematic Eq. 18, the workspace of this hybrid leg can be plotted by Matlab which is shown in Fig. 6. From the result, we found the workspace looks like a mushroom and the $z_0 max = 206.27$ mm. It is clearly that the workspace of this hybrid leg is larger than the traditional 3-DOF parallel robot with same geometric parameters.

5.2   Verification

The 3D model of the hybrid leg designed by Soildworks was imported into Adams to verify the results of our analysis. In Adams, the complete constraints were added to this leg and the result is in Fig. 7(a) shows that the DOF of this structure is 3, which is consistent with the DOF analysis before. We planned a backwards movement in the workspace for this structure which lasts 25 s and the foot movement track is:

$$\begin{cases} x_0 = -t \\ y_0 = 0 \\ z_0 = 206.27 - t \end{cases} \tag{19}$$

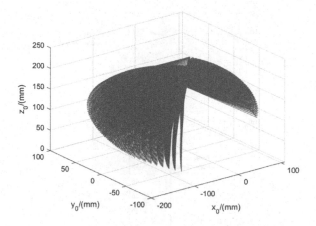

Fig. 6. Workspace of this hybrid leg.

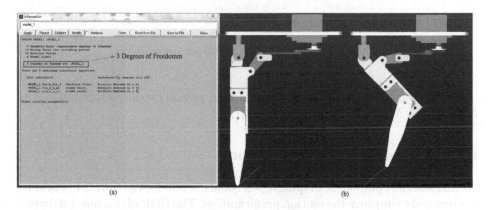

Fig. 7. Adams simulation.

Next, the result of inverse kinematics calculated by Matlab was imported into Adams to drive this leg. The beginning and end of the simulation positions were shown in Fig. 7(b).

From the equation of the track, the joint angles $(\theta_1, \theta_2, \theta_3)$ and the driving angles $(\beta_1, \beta_2, \beta_3)$ can be obtained by inverse kinematics, which the $\theta_1 = 0, \beta_1 = \beta_2$ in this track. So, we just needed to focus on $(\beta_1, \theta_2, \theta_3)$. The simulation results of $(\beta_1, \theta_2, \theta_3)$ were shown in Fig. 8. The green full curve represented the results calculated by Matlab and the red dummy curve was the results from Adams. And, it was easy to find that the angles $(\beta_1, \theta_2, \theta_3)$ in Fig. 8 were almost identical.

For the forward kinematic, we chose the point when $t = 10\,\mathrm{s}$ to prove the correctness. At this point, $\theta_1 = 0°, \theta_2 = -113.96°, \theta_3 = 38.77°$ and $x_0 = -10, y_0 = 0, z_0 = 196.27$ by Eq. (19). Bring the joint angles into Eq. (18), the position of $\hat{P}$ was: $\hat{x}_0 = -9.998, \hat{y}_0 = 0, \hat{z}_0 = 196.277$ which was almost the same with (x_0, y_0, z_0).

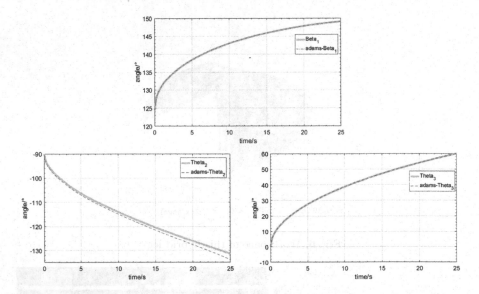

Fig. 8. Co-simulation results. (Color figure online)

Above all, our kinematic analysis was right proved by the co-simulation with Matlab and Adams.

6   Conclusion and Future Work

As an essential component of quadruped robots, a novel serial-parallel hybrid leg is proposed to improve the motion performances. The DOF of this novel structure is 3 which is proved later. A prototype 3D model is designed, and analytical equations of inverse and forward kinematics are derived. The workspace for this hybrid leg is also plotted. By Matlab and Adams co-simulation, the analysis is verified. These analysis results show that this hybrid leg combines the advantages of both serial and parallel mechanisms: high stiffness, high bearing capacity, low structural inertia and large workspace. The manufacturing cost of this hybrid leg is low, which means it is easy to be popularized and applied.

The future work includes velocity analysis, dynamic analysis and kinematic parameter optimization to realize the desired motion-force relationship. A prototype hardware should be implemented and experimental verified.

Acknowledgment. This research is supported by the national key development plan project of intelligent robot (No. 2018YFB4505), ministry of science and technology of China.

References

Ananthanarayanan, A., Azadi, M., Kim, S.: Towards a bio-inspired leg design for high-speed running. Bioinspir. Biomim. **7**(4), 046,005 (2012)

Chai, H., Meng, J., Rong, X., Li, Y.: Design and implementation of scalf, an advanced hydraulic quadruped robot. Robot **36**(4), 385–391 (2014)

Ding, L., Wang, R., Feng, H.: Key technology analysis of bigdog quadruped robot. J. Mech. Eng. **51**(7), 1–23 (2015)

Gao, J., Li, M., Hou, B., Wang, B.: Kinematics analysis on the serial-parallel leg of a novel quadruped walking robot. Opt. Precis. Eng. **23**(11), 3147–3160 (2015)

Gehring, C., et al.: Practice makes perfect: an optimization-based approach to controlling agile motions for a quadruped robot. IEEE Robot. Autom. Mag. **23**(1), 34–43 (2016)

Kenneally, G., De, A., Koditschek, D.E.: Design principles for a family of direct-drive legged robots. IEEE Robot. Autom. Lett. **1**(2), 900–907 (2016)

Rong, Y., Jin, Z.L., Qu, M.K.: Design of parallel mechanical leg of six-legged robot. Guangxue Jingmi Gongcheng (Opt. Precis. Eng.) **20**(7), 1532–1541 (2012)

Semini, C., Tsagarakis, N.G., Guglielmino, E., Focchi, M., Cannella, F., Caldwell, D.G.: Design of HyQ-a hydraulically and electrically actuated quadruped robot. Proc. Inst. Mech. Eng. Part I: J. Syst. Control Eng. **225**(6), 831–849 (2011)

Seok, S., et al.: Design principles for energy-efficient legged locomotion and implementation on the mit cheetah robot. IEEE/ASME Trans. Mechatron. **20**(3), 1117–1129 (2015)

Sugahara, Y., et al.: Walking control method of biped locomotors on inclined plane. In: Proceedings of the 2005 IEEE International Conference on Robotics and Automation, pp. 1977–1982. IEEE (2005)

Xianbao, T.X.G.F.C., Chenkun, Q.: Mechanism design and comparison for quadruped robot with parallel-serial leg. J. Mech. Eng. **6** (2013)

A Novel 5-DOF Hybrid Robot Without Singularity Configurations

Xin Tian[1,2], Tieshi Zhao[1,2(✉)], and Erwei Li[1,2]

[1] Hebei Provincial Key Laboratory of Parallel Robot and Mechatronic System,
Yanshan University, Qinhuangdao 066004, China
tszhao@ysu.edu.cn
[2] Key Laboratory of Advanced Forging and Stamping Technology and Science,
Yanshan University, Ministry of Education of China,
Qinhuangdao 066004, China

Abstract. This paper deals with the kinematics of a novel 5 degrees of freedom (5-DoF) hybrid robot without singularity configurations, which is composed of a 4-DoF parallel robot plus an X table. The 4-limb parallel robot is especially designed as cross-arranged 2-PRU/2-PUS without singularity configurations during moving. Based on the Grassmann linear geometry principle, the residual degree of freedom singularity at the initial position of the 5-DoF robot is studied. Then considering the constraint screws of the parallel robot, the DoF of the hybrid robot is analyzed. On the basis of screw theory, the complete Jacobian matrix is established. And the theoretical model is verified by the numerical example. The complete Jacobian matrix is helpful for further analysis of the complete performance of the hybrid robot.

Keywords: Hybrid robot · Singularity configuration · Screw theory · Complete Jacobian matrix

1 Introduction

With reduced set up work, accuracy and better surface finishes, the 5-DoF robot is considered to be the most important equipment for manufacturing key components in the fields of aeronautics, astronautics, shipping, and railroad, etc. in recent years [1].

Compared with the serial robot, the parallel robot has the higher speed and rapider acceleration, higher stiffness and carrying capacity, and greater precision. So, the parallel robot obtains a great development in the processing field [2]. Most parallel kinematics machines (PKMs) such as VARIAX presented by Giddings & Lewis in 1994 [3] and the Hexapod [4] have a very limit proceeding space due to the small workspace of the parallel mechanism. The PKM METROM [5] with pentapod parallel mechanism is used to solve the problem of the small workspace, but has complicated and difficult calibration and homing processes. Another kind of machining equipment is composed of a lower-mobility parallel mechanism and a serial mechanism such as turntable, swing head and so on. For instance, the Tricept [6], the Exechon [7], and others shown in the literatures [8, 9] are 3-DoF parallel mechanism combined with two serial rotary axes. Due to the complex structure and large size of the multiple axes

© Springer Nature Switzerland AG 2019
H. Yu et al. (Eds.): ICIRA 2019, LNAI 11742, pp. 448–457, 2019.
https://doi.org/10.1007/978-3-030-27535-8_40

rotary spindle head, the hybrid robot turns larger in order to meet the stiffness requirements. What's more, the Ecospeed of Sprint Z3 head with one translation and two rotations (1T2R) [10, 11] plus a serial XY table is achieved within the processing field, however, the limitation is that the XY table affects the overall dynamic characteristics. Considering the negative effects of swing head, XY table, etc., the 5-DoF hybrid kinematics machine with 4-DoF parallel mechanism is significant. The example of such concept, 4-DoF parallel mechanisms used for 5-DoF hybrid kinematics machine are proposed in literatures [12, 13].

To widen and enrich the applications of series-parallel hybrid mechanism in five-axis machining, a novel 5-DoF hybrid robot is proposed, which is composed of a 4-DoF 2-PRU/2-PUS parallel robot plus an X table. Here, R, P, U and S represent revolute, prismatic, universal, and spherical pair, respectively. In Sect. 2, the DoF of the hybrid robot is analyzed. After that, based on the Grassmann linear geometry principle, the singularity at the initial position of the 5-DoF robot is studied. In Sect. 3, kinematics of the novel 5-DoF hybrid robot and the complete Jacobian matrix are established. In Sect. 4, a numerical example is given to verify the theoretical model before conclusions are drawn in Sect. 5.

2 Structure of the Hybrid Robot

Figure 1 shows the structure of the 5-DoF hybrid robot with 4-DoF parallel robot plus the X table, which the parallel robot can translate along. And the tool is fixed on the moving platform.

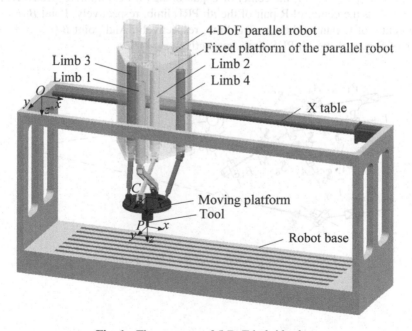

Fig. 1. The structure of 5-DoF hybrid robot

As shown in Fig. 2, the 4-DoF parallel robot has four limbs between the fixed platform and the moving platform, each limb mainly consists of one prismatic actuator and one link. The actuators in limb 1, limb 3 and limb 4 are fixed on the same circumference, and the limb 2 is assembled inside the circle. The plane of limb1 and limb 2 is vertical to the plane spanned by the axes of actuators in limb 3 and limb 4. The links in limb 1 and limb 2 cross with each other.

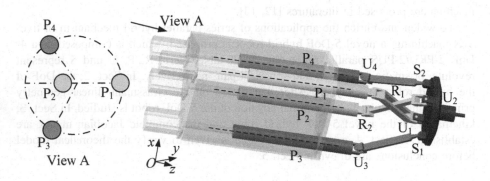

Fig. 2. The structure of 4-DoF parallel robot

2.1   Degrees of Freedom

The parallel robot with two unconstraint PUS limbs and two PRU limbs is shown in Fig. 3. Point $A_i(i = 1, 2)$ is the center of U pair of the ith PUS limb, respectively; Point $A_i(i = 3, 4)$ is the center of R pair of the ith PRU limb, respectively; Point $B_i(i = 1, 2)$ is the center of U pair of the ith PRU limb, respectively. And point $B_i(i = 3, 4)$ is the center of S pair of the ith PUS limb, respectively.

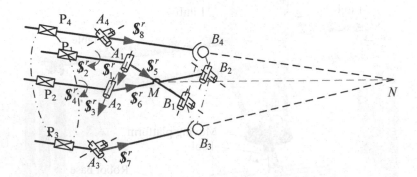

Fig. 3. Constraint screws of the 4-DoF parallel robot

The constraint screw group is expressed as

$$\$_1^r = (1,0,0;0,0,a), \$_2^r = (0,0,0;0,0,1),$$
$$\$_3^r = (1,0,0;0,0,b), \$_4^r = (0,0,0;0,0,1)$$

(1)

Its linear independent group is

$$\$_1^r = (1,0,0;0,0,a), \$_2^r = (0,0,0;0,0,1)$$

(2)

Based on the analysis about constraint screw, there are no common constraints, but two redundant constraints. According to the modified Kutzbach-Grübler formulae [14], the DoF of parallel robot is

$$M = d(n-g-1) + \sum_{i=1}^{g} f_i + v - \zeta = 4$$

(3)

It can be seen from Eq. (2) that the translation along the x-axis and the rotation around the z-axis are constrained. So, the moving platform can translate along the axes of y and z, and rotate around the axes of x and y. Combined with the translation along X table, this hybrid robot P(2-PRU/2-PUS) can translate along the axes of x, y and z, and rotate around the axes of x and y.

2.2   Singularity

Based on the Grassmann linear geometry principle [15], the singularity of the parallel robot is studied.

As shown in Fig. 3, under the constraint wrenches $\$_5^r, \$_6^r, \$_7^r, \$_8^r$ from the actuators, the robot can rotate around the public line MN. However, the constraint wrenches $\$_1^r, \$_3^r$ can limit this rotation. At the same time, the robot can rotate around the public line A_1A_2 of the constraint wrenches $\$_1^r, \$_3^r, \$_5^r, \$_6^r$. However, the constraint wrenches $\$_7^r, \$_8^r$ can limit this rotation. Because the lines MN and A_1A_2 are always steady, the robot can effectively avoid the singular configuration.

3   Kinematics of the 5-DoF Hybrid Robot

At the initial position, the moving platform is horizontal. The tool is vertically downward. And the axes of fixed platform frame, moving platform and tool frame are in the same directions. As shown in Fig. 1, the frames are defined as follows:

(1) Fixed platform frame $\{O\}$. As the reference frame, it is located at the beginning of the X table, with its x-axis along the X table and z-axis vertically down.
(2) Moving platform frame $\{C\}$. Its origin is established at the center of the moving platform C; x-axis is along the B_3B_4, and y-axis is along the B_1B_2.

(3) Tool frame $\{P\}$. Its origin is established at the center of the tool tip P, with its z-axis along the tool.

3.1 Inverse Kinematic Analysis

Let the coordinate of the tool tip be $P(P_x P_y P_z)$, the precession angle α, and nutation angle β, the direction vector of tool is

$$z_P = (\sin\beta\cos\alpha \ \sin\beta\sin\alpha \ \cos\beta) \tag{4}$$

Assuming the distance of origins between moving platform frame and tool frame CP is l, the coordinate of the moving platform frame is expressed as

$$C = P + lz_P \tag{5}$$

According to the analysis above, the rotation matrix of the moving platform frame $\{C\}$ with respect to fixed platform frame $\{O\}$ is

$$T = [x_C \, y_C \, z_C] = \begin{bmatrix} \frac{y_C \times z_P}{|y_C \times z_P|} & z_P \times \frac{\overline{A_2C} \times \overline{A_1C}}{|\overline{A_2C} \times \overline{A_1C}|} & z_P \\ & z_P \times \frac{\overline{A_2C} \times \overline{A_1C}}{|\overline{A_2C} \times \overline{A_1C}|} & \end{bmatrix} \tag{6}$$

Based on the geometrical relationship, the coordinates $B_i^O(i=1,2,3,4)$ and $A_{0i}(i=1,2,3,4)$ of points $B_i(i=1,2,3,4)$ and $A_i(i=1,2,3,4)$ relative to the fixed platform frame $\{O\}$ during moving, respectively, are

$$\begin{cases} B_i^O = TB_i^C + C \\ (A_{0i} - B_i^O)^2 = (l_i)^2 \\ (A_{0i})_x = (A_i)_x \\ (A_{0i})_y = (A_i)_y \end{cases} \tag{7}$$

Where, the coordinates B_i^C donate the points $B_i(i=1,2,3,4)$ relative to the moving platform frame $\{C\}$, respectively, and l_i is the length between the joints of the ith limb. Then, the displacement of actuators $d_i(i=1,2,3,4,5)$ can be obtained as follows:

$$d_i = \begin{cases} |A_{0i} - A_i|_z, i = 1,2,3,4 \\ |C - O|_x, i = 5 \end{cases} \tag{8}$$

3.2 Complete Jacobian Matrix and Velocity Mapping

In order to establish the velocity relationship between actuators and the tool tip, let the cP(2-PRU/2PUS) hybrid mechanism equivalent to the mechanism (see Fig. 4), whose $S_{13}, S_{14}, S_{23}, S_{24}$ are imaginary Rs.

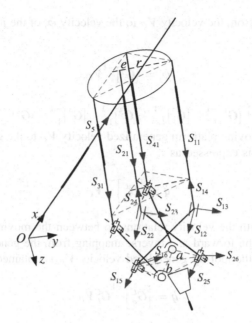

Fig. 4. Geometric parameters of hybrid robot and its equivalent mechanism P(2PSU/2PUS)

The generalized velocity mapping of the hybrid robot from the tool tip to the moving platform can be obtained as,

$$V_C = G_P^C V_P \qquad (9)$$

Where,

$$V_P = \begin{bmatrix} w_{Px} & w_{Py} & w_{Pz} & v_{Px} & v_{Py} & v_{Pz} \end{bmatrix}^T, G_P^C = \begin{bmatrix} I_{3\times3} & \mathbf{0}_{3\times3} \\ 0 & 1 & 0 & 0 & 0 & 0 \\ 0 & 0 & 0 & 0 & 1 & 0 \\ 0 & 0 & 0 & 0 & 0 & 1 \end{bmatrix}.$$

The velocity mapping from each joint $\dot{\varphi}_j$ to the moving platform V_C of the jth limb is expressed as

$$V_C = G^j \dot{\varphi}_j \qquad (10)$$

Where,

$$\begin{cases} G^j = \begin{bmatrix} 0 & S_{j2} & S_{j3} & S_{j4} & S_{j5} & S_{j6} \\ S_{j1} & S_{j2} \times \overline{A_{0j}C} & S_{j1} \times \overline{A_{0j}C} & S_{j4} \times \overline{A_{0j}C} & S_{j5} \times \overline{B_jC} & S_{j6} \times \overline{B_jC} \end{bmatrix}, j = 1, 2 \\ G^j = \begin{bmatrix} 0 & S_{j2} & S_{j3} & S_{j4} & S_{j5} & S_{j6} \\ S_{j1} & S_{j2} \times \overline{A_{0j}C} & S_{j1} \times \overline{A_{0j}C} & S_{j4} \times \overline{B_jC} & S_{j5} \times \overline{B_jC} & S_{j6} \times \overline{B_jC} \end{bmatrix}, j = 3, 4 \end{cases}$$

So the mapping from the velocity V_C to the velocity $\dot{\varphi}_j$ of the jth limb is expressed as

$$\dot{\varphi}_j = \left[G^j\right]^{-1} V_C \tag{11}$$

Let $\left[G_q^C\right]^{-1} = \left[\ [G^1]_{1,:}^{-1}\ \ [G^2]_{1,:}^{-1}\ \ [G^3]_{1,:}^{-1}\ \ [G^4]_{1,:}^{-1}\ \ [G^1]_{3,:}^{-1}\ \ [G^2]_{3,:}^{-1}\ \right]^T$, the mapping from the moving platform generalized velocity V_C to the generalized velocity of actuated joints $\dot{q}$ is expressed as

$$\dot{q} = \left[G_q^C\right]^{-1} V_C \tag{12}$$

By combined with the velocity relationship between the moving platform and the tool tip as Eq. (9), the forward and inverse mapping from the generalized velocity of actuated joints $\dot{q}$ to the tool tip generalized velocity V_P is obtained as

$$\dot{q} = \left[G_q^C\right]^{-1} G_P^C V_P \tag{13}$$

The velocity mapping from the tool tip V_P to the X table $\dot{q}_5$ is expressed as

$$\dot{q}_5 = \left[G_{q5}^P\right]^{-1} V_P \tag{14}$$

Where, $\left[G_{q5}^P\right]^{-1} = \begin{bmatrix} 0 & -l & 0 & 1 & 0 & 0 \end{bmatrix}$.

Consequently, let $\left[G_q^P\right]^{-1} = \begin{bmatrix} \left\{\left[G_q^C\right]^{-1} G_P^C\right\}_{1:4,:} \\ \left[G_{q5}^P\right]^{-1} \end{bmatrix}$, a matrix with five rows and six columns, the velocity mapping of the P(2-PRU/2-PUS) hybrid mechanism is obtained as

$$\dot{q} = \left[G_q^P\right]^{-1} V_p \tag{15}$$

Where, $\left[G_q^P\right]^{-1}$ is the complete mapping matrixes from the tool tip to the actuators of the hybrid robot.

4   Numerical Example

As shown in Fig. 4, the mechanism dimensions of the hybrid robot are set as $a = b = 0.16\,\text{m}$, $r = 0.125\,\text{m}$, $e = 0.035\,\text{m}$, $l_1 = l_2 = 0.22\,\text{m}$, $l_3 = l_4 = 0.19\,\text{m}$. The path of tool tip is set as formulae:

$$\begin{cases} P_x = 400 + 100 \times \sin(\frac{\pi}{2} \times t) \\ P_y = 20 \times \sin(\pi \times t) \\ P_z = 500 + 80 \times \sin(\frac{\pi}{2} \times t) \\ \alpha = 0 \\ \beta = \frac{\pi}{6} \times \sin(\frac{\pi}{2} \times t) \end{cases} \tag{16}$$

Substituting numerical example and structure parameters into Eqs. (8) and (15), respectively, we obtained the theory results of displacement and velocity of each actuator. Importing the 3D configuration of the hybrid robot into Adams, the simulation results of displacement and velocity are obtained, respectively. By comparison, the results of the theoretical model and the simulation model are consistent, which validates the accuracy of the theoretical model and simulation model. The results are shown in Fig. 5 for displacement and Fig. 6 for velocity of each actuator.

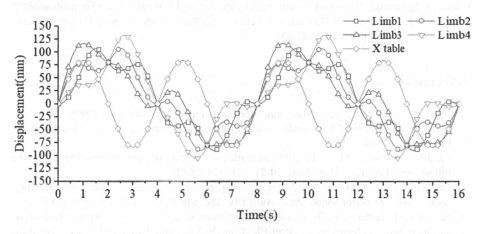

Fig. 5. Displacement of each actuator

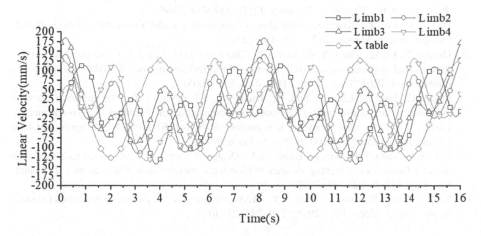

Fig. 6. Velocity of each actuator

5   Conclusion

In this paper, the configuration of a novel 5-DoF hybrid robot is proposed as Fig. 1. The conclusions are drawn as follows:

(1) The 4-DOF parallel robot with 2R2T effectively avoid the singularity configuration, based on the Grassmann linear geometry principle.
(2) Mainly drawing on screw theory, the complete Jacobian matrix of hybrid robot is established, which provides the basis for studying the complete performance of the hybrid robot. The correctness of the theoretical model is verified by numerical examples.

The hybrid robot has much potential in industrial application, especially for slender pieces.

Acknowledgements.   This work is supported by the National Natural Science Foundation of PR China (NSFC) (Grant no. 51875496), and Science and Technology Planning Project of Hebei Province, China (Grant no. 18961828D).

References

1. Apro, K.: Secrets of 5-Axis Machining. Industrial Press Inc., New York (2008)
2. Patel, Y.D., George, P.M.: Parallel manipulators applications—a survey. Modern Mech. Eng. **2**(03), 57–64 (2012)
3. Pandilov, Z., Dukovski, V.: Parallel kinematics machine tools: overview-from history to the future. Ann. Fac. Eng. Hunedoara **10**(2), 111–124 (2012)
4. Gough, V.E.: Contribution to discussion of papers on research in automobile stability, control and tyre performance. Proc. Auto Div. Inst. Mech. Eng. **171**, 392–395 (1957)
5. Schwaar, M., Jaehnert, T., Ihlenfeldt, S.: Mechatronic design, experimental property analysis and machining strategies for a 5-strut-PKM. In: 3rd Chemnitz Parallel Kinematics Seminar, vol. 23, no. 25.5 (2002)
6. Siciliano, B.: The Tricept robot: inverse kinematics, manipulability analysis and closed-loop direct kinematics algorithm. Robotica **17**(4), 437–445 (1999)
7. Bi, Z.M., Jin, Y.: Kinematic modeling of Exechon parallel kinematic machine. Robot. Comput.-Integr. Manuf. **27**(1), 186–193 (2011)
8. Huang, T., Li, M., Zhao, X.M., Mei, J.P., Chetwynd, D.G., Hu, S.J.: Conceptual design and dimensional synthesis for a 3-DOF module of the TriVariant-a novel 5-DOF reconfigurable hybrid robot. IEEE Trans. Rob. **21**(3), 449–456 (2005)
9. Dong, C., Liu, H., Liu, Q., Sun, T., Huang, T., Chetwynd, D.G.: An approach for type synthesis of overconstrained 1T2R parallel mechanisms. In: Zeghloul, S., Romdhane, L., Laribi, M.A. (eds.) Computational Kinematics. MMS, vol. 50, pp. 274–281. Springer, Cham (2018). https://doi.org/10.1007/978-3-319-60867-9_31
10. Liu, X.J., Wang, L.P., Xie, F., Bonev, I.A.: Design of a three-axis articulated tool head with parallel kinematics achieving desired motion/force transmission characteristics. J. Manuf. Sci. Eng. **132**(2), 021009 (2010)
11. Ni, Y., Zhang, B., Sun, Y., Zhang, Y.: Accuracy analysis and design of A3 parallel spindle head. Chin. J. Mech. Eng. **29**(2), 239–249 (2016)

12. Kim, S.M., Kim, W., Yi, B.J.: Kinematic analysis and design of a new 3T1R 4-DOF parallel mechanism with rotational pitch motion. In: 2009 IEEE/RSJ International Conference on Intelligent Robots and Systems, pp. 5167–5172 (2009)
13. Xie, H., Li, S., Shen, Y.F., Cao, S.W., Cai, W.: Structural synthesis for a lower-mobility parallel kinematic machine with swivel hinges. Robot. Comput.-Integr. Manuf. **30**(5), 413–420 (2014)
14. Huang, Z., Li, Q.C., Ding, H.F.: Theory of Parallel Mechanisms. Springer, London (2013)
15. Merlet, J.P.: Singular configurations of parallel manipulators and Grassmann geometry. Int. J. Robot. Res. **8**(5), 45–56 (1989)

Human-Robot Collaboration

Select and Focus: Action Recognition with Spatial-Temporal Attention

Wensong Chan[1], Zhiqiang Tian[1(✉)], Shuai Liu[1], Jing Ren[2], and Xuguang Lan[3]

[1] School of Software Engineering,
Xi'an Jiaotong University, Xi'an, China
zhiqiangtian@xjtu.edu.cn
[2] Xi'an Aeronautical University, Xi'an, China
[3] Institute of Artificial Intelligence and Robotics,
Xi'an Jiaotong University, Xi'an, China

Abstract. With the rapid development of neural networks, human action recognition has been achieved great improvement by using convolutional neural networks (CNN) or recurrent neural networks (RNN). In this paper, we propose a model based on weighted spatial-temporal attention for action recognition. This model selects the key parts in each video frame and important frames in each video sequence. Then the model focuses on analyzing these key parts and frames. Therefore, the most important tasks of our model is to find out the key parts spatially and the important frames temporally for recognizing the action. Our model is trained and tested on three datasets including UCF-11, UCF-101, and HMDB51. The experiments demonstrate that our model can achieve a satisfactory result for human action recognition.

Keywords: Human action recognition · Deep learning · Attention

1 Introduction

Human action recognition gets more and more attention in recent years. Researchers have developed many different methods for human action recognition. For example, there are some models based on Support Vector Machine (SVM) [1], CNN [2] or RNN [3]. Some of them achieve pretty great performances in human action recognition.

The methods in human action recognition can be split into two main categories, which are the traditional machine-learning based and the deep learning based method.

As for traditional machine-learning based methods, SVM combined with the improved Dense Trajectories (iDT) [1] method performs pretty well before the rapid development of deep learning. Because of the low speed of the iDT, there are some improved methods based on iDT. Stacked Fisher Vectors (SVF) [4] is thought as one of the best improvement of IDT. Actually, many new deep learning based methods of action recognition would use iDT to capture the

© Springer Nature Switzerland AG 2019
H. Yu et al. (Eds.): ICIRA 2019, LNAI 11742, pp. 461–471, 2019.
https://doi.org/10.1007/978-3-030-27535-8_41

motion in video. As for deep learning, there are lots of methods proposed recently which are classical and useful. There are three main deep learning methods which are based on CNN, RNN or both of them.

With respect to CNN, in order to remind the temporal messages in videos, C3D [5] obtains good performance which adds the temporal information by extending the 2D CNN to 3D CNN. Long-term Temporal Convolutions networks [6] is demonstrated with increased temporal extents, it improves the performance in action recognition. Two-stream CNN [7,8] is made up of two deep networks, one is used as temporal networks and another is used as spatial networks. Pose-based CNN [9] uses RGB frames and optical flow to recognize actions. Two-stream Inflated 3D ConvNet (I3D) [2] gives a state-of-art performance in human action recognition, it uses a more advanced architecture, and the model is trained on bigger data sets.

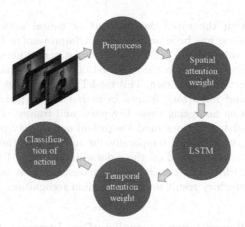

Fig. 1. The architecture of our spatial-temporal model. We preprocess each video by dividing it into images and extract features by feeding those images into CNN. Then the model calculates the spatial attention and weights the feature map. After this step, the weighted feature map will be put into the LSTMs. Via LSTMs, the model gets the outputs of the hidden layer. In order to get the final result, temporal attention will be used to weight the outputs. Finally, our model will output the classification of action in the video.

Other popular method uses RNNs as the main networks in RGB videos, usually it also uses CNN as one part of the whole model. In this kind of model, CNNs are used to preprocess the video clips by extracting the convolutional features. The Long-term recurrent convolutional networks (LRCN) model [10] is a classical architecture, it combines RNNs and CNNs organically. Based on CNN and RNN, Sharma [11] propounds a better model with visual attention mechanism, this model can focus on the important parts in each frame, it improves the accuracy of recognition.

RNN with attention mechanism works very well in machine translation tasks [12]. The attention in videos includes spatial attention and temporal attention. The spatial attention in each frame shows the saliency of every part, but it's not very easy to generate attention automatically in images. Inspired by the success of attention in machine translation, Xu and his group [13] come up with the attention mechanism including soft attention and hard attention in single still image, then their model generates the caption of the image by using soft or hard attention. But their attention mechanism still only works in still images until Sharma [11] apply their soft attention mechanism to human action recognition in videos, it shows a improvement compared with the model without attention mechanism.

However, in addition to adopting attention in space, we also think that selecting the key frames in video clips by using temporal attention is necessary. In this paper, our model pays attention to the key parts on the frames and also the key frames on the video clips automatically. The architecture of our model is illustrated in Fig. 1. It shows the progress of how our model dealing with the data. By using LSTM and spatial-temporal attention mechanism, we obtain satisfactory results in UCF11, UCF101, and HMDB51.

The contributions of this paper are listed as follows:

1. We propose a model with spatial and temporal attention for human action recognition in RGB videos.
2. Compared with the baseline method, the proposed model obtains better results, which increases about 7% on UCF11 and 15% on HMDB51. In addition, our results also has improvement compared with other state-of-the-art methods.

In Sect. 2, we will introduce our method in detail. Then we plan to show the details of the experiment and also the results in Sect. 3. We make a conclusion of our model in Sect. 4.

2 Spatial-Temporal Attention Mechanism

In this section, we will demonstrate our model in detail. First, we are going to introduce how our model encodes the video clips. Then we will present how our model figures out the spatial attention in each frames and select the key frames in the videos. Next, we will show the progress of the decoder and the production of results. Finally, we will introduce the loss function chosen in our model.

2.1 Encoder of the Model

We encode these frames by using CNN to extract feature. As showed in Fig. 3, in our model, the VGG19 [14] network pre-trained on Imagenet is used to extract the features of each video frames. After this step, we will get the feature cube with shape of $L \times L \times D$ ($14 \times 14 \times 512$). For the purpose of easier calculation in the following step, we flatten the feature map from 3D to 2D of shape $L^2 \times D$(196×512). The flat feature map can be expressed as follows,

$$X_t = [x_{t,1}, x_{t,2}, ..., x_{t,i}, ...]$$ (1)

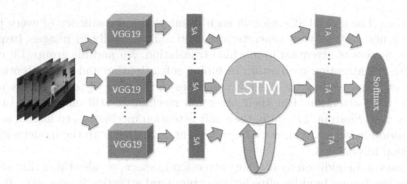

Fig. 2. The architecture of the proposed model. It shows the overall architecture of our model, and there are three main parts in the model, which are spatial attention weight part (SA), LSTM networks and temporal attention weight part (TA).

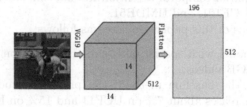

Fig. 3. The schematic diagram of extracting feature. We use Vgg19 to extract the feature from the RGB images of the video. After getting the feature maps, we flatten them into 2D matrix.

where the t denotes the time that means the frame number in the videos. For example, if we extract twenty images in each video evenly, that means t should be in the range of 1 to 20. The frame is divided into 14×14 parts. The i represents the localization in each single image, so the i should be in the range of 1 to 196.

2.2 Spatial Attention Mechanism

The overall architecture is showed by Fig. 2, SA part presents the spatial attention weighting operation. $\alpha = \{\alpha_1, \alpha_2, ..., \alpha_t, ...\}$ denotes the spatial attention in the frames t (the range of t is 1 to T, T is the time steps of LSTMs). Since in each time, the frame is divided into L^2 (14×14) parts, α_t is a matrix with shape L^2 (14×14). In this paper, we adopt the soft attention mechanism demonstrated by Xu et al. [13] and Sharma et al. [11]. The soft attention mechanism can be formulated as follows,

$$e_{t,i} = W_h^T \times h_{t-1} + W_x \times X_t + b$$
$$\alpha_{t,i} = \frac{\exp(e_{t,i})}{\sum_{j=1}^{L^2} \exp(e_{t,j})} \tag{2}$$

where the h_{t-1} is the hidden state of LSTM in previous time $t-1$, and the X_t is the feature matrix in present frame t. After the $e_{t,i}$ is calculated, the model will use the softmax function to compute $\alpha_{t,i}$. $\alpha_{t,i}$ is the probability that means the spatial attention weight of the ith part in the frame t. After computing the spatial attention weights, the model will weight the feature. Then the weighted feature maps will be the inputs of LSTMs formulated in Eq. 3.

$$Y_t = \sum_{i=1}^{L^2} \alpha_{t,i} x_{t,i} \tag{3}$$

In previous section, we have already known the meaning of variable $x_{t,i}$. After the attention weights each parts in time t, Y_t is computed as the input of LSTM in time t. This spatial weight will make our model pick up the important parts in each frames and focus on them.

The initialize of the memory state and the hidden state of LSTM we adopt refers to the strategy used by Xu et al. [13]. It can be formulated as follows,

$$c_0 = f_{init,c}\left(\frac{1}{T}\sum_{t=1}^{T}\left(\frac{1}{L^2}\sum_{i=1}^{L^2} x_{t,i}\right)\right)$$
$$h_0 = f_{init,h}\left(\frac{1}{T}\sum_{t=1}^{T}\left(\frac{1}{L^2}\sum_{i=1}^{L^2} x_{t,i}\right)\right) \tag{4}$$

The $f_{init,c}()$ and $f_{init,h}()$ are both the multilayer perceptrons. T is the number of the time steps of LSTMs. The c_0 and h_0 will be used as the initial state of LSTMs. In addition, these two values will be also used for calculated α_1, the spatial attention of the first frame.

2.3 Temporal Attention Mechanism

After obtaining the output of LSTMs, temporal attention mechanism is used to select the key frames. The temporal attention used in our paper is proposed by Song et al. [15].

In Fig. 2, TA part denotes the temporal attention weighting operation. $\beta = \{\beta_1, \beta_2, ..., \beta_t, ...\}$ is the temporal attention used in our model. β_t denotes the temporal attention in time t, it can be calculated by the equation showed as follows,

$$\beta_t = ReLU(W_h \times h_{t-1} + W_x \times X_t + b) \tag{5}$$

where the meaning of h_{t-1} is the hidden state of LSTM in previous time $t-1$. The X_t is the feature map in present frame t. The ReLU function is used to compute the temporal attention β_t. The β_t for frame t is a scalar. It's worth mentioning that the initialize of h_{t-1} used here also adopts the strategy demonstrated in Eq. 4. After this step, the model will weight the output in each time step of the LSTMs as follows,

$$o = \sum_{t=1}^{T} \beta_t tanh(h_t) \tag{6}$$

The vector $o = (o_1, o_2, ..., o_C)$ will be used to calculate the final output, in which C is the total action classes of the video sets. At each time t, the spatial attention β_t will be used to weight the corresponded output of LSTM networks in time t. Then this weighted vector in each frames will be added together as one vector o. Finally, the softmax function will be used to figure out the probability of each action as follows,

$$\hat{z}_i = \frac{\exp(o_i)}{\sum_{j=1}^{C} \exp(o_j)} \tag{7}$$

In Eq. 7, $\hat{z}_i$ denotes the probability of the action belonging to the class i in the video. The i is in the range of 1 to C. C is the total classifications of action. So the final class will be given based on $\hat{z} = (\hat{z}_1, \hat{z}_2, ..., \hat{z}_C)$, our model will output the class which has the maximum probability.

2.4   Loss Function

In order to train our model effectively, we formulate the loss function by using cross-entropy as follows,

$$L = -\sum_{i=1}^{C} z_i \log \hat{z}_i + \lambda_1 \sum_{i=1}^{L^2} (1 - \sum_{t=1}^{T} \alpha_{t,i}) + \lambda_2 \sum_{t=1}^{T} \|\beta_t\| \tag{8}$$

where the $z = (z_1, z_2, ..., z_C)$ is the one-hot vector, it is the groundtruth of the action. The $\hat{z} = (\hat{z}_1, \hat{z}_2, ..., \hat{z}_C)$ is the vector of probability that we have already talked before. λ_1 and λ_2 are the penalty coefficient of spatial and temporal attention which decide the contribution of them. The first term which uses cross-entropy makes our model predict more precisely. The second term is applied to force the model pay more spatial attention on more relevant parts in the frame automatically, then we also force $\sum_{t=1}^{T} \alpha_{t,i} = 1$. The third term is used to restrict the unlimited increasing of temporal attention.

3   Experimental Results

3.1   Data Sets

In this paper, the proposed method is evaluated on three public data sets, which are UCF11, UCF101, and HMDB51.

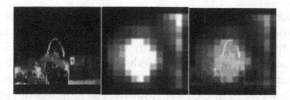

Fig. 4. The spatial attention in the frame. In this frame, a man raises up his hand. After putting the video frames into our model, we got the spatial attention weights of this frame, then we visualized the spatial attention. Obviously our model focus on the man and his hand in the picture.

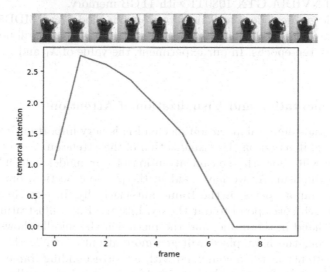

Fig. 5. The temporal attention weight in frames. This is the temporal attention curve of the action 'brush hair'. Our model selects the key frames that is relevant to the action.

UCF11 [16]: this data set is also called YouTube action. It is the RGB video set which contains 11 action categories. For each category, there are 25 groups with more than 4 clips in each group.

UCF101 [17]: this data set is the expansion of UCF11. It contains 101 action categories, which can be divided into Human-Object Interaction, Body-Motion Only, Human-Human Interaction, Playing Musical Instruments, and Sports. These videos all come from realistic action videos from YouTube. That's a very challenging job for action recognition in this data set, obviously it's much more bigger and complex than UCF11.

HMDB51 [18]: this data set contains 51 action categories with five groups: General facial actions, Facial actions with object manipulation, General body movements, Body movements with object interaction, and Body movements for human interaction. These videos are collected from movies and public databases, many of them have complex background, shifty lighting, miscellaneous actions. In fact, it's more difficult to deal with HMDB51 than UCF101 and UCF11.

We implement the proposed model by using Python. The video clip is split into separated images. All images are reshaped to the size of 224×224. A pre-trained VGG19 model is used to extract the feature from each images. The time steps of LSTM is set as 30 in UCF11. However, the numbers of videos of UCF101 and HMDB51 are much bigger. Therefore, we choose smaller steps of 20 or 10 in UCF101 and HMDB51. We have tried different number of layers. They have no much difference. In addition, in order to avoid over-fitting of our model in the training process, dropout is used in the proposed model. Our model was trained on a GPU of NVIDIA GTX 1080TI with 11 GB memory.

Stochastic gradient descent is used to train our model on HMDB51 data set. The epoch was set as 500. The learning rate was set as 10^{-5}. It will be multiplied by 10^{-1} every ten epochs. In our experiment, the value of λ_1 and λ_2 was set as 0.1 and 0.01.

3.2   Implementation and Visualization of Attention

Since the spatial-temporal attention mechanism is very important in our model, we will analyze it based on the visualization of the attention.

First, we will show the spatial attention of our model, which is the soft attention mechanism. As we have said in the previous section, our model will focus on the import parts in the frame automatically. In experiment, we get the results which correspond to our theory. Like the Fig. 4 illustrating, the man raises up his hand in the frame, and the picture in the middle shows where our model focus on, the light place will get more attention while the dark place will get less attention, when combined with its corresponding frame, as we have expected, the model focus on the man and his hand automatically. It indicates the correctness of the spatial attention in our model.

The temporal attention is shown in Fig. 5 with original images from HMDB51 data set. For the action 'brush hair', some frames with high spatial attention weights are selected. Then the model focuses on these selected frames to recognize the actions. When the woman raise up the comb, our model pays more attention on the frames. After the woman putting down the comb, our model gives a less attention on the frames. Sometimes, we could recognize the actions by only watching the first serval frames. Therefore, we have no necessary to read the whole video. If the videos contain a repetitive action, our model has the ability to recognize the actions by watching only the first serval frames.

The visualization of the attention shows that our model can pick up the important parts in the frame and the key frames in the video sequence automatically. It also shows the correctness of the spatial and temporal attention.

3.3   Comparison and Evaluation

The proposed model was compared with LRCN and soft attention model on UCF101. The results are showed in Table 1. LRCN is the model which uses

CNN and LSTM without any attention mechanism, while soft attention model uses the spatial attention mechanism based on LRCN. The result of the soft attention model on UCF101 was obtained from Li's work [19]. Our model used both spatial and temporal attention. Obviously, our model achieves a much better result. Our model is trained and tested on three data sets, it achieves the accuracy of 91.67% on UCF11, which improves about 7% compared with the baseline(soft attention model). For the data set HMDB51, we get nearly 15% improvement which achieves the accuracy of 56.77%. For UCF101, we get the accuracy of 90.25%. For UCF11 and HMDB51, our model both makes great improvement in the accuracy.

Table 1. Ablation experiments.

Method	LRCN [10]	Soft attention [11]	Spatial-temporal attention (ours)
Accuracy	82.34%	75.8%	90.25%

Comparison results are shown in Table 2. It shows that our model has the highest accuracy on all three data sets.

Table 2. The comparison with other methods in accuracy.

Methods	Action-VLAD (RGB) [20]	C3D (RGB) [21]	Attention pooling [22]	Res3D [23]	Two-Stream +LSTM [24]	Video-LSTM [19]	Spatial-temporal attention (Ours)
UCF11	-	-	-	-	-	-	91.67%
UCF101	-	85.20%	-	88.00%	88.60%	88.90%	90.25%
HMDB51	49.80%	-	52.20%	54.90%	-	56.40%	56.77%

4 Conclusion

In this paper, we propose a human action recognition model based on the spatial and temporal attention mechanism. We adopt the soft attention mechanism to select the relevant parts automatically in the frame, while use the temporal attention gates to pick up the key frames in the video clips. Compared with the baseline method, our model makes great improvement in human action recognition in RGB videos. To verify the correctness of the spatial-temporal attention, we visualize the spatial and temporal attention by plotting them individually. Our model was compared with other state-of-the-art methods on three data sets. The experimental results shows that the proposed model outperforms all of these methods. It indicates the effectiveness of the spatial-temporal attention mechanism.

However, there are still some weaknesses in our model. The proposed model is little simple. Therefore, the spatial attention and temporal attention not always pick up the key parts and the important frames. In the future, we plan to improve it by using more sophisticated attention algorithms.

Acknowledgements. This work was supported in part by the National Natural Science Foundation of China under grant No. 61876148 and No. 61703328. This work was also supported in part by the key project of Trico-Robot plan of NSFC under grant No. 91748208, key project of Shaanxi province No. 2018ZDCXL-GY-06-07, the Science and Technology Bureau of Xi'an under No. 2017076CG/RC039 (XAHK005), the Fundamental Research Funds for the Central Universities No. XJJ2018254 and No. XJJ2018253, and China Postdoctoral Science Foundation NO. 2018M631164 and No. 2018M631165.

References

1. Wang, H., Schmid, C.: Action recognition with improved trajectories. In: Proceedings of the IEEE International Conference on Computer Vision, pp. 3551–3558 (2013)
2. Carreira, J., Zisserman, A.: Quo vadis, action recognition? A new model and the kinetics dataset. In: Proceedings of the IEEE Conference on Computer Vision and Pattern Recognition, pp. 4724–4733 (2017)
3. Zhu, W., et al.: Co-occurrence feature learning for skeleton based action recognition using regularized deep LSTM networks. In: AAAI Conference on Artificial Intelligence, p. 6 (2016)
4. Peng, X., Zou, C., Qiao, Y., Peng, Q.: Action recognition with stacked fisher vectors. In: Fleet, D., Pajdla, T., Schiele, B., Tuytelaars, T. (eds.) ECCV 2014. LNCS, vol. 8693, pp. 581–595. Springer, Cham (2014). https://doi.org/10.1007/978-3-319-10602-1_38
5. Ji, S., Xu, W., Yang, M., Yu, K.: 3D convolutional neural networks for human action recognition. IEEE Trans. Pattern Anal. Mach. Intell. **35**, 221–231 (2013)
6. Varol, G., Laptev, I., Schmid, C.: Long-term temporal convolutions for action recognition. IEEE Trans. Pattern Anal. Mach. Intell. **40**, 1510–1517 (2018)
7. Simonyan, K., Zisserman, A.: Two-stream convolutional networks for action recognition in videos. In: Advances in Neural Information Processing Systems, pp. 568–576 (2014)
8. Feichtenhofer, C., Pinz, A., Zisserman, A.: Convolutional two-stream network fusion for video action recognition. In: Proceedings of the IEEE Conference on Computer Vision and Pattern Recognition, pp. 1933–1941 (2016)
9. Chéron, G., Laptev, I., Schmid, C.: P-CNN: pose-based CNN features for action recognition. In: Proceedings of the IEEE International Conference on Computer Vision, pp. 3218–3226 (2015)
10. Donahue, J., et al.: Long-term recurrent convolutional networks for visual recognition and description. In: Proceedings of the IEEE Conference on Computer Vision and Pattern Recognition, pp. 2625–2634 (2015)
11. Sharma, S., Kiros, R., Salakhutdinov, R.: Action recognition using visual attention. In: ICLR Workshop (2016)
12. Luong, M.-T., Pham, H., Manning, C.D.: Effective approaches to attention-based neural machine translation. arXiv preprint arXiv:1508.04025 (2015)

13. Xu, K., et al.: Show, attend and tell: neural image caption generation with visual attention. In: International Conference on Machine Learning, pp. 2048–2057 (2015)
14. Simonyan, K., Zisserman, A.: Very deep convolutional networks for large-scale image recognition. arXiv preprint arXiv:1409.1556 (2014)
15. Song, S., Lan, C., Xing, J., Zeng, W., Liu, J.: An end-to-end spatio-temporal attention model for human action recognition from skeleton data. In: AAAI Conference on Artificial Intelligence, pp. 4263–4270 (2017)
16. Liu, J., Luo, J., Shah, M.: Recognizing realistic actions from videos "in the wild". In: Proceedings of the IEEE Conference on Computer Vision and Pattern Recognition, pp. 1996–2003 (2009)
17. Soomro, K., Zamir, A.R., Shah, M.: Ucf101: a dataset of 101 human actions classes from videos in the wild. arXiv preprint arXiv:1212.0402 (2012)
18. Kuehne, H., Jhuang, H., Garrote, E., Poggio, T., Serre, T.: HMDB: a large video database for human motion recognition. In: Proceedings of the IEEE International Conference on Computer Vision, pp. 2556–2563 (2011)
19. Li, Z., Gavrilyuk, K., Gavves, E., Jain, M., Snoek, C.G.M.: Videolstm convolves, attends and flows for action recognition. Comput. Vis. Image Underst. **166**, 41–50 (2018)
20. Girdhar, R., Ramanan, D., Gupta, A., Sivic, J., Russell, B.: ActionVLAD: learning spatio-temporal aggregation for action classification. In: Proceedings of the IEEE Conference on Computer Vision and Pattern Recognition, p. 3 (2017)
21. Tran, D., Bourdev, L., Fergus, R., Torresani, L., Paluri, M.: Learning spatiotemporal features with 3D convolutional networks. In: Proceedings of the IEEE International Conference on Computer Vision (2015)
22. Girdhar, R., Ramanan, D.: Attentional pooling for action recognition. In: Advances in Neural Information Processing Systems, pp. 34–45 (2017)
23. Tran, D., Ray, J., Shou, Z., Chang, S.-F., Paluri, M.: Convnet architecture search for spatiotemporal feature learning. arXiv preprint arXiv:1708.05038 (2017)
24. Yue-Hei Ng, J., Hausknecht, M., Vijayanarasimhan, S., Vinyals, O., Monga, R., Toderici, G.: Beyond short snippets: deep networks for video classification. In: Proceedings of the IEEE Conference on Computer Vision and Pattern Recognition (2015)

Real-Time Grasp Type Recognition Using Leap Motion Controller

Yuanyuan Zou[1,2](✉) 📵, Honghai Liu[3], and Jilong Zhang[4]

[1] School of Mechanical Engineering,
Shenyang Jianzhu University, Shenyang 110168, China
yyzou@sjzu.edu.cn
[2] National-Local Joint Engineering Laboratory of NC Machining Equipment
and Technology of High-Grade Stone, Shenyang 110168, China
[3] School of Computing, University of Portsmouth, Portsmouth PO1 3HE, UK
[4] Shenyang Institute of Automation, Chinese Academy of Sciences,
Shenyang 110016, China

Abstract. The recognition of grasp type is essential for a more detailed analysis of human action. In this paper, we propose a novel method for real-time grasp type recognition using Leap motion controller (LMC). Our proposal is based on the tracking data provided by the LMC sensor and a series of feature descriptors are introduced and extracted from LMC data. Combining the feature descriptors of relative positions of thumb, finger joint angles and finger directions lead to the best representation of the arrangement of the fingers. And then the grasp type classification can be achieved by using a SVM classifier. An experimental study of our approach is addressed and we show that recognition rate could be improved. The current implementation is also can satisfy the real-time requirements.

Keywords: Grasp type recognition · Feature representation · SVM · Leap motion controller

1 Introduction

Human hand action recognition is the key for many research areas such as human computer interaction, robot control, robotic action planning, etc., and is attracting more and more research interest. Understanding human hand usage is one of the richest information source to recognize manipulation actions [1]. Human uses various types of hand grasp in daily living activities and industrial manipulations. Hand grasp types are important for understanding hand manipulation since they characterize how hands hold the objects during manipulation [2]. Therefore, the recognition of grasp types is essential for a more detailed analysis of human action. Various methods of the grasp recognition have been explored, including EMG-based [3] and vision-based [4] etc. Among these methods, vision-based methods are used widely since they can be less cumbersome uncomfortable than the other methods due to no physical contact with users.

© Springer Nature Switzerland AG 2019
H. Yu et al. (Eds.): ICIRA 2019, LNAI 11742, pp. 472–480, 2019.
https://doi.org/10.1007/978-3-030-27535-8_42

Leap motion controller (LMC) is a recently introduced sensor which is based on vision techniques for hand gesture recognition [5–7]. Comparing to depth cameras such as the Microsoft Kinect [8], LMC is working on a smaller 3D region and extracts data with higher accuracy [9]. It can be exploited for accurate gesture recognition. In this paper, we present a real-time grasp types recognition approach using LMC, where the main advantage is the extraction of a set of relevant features that can effectively recognize the grasp types.

This paper is structured as follows. Section 2 presents the architecture of the proposed hand grasp type recognition system and the grasp types selected for recognition in this work. Our recognition approach is described in Sect. 3. The following section highlights the experimental results. The paper is enclosed by a conclusion and future perspectives.

2 System Description

2.1 System Architecture

The general architecture of the system presented in this paper is shown in Fig. 1. The LMC is used for capturing the hand gestures. The LMC is composed of two cameras and three LEDS, which can infer the 3D position of a subject's hand. The features are extracted from 3D hand data and then are processed with the classification method of Support Vector Machines (SVM).

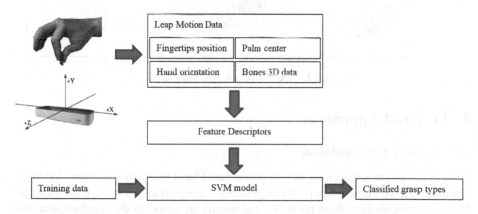

Fig. 1. Proposed hand grasp type recognition system architecture.

2.2 Grasp Types

The grasp taxonomy of human hand grasp type is important for understanding the way human grasp objects and knowing common use patterns. A number of work have investigated the categorization of hand grasp. Feix et al. [10] compares the existing taxonomies and extracts 33 grasp types which are arranged in a novel taxonomy according to the number of fingers in contact with the object and the position of the thumb. Heumer et al. [11] identifies six different grasp types, including power, palm-up, hook, oblique, precision and pinch which are sufficient for grasping strategies in daily living activities.

In this work, we select six types of hand grasps based on functionality which are usually in daily life activities and industrial in-hand manipulations. The list of selected grasp types is shown in Fig. 2.

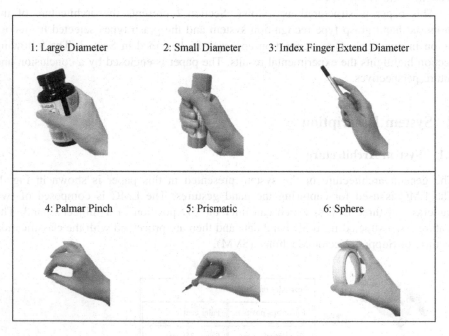

Fig. 2. The list of selected grasp types.

3   Proposed Approach

3.1   Feature Representation

Feature extraction is the major step in vision based hand gesture recognition system. To represent the characteristics of hand gestures, various features have been extracted. Many approaches have been presented and mostly are based on the standard scheme of extracting relevant features from the RGB depth data [12]. Hand shape are represented with Histogram of Oriented Gradient (HOG) features which are image descriptors based on collected local distributions of intensity gradients. Cai et al. extracts three HOG features for palm regions which encodes the shape of different hand postures [13]. The LMC captures the skeletal data of hand gesture and mainly provide the following data such as Number of detected fingers, Position of the fingertips, Palm center, Hand orientation, Hand radius, Bones data etc. Some data acquired by LMC are shown in Fig. 3. The device provides directly some of the most relevant points for gesture recognition and allows avoiding complex computations needed for their extraction from depth and color data.

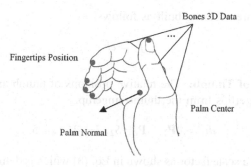

Fig. 3. Data acquired by LMC.

However, these absolutely position of the hand and fingers are not relevant as gesture features, but they can be used to obtain other meaningful features. Therefore, to represent the hand grasp types in Fig. 2 entirely, we extract 5 features, including the feature descriptors of Fingertip distances proposed by [14], the feature descriptors of Extended index finger representation, Relative positions of thumb and Finger joint angles proposed in this paper, and Finger directions.

Let i be the index of a finger, Vectors $\mathbf{P}_i$ containing the 3D positions of each of the detected fingertips, the center of the hand palm is $\mathbf{C}$, the normal to the plane that corresponds to the palm region pointing downward from the palm center is $\mathbf{n}$.

Fingertip Distances: The fingertip distances are defined as the 3D distance of the fingertips from the palm center. The vector of finger i is computed by:

$$\mathbf{v}_i = \mathbf{P}_i - \mathbf{C}, \; i = 1, \ldots, 5 \tag{1}$$

$$d_i = \|\mathbf{P}_i - \mathbf{C}\|/S_1, \; i = 1, \ldots, 5 \tag{2}$$

Where S_1 is the scale factor as shown in Eq. (3), which is to make the approach robust to people with hands of different size. It is defined as the maximum distance between the palm center and the fingertips. The feature values are normalized in the interval [0, 1] by dividing the value.

$$S_1 = \max(\|\mathbf{P}_i - \mathbf{C}\|) \tag{3}$$

Then the first feature vector is built as follows:

$$f_1 = [d_1, \, d_2, \, d_3, \, d_4, \, d_5] \tag{4}$$

Extended Index Finger Binary Representation: The Extended index finger binary representation is defined as if the index finger is extended for the grasp gesture.

$$eb = \begin{cases} 1, & extended \\ 0, & otherwise \end{cases} \tag{5}$$

The second feature vector is built as follows:

$$f_2 = eb \tag{6}$$

Relative Positions of Thumb: The relative positions of thumb are defined as the 3D distances of the fingertips from the thumb fingertip.

$$dr_i = \|\mathbf{P}_1 - \mathbf{P}_i\|/S_2, \ i = 2, \ \ldots, \ 5 \tag{7}$$

Where S_2 is also a scale factor as shown in Eq. (8) which is defined as the maximum value of the distances of the other fingertips from the thumb fingertip. The feature values are normalized in the interval [0, 1] by dividing the value.

$$S_2 = \max(\|\mathbf{P}_1 - \mathbf{P}_i\|) \tag{8}$$

Then the third feature vector is built as follows:

$$f_3 = [dr_2, \ dr_3, \ dr_4, \ dr_5] \tag{9}$$

Finger Joint Angles: The Finger joint angles are defined as the angles of every finger joint. The LMC can capture bones 3D data, so the joint angles of each finger can be calculated respectively. For three joints are present on each finger, with the exception of the thumb, which possesses only two. Therefore, the fourth feature vector is built as follows:

$$f_4 = \begin{bmatrix} 0, & c_{11}, & c_{12} \\ c_{21}, & c_{22}, & c_{23} \\ c_{31}, & c_{32}, & c_{33} \\ c_{41}, & c_{42}, & c_{43} \\ c_{51}, & c_{52}, & c_{53} \end{bmatrix} \tag{10}$$

Finger Directions: The finger directions are identified as the angles between the finger vector and the normal.

$$a_i = \angle(\mathbf{v}_i, \mathbf{n}) \ , \ i = 1, \ \ldots, \ 5 \tag{11}$$

Then the fifth feature vector is built as follows:

$$f_5 = [a_1, \ a_2, \ a_3, \ a_4, \ a_5] \tag{12}$$

3.2 Grasp Types Classification

The Support Vector Machine (SVM) is used as the classifier for grasp types classification. The SVM is a powerful tool for classification and is widely used in object detection and recognition [15].

The SVM model is established by using the different feature descriptors as the input of the network. In order to realize the accurate recognition under the condition of small sample as far as possible, cross validation test is used. The training samples are divided into n parts, where m copies as the part retained, the remaining n-m as parts of training. The training part is used to probability estimation as training set, and the retained part is used to test as test set. The parameters to be chosen mainly include penalty factor and kernel function parameter, which are determined by the method of grid search.

4 Experiments and Analysis

The experiments are designed and conducted to evaluate the proposed approach. We acquire a set of grasp gesture type (GGT) database with a LMC device. It consists of 6 different gestures performed by 6 different subjects a total of 20 times each for 720 different samples. LMC images of grasp gestures in GGT database from different people are shown in Fig. 4.

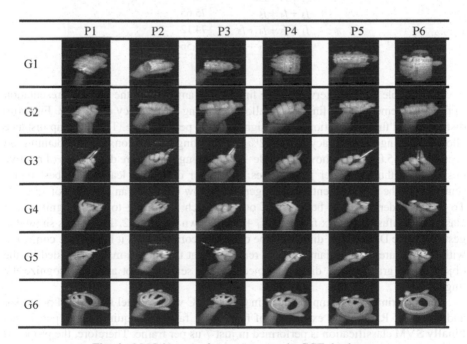

Fig. 4. LMC images of grasp gestures in GGT database.

We split the dataset in a train set and a test set. We place in the train set the data from all the subjects except one and in the test set the data from the remaining subject. To assess the effectiveness of our approach to classify the grasp gesture of GGT dataset into 6 classes, we execute 6 completely independent tests changing the subject each time in the test set. In each test, a train set with 5 persons and a test set with a single person are used. The final recognition accuracy is obtained by averaging the results of the 6 tests.

For all following experiments, we compare the results by using each feature descriptor independently and by reconstructing different feature descriptors. The Table 1 presents the results obtained by using different descriptors.

Table 1. Results of using different descriptors.

Features	Accuracy
f_1	66.72
f_2	30.60
f_3	53.12
f_4	73.15
f_5	65.09
$f_1+f_3+f_4$	74.95
$f_1+f_4+f_5$	72.87
$f_3+f_4+f_5$	75.65
$f_1+f_3+f_4+f_5$	74.12
$f_1+f_2+f_3+f_4+f_5$	73.56

From Table 1, we observe that the finger joint angles give the better representation of the arrangement of the fingers and allow obtaining an accuracy of 73.15%. Fingertip distances and finger directions have slightly lower performance. The fingertip distance allow obtaining an accuracy of 66.72% and the finger directions allow obtaining an accuracy of 65.09%. As shown in Table 1, combining the feature descriptors of relative positions of thumb, finger joint angles and finger directions lead to the best representation of the arrangement of the fingers and allow obtaining an accuracy of 75.65%. To better understand the behavior of our approach according to the recognition per class, the confusion matrix from $f_3+f_4+f_5$ is shown in Table 2. The results show that gesture Large Diameter is difficult to be classified correctly and it has a wide confusion with the gesture Small Diameter. The reason is that the fingers maybe shielded by the object when grab a large diameter object, so the sensor is not able to recognize the fingers.

The experiments are implemented in C# on a PC with an Intel I5-3210 M processor and 8 GB of RAM. The extraction of features is fast and requires 10 us per frame. Finally SVM classification is performed in just 7 us per frame. Therefore, the proposed approach is particularly suitable for real time gesture recognition.

Table 2. The confusion matrix of the proposed approach for GGT database

	G_1	G_2	G_3	G_4	G_5	G_6
G_1	4	15	1	0	0	0
G_2	3	17	0	0	0	0
G_3	1	2	17	0	0	0
G_4	0	0	0	20	0	0
G_5	1	0	0	2	17	0
G_6	0	0	0	0	0	20

5 Conclusions

In this paper, we mainly presented a real-time grasp type recognition system using LMC and investigated the feature extraction of LMC tracking data for selected six types of hand grasp. We proposed the new feature descriptors called relative positions of thumb and finger joint angles which can describe the hand grasp type more effectively. Finally, the experimental results have shown a higher recognition accuracy can be obtained by combining the two new features with finger directions.

As future work, the approach can be studied to be able to utilize two hands and to recognize dynamic grasp. In addition, skeleton-based features can be combined with the sensor images to provide more effective description and to obtain better recognition.

Acknowledgements. The authors would like to acknowledge the support from the Natural Science Foundation of China under Grant No. 51405481 and the Natural Science Foundation of Liaoning Province under Grant No. 20180551124.

References

1. Kim, J.W., You, S., Ji, S.H., Kim, H.S.: Real-time hand grasp recognition using weakly supervised two-stage convolutional neural networks for understanding manipulation actions. In: 2017 IEEE Conference on Computer Vision and Pattern Recognition (CVPR) Workshops, pp. 10–11 (2017)
2. Yang, Y., Guha, A., Fermuller, C., Aloimonos, Y.: A cognitive system for understanding human manipulation actions. Adv. Cogn. Syst. **3**, 67–86 (2014)
3. Kakoty, N.M., Hazarika, S.M.: Recognition of grasp types through principal components of DWT based EMG features. In: 2011 IEEE International Conference on Rehabilitation Robotics, pp. 1–6 (2011)
4. Cai, M.J., Kitani, K.M., Sato, Y.: A scalable approach for understanding the visual structures of hand grasps. In: 2015 IEEE International Conference on Robotics and Automation (ICRA), pp. 1360–1366 (2015)
5. Khelil, B., Amiri, H.: Hand gesture recognition using leap motion controller for recognition of arabic sign language. In: Proceedings of the 3rd International Conference on Automation, Control, Engineering and Computer Science, ACECS 2016, pp. 20–22 (2016)

6. De Smedt, Q., Wannous, H., Vandeborre, J.: Skeleton-based dynamic hand gesture recognition. In: Proceedings of the IEEE Conference on Computer Vision and Pattern Recognition Workshops, pp. 1–9 (2016)
7. Bachmann, D., Weichert, F., Rinkenauer, G.: Review of three-dimensional human-computer interaction with focus on the leap motion controller. Sensors 18(7), 2194–2232 (2018)
8. Du, H., To, T.: Hand gesture recognition using Kinect, Boston University (2011)
9. Guna, J., Jakus, G., Pogačnik, M., et al.: An analysis of the precision and reliability of the leap motion sensor and its suitability for static and dynamic tracking. Sensors 14(2), 3702–3720 (2014)
10. Feix, T., Romero, J., Schmiedmayer, H., et al.: The grasp taxonomy of human grasp types. IEEE Transact. Hum. Mach. Syst. 46(1), 66–77 (2016)
11. Heumer, G., Amor, H.B., Jung, B.: Grasp recognition for uncalibrated data gloves: a machine learning approach. Presence Teleoperators Virtual Environ. 17(2), 121–142 (2008)
12. Yang, Y., Fermuller, C., Li, Y., et al.: Grasp type revisited: a modern perspective on a classical feature for vision. In: Proceedings of the IEEE Conference on Computer Vision and Pattern Recognition, pp. 400–408 (2015)
13. Cai, M.J., Kitani, K.M., Sato, Y.: Understanding hand-object manipulation with grasp types and object attributes. In: Robotics: Science and Systems (2016)
14. Marin, G., Dominio, F., Zanuttigh, P.: Hand gesture recognition with jointly calibrated leap motion and depth sensor. Multimedia Tools Appl. 75(22), 14991–15015 (2016)
15. Dutt, V., Chaudhry, V., Khan, I.: Pattern recognition: an overview. Am. J. Intell. Syst. 2(1), 23–27 (2012)

Speaker-Independent Speech Emotion Recognition Based on CNN-BLSTM and Multiple SVMs

Zhen-Tao Liu[1,2(✉)], Peng Xiao[1,2], Dan-Yun Li[1,2], and Man Hao[1,2]

[1] School of Automation, China University of Geosciences,
Wuhan 430074, Hubei, China
liuzhentao@cug.edu.cn

[2] Hubei Key Laboratory of Advanced Control and Intelligent Automation
for Complex Systems, Wuhan 430074, Hubei, China

Abstract. Speaker-independent speech emotion recognition (SER) is a complex task because of the variations among different speakers, such as gender, age and other emotional irrelevant factors, which may lead to a tremendous difference among emotional features' distribution. To alleviate the adverse effect generated by emotional irrelevant factors, we propose a SER model that consists of convolutional neutral networks (CNN), attention-based bidirectional long short-term memory network (BLSTM), and multiple linear support vector machines. The log Mel-spectrogram with its velocity (delta) and acceleration (double delta) coefficients are adopted as the inputs of our model since they can apply sufficient information for feature learning by our model. Several groups of speaker-independent SER experiments are performed on the Interactive Emotional Dyadic Motion Capture Database (IEMOCAP) database to improve the credibility of the results. Experimental results show that our method obtains unweighted average recall of 61.50% and weighted average recall of 62.31% for speaker-independent SER on IEMOCAP database.

Keywords: Speech emotion recognition · Speaker-independent
Long short-term memory network · Support vector machine

1 Introduction

To provide users with a more natural and friendly human-machine interaction, human emotional recognition has become a research hotspot in the field of human-machine interaction. Generally, humans transmit emotional information through speech signal [1], gesture [2], facial expression [3], and EEG signal [4]. Speech signal contains rich emotional information, not only that, compared with other signals, it conveys emotions in a faster and more direct way. Therefore, speech emotion recognition (SER) has drawn more widespread attention. Speech emotional features extraction and speech emotion classification are the two indispensable steps in the process of SER.

For speech emotional features extraction, researchers always concentrate on obtaining an ideal set of speech emotion features to improve the accuracy of SER in the past. For this reason, many hand-crafted features based on personal characteristics had

© Springer Nature Switzerland AG 2019
H. Yu et al. (Eds.): ICIRA 2019, LNAI 11742, pp. 481–491, 2019.
https://doi.org/10.1007/978-3-030-27535-8_43

been designed and extracted, including fundamental frequency, short-time energy, short-time average cross zero ratio and short-time maximum amplitude etc. [5], which have actual physical meanings generally. These hand-crafted features have achieved great performance in speaker-dependent SER. However, most of the SER tasks are conducted among different speakers in actual human-machine interaction, their performance in speaker-independent SER task, however, is not satisfactory while only using hand-crafted features. In recent years, with the rapid development of deep learning, deep neural networks including deep belief network [6, 7], convolutional neural networks (CNN) [8–10], recurrent neural networks [11–13] etc., have been used for speaker-independent speech emotion recognition because of their powerful feature extraction ability. The features extracted by deep neural networks can make up for the defects of hand-crafted features in speaker-independent SER to some extent.

For speech emotion classification, traditional classifiers such as hidden Markova model [14], support vector machine (SVM) [15] and decision tree [16], have been used in SER. To improve the accuracy of SER, researchers have made lots of attempts when using traditional classifiers. For example, Genetic Algorithm was employed to improve the original weights updating method of the original brain emotion learning model [17]. According to the confusion degree among six basic emotion status, Liu et al. [5] proposed a SER method named extreme learning machine decision tree. Based on the idea of ensemble learning, Li et al. [18] employed different basic classifiers for different emotion feature, after obtaining the results from each individual classifier, the results with different weights are fused in decision level to get the predictions.

In this paper, a new SER model is proposed, which mainly consists of CNN, attention-based bidirectional long short-term memory network (BLSTM), and multiple linear SVMs. Firstly, zero mean, unit variance, framing, and windowing etc. are conducted on the original speech signal to get the log Mel-spectrogram with its delta and double delta coefficients as the inputs of our model. Then features are discovered automatically by CNN and attention-based BLSTM from the inputs. Finally, we get the predictions through the multiple linear SVMs classifier. Experimental results of speaker-independent speech emotion recognition on IEMOCAP database show that the proposed model is superior to the baseline model [19].

The rest of this paper is organized as follows. The overall architecture and the details setting of the proposed model are introduced in Sect. 2. The experiments and discussion are summarized in Sect. 3.

2   Architecture of the SER Model

The overall architecture of the proposed model is shown in Fig. 1. The model consists of three parts, i.e., speech signal preprocessing, feature extraction by CNN and attention-based LSTM, and speech emotion classification by multiple linear SVMs classifier.

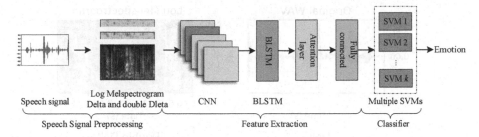

Fig. 1. Overall architecture of the proposed model

2.1 Speech Signal Preprocessing

The procedures to get the log Mel-spectrogram are shown in Fig. 2. Firstly, zero mean and unit variance are done for speech signal, which can reduce the variations among different speakers [11]. After that, we divide the speech signal into short frames and multiply them by hamming window. Then the fast Fourier Transform is applied to the windowed frame to get the power spectrum. Finally, we get Mel-spectrogram by making the power spectrum pass through the Mel-filter bank, and log Mel-spectrogram is acquired by applying the logarithm to Mel-spectrogram.

With the purpose of alleviating the influence of speaker's personal characteristics and improving speaker-independent SER accuracy, a common strategy is to calculate the derivative of speaker-dependent features. Therefore, we choose the original log Mel-spectrogram along with its delta and double delta coefficients as inputs of our model. An example of original WAV with its static, delta, and double delta coefficients log Mel-spectrogram are shown in Figs. 3 and 4 shows log Mel-spectrogram examples of four emotions, i.e., angry, sad, happy, and neutral.

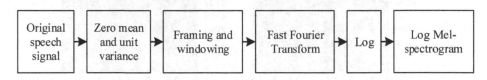

Fig. 2. Procedures of obtaining the log Mel-spectrogram

2.2 Feature Extraction by CNN and Attention-Based LSTM

In this section, CNN and attention-based BLSTM are employed for feature learning. We first use CNN to extract low-level features. Then we obtain utterance-level features by using the attention-based BLSTM layer.

We build the CNN according to AlexNet [20], in which there are five convolution layers and one pooing layer. The architecture of CNN is shown in Table 1.

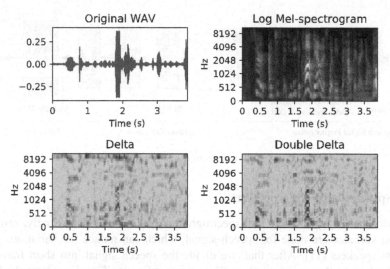

Fig. 3. An example of Original WAV with its static, First-order and Second-order differential Log Mel-spectrogram

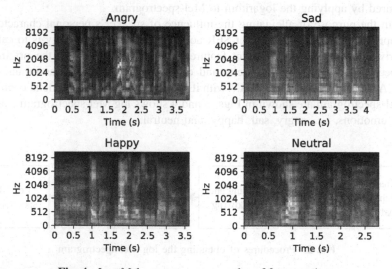

Fig. 4. Log Mel-spectrogram examples of four emotions

Followed by the CNN layer, we employ an attention-based BLSTM layer to alleviate the negative effects of emotional irrelevant factors and generate utterance-level features. BLSTM architecture is a variant of recurrent neural networks (RNN), aiming to overcome two shortcomings of RNN. The first one is RNN's underperformance in Long-Term dependencies. Another is that RNN only makes use of previous information, while future information may have the same influence on the current state with previous information. Generally, the outputs of LSTM are obtained by [12]

$$i_t = \sigma(W_{xi}x_t + W_{hi}h_{t-1} + W_{ci}c_{t-1} + b_i), \tag{1}$$

$$f_t = \sigma(W_{xf}x_t + W_{hf}h_{t-1} + W_{cf}c_{t-1} + b_f), \tag{2}$$

$$c_t = f_t c_{t-1} + i_t \tanh(W_{xc}x_t + W_{hc}h_{t-1} + W_{cf}c_{t-1} + b_c), \tag{3}$$

$$o_t = \sigma(W_{xo}x_t + W_{ho}h_{t-1} + W_{co}c_{t-1} + b_o), \tag{4}$$

$$h_t = o_t \tanh(c_t), \tag{5}$$

where i, f, c, o and h represent the input gate, forget gate, cell state, output gate and hidden vector, respectively. $W_{xi}, W_{hi}, \ldots, W_{co}$ are the weight matrices. σ is the logistic sigmoid function. BLSTM contains two sub networks which process the features forward and backward, respectively. In our experiments, each direction contains 128 cells. Hence, we can get 256-dimensional outputs from two directions

$$h_t = \left[\overrightarrow{h_t}, \overleftarrow{h_t} \right]. \tag{6}$$

In this paper, attention layer is employed after BLSTM to generate utterance-level features. The application of attention layer is illustrated in Fig. 5. The attention weight α_t and the utterance-level features C are obtained by

$$\alpha_t = \text{softmax}(w \cdot h_t), \tag{7}$$

$$C = \sum_{t=1}^{T} \alpha_t h_t, \tag{8}$$

where w is a learnable parameter. Finally, these utterance-level features C are fed into two fully connected layers to produce higher-level features for the multiple linear SVMs classifier.

Table 1. CNN architecture details.

Layer	Dimension
First convolution layer	11×11 (64 filters)
Max pooing layer	2×4
Second convolution layer	5×5 (192 filters)
Third convolution layer	3×3 (384 filters)
Fourth convolution layer	3×3 (256 filters)
Fifth convolution layer	3×3 (256 filters)

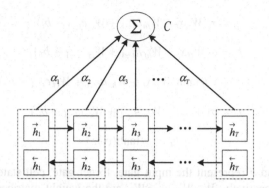

Fig. 5. Outputs of BLSTM linking to the attention layer

2.3   Emotion Classification Based on Multiple Linear SVMs

SVM has been adopted to be the top layer in a deep learning classification model, and achieving a superior performance while compared with using SoftMax layer as the top layer [22]. Therefore, multiple linear SVMs are employed for classification in our model.

Give training data

$$\{(x_1, y_1), (x_2, y_2), \cdots, (x_i, y_i), \cdots, (x_N, y_N)\}, \\ \text{s.t. } x_i \in \mathbb{R}^D, y_i \in \{-1, +1\}, \tag{9}$$

where x_i and y_i representing for the i-th training data's feature vector and corresponding labels respectively, and N represents the number of training data.

All the samples are classified into 2 categories by separating hyperplane:

(1) Class 1 located on the outside of separating hyperplane, which can be classified by SVM.
(2) Class 2 located on the separating hyperplane, which determines the separating hyperplane.

The linear SVM model is demonstrated as

$$\min_{\omega, b} \frac{1}{2} \|\omega\|^2, \\ \text{s.t. } y_i(\omega x + b) \geq 1, \ i = 1, 2, \ldots, N, \tag{10}$$

where ω and b are the parameters of the separating hyperplane.

However, the training data are not linearly separable completely in the actual process. Facing this problem, slack variables are set up to penalize data points which violate the margin requirements and we can get the following constrained optimization,

$$\min_{\omega,b,\zeta} \frac{1}{2}\|\omega\|^2 + C\sum_{i=1}^{N}\zeta_i,$$
$$\text{s.t. } y_i(\omega x + b) \geq 1 - \zeta_i, \, i = 1,2,\ldots,N, \tag{11}$$
$$\zeta_i \geq 0, \, i = 1,2,\ldots,N,$$

where ζ_i are slack variables and C is the penalty term. Since there are constraints in the objective function, it is difficult to get the optimal parameters. The process of getting the optimal parameters of the model can be simplified by introducing the hinge loss function into the objective function. The unconstrained objective function is demonstrated as

$$\min_{\omega,b,\zeta} L(\omega,b) = \frac{1}{2}\|\omega\|^2 + C\sum_{i=1}^{N}\max(0, 1 - y_i(\omega x + b)). \tag{12}$$

The Eq. (12) is known as the primal form of L1-SVM. Since it is too complex to get the differential of the Eq. (12), a popular variation of L1-SVM was proposed which is named of L2-SVM. L2-SVM is differentiable because of the quadratic function. The formula of the L2-SVM is

$$\min_{\omega,b,\zeta} L(\omega,b) = \frac{1}{2}\|\omega\|^2 + C\sum_{i=1}^{N}\max(0, 1 - y_i(\omega x + b))^2. \tag{13}$$

In this paper, one-vs-rest (OVR) approach is adopted in multiple SVMs for multiple emotion classification. For k class problems, each value is acquired by individual linear SVM, and OVR strategy makes the final decision by Eq. (14) as output of the multiple SVMs

$$\underset{K}{\text{argmax}} \ \omega_K^T x + b_K. \tag{14}$$

3 Experiments and Discussion

3.1 Experiment Setting

In this paper, speaker-independent experiments are done on the Interactive Emotional Dyadic Motion Capture Database (IEMOCAP) [23] to evaluate our model. IEMOCAP is an audio-visual database and we only choose the audio part of the database. The audio data in the IEMOCAP database are divided into 5 sessions. Each session consists of a series of dialogues recorded by an actor and an actress. Every dialogue is divided into utterances and the database has a total number of 10039 utterances, with an average duration of 4.5 s and 11.4 words per segment. Each segment is labeled by three human annotator using discrete emotional labels and dimension emotional labels. The discrete emotional labels are composed by nine emotional labels, only the improvised audio with the following emotional label are adopted in our speaker-independent SER experiment, i.e., angry, sadness, happy and neutral.

Since the IEMOCAP database include 10 speakers, for the purpose of getting a credible conclusion, 10-fold cross-validation is conducted to evaluate our results of experiments in our letter. The procedures are as follow. For each experiment, we choose four sessions including 8 speakers' audio as our training data, and two speakers' audio in the remaining session is employed to be validation set and test set respectively. For speaker-independent SER, both the unweighted average recall (UAR) with weighted average recall (WAR) are adopted to evaluate our model's performance. To obtain test set's UAR, firstly, we get our model's optimal parameters by monitoring the validation data's UAR, we record the parameters of the model when the validation set got a best UAR. Then, we use these parameters to initialize our model. Finally, we get test set's UAR by running this model with test set. The same operations are conducted to get the test set's WAR.

Experiments are performed on a computer which is equipped with two Intel Xeon E5-2620 CPU, 64 GB memory, and a GTX 1080Ti GPU which compute capability is 6.1. Our model is implemented with TensorFlow [24] framework with a batch size of 60. 40 Mel-filter banks are adopted to extract log Mel-spectrogram. L_2 Regularization [25] is applied to CNN to avoid over-fitting and four linear SVMs are employed in our model for four kinds of emotional classification.

3.2 Experimental Results and Discussion

We compare our method with [19] in terms of UAR and WAR, and the results are illustrated in Table 2. Several architectures were proposed by [19], one of which is selected since it achieved the best results as the baseline. From the Table 2, it shows that our proposed method improves UAR from 49.50% to 61.50%, and improves WAR from 59.33% to 62.31%.

To further analyze the classification distribution of each emotion, one of the confusion matrixes during our speaker-independent SER experiment is shown in Table 3. It can be seen that angry, sad, and happy are easily misclassified to neutral, while neutral is more likely to be misclassified to happy. We can also see that 16.22% of angry are misclassified to happy, 14.29% of happy are misclassified to sad, these misclassifications shouldn't appear in practical application since they totally are inconsistent with the user's emotional state. We'll focus on finding the reason for these phenomena and solving them in the future.

During our SER experiments, we find that the results are different while choosing male and female as the test set respectively. Therefore, we calculate the UAR and WAR separately according to gender, whose results are listed in Table 4. It shows that male obtains 3.76% and 1.29% higher results than female in terms of UAR and WAR, respectively. Investigation and relativity study on gender-based SER will be conducted in our future works to improve the performance of speaker-independent SER.

Table 2. Comparison of different methods on IEMOCAP in terms of UAR and WAR.

Method	UAR (%)	WAR (%)
Proposal	61.50	62.31
Greedy + Dropout + Att. + MLP [19]	49.96	59.33

Table 3. Confusion matrix of speaker-independent experiment on IEMOCAP database

	Angry	Sad	Happy	Neutral
Angry	59.46	5.4	16.22	18.92
Sad	2.5	85	0	12.5
Happy	4.76	14.29	57.14	23.81
Neutral	8.13	6.51	25.2	60.16

Table 4. Comparison of different gender on IEMOCAP in terms of UAR and WAR.

Gender	UAR (%)	WAR (%)
Male	63.38	62.95
Female	59.62	61.66

4 Conclusion

A novel speaker-independent SER model composed by CNN, attention-based BLSTM and multiple SVMs was proposed. Log Mel-spectrogram with its delta and double delta coefficients are extracted from speech signals as our model input. Speaker-independent SER experiments on the IEMOCAP database indicate that our model achieves 12% and 2.98% higher in terms of UAR and WAR compared with the baseline. Male achieves a superior performance on SER experiments to female in terms of both UAR and WAR.

In future work, we'll first figure out the problem that angry misclassified to happy and happy misclassified to sad. After that, we'll construct a gender-based speaker-independent SER model after investigating the influence of gender to SER.

Acknowledgements. This work was supported in part by the National Natural Science Foundation of China under Grants 61403422, 61703375 and 61273102, the Hubei Provincial Natural Science Foundation of China under Grants 2018CFB447 and 2015CFA010, the Wuhan Science and Technology Project under Grant 2017010201010133, the 111 project under Grant B17040, and the Fundamental Research Funds for National University, China University of Geosciences (Wuhan) under Grant 1810491T07.

References

1. El Ayadi, M., Kamel, M.S., Karray, F.: Survey on speech emotion recognition: Features, classification schemes, and databases. Pattern Recognit. **44**(3), 572–587 (2011)
2. Gunes, H., Piccardi, M.: Bi-modal emotion recognition from expressive face and body gestures. J. Netw. Comput. Appl. **30**(4), 1334–1345 (2007)
3. Calvo, M.G., Nummenmaa, L.: Perceptual and affective mechanisms in facial expression recognition: an integrative review. Cogn. Emot. **30**(6), 1081–1106 (2016)
4. Mohammadi, Z., Frounchi, J., Amiri, M.: Wavelet-based emotion recognition system using EEG signal. Neural Comput. Appl. **28**(8), 1985–1990 (2017)
5. Liu, Z.T., Wu, M., Cao, W.H., et al.: Speech emotion recognition based on feature selection and extreme learning machine decision tree. Neurocomputing **273**, 271–280 (2018)
6. Shi, P.: Speech emotion recognition based on deep belief network. In: 15th International Conference on Networking, Sensing and Control. IEEE, Zhuhai (2018)
7. Zhu, L., Chen, L., Zhao, D., et al.: Emotion recognition from Chinese speech for smart affective services using a combination of SVM and DBN. Sensors **17**(7), 1694 (2017)
8. Mao, Q., Dong, M., Huang, Z., et al.: Learning salient features for speech emotion recognition using convolutional neural networks. IEEE Trans. Multimed. **16**(8), 2203–2213 (2014)
9. Hossain, M.S., Muhammad, G.: Emotion recognition using deep learning approach from audio–visual emotional big data. Inf. Fusion **49**, 69–78 (2019)
10. Zhang, S., Zhang, S., Huang, T., et al.: Learning affective features with a hybrid deep model for audio–visual emotion recognition. IEEE Trans. Circuits Syst. Video Technol. **28**(10), 3030–3043 (2018)
11. Chen, M., He, X., Yang, J., et al.: 3-D convolutional recurrent neural networks with attention model for speech emotion recognition. IEEE Signal Process. Lett. **25**(10), 1440–1444 (2018)
12. Graves, A., Jaitly, N., Mohamed, A.: Hybrid speech recognition with deep bidirectional LSTM. In: 2013 Proceedings of Workshop on Automatic Speech Recognition and Understanding, pp. 273–278. IEEE, Olomouc (2013)
13. Zhao, J., Mao, X., Chen, L.: Speech emotion recognition using deep 1D & 2D CNN LSTM networks. Biomed. Signal Process. Control **47**, 312–323 (2019)
14. New, T.L., Foo, S.W., De Silva, L.C.: Speech emotion recognition using hidden Markov models. Speech Commun. **41**(4), 603–623 (2003)
15. Pan, Y., Shen, P., Shen, L.: Speech emotion recognition using support vector machine. Int. J. Smart Home **6**(2), 101–108 (2012)
16. Lee, C.C., Mower, E., Busso, C., et al.: Emotion recognition using a hierarchical binary decision tree approach. Speech Commun. **53**(9–10), 1162–1171 (2011)
17. Liu, Z.T., Xie, Q., Wu, M., et al.: Speech emotion recognition based on an improved brain emotion learning model. Neurocomputing **309**, 145–156 (2018)
18. Li, P., Song, Y., Wang, P., et al.: A multi-feature multi-classifier system for speech emotion recognition. In: 2018 First Asian Conference on Affective Computing and Intelligent Interaction, Beijing, China (2018)
19. Huang, C.W., Narayanan, S.S.: Attention assisted discovery of sub-utterance structure in speech emotion recognition. In: 17th Proceedings of Annual Conference of the International Speech Communication Association, pp. 1387–1391. International Speech Communication Association, San Francisco (2016)
20. Krizhevsky, A., Sutskever, I., Hinton, G.E.: Imagenet classification with deep convolutional neural networks. In: Proceedings of Advances in Neural Information Processing Systems, pp. 1097–1105. Neural Information Processing Systems, Nevada (2012)

21. Zhou, P., Shi, W., Tian, J., et al.: Attention-based bidirectional long short-term memory networks for relation classification. In: 54th Proceedings of the Annual Meeting of the Association for Computational Linguistics, Short Papers, vol. 2, pp. 207–212. Association for Computational Linguistics, Berlin (2016)
22. Tang, Y.: Deep learning using linear support vector machines. In: 30th International Conference on Machine Learning, Atlanta, Georgia, USA (2013)
23. Busso, C., Bulut, M., Lee, C.C., et al.: IEMOCAP: interactive emotional dyadic motion capture database. Lang. Resour. Eval. **42**(4), 335 (2008)
24. Abadi, M., Barham, P., Chen, J., et al.: TensorFlow: a system for large-scale machine learning. In: 12th Proceedings of USENIX Symposium on Operating Systems Design and Implementation (OSDI 2016), pp. 265–283. USENIX Association, Savannah (2016)
25. Ng, A.Y.: Feature selection, L_1 vs. L_2 regularization, and rotational invariance. In: 21st Proceedings of International Conference on Machine Learning. ACM, Banff (2004)

On-Line Identification of Moment of Inertia for Permanent Magnet Synchronous Motor Based on Model Reference Adaptive System

Yujian Zhou[1,2], Jinhua She[1,2,3(✉)], Wangyong He[1,2], Danyun Li[1,2],
Zhentao Liu[1,2], and Yonghua Xiong[1,2]

[1] School of Automation, China University of Geosciences,
Wuhan 430074, People's Republic of China
j_she@cug.edu.cn
[2] Hubei Key Laboratory of Advanced Control and Intelligent Automation for
Complex Systems, Wuhan 430074, People's Republic of China
[3] School of Engineering, Tokyo University of Technology, Tokyo 192-0982, Japan

Abstract. Moment of inertia is an essential parameter that has to be identified for satisfactory control performance for a permanent magnet synchronous motor (PMSM). In this paper, an on-line identification method for moment of inertia is presented, featuring high accuracy and short convergence time. A model reference adaptive system (MRAS) consists of three parts: a reference model, an adaptive model, and an adaptive law. In this paper, the practical and mathematical models of a PMSM are used as the reference and adaptive models of an MRAS, respectively. Then, an adaptive law is presented to adjust the adaptive model to approach the reference model. Simulations and a comparison of the presented method with a conventional MRAS-based method were carried out and showed that the presented method improved both accuracy and identification speed.

Keywords: Permanent magnet synchronous motor (PMSM) ·
Moment of inertia · Parameter identification ·
Model reference adaptive system (MRAS)

1 Introduction

Permanent magnet synchronous motors (PMSMs) are a kind of widely used industrial equipment for high reliability, broad adjustable ranges and simple control strategies [1–3]. Vector control (VC) [4,5] and direct torque control (DTC)

This work was supported by the National Key R&D Program of China under Grant 2017YFB1300900; by the National Natural Science Foundation of China under Grants 61873348 and 61703375; by the 111 Project, China under Grant B17040; and by the Hubei Provincial Natural Science Foundation, China under Grant 2015CFA010.

© Springer Nature Switzerland AG 2019
H. Yu et al. (Eds.): ICIRA 2019, LNAI 11742, pp. 492–498, 2019.
https://doi.org/10.1007/978-3-030-27535-8_44

[6] are two kinds of widely used control methods. With the increasing applications of PMSMs in different fields, a more strict control requirement is needed. The accuracies of the parameters play an important role in the design of real-time control algorithms. Several studies have been conducted by researchers on parameter identification of PMSMs [7–9].

Among those parameters, the moment of inertia is considered significant for the design of the speed-loop controller in VC [10]. Generally, the moment of inertia cannot be obtained directly. Therefore, identification methods are necessary. Methods based on the Kalman observer and least squares have advantages where the computation is relatively small and the speed is high as well as accurate, but they are complex to design [11]. Methods based on the model reference adaptive system (MRAS) can provide accurate results if the models are built reasonably, but the speed is lower.

In this paper, a new MRAS-based identification method is presented. The simulation results using the presented method are compared with those of the conventional MRAS-based method [12] to demonstrate the improvements.

2   Vector Control of PMSM

PMSMs use permanent magnets created from rare materials and are different from three-phase synchronous motors with electrical excitation. However, the stator of a PMSM is essentially the same as that of the three-phase synchronous motor with electrical excitation. That fact enables the model of the PMSM to be greatly simplified.

There are three different kinds of PMSM models. The first one is a model in the three-phase (ABC) reference frame. The second one uses the Clark transformation to recalculate the first model in the $\alpha - \beta$ stationary reference frame. The last one uses the Park transformation to further recalculate to the $d - q$ rotating reference frame. In this paper, the $d - q$ model is used, and can be described by Eqs. (1) and (2).

The voltage equations for $d - q$ rotating reference frame are given by

$$\begin{cases} u_d = Ri_d + L_d\frac{di_d}{dt} - \omega L_q i_q \\ u_q = Ri_q + L_q\frac{di_q}{dt} - \omega L_d i_d + \omega\psi_f \end{cases}, \tag{1}$$

where u_d, u_q, i_d, i_q, L_d, and L_q are the voltages, currents and inductances under $d - q$ axis separately, ψ_f represents the linkage of the stator, and ω stands for the rotor angular speed.

The equation of mechanical motion is given by

$$J\frac{d\omega}{dt} = T_e - T_L + B\omega, \tag{2}$$

where T_L and T_e indicate the load and electromagnetic torques separately, B represents the viscous damping, and J represents the moment of inertia.

Since a salient-pole PMSM is characterized by $L_d = L_q = L$, the control methods can be simplified. Among those control methods, $i_d = 0$ control is used more often. This method set $i_d = 0$ so that the stator current only has the quadrature component, and both demagnetizing effect and excitation effect are depressed. Thus the current-loop and speed-loop controllers can be designed more easily.

3   MRAS-Based Identification Algorithm

The moment of inertia is an important parameter in the design of the speed-loop controller, but it may change with environmental effects or machine aging. Thus, the moment of inertia should be identified or estimated during the working process in order to improve the performance of a servo system.

3.1   Model Reference Adaptive System (MRAS)

MRAS consists of three parts, reference model, adaptive model and adaptive law. Its structure is shown in Fig. 1.

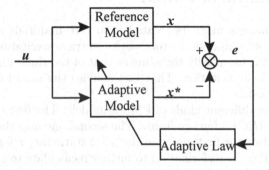

Fig. 1. Basic structure of the MRAS.

Usually, the practical model is used as the reference model, and a mathematical model is used as the adaptive model. The adaptive law is designed to adjust the output error between the two models to zero, which means the parameters of the adaptive model converge to the real one. In this paper, the presented MRAS-based method is called IMRAS to distinguish it from the conventional MRAS-based method in simulations and comparisons.

3.2   Design of Algorithm

The equation of mechanical motion shows the relationship between J, T_e, and T_L. In this paper, this equation will be used to obtained the adaptive law.

First, make a discretization on the left side of the equation to obtain the discrete output, that is

$$J\frac{d\omega}{dt} \approx J\frac{\omega(k) - \omega(k-1)}{\Delta t} = J\frac{\omega(k) - \omega(k-1)}{T_s}, \tag{3}$$

where T_s is the sampling period. Then the discrete mechanical motion equation is obtained as

$$J\frac{\omega(k) - \omega(k-1)}{T_s} = T_e(k) - T_L(k) + B\omega(k). \tag{4}$$

Rearranging Eq. (4), the estimated ω at moment k is given by

$$\omega(k) = (1 - B\frac{T_s}{J})\omega(k-1) + \frac{T_s}{J}[T_e(k-1) - T_L(k-1)]. \tag{5}$$

Considering the fact that viscous damping B will be designed to be small to guarantee the working performance of a PMSM, and that the sampling period T_s is also small to ensure that the analog to digital (A/D) process will not lose too much information, the value of $B\frac{T_s}{J}$ will be much smaller than 1. Therefore it can be ignored, and Eq. (5) is changed to

$$\omega(k) = \omega(k-1) + \frac{T_s}{J}[T_e(k-1) - T_L(k-1)]. \tag{6}$$

Therefore, the estimated ω at $k-1$ is

$$\omega(k-1) = \omega(k-2) + \frac{T_s}{J}[T_e(k-2) - T_L(k-2)]. \tag{7}$$

Subtracting Eq. (6) from Eq. (7) and rearranging it, it yields

$$\omega(k) = 2\omega(k-1) - \omega(k-2) + \frac{T_s}{J}[\Delta T_e(k-1) - \Delta T_L(k-1)], \tag{8}$$

where $\Delta T_e(k-1) = T_e(k-1) - T_e(k-2)$, $\Delta T_L(k-1) = T_L(k-1) - T_L(k-2)$.

Since the change period of the load torque is larger than the sampling period, T_L can be considered as a constant value. Thus, $\Delta T_L(k-1)$ is ignored. Then, the reference model is given as

$$\omega(k) = 2\omega(k-1) - \omega(k-2) + \beta\Delta T_e(k-1), \tag{9}$$

where $\beta = \frac{T_s}{J}$, and the adaptive model is

$$\hat{\omega}(k) = 2\omega(k-1) - \omega(k-2) + \hat{\beta}\Delta T_e(k-1). \tag{10}$$

A conventional MRAS-based identification method was given by [12]

$$\hat{\beta}(k) = \hat{\beta}(k-1) + \frac{b\Delta T_e(k-1)}{1 + b\Delta T_e^2(k-1)}\Delta\omega(k), \tag{11}$$

where $\Delta\omega(k) = \omega(k) - \hat{\omega}(k)$, and b is a positive real number that represent gain factor. Thus, the estimated value of the moment of inertia is given by

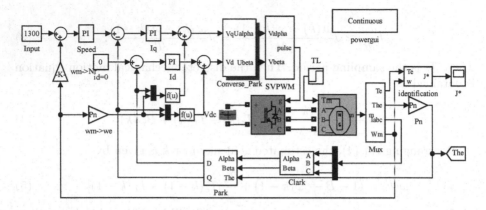

Fig. 2. Identification model.

$$J^* = \frac{T_s}{\hat{\beta}}. \tag{12}$$

However, there is a room to improve the accuracy and convengent speed by adjusting β.

Since the reference model is a recursive SISO system, applying the design laws for discrete SISO systems (see [13]), the following improved identification method is devised for β in this study.

$$\hat{\beta}(k) = \hat{\beta}(k-1) + \frac{b\Delta T_e(k-1)}{1 + \sum_{i=1}^{2} a_i \omega^2(k-i) + b\Delta T_e^2(k-1)} \Delta\omega(k), \tag{13}$$

where a_1 and a_2 are all positive real numbers that represent gain factors, too. Through adjusting three gain factors, satisfactory results were obtained in simulations.

4   Simulation Verification

Simulations were conducted using MATLAB/Simulink, and the identification model was built based on a VC model. VC models are widely used in practical control, they contain three PI controllers for the speed loop, and $d-q$ current loops. The moment of inertia is important for the design of the speed-loop controller. The complete model is shown in Fig. 2.

The values of this model were set as $B = 0.008\,\mathrm{N\,m\,s}$, $T_s = 0.0001\,\mathrm{s}$, and input rotation speed $= 1300\,\mathrm{rpm}$. Two values of the moment of inertia were identified in the simulations where $J = 0.005\,\mathrm{kg\,m^2}$ and $J = 0.008\,\mathrm{kg\,m^2}$. The results of the simulations are shown in Fig. 3.

In Fig. 3, the CMRAS represents the conventional MRAS identification method, and IMRAS represents the improved MRAS identification method. For $J = 0.005\,\mathrm{kg\,m^2}$, the identified results are $5.048 \times 10^{-3}\,\mathrm{kg\,m^2}$ and $6.153 \times$

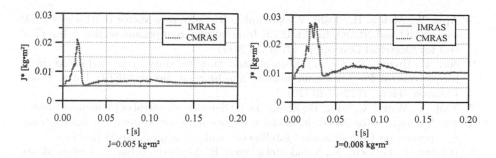

Fig. 3. Identification results of J.

10^{-3} kg m^2 by IMRAS and CMRAS respectively. For $J = 0.008$ kg m^2, the iden tified results are 8.100×10^{-3} kg m^2 and 1.010×10^{-3} kg m^2. The corresponding errors are 0.96% and 1.25% by IMRAS and, 23.06% and 25.13% by CMRAS. Identification time by the IMRAS is approximately 0.003 s, which is much shorter compared with that of IMRAS of about 0.15 s. These results demonstrate that the method presented in this paper provides much better performance than the conventional method.

5   Conclusion

This paper presented an on-line identification method for the moment of iner-tia of a PMSM based on MRAS. The presented method was compared with a conventional MRAS-based identification scheme, and the results by simulations presented significant improvements in terms of speed and accuracy.

However, there are still some aspects that could be further improved. On the one hand, simulations are performed for a condition where the sampling period is very short, which makes it hard to apply in practical situations. On the other hand, application of the identified value to parameter-tuning is still lacking, so the future works may focus on these aspects.

References

1. Cao, H., Huang, D.: O ncomposite position control of CNC system feeding PMSM based on position feedforward and SVPWM. In: IEEE Interference on Mechatronics and Automation, pp. 735–740 (2010)
2. Jang, J.H., Sul, S.K., Ha, J.I.: Sensorless drive of surface-mounted permanent-magnet motor by high-frequency signal injection based on magneric saliency. IEEE Trans. Ind. Appl. **39**, 1031–1039 (2003)
3. Inoue, Y., Morimoto, S., Sanada, M.: Comparative study of PMSM drive systems based on current control and direct torque conrtol in flux-weakening control. IEEE Trans. Ind. Appl. **48**(6), 2382–2389 (2013)
4. Sharma, R.K., Sanadhya, V., Behera, L., Bhattacharya, S.: Vector control of a permanent magnet synchronous motor. In: IEEE Conference and Exhibition on Control, Communications and Automation, pp. 81–86 (2008)

5. Apte, A., Mehta, H., Joshi, V., Walambe, R.: Sensorless vector control of PMSM using SMO and NLDO. In: 8th IEEE International Symposium on Sensorless Control for Electrical Drives, pp. 127–131 (2017)
6. Niu, F., Huang, X., Ge, L.: A simple and practical duty cycle modulated direct torque control for permanent magnet synchronous motors. IEEE Trans. Power Electron. **34**(2), 1572–1579 (2019)
7. Xing, Y., Wang, X., Yang, D., Zhang, D.Y.: Sensorless control of permanent magnet synchronous motor based on model reference adaptive system. In: International Symposium on Computational Intelligence and Design, pp. 20–23 (2017)
8. Boileau, T., Leboeuf, N., Nahid-Mobarakeh, B., Meibody-Tabar, F.: Online identification of OMSM parameters: parameter identifiability and estimator cmparative study. IEEE Trans. Ind. Appl. **47**(4), 1944–1957 (2011)
9. Zhang, Y., Yin, Z., Sun, X., Zhong, Y.: On-line identification methods of parameters for permanent magnet synchronous motors based on cascade MRAS. In: International Conference on Power Electronics, pp. 345–350 (2015)
10. Liu, K., Zhu, Z.: Fast determination of moment of inertia of permanent magnet synchronous machine drives for design of speed loop regulator. IEEE Trans. Control Syst. Technol. **25**(5), 1816–1824 (2017)
11. Yang, M., Liu, Z., Long, J., Qu, W., Xu, D.: An algorithm for online inertia and load torque observation via adaptive Kalman observer-recursive least squares. Energies **11**(4), 778 (2018)
12. Dong, H., Duan, J.: Inertia identification and its improvement of servo system based on MRAI. J. Mech. Electr. Eng. **35**(9), 959–963 (2018)
13. Landau, I.D.: Adaptive Control: The Model Reference Approach. Marcel Dekker, Inc., New York (1979)

Multi-point Interaction Force Estimation for Robot Manipulators with Flexible Joints Using Joint Torque Sensors

Xing Liu[1,2], Fei Zhao[1,2(✉)], Baolin Liu[1,2], and Xuesong Mei[1,2]

[1] Shaanxi Key Laboratory of Intelligent Robots, Xi'an Jiaotong University,
Xi'an 710094, Shaanxi, People's Republic of China
liuxing1990.ok@163.com, ztzhao@mail.xjtu.edu.cn, xsmei@xjtu.edu.cn
[2] School of Mechanical Engineering, Xi'an Jiaotong University,
Xi'an 710094, Shaanxi, People's Republic of China

Abstract. In this paper, multi-point interaction forces of the robot manipulators with flexible-joints are separated and estimated by using the backward method and link-side generalized momentum observer method. Similar to the Newton-Euler method, the backward method is utilized to separate and compute the contact forces exerted on the links. To avoid the use of the acceleration signals, the generalized momentum observer is employed to estimate the external forces. For robot manipulators with flexible-joints, the joint torque data rather than the motor command torque data are used to obtain accurate estimation results. Experimental results show that the multi-point contact forces are accurately separated and estimated using the presented method.

Keywords: Multi-point physical interaction · Force estimation · Link-side generalized momentum observer · Backward method

1 Introduction

Physical human-robot interaction has attracted the attention of many researchers and is becoming popular on development side, due to more and more demands and needs of collaborative robots (cobots). In a highly unstructured environment or social environment, the physical interaction, such as handshaking, and human-robot cooperation, is important in the sense that human lives are improved by integration of the intelligent robots into human society Li et al. (2011).

Most research works on physical interaction control focus only on single-point interaction problems (Damme et al. 2011; Le et al. 2013; Colomé et al. 2013; Cho et al. 2012). However, in many social scenarios multi-point physical interaction will be more and more common. For example, when a robot is taking care of a patient or collaborating with the human worker in an assembly cell, the interaction may happen at not only one single point but several others. Multi-point interaction force perception is critical for multi-point physical interaction

© Springer Nature Switzerland AG 2019
H. Yu et al. (Eds.): ICIRA 2019, LNAI 11742, pp. 499–508, 2019.
https://doi.org/10.1007/978-3-030-27535-8_45

control. How to accurately estimate or measure the multi-point contact forces is still a problem and there are few studies in this area Vorndamme et al. (2017). At present, the research on estimation of multi-point contact forces is mainly aimed at humanoid robot (Vorndamme et al. 2017; Manuelli and Tedrake 2016), but there is little research on robot manipulators.

Among commonly used force perception methods, the robot electronic skin is effective for multi-point interaction force perception but very expensive. The multi-dimensional force/torque sensor can only be used to measure the single-point interaction force. When motor current is used, the estimation accuracy is not very high because of many factors affecting the estimation accuracy, especially for the robot manipulators with flexible joints Liu et al. (2019). Therefore, the joint torque sensor is commonly used to estimate the contact forces accurately because it can separate the dynamics of the link side from the motor side (Liu et al. 2019; Luca et al. 2006). In addition, multi-point force estimation can also be realized by using joint torque sensors. Therefore, joint torque sensors are utilized in this paper and the backward estimation algorithm is presented to estimate the multi-point contact forces.

The rest of this paper is organized as follows. In Sect. 2, the description of the multi-point interaction problems is given. In Sect. 3, the proposed multi-point interaction force estimation method is derived in detail, and the implementation procedure of the presented algorithm is also given. In Sect. 4, experimental studies and the corresponding results are shown. Then, the conclusion of this paper is given in Sect. 5.

2   Problem Description

As shown in Fig. 1, we suppose that there are m interaction points along the robot arm. In what follows, the dependence of the system parameters and signals on time is implied unless otherwise specified.

$$M(q)\ddot{q} + C(q,\dot{q})\dot{q} + G(q) = \tau + \sum_{i=1}^{m} J_i^T(q)F_i, \tag{1}$$

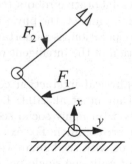

Fig. 1. Multi-point contact between the robot manipulator and the environment.

where $q \in \mathbb{R}^n$ denotes the coordinate of the robot manipulator and n is the DOF of the robot arm; $M(q) \in \mathbb{R}^{n \times n}$ is the symmetric and positive definite inertia matrix, $C(q, \dot{q}) \in \mathbb{R}^{n \times n}$ denotes the centrifugal-Coriolis matrix, $G(q) \in \mathbb{R}^n$ is the gravitational term, $\tau \in \mathbb{R}^n$ denotes the input torque vector, and $\tau_d \in \mathbb{R}^n$ denotes the torque generated by the multi-point interaction, which may be directly measured by the torque sensors mounted on the joints or indirectly calculated by the force sensors mounted at the interaction points, $J_i^T(q)$ denotes the Jacobian matrix of the robot manipulator, F_i denotes the interaction force between the robot and the environment at the ith point, which will be estimated in this paper.

3 The Multi-point Interaction Force Estimation Algorithm

3.1 The Backward Method for Multi-point External Force Estimation

For simplicity and ease of computation, assume that there exists at most one contact point on each link of the robot manipulator. We also assume that the contact locations and directions of the contact points are all clearly known.

For robot dynamics modeling methods, Newton-Euler method is widely used, which is a forward-backward method to establish the relationship between the robot motions and the generalized forces. In particular, the backward method is utilized to compute the generalized forces on each link. Here, we take advantage of this method to calculate the interaction forces acting on each link step by step.

For the multi-DOF serial robot manipulators with joint elasticity, the dynamics model of the robot manipulator in the joint space can be rewritten as Luca et al. (2006)

$$M(q)\ddot{q} + C(q, \dot{q})\dot{q} + G(q) + F_q(\dot{q}) = \tau_J + DK^{-1}\dot{\tau}_J + \tau_{ext} \qquad (2)$$

$$B(\theta)\ddot{\theta} + F_\theta(\dot{\theta}) + \tau_J + DK^{-1}\dot{\tau}_J = \tau \qquad (3)$$

where q, θ denote the joint positions on the link side and motor side, respectively, F_q and F_θ denote the friction terms on the link side and motor side, respectively, τ_J denotes the joint torque signal, D and K denote the damping and stiffness coefficients of the joint, respectively, τ_{ext} equals to $J^T F_{ext}$, $B(\theta)$ is the inertia matrix of the robot joint.

Here, we take advantage of the joint torque sensors available on our robot manipulator, which is shown in Fig. 2. Actually, every joint is equipped with a high-resolution absolute position encoder on the motor side and a built-in joint torque sensor, so that q and τ_J are available. Therefore, the interaction forces can be solved only by taking advantage of (2).

For the sake of convenience and without losing generality, we take a two-degree-of-freedom manipulator for example. Then, decompose (2) and obtain:

$$
\begin{bmatrix} M_{11} & M_{12} \\ M_{21} & M_{22} \end{bmatrix} \begin{bmatrix} \ddot{q}_1 \\ \ddot{q}_2 \end{bmatrix} + \begin{bmatrix} C_{11} & C_{12} \\ C_{21} & C_{22} \end{bmatrix} \begin{bmatrix} \dot{q}_1 \\ \dot{q}_2 \end{bmatrix} + \begin{bmatrix} G_1 \\ G_2 \end{bmatrix} + \begin{bmatrix} F_{q1} \\ F_{q2} \end{bmatrix} = \begin{bmatrix} \tau_{J1} \\ \tau_{J2} \end{bmatrix} + \begin{bmatrix} D_1 K_1^{-1} \dot{\tau}_{J1} \\ D_2 K_2^{-1} \dot{\tau}_{J2} \end{bmatrix}
$$
$$
+ \begin{bmatrix} J_1^T F_1 + J_2^T F_2 \\ J_2^T F_2 \end{bmatrix}
$$

(4)

It is very clear that Eq. (2) can be decomposed into two equations for the two joints, respectively. Then, utilizing the backward method, the multiple contact forces can be obtained as follows:

Firstly, employ the joint torque data τ_{J2} as well as q_1, $\dot{q}_1$, $\ddot{q}_1$, q_2, $\dot{q}_2$, $\ddot{q}_2$ to calculate the external force exerted on the second link F_2;

Secondly, substitute F_2 into the first row of Eq. (2) and employ the joint torque data τ_{J1} as well as q_1, $\dot{q}_1$, $\ddot{q}_1$, q_2, $\dot{q}_2$, $\ddot{q}_2$ to calculate the external force exerted on the first link F_1.

The detailed execution process of the algorithm will be introduced in the latter section and this method can be easily extended to the robot manipulators with n degrees of freedom.

3.2   The Link-Side Generalized Momentum Observer

In our previous work Liu et al. (2019) and the works of (Haddadin et al. 2017; Luca et al. 2006), the link-side generalized momentum observer was derived and utilized to estimate the external force exerted on the robot manipulators with flexible joints. Specifically, we take advantage of the joint torque sensor available on our robot, which is shown in Fig. 2.

Then, we can consider only (2) and use the measured joint torque τ_J to replace the motor command torque signal τ in (1). More specifically, substituting τ with $\tau_J + DK^{-1}\dot{\tau}_J$, we can obtain the link-side generalized momentum obserer. The external forces $r_{EJ} \in \Re^n$ for the flexible joint case is computed as Luca et al. (2006)

$$
r_{EJ}(t_c) = K_I[p(t_c) - \int_0^{t_c} (\tau_J(t) + DK^{-1}\dot{\tau}_J(t) - F_q(\dot{q}(t))
$$
$$
+ C^T(q(t), \dot{q}(t))\dot{q}(t) - G(q(t)) + r_{EJ}(t))\mathrm{d}t - p(0)]
$$

(5)

with $p = M(q)\dot{q}$ denotes the generalized momentum of the robot manipulator, $r_{EJ}(0) = 0$ and a diagonal matrix $K_I > 0$.

3.3   Implementation Procedure of the Presented Algorithm

In this article, for the robot manipulator with 2 degree of freedom, using the joint torque sensors (mounted inside the robot joint), the contact forces exerted on the two links are separated and estimated accurately.

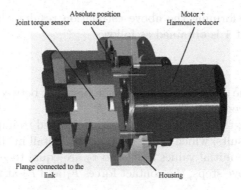

Absolute position
Joint torque sensor   encoder   Motor +
                                                Harmonic reducer

Flange connected to the
        link   Housing

Fig. 2. Schematic diagram of the flexible joint.

As can be seen from the above, the implementation procedure of the external force sensing scheme presented for two-point interaction scenarios is shown as follows:

Step 1: By substituting the joint torque signal of the second joint τ_{J2} into the link-side generalized momentum observer, the external force of the joint space caused by the contact force F_2 can be obtained as below.

$$
r_2 = K_{I2}[p_2(t) - \int_0^t (\tau_{J2} + D_2 K_2^{-1} \dot{\tau}_{J2} + C_2^T(q,\dot{q})\dot{q} \\
- F_{q2}(\dot{q}_2) - G_2(q) + r_2)\mathrm{d}s - p_2(0)].
\tag{6}
$$

Step 2: By transforming the above estimation results, the contact force exerted on the second link is obtained as follows,

$$
F_2 = J_2{}^T r_2.
\tag{7}
$$

where J_2 denotes the Jocabian matrix of the second link between the second interaction point and the center of the second joint.

Step 3: The residual joint torque signal of the first joint is obtained by subtracting the joint torque signals τ_{J1,F_2} cause by F_2 from the measured joint torque signal τ_{J1},

$$
\tau_{J1,res} = \tau_{J1} - \tau_{J1,F_2},
\tag{8}
$$

where τ_{J1} denote the joint torque signal of the first robot joint, $\tau_{1,res}$ denote the residual joint torque signal of the first joint, which can be utilized to estimate the contact force F_1.

Step 4: By substituting the residual torque signal of the joints into the link-side generalized momentum observer, the external force of the joint space caused by the contact force F_1 can be obtained.

$$
r_1 = K_{I1}[p_1(t) - \int_0^t (\tau_{J1,res} + D_1 K_1^{-1} \dot{\tau}_{J1,res} + C_1^T(q,\dot{q})\dot{q} \\
- F_{q1}(\dot{q}_1) - G_1(q) + r_1)\mathrm{d}s - p_1(0)]
\tag{9}
$$

Step 5: By transforming the above estimation results, the contact force at the interaction point 1 is obtained as follows,

$$F_1 = J_1^{-T} r_1 \tag{10}$$

where J_1 denotes the Jocabian matrix of the first link between the first interaction point and the center of the first joint.

In Steps 2 and 5, the Kalman filter is also employed to improve the accuracy of the estimation results, which is not explained in detail in this article. It is also noteworthy that the initial values of r_1 and r_2 are equal to zero.

Through the above steps, the contact forces F_1 and F_2 at the two interaction points are obtained.

4   Experimental Study

4.1   Experimental Setup

To verify the effectiveness of the proposed method, force estimation experiments using the presented algorithm are also carried out on a 2-DOF robot manipulator, which is shown in Fig. 4 with the dynamics parameters shown in Table 1. The dSPACE control platform, in particular, the DS1005 board, is employed as the control system of the robot manipulator. MATLAB/Simulink is used to design and implement the presented algorithm in this paper. The coefficients K_{I1} and K_{I1} are both set to be 10π. The execution and sampling interval for our experiments are chosen as 1 ms.

The experimental work is composed of two parts. In the first part, the robot manipulator is in free motion. The proposed multi-point contact force estimation algorithm is utilized to estimate the contact force. Then the estimation results are compared with the actual forces which are zero in free motion. In the second part, the robot manipulator is running with 2 contact forces exerted on the 2 links, simultaneously. The proposed multi-point interaction force estimation method is employed to estimate the contact forces. Then the estimation results are compared with the measurement results of the force sensors and the estimation accuracy are obtained.

For convenience and without loss of generality, we assume that the motion of the robot manipulator is along the x direction with sinusoidal velocity curves and the position along the y axis remains constant. In addition, the contact forces are assumed to be exerted on the ends of the two links respectively and the directions are both along the x axis (Fig. 3).

4.2   Experimental Results and Discussion

Firstly, the first-part experimental results without contact forces are shown in Fig. 4. It can be seen from the figure that at contact points 1 and 2, the error ranges of the force estimation results are within $[-2.5, 2.5]$ N and $[-1, 1]$ N.

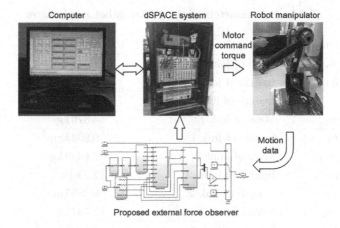

Fig. 3. 2-DOF robot manipulator and the dSPACE control system.

From the results, we can see that the proposed algorithm can realize the contact forces accurately as the estimation results are both around zero when the robot manipulator moves without contact forces.

Secondly, the second-part experimental results with contact forces exerted on the two links of the robot manipulator are shown in Figs. 5 and 6, respectively. Specifically, in Fig. 5, it shows the estimation results of the contact force on the first link. It can be seen from the figure that at contact point 1, the error ranges of the force estimation results is within $[-4, 2.5]$ N. In Fig. 6, the estimation results of the contact force on the second link are given. At this contact point, the error ranges of the force estimation results is within $[-3.5, 3]$ N. From the results, we can see that the proposed algorithm can realize accurate multi-point contact force estimation as the estimation errors are relatively small when the robot manipulator moves with two contact forces. It is worth mentioning that

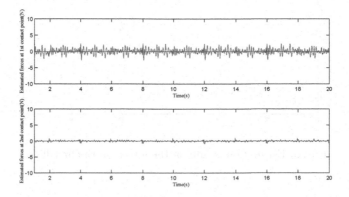

Fig. 4. Estimation results of the forces when there does not exist external forces.

Table 1. Parameters of the 2-DOF robot manipulator

Parameter	Description	Value
m_{r1}	Mass of joint 1	7.6489 kg
I_{r1}	Inertia of joint 1	2.2 kgm^2
l_1	Length of link 1	0.51 m
m_{l1}	Mass of link 1	8.879 kg
I_{l1}	Inertia of link 1	0.993 kgm^2
m_{r2}	Mass of joint 2	7.6489 kg
I_{r2}	Inertia of joint 2	2.2 kgm^2
l_2	Length of link 2	0.4655 m
m_{l2}	Mass of link 2	1.587 kg
I_{l2}	Inertia of link 2	0.1507 kgm^2
K	Stiffness of joint torque sensor	2864.789 N m/rad
D	Damping of joint torque sensor	258 N m s/rad

even if the contact forces change rapidly, the presented algorithm can also achieve relatively accurate estimation. When the estimation errors are large, there are two main reasons. Firstly, the estimation errors are caused at the beginning moment of the contact forces because the contact forces are not stably applied. Secondly, at the motion reversal moment the estimation errors are relatively larger because that the friction at this moment is more complex and the modeling accuracy of the friction is not very good. These are also the focus of our future research work.

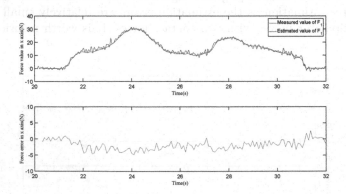

Fig. 5. Estimation results of the forces on the first link.

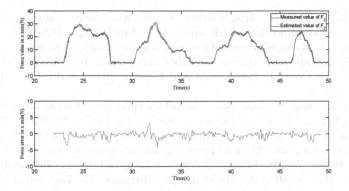

Fig. 6. Estimation results of the forces on the second link.

5 Conclusion

Multi-point physical interactions are becoming more and more common in robot-environment interactions, especially in the unstructured environments or social environments. To obtain the multi-point contact forces of the robot manipulators with flexible-joints, these forces are separated and estimated using the backward method and the link-side generalized momentum observer method. The backward method is utilized to separate and compute the contact forces exerted on different links. To avoid the use of the acceleration signals, the generalized momentum observer is employed to estimate the interaction forces. For robot manipulators with flexible-joints, the joint torque data rather than the motor command torque data are used to obtain accurate estimation results. Experimental studies have shown that accurate multi-point interaction force estimation have been realized via the proposed method in this paper.

Acknowledgement. This work was supported in part by the National Natural Science Foundation of China under Grant 91748208, and the Department of Science and Technology of Shaanxi Province under Grant 2017ZDL-G-3-1.

References

Cho, C.N., Kim, J.H., Lee, S.D., Song, J.B.: Collision detection and reaction on 7 DOF service robot arm using residual observer. J. Mech. Sci. Technol. **26**(4), 1197–1203 (2012)

Colomé, A., Pardo, D., Alenya, G., Torras, C.: External force estimation during compliant robot manipulation. In: 2013 IEEE International Conference on Robotics and Automation, pp. 3535–3540. IEEE (2013)

Van Damme, M., Beyl, P., Vanderborght, B., Grosu, V., Van Ham, R., Vanderniepen, I.: Estimating robot end-effector force from noisy actuator torque measurements. In: 2011 IEEE International Conference on Robotics and Automation, pp. 1108–1113 (2011)

Haddadin, S., De Luca, A., Albu-Schäffer, A.: Robot collisions: a survey on detection, isolation, and identification. IEEE Trans. Rob. **33**(6), 1292–1312 (2017)

Le, D.P., Choi, J., Kang, S.: External force estimation using joint torque sensors and its application to impedance control of a robot manipulator. In: 2013 13th International Conference on Control, Automation and Systems (ICCAS 2013), pp. 1794–1798. IEEE (2013)

Li, Y., Ge, S.S., Yang, C.: Impedance control for multi-point human-robot interaction. In: 2011 8th Asian Control Conference (ASCC), pp. 1187–1192. IEEE (2011)

Liu, X., Zhao, F., Ge, S.S., Wu, Y., Mei, X.: End-effector force estimation for flexible-joint robots with global friction approximation using neural networks. IEEE Trans. Ind. Inf. **15**(3), 1730–1741 (2019). https://doi.org/10.1109/TII.2018.2876724

Luca, A.D., Albu-Schäffer, A., Haddadin, S., Hirzinger, G.: Collision detection and safe reaction with the DLR-III lightweight manipulator arm. In: 2006 IEEE/RSJ International Conference on Intelligent Robots and Systems, pp. 1623–1630 (2006)

Manuelli, L., Tedrake, R.: Localizing external contact using proprioceptive sensors: the contact particle filter. In: 2016 IEEE/RSJ International Conference on Intelligent Robots and Systems (IROS), pp. 5062–5069. IEEE (2016)

Vorndamme, J., Schappler, M., Haddadin, S.: Collision detection, isolation and identification for humanoids. In: 2017 IEEE International Conference on Robotics and Automation (ICRA), pp. 4754–4761. IEEE (2017)

An Insulator Image Segmentation Method for Live Working Robot Platform

Wenpeng He[1,2], Xin Chen[1,2(✉)], and Xu Jian[1,2]

[1] School of Automation, China University of Geosciences,
Wuhan 430074, People's Republic of China
chenxin@cug.edu.cn
[2] Hubei Key Laboratory of Advanced Control and Intelligent Automation
for Complex Systems, Wuhan 430074, People's Republic of China

Abstract. Current methods for insulator extraction are mostly used for aerial imagery. There are few insulator extraction methods suitable for live working robots on mobile platforms. This paper proposes an insulator segmentation method based on depth image and color image (ISBDC). Firstly, ISBDC divides the image according to the depth information acquired by the depth camera, and removes the background image with a long distance to obtain the approximate position of the insulator in the image. Then, using OSTU to extract contours of the insulator. Finally, according to the distribution of the pixels, the background noise is further removed and the small connected region is deleted to get the final result. Compared with other algorithms, ISBDC can suppress more background noise (especially when there are multiple interference insulators in the image) and obtain enough insulator details while ensuring simple structure and not requiring much data to train.

Keywords: Insulator extraction · Live working robot · Image segmentation · Depth image

1 Introduction

With the advancement of society, people have higher and higher requirements for the safety and stability of power supply, so it is necessary to regularly maintain the power supply line. The traditional method of operation is manual powered or unpowered maintenance. Although live maintenance can ensure the stability of power transmission, it may pose a huge threat to the operator's personal safety. Similarly, although the safety factor of power-off maintenance is high, it may affect the stability of power transmission and cause huge economic losses [1,2]. Therefore, it is an inevitable requirement to vigorously develop live-working robots.

1.1 Working Object

As shown in Fig. 1, the insulator is a common physical component in the substation, and its main function is to support conductors or grounding members.

© Springer Nature Switzerland AG 2019
H. Yu et al. (Eds.): ICIRA 2019, LNAI 11742, pp. 509–518, 2019.
https://doi.org/10.1007/978-3-030-27535-8_46

Fig. 1. Insulators on the transmission line

Therefore, the insulator needs to have certain mechanical strength and insulation properties. Insulators are generally located outdoors, and prone to damage after prolonged operation. Icicles will be formed between different layers of the insulator, especially when it rains or snow in winter, which seriously affects the insulation performance of the insulator, causing accident. So the insulators need to be regularly inspected.

Figure 2a is the platform we designed for the cleaning of insulators and Fig. 2b is the actual working scenarios. The working platform mainly includes robot arm system, vision system, battery system, and also working tool system. Before the insulator cleaning operation is performed, the working platform is sent to sky by the arm vehicle. Then, the platform needs to position the insulator to obtain its spatial position. Finally, the robot arm drives the tool for insulator cleaning. Since the design margin of the working tool is limited, the accuracy of position should be controlled within 10 mm.

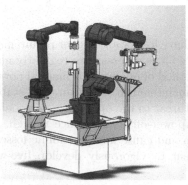   

(a) Robotic arm platform   (b) Indoor simulation site

Fig. 2. Working platform

In the actual project, we use the depth camera as the positioning camera. When positioning the insulator, the outline of the insulator needs to be extracted first so that the camera can calculate the axis coordinates of the insulator. Therefore, if the hardware performance is determined, the accuracy of the insulator contour extraction basically determines its positioning accuracy. This paper is mainly about how to extract the insulator contours.

All relevant pictures used in this paper are taken in Fig. 2b, and the software platform is OpenCV 3.1 and Microsoft Visual Studio 2017. Using Intel RealSense D435 as a shooting camera.

1.2 Research Background

Current methods for detecting insulators are mainly divided into two categories. One is to use digital image processing techniques to segment and identify insulator images according to the characteristics of the insulator, such as color [6–10], shape [5,9], and texture [3,4]. The disadvantage of this method is that only the pixel information is used, so the interference problem when there are multiple insulators in the image can not be eliminated. Another common type of insulator identification method is based on deep learning, as shown in the literature [11–14]. Compared with the traditional method, the deep learning method has higher stability for insulator extraction when the amount of data is sufficient. But for this robot platform, it is difficult to provide so much data, so the method of deep learning is not suitable for the environment referred to in this article too.

In addition, the existing insulator detection is mostly for aerial image, the background of the picture is mostly ground or tree. In the environment indicated in this paper, the camera is only about 1 m away from the insulator, and the height is basically equal to the insulator. Therefore, the background of the image is no longer the ground, but most likely other equipment in the substation, so the traditional method can not adapt well to the environment referred in this paper. The Intel RealSense D435 used in this paper can output both depth image and color image, and filtering with depth image can effectively suppress the segmentation error caused by multiple insulator. Therefore, a method based on depth image and color image for insulator positioning is proposed.

2 Method of ISBDC

The depth map can provide most of the depth information in the camera's field of view, but because there may be other objects with similar distance around the insulator, the insulator cannot be accurately positioned by the depth map alone. At the same time, due to the shape of the insulator and the external light, the edge information of the insulator in the image is severely missing (as shown in Fig. 3a). This also creates great difficulties for the edge extraction of the insulator. In order to solve these problems, we introduce color image. As shown in Fig. 3b, the color image can completely extract the contours of the insulator.

(a) Filter only by depth map   (b) Filter only by color map

Fig. 3. Single image filtering results (Color figure online)

2.1 Method of Depth Map Segmentation

The depth map and color map provided by the camera are both 1280×720. However, the depth information is composed of two bytes, so the size of the depth matrix is 2560×720. If $v_{i,j}$ is used to represent the value in the depth matrix in ith row and jth column, then the depth information in ith row and jth column is

$$d_{i,j} = v_{i,2 \times j} + v_{i,2 \times j+1} \times 256 \tag{1}$$

In actual work, the distance between the insulator and the camera is about 0.9 m. Considering the initial position error of the working platform, we set the depth range to 500 mm–1200 mm. Therefore, the basic formula for depth image segmentation is as follows:

$$v_{i,j} = \begin{cases} 0 & if \quad d_{i,j} < 500 \quad or \quad d_{i,j} > 1200 \\ v_{i,j} & otherwise \end{cases} \tag{2}$$

where $d_{i,j}$ represents the pixel depth in ith row and jth column.

After the segmentation of Eq. (2), the image will generate multiple connected components. In general, the insulator will be in the largest connected components, however, due to the error of the depth map, the edge portion of the insulator may be missing or depth error, as shown in Fig. 3a. So the smallest rectangle where the largest connected domain located is selected as the depth image segmentation result, as shown in Fig. 4.

2.2 Method of Color Map Segmentation

Color map segmentation mainly includes three steps: first, transform the result of depth map segmentation to HSV space; secondly, use OSTU algorithm to segment the image in S channel of HSV space to remove part of the background; finally, use the minimum value of gray distribution to segment the image in V channel to further remove the background.

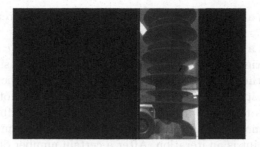

Fig. 4. Result of first step

The three channels of HSV color space represent hue, saturation, value respectively. Compared with RGB color space, HSV color space is more intuitive. The formulas for converting RGB color space to HSV color space are as follows:

$$V = \max(R, G, B)$$

$$S = \frac{\max(R, G, B) - \min(R, G, B)}{\max(R, G, B)}$$

$$H_t = \begin{cases} \frac{G-B}{\max(R,G,B)-\min(R,G,B)} \times 60, & if \ R = \max(R, G, B) \\ 120 + \frac{(B-R)}{\max(R,G,B)-\min(R,G,B)} \times 60, & if \ G = \max(R, G, B) \\ 240 + \frac{(R-G)}{\max(R,G,B)-\min(R,G,B)} \times 60, & if \ B = \max(R, G, B) \end{cases} \qquad (3)$$

$$H = \begin{cases} H_t & if \ H_t > 0 \\ 360 + H_t & if \ H_t < 0 \end{cases}$$

Maximum between-cluster variance algorithm (OSTU) is an adaptive threshold determination algorithm. The algorithm divides the gray image into two categories: background and object, and finds the appropriate threshold by maximizing the variance between classes. Its basic idea is that dividing the image into background and object according to a threshold $t(t \in [0,255])$. If the average gray value of background is represented by μ_1, the average gray value of object is represented by μ_2, and the global average gray value is represented by μ, then the formula for calculating the inter-class variance g is as follows:

$$g = \omega_1 \times (\mu - \mu_1)^2 + \omega_2 \times (\mu - \mu_2)^2 \qquad (4)$$

where ω_1 represents the probability of background pixels occurrence and ω_2 represents the probability of object pixels occurrence. The maximum variance between classes can be obtained by traverse t, and the corresponding t_0 is the optimal threshold.

After the segmentation OSTU, insulators have been basically extracted, as shown in Fig. 5. But in some pictures, there are still some background pixels (such as the banner in Fig. 5). ISBDC assumes that the insulator body presents a single peak distribution on V channel in HSV space. When there are background pixels in the image, the gray distribution of the image will be disturbed, so the background pixels after OSTU segmentation can be further removed by its gray distribution.

In order to get a smooth gray distribution curve, ISBDC calculates the average value of the original distribution map in a fixed window size, and takes this average value as the value of midpoint of the window in the new distribution map. Since the endpoint value of the distribution map can not calculate by this method, it assigns the value directly from the original distribution map to the new distribution map. The process of the window moves from the left endpoint to the right endpoint is an iteration. After a certain number of iterations, a new smooth distribution map corresponding to the initial distribution map can be obtained, as shown in Algorithm 1.

Algorithm 1. Method of Smothing Distribution Map

Input:
 The gray value distribution of a map, P_i;
 Window Length(must be odd) L;
 Number of iterations, $maxIters$;

Output:
 New distribution map, N_i;

1: Place the window at the leftmost end of the distribution map, and assign $(L-1)/2$ pixels at the leftmost and rightmost end to the corresponding N_i directly;

2: Calculate the average value of the distribution map corresponding to the current window and assign it to the corresponding N_i;

3: If the window reaches the rightmost end, goes to step5; otherwise, goes to the next step;

4: Move the window one bit to the right and step to step2;

5: If it reaches $maxIters$, the algorithm ends. Otherwise, let $P_i = N_i$ and goes to step 1.

6: **return** N_i;

After getting the smooth curve, in order to remove redundant peaks, ISBDC needs to find the minimum point t in the curve, which satisfies the following formula:

$$v_t < \min(v_{t-2}, v_{t-1}, v_{t+1}, v_{t+2}) \tag{5}$$

Generally speaking, there is only an integer i that satisfies the condition. When i is determined, the gray distribution map is divided into two parts again. ISBDC regards the part with more pixels as the object and the other part as the background.

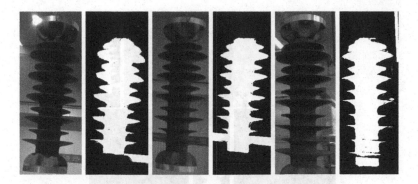

Fig. 5. OSTU result based on depth segmentation

3   Segmentation Results of ISBDC

To sum up, ISBDC divides the insulator image mainly include 3 steps: First, use depth map to remove most of the pixels that do not contain the object. Second, on the basis of the first step, ISBDC uses OSTU algorithm to remove background information again on S-channel in HSV space. Finally, by removing the redundant peaks on the gray distribution and deleting the small connected components, the final result will be obtained.

For practical work, the range of distance is set to [600, 1200] in step 1, and the iteration times of histogram smoothing is set to 50 in color image segmentation. The final results are shown in Figures 6, 7 and 8:

Fig. 6. Result of image-1, the image represent the original image, the depth segmentation result, the OSTU segmentation result, the OSTU segmentation histogram, the final result and the final result histogram representatively. (Color figure online)

Fig. 7. Result of image-2, the image represent the original image, the depth segmentation result, the OSTU segmentation result, the OSTU segmentation histogram, the final result and the final result histogram representatively. (Color figure online)

Fig. 8. Result of image-3, the image represent the original image, the depth segmentation result, the OSTU segmentation result, the OSTU segmentation histogram, the final result and the final result histogram representatively. (Color figure online)

It can be seen from the results that ISBDC can extract insulators on the basis of retaining enough details, and by removing the second peak of the gray distribution, the background pixels of the image is further removed, which enhances the accuracy of image segmentation. It should be pointed out that, because of the introduction of depth image, when there are multiple insulators in the image, it is also very easy to remove the insulators which are belong to the background, so as to achieve a more accurate segmentation effect.

4 Discussion

In this paper, an insulator image segmentation method based on depth image and color image (ISBDC) is proposed. This method is mainly used to extract insulators captured on mobile platforms. Compared with traditional algorithms, ISBDC has better segmentation effect while maintaining simple structure. At the same time, ISBDC can effectively overcome the failure of image segmentation caused by the presence of multiple insulators by introducing depth map at the first step.

The disadvantage of ISBDC is that the final segmentation result depends on the OSTU segmentation effect, which challenges the adaptability of the method, so more data are needed for further testing.

Acknowledgments. This work is supported by the National Natural Science Foundation of China under Grants 61873248, the Hubei Provincial Natural Science Foundation of China under Grant 2017CFA030 and Grant 2015CFA010, and the 111 project under Grant B17040, the Science and Technology Project of State Grid Corporation of China under Grant 52153216000R.

References

1. Yan, G., et al.: Automatic extraction of power lines from aerial images. IEEE Geosci. Remote Sens. Lett. **4**, 387–391 (2007)
2. Liu, W., et al.: Review of research on smart grid technical standard system. Power Syst. Prot. Control **40**, 120–126 (2012)
3. Zhang, X., et al.: Method for recognizing insulator from airborne image. In: Fifth International Conference on Intelligent Computation Technology and Automation. IEEE Computer Society (2012)
4. Zhang, J., et al.: Insulators recognition for 220 kV/330 kV high-voltage live-line cleaning robot. In: International Conference on Pattern Recognition. IEEE Computer Society (2006)
5. Zhao, Z., et al.: Localization of multiple insulators by orientation angle detection and binary shape prior knowledge. IEEE Trans. Dielectr. Electr. Insul. **22**, 3421–3428 (2015)
6. Yuan, J., et al.: Identification and location of insulator video images based on ASIFT algorithm. Electr. Meas. Instrum. **52**, 106–112 (2015)
7. Ma, S., et al.: Segmentation of insulator images based on HSI color space. J. Dalian Natl. Univ. **12**, 481–484 (2010)
8. Gao, Q., et al.: Features description of difference-based image and its application in insulator recognition. Electr. Meas. Instrum. **52**, 117–122 (2015)
9. Huang, X., et al.: Composite insulator images segmentation technology based on improved color difference. High Volt. Eng. **44**, 2493–2500 (2018)
10. Zhu, S., et al.: Identification and location of insulator string based on frequency-tuned. Trans. China Electrotech. Soc. **33**, 5573–5580 (2018)
11. Liu, Y., et al.: The method of insulator recognition based on deep learning. In: IEEE (2016)

12. Wang, X., et al.: Insulator identification from aerial images using Support Vector Machine with background suppression. In: International Conference on Unmanned Aircraft Systems. IEEE (2016)
13. Peng, X., et al.: An automatically locating method for insulator object based on CNNs. Geomat. Inf. Sci. Wuhan Univ. **44**, 563–569 (2019)
14. Kazemi, A., et al.: Artificial neural network for insulator leakage currents prediction from environmental data. In: IEEE International Conference on Power and Energy. IEEE (2008)

Swarm Intelligence and Multi-robot Cooperation

Multi-robot Collaborative Assembly Research for 3C Manufacturing–Taking Server Motherboard Assembly Task as an Example

Jinyu Xu, Yanpu Lei, Jiawei Luo, Yue Wu, and Hai-Tao Zhang[✉]

School of Artificial Intelligence and Automation,
Huazhong University of Science and Technology, Wuhan 430074, China
zht@mail.hust.edu.cn
http://imds.aia.hust.edu.cn/

Abstract. In the multi-robot collaborative manufacturing, such as the server motherboard assembly task in the 3C industry, the characteristic of the operating process and the uncertainty of the assembly environment make this problem difficult to be solved in an efficient way. This paper addresses the key points of this problem. Firstly, a series of end effectors for 3C assembly operation is designed. After analyzing precision and scope for different steps in the assembly process, the positioning systems with different precision and scope are designed and are chosen for better performance in different operations. Finally, compliant control is introduced in the inserting process where the positioning system does not perform well to further increase the success rate. Experiments illustrate the superiority of our ideas. Due to its convenience and generality, the present approach can be expected to apply to more general industrial scenarios.

Keywords: Robotic assembly · Changeable precision and scope · Compliant control

1 Introduction

In robotics research, developed countries take multi-robot assembly and manufacturing technology as one of the priorities. In recent years, developed countries and economies have proposed roadmaps for robot technology development in order to step up the layout and mastered the multi-robot manufacturing technology [1]. Task-driven, low cost, good flexibility, large operating space, and cross-scale, the advantages of multi-robot collaborative assembly technology are countless. At the same time, with the development of sensing technologies such as vision and force feedback, we take the multi-robot system as the actuator supplement by real-time condition sensing and muti-source sensor fusion. That will break through the single tasks limitations and play an important role in the

© Springer Nature Switzerland AG 2019
H. Yu et al. (Eds.): ICIRA 2019, LNAI 11742, pp. 521–532, 2019.
https://doi.org/10.1007/978-3-030-27535-8_47

robotic automated assembly line. What's more, it is especially suitable for the agile assembly of complex parts with small batches and multiple varieties, which meets the production needs of the 3C industry and may becomes one of the core technologies for 3C assembly in the future.

In this paper, we present a multi-robots system to assemble 3C server motherboard equipped with muti-source Sensor fusion in a different scale. Some key problems were solved in the multi-robot application in 3C assembly. Our contributions are:

- A series of end effectors were designed to suit for 3C assembly tasks, which solves the basic needs of the robot in 3C operation.
- Collaborative algorithms and positioning methods for multi-robot 3C assembly in the different process with changeable scope and accuracy.
- Greatly improve the system's robustness, positioning accuracy and success rate, makes it possible to apply to the real 3C assembly production environment and more general industrial scenarios.

2   Related Works

At the beginning, in multi-scale collaborative assembly, early work focused on the coordinated handling, construction, and assembly of brick or truss structures. For example, Desai et al. [2] designed a multi-robot moving strategy for autonomous transport in multiple obstacle environments; Khatib et al. [3] proposed a cooperative control method to operate several six-degree-of-freedom robots; Reinhart et al. [4] developed a method to make robots autonomous collaborative assemble the factory floors; Worcester et al. [5] achieved the parallel assembly and instability recovery of multi-robots in complex large structures assembly tasks based on real-time collaborative detection of RGB-D cameras; Lindsey et al. [6] and Willmann et al. [7] used UAV formation to assemble and construct complex structures; Heger et al. [8] designed the robot assembly method of mesh-shaped structures; Petersen et al. [9] designed the formation of autonomous mobile robots on the ground, which realized constructing much larger than the ontology scale buildings; Yun et al. [10] designed the multi-robot self-assembly and stability control method for the truss structure. However, the above methods are mainly used for the assembly of bricks or truss structures with uniform size. Facing the increasingly complex needs of the manufacturing industry, researchers later turned to multi-robot assembly systems which can operate multiple discrete components of varying sizes. For example, Kume et al. [11] and Li et al. [12] proposed a method of cross-scale cooperative handling, alignment, and assembly using robot formations; MIT's Dogar et al. [13] used four KUKA youBot mobile robots to cooperatively assemble more than ten different wing parts through the visual sensing based on different scales and precisions.

In summary, at present, the efficiency, synergy and flexibility of multi-robots in 3C assembly are still insufficient, and there is still much space to improve in the performance of collaborative assembly.

3   Problem Description and Solution Overview

3.1   Task Solution Overview

At the beginning, we will clarify the details of the tasks. We present the server motherboard assembly task as an instantiation of the problem specification. The experiment platform is shown in Figs. 1, 2, 3 and 4.

Sensor: According to the characteristics of the muti-robots' performing during the tasks, firstly, we take a positioning system like Optitrack with a large scope and relatively low precision to meet the demand. Then the operation area in the workspace can be located by using the marker-based positioning method. Of course, this positioning method has its corresponding shortcomings, such as occlusion problems, insufficient accuracy of subsequent operations and so on. The main function of this system is to locate the position of the assembly part initial position and server motherboard operate table. In addition, the robot's end effectors could be moved above the target according to the location information, waiting to switch next positioning system. Then we use CMOS industrial camera and image-based visual servoing method to achieve narrow scope but high positioning precision. It was used to connect the previous step and improve the positioning precision further. Finally, before the inserting operation, the alignment process is completed with sufficient precision compensation operation. In order to further improve the assembly success rate and accuracy in the final assembly process, we refer to the method and rules in human's perspective, and we introduce impedance control to realize the interaction feedback between the part and the motherboard during the final insertion process.

Robot's End Effectors: The end effect effectors for the server board assembly process were designed to pick up the 3C parts and fix the server motherboard's position and freedom. We used pneumatics to drive them working.

We need to meet the following points during the whole assembly process:

Assembly Flexibility: 3C assembly line has a short change cycle, high production efficiency requirements, and high reworkability requirements for tasks. Therefore, the entire assembly system needs sufficient task flexibility to meet the task production needs.

Collaboration: Robots need to complete a large number of data interaction and time synchronization tasks. At the same time, in the collaborative work, it is necessary to ensure that the assembly precision meets the requirements, and on the basis of synergy, the actions of capture and fix. should adapt a series of sizes of server motherboards.

Accuracy and Speed: It is necessary to adapt to a series of precision and scope of view changes in different operation process and the time-consuming requirements of the entire operation process. At the same time, the task time arrangement needs to be well planned so that the entire task can be balanced in both accuracy and time requirement.

Robustness: The task consists of multiple steps, and the environment changes during the assembly process. The entire assembly system needs to be robust enough to adapt to the changing assembly environment.

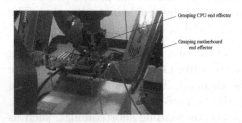

Fig. 1. Platform composition 1.   **Fig. 2.** Platform composition 2.

Fig. 3. Platform composition 3.   **Fig. 4.** Platform composition 4.

3.2   Example Task

Our experimental platform used three industrial robots to complete a series of collaborative assembly tasks. While working, it contains synchronous coordination, asynchronous coordination, asynchronous independent actions and so on between the robots. In Fig. 5, all the steps have been described clearly. We use R1, R2 to grab and fix the server motherboard, and R3 performs the assembly operations with several sensors on its end effectors to satisfy the location demand in the task. The whole task can be described as follows.

Optitrack and industrial camera are combined to locate the position of the server motherboard with high precision and large scope, making up for their shortcoming in their respective use. Then R1, R2 cooperate to grab and lift the server motherboard to the target position waiting for the next step.

R3 uses the same way to get the CPU position and then pick it up with CPU operation end effectors.

R3 locates the CPU socket position on the server motherboard and moves above it, then inserts the CPU into the socket to the correct position and judges whether the installation is in place through the assembly contact force data feedback by the force sensor. After confirming that the CPU has been successfully installed, R3 release the CPU and completes the CPU installation steps.

Change R3 end effectors to the memory module one. Repeat the above process. The difference from the CPU installation is that due to the special design of the memory strip slot, there will be a series of changes in the contact force during the final insertion process. The installation uses a six-axis sensor(Optiforce) to sense whether the CPU was contacted with the slot. We changed the control strategy so that the memory module will track the target force in target position during inserting process, so that the memory module can guarantee to be assembled into the memory slot successfully.

R1, R2 put the server motherboard back, waiting for the next task cycle.

The above is the general flow of our assembly task, which we will describe in detail below.

R1	R2	R3
Navigate and move gripper to server motherboard		
Collaboratively grab and fix the sever motherboard,then lift it up		Help to locate the sever motherboard
		Navigate the CPU and move gripper
		Pick up CPU then localize the CPU socket on the server motherboard
		Insert CPU using impedance control
		Change the end effectors to perform the next step.
		....
Put the server motherboard back on the table		Assembly tasks complete
Move out of the away		

Fig. 5. Task flow table. Time flows from top to bottom. Cell colors indicate different localization methods used in each action. Blue cells indicated Optitrack with a large scope and relatively low precision. Yellow cells indicate CMOS industrial camera and image-based visual servoing method with a narrow scope but high positioning precision. Red cells indicate impedance control with force feedback. (Color figure online)

4   Multi-robot Manipulation with Multi-source Sensor in Different Scale

4.1   Collaborative Process with a Large Scope and Low Accuracy Requirements

The server motherboard has a large layout and the substrate is PCB. This material has low bending rigidity and is prone to bending of the board under unconstrained and unsupported conditions. Therefore, at the beginning of the assembly tasks, providing support on its bottom and limiting its freedom provide the foundation for subsequent part assembly operations.

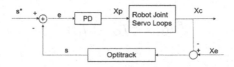

Fig. 6. Optitrack positioning system block diagram.

Based on the server motherboard structure, we design a grasping end effector that could adapt to a series of size changes. Under the synchronous operation of two industrial robots, we can complete the precise grasping. On the motherboard console, we have set marker balls for Optitrack global positioning. When the system obtains the position of the motherboard, R3 moves above the motherboard console to position the motherboard into the camera field of view, locates the center coordinates of the motherboard in the multi-robot world coordinate system. According to the center coordinates of the motherboard and the motherboard size data, robots can calculate the Cartesian coordinates of the two robot ends. With the current Cartesian coordinates and expected coordinates of the two robots, we hope that they can complete the autonomous path planning to complete the grab. Here we use a cylinder envelope to simplify the modeling of robots and the obstacle. The gradient descent envelope method was used to search planning path with repulsive attracting potential energy function under the C-space mapping condition. We can summarize it as Algorithm 1.

Algorithm 1. MotherBoard grasping algorithm(i, n)

Function Grasping Control(i, n)

Require:

  i-index of this robot;

  n-number of robot;

  $P_i c$-this robot current Pose;

  $P_i e$-this robot expected Pose;

1: $P \leftarrow$ GetCurrentMotherboardPosition()
2: $P_i e \leftarrow$ ComputeExpectPose(i, n)
3: $T_i \leftarrow$ ComputeTrajectoryWithSelf-collisionAvoidance$(P_i c, P_i e)$
4: **Publish** T_i to robot arm control system

In this case, PD control can meet demand in Fig. 6. After Optitrack is used to obtain the coordinates of the current target in the robot world coordinate system, the robot can move to the target position with the target pose. The work we need to do here is to pre-calibrate the relationship between the Optitrack coordinate system and the robot world coordinate system and obtain the rotation matrix between the two coordinate systems. So after obtaining the coordinates of the target in the Optitrack coordinate system, the coordinates in the robot world coordinate system can be gotten as Eqs. (1) and (2), $^{E}T_O, ^{E}R_V, ^{V}T_O \in SE(3)$.

$$^{E}T_O = {}^{E}R_V \cdot {}^{V}T_O \tag{1}$$

$$^{E}R_V = {}^{E}T_O \cdot ({}^{V}T_O)^{-1} \tag{2}$$

4.2 Collaborative Process with a Small Scope and High Accuracy Requirements

After acquiring the target position in the current large space through the global positioning system, we add an image-based visual servoing method to achieve narrow-field high-precision positioning combined with the industrial camera. When the operating robot needs to perform the high-precision operation and the current positioning system cannot meet its precision requirements, the positioning method will be switched to meet the different requirements of the robot's sensing scope and precision under different processes.

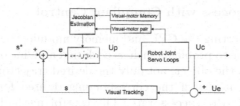

Fig. 7. Visual-base servoing system block diagram.

The image-based visual servoing is wildly applied to 3D positioning in Fig. 7, but the image Jacobian matrix is nonlinearly time-varying during servo positioning in Eq. (3). If real-time servoing is realized in 3D space, the model in the Cartesian coordinate system is six-dimensional variable model needs to identify the image Jacobian matrix in the current tracking field simultaneously, which leads the model to become complex and inefficient. We simplify the above problem and stipulate that the spatial position of the current console is obtained under the premise of a large scope positioning system, and the console is placed vertically horizontally. The camera is working at a fixed height relative to the console, and the dimension is reduced from 6-dimensional to 3D. In Eqs. (4) and (5), U_A is target's two-dimensional coordinates and rotation angle obtained from pre-calibrated images. X_A is the X, Y axis coordinate and Z-axis rotation component of the object after dimensionality reduction. So while we get the image of the target B, the relative position ΔX of the robot that needs to move can be calculated according to the Eq. (9). Assembled parts' mage feature is extracted in advance, so all we need to do is to take 9-point calibration. We can summarize above as Algorithm 2.

$$u = -\lambda \hat{J}_u^+ (s - s^*) \tag{3}$$

$$\begin{bmatrix} x \\ y \\ r \end{bmatrix} = T \begin{bmatrix} X \\ Y \\ R_Z \end{bmatrix} \tag{4}$$

$$U_A = T X_A \tag{5}$$

$$\Delta X = T^{-1} U_B - X_A \tag{6}$$

Algorithm 2. Locate target position algorithm(T, i)

Function Visual Servoing Control(T, i)

Require:

    T-Target with pre-calibrated features and target images;

    i-Current image;

    P-The relative displacement of the robot that needs to be moved;

1: $P \leftarrow$ CalculateTheRelativeDisplacement(i,T.targetImage)

2: $T_i \leftarrow$ ComputeTrajectory(P)

3: **Publish** T_i to robot arm control system

4.3   Insertion Process with Compliant Control

In the process of inserting the CPU and memory module, the above two systems can no longer use due to problems such as occlusion and line of sight. In addition, the robot assembles the object, not only the desired trajectory movement needs to be performed, but also if the corresponding desired force can be applied will further increase the success rate. The control method that achieves the above-mentioned object so that the manipulator produces flexibility is compliant control. Impedance control is a compliant control method that allows the robotic arm to exhibit compliance with the external environment by adjusting the target impedance. By using the compliant control in Fig. 8, we can improve the success rate in the final insertion step, and judge the success or failure of the assembly according to the value of the force feedback, so as to judge the next step.

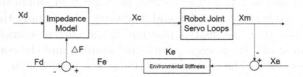

Fig. 8. Compliant control system block diagram.

We simplified the insertion operation as a stiffness model with stiffness K_e. X_d is the reference trajectory information corresponding to the desired tracking force, X_c is the trajectory information sent to the robot, X_e is environmental location information, and X_m is the trajectory information actually arrived by the robot. F_e can be accurately obtained by a force sensor, and F_d is the desired tracking force.

$$K_e(X_d - X_m) = F_e - F_d \tag{7}$$

$$K_e(X_m - X_e) = F_e \tag{8}$$

In order to achieve the desired force contact, combined with the above equations, we can update the desired trajectory to:

$$X_d = \frac{F_d(X_m - X_e)}{F_e} + X_e \tag{9}$$

Here, we introduce an impedance model in which M, B, and K represent the mass coefficient, damping coefficient, and stiffness coefficient.

$$m\ddot{e} + b\dot{e} + (k + k_e)e = -f_d \tag{10}$$

Here, $e = x_e - x_m$, but x_e is to get accurate values, so we use x'_e indicates the estimated environmental location. Define $\delta x_e = x'_e - x_m$, $e' = e + \delta x_e$. Bring it into equation and add adaptive adjustment $Omega$ to ensure the force error is stable and convergent, λ is sampling period, η is learning rate, and we get:

$$m\ddot{e}' + b\dot{e}' + k(e' + \Omega(t)) = f_e - f_d \tag{11}$$

$$\Omega(t) = \Omega(t - \lambda) + \eta\frac{(f_d(t - \lambda) - f_e(t - \lambda))}{k} \quad \eta > 0 \tag{12}$$

From $f_e = k_e(x_m - x_e)$ we can get the following relationship:

$$x_m = x_e + \frac{f_e}{k_e}; \dot{x}_m = \dot{x}_e + \frac{\dot{f}_e}{k_e}; \ddot{x}_m = \ddot{x}_e + \frac{\ddot{f}_e}{k_e} \tag{13}$$

Bring Eq. 13 and $\delta x_e = x'_e - x_m$, $e' = e + \delta x_e$ into Eq. (10) and consider Ω as the sum of the sequences of p elements, and the first one is 0, let's define $\varepsilon(t) = f_d(t) - f_e(t)$, $f'_e = k_e\delta x_e$, $v = f_d - f'_e$ and bring them into Eq. (10) so we get:

$$m\ddot{\varepsilon}(t) + b\dot{\varepsilon}(t) + (k + k_e)\varepsilon(t) + \eta k_e(\varepsilon(t - (p - 1)\lambda) + ... + \varepsilon(t - \lambda))$$
$$= m\ddot{v} + b\dot{v} + kv \tag{14}$$

After the transfer function is obtained by Laplace transform, consider that when the delay of the system is λ, $0 < \lambda < 1$ and p is large enough, the characteristic equation is obtained by Taylor expansion:

$$\lambda m s^3 + \lambda b s^2 + \lambda(k + k_e - k_e\eta)s + k_e\eta = 0 \tag{15}$$

According to the Rolls criterion, the system must be satisfied Eq. (16) if it want to be stable:

$$\frac{\lambda b \cdot \lambda(k + k_e - k_e\eta)}{\lambda b} > 0, k_e\eta > 0 \tag{16}$$

And the environmental stiffness is usually much larger than the impedance control stiffness, so $k_e \gg k$, and we can get when η satisfy Eq. (17) can ensure the system stable.

$$0 < \eta < \frac{\lambda b}{\lambda b + m} \tag{17}$$

5   Experiment

We use the ODG JLRB20 manipulator arm equipped with Optitrack, industrial camera and Optiforce force/torque sensor. The robots, positioning system and sensors communicate through TCP/IP. The position systems' properties is shown in Table 1. The experimental process is mentioned in Sect. 3.2.

Table 1. Comparison of the performance of different location system.

Sensor	Scope (m)	Error (m)	
		Sensor	Indirection
Optitrack	100	0.001	0.1
CMOS industrial camera	1	0.001	0.01

In final inserting process, we assume $K_e = 5000\,(\text{N/m})$, and because robot's inserting pose is vertical to the horizontal, all we need to control is Z axis force to make it reach the desired force at the desired position. The control parameters are given by: $K = 20, B = 50, M = I, F_d = 30\,\text{N}, \lambda = 0.01$. According to the Eq. 17, η need to less than:

$$\frac{0.01 \times 50}{0.01 \times 50 + 1} \approx 0.33 \tag{18}$$

So we set the initial $\eta = 0.1$. We can get the force/torque trajectory in Z axis in Fig. 9 and tracking error in Fig. 10. In order to show our system's superiority, we repeat the experiment several times in different condition to compare the success rate. We design another two conditions, one is entirely open loop, another is equipped with Optitrack. It is clear that the first one will not work once the position changes. The result is in Table 2.

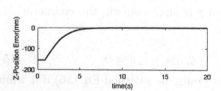
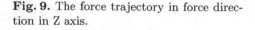

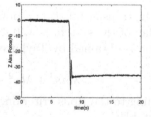

Fig. 9. The force trajectory in force direction in Z axis.

Fig. 10. The position tracking error of the robot.

Our system is obviously better than the others. Because the positioning, image processing, and information transferring need time to do, time efficiency is relatively lower, but the outstanding success rate can make up for the shortfall.

Table 2. Experiments result

Config	Success	Total time	Note
Open loop	25%	119 s	Only can be used while the position is not changed
With Optitrack	50%	149 s	There is a big chance that it will not be aligned
Our system	80%	180 s	In a few cases, the inserting process is failed

6 Insights and Conclusion

In this paper, the research about muti-robots assemble the 3C parts equipped with muti-source Sensor fusion in different scale improves the system's robustness greatly, and this approach can be extended to other industrial areas such as vehicle manufacturing and else. What's more, the cases of failure during the experiment are not solved, which can be a new research direction in the future.

Funding. This work is supported by National Natural Science Foundation (NNSF) of China under Grant U1713203 and 61803168 and the MOE Key Laboratory of Image Processing and Intelligence Control, Wuhan, China under Grant IPIC2016-05.

References

1. Lehmann, C., Pellicciari, M., Drust, M., Gunnink, J.W.: Machining with industrial robots: the COMET project approach. In: Neto, P., Moreira, A.P. (eds.) WRSM 2013. CCIS, vol. 371, pp. 27–36. Springer, Heidelberg (2013). https://doi.org/10.1007/978-3-642-39223-8_3
2. Desai, J.P., Kumar, V.: Motion planning for cooperating mobile manipulators. J. Robot. Syst. **16**(10), 557–579 (1999)
3. Khatib, O., Yokoi, K., Chang, K., Ruspini, D., Holmberg, R., Casal, A.: Coordination and decentralized cooperation of multiple mobile manipulators. J. Robot. Syst. **13**(11), 755–764 (1996)
4. Reinhart, G., Zaidan, S.: A generic framework for workpiece-based programming of cooperating industrial robots. In: 2009 International Conference on Mechatronics and Automation, pp. 37–42. IEEE (2009)
5. Worcester, J., Ani Hsieh, M., Lakaemper, R.: Distributed assembly with online workload balancing and visual error detection and correction. Int. J. Robot. Res. **33**(4), 534–546 (2014)
6. Lindsey, Q., Mellinger, D., Kumar, V.: Construction with quadrotor teams. Auton. Robot. **33**(3), 323–336 (2012)
7. Willmann, J., Augugliaro, F., Cadalbert, T., D'Andrea, R., Gramazio, F., Kohler, M.: Aerial robotic construction towards a new field of architectural research. Int. J. Archit. Comput. **10**(3), 439–459 (2012)
8. Heger, F.W., Singh, S.: Robust robotic assembly through contingencies, plan repair and re-planning. In: 2010 IEEE International Conference on Robotics and Automation, pp. 3825–3830. IEEE (2010)

9. Petersen, K.H., Nagpal, R., Werfel, J.K.: Termes: an autonomous robotic system for three-dimensional collective construction (2011)
10. Yun, S., Rus, D.: Adaptation to robot failures and shape change in decentralized construction. In: 2010 IEEE International Conference on Robotics and Automation, pp. 2451–2458. IEEE (2010)
11. Kume, Y., Hirata, Y., Kosuge, K.: Coordinated motion control of multiple mobile manipulators handling a single object without using force/torque sensors. In: 2007 IEEE/RSJ International Conference on Intelligent Robots and Systems, pp. 4077–4082. IEEE (2007)
12. Li, Z., Ge, S.S., Wang, Z.: Robust adaptive control of coordinated multiple mobile manipulators. Mechatronics 18(5–6), 239–250 (2008)
13. Dogar, M., Knepper, R.A., Spielberg, A., Choi, C., Christensen, H.I., Rus, D.: Multi-scale assembly with robot teams. Int. J. Robot. Res. 34(13), 1645–1659 (2015)
14. Collet, A., Martinez, M., Srinivasa, S.S.: The moped framework: object recognition and pose estimation for manipulation. Int. J. Robot. Res. 30(10), 1284–1306 (2011)
15. Ilonen, J., Bohg, J., Kyrki, V.: Fusing visual and tactile sensing for 3-D object reconstruction while grasping. In: 2013 IEEE International Conference on Robotics and Automation, pp. 3547–3554. IEEE (2013)
16. Jung, S., Hsia, T.C., Bonitz, R.G.: Force tracking impedance control of robot manipulators under unknown environment. IEEE Trans. Control Syst. Technol. 12(3), 474–483 (2004)
17. Xu, J., Hou, Z., Wang, W., Xu, B., Zhang, K., Chen, K.: Feedback deep deterministic policy gradient with fuzzy reward for robotic multiple peg-in-hole assembly tasks. IEEE Trans. Ind. Inform. 15(3), 1658–1667 (2019)
18. Zhang, K., Xu, J., Chen, H., Zhao, J., Chen, K.: Jamming analysis and force control for flexible dual peg-in-hole assembly. IEEE Trans. Ind. Electron. 66(3), 1930–1939 (2019)

Multiagent Reinforcement Learning
for Swarm Confrontation Environments

Guanyu Zhang[1], Yuan Li[2(✉)], Xinhai Xu[2], and Huadong Dai[2]

[1] National University of Defense Technology, Changsha 410073, Hunan, China
[2] Artificial Intelligence Research Center,
National Innovation Institute of Defense Technology, Beijing 100071, China
yuan.li@nudt.edu.cn

Abstract. The swarm confrontation problem is always a hot research topic, which has attracted much attention. Previous research focuses on devising rules to improve the intelligence of the swarm, which is not suitable for complex scenarios. Multi-agent reinforcement learning has been used in some similar confrontation tasks. However, many of these works take centralized method to control all entities in a swarm, which is hard to meet the real-time requirement of practical systems. Recently, OpenAI proposes Multi-Agent Deep Deterministic Policy Gradient algorithm (MADDPG), which can be used for centralized training but decentralized execution in multi-agent environments. We examine the method in our constructed swarm confrontation environment and find that it is not easy to deal with complex scenarios. We propose two improved training methods, scenario-transfer training and self-play training, which greatly enhance the performance of MADDPG. Experimental results show that the scenario-transfer training accelerate the convergence speed by 50%, and the self-play training increases the winning rate of MADDPG from 42% to 96%.

Keywords: Swarm confrontation · Multiple reinforcement learning · Transfer leaning · Self-play

1 Introduction

The swarm confrontation problem is a challenging task, which has attracted many interests [1–3]. However it is difficult to develop an effective strategy as the combat process is dynamic and uncertain. For a long time, people try to summarized human knowledge to find tactical rules for such system. However, the knowledge that people can accumulate are limited after all. When the constraint conditions of a scenario are unknown, formulating perfect rules is also a hard work.

In recent years, reinforcement learning has gained great success in single-agent confrontation environment, for example, in Go game [4] and Atari games [5]. However, traditional reinforcement learning methods, such as Q-learning [6]

© Springer Nature Switzerland AG 2019
H. Yu et al. (Eds.): ICIRA 2019, LNAI 11742, pp. 533–543, 2019.
https://doi.org/10.1007/978-3-030-27535-8_48

and Policy Gradient Learning [7], are not suitable for multi-agent environments. Firstly, with the number of agents increasing, the state-action space expands exponentially, resulting in the curse of dimensionality. Secondly, in the multi-agent environment, all agents learn at the same time. When the strategy of one agent changes, the optimal strategy of other agents may also change, which will affect the convergence of the algorithm [8]. In order to solve the problem, researchers extend reinforcement learning to multi-agent setting. The most common practice is to assign the single-version reinforcement learning method such as Q-learning to each agent [9]. Tampuu et al. [10] used the DQN algorithm instead of Q-learning algorithm to train each agent individually. However, the separate training mechanism does not consider the cooperation and the competition among multiple agents. In addition, these algorithms are mainly applicable to discrete-action environment. The continuous action space is too large to explore.

Lowe et al. [11] proposes multi-agent deep deterministic policy gradient (MADDPG) algorithm, which is an extension of the DDPG algorithm. MADDPG takes the actor-critic framework, which can be used for centralized learning and decentralized execution in multi-agent environments. It allows agents to learn to collaborate and compete with each other. Although it is an advanced algorithm that can effectively cope with continuous-action problems, it has not been applied in the field of swarm confrontation at present.

In this paper we construct a swarm confrontation simulation environment which originates from multiple unmanned aerial vehicle combatant scenarios [12]. We find that MADDPG does not perform well for this kind of problems, i.e., the convergence speed is slow and the combat ability is week. Therefore, we propose two improved training methods:scenario-transfer training method and self-play training. The scenario-transfer training transfers the knowledge that agents learnt in simple scenarios to complex scenarios. The self-play training is letting the agent learn from competing itself and finally surpass itself.

With the two training methods, we make tens of thousands of training times based on the swarm confrontation environment. It is remarkable to see that the convergence speed of MADDPG is accelerated by around 50% by scenario-transfer training. Surprisingly, the winning rate of agents equipped with MADDPG in increases from 42% to 96% by the self-play training.

2   Problem Description and Modeling

2.1   Problem Description

In this paper we construct a swarm confrontation environment based on a multi-UAV combatant scenario [13]. We call an UAV as an agent in the sequel. This combatant scenario contains two teams: red team and blue team. The team which wipes out all agents in the other team will win the game. Each agent is associated with 5 properties: speed v, direction ϕ, attacking zone, unprotected zone, and position (x, y). The attacking zone is in front of the vehicle, covering a sector of θ_1-degrees. The unprotected zone is a θ_2-degree sector behind the agent.

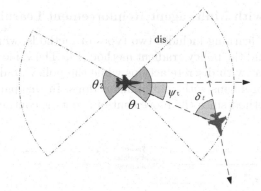

Fig. 1. An illustration of an attacker-target pair (Color figure online)

Figure 1 shows a simple scenario of an attacker (blue)-target (red) pair. At any time instance t, the relation of any attacker-target pair can be characterized by a quaternion, $s(t) = [\omega(t), \psi(t), d(t), \delta(t)]^T$. $\omega(t)$ is a distance vector between the two agents. $\psi(t)$ is the attacking angle of the attacker and $\delta(t)$ is unprotected angle of the target. $d(t)$ is the Euclidean distance between the two agents. The coordinate of the attacker i is (x_i, y_i), and that of the target is (x_j, y_j). Each element of the quaternion is computed by formulations (1a), (1b), (1c) and (1d).

$$\omega(t) = (\omega_0(t), \omega_1(t)) = (x_i - x_j, y_i - y_j) \tag{1a}$$

$$d(t) = \sqrt{(x_i - x_j)^2 + (y_i - y_j)^2} \tag{1b}$$

$$\psi(t) = \arg\cos\frac{x_i\omega_0(t) + y_i\omega_1(t)}{d_{ij}\sqrt{x_i^2 + y_i^2}} \tag{1c}$$

$$\delta(t) = \arg\cos\frac{-x_j\omega_0(t) - y_j\omega_1(t)}{d_{ij}\sqrt{x_j^2 + y_j^2}} \tag{1d}$$

In the considered scenario, each agent has the same size of attacking zone, unprotected zone, and attacking distance. A target can be killed by an attacker when three conditions are satisfied: **(a)** the distance between the attacker and the target is smaller than the distance; **(b)** the target is in the attacking zone of the attacker; **(c)** the attacker is located in the unprotected area of the target. These condition can be formulated as (2a), (2b) and (2c).

$$d_{ij} \leq d_{attacking} \tag{2a}$$

$$\delta(t) \times 180/\pi > 180 - \theta_2/2 \tag{2b}$$

$$\delta(t) \times 180/\pi < \theta_1/2 \tag{2c}$$

2.2   Modeling with Multi-agent Reinforcement Learning

The reinforcement learning includes two types of methods, which are the value function method and the policy gradient method [14]. The value function method is used for problems with discrete actions while the policy gradient method can be applicable for problems with continuous actions. In this paper we adopt the policy gradient method since the movement of agents is continuous.

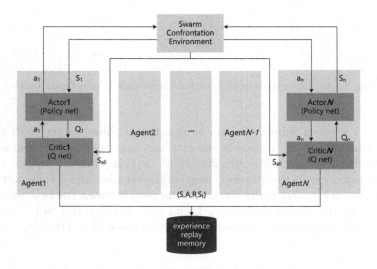

Fig. 2. The training framework.

We model the problem by the state-of-art multi-agent reinforcement learning method, MADDPG, which is a kind of policy gradient method. The training framework is shown in Fig. 2. Each agent corresponds to two neural networks, i.e., an actor network and a critic network. The actor network is used to compute the action of agent based on the observed state while the critic network is used to evaluate the action computed by the actor network which helps to improve the performance of the actor network. The experience replay buffer is used to collect experiences obtained from the environment. During the training, the input for the actor network of an agent is only the observation belonged to it. For the critic network, the input includes not only the observation of the corresponding agent but also observations of all other agents. The critic network computes the Q value for the state-action pair of the actor network, which is used as the loss value to update the parameters in the actor network. In this way, the actor network is trained with whole information (centralized training) and executed with its own observation (decentralized execution). Therefore, each actor network has a god-viewing instructor who can observe all the information to improve the strategy. With the trained model, each agent uses the actor network to interact with the environment. Even if an agent only has partial state information, it can still make a proper decision.

We use $\eta = \{\eta_1 \dots \eta_n\}$ to parameterize policy, and $\pi = \{\pi_1, \dots, \pi_n\}$ to represent policy. $J(\eta_i) = E_{s \sim \rho^\pi, a_i \sim \pi_{\eta_i}} \left[\sum_{t=0}^{\infty} \gamma^t r_{i,t} \right]$ is the cumulative expected reward for agent i. For the deterministic policy μ_{η_i}, the policy gradient for each agent i can be described as (3). In (3), $x = [o_1, \cdots, o_n]$ represents the state, $Q_i^\mu(x, a_1, \dots, a_n)$ is the Q-value.

$$\nabla_{\eta_i} J(\mu_i) = E_{x,a \sim D} \left[\nabla_{\eta_i} \mu_i(a_i|o_i) \nabla_{a_i} Q_i^\mu(x, a_1, \cdots, a_n)|_{a_i = \mu_i(o_i)} \right] \quad (3)$$

Taking experiences from the experience replay buffer, the critic network is updated based on the loss function (4).

$$\mathcal{L}(\eta_i) = \mathbb{E}_{\mathbf{x},a,r,\mathbf{x}'} \left[(Q_i^\mu(\mathbf{x}, a_1, \dots, a_N) - y)^2 \right],$$
$$where \quad y = r_i + \gamma Q_i^{\mu'}(\mathbf{x}', a_1', \dots, a_N')|_{a' = \mu_j'(o_j)} \quad (4)$$

The actor network is updated by minimizing the policy gradient of each agent which is formulated in (5).

$$\nabla_{\eta_i} J \approx \frac{1}{T} \sum_j \nabla_{\eta_i} \mu_i \left(o_i^j \right) \nabla_{a_i} Q_i^\mu \left(\mathbf{x}^j, a_1^j, \dots, a_N^j \right) \Big|_{a_i = \mu_i(o_i^j)} \quad (5)$$

3 Improved Training Techniques

3.1 Scenario-Transfer Training Method

Reinforcement learning improves the intelligence of an agent by adjusting rewards through trial and error. However, a common problem is that the agent is hard to get effective rewards when learn from scratch in a complex scenario. Inadequate reward accumulation leads to slow convergence of learning and poor final results [15].

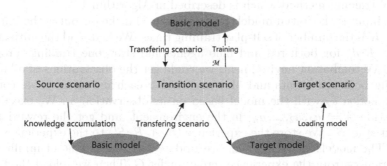

Fig. 3. The schematic diagram of scenario-transfer training.

Transfer Learning is a machine Learning method that applies experience obtained in one scenario to other scenarios [16]. In fact for the problem in this paper, it is hard to train a good model directly. Thus we consider to train a model for simple combat scenarios and then transfer the obtained experience to complex scenarios. We propose a scenario-transfer training method, of which the principle is shown in Fig. 3. The training for a task can be achieved by the training in several simple but similar transition scenarios, in which the first one is called source scenario and the last one is called target scenario. A reinforcement learning model could be firstly trained in the source scenario, then in several transition scenarios, and finally in the target scenario. The experience trained in each scenario is memorized in the model which is used as the base model for subsequent training.

In this paper we will use a two-step transfer training. We firstly train the red agents when the blue agents keep still. With the trained model, we go on training red ones for scenarios when blue ones move at the same speed with red ones. The experiment results are described in Sect. 4.

3.2 Self-play Training Method

With scenario-transfer training method, we could obtain a basic trained model. It is hard to further improve the ability of the model since it is not easy to design good transition scenarios [17]. Here we consider another training technique, self-play training method, which has been successfully applied in as Go game, chess and shogi game [4]. The main idea of self-play is to put the trained model for one agent to its opponent and train the agent to against the opponent iteratively to improve the ability of the trained model. The scenario-transfer training method and the self-play training method are complementary. The former one could provide a good initial model while the latter one could continuously improve the model [18].

Previously, the self-play training is mainly used in single-agent environments. In this paper we consider to use self-play training method for multi-agent environments. For the multi-UAV combatant problem in this paper, we propose a self-play training method which is described in Algorithm 1.

The input is the initial models for red agents and the output is the improved models. K is the number of self-play training times. We first load the initial model $Red_1, ..., Red_n$ for both red and blue agents and start one training. From the multi-UAV combatant environment, we could get the observations of all agents, including both red agents and blue agents. For each red agent i, we compute its next action a_i with the model based on its observation s_i. We execute the joint action $A = [a_1, a_2, ..., a_n]$ in the environment, and get the reward R and the next state S'. We store the experience (S, A, R, S') to the experience replay buffer. The models $Red_1, ..., Red_n$ are updated with a sample of minibatch of T experiences from the experience replay buffer G. Then we reload the trained model and start a training again.

Algorithm 1. Self-play training

Input: The initial models for red agents: $Red_1, Red_2, ..., Red_n$
Output: Generated model by self-play: $Red_1, Red_2, ..., Red_n$
   $k=1$;
   for $k <= K$ **do**
     for $i <= n$ **do**
       Load Red_i to red agent i
       Load Red_i to blue agent i
     end for
     while training not finished **do**
       for steps in each episode **do**
         for $i <= n$ **do**
           Get observations S for all agents (including red agent and blue agent)
           For each red agent i, compute action a_i
         end for
         Take the joint action $A = [a_1, a_2, ..., a_n]$
         Execute action A in the environment
         Get observation of next time S_t and reward R
         Store (S,A,R,S_t) in experience replay buffer G
         Sample a minibatch of T experiences from G
         Update $Red_1, Red_2, ..., Red_n$
       end for
     end while
   end for

---

4 Experiments

In this experiment, we construct an UAV combatant scenario (3 red agents combat with 3 blue agents) based on the multi-agent particle environment of OpenAI, which can simulate the combatant scenario described in Sect. 2. We firstly examine the performance of the original MADDPG for the UAV combatant environment, which is used as the baseline. Then we train red agents with scenario-transfer training method and self-play training method, which greatly improves the performance of MADDPG.

The actor network used in MADDPG contains 2 hidden layers with 50 hidden units each and ReLU activations. The critic network has the same hidden layers, however, the input layer contains more number of units for accepting states of all agents and all actions. The output activation for each network is a sigmoid. For the training of the neural network, we take the Adam optimizer and the learning rate is set to be 0.01. The gamma value is 0.95 and the batch-size is 1024. During training, the maximum steps for each episode is 100. The agent getting away from the combatant border will receive a negative reward -60, and the agent that wipes out an enemy will receive a positive reward 40. A combatant round, also called an episode, is terminated when red agents or blue agents are all wiped out, or the execution step in one episode exceeds 100.

4.1   The Performance of Scenario-Transfer Training

For the multi-UAV combatant task, we could firstly construct a source scenario, named as the target assignment task [19], in which blue agents do not move and do not have the attacking ability. We firstly apply MADDPG on the target assignment task. The training results are shown in Fig. 4, which shows the reward and the win rate. In the figure, each episode represents a training combatant round. The reward for each episode is the sum of rewards of all red agents. For every 100 training episode, we make a test in which red agents equipped with the trained model to combat the blue agents for 100 rounds, and record the win rate. We can see that MADDPG is convergent in the target assignment task, and achieves a good win rate (around 90%) when blue agents does not move.

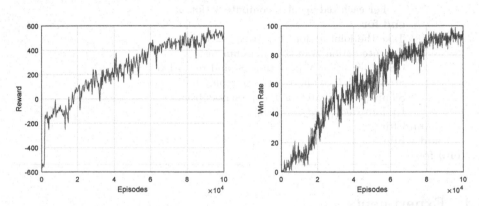

Fig. 4. Performance of baseline MADDPG for the target assignment task. (Color figure online)

We use M_1 to represent the trained model for the target assignment task. Now we consider the case when blue agents move randomly and can attack red ones, named as the random combatant task. We compare the performance of MADDPG based on scenario-transfer training and baseline MADDPG. The scenario-transfer training method firstly loads M_1 to red agents and then starts new trains. The baseline MADDPG trains red agents from the scratch. We make 100,000 training times and the results are shown in Fig. 5. As we can see, both methods are convergent for the random combatant task. It is interesting to see that the scenario-transfer training needs only 30,000 training episodes to converge while the baseline MADDPG needs around 60,000 training episodes, which means that the convergence speed is saved around 50% by the scenario-transfer training.

4.2   The Performance of Self-play Training

The scenario-transfer training already gains good performance for the random combatant task. To further improve the ability of the model, it is not easy to

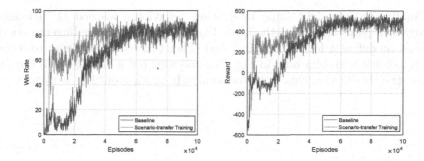

Fig. 5. Comparison of scenario-transfer training and baseline MADDPG for the random combatant task. (Color figure online)

continuously increase the complexity of the scenario. Therefore, we consider to use the self-play training method. Let M_2 represent the trained model from the scenario-transfer training. We load M_2 for both red and blue agents, and train the red agents to combat with the blue ones. The results of the first training with 100,000 episodes is shown in the first two pictures in Fig. 6. As we can see, the training process for red agents is convergent when combat with blue agents equipped with M_2. The wining rate of red agents is convergent to around 70%. This illustrates that the self-play training is a feasible way to improve the ability of the model for this multi-UAV combatant problem.

Next, we make another experiment to show the superiority of the self-play training method. We carry out 50 times of self-play ($K \doteq 50$ in Algorithm 1). Each training of self-paly contains 50,000 episodes. For every 100 episodes, we make a test in which the red agents equipped with the lasted trained model combat with blue agents equipped with M_2 for 100 rounds. The results are shown in the third picture in Fig. 6. With the increasing number of self-play times, the combatant ability of red agents becomes stronger and stronger. It is surprise to see that through self-play, the win rate of red agents could achieve 96% when combat with blue agents equipped with M_2. This is a great improvement compared to the initial win rate of 42%.

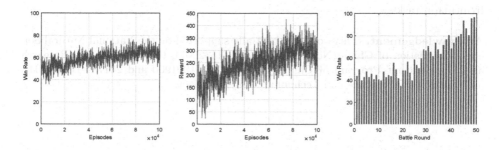

Fig. 6. Performance of self-play training. (Color figure online)

Finally, we introduce some interesting behaviours learned by red agents through self-play training method, see Fig. 7. Initially three red agents are distributed on different locations in Fig. 7(a). Then two red agents learn to cooperatively combat with blue ones in Fig. 7(b) and wipe out a blue agent in Fig. 7(c). At last the three red agents work cooperatively to wipe out the last agent.

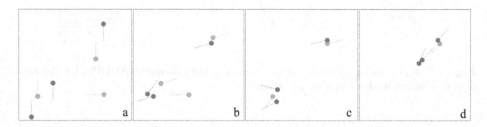

Fig. 7. The cooperative behaviour learned by red agents to combat with blue agents. (Color figure online)

5   Conclusion

In this paper we study a swarm confrontation problem with the multi-agent reinforcement learning method. By constructing a swarm confrontation environment, we show that the state-of-art method MADDPG could gain good performance for some simple scenarios. To deal with complex scenarios, we propose the scenario-transfer training method and the self-play training method. The scenario-transfer training method makes use of the model trained from simpler tasks and trains the new model on base of that, which can significantly accelerate the converge speed. The self-play training method train agents by iteratively equipping the trained model to opponents, which greatly improve the combating ability of the agent with the new model. It is also interest to see that intelligent behaviours could be leaned for agents with multi-agent reinforcement learning, which sheds a light for applying learning methods for more complex swarm confrontation tasks.

Acknowledgement. This work was partially supported by the National Natural Science Foundation of China (No. 91648204 and 61532007), the National Key Research and Development Program of China (No. 2017YFB1001900 and 2017YFB1301104), and the National Science and Technology Major Project.

References

1. Peng, P., Quan, Y., Ying, W., Yang, Y., Wang, J.: Multiagent bidirectionally-coordinated nets for learning to play StarCraft combat games (2017)
2. Besada-Portas, E., Torre, L.D.L., Cruz, J.M.D.L., Andrés-Toro, B.D.: Evolutionary trajectory planner for multiple uavs in realistic scenarios. IEEE Trans. Robot. **26**(4), 619–634 (2010)
3. Fields, M.A., Haas, E., Hill, S., Stachowiak, C., Barnes, L.: Effective robot team control methodologies for battlefield applications. In: IEEE/RSJ International Conference on Intelligent Robots & Systems (2009)
4. Silver, D., et al.: Mastering the game of go without human knowledge. Nature **550**(7676), 354–359 (2017)
5. Volodymyr, M., et al.: Human-level control through deep reinforcement learning. Nature **518**(7540), 529 (2015)
6. Watkins, C.J.C.H., Dayan, P.: Q-learning. Mach. Learn. **8**(3–4), 279–292 (1992)
7. Peters, J., Bagnell, J.A.: Policy gradient methods. Encycl. Mach. Learn. **5**(11), 774–776 (2010)
8. Buşoniu, L., Babuška, R., De Schutter, B.: Multi-agent reinforcement learning: an overview. In: Srinivasan, D., Jain, L.C. (eds.) Innovations in Multi-Agent Systems and Applications - 1. SCI, vol. 310, pp. 183–221. Springer, Heidelberg (2010). https://doi.org/10.1007/978-3-642-14435-6_7
9. Matignon, L., Laurent, G.J., Fort-Piat, N.L.: Independent reinforcement learners in cooperative Markov games: a survey regarding coordination problems. Knowl. Eng. Rev. **27**(1), 1–31 (2012)
10. Tampuu, A., et al.: Multiagent cooperation and competition with deep reinforcement learning. Plos One **12**(4), e0172395 (2017)
11. Lowe, R., Wu, Y., Tamar, A., Harb, J., Abbeel, P., Mordatch, I.: Multi-agent actor-critic for mixed cooperative-competitive environments. In: Neural Information Processing Systems (NIPS) (2017)
12. Luo, D., Yang, X.U., Zhang, J.: New progresses on UAV swarm confrontation. Sci. Technol. Rev. **35**, 26–31 (2017)
13. Yan, J., Minai, A.A., Polycarpou, M.M.: Cooperative real-time search and task allocation in UAV teams. In: IEEE Conference on Decision & Control (2003)
14. Busoniu, L., Babuska, R., De Schutter, B.: A comprehensive survey of multiagent reinforcement learning. IEEE Trans. Syst. Man Cybern. Part C **38**(2), 156–172 (2008)
15. Pan, S., Yang, Q.: A survey on transfer learning. IEEE Trans. Knowl. Data Eng. **22**, 1345–1359 (2010)
16. Taylor, M.E., Stone, P.: Transfer learning for reinforcement learning domains: a survey. J. Mach. Learn. Res. **10**(10), 1633–1685 (2009)
17. Genesereth, M.R., Love, N., Pell, B.: General game playing: overview of the aaai competition. AI Mag. **26**(2), 62–72 (2005)
18. Heinrich, J., Silver, D.: Deep reinforcement learning from self-play in imperfect-information games (2016)
19. Babel, L.: Coordinated target assignment and UAV path planning with timing constraints. J. Intell. Robot. Syst. **94**, 1–13 (2018)

Distributed Adaptive Formation Control of a Team of Aerial Robots in Cluttered Environments

Zhipeng Xie, Youlian Long, and Hui Cheng$^{(\boxtimes)}$

School of Data and Computer Science, Sun Yat-sen University,
No. 135, Xingang Xi Road, Guangzhou 510275, People's Republic of China
chengh9@mail.sysu.edu.cn

Abstract. Multi-robot system coordinated navigation in obstacle populated environment is likely to raise conflict between collision avoidance and local formation maintenance. In this paper, we explored a model predictive control based framework to achieve control of aerial robot swarm moving in a cluttered environment by introducing a local formation transform approach to reconfigure the formation topology locally, while guaranteeing collision-free with static and dynamic obstacles. Finally, the effectiveness of the proposed approach is validated by simulations and realistic experiments.

Keywords: Multi-robot system · Coordinated navigation · Formation reconfiguration · Model Predictive Control

1 Introduction

It has been witnessed that multi-robot systems (MRSs) have received extensive attention for the past several years. Compared to the individual robot, having a team of robots coordinate together to complete a mission has numerous advantages. Therefore, multi-robot coordination has a good application prospect in transportation [1,2], tracking [3], surveillance [4] and other fields. A particular type of MRS known as a *robotic swarm* is a system whose members have access to local information, neighbor-only sensing and simple reactive control laws. The locality of the information required for execution by swarm members makes robotic swarms more scalable than other types of MRS because members can be inserted or removed easily.

However, coordinating teams of mobile robots is much more challenging than controlling a single robot. Teams of robots are required to maintain a predetermined geometric shape while adapting to the environmental constraints, such

This work was supported by Major Program of Science and Technology Planning Project of Guangdong Province (2017B010116003), NSFC-Shenzhen Robotics Projects (U1613211) and Guangdong Natural Science Foundation (1614050001452, 2017A030310050).

© Springer Nature Switzerland AG 2019
H. Yu et al. (Eds.): ICIRA 2019, LNAI 11742, pp. 544–558, 2019.
https://doi.org/10.1007/978-3-030-27535-8_49

as obstacles avoidance and inter-robot collision-free. To this extent, the Model Predictive Control (MPC) [5] is an effective approach to deal with this problem.

In the existing literature, many control approaches have been put forward to solve the problems in formation control, such as, leader-follower strategy [6], behavior-based method [7] and virtual structure approach [8]. Various works have proposed successful trajectory tracking and coordinated navigation for multi-robot in the scenario with obstacles. The author in [9] proposed a method to address the cooperative motion coordination of leader-follower formations under sensory and communication constraints in polygonal obstacle environments. In [10], a neural-dynamic optimization-based NMPC is applied to trajectory tracking and formation maintenance for the multiple nonholonomic mobile robots. A similar work was presented in [11,12] where formulates a MPC based method for trajectory planning and heterogeneous formation control by the use of visual top-view feedback from MAV.

Formation reconfiguration is a challenging work and has recently aroused great interest. Local Formation Transformation (LFT) algorithm is proposed in [13] where robots can change local formation shape without impose a global reconfiguration. The method introduced in [14,15] is composed of computing optimal group formation via sequential convex optimization and assigning optimal target positions of robots, achieving formation reconfiguration and collision-free. However, the target formation shapes are predefined by human. In [16–18], authors construct a decentralized navigation functions based controller that navigate multi-robot system to the goal and formulate the reconfiguration problem as a Distributed Constraint Satisfaction Problem under local communication. These approach are evaluated only in simulation. Other approaches to formation geometry changes include scaling [19], using a transition matrix [20] and using a stress matrix [21].

In this work, we present a Nonlinear Model Predictive Control (NMPC) based distributed framework to achieve aerial robotic swarm coordinated navigation and collision-free in cluttered environment. The navigation task includes two aspects, path tracking and formation control. The waypoints, given by path planning algorithm or human being, enable leader navigating from the initial location to a final location by the use of Potential Fields (PF) as described in [22]. The remaining robots, namely followers, are controlled indirectly through interaction between neighbors while the leader is making progress towards the goal. The strategy enables a waypoint navigation of a team of robots while remains individual flexibility.

Taking into account the robotic kinematics and the physical limitations, a potential field-like term is included to the cost function to penalizes collision with obstacles. For inter-robot collision avoidance, we introduce adaptive weight assignment algorithm and graph-based dynamic formation reconfiguration approach, then robots adapt their configuration via their individual controller to achieve collision-free. The main contribution of this paper can be concluded as follows. First, a distributed framework is proposed for coordinated navigation of a team of aerial robots while collision-free is guaranteed based on NMPC computed within a neighborhood of the robots. Second, a graph-based adaptive formation transform approach activated in obstacle dense area is proposed.

The remainder paper is structured as follows. Section 2 introduces the kinematics model and some notation of graph theory. In Sect. 3, we formulate the framework of our controllers. Section 4 introduces adaptive formation transform algorithm proposed in this paper. Section 5 presents simulation and experimental results. Finally, some concluding remarks are given in Sect. 6.

2 Preliminaries

2.1 Graph Theory

Since information exchange is fundamental to cooperative control, graphs are used to represent the network topology of a group of robots. In this paper we restrict our focus on directed graphs. Therefore, we provide some definition and notation of graphs referring to [23].

A directed graph, denote by $\mathcal{D} = (\mathcal{V}, \mathcal{E})$, consists of a finite set of vertices $\mathcal{V}$ and the set of directed edges $\mathcal{E} \subset \mathcal{V} \times \mathcal{V}$. An edge (v_i, v_j) between two vertices v_i, v_j in a directed graph represents the flow of information, then v_i is said to be the tail, while v_j is its head. For each vertex $v_i \in \mathcal{V}$ we define the set of *neighbors* $\mathcal{N}_i(\mathcal{D}) \triangleq \{v_j \in \mathcal{V} | (v_j, v_i) \in \mathcal{E}\}$. The directed graph is called *weakly connected* if it is connected when viewed as a undirected graph. An edge $e \in \mathcal{E}$ of a weakly connected graph $\mathcal{D}$ is called a *critical edge* if the graph $(\mathcal{V}, \mathcal{E} \backslash \{e\})$ is disconnected. We achieve determining whether an edge $e = (v_i, v_j)$ is critical in a distributed way by using *Distributed Breadth-First Search* algorithm [24]. The *distance* of two vertices u, v of a connected graph, denoted by $\text{dist}(u, v)$ is equal to the length of the shortest path in the graph that contains both vertices.

The *adjacency matrix* of a directed graph $\mathcal{D}$ with n vertices is an $n \times n$ matrix, the element (i, j) of which is 1 if there is a directed edge (v_i, v_j) and 0 otherwise [25]. A *weighted graph* is a graph with weights assigned to each edge. The (i, j) entry ω_{ij} in the adjacency matrix of weighted directed graph represents the weights of a directed edge (v_i, v_j).

2.2 Formation Graph

Inspired by [16], a group of n mobile agents can be formulated as a directed time-varying graph $\mathcal{D}_f(t) = (\mathcal{V}, \mathcal{E}_f(t), \mathcal{S}_f(t), \mathcal{B}_f(t))$. The first agent v_1 is the leader, while the remaining $n - 1$ agents are followers. The *priority* of agent v_j is given by its distance to the v_1, i.e., $\text{dist}(v_1, v_j)$ in the initial formation graph $\mathcal{D}_f(0)$. It is assume that the edge starts from the higher priority agent to the equal or lower one, meaning that the lower priority agent may have desired separation with respect to the higher one but not *vice versa*. In addition, each agent has an unique ID for identification which is given by breadth-first search for initial formation graph $\mathcal{D}_f(0)$, as illustrated in Fig. 1.

Direction of edges indicate the direction of flow of information, that is if v_j can be perceived by v_i by means of sensory observation or direct communication at time t, then there exists an edge $(v_i, v_j) \in \mathcal{E}_f(t)$. For each $(v_i, v_j) \in \mathcal{E}_f(t), s_{ij}(t), b_{ij}(t) \in \mathbb{R}$ denotes the desired separation and desired bearing of agent v_j with respect to agent v_i at time t respectively. An agent at least has one neighbor with a desired separation and relative bearing, denoted SBC, or two neighbor with two desired separations, denoted SSC [26].

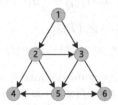

Fig. 1. Formation control graph for six agents.

3 NMPC Framework Formulation

3.1 Problem Formulation

This paper considers the coordinated waypoint navigation of aerial robotic swarm with holonomic kinematics in cluttered environments. Leader of swarm performs waypoint navigating and the followers are controlled indirectly through interaction between neighbors to achieve formation maintenance. At the meantime, robots have to avoid obstacles and prevent collision with higher or equal priority robots.

The swarm formation is formulated as formation graph proposed in Sect. 2.2, which should remain weakly connected for all time to prevent swarm splitting. In this work, we consider $\mathcal{B}_f$ is a singleton set with single element b_{12}. To guarantee the uniqueness of position, robot v_2 follows v_1 with a desired separation s_{12} and relative bearing b_{12}, which controls the rotation of formation shape, while other followers have at least two neighbors with two desired separations.

3.2 Kinematics Model

We regard the robot as a holonomic model. The robot configuration is described by the position of the center of gravity in the inertial frame $\boldsymbol{p} = [x \ y \ z]^T$, the velocity in the body frame $\boldsymbol{v} = [v_x \ v_y \ v_z]^T$, the yaw θ and body yaw rate ω. Let $\boldsymbol{x} = [\boldsymbol{p}^T, \theta]^T$ and $\boldsymbol{u} = [\boldsymbol{v}^T, \omega]^T$. The single-integrator model $\dot{\boldsymbol{x}} = f(\boldsymbol{x}, \boldsymbol{u})$ can be described as

$$\dot{x} = v_x \cos\theta - v_y \sin\theta, \ \dot{y} = v_x \sin\theta + v_y \cos\theta, \ \dot{z} = v_z, \ \dot{\theta} = \omega. \qquad (1)$$

3.3 Nonlinear Model Predictive Control

The proposed coordination navigation system is divided into two blocks. In the leader part, leader performs waypoints navigation to the goal. In the follower part, controller computes a optimal control input according to the information of local neighbors to realize swarm navigation. At each sampling instant t_0, leader attempt to solve the following cost function online:

$$\arg\min_u \int_0^T \left[\|\boldsymbol{x}(t) - \boldsymbol{x}_r(t)\|_{\boldsymbol{Q}}^2 + \|\boldsymbol{u}(t) - \boldsymbol{u}_r(t)\|_{\boldsymbol{R}}^2 + J_o(t) \right] dt$$
$$+ \|\boldsymbol{x}(T) - \boldsymbol{x}_r(T)\|_{\boldsymbol{Q}_N}^2$$
$$\text{subject to} \quad \dot{\boldsymbol{x}} = f(\boldsymbol{x}, \boldsymbol{u}); \boldsymbol{u}(t) \in \mathcal{U}; \boldsymbol{x}(t) \in \mathcal{X}; \boldsymbol{x}(0) = \boldsymbol{x}(t_0), \tag{2}$$

where $\boldsymbol{Q}, \boldsymbol{R}$ and $\boldsymbol{Q}_N$ are positive semi-definite symmetric matrix of appropriate dimensions. System equation $\dot{\boldsymbol{x}} = f(\boldsymbol{x}, \boldsymbol{u})$ is given by (1). T is prediction time horizon, $\boldsymbol{x}_r$ and $\boldsymbol{u}_r$ are reference state and reference input at time t respectively. Collision cost function $J_o(t)$ is define as

$$J_o(t) = \sum_{i \in \mathcal{O}_{obs}} \exp\left(-(\|\boldsymbol{p}(t) - \boldsymbol{p}_{o,i}(t)\| - r_s - r_{o,i})/\tau \right), \tag{3}$$

where $0 < \tau \ll 1$ is a tuning parameter, r_s is safe radius which strictly not less than the radius of robot. $\boldsymbol{p}_{o,i}(t)$ and $r_{o,i}$ are position and radius of the i-th nearest obstacles respectively. It is the first term of cost function that enables leader to make progress to the next waypoint. The second term is to make trajectory more smooth. $\mathcal{U}$ and $\mathcal{X}$ are admissible set of state variables and input variables respectively. $\mathcal{U}$ is defined as

$$\mathcal{U} = \left\{ \boldsymbol{u} \in \mathbb{R}^4 \mid \boldsymbol{u}_{min} \leq \boldsymbol{u} \leq \boldsymbol{u}_{max} \right\}. \tag{4}$$

where $\boldsymbol{u}_{min} = [v_{x,min}, v_{y,min}, v_{z,min}, w_{min}]^T$, $\boldsymbol{u}_{max} = [v_{x,max}, v_{y,max}, v_{z,max}, w_{max}]^T$. The set $\mathcal{X}$ is supposed to guarantee collision avoidance with obstacles and other robots, Thus $\mathcal{X}$ of the j-th robot can be defined as

$$\mathcal{X} = \mathcal{X}_o \cap \mathcal{X}_c, \tag{5}$$

where $\mathcal{X}_o = \{\boldsymbol{x} \in \mathbb{R}^4 \mid \|\boldsymbol{p} - \boldsymbol{p}_o\| \geq r_o + r\}$ and $\mathcal{X}_c = \{\boldsymbol{x} \in \mathbb{R}^4 \mid \|\boldsymbol{p}_i - \boldsymbol{p}_j\| \geq 2r, \forall v_i \in \mathcal{N}_i\}$ are obstacle avoidance set and inter-robot collision-free set respectively. r is the radius of robot, $\boldsymbol{p}_o$ and r_o are the position and radius of the nearest obstacle among all detected obstacles.

The formation maintenance problem for j-th follower of the formation is formulated also as an MPC problem:

$$\arg\min_u \int_0^T \left[\|\boldsymbol{x}(t) - \boldsymbol{x}_r(t)\|_{\boldsymbol{Q}}^2 + \|\boldsymbol{u}(t)\|_{\boldsymbol{R}}^2 + \sum_{i \in \mathcal{N}_j} w_{ij}(d_{ij}(t) - s_{ij}(t))^2 + J_o(t) \right] dt$$
$$+ \|\boldsymbol{x}(T) - \boldsymbol{x}_r(T)\|_{\boldsymbol{Q}_N}^2$$
$$\text{subject to} \quad \dot{\boldsymbol{x}} = f(\boldsymbol{x}, \boldsymbol{u}); \boldsymbol{u}(t) \in \mathcal{U}; \boldsymbol{x}(t) \in \mathcal{X}; \boldsymbol{x}(0) = \boldsymbol{x}(t_0), \tag{6}$$

where $d_{ij}(t) = \|\boldsymbol{p}_j(t) - \boldsymbol{p}_i(t)\|$ is the separation between i-th robot and j-th robot. Different to (2), the third term is *synchronous position term* used to penalize deviation from the desired separation s_{ij} to achieve formation maintenance, and ω_{ij} is the corresponding weight. The other terms and constraints are analogous to that of leader module.

4 Technical Approaches

4.1 Adaptive Weight Assignment

Algorithm 1. Weight Assignment Algorithm

   Result: Update the weight ω_{ij}
1   initialize $w \leftarrow j$-th column of adjacency matrix of $\mathcal{D}_f(t)$
2   **foreach** $i \in \mathcal{N}_j(\mathcal{D}_f)$ **do**
3   Find set $\mathcal{P}$ of robot within danger range of j
4   **if** $\mathcal{P} = \varnothing$ **then**
5   return
6   **else**
7   **foreach** $i \in \mathcal{P}$ **do**
8   Calculate time to collision δt_{ij}
9           $w_{ij} \leftarrow k e^{-\delta t_{ij}^2 / \sigma^2}$
10   **end**
11   **end**
12 **end**

In order to prevent inter-robot collision, a naive way is to add hard constraints to the MPC controller, with high solving complexity. In this work, we ensure that the separation between robots $\mathcal{R}_i$ and $\mathcal{R}_j$ is above a threshold to prevent collision. We consider the rate of change of this separation and ensure that relative motion between the robots do not cause this separation to decrease below the threshold rapidly. Suppose $\mathcal{R}_i$ is one of the leader of $\mathcal{R}_j$, then $\mathcal{R}_j$ has to maintain desire separation with respect to $\mathcal{R}_i$. Referring to [26], we define a metric for the rate of change of separation of $\mathcal{R}_j$ relative to $\mathcal{R}_i$. Consider the position constraint in (5), the *distance margin* is given by $l_{ij} = \|\boldsymbol{p}_i - \boldsymbol{p}_j\| - 2r$. We know

$$\dot{l}_{ij} = \frac{\partial l_{ij}}{\partial \boldsymbol{p}_i} \dot{\boldsymbol{p}}_i + \frac{\partial l_{ij}}{\partial \boldsymbol{p}_j} \dot{\boldsymbol{p}}_j. \tag{7}$$

Then $\mathcal{R}_j$ can estimate the *time to collision* with $\mathcal{R}_i$ as:

$$\delta t_{ij} = \frac{l_{ij}}{\dot{l}_{ij}}. \tag{8}$$

Since $\mathcal{R}_i$ is a leader of $\mathcal{R}_j$, therefore $\mathcal{R}_j$ knows $\mathcal{R}_i$ accurately, then $\mathcal{R}_j$ can estimate $\dot{p}_i$ by the use of a Luenberger observer or extended Kalman filter. Both the magnitude and sign of δt_{ij} can be used to identify pairs of robots $(\mathcal{R}_i, \mathcal{R}_j)$ that are on a collision course. $\delta t_{ij} = 0$ means violation has occurred. The sign of δt_{ij} tells us if $\mathcal{R}_j$ is headed towards or away from $\mathcal{R}_i$. A small magnitude of δt_{ij} means violation is about to happen. For collision avoidance, we neglect the sign and assume the magnitude is matter.

If a pair of robots $(\mathcal{R}_i, \mathcal{R}_j)$ which is adjacent in the formation graph $\mathcal{D}_f(t)$ has small magnitude of δt_{ij}, the weight of their desired separation, i.e., w_{ij} of the adjacency matrix should increase instantaneously for safety sake. If there is no edge between $\mathcal{R}_i$ and $\mathcal{R}_j$, $\mathcal{R}_j$ can estimate $\mathcal{R}_i$ by virtue of sensory observation within sensing radius. Then the edge (v_i, v_j) should be established with a large weight when the magnitude of δt_{ij} is small. As changing weights on edges triggers a different behavior, we formulate the change of weight of formation graph w_{ij} as a scaled zero-mean Gaussian density function

$$w_{ij} = k \exp\left(-\frac{\delta t_{ij}^2}{\sigma^2} \right), \tag{9}$$

where $k > 0$ is tuning parameter, the peak of the Gaussian function, and σ is a parameter define the sensitive of the time to collision δt_{ij}, the smaller the value of σ, the more sensitive to δt_{ij}.

Algorithm 1 describes the weight assignment process performed by robot j. The adjacency matrix is of global nature of which each robot has access to one column locally, as stated in step 1 of Algorithm 1. Therefore, Algorithm 1 can be executed in distributed way by each robot resulting in the change of adjacency matrix and weight of synchronous position term in (6).

4.2   Formation Reconfiguration

When navigating in cluttered or narrow environment, presence of static obstacles renders shrinkage of feasible region of controller, and even makes the problem infeasible. As an example, consider the case illustrated in Fig. 2. Given a formation graph as the one illustrated in Fig. 2(a), the left robot a (the orange one) has the possibility of colliding with right robot b (the green one), due to b's evasive maneuver toward obstacle. Intuitively, Adding a separation constraints between robot a and b can avoid this problem (see Fig. 2(b)). From the precessing discussion, it becomes apparent that reconfiguration of the formation graph is of paramount importance.

Consider the other case illustrated in Fig. 3. Given a formation graph as the one depicted in Fig. 3(a), it is difficult for the system to pass through. However, for a different formation graph and consequently different connectivity constraints and desired separations, this is no longer a case (see Fig. 3(b)).

We call the state discussed above as *conflict state*, which occurs in obstacles populated environment. The *separation distortion* of robot $\mathcal{R}_j$ is given by

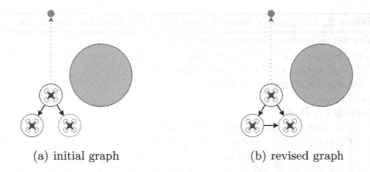

(a) initial graph   (b) revised graph

Fig. 2. An example of three robots avoid the obstacle by means of reconfiguring formation graph adaptively. (Color figure online)

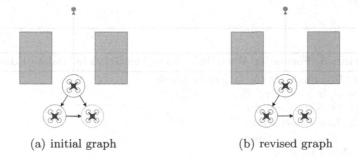

(a) initial graph   (b) revised graph

Fig. 3. An example of three robots coordinately pass through a long corridor with different formation graph.

$$\eta_{ij} = \frac{d_{ij} - s_{ij}}{s_{ij}}, \tag{10}$$

where $s_{ij} \in \mathcal{S}_f$ is desired separation with respect to $\mathcal{R}_i$, d_{ij} is the distance between robot $\mathcal{R}_j$ and robot $\mathcal{R}_i$. $\eta_{ij} = 0$ means the constraint is maintained as expected. The positive sign of η_{ij} tells us $\mathcal{R}_i$ is pulling $\mathcal{R}_j$, and opposite situation tells us $\mathcal{R}_i$ is pushing $\mathcal{R}_j$.

Suppose robot $\mathcal{R}_j$ have edge (v_i, v_j) and (v_k, v_j) in $\mathcal{D}_f$ with $\eta_{ij} < 0$ and $\eta_{kj} > \eta_{threshold}$, we define $\mathcal{R}_j$ is in conflict state. In this situation, $\mathcal{R}_j$ need to delete the edge (v_k, v_j) to slack the constraints. Another possible situation of conflict state occurs is where $\mathcal{R}_j$ observe a robot $\mathcal{R}_u$, which is not a neighbor member of $\mathcal{R}_j$ in formation graph with $\delta t_{ju} < 0$ within its sensing range. It means that an prior unknown member $\mathcal{R}_u$ is headed towards $\mathcal{R}_j$. In this situation, the edge (v_u, v_j) and desired separation s_{uj} should be established to prevent collision by maintaining a given distance.

The concrete step of formation reconfiguration process for robot $j(j \neq 1)$ is shown as Algorithms 2 and 3, which can be executed in distributed way because the requirement is neighbor members of robot j. In regard to perception part, decision of adding edges is in virtue of sensory observation with limited sensing range while deleting an edge relies on local communication.

Algorithm 2. Formation Reconfiguration Algorithm by Add Edge

Result: Reconfigurate the formation graph

1 Initialize $\mathcal{E}_f(\tau') \leftarrow \mathcal{E}_f(\tau)$, $\mathcal{S}_f(\tau') \leftarrow \mathcal{S}_f(\tau)$

2 Find set $\mathcal{P}$ of robot within sensing range of j

3 $d_j \leftarrow$ distance of v_1 and v_j of $\mathcal{D}_f(0)$

4 **if** $\mathcal{P} \neq \varnothing$ **then**

5   **foreach** $i \in \mathcal{P}$ **do**

6        $d_i \leftarrow$ distance of v_1 and v_i of $\mathcal{D}_f(0)$

7   **if** $i \notin \mathcal{N}_j(\mathcal{D}_f(\tau))$ *and* $d_i \leq d_j$ **then**

8          $\mathcal{E}_f(\tau') \leftarrow \mathcal{E}_f(\tau) \bigcup (v_i, v_j)$

9          $\mathcal{S}_f(\tau') \leftarrow \mathcal{S}_f(\tau) \bigcup s_{ij}$

10          $\mathcal{D}_f(\tau') \leftarrow (\mathcal{V}, \mathcal{E}_f(\tau'), \mathcal{S}_f(\tau'), \mathcal{B}_f(\tau'))$

11   **end**

12   **end**

13 **end**

Algorithm 3. Formation Reconfiguration Algorithm by Delete Edge

---

Result: Reconfigurate the formation graph

1 Initialize $\mathcal{E}_f(\tau') \leftarrow \mathcal{E}_f(\tau)$, $\mathcal{S}_f(\tau') \leftarrow \mathcal{S}_f(\tau)$

2 **foreach** $i \in \mathcal{N}_j(\mathcal{D}_f(\tau))$ **do**

3   Calculate distortion η_{ij}

4   **if** $\eta_{ij} > \eta_{thershold}$ **then**

5   Add i to set $\mathcal{G}$

6   **else**

7   Add i to set $\mathcal{L}$

8   **end**

9 **end**

10 **if** *exist negative element in* $\mathcal{L}$ **then**

11   **while** $\mathcal{G} \neq \varnothing$ **do**

12   exist$i \leftarrow \arg\max_{i \in \mathcal{G}} \eta_{ij}$

13   **if** (v_i, v_j) *is not a critical edge of* $\mathcal{D}_f(\tau)$ **then**

14          $\mathcal{E}_f(\tau') \leftarrow \mathcal{E}_f(\tau) \setminus (v_i, v_j)$

15          $\mathcal{S}_f(\tau') \leftarrow \mathcal{S}_f(\tau) \setminus s_{ij}$

16          $\mathcal{D}_f(\tau') \leftarrow (\mathcal{V}, \mathcal{E}_f(\tau'), \mathcal{S}_f(\tau'), \mathcal{B}_f(\tau'))$

17   **return**

18   **else**

19          $\mathcal{G} \leftarrow \mathcal{G} \setminus i$

20   **end**

21   **end**

22 **end**

5   Simulation and Experiment

5.1   Performance Metrics

We adopt two criteria similar to that proposed in [13] to evaluated the performance of the system.

$$E_D = \frac{1}{N_F} \sum_{j=1}^{N_F} \left(\frac{1}{|\mathcal{N}_j|} \sum_{i \in \mathcal{N}_j} |\eta_{ij}| \right),$$
$$E_O = \frac{1}{\pi N_F} \sum_{j \in \mathcal{N}_i} \left(\frac{1}{|\mathcal{N}_j|} \sum_{i \in \mathcal{N}_j} |\theta_i - \theta_j| \right),$$

(11)

where N_F is the number of followers. E_D assesses the formation maintenance by averaging the separation distortion of every edge in formation graph. E_O evaluates the orientation control by verifying differences in yaw between neighbors.

5.2   Simulation Results

The simulations are carried out using MATLAB R2017b on Intel i7 2.6 GHz CPU with 8 GB RAM. The efficient solver for MPC problem is generated by FORCES Pro toolkit [27]. In the simulation, the quadrotor radius is set to 0.3 m, the sensing range is set to 1.5 m and the maximum speed is taken equal to 1.0 m/s. The prediction time horizon is 0.5 s and the control interval is 0.05 s.

The first simulation is to reveal behavior of the swarm maneuvering in cluttered environment and especially encountering a dynamic obstacle. In the first scenario we consider a swarm for four quadrotors with initial adjacency matrix

$$\begin{bmatrix} 0 & 1 & 1 & 0 \\ 0 & 0 & 1 & 1 \\ 0 & 0 & 0 & 1 \\ 0 & 0 & 0 & 0 \end{bmatrix}$$

and each side is 1 m long. Swarm need to maneuver following waypoints in a severely obstacle-populated environment with a dynamic obstacle moves left and right reciprocally at 1.5 m/s (see Fig. 4(a)).

The swarm succeeds to pass through the obstacles clutter as presented in snapshots in Fig. 4(a). Approaching obstacles and robot 3 around 5.25 s, robot 2 locally modifies the formation by the means of formation reconfiguration algorithm to enlarge its free space. Similarly, edge (v_3, v_4) is disconnected by time 10.5 s. The two valleys (near 5 and 10 s) of E_D in Fig. 4(b) correspond to the two times formation reconfiguration, and two peaks (at $t = 7.4$ s and $t = 13.15$ s) correspond to the quadrotors avoid the static and dynamic obstacles.

The second scenario we consider a swarm for six quadrotors with initial formation shape as Fig. 1 in a complex polygonal environment. Swarm performs a waypoint patrolling task designed so that it is necessary for the quadrotors to change the formation as well as rotate when passing through the narrow passages.

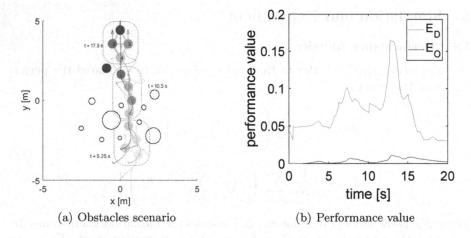

(a) Obstacles scenario   (b) Performance value

Fig. 4. Diamond formation to line formation switch to avoid obstacle.

We observe how the quadrotors cope with the complex polygonal environment in Fig. 5(a). The swarm starts in a triangular formation, which then reconfigures as snapshot shown at $t = 7.45\,\mathrm{s}$. At the waypoints ($t = 9.35\,\mathrm{s}$ and $t = 13.25\,\mathrm{s}$), the formation has to rotate around the leader in a narrow area with the diameter of the free space smaller than the diameter of the desired formation, resulting in two peaks of E_O. During negotiation of the obstacles clutter, a peak of E_D (see Fig. 5(b)) occurs but it has no significant impact on formation maintenance (<0.07).

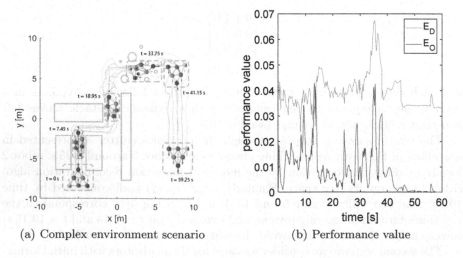

(a) Complex environment scenario   (b) Performance value

Fig. 5. Six robots navigate to a goal position in complex environment, moving along a narrow corridor and passing through an occluded obstacles.

Fig. 6. An instance of experimental environment. The radius of 1*st* obstacle is 0.3 m, that of 2*nd* and 3*rd* obstacle are both 0.5 m.

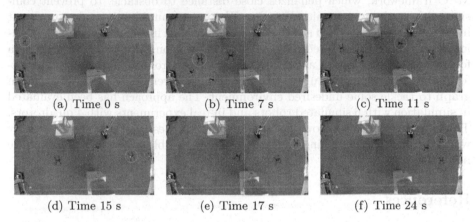

| (a) Time 0 s | (b) Time 7 s | (c) Time 11 s |

| (d) Time 15 s | (e) Time 17 s | (f) Time 24 s |

Fig. 7. Four MAVs navigate to a goal position in the other side of the room in formation. When passing through the narrow opening, they perform adaptive formation transformation to avoid the obstacles and arrive at the goal successfully.

5.3   Experimental Results

The realistic indoor experiments are performed on Parrot Bebop 2, equipped with an Raspberry Pi 3 single-board computer running Robot Operating System (ROS) and tuned controller. The MPC controller has been implemented in C++ with solver generated by ACADO toolkit [28]. The on-board computer communicates with the Bebop built-in flight controller via WiFi. OptiTrack, a motion capture and 3D tracking system, is used to measure the pose of quadrotor at 120 Hz. The flow of information between quadrotors is achieve by ROS third-party *multimaster_fkie package*[1].

In the indoor environment, three obstacles are scattered on the way of quadrotors while they navigating from the initial position to the last waypoint. The radii of obstacles are 0.3 m, 0.5 m and 0.5 m respectively as shown in Fig. 6.

We experimentally evaluates the proposed approach with four Parrot Bebop2 in the obstacles environment as shown in Fig. 6. In the experiment, four MAVs

---

[1] multimaster_fkie (http://wiki.ros.org/multimaster_fkie).

have an initial diamond formation navigating to a goal position, passing through the obstacles environment with reconfigurated formation. A serial of snapshots shown in Fig. 7 shows the process of four MAVs maintaining formation while locally avoiding three obstacles during the experiment.

6   Conclusion

In this work, we presents a MPC based formation control framework with graph based method to enable a swarm cooperative navigating in formation in an uncertain environment with static and dynamic obstacles. We combine PF into MPC framework, which penalizes close distance to obstacle, to prevent collision with static or dynamic obstacles. We present an adaptive rule to prevent inter-robot collision, which adjusts the weight of edge in formation graph dynamically according to the prediction of time to collision. Moreover, we propose a formation reconfiguration algorithm which enables robotic individual to transform the formation structure locally by adding or removing edge of formation graph to tackle some undesired environment. The approach has been evaluated in simulation with 6 simulated robots and in real experiments with 4 quadrotors. The experiment results showed that the approach preserved swarm connectivity when cooperative navigating while maintaining flexible collision-free during the negotiation.

References

1. Jiang, Q., Kumar, V.: The inverse kinematics of cooperative transport with multiple aerial robots. IEEE Trans. Robot. **29**(1), 136–145 (2013)
2. Ebel, H., Ardakani, E.S., Eberhard, P.: Distributed model predictive formation control with discretization-free path planning for transporting a load. Robot. Auton. Syst. **96**, 211–223 (2017)
3. Morbidi, F., Mariottini, G.L.: Active target tracking and cooperative localization for teams of aerial vehicles. IEEE Trans. Control Syst. Technol. **21**(5), 1694–1707 (2013)
4. Nigam, N., Bieniawski, S., Kroo, I., Vian, J.: Control of multiple UAVs for persistent surveillance: algorithm and flight test results. IEEE Trans. Control Syst. Technol. **20**(5), 1236–1251 (2012)
5. Christofides, P.D., Scattolini, R., de la Pena, D.M., Liu, J.: Distributed model predictive control: a tutorial review and future research directions. Comput. Chem. Eng. **51**, 21–41 (2013)
6. Xiao, H., Li, Z., Chen, C.P.: Formation control of leader–follower mobile robots' systems using model predictive control based on neural-dynamic optimization. IEEE Trans. Ind. Electron. **63**(9), 5752–5762 (2016)
7. Lee, G., Chwa, D.: Decentralized behavior-based formation control of multiple robots considering obstacle avoidance. Intel. Serv. Robot. **11**(1), 127–138 (2018)
8. Roy, D., Chowdhury, A., Maitra, M., Bhattacharya, S.: Multi-robot virtual structure switching and formation changing strategy in an unknown occluded environment. In: 2018 IEEE/RSJ International Conference on Intelligent Robots and Systems (IROS), pp. 4854–4861. IEEE (2018)

9. Panagou, D., Kumar, V.: Cooperative visibility maintenance for leader–follower formations in obstacle environments. IEEE Trans. Robot. **30**(4), 831–844 (2014)
10. Li, Z., Yuan, W., Chen, Y., Ke, F., Chu, X., Chen, C.P.: Neural-dynamic optimization-based model predictive control for tracking and formation of nonholonomic multirobot systems. IEEE Trans. Neural Netw. Learn. Syst. **29**, 6113–6122 (2018)
11. Saska, M., Vonásek, V., Krajník, T., Přeučil, L.: Coordination and navigation of heterogeneous UAVs-UGVs teams localized by a hawk-eye approach. In: 2012 IEEE/RSJ International Conference on Intelligent Robots and Systems (IROS), pp. 2166–2171. IEEE (2012)
12. Saska, M., Vonásek, V., Krajník, T., Přeučil, L.: Coordination and navigation of heterogeneous MAV–UGV formations localized by a 'hawk-eye'-like approach under a model predictive control scheme. Int. J. Robot. Res. (IJRR) **33**(10), 1393–1412 (2014)
13. Wasik, A., Pereira, J.N., Ventura, R., Lima, P.U., Martinoli, A.: Graph-based distributed control for adaptive multi-robot patrolling through local formation transformation. In: 2016 IEEE/RSJ International Conference on Intelligent Robots and Systems (IROS), pp. 1721–1728. IEEE (2016)
14. Alonso-Mora, J., Baker, S., Rus, D.: Multi-robot navigation in formation via sequential convex programming. In: 2015 IEEE/RSJ International Conference on Intelligent Robots and Systems (IROS), pp. 4634–4641. IEEE (2015)
15. Alonso-Mora, J., Montijano, E., Schwager, M., Rus, D.: Distributed multi-robot formation control among obstacles: a geometric and optimization approach with consensus. In: 2016 IEEE International Conference on Robotics and Automation (ICRA), pp. 5356–5363. IEEE (2016)
16. Vrohidis, C., Bechlioulis, C.P., Kyriakopoulos, K.J.: Safe decentralized and reconfigurable multi-agent control with guaranteed convergence. In: IEEE International Conference on Robotics and Automation (ICRA), pp. 267–272 (2017)
17. Vrohidis, C., Vlantis, P., Bechlioulis, C.P., Kyriakopoulos, K.J.: Reconfigurable multi-robot coordination with guaranteed convergence in obstacle cluttered environments under local communication. Auton. Robots **42**(4), 853–873 (2018)
18. Vrohidis, C., Bechlioulis, C.P., Kyriakopoulos, K.J.: Decentralized reconfigurable multi-robot coordination from local connectivity and collision avoidance specifications. IFAC-PapersOnLine **50**(1), 15798–15803 (2017)
19. Han, Z., Wang, L., Lin, Z., Zheng, R.: Formation control with size scaling via a complex Laplacian-based approach. IEEE Trans. Cybern. **46**(10), 2348–2359 (2016)
20. Desai, J.P., Ostrowski, J.P., Kumar, V.: Modeling and control of formations of nonholonomic mobile robots. IEEE Trans. Robot. Autom. **17**(6), 905–908 (2001)
21. Zhao, S.: Affine formation maneuver control of multi-agent systems. IEEE Trans. Autom. Control **63**, 4140–4155 (2018)
22. Kamel, M., Alonso-Mora, J., Siegwart, R., Nieto, J.: Robust collision avoidance for multiple micro aerial vehicles using nonlinear model predictive control. In: 2017 IEEE/RSJ International Conference on Intelligent Robots and Systems (IROS), pp. 236–243. IEEE (2017)
23. Mesbahi, M., Egerstedt, M.: Graph Theoretic Methods in Multiagent Networks, vol. 33. Princeton University Press, Princeton (2010)
24. Yoo, A., Chow, E., Henderson, K., Mclendon, W., Hendrickson, B., Catalyurek, U.: A scalable distributed parallel breadth-first search algorithm on BlueGene/L. In: Proceedings of the ACM/IEEE SC 2005 Conference on Supercomputing, p. 25 (2005)

25. Desai, J.P.: A graph theoretic approach for modeling mobile robot team formations. J. Robot. Syst. **19**(11), 511–525 (2002)

26. Fierro, R., Das, A.K.: Hybrid control of reconfigurable robot formations. In: Proceedings of the American Control Conference, vol. 6, pp. 4607–4612 (2003)

27. Domahidi, A., Zgraggen, A.U., Zeilinger, M.N., Morari, M., Jones, C.N.: Efficient interior point methods for multistage problems arising in receding horizon control. In: 2012 IEEE 51st Annual Conference on Decision and Control (CDC), pp. 668–674. IEEE (2012)

28. Houska, B., Ferreau, H.J., Diehl, M.: ACADO toolkit–an open source framework for automatic control and dynamic optimization. Optim. Control Appl. Methods **32**(3), 298–312 (2011)

Resource Planning for UAV Swarms Based on NSGA-II

Jinge Li$^{(\boxtimes)}$, Yuan Yao, Gang Yang, and Xingshe Zhou

Northwestern Polytechnical University, Xi'an 710072, China
lijinge@mail.nwpu.edu.cn

Abstract. With the development of unmanned systems, the scale and application scenarios of unmanned swarms have greatly expanded. At present, the research on swarms mainly focuses on the swarm intelligent bionic strategy and the implementation of obstacle avoidance algorithms for specific task scenarios. In the process of swarm control, due to the complex natural environment and limited number of base station connections, the size of the swarm for specific task scenarios needs to be explored and studied. Different mission scenarios have different requirements for the capability of the drone. How to organize the unmanned nodes that meet the mission capability requirements, and how large the swarm size is the best for the mission completion revenue. This article mainly addresses the above two issues. Based on the target search task, the task requirements and the capability of the UAV group are formally modeled, the mapping between the task requirements and the UAV capability is matched, and the multiobjective optimization problem is solved by the NSGA-II algorithm. The unmanned nodes that meet the mission requirements are organized to form alliances. This model is also applicable to mission scenarios where area coverage is required.

Keywords: UAV swarms · Resource planning · Target search

1 Introduction

With the development of unmanned systems, the scale of unmanned swarms has expanded from several to hundreds of thousands. At the same time, due to the complex natural environment, limited communication range and the number of base station connections and many other factors, the control of unmanned swarm has formed a challenge. However, for different scenarios, the size of the unmanned swarm is not as large as possible. In face of a specific task scenario, we pursue the goal of selecting the UAV that is suitable for the task requirements to form a coalition to execute the task and achieving the maximization of the efficiency of completing the task with the least number of nodes.

The main military applications of unmanned swarm are target search, reconnaissance, patrol, surveillance and other dangerous and complex scenarios. In the civil aspect, it is mainly used for camera measurement [8], agricultural plant

© Springer Nature Switzerland AG 2019
H. Yu et al. (Eds.): ICIRA 2019, LNAI 11742, pp. 559–568, 2019.
https://doi.org/10.1007/978-3-030-27535-8_50

protection and other labor consuming scenes. Most of the application scenarios of unmanned swarm need to be carried out in the widearea space, but different mission scenarios have different requirements for the capability and scale of agent. There is little research on how to adjust the swarm size according to specific task requirements in the available literature [6]. A task synchronization resource scheduling model based on single objective nonlinear integer programming is proposed. The scales of the target swarms are considered as the constraints for the scales of the cooperative teams to make them match in scale [4]. A distributed multiagent system in the precision agriculture scenario is proposed, which is based on the enhanced random walk mechanism with suppression return for field coverage [7]. This paper is mainly based on heuristic algorithm to reduce the turn to energy saving optimization target path planning. The comparison experiment proves that the larger the size of the single agent load area, the smaller the energy saving. However, in reality, the scale is not necessarily as large as possible, and the ideal swarm size should be set in combination with the task revenue. On the issue of resource scheduling, many jobs are using NSGA-II to solve multiobjective optimization problems [1, 10]. At present, most of the research on unmanned swarms mainly focuses on group strategy and communication topology research in specific scenarios. However, some of the reasonable assumptions of these studies have the following two problems: (1) The description of task requirements and environment is still vague. Moreover, the performance problem of the agent itself (mainly the endurance problem) is not considered, and (2) how to qualitatively and even quantitatively describe the relationship between the number of UAV swarms and the coverage efficiency. The main research contents and results of this paper are as follows:

(1) By analyzing the requirements of the target search task and the agent capability, extracting the characteristic requirements corresponding to the agent resources, and formalizing the description of the task requirements and agent capabilities. The multiobjective optimization problem is solved using the NSGA-II algorithm. Complete mapping matching of task requirements to agent resources.
(2) The cluster organization structure of "hierarchical alliance" is proposed, and the nodes that meet the task requirements are organized.

In the remainder of the paper, we formalized the task requirements and the ability matching of agents. Thereafter, in Sect. 3, we solved the resource planning problem based on NSGA-II. In Sect. 4, we mainly to instantiate the task an realize resource planning.

2   Problem Definition

This section takes the search task as the scene, defines the task requirements and agent capabilities that are required as background and reference for other sections.

In this paper, the alliance is defined as finding an optimal agent combination that meet the requirements of the task. Considering two objectives: coverage area and loads.

2.1 Definition of Search Task

This paper describes the mission area as a regular rectangle. For the target search mission, there are four requirements for the UAV capability:

- Perception: UAVs can carry a variety of sensors, such as PTZ cameras, radar rangefinders, infrared rangefinders, etc.
- Endurance: refers to the capacity of the UAV battery, Maximum flight time (minutes).
- Load capacity: maximum load weight (kg).
- Mobility: Maximum smooth flight speed under ideal conditions (m/s).

Formal Description of Task Requirements. In order to match the UAV resources suitable for specific missions, it is necessary to describe the mission requirements and quantify the abstraction capabilities as much as possible. The search mission is described in the following five tuple form:

$$SearchTask = <Task\_id, Type, Location, Time, Capability> \qquad (1)$$

- $Task\_id$ is mark.
- Type include search, reconnaissance, search and rescue, surveillance.
- $Location = <longitude, latitude, R>$, describe the center point and radius of the mission area.
- $Time = <LST(Latest\ start\ time), LET(Latest\ end\ time)>$
- $Capability = <Perception, Endurance, Loads, Mobility>$ describe the capabilities required to complete a mission.

The specific definition is shown in Table 1. The Perception field in Capability means that each bit represents a different sensor device. This field is extensible (see Table 2).

Table 1. Task description field definition

Attributes	Value
Task_id	id
Type	[search, reconnaissance...]
Location	[Latitude, longitude, R]
Time	[LST, LET]
Capability	[Perception, Endurance, Load, Mobility]

Table 2. Perceptibility field definition

Perception field							
0	0	0	0	0	1	1	1
...	...	...	...	extend	Infrared	Rangefinder	Camera

Formal Description of the UAV. Agent has a global tag. The capabilities of the agent include perception, endurance, load capacity, mobility. These four capabilities describe the heterogeneity of drones. The agent is described in the following four tuple form:

$$agent = <id, State, Capability, TaskList> \qquad (2)$$

- $State = <Location, power, load, height, speed, status, updata\_time>$ These parameters are used to indicate the current status of the agent. Where the $updata\_time$ indicates the status update time, and status indicates the mission status. The specific definition is shown in Table 3.

Table 3. UAV parameter description field definition

Attributes	Value
UAV_id	id
State	[Latitude, longitude, Power, Load, Height, Speed, Status, Updata_time]
Capability	[Perception, Endurance, Load, Mobility]
Task_list	[task_filename, ...]

2.2 Problem Modeling

The completion benefit of the task is difficult to quantify, so we mainly consider completely covering the task area with the least number of drones and meeting the load requirements of the task.

Swarm Capability. A swarm consists of a group of agent. Agent has ability vector $<Perception, Endurance, Loads, Mobility>$. The combination of swarm capabilities is not a simple overlay. The basic principles should be met between swarm capability combinations. Specifically summarized as four combinations of capabilities: superposition, union, optimal, and equivalent. About union, such as the value of perception. The mission does not require all agents to have a camera and rangefinder. Only the load can be superimposed. The mobility of an agent must match the mobility of the swarm under certain circumstances. The following picture gives a simple example (Fig. 1). The follow table gives a simple description (Table 4).

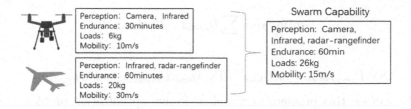

Fig. 1. Swarm capability combination example

Table 4. Swarm capability description rule

Capability	Reference	Combination method
Perception	sensor	Union
Endurance	Maximum flight time	Maximum
Loads	Maximum load weight	Add
Mobility	Maximum flight speed	Minimum

Optimize the Target. There are multiple drones in the swarm, but we need to give which drones are suitable for search tasks. This can be seen as a multiobjective optimization problem. In order to make the model compatible, the goal of optimization mainly considers two aspects.

– The drone group should be able to completely cover the mission area.
– The load of the drones meets the mission requirements.

Here we give some notations:

– $U = [Perception, Endurance, Load, Mobility]$
– $Task = [Latitude, longitude, R, Perception, Endurance, Load, Mobility, t]$
– d is the distance from the agent base to the mission area.
– L is the distance required for the full coverage of the agent.

Objective function

$$\sum_{i=0}^{n}(U_{i,mobility} \times Task_{time} - d) \geq L \tag{3}$$

$$\sum_{i=0}^{n} U_{i,load} \geq Task_{load} \tag{4}$$

Can be Converted to

$$min(f_1) = \sum_{i=0}^{n}(U_{i,mobility} \times Task_{time} - d) - L \tag{5}$$

$$min(f_2) = \sum_{i=0}^{n} U_{i,load} - Task_{load} \tag{6}$$

$$S.t. \ U_{perception} \geq 0, U_{load} \geq Task_{load}, U_{mobility} \geq Task_{mobility} \tag{7}$$

We can see this problem as a multiobjective optimization problem. In the end, we should choose UAV swarms that meets the capability requirements and has the fewest number of. The specific problem solving see the Sect. 3.

3   Resource Planning Based on NSGA-II

3.1   An Agent-Based Framework for Resource Planning

Contrasting centralized and distributed [5], hierarchical is the most suitable control structure for large scale swarms [9,12]. The layered structure is shown below Fig. 2.

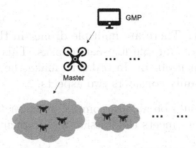

Fig. 2. GMP (Ground management planning), Master as the management of the alliance responsible for communication between the swarm and the GMP.

Hierarchical organization allows a agent fleet to accomplish more complex tasks. The master acts as the "supervisor" role. It is mainly responsible for maintaining the information of the UAV in the group, monitoring the status of the UAV, monitoring the progress of the tasks performed by the members, and coordinating the communication cooperation between the multiple alliances, constructing a partial status list, and the local master list. Report the status of UAV and the progress of task execution in the federation. The alliance has the following characteristics:

- The node with the strongest computing and storage capacity will serve as the master of the federation.
- The life cycle of the alliance begins with the start of the mission and ends with the end of the mission.

The hierarchical structure simplifies the management of agent, reduces the coordination difficulty of the agent group, improves the management control efficiency of the swarm for all UAV.

3.2 NSGA-II to Solve Multiobjective Optimization

NSGA is a fast and elitist multiobjective genetic algorithm. Here we give some notations:

- N is the length of the chromosome, which is the number of all available agents.
- P is the number of population genes.
- M is the number of objective functions.
- $G = [u_1, u_2, ..., u_N]$, $u_i \in \{1, 0\}$, G stands for the alliance, where 1 represents the drone joining the alliance.

Initial Population. First, Set the initial population in conjunction with current optimization issues. Each line represents an alliance. The solution matrix of the initial population is as follows Chrom:

$$\mathbf{Chrom_{P,N}} = \begin{bmatrix} C_{00} & \cdots\cdots & C_{0n} \\ \vdots & \vdots & \vdots & \vdots \\ C_{p0} & \cdots\cdots & C_{pn} \end{bmatrix}$$

Definition 1. *Pareto Optimal Solution.*

An alliance p, when compared with any other alliance q, its objective vector satisfies the following conditions:

$$f_i(Chrom\,[p]) \leq f_i(Chrom\,[q]), \forall i \in [1, M]$$
$$\exists i \in [1, M], f_i(Chrom\,[p]) \leq f_i(Chrom\,[q]) \tag{8}$$

For each solution we calculate two entities: (1) domination count n_p, the number of solutions which dominate the solution p, and (2) S_p, a set of solutions that the solution p dominates [1]. This requires $O(MN^2)$ comparisons. Second, each solution can be compared with every other solution in the population to find if it is dominated. Because we want to minimize the objective function, the solution that minimizes the value of all objective functions is the nondominant solution. In order to find the individuals in the next nondominated front, the solutions of the first front are discounted temporarily and the above procedure is repeated.

Diversity Preservation. In order to maintain a good solution scalability in the obtained solution set. We use a crowded comparison approach. The crowded distance of each individual is obtained by calculating the sum of the distance differences between the two individuals adjacent to each of the subobjective functions.

1. For each objective function f_m: Sorting different levels of individuals according to the objective function, f_m^{max} is the maximum value of the f_m.

$$n_d = n_d + (f_m(i + 1) - f_m(i - 1))/(f_m^{max} - f_m^{min}) \tag{9}$$

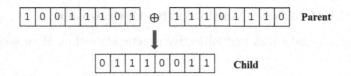

Fig. 3. Generate new progeny chromosomes based on the parent

2. Randomly select two parent genes for XOR operation to generate new Child (see Fig. 3).

Combine the parent population C_i and the child population D_i to synthesize the population R_i. Arrange each layer of individuals according to the degree of congestion from big to small. Put in the parent population in turn until the parent population is filled. And so on, until the conditions for the end of the program are met.

4 Experiment

4.1 Task Setting

Use the search task as an instance of the scene, where the specific task definition is described in the Sect. 2. The following Table 5 defines and describes the specific fields of the search task:

Table 5. Task setting

Attributes	Value
$Task\_id$	1
Type	[1]
Location	$[120.729933, 38.046055, 500]$
Time	$[2019/04/10\ 02:00:00, 2019/04/10\ 02:25:00]$
Capability	$[1, 15, 20, 8]$

The mission area is around $785,000\,\mathrm{m}^2$. Task type is search. The perceptual ability requirement is 1, which means that the drone is required to have a camera. The endurance value is 15, which means that the required drone flight time is at least 15 min. The load requirement is 20, which means the alliance needs to bear 20 kg load. 8 represents a minimum flight speed. 25 is the time window of the task. The location of the task is marked by latitude and longitude. The agent alliance we provide can cover the task area completely under the parallel scanning strategy [7]. Since the main task of the model is to plan the resources of the drone according to the task requirements, one of the basis is that the swarm in the alliance can completely cover the task area, so the target information to be searched is temporarily not considered.

4.2   UAV Resource Settings

Initialize the UAV swarm: $UAV_N = 400$, For simulation experiments, we need to set the agent parameter. $Perception \in [0, 9], Endurance \in [20, 35], load \in [0, 4], Mobility \in [8, 15]$. (The above parameter range refers to the DJI UAV) Generate initial UAV information randomly based on these parameter ranges. The initial population matrix established is as follows UAV:

$$
\mathbf{UAV} = \begin{bmatrix} Perception & Endurance & loads & Mobility \\ \vdots & \vdots & \vdots & \vdots \\ U_{i0} & U_{i1} & U_{i2} & U_{i3} \end{bmatrix}
$$

4.3   Result

According to the constraint setting of the objective function, the nodes that meet the constraint conditions are selected as available nodes. Number of agent selected according to constraints is N. Then, initialize the population solution $Chrom [P, N]$. The number of iterations is set to 40. After iteration, the final optimal solution is shown in the Fig. 4.

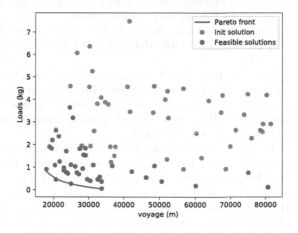

Fig. 4. Initial solution to optimal solution

The horizontal axis represents the portion of the coverage area beyond the mission requirements after the alliance capability combination. The vertical axis represents the portion of the alliance's load capacity that exceeds the mission requirements. According to the experimental results, the alliance form of the optimal solution is composed of 9 unmanned nodes. Each node is independent and different from the other nodes.

Therefore, we can analyze and model the task requirements, and based on meeting the coverage area and load requirements, we can give the appropriate swarm size.

5   Conclusion

Through the formal description of task scenario requirements and heterogeneous node resources, advanced abstract tasks are no longer just conceptual definitions. The size of the swarm must also be considered in terms of the economics of task completion. In the process of describing the mission scenario, its universality should also be considered. In this paper, the description of heterogeneous unmanned node resources is not detailed enough. Further research is needed. By encapsulating the description of node resources, it can further provide more detailed data for control of the GMP, making the whole intelligent unmanned system more controllable and controllable.

References

1. Deb, K., Pratap, A., Agarwal, S., et al.: A fast and elitist multiobjective genetic algorithm: NSGA-II. IEEE Trans. Evol. Comput. **6**(2), 182–197 (2002)
2. Dasgupta, P.: A multiagent swarming system for distributed automatic target recognition using unmanned aerial vehicles. IEEE Trans. Syst. Man Cybern. - Part A: Syst. Hum. **38**(3), 549–563 (2008)
3. Marinho, J.: Limited pre-emptive global fixed task priority. In: IEEE Real Time Systems Symposium. IEEE Computer Society (2013)
4. Mathews, E., Graf, T., Kulathunga, K.S.S.B.: Biologically inspired swarm robotic network ensuring coverage and connectivity. In: IEEE International Conference on Systems. IEEE (2012)
5. Shuyan, T., Zheng, Q., Jiankuan, X.: Collaborative task assignment scheme for multi-UAV based on swarm structure. In: Second International Conference on Intelligent Human-machine Systems and Cybernetics. IEEE Computer Society (2010)
6. Zeng, J.: Modeling for UAV resource scheduling under mission synchronization. J. Syst. Eng. Electron. **21**(5), 821–826 (2010)
7. Modares, J., Ghanei, F., Mastronarde, N., et al.: UB-ANC planner: energy efficient coverage path planning with multiple drones. In: 2017 IEEE International Conference on Robotics and Automation (ICRA). IEEE (2017)
8. Albani, D., Nardi, D., Trianni, V.: Field coverage and weed mapping by UAV swarms. In: IEEE/RSJ International Conference on Intelligent Robots and Systems. IEEE (2017)
9. Sampedro, C., Bavle, H., Sanchez-Lopez, J.L., et al.: A flexible and dynamic mission planning architecture for UAV swarm coordination. In: International Conference on Unmanned Aircraft Systems, pp. 355–363. IEEE (2016)
10. Li, H.L.H., Zhang, Q.Z.Q.: Multiobjective optimization problems with complicated pareto sets, MOEA/D and NSGA-II. IEEE Trans. Evol. Comput. **13**(2), 284–302 (2009)
11. Wei, Y., Madey, G.R., Blake, M.B.: Agent-based simulation for UAV swarm mission planning and execution. In: Agent-Directed Simulation Symposium (2013)
12. Roldán, J.J., Lansac, B., del Cerro, J., Barrientos, A.: A proposal of multi-UAV mission coordination and control architecture. Robot 2015: Second Iberian Robotics Conference. AISC, vol. 417, pp. 597–608. Springer, Cham (2016). https://doi.org/10.1007/978-3-319-27146-0_46

An Improved OLSR Protocol Based on Task Driven Used for Military UAV Swarm Network

Yuqing Jiang, Zhichao Mi$^{(\boxtimes)}$, and Hai Wang

College of Communications Engineering, Army Engineering University of PLA,
Nanjing, China
joyceginger@126.com, icemizc@126.com,
hai.wang@gmail.com

Abstract. Modern military warfare is inseparable from the tactics of UAV Ad-hoc network (UANET). Large-scale unmanned aerial vehicles (UAVs) can form an intelligence communication network to monitor, chase and surround targets. However, the network performance of UAVs is highly susceptible to the fast transformation of network topology in the battlefield environment. This paper designs and implements a task-driven OLSR protocol (Td-OLSR) for this problem. It pre-plans the tasks with time and geography, and dynamically adjusts the parameters of the routing protocol according to different tasks. Through the experiment and comparison of the Exata simulation platform, the network performance of Td-OLSR is better and more stable than that of OLSR for UANET.

Keywords: UAV Ad-hoc network · Routing protocol · Td-OLSR ·
Task driven

1 Introduction

In modern military warfare, the use of unmanned machines instead of manpower for reconnaissance and attack has been widely applied [1]. With the development of communication technology, unmanned aerial vehicles (UAVs) that connect the air and space stand out. Concealed and adaptable military UAVs can not only detect enemy situations and carry out air raids, but also command the ground army's actions, promptly issue early warnings and conduct electronic interference [2, 3]. At present, the tactical strategy of UAVs has also evolved from the decent single UAV's inspection to a group of UAVs cooperative network operation [4]. UAVs of different levels and uses are deployed in different locations in the air to form a large-scale tactical intelligence communication network [5]. It effectively helps the investigation of the battlefield intelligence, and facilitates a wide range of surveillance, pursuit and rounding up targets in the battlefield.

Flexible tactical strategies require the use of the non-central Ad Hoc network to adapt to the dynamically changing network topology of battlefield UAVs and to support the multi-hop wireless transmission [6]. Therefore, the UAV Ad-hoc network

© Springer Nature Switzerland AG 2019
H. Yu et al. (Eds.): ICIRA 2019, LNAI 11742, pp. 569–581, 2019.
https://doi.org/10.1007/978-3-030-27535-8_51

(UANET) came into being. UANET extends the Mobile Ad-hoc network (MANET) and the Vehicular Ad-hoc network (VANET) to solve the defects of centralized and cellular network communication [7]. The "bee colony" of UAVs changes the UANET's topology when it performs the specific tasks, especially in the military system. The tasks of UAVs' military system are usually pre-planned, rather than free-random walking. For example, in the Vietnam War of the 1960s, the US military used more than 3,400 "QH-50" series of UAVs and "Fire Bee" UAVs for the first time to perform tasks such as aerial reconnaissance and electronic intelligence gathering according to the prescribed network topology. It achieved outstanding results finally. During the 1991 Gulf War, the multinational forces used the UAVs' swarm tactics extensively to provide the main basis for grasping the distribution, deployment, threat assessment and damage assessment of Iraq's military targets in real time. In the Afghan war on terrorism, the UAVs' colony system achieved the first actual combat attack. In the 2003 Iraq war, the US and British forces used a total of more than a dozen UAVs on the battlefield, three times as many as those in the Afghan war. Today, the Defense Advanced Research Projects Agency's (DARPA) "Elves" project was announced in September 2015 with plans to develop the UAVs' bee colony for partially recyclable reconnaissance and electronic warfare. This UAVs' bee colony can quickly enter the undetected enemy and defeat the enemy by suppressing missile defense, cutting off communications, influencing internal security, and even possibly using computer viruses to attack enemy's data networks. Therefore, in the design process of the routing protocol in such systems, it is necessary to make full use of this information: task planning information (time point) to reduce routing overhead and adapt to the real-time and reliability requirements of network services.

The traditional routing protocol of Ad Hoc network cannot continue to guarantee good communication performance under such circumstances. The OLSR protocol is widely used in the Ad Hoc network. It is a typical proactive routing protocol and makes nodes actively discover and update the route by periodically broadcasting the packets with its own routing information. The important message packets of the OLSR protocol are Hello packets and TC packets. Hello packets are used to detect the continuity of link (neighbor broadcast), and TC packets are made up of topology control messages just like link status advertisement messages (full network broadcast) [8]. However, in the case that the network structure changes frequently, the Hello and TC messages' broadcast period that cannot be adaptively changed makes the routing table unable to update in time. It may result in the waste of resources and the degradation of network performance. In response to this challenge, we improve the traditional Optimized Link State Routing (OLSR) protocol and design a task-driven OLSR protocol (Td-OLSR) to enhance the performance in UANET. The research provides support for subsequent UAV tactical applications.

In this paper, we compare the network performance of large-scale UAVs in static and dynamic topologies through actual UAV experiments and simulations in Exata platform. The comparison includes the network response time, the packet loss rate and the network bandwidth capacity under the different broadcast period of Hello and TC messages, the different flight speed of the UAVs and the different number of nodes. After analyzing the data, we propose an improved algorithm of OLSR protocol which balances the instability of dynamic topology network. It can improve the overall network performance of the UANET, and look forward to the more advanced routing protocol for future battlefield UANET.

The main contributions are listed below:

1. We design and implement a task-driven OLSR protocol (Td-OLSR) for UANET. The improved routing protocol can dynamically adjust the interval for sending Hello and TC messages according to the changes in the task topology of the UANET. When the UAVs are moving relatively statically, it shorten the broadcast interval of Hello and TC messages to avoid the congestion of the channel and the degradation of the network performance. When the UAVs' network topology changes frequently, it increases the broadcast interval of Hello and TC messages to update the route table in time, which reduces the packet loss rate and ensures the network performance stable.

2. We use the Exata simulation platform to verify the feasibility of the improved routing protocol and compare the network performance with the original OLSR protocol. We pre-set a military tactical scenario and use time and coordinate position to plan the task topology of a large-scale UAV group. The simulation results show that the improved routing protocol can improve the throughput of the UAV nodes, reduce the end-to-end delay and packet loss rate when the network topology is relatively static or fast changing. It enhances the stability of the overall network.

The rest of this article is organized as follows. In Sect. 2, we review the current related work and analyze the direction and feasibility of the improvement. In Sect. 3, we introduce the task-driven OLSR protocol for UANET. In Sect. 4, we provide and analyze the results of Exata simulation. Finally, in Sect. 5, we summarize the development trend of the battlefield UANET and the necessary for the routing protocol improvements.

2 Related Work

The core of the OLSR protocol is to use the Multipoint reply (MPR) concept [9]. The MPR means that the source node will pick several best forwarding broadcast nodes when it's in the process of finding route with broadcast flood. The selected nodes only forward the link state information. This can reduce the flooding of redundant messages and alleviate channel pressure in large and dense networks. The OLSR protocol mainly uses Hello packets and TC packets to control packets.

2.1 Static Topology Test

We use the traditional OLSR protocol to perform network performance testing in a large-scale UAVs static topology. As a communication board of the UAV, the Raspberry Pi completes the multi-hop communication task between UAVs [10]. Since the indoor test is much less disturbing than the outdoor one and the measured data is relatively stable, the UAVs' static topology test is based on the Raspberry Pis' test. We use 40 Raspberry Pis (a microcomputer based on Linux) to test the network's bandwidth, jitter and packet loss rate for 1 to 3 hops. The network topology of indoor test is shown in Fig. 1. The test results are shown in the Fig. 2, the bandwidth decreases and the jitter and packet loss rate increases as the number of nodes or hops increases. The bandwidth, jitter and packet loss rate of interval2 are all better than that of interval1. Interval2 means Hello message interval is 2 s and interval1 means Hello message interval is 1 s. Therefore, the higher the node density is, the worse the network performance is. The larger the broadcast period of Hello and TC messages is, the better the network performance is [11].

Fig. 1. The network topology of indoor multi-node one-hop test.

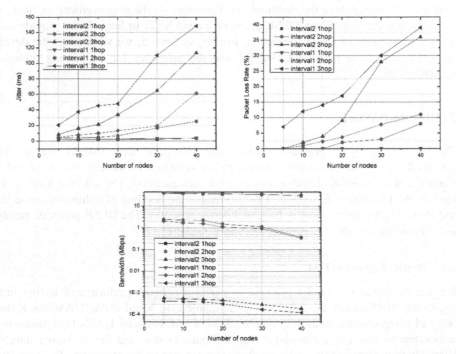

Fig. 2. Network performance of UAVs' static topology, interval2 means Hello message interval is 2 s, interval1 means Hello message interval is 1 s.

2.2 Dynamic Topology Test

We use the Exata simulation platform to perform dynamic topological motion simulation experiments of 50 UAVs randomly traveling at different speeds. The test results are shown in Fig. 3. The greater the node moving speed is, the worse the network performance is. The larger the broadcast period of Hello and TC messages is, the worse the network performance is. That because when Hello and TC control messages get more, the channel will be occupied more easily and the efficiency of sending service data will become lower. This is contrary to the test results of the static topology.

In a static topology, the topology convergence time has little effect on the network. Therefore, the larger the broadcast period of Hello and TC messages is, the better the network performance is. However, in the dynamic topology, the topology convergence time greatly affects the network performance. Therefore, in the UANET with a large topology change, it's reasonable to flexibly adjust the broadcast period of Hello and TC messages to maintain the network stability.

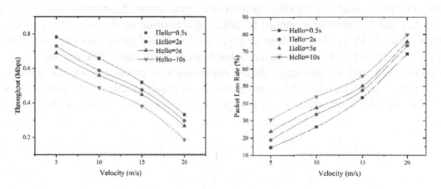

Fig. 3. Network performance of UAVs' randomly traveling.

3 Design of the Improved Routing Protocol

In the battlefield UAVs scenario, we pre-deploy the flight mission schedule for the UAVs. The design of a task-driven routing protocol is based on the calculated time between local to destination. The significance of this design is to avoid the waste of resources caused by blind operations in the battlefield, and when the UAVs group is close to the enemy target, we need to silence the radio of the UAVs group, otherwise too much broadcast information will expose our combat operations.

The design of a task-driven routing protocol is improved on the OLSR protocol because the OLSR protocol uses MPR technology and is suitable for the large mobile network, and it discovers and maintains link information by broadcasting Hello and TC messages at the fixed period over the whole network [12]. Although the operation of the original OLSR is simple, the nodes' routing table cannot be updated in time if the broadcast period of Hello and TC messages is too large when the UANET's topology changes at a high speed. That may increase the packet loss rate and reduce the communication quality. When the UANET's topology is relatively static, too small broadcast period of Hello and TC messages will cause too much redundant information to occupy the communication channel, which conflicts with the really required communication messages and weakens the network performance. Therefore, we make the following improvements to the original OLSR protocol:

3.1 Design of Mission Planning

The mission of the UAVs' group can be divided into three time slices, as shown in Fig. 4. Mission can be arbitrarily combined according to the above three types. In each type, the sending frequency of Hello and TC messages is different. We discuss the frequency strategies of the three phases with its types separately. For the first type of mission: Hello and TC messages can follow the default transmission frequency. During the period from T_0 to T_1, there are no strict time requirements for the topology changes of the UAVs' group. The task is completed as much as possible during this time because the main purpose is to discover the neighbor nodes and form a stable routing table. For the second type of mission with strict time limits, the transmission frequency of Hello and TC messages should be adjusted according to the deadline. During the period from T_1 to T_2, the topology changes of the UAVs' group has strict time limits, and the specified tasks must be completed within this time. For the third type of mission, Hello and TC messages should maximize their broadcast periods. During the period from T_2 to T_3, the UAVs' group moves in a quasi-static mode with the aim of reducing broadcast messages to avoid exposing our operations. Time can be controlled

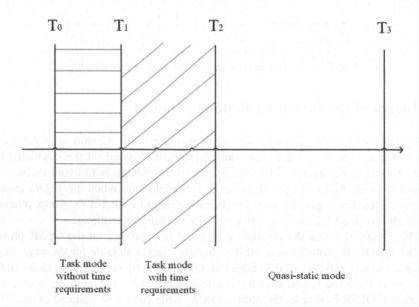

Fig. 4. Mission time slices of the UAVs' group.

by the relative position of the UAVs and the speed of them. For example, in a military war, the UAVs will conduct decentralized investigations in the early stage and there is no strict planning for the topology. At this time, the first type of mission will be performed. When the UAVs suddenly receive an instruction and must round up the target within the specified time, the second type of mission will be performed. When the UAVs complete the battle, the third type of mission is performed to conceal itself.

3.2 Specific Design of the Td-OLSR Protocol

We change the mechanism for broadcasting constant period of control messages (Hello packets and TC packets) in the original OLSR protocol. According to the known time and location information, the broadcast period of Hello and TC messages is set to three threshold modes from small to large: Hmin, Hmid and Hmax. The location information of the UAVs can be obtained by the GPS call information encapsulated in the Hello messages [13]. T is the time of UAVs' flight and obtained by the flight distance and the relative speed.

- When $T_0 < T < T_1$, the network topology of the UAVs does not need to change rapidly at this time. If the Hello and TC messages' broadcast period is too small, it will make redundant messages congest channel. If the Hello and TC messages' broadcast period is too large, it will not find enough neighbor nodes to form a network during this time. Therefore, the Hello and TC messages use the Hmid mode;

- When $T_1 < T < T_2$, the network topology of the UAVs changes drastically. If the Hello and TC messages' broadcast period is too large, it will cause the routing table cannot be updated in time, which greatly affects the network performance. Time T_2 is equal to the time which the neighbor changes are completely detected in three broadcast periods of Hello messages, plus the time when the TC messages are delivered to the farthest node.

The formula for calculating time T_2 is as follows:

$$T_2 = 3 * T_{Hello} + \frac{Distance_{max}}{C} + T_{transfer} \cdot Hop_{max} \tag{1}$$

C stands for the speed of light, and the maximum hop count and maximum distance value can be obtained by position information. Therefore, we can estimate the transmission period of Hello messages according to the time T_2. This is called Hmin mode;

- When $T_2 < T < T_3$, the network topology of the UAVs tends to be a quasi-static mode, so the Hello and TC messages' transmission frequency should not be too fast. Otherwise, the messages' conflict in the channel increases and the valid data cannot be transmitted correctly and in time. The network performance deteriorates and it is also detected by the enemy. Therefore, the Hello and TC messages adopt the Hmax mode.

The purpose of the above Td-OLSR protocol is to switch the appropriate broadcast period of Hello and TC messages in time by mastering the pre-set motion trajectory of the UAVs, so that the performance of the UANET will be optimally independent of topological changes. The traditional OLSR protocol uses a fixed frequency to broadcast control messages and is not suitable for the complex and variable military network environment.

4   Exata Simulation Experiment and Analysis

Since the UAVs' group flight experiment is difficult to implement in the actual environment, the improved routing protocol is simulated and verified in the computer by Exata5.1 simulation software. The original OLSR protocol is simulated to compare the experiment results with the improved routing protocol. The simulation experiment composes 50 UAV nodes into a wireless network. The UAVs use an omnidirectional antenna with a channel bandwidth of 2Mbps and a communication range of 340 m. The MAC layer uses the IEEE 802.11 protocol and is accessed in CSMA/CA mode. The nodes adopt a preset waypoint movement model. The nodes move along the specified path during 0 s to 15 s without strict time constraints. Then they start to change the network topology significantly within 15 s to 55 s and the topology of the mission plan must be formed within this time, such as a circle. Finally, the topology is maintained for the relatively static motion in 55 s to 85 s. In Exata, the broadcast period of Hello messages in original OLSR protocol is 2 s by default, and the broadcast period of TC messages is 5 s. We use the default value as a reference standard to determine the first two thresholds for controlling the messages' transmission period. In Hmid mode, the Hello messages' broadcast period is 2 s and the TC messages' broadcast is 5 s. In Hmax mode, the Hello messages' broadcast period is 10 s and the TC messages' broadcast period is 25 s. In the Hmin mode, we bring the data in the above scenario into (1) and calculate that the Hello messages' broadcast period is 0.5 s, and the TC messages' broadcast period is 1.5 s. Within the simulation scenario range of 1 km * 1 km, the two most remote nodes in the topology are selected for VBR service with a traffic size of 1 Mbps. Traffic is generated from the first second, the duration is 85 s, the simulation lasts for 200 s, and each routing protocol is simulated 100 times independently to compare the protocol performance. Specific experimental parameters are shown in Table 1.

Table 1. Simulation parameter configuration.

Item category	Value
Antenna type	Omnidirectional antenna
Moving model	Waypoint movement model
Communication range	340 m
Simulation scenario range	1 km * 1 km
Service data type	VBR (1 Mbps)
Channel bandwidth	2 Mbps
Number of UAVs	50

In this simulation experiment, we carry out simulation experiments on node throughput, network delay and packet loss rate under different node moving speeds. We compare the performance difference between OLSR protocol and Td-OLSR protocol. The experimental results are respectively shown in Figs. 5, 6 and 7.

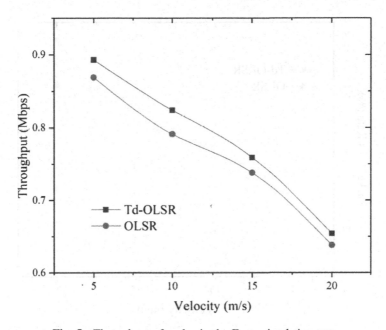

Fig. 5. Throughput of nodes in the Exata simulation test.

As is shown, on the one hand, both the OLSR protocol and the improved Td-OLSR protocol display that the network performance is worse when the nodes are flying faster. For example, when the nodes' speed is 5 m/s, the throughput of Td-OLSR is 0.893Mbps, the packet loss rate is 10.78% and the end-to-end delay is 26.15 ms. When the nodes' speed is 20 m/s, the throughput of Td-OLSR is just 0.654 Mbps, the packet loss rate is almost 61.69% and the end-to-end delay is 33.32 ms. We analyze that when the flight speed of the UAVs increases, the network topology changes more severely, which makes the network performance inevitably decline.

On the other hand, when the nodes' flight speed is the same, the overall network performance of Td-OLSR protocol is better than that of OLSR protocol. The nodes' throughput of the Td-OLSR protocol is increased by 4.17% over that of the OLSR protocol. The data packet loss rate of the Td-OLSR protocol is 42.87% lower than that of the OLSR protocol. The network delay of the Td-OLSR protocol is decreased by 8.58% compared to that of the OLSR protocol. It can be seen that in the same scenario, the node throughput of Td-OLSR protocol is larger than that of OLSR protocol and the network delay and packet loss rate are smaller. We analyze that it's because the broadcast period of Hello and TC messages is adjusted according to different task topologies. When the network topology of the UAVs is relatively stationary, increasing the transmission period can reduce invalid messages and waste of resources. When the network topology of the UAVs changes frequently, the routing table can be updated in time by decreasing the transmission period to reduce the packet loss rate and ensure the stability of the network performance.

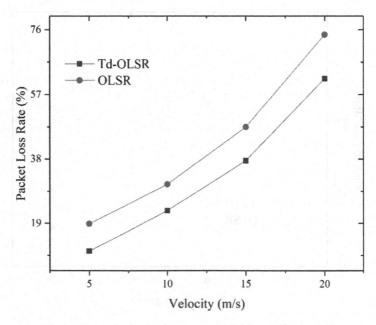

Fig. 6. Packet Loss Rate of nodes in the Exata simulation test.

After the topology of randomly distributed nodes are relatively stationary, we plan different task topologies for simulation experiments, such as circle, diamond and linear. The nodes are simulated according to the above path at the same speed and different Hello and TC messages' transmission periods. The simulation results are shown in Fig. 8. The packet loss rate of the messages and the throughput of nodes are not very different in different changing topologies, so the simulation comparison of the impact of different topological changes on the network performance is not performed. Figure 8 also from the side reflects that the network performance decreases with the increase of Hello and TC messages' transmission periods in dynamic topology.

In summary, the simulation experiments in this section prove the feasibility of Td-OLSR protocol in a large UANET. In addition, we compare the simulation performance of Td-OLSR protocol and OLSR protocol respectively by simulating military scenarios, and find the Td-OLSR protocol is better. Our future work needs to further optimize the routing protocol to enable it to adaptively sense changes in the dynamic topology of the UANET. At the same time, we also need to study the ways to overcome the impact of UAVs' flight speed on network performance.

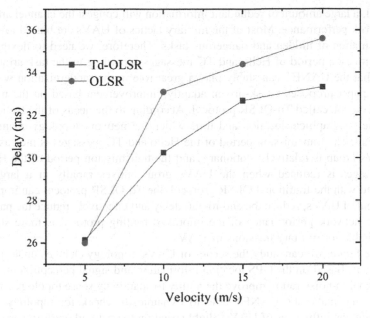

Fig. 7. Delay of nodes in the Exata simulation test.

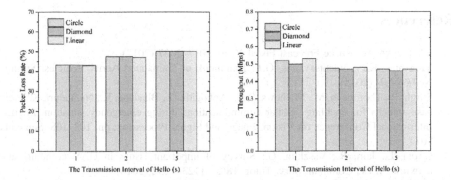

Fig. 8. Network performance of different topological changes in the Exata simulation test.

5 Conclusion and Outlook

Traditional OLSR protocol uses Hello and TC messages in the fixed period to maintain routing and detect link disruption. This method is too simple in the military tactics of the UANET. When the network topology of the UAVs group changes frequently, if the broadcast period of Hello and TC messages is too large, the routing table will not be updated in time, which leads that the lost data is significantly increased and the network performance becomes extremely unstable. When the network topology of the UAVs group needs to be relatively static, if the broadcast period of Hello and TC messages is too small, a large amount of redundant information will congest the channel and reduce the network performance. Most of the military tactics of UAVs are biased towards the implementation of hidden and dangerous tasks. Therefore, we need to flexibly adjust the transmission period of Hello and TC messages according to the task arrangement. Ensure that the UANET can stably play a great role in the modernization war.

This paper proposes a task-driven adaptive improvement based on the traditional OLSR protocol, called Td-OLSR protocol. According to the needs of the tactical tasks, preset the geographical location and time which the network topology changes from start to end. The transmission period of the Hello and TC messages is increased when the UAVs group is relatively stationary, and the transmission period of the Hello and TC messages is reduced when the UAVs group moves rapidly in a large range. Compared with the traditional OLSR protocol, the Td-OLSR protocol can improve the throughput of UAVs, reduce the end-to-end delay and effectively reduce the packet loss rate. The network performance of the improved routing protocol is more stable and more suitable for military missions of UAVs.

In the future, we can study the scenes of UAVs' topology changes under unknown air missions. Based on the GPS location information and signal perception information of the signal-to-noise ratio, improve the ability to adaptively sense topology for routing protocol, and make the UANET able to dynamically check for topology changes. Meanwhile, the influences of UAVs' flight speed on the network performance needs to be researched continuously.

References

1. FAA: FAA Aerospace Forecast Fiscal Years 2017–2037 (2017)
2. Valavanis, K.P., Vachtsevanos, G.J.: Handbook of Unmanned Aerial Vehicles. Springer, Netherlands (2015)
3. Singh, R., Thompson, M., Mathews, S.A., Agbogidi, O., Bhadane, K., Namuduri, K.: Aerial base stations for enabling cellular communications during emergency situation. In: IEEE International Conference on Vision, Image and Signal Processing, pp. 103–108, September 2017
4. Gupta, L., Jain, R., Vaszkun, G.: Survey of important issues in UAV communication networks. IEEE Commun. Surv. Tutor. 18(2), 1123–1152 (2016)
5. Noble, J., et al.: Battalion-organic electronic fires: a tactical application of commercial unmanned systems and software-defined radios. In: Defence Technology IEEE (2017)
6. Fan, X., Cai, W., Lin, J.: A survey of routing protocols for highly dynamic mobile ad hoc networks. In: 2017 IEEE 17th International Conference on Communication Technology (ICCT), Chengdu, pp. 1412–1417 (2017)
7. Bekmezci, I., Sahingoz, O.K., Temel, S.: Flying ad-hoc networks (FANETs): a survey. Ad Hoc Netw. 11(3), 1254–1270 (2013)
8. Hiyama, M., Kulla, E., Ikeda, M., Barolli, L., Takizawa, M.: Performance analysis of OLSR with ETX_ff for different HELLO packet interval in a MANET testbed. In: Park, J., Barolli, L., Xhafa, F., Jeong, H.Y. (eds.) Information Technology Convergence. LNEE, vol. 253, pp. 77–88. Springer, Dordrecht (2013). https://doi.org/10.1007/978-94-007-6996-0_9
9. Clausen, T., Jacquet, P.: RFC 3626: Optimized link state routing protocol (OLSR). IETF, October 4 2003

10. Vega, A., Lin, C.C., Swaminathan, K., et al.: Resilient, UAV-embedded real-time computing. In: 2015 IEEE 33rd International Conference on Computer Design (ICCD), New York City, NY, USA, pp. 736–739 (2015)
11. Jiang, Y., Mi, Z., Wang, H., et al.: The experiment and performance analysis of multi-node UAV ad hoc network based on swarm tactics. In: International Conference on Wireless Communications and Signal Processing (WCSP), Hangzhou (2018)
12. Ladas, A., Pavlatos, N., Weerasinghe, N., Politis, C.: Multipath routing approach to enhance resiliency and scalability in ad-hoc networks. In: 2016 IEEE International Conference on Communications (ICC), Kuala Lumpur, pp. 1–6 (2016)
13. Trotta, A., D'Andreagiovanni, F., Di Felice, M., Natalizio, E., Chowdhury, K.R.: When UAVs ride a bus: towards energy efficient city-scale video surveillance. In: IEEE International Conference on Computer Communications (2018)

A Semantic Segmentation Based Lidar SLAM System Towards Dynamic Environments

Rui Jian[1,2], Weihua Su[1,2(✉)], Ruihao Li[1,2], Shiyue Zhang[2],
Jiacheng Wei[3], Boyang Li[1,2], and Ruqiang Huang[1,2]

[1] National Innovation Institute of Defense Technology,
Academy of Military Sciences, Beijing, China
directorsu@126.com
[2] Tianjin Artificial Intelligence Innovation Center (TAIIC), Tianjin, China
[3] Department of Electrical and Computer Engineering, University of Pittsburgh
Swanson School of Engineering, 3700 O'Hara Street,
Benedum Hall of Engineering, Pittsburgh, PA 15261, USA

Abstract. The Simultaneous Localization and Mapping (SLAM) ability is essential for autonomous driving and intelligent mobile robots. A large number of methods have been proposed to solve this problem, and outliers rejection in dynamic environments plays an important role in SLAM system. In this paper, we propose a semantic segmentation based Lidar SLAM system, which introduces semantic segmentation into Lidar SLAM system and improves the accuracy of the SLAM system in dynamic environment. A CNN based deep learning method is adopted for semantic segmentation and understanding of the environment. We use semantic segmentation to get rid of dynamic outliers, and then achieve motion estimation and environment reconstruction. We evaluate our method on the public KITTI dataset, and the results show that our proposed method can efficient reject the dynamic outlier and improve the performance in terms of accuracy.

Keywords: SLAM · Semantic segmentation · Dynamic environment ·
Outliers rejection

1 Introduction

The Simultaneous Localization and Mapping problem is vitally important, especially in such an age with the growth of automatic driving. Many sensors such as mono, stereo cameras and depth sensors are widely used in SLAM research [1–4]. Many impressive methods have been proposed and achieved good performance in localization and mapping. Lidar has played an important role in depth sensor used in SLAM over the decades, especially the 3D Lidar, which would push the automatic driving industry. Lidar acquires more precise and robust data. As a result, Lidar-SLAM preformed satisfactory in odometry and mapping under certain circumstances. Many methods such as LOAM [5], LeGO-LOAM [6] gain low rotation errors and translation errors in motion estimation and environment reconstruction.

© Springer Nature Switzerland AG 2019
H. Yu et al. (Eds.): ICIRA 2019, LNAI 11742, pp. 582–590, 2019.
https://doi.org/10.1007/978-3-030-27535-8_52

In respect to those achievements, there is still some problems existed. For example, when the extraordinarily environment have some moving objects such as high speed car and the walking pedestrians, results will be affected. In other words, the accuracy of motion estimation and environment reconstruction can be easily influenced by dynamic objects, even if the mature Lidar-SLAM would suffer a little challenge.

The typical Lidar-SLAM approach for motion estimation is iterative closest point [7] through the feature point, which loses sight of the noisy point. Some new novel methods appeared. LIMO [8] present a frame which combined Lidar and camera. They used semantic label to get rid of the ground filters and vegetable landmarks. LeGO-LOAM concentrates on feature extraction and motion estimation by using segmentation method. SegMatch focuses on place recognition, loop-closrue detection and localization. None of them pays attention to the moving objects.

We address a novel frame using the sematic segmentation methodto eliminate the pose estimation error and mapping error caused by moving objects. We combine a 3D Lidar data and camera frames. We use camera data through deep learning method to detect the moving objects, then get rid of the points, which was labeling as dynamic. After that, we do motion estimation and environment reconstruction. More specifically, our contributions in this paper can be summarized as below:

1. We introduce the semantic segmentation method into the Lidar SLAM system to get rid of the dynamic outliers in the process of localization and mapping. The combination can reject dynamic objects, and at the same time yields semantic scene understanding.
2. We implement the proposed algorithm in C++ and evaluate it on then KITTI dataset. The results show that our method achieves better performance in terms of accuracy.

The paper is structured as follows: Sect. 2 provides an overview of the related works in the respects of 3D Lidar-SLAM in the rough environment. Section 3 presents the details of the whole SLAM system's framework. The experiments and evaluation of the algorithm are then described in Sect. 4. Finally, a brief conclusion and discussion are given in Sect. 5.

2   Related Work

There are thousands of engineers working on Simultaneous Localization and Mapping problems. All of them invest their time and energy to improve the accuracy and robustness of motion estimation and environment reconstruction. Here we present some representative methods of 3D Lidar-SLAM.

LeGO-LOAM presents a novel framework for real six-degree-of-freedom pose estimation with ground vehicles [6]. They take scan's point cloud and projects it onto a range image for segmentation. The segmentation point cloud is performed to filter out noise which would disturb the motion estimation. This step would discard some points which are obtained from surrounding vegetation that may yield unreliable features. They make a loop closure detection by using of the labeled point cloud to eliminate drift. They mainly aim at the surrounding noisy like tree in the forest and grasses in the ground. A better accuracy with low computational expense rewarded. LIMO is a multiple sensor framework which combined Lidar and camera. They transform the Lidar point cloud into the camera frame, and then extract the local plane around the point cloud. They segment the foreground and get rid of some points on the background tilt the estimated local plane, causing a wrong depth estimate. This step is to guarantee the feature points which lie on edges or corners be selected correctly. A high accuracy frame-to-frame odometry will be ensured in the end. They are absorbed in noisy like the vegetation landmarks by combination of Lidar and Monocular.

SegMatch [9] presents a segmentation based algorithm to perform place recognition in 3D point cloud and a real-time loop closure detection and localization to ensure an improvement of accuracy. In this method, they don't depend on a premise of 'perfect segmentation' or a suitable object of environment. They use a good compromise between local and global descriptions. A real-time loop closure detection is made to achieve an online accurate localization. Huang [10] propose a framework which uses a camera to determine orientation well and a laser range finders to estimate the scale. They estimate relative orientation from image pairs through point feature and formulate the scale estimation of iterative closet point. They constrain the data association between laser points with the use of camera information. Their approach is able to accurately estimate the ego-motion though the merging data of laser and camera. Zhang [11] and Sanjiv Singh presents a general framework for combining visual odometry and lidar odometry. They make a visual odometry in frequency, and a low frequency lidar odometry to eliminate the drift of visual odometry. They gain a higher precision than a single sensor. Above all, none of them concerns the influence of noisy like move object.

Therefore, we present a novel method for the combination of laser scan and camera data. The use of deep learning method provides information of moving objects. We aim at noises like moving car, person and so on, and we evaluate the method with experiment and gain an improvement of accuracy.

3   System Introduction

In this section, our system will be introduced in detail. There are four parts. First and the foremost, a brief introduction of the framework is essential. Second, we introduce the way to get the semantic segmentation data from the camera frame. After that, we get the target noisy in laser scan though the calibration of camera frame and laser scan. We simply introduce the way of odometry and mapping.

3.1   A Framework of Our Algorithm

Pose estimation and mapping are key capabilities of most autonomous robots in real-world applications. The LOAM has a high accuracy in KITTI [12] odometry and a satisfied performance in Lidar-SLAM. We reach higher accuracies by the way of standing on the shoulder of giants. Hence, our algorithm takes part of LOAM as main sector. We make use of the combination of a Lidar and a camera. Camera data enables us to detect dynamic objects. Lidar data provide us motion estimation and environment reconstruction. The overview of our framework is shown in Fig. 1.

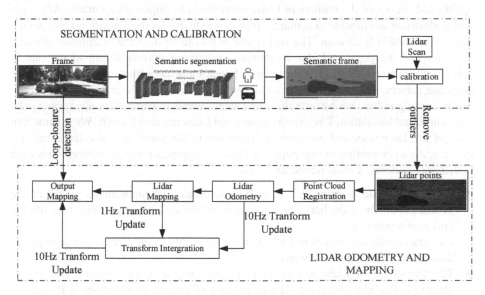

Fig. 1. The framework of our algorithm. We have the similar strategy to LOAM in Lidar odometrty and mapping thread. The segmentation and calibration thread is a new attempt to use camera data and deep learning method.

There are two threads in parallel in our algorithm: segmentation and calibration, Lidar odometry and mapping. The raw RGB frames captured by camera are processed in semantic segmentation part. After that, we calibrate the semantic frame and laser scan to get the dynamic objects in laser point cloud. The points cloud data removed outlies motivate the Lidar and mapping thread. After a Point Cloud Registration, we do a high frequency motion estimation and a low frequency environment reconstruction. We transform integration the data and then output a map.

3.2 Semantic Segmentation

In this part, we should care about the balance of real-time and accuracy, for the reason that our algorithm will be applied in real-world. There many methods in semantic segmentation era. We use a deep fully convolutional neural network architecture for semantic pixel-wise segmentation termed SegNet [12]. Because it is designed to be efficient both in terms of memory and computational time during inference. The SegNet based on caffe [13] is trained on the CityScapes [14] dataset, which has 11 class version including car and pedestrian. We adjust camera frame's size to suit for SegNet Model. In real automatic robot applications, the moving cars and pedestrians are most possibly to be dynamic objects. And we assume that feature points using in odometry and mapping located in cars and pedestrians are most likely to be outliers. Therefore, we use caffe-SegNet to detect moving cars and pedestrians in the camera data.

3.3   Calibration and Outliers Noisy

Lidar point cloud is vital in motion estimation and environment reconstruction. Hence, we should get out of the outliers in Lidar point cloud to improved accuracy. After cars and pedestrians are labeled in semantic frame, we should let the algorithm know which point is labeled in laser scan. The real world point can be detected in different sensors. We can find the point in Lidar coordinate system are corresponding to the one in camera coordinate system. Therefore, we choose Lidar coordinate system to coincide with the camera coordinate system to label the points in laser scan.

In our algorithm, we assume that the camera intrinsic parameters are known. The rotation R and translation T between camera and Lidar are also known. We assume that we get the laser scan and the camera frame are in the same time use the same frequency. As a convention of this paper, we use left uppercase superscription to indicate coordinate systems. Let us define as follows:

- Lidar coordinate system {X} is a 3D coordinate system with its origin at the geometric center of the liar. The x-axis points forwards, the y-axis points to the left and z-axis points up.
- Camera coordinate system is {Y}. The x-axis points to the right, the y-axis points down and z-axis points forward.
- The translation of Lidar to camera is T_(lidar_to_cam). The rotation of Lidar to camera is R_(lidar_to _cam). The calibration of camera to distortion is P_rect.

We project all Lidar points into the camera coordinate system on receiving as follows:

$$Y = P\_rect * R\_(lidar\_to\_cam) * T\_(lidar\_to\_cam) * X$$

We gain Lidar points' corresponding coordinate in camera coordinate system. There are some labeled pixel points and unlabeled laser points in the camera. We set a threshold value. If the Lidar points' pixel value is surrounded by labeled camera's pixel points, we give the same label to Lidar points as the pixel points. All the Lidar points should be estimated. Dynamic objects like moving car and pedestrians would be detected in laser scan. Remove all the labeled Lidar points before the Lidar odometry and mapping thread. The algorithm to calibration and outliers noisy is shown in Algorithm 1 (Table 1).

3.4   Odometry and Mapping

The Lidar odometry estimates the sensor motion between two consecutive scans. We use the same strategy as LOAM. We extract edge and flat points in Point Cloud Registration step. A transformation between two scans is found by performing point-to-edge and point-to-plane at a high frequency. Then the L-M [15] method is used to get an optimal transformation. We match features to a surrounding point cloud map after pose transformation at low frequency with the similar strategy as LOAM. If you want to know more about matching and optimization procedure, you can refer from the LOAM for detailed description.

Table 1. Algorithm 1: calibration and outliers noisy

Algorithm 1 Calibration And Outliers Noisy

Input: semantic segmentation camera frames and laser scan
Output: laser scan without dynamic objects

1 load laser scan $\{X\}$ and semantic segmentation camera frames $\{Z\}$

2 load the translation of Lidar to camera $T_{lidar\_to\_cam}$, the rotation of Lidar to camera $R_{lidar\_to\_cam}$, the calibration of camera to distortion P_{rect}.

3 Lidar points in camera coordinate system:
$$Y = P_{rect} * R_{lidar\_to\_cam} * T_{lidar\_to\_cam} * X$$

4 for i in Y

5. if $Y - Z < threshold$

6    $label\_Z = label\_Y$

7 end if

9 end for

10 $label\_Y\_dynamic\_objects = [0,0,0,0]$

---

4 Experiments

The main purpose of our algorithm is to increase the accuracy of odometry and mapping. We test our algorithm on the KITTI dataset as it is a standard dataset for this type of problems. In this section, we first introduced the KITTI dataset and my experiment computer. Then an illustration of experiment in detail is essential. We analyze the result of our experiments.

The KITTI is logged with many sensors on the top of a Volkswagenwerk vehicle in the road driving scenarios. The vehicle is mounted with color stereo cameras, a Velodyne HDL-64E Lidar and a high accuracy GPS/IMU. The calibration between color camera and Velodyne Lidar is provided. The datasets have 11 tests sequences with GPS/IMU ground truth.

Urban, Highway, Country, Country+Ubran scenes are contained in the dataset. Some of them have dynamic objects like moving cars and pedestrians are suitable for our evolution. All the experiments are performed on a computer with intel i7 CPU, 1080Ti GPU with 11 GB memory (Fig. 2).

We use the camera frame and corresponding laser scan to evaluate our algorithm. LOAM as an essential part of our framework, which is a standard of KITII odometry dataset at present. Though code is available, it is still hard to get the same result as LOAM. They have their own special engineering skills. Therefore, we make a comparison between our algorithm and the reproduction of LOAM. We compare the relative absolute transformational and rotational errors of two method to evaluate the estimation accuracy.

We use the KITTI official tools to evaluate our algorithm. As shown in Table 2, the translation error and rotation error of our algorithm are generally lower than LOAM.

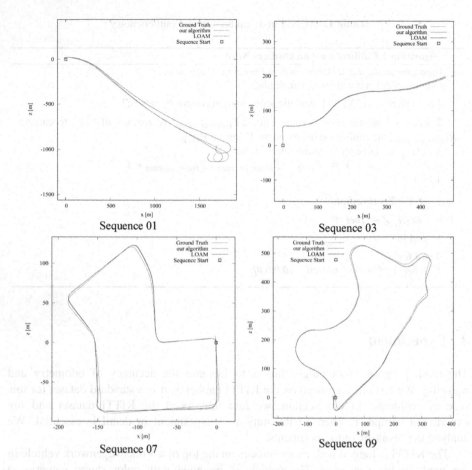

Fig. 2. As shown above, red is on behalf of ground truth, blue is our algorithm and black is LOAM. The improvement of result is macroscopic between our algorithm and LOAM, especially on highways like sequence 01. (Color figure online)

Table 2. Translation error and rotation error between our algorithm and LOAM

Sequence	Sequence01		Sequence03		Sequence07		Sequence09	
Method	Our algorithm	LOAM	Our algorithm	LOAM	Our algorithm	LOAM	Our algorithm	LOAM
Translation error %	3.2037	**3.0007**	**2.0205**	2.1983	**0.9063**	0.9402	**1.8619**	2.0018
Rotation error %	**0. 0120**	0.0135	**0.0185**	0.0193	**0.0115**	0.0121	**0.0151**	0.0160

5 Conclusion

We propose a navel framework with the combination of Lidar scan and camera frame, and make use of deep learning method to get rid of dynamic objects like moving car and pedestrians. Then we evaluate our algorithm in KITTI dataset. We gain a good improvement in some sequence; however, in some complicated sequences which have many corners, we have not get satisfied results. I think the reason is that feature points would be selected incorrectly in the corners. The current method have no recognize loop closure and relocation, our future work is to detect loop closure and relocation by the use of labeled camera frame and laser scan.

References

1. Mur-Artal, R., Tardós, J.D.: ORB-SLAM2: An open-source SLAM system for monocular, stereo, and RGB-D cameras. IEEE Transact. Robot. **33**(5), 1255–1262 (2017)
2. Lowry, S., et al.: Visual place recognition: a survey. IEEE Transact. Robot. **32**(1), 1–19 (2016)
3. Sun, Y., Liu, M., Meng, M.Q.-H.: Improving RGB-D SLAM in dynamic environments: a motion removal approach. Robot. Auton. Syst. **89**, 110–122 (2017)
4. Deschaud, J.E.: IMLS-SLAM: scan-to-model matching based on 3D data. In: IEEE International Conference on Robotics and Automation (ICRA), pp. 2480–2485 (2018)
5. Zhang, J., Singh, S.: LOAM: lidar odometry and mapping in real-time. In: Proceedings of Robotics: Science and Systems (2014)
6. Shan, T., Englot, B.: LeGO-LOAM: lightweight and ground optimized lidar odometry and mapping on variable terrain. In: 2018 IEEE/RSJ International Conference on Intelligent Robots and Systems (IROS), pp. 4758–4765. IEEE (2018)
7. Geiger, A., Lenz, P., Urtasun, R.: Are we ready for autonomous driving? The KITTI vision benchmark suite. In: Proceedings of the IEEE International Conference on Computer Vision and Pattern Recognition, pp. 3354–3361 (2012)
8. Graeter, J., Wilczynski, A., Lauer, M.: LIMO: lidar-monocular visual odometry. In: 2018 IEEE/RSJ International Conference on Intelligent Robots and Systems (IROS), pp. 7872–7879. IEEE (2018)
9. Dube, R., Dugas, D., Stumm, E., Nieto, J., Siegwart, R., Cadena, C.: SegMatch: segment based place recognition in 3D point clouds. In: Proceedings of the IEEE International Conference on Robotics and Automation (ICRA), pp. 5266–5272 (2017)
10. Huang, K.H., Stachniss, C.: Joint ego-motion estimation using a laser scanner and a monocular camera through relative orientation estimation and 1-DoF ICP. In: 2018 IEEE/RSJ International Conference on Intelligent Robots and Systems (IROS) (2018)
11. Zhang, J., Singh, S.: Visual-lidar odometry and mapping: low-drift, robust, and fast. In: 2015 IEEE International Conference on Robotics and Automation (ICRA), pp. 2174–2181. IEEE (2015)
12. Jia, Y., et al.: Caffe: Convolutional architecture for fast feature embedding, pp. 675–678 (2014)
13. Badrinarayanan, V., Kendall, A., Cipolla, R.: SegNet: a deep convolutional encoder-decoder architecture for scene segmentation. In: 2017 IEEE Transactions on Pattern Analysis and Machine Intelligence (2017)

14. Cordts, M., et al.: The cityscapes dataset for semantic urban scene understanding. In: 2016 IEEE Conference on Computer Vision and Pattern Recognition (CVPR) (2016)
15. Moré, J.J.: The Levenberg-Marquardt algorithm: implementation and theory. In: Watson, G. A. (ed.) Numerical Analysis. LNM, vol. 630, pp. 105–116. Springer, Heidelberg (1978). https://doi.org/10.1007/BFb0067700

Adaptive and Learning Control System

Fault-Tolerant Control of Robotic Manipulators With/Without Output Constraints

Ting Lei, Ye He$^{(\boxtimes)}$, Xiaoan Chen, and Xue Zhao

The State Key Laboratory of Mechanical Transmission,
Chongqing University, Chongqing 400044, China
260413967@qq.com

Abstract. This paper investigates the tracking control problem of rigid robot manipulators with asymmetric output constraints and actuation faults. To lower the rigorous requirements on the initial conditions of system output, a novel output-dependent universal barrier function (UBF) is developed such that the normally employed conservative design of converting the output constraint into tracking error related constraint is removed. In addition, such control is also able to the robot free from output constraints without changing the control structure; To solve the time-varying yet undetectable faults of robotic manipulators in the long term operation, a robust method based fault-tolerant control (FTC) is proposed such that neither fault detection and diagnosis(FDD)/fault detection and identification (FDI) nor controller reconfiguration is required. Both theoretical analysis and numerical simulation verify the effectiveness and benefits of the proposed method.

Keywords: Robotic manipulators · Output constraints ·
Actuation faults · Universal barrier function

1 Introduction

The robotic manipulator plays a pivotal role in practical systems during the past several years due to its wide applications in a variety of industrial processes, then the control of such systems is of great theoretical significance and engineering guidance value. Furthermore, note that robots belong to the multi-input multi-output (MIMO) nonlinear systems and there exist some structured and unstructured uncertainties (such as payload variation, friction, external disturbances), then it is evident that the existence of nonlinear property and uncertainty makes the controller design more complicated and more challenging.

Much effort has been made to seek advanced methods in the literature, such as computed torque control [6], adaptive control [3,5], neural network control [4], and sliding mode control [24]. However, due to the complexity and diversity of the environment in practical industrial systems, various kinds of constraints are inevitable [8,18,26], in which the form of output constraints is one of the most common constraints, i.e., there always exist certain limited operational range for the joint of uncertain robotic manipulators (i.e., Fig. 1 shows that there exist output constraints on robots), which, if

© Springer Nature Switzerland AG 2019
H. Yu et al. (Eds.): ICIRA 2019, LNAI 11742, pp. 593–604, 2019.
https://doi.org/10.1007/978-3-030-27535-8_53

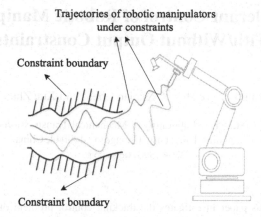

Fig. 1. Schematic illustration of the rigid robotic manipulator under output constraints.

not properly accommodated, might result in control inaccuracy, system instability, or even accident, therefore, the development of advanced control schemes for uncertain robotic manipulators with constraints has been a task of major practical interest as well as theoretical significance [16–18].

During the past several years, there are numerous methods for dealing with output constraints, including model predictive control (MPC) [19], reference governors (RG) [20], set invariance notions (SIN) [21], and the typical barrier Lyapunov Function (BLF)-based methods [7, 11–14]. However, MPC and RG based approaches require large computable burden and the SIN method is applicable to linear systems. In [17], a BLF-based intelligent method was proposed for uncertain robotic manipulators with state constraints such that such constraints can be ensured. Subsequently, by utilizing the piecewise yet asymmetric BLF (ABLF), the authors in [22] developed a ABLF-based control for uncertain robots to handle the problem of time-varying output constraints. Ref. [15] also developed an advanced method for rigid manipulators such that not only state constraints were not violated, but also the prescribed performance index was ensured. Moreover, a iterative learning control (ILC) algorithm for a class of unicycle-type mobile robots without output constraints and actuation faults was investigated [16]. Although the aforementioned BLF-based approaches deal with the problem of output constraints for robotic manipulators, it requires rigorous initial conditions. Specifically speaking, under the BLF-based methods, the original output constraints of robots are enforced indirectly by imposing transformed constraints on the errors, which leads to more conservative initial conditions (see the detailed analysis in [18]). Although Integral BLF (IBLF)-based methods [23, 27] can deal with the output constraints directly, the aforementioned developed approaches cannot be extended to discuss the general case without constraint requirements, namely, those methods cannot deal with the cases with or without output constraints in a unified manner. Although the author in [1] developed a UBF based algorithm dealing with the case with or without constraint simultaneously, such method still needs a strict initial conditions on output.

Therefore, how to directly deal with uncertain robotic manipulators with or without asymmetric output constraints in a unified manner is still an open problem.

Furthermore, it is worth mentioning that actuator failures might occur for robots. Controller reconfiguration is a common method to cope with actuator faults. In [10] a reconfigurable control scheme was proposed based on fault detection and diagnosis, such that the impacts of failures was compensated and the stability of the system was maintained. In addition, a reconfigurable fault tolerant control architecture in [24] was presented for a class of uncertain mechanical systems by using an observer technique. However, the aforementioned methods explicitly require that the faults change with time slowly to allow for fault identification and diagnosis. If the actuation faults are time-varying and completely undetectable, the fault detection and diagnosis(FDD)/fault detection and identification (FDI) and controller reconfiguration are difficult to implementation. In [2], a robust based method was developed for uncertain robotic manipulators under actuation faults such that FDD/FDI and controller reconfiguration are not required for control design. But, how to use such fault-tolerant method to cope with the problem of asymmetric output constraints is still unknown.

In this paper, we present a fault-tolerant control scheme for uncertain robotic manipulators to solve the actuation faults and output constraints simultaneously. Firstly, to reduce the requirement on initial conditions of output and to cope with asymmetric output constraints directly, borrowing from [1,29], we construct a output-dependent universal barrier function such that the normally employed design of converting the output constraint into error constraint is removed; It should be emphasized that the proposed UBF can deal with the cases with or without output constraints in a unified manner such that the process of redesigning controller is not required; Secondly, to deal with the time-varying yet undetectable faults of robotic manipulators in the long term operation, a robust method based fault-tolerant control (FTC) is proposed such that neither FDD/FDI nor controller reconfiguration is required. The system stability of robotic manipulators is established and the output constraints are not violated. In addition, the effectiveness of the developed FTC is verified by the simulation.

2 Problem Formulation and Preliminaries

2.1 System Description

We consider a general m degree of freedom robot manipulator systems under output constraints described by the following dynamics:

$$M(q)\ddot{q} + C(q,\dot{q})\dot{q} + G(q) + \tau_d = u \tag{1}$$

where $q = [q_1, \cdots, q_m] \in R^m$ are joint variables, which are required to satisfy the following asymmetric constraints:

$$-\underline{F}_{1k} < q_k < \overline{F}_{1k}, \ k = 1, \cdots, m \tag{2}$$

where $\underline{F}_{1k}$ and $\overline{F}_{1k}$ are positive constants. $M(q) \in R^{m \times m}$ denotes the inertia matrix, $C(q,\dot{q}) \in R^{m \times m}$ denotes the centripetal-coriolis matrix, $G(q) \in R^m$ represents the gravitation vector, $\tau_d \in R^m$ is the disturbance vector including unstructured and unmodelled dynamics, $u \in R^m$ is the control input[1]. In addition, some of the basic properties for robot manipulators are given as follows [5]:

(P_1) The matrix $M(q)$ is positive definite and symmetric, so is $H(q) = M^{-1}(q)$.
(P_2) The matrix norm of $M(q)$ is bounded by some positive and bounded constants λ_m and λ_M such that[2]:

$$\lambda_m \leq \|M\| \leq \lambda_M, \text{ and } \lambda_m \|x\|^2 \leq x^T M x \leq \lambda_M \|x\|^2, \; \forall x \in R^m \tag{3}$$

(P_3) The skew-symmetry property holds: $x^T(\dot{M} - 2C)x = 0$ for any $x \in R^m$; and
(P_4) There exist some positive constants, k_c, k_g, and k_d, such that for $\forall q \in R^m$, $\forall \dot{q} \in R^m$, we have

$$\|C(q,\dot{q})\| \leq k_c\|\dot{q}\|, \; \|G(q)\| \leq k_g, \; \|\tau_d\| \leq k_d \tag{4}$$

For control design, we define that $q = x_1 = [x_{11}, \cdots, x_{1m}]^T \in R^m$ and $\dot{q} = x_2 = [x_{21}, \cdots, x_{2m}]^T \in R^m$, then (1) can be rewritten as

$$\begin{cases} \dot{x}_1 = x_2 \\ \dot{x}_2 = Hu + F(\cdot) \end{cases} \tag{5}$$

where $F(\cdot) = H(-Cx_2 - G - \tau_d)$.

Furthermore, unexpected actuation faults might occur in practice during system operation, rendering the actual control input of the system u and the designed input u_d unequal and leading to the following relationship between u and u_d:

$$u = \rho(t)u_d + u_r(t) \tag{6}$$

where $\rho = \text{diag}\{\rho_j\} \in R^{m \times m}$, $j = 1, \cdots, m$, is the "healthy indicator" reflecting the effectiveness of the actuator, $u_r = [u_{r1}, \cdots, u_{rm}]^T \in R^m$ is the uncontrollable portion of actuator input. Both $\rho(t)$ and $u_r(t)$ are assumed to be unknown bounded, time-varying, and undetectable.

Substituting the expression of actuation fault as given in (6) into (7), we have

$$\begin{cases} \dot{x}_1 = x_2 \\ \dot{x}_2 = H(\rho u_d + u_r) + F(\cdot) \end{cases} \tag{7}$$

2.2 Objectives

Define the tracking error as $E = x_1 - y_d = [e_1, \cdots, e_m]^T$ with $y_d = [y_{d1}, \cdots, y_{dm}]^T$ being the desired trajectory. In this work, we seek for a fault-tolerant control approach capable of achieving the following objectives: (1) all signals in the closed-loop systems are bounded; (2) the output constraints can be directly handled and the cases with or without output constraints can be addressed in a unified manner without changing the control structure; and (3) the actuation fault can be easily compensated without the need for fault information.

To achieve such control objective, the following Assumptions are introduced.

---

[1] R denotes the set of real numbers, $R^{n \times n}$ denotes the set of $n \times n$ real matrices, and R^n denotes the set of n–dimensional real vectors.
[2] Let $\|\bullet\|$ represent the Frobenius norm of matrix ($\bullet$) and Euclidean norm of vector ($\bullet$), $|\bullet|$ be the absolute value of a real number.

Assumption 1. *The desired trajectory* $y_d(t) = [y_{d1}, \cdots, y_{dm}]^T \in R^m$ *and its derivatives* $y_d^{(i)}(t)$ $(i = 1, 2)$ *are known and bounded. In addition, the system state vectors q and $\dot{q}$ are measurable.*

Assumption 2. $\rho_i(\cdot)$ $(i = 1, \cdots, m)$ *and* $u_r(\cdot)$ *are unknown, possibly fast time-varying and unpredictable but bounded, i.e. there exist some unknown positive constants* $\underline{\rho}_i$ *and* k_r *such that*

$$0 < \underline{\rho}_i \leq \rho_i(\cdot) \leq 1, \|u_r(\cdot)\| \leq k_r \tag{8}$$

then there exists a positive constant $\underline{\rho}$ such that $0 < \underline{\rho} \leq \|\rho\| \leq 1$.

Assumption 3. *There exist positive constants* $\overline{F}_{dk}$ *and* $\underline{F}_{dk}$ *satisfying* $\overline{F}_{dk} < \overline{F}_{1k}$ *and* $\underline{F}_{dk} < \underline{F}_{1k}$ *such that* $y_{dk} \in D_{dk} := \{y_{dk} \in R \mid -\underline{F}_{dk} \leq y_{dk} \leq \overline{F}_{dk}\}$ *with* $k = 1, \cdots, m$.

3 UBF-Based Fault-Tolerant Control

3.1 Universal Barrier Function

To guarantee the asymmetric output constraints are not violated and to deal with the cases with or without output constraints in a unified manner, a output-dependent universal barrier function (UBF) is given in the following form:

$$\zeta_{1k} = \frac{\underline{F}_{1k}\overline{F}_{1k}x_{1k}}{(\underline{F}_{1k} + x_{1k})(\overline{F}_{1k} - x_{1k})} = \mu_{1k}x_{1k} \tag{9}$$

where $\mu_{1k} = \frac{\underline{F}_{1k}\overline{F}_{1k}}{(\underline{F}_{1k} + x_{1k})(\overline{F}_{1k} - x_{1k})}$. It is shown from (9) that ζ_{1k}, $k = 1, \cdots, m$, tend to infinity when x_{1k} approach the boundaries of $D_{1k} := \{-\underline{F}_{1k} < x_{1k} < \overline{F}_{1k}\}$. Therefore, it is obviously seen that, under the initial conditions x_{1k} within the subsets of D_{1k}, if $\zeta_{1k} \in L_\infty$ for $\forall t \geq 0$, one has $x_{1k} \in D_{1k}$, namely, as long as ζ_{1k}, $k = 1, \cdots, m$, are made bounded, the output constraints are not violated. Then, the problem of maintaining the output constraints boils down to ensuring the boundedness of ζ_{1k}.

Remark 1. It should be emphasized that if there are no constraints on output, one has $\underline{F}_{1k} = \overline{F}_{1k} \to \infty$. Upon utilizing the L'Hospital's rule, we obtain

$$\lim_{\underline{F}_{1k} = \overline{F}_{1k} \to \infty} \zeta_{1k} = \frac{\underline{F}_{1k}\overline{F}_{1k}x_{1k}}{(\underline{F}_{1k} + x_{1k})(\overline{F}_{1k} - x_{1k})} = x_{1k} \tag{10}$$

implying that when there are no output constraints, UBF ζ_{1k} $(i = 1, \cdots, m)$ revert to output x_{1k}, which means that the UBF proposed in (9) can be utilized to deal with the systems with and without output constraints concurrently and uniformly.

Taking the derivative of ζ_{1k} with respect to (w.r.t.) time yields

$$\dot{\zeta}_{1k} = \frac{\underline{F}_{1k}\overline{F}_{1k}(\underline{F}_{1k}\overline{F}_{1k} + x_{1k}^2)}{(\underline{F}_{1k} + x_{1k})^2(\overline{F}_{1k} - x_{1k})^2}\dot{x}_{1k} = \eta_{1k}\dot{x}_{1k}, \quad k = 1, \cdots, m \tag{11}$$

where $\eta_{1k} = \frac{E_{1k}\overline{F}_{1k}(E_{1k}\overline{F}_{1k}+x_{1k}^2)}{(E_{1k}+x_{1k})^2(\overline{F}_{1k}-x_{1k})^2}$ are computable for control design in the open sets D_{1k}.
Then (11) can be written in compact form as

$$\dot{\zeta}_1 = \eta_1 \dot{x}_1 = \eta_1 x_2 \tag{12}$$

where $\eta_1 = \text{diag}\{\eta_{1k}\} \in R^{m \times m}$ is available in the sets D_{1k}, $\zeta_1 = [\zeta_{11}, \cdots, \zeta_{1m}]^T$, and $x_2 = [x_{21}, \cdots, x_{2m}]^T$.

According to the definitions of η_{1k}, it is easily seen that there exist positive constants $\underline{\eta}_{1k}$ $(k = 1, \cdots, m)$ such that $0 < \underline{\eta}_{1k} \leq \eta_{1k} < \infty$ in the open set D_{1k}, which implies that the diagonal matrix η_1 is positive definite for $x_{1k} \in D_{1k}$, which further indicates that there exist a positive constant $\eta_{1\min}$ such that $0 < \eta_{1\min} \leq \min\{eig(\eta_1\eta_1)\}^3$.

3.2 Controller Design and Stability Analysis for Robotic Manipulators

Different from the normally used coordinate transformation in backstepping technique [28], by making use of the output-dependent UBF ζ_{1k}, a different coordinate transformation is developed as follows:

$$z_1 = \zeta_1 - \alpha_0 \tag{13}$$
$$z_2 = x_2 - \alpha_1 \tag{14}$$

where $\alpha_0 = [\alpha_{01}, \cdots, \alpha_{0m}]^T$ and $\alpha_{0k} = \frac{E_{1k}\overline{F}_{1k}y_{dk}}{(E_{1k}+y_{dk})(\overline{F}_{1k}-y_{dk})}$ are bounded and computable functions in the compact sets D_{dk}, and α_1 is the virtual controller which will be given later. Now, we carry out the control design by utilizing the backstepping technique.

Step 1. Taking the derivative of z_1 as defined in (13) yields

$$\dot{z}_1 = \eta_1 x_2 - \dot{\alpha}_0 = \zeta_1 x_2 - \eta_d \dot{y}_d \tag{15}$$

where $\eta_d = [\eta_{d1}, \cdots, \eta_{dm}]^T$ and $\eta_{dk} = \frac{E_{1k}\overline{F}_{1k}(E_{1k}\overline{F}_{1k}+y_{dk}^2)}{(E_{1k}+y_{dk})^2(\overline{F}_{1k}-y_{dk})^2}$ are computable for control design.

As $x_2 = z_2 + \alpha_1$, then (15) can be rewritten as

$$\dot{z}_1 = \eta_1(z_2 + \alpha_1) - \eta_d \dot{y}_d \tag{16}$$

Choosing the Lyapunov function candidate as $V_1 = \frac{1}{2}z_1^T z_1$, then the derivative of V_1 is

$$\dot{V}_1 = z_1^T \dot{z}_1 = z_1^T \eta_1 z_2 + z_1^T \eta_1 \alpha_1 - z_1^T \eta_d \dot{y}_d \tag{17}$$

Note that $-z_1^T \eta_d \dot{y}_d \leq \eta_{1\min}\|z_1\|^2\|\eta_d\|^2\|\dot{y}_d\|^2 + \frac{1}{4\eta_{1\min}}$, so (17) can be expressed as

$$\dot{V}_1 \leq z_1^T \eta_1 \alpha_1 + z_1^T \eta_1 z_2 + \eta_{1\min}\|z_1\|^2\|\eta_d\|^2\|\dot{y}_d\|^2 + \frac{1}{4\eta_{1\min}} \tag{18}$$

Designing the virtual controller α_1 as

$$\alpha_1 = -\left(c_1 + \|\dot{y}_d\|^2\|\eta_d\|^2\right)\eta_1 z_1 \tag{19}$$

---

^{3} $\min\{eig(\bullet)\}$ denotes the minimum eigenvalue of positive definite matrix $\bullet$.

where c_1 is a positive design parameter. Then substituting the virtual controller as defined in (19) into the first term of right-hand side of (18), one has

$$z_1^T \eta_1 \alpha_1 = -(c_1 + \|\dot{y}_d\|^2 \|\eta_d\|^2) z_1^T \eta_1 \eta_1 z_1 \le -\eta_{1\min}(c_1 + \|\dot{y}_d\|^2 \|\eta_d\|^2) \|z_1\|^2 \quad (20)$$

Therefore, (18) can further express as

$$\dot{V}_1 \le -\eta_{1\min} c_1 \|z_1\|^2 + z_1^T \eta_1 z_2 + \frac{1}{4\eta_{1\min}} \quad (21)$$

Step 2. Taking the derivative of z_2 as given in (14), we obtain

$$\dot{z}_2 = \dot{x}_2 - \dot{\alpha}_1 = H(\rho u_d + u_r - Cx_2 - G - \tau_d) - \dot{\alpha}_1 \quad (22)$$

Then the derivative of quadratic function $V_{21} = \frac{1}{2} z_2^T M z_2$ is

$$\dot{V}_{21} = z_2^T M \dot{z}_2 + \frac{1}{2} z_2^T \dot{M} z_2 = z_2^T \rho u_d + z_2^T (u_r - Cx_2 - G - \tau_d - M\dot{\alpha}_1 + \frac{1}{2}\dot{M} z_2) \quad (23)$$

According to the property (P_3) of uncertain robotic manipulators, (27) can be rewritten as

$$\dot{V}_{21} = z_2^T \rho u_d + z_2^T (u_r - Cx_2 - G - \tau_d - M\dot{\alpha}_1 + Cz_2) \quad (24)$$

Defining $V_2 = V_1 + V_{21}$, then together with (21), the derivative of V_2 is

$$\dot{V}_2 \le -\eta_{1\min} c_1 \|z_1\|^2 + \frac{1}{4\eta_{1\min}} + z_2^T \rho u_d + \Xi \quad (25)$$

where $\Xi = z_2^T (\eta_1 z_1 + u_r - Cx_2 - G - \tau_d - M\dot{\alpha}_1 + Cz_2)$.

By employing the properties (P_2) and (P_4) and utilizing the Young's inequality, we have

$$\Xi \le a\|z_2\|^2 \Phi + \frac{3}{2} \quad (26)$$

where $a = \max\{1, k_r^2, k_c^2, k_g^2, k_d^2, k_m^2, k_c\}$ is a constant and $\Phi = 3 + \|\eta_1\|^2 \|z_1\|^2 + \|x_2\|^4 + \|\dot{\alpha}_1\|^2 + \|x_2\|$ is an available function. Therefore, (25) can be further expressed as

$$\dot{V}_2 \le -\eta_{1\min} c_1 \|z_1\|^2 + \frac{1}{4\eta_{1\min}} + z_2^T \rho u_d + a\|z_2\|^2 \Phi + \frac{3}{2} \quad (27)$$

To proceed, we construct the following controller and adaptive law:

$$u_d = -(c_2 + \hat{a}\Phi) z_2 \quad (28)$$

$$\dot{\hat{a}} = \gamma \|z_2\|^2 \Phi - \sigma \hat{a}, \ \hat{a}(0) \ge 0 \quad (29)$$

where c_2, γ, and σ are positive design parameters. It should be noted that as $\gamma \|z_2\|^2 \Phi \ge 0$ for $\hat{a}(0) \ge 0$, it holds that $\hat{a}(t) \ge 0$ for $t \in [0, \infty)$.

Theorem 1. *Consider the robotic manipulators (1) with output constraints (2) and actuation fault (6). Under Assumptions 1, 2 and 3, if the fault-tolerant controller (28) with the adaptive law (29) is used, then it is ensured that (1) all signals in the closed-loop systems are bounded; and (2) the cases with or without output constraints can be handled in a unified manner.*

Proof. Choose the Lyapunov function candidate as $V = V_2 + \frac{1}{2\rho\gamma}\tilde{a}^2$, where $\tilde{a} = a - \rho\hat{a}$ is the parameter estimate error, $\gamma > 0$ is a positive constant, and ρ is an unknown constant, which will be given later. The derivative of V w.r.t time is

$$\dot{V} \leq -\eta_{1\min}c_1\|z_1\|^2 + \frac{1}{4\eta_{1\min}} + z_2^T\rho u_d + a\|z_2\|^2\Phi + \frac{3}{2} - \frac{1}{\gamma}\tilde{a}\dot{a} \qquad (30)$$

Substituting the control law as defined in (28) into (30), we have

$$\dot{V} \leq -\eta_{1\min}c_1\|z_1\|^2 + \frac{1}{4\eta_{1\min}} - (c_2 + \hat{a}\Phi)z_2^T\rho z_2 + a\|z_2\|^2\Phi + \frac{3}{2} - \frac{1}{\gamma}\tilde{a}\dot{a} \qquad (31)$$

Note that $-(c_2 + \hat{a}\Phi)z_2^T\rho z_2 \leq -\underline{\rho}(c_2 + \hat{a}\Phi)\|z_2\|^2$, then (31) can be expressed as

$$\dot{V} \leq -\eta_{1\min}c_1\|z_1\|^2 - \underline{\rho}c_2\|z_2\|^2 + \frac{1}{4\eta_{1\min}} + \tilde{a}\|z_2\|^2\Phi + \frac{3}{2} - \frac{1}{\gamma}\tilde{a}\dot{a} \qquad (32)$$

Invoking the adaptive law for $\hat{a}$ as defined in (29) into (32), we have

$$\dot{V} \leq -\eta_{1\min}c_1\|z_1\|^2 - \underline{\rho}c_2\|z_2\|^2 + \frac{1}{4\eta_{1\min}} + \frac{\sigma}{\gamma}\tilde{a}\hat{a} + \frac{3}{2} \qquad (33)$$

As $\frac{\sigma}{\gamma}\tilde{a}\hat{a} = \frac{\sigma}{\gamma\rho}\tilde{a}(a - \tilde{a}) \leq \frac{\sigma}{2\gamma\rho}(a^2 - \tilde{a}^2)$, then (33) can be described as

$$\dot{V} \leq -\eta_{1\min}c_1\|z_1\|^2 - \underline{\rho}c_2\|z_2\|^2 - \frac{\sigma}{2\gamma\rho}\tilde{a}^2 + \frac{1}{4\eta_{1\min}} + \frac{3}{2} \leq -\Gamma_1 V + \Gamma_2 \qquad (34)$$

where $\Gamma_1 = \min\{2\eta_{1\min}c_1, \frac{2\rho c_2}{\lambda_{\max}}, \sigma\} > 0$ and $\Gamma_2 = \frac{1}{4\eta_{1\min}} + \frac{3}{2} + \frac{\sigma}{2\gamma\rho}a^2 < \infty$.

From (34) it is seen that $V(t)$ is bounded for $\forall t \geq 0$, which implies that the boundedness of z_1, z_2, and $\hat{a}$ are ensured. According to the definition of z_1 as given in (13) and the expression of α, it is seen that ζ_1 is bounded. Therefore, according to (9) and for any given initial conditions $x_{1k}(0) \in D_{1k}$, $k = 1, \cdots, m$, it is concluded that $x_{1k}(t)$ remain in the open sets D_{1k} for $t \geq 0$, namely, the output constraints are not violated. Then according to the expressions of η_1 and η_d, it is ensured that such two computable functions are bounded, then it is indicated from (19) that the virtual controller α_1 is bounded. Note that $z_2 = x_2 - \alpha_1$, then it is shown that x_2 is bounded, which further implies that $\dot{\alpha}_1$ and Φ are bounded for $t \geq 0$, then it follows from (28) that the proposed fault-tolerant controller u_d is bounded.

Furthermore, recall the definition of z_1, the component elements z_{1k}, $k = 1, \cdots, m$, can be expressed as $e_k = \delta_k z_{1k}$, where e_k are component elements of the tracking error and $\delta_k = \frac{(\underline{F}_{1k} + x_{1k})(\overline{F}_{1k} - x_{1k})(\underline{F}_{1k} + y_{dk})(\overline{F}_{1k} - y_{dk})}{\underline{F}_{1k}\overline{F}_{1k}(\underline{F}_{1k}\overline{F}_{1k} + x_{1k}y_{dk})} > 0$, $k = 1, \cdots, m$. As x_{1k} are within the subsets of D_{1k}, then it indicates that there exist positive constants $\underline{\vartheta}_k$, $\overline{\vartheta}_k$, $\underline{v}_k$, and $\overline{v}_k$, such that $0 < \underline{\vartheta}_k \leq (\underline{F}_{1k} + x_{1k})(\overline{F}_{1k} - x_{1k})(\underline{F}_{1k} + y_{dk})(\overline{F}_{1k} - y_{dk}) \leq \overline{\vartheta}_k$ and $0 < \underline{v}_k \leq \underline{F}_{1k}\overline{F}_{1k}(\underline{F}_{1k}\overline{F}_{1k} + x_{1k}y_{dk}) \leq \overline{v}_k$, which implies that there exist positive constants $\underline{\delta}_k$ and $\overline{\delta}_k$ such that $0 < \underline{\delta}_k \leq \delta_k \leq \overline{\delta}_k$, then it follows that e_k are bounded. The proof is completed. $\square$

Remark 2. It is interesting to note that the FDI/PDD based fault tolerant controls normally require that the faults change with time slowly such that the fault identification and diagnosis can be obtained [9], whereas the proposed method in such paper has no such demanding conditions, making the control design more reliable.

Remark 3. Under the existing BLF-based control methods for uncertain robotic manipulators in the literature, the original output constraints are enforced indirectly by imposing transformed constraints on the tracking errors, which leads to more conservative initial conditions [15–17]. However, in this paper, with the aid of the output-dependent UBF (9), the developed control scheme is able to directly deal with output constraints without the need for converting the constraints into new bounds on tracking errors, resulting in a control scheme capable of handling wider initial conditions.

4   Simulation Verification

To show the applicability of the proposed control method, let us consider the following 2-link robotic manipulator (1) under output constraint and actuation fault and the detailed expressions are as follows [15,25]:

$$M(q) = \begin{bmatrix} p_1 + p_2 + 2p_3\cos(q_2) & p_2 + p_3\cos(q_2) \\ p_2 + p_3\cos(q_2) & p_2 \end{bmatrix};$$

$$C(q,\dot{q}) = \begin{bmatrix} -p_3\dot{q}_2\sin(q_2) & -p_3(\dot{q}_1 + \dot{q}_2)\sin(q_2) \\ p_3\dot{q}_1\sin(q_2) & 0 \end{bmatrix};$$

$$G(q) = \begin{bmatrix} p_4 g\cos(q_1) + p_5 g\cos(q_1 + q_2) \\ p_5 g\cos(q_1 + q_2) \end{bmatrix};$$

and $\tau_d = [\sin(t), \sin(t)]^T \in R^2$, where p_k $(1 \leq k \leq 5)$ are unknown system parameters and are given as $[p_1, p_2, p_3, p_4, p_5] = [2.9, 0.76, 0.87, 3.04, 0.87]$. Furthermore, for the actuation fault, the "healthy indicator" are $\rho_1 = 0.6 + 0.4\cos(\pi t)$, $\rho_2 = 0.8 + 0.2\cos(t)$ and the uncertain partition are $u_{r1} = 0.2\cos(t)$, $u_{r2} = 0.2\sin(t)$.

In this paper, the control objective is to design a fault-tolerant controller such that: (1) the output $q = x_1$ can track the desired reference signal $y_d(t) = [\sin(t), \sin(t)]^T$ as closely as possible; (2) all signals remain bounded; and (3) the output constraints x_{11} and x_{12} are within the following open sets:

$$D_{1k} = \{-\underline{F}_{1k} < x_{1k} < \overline{F}_{1k}\} \tag{35}$$

where $\underline{F}_{11} = 0.6$, $\overline{F}_{11} = 0.7$, $\underline{F}_{12} = 0.7$, and $\overline{F}_{12} = 0.8$. To complement the proposed control, we use the following initial conditions: $q_1(0) = x_1(0) = [0.4, 0.3]^T$, $q_2(0) = x_2(0) = [0,0]^T$, $\hat{a}(0) = 0$.

Test A: To verify that under the proposed control (28), the cases of output constraints and actuation faults can be handled. In such case, we select design parameters to produce similar control efforts between the proposed control with $c_1 = 5$, $c_2 =$

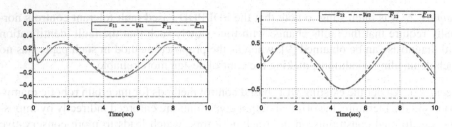

Fig. 2. The evolutions of x_{1k} and $y_{dk}, k = 1, 2$, with output constraints.

80, $\gamma = 0.001$, $\sigma = 0.1$, the simulation results are shown in Figs. 2 and 3, where Fig. 2 is the evolutions of the components of output (x_{11} and x_{12}) and desired signal (y_{d1} and y_{d2}), showing that although the actuation faults are involved in the uncertain robotic manipulators, the developed fault-tolerant control can still ensure that the output constraints are not violated. The control torques u_{d1} and u_{d2} are presented in Fig. 3.

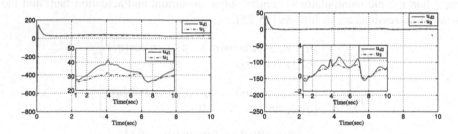

Fig. 3. The evolutions of control inputs u_{d1} and u_{d2} with output constraints.

Test B: To show that under the proposed control (28), the case without output constraints can be dealt with without changing the control structure. We use the identical controller and the same design parameters with Test A. The simulation results are shown in Figs. 4 and 5. Apparently, it is seen that under the proposed control method, all signals are still bounded without changing the control structure.

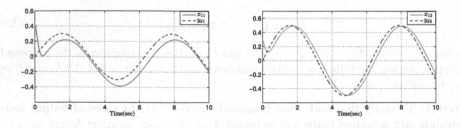

Fig. 4. The evolutions of x_{1k} and $y_{dk}, k = 1, 2$, with output constraints.

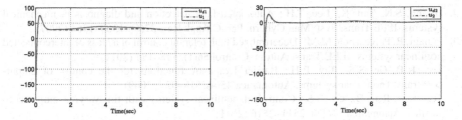

Fig. 5. The evolutions of control inputs u_{d1} and u_{d2} with output constraints.

5 Conclusion

An advanced fault-tolerant control of uncertain robotic manipulators subject to asymmetric output constraints has been investigated in this paper. By employing the output-dependent UBF, the rigorous requirements on the initial conditions of system output; Furthermore, it is worth mentioned that the developed method can applicable to the case without constraint requirements on output without redesigning controller; Furthermore, the robust control based fault-tolerant algorithm can solve the time-varying yet undetectable faults of robotic manipulators without FDD/FDI and controller reconfiguration. The feasibility and applicability of the proposed method to uncertain robotic systems have been demonstrated.

Acknowledgment. This work was supported by the National Key Research and Development Program of China (No. 2017YFB1301401).

References

1. Jin, X.: Adaptive fixed-time control for MIMO nonlinear systems with asymmetric output constraints using universal barrier functions. IEEE Trans. Autom. Control (2018). https://doi.org/10.1109/TAC.2018.2874877
2. Cao, Y., Song, Y.D.: Adaptive PID-like fault-tolerant control for robot manipulators with given performance specifications. Int. J. Control. https://doi.org/10.1080/00207179.2018.1468928
3. Craig, J.J.: Adaptive Control of Mechanical Manipulators. Addison-Wesley, New York (1998)
4. Lewis, F.L., Yesildirak, A., Jagannathan, S.: Neural Network Control of Robot Manipulators and Nonlinear Systems. Taylor & Francis, London (1999)
5. Slotine, J.J.E., Li, W.: Composite adaptive control of robot manipulators. Automatica 25(4), 509–519 (1989)
6. Spong, M.W., Hutchinson, S., Vidyasagar, M.: Robot Modeling and Control. Wiley, New York (2006)
7. Zhao, K., Song, Y.D., Shen, Z.: Neuro-adaptive fault-tolerant control of nonlinear systems under output constraints and actuation faults. IEEE Trans. Neural Netw. Learn. Syst. 29(2), 286–298 (2018)
8. Jin, X.: Adaptive fault tolerant control for a class of input and state constrained MIMO nonlinear systems. Int. J. Robust Nonlinear Control 26(2), 286–302 (2015)

9. Huang, S.N., Tan, K., Lee, T.H.: Automated fault detection and diagnosis in mechanical systems. IEEE Trans. Syst. Man Cybern. Part C Appl. Rev. **37**(6), 1360–1364 (2007)

10. Panagi, P., Polycarpou, M.M.: Decertralized fault tolerant control of a class of interconnected nonlinear systems. IEEE Trans. Autom. Control **56**(1), 178–184 (2011)

11. Tee, K.P., Ge, S.S., Tay, E.H.: Barrier Lyapunov functions for the control of output-constrained nonlinear systems. Automatica **45**(4), 918–927 (2009)

12. Tee, K.P., Ren, B., Ge, S.S.: Control of nonlinear systems with timevarying output constraints. Automatica **47**(11), 2511–2516 (2011)

13. Liu, Y.J., Tong, S.: Barrier Lyapunov functions-based adaptive control for a class of nonlinear pure-feedback systems with full state constraints. Automatica **64**, 70–75 (2016)

14. Liu, Y.J., Li, J., Tong, S., Chen, C.L.P.: Neural network controlbased adaptive learning design for nonlinear systems with full-state constraints. IEEE Trans. Neural Netw. Learn. Syst. **27**(7), 1562–1571 (2016)

15. Zhao, K., Song, Y.D., Ma, T.D., He, L.: Prescribed performance control of uncertain Euler-Lagrange systems subject to full-state constraints. IEEE Trans. Neural Netw. Learn. Syst. **29**(8), 3478–3489 (2018)

16. Jin, X.: Fault-tolerant iterative learning control for mobile robots non-repetitive trajectory tracking with output constraints. Automatica **94**, 63–71 (2018)

17. He, W., Chen, C.L.P., Yin, Z.: Adaptive neural network control of an uncertain robot with full-state constraints. IEEE Trans. Cybern. **46**(3), 620–629 (2016)

18. Zhao, K., Song, Y.D.: Removing the feasibility conditions imposed on tracking control designs for state-constrained strict-feedback systems. IEEE Trans. Autom. Control **64**(3), 1265–1272 (2019)

19. Mayne, D.Q., Rawlings, J.B., Rao, C.V., Scokaert, P.O.M.: Constrained model predictive control: stability and optimality. Automatica **36**(6), 789–814 (2000)

20. Bemporad, A.: Reference governor for constrained nonlinear systems. IEEE Trans. Autom. Control **43**(3), 415–419 (1998)

21. Liu, D., Michel, A.N.: Dynamical Systems with Saturation Nonlinearities. Springer, London (1994). https://doi.org/10.1007/BFb0032146

22. He, W., Huang, H., Ge, S.S.: Adaptive neural network control of a robotic manipulator with time-varying output constraints. IEEE Trans. Cybern. **47**(10), 3136–3147 (2017)

23. Tang, Z., Ge, S.S., Tee, K.P., He, W.: Robust adaptive neural tracking control for a class of perturbed uncertain nonlinear systems with state constraints. IEEE Trans. Syst. Man Cybern. Syst. **46**(12), 1618–1629 (2016)

24. Xiao, B., Yin, S., Gao, H.J.: Reconfigurable tolerant control of uncertain mechanical systems with actuator faults: a sliding mode observer-based approach. IEEE Trans. Control Syst. Technol. **26**(4), 1249–1258 (2018)

25. Zhao, K., Song, Y.D., Qian, J., Fu, J.: Zero-error tracking control with pre-assignable convergence mode for nonlinear systems under nonvanishing uncertainties and unknown control direction. Syst. Control Lett. **115**(5), 34–40 (2018)

26. Wen, C., Zhou, J., Liu, Z.T., Su, H.: Robust adaptive control of uncertain nonlinear systems in the presence of input saturation and external disturbance. IEEE Trans. Autom. Control **56**(7), 1672–1678 (2011)

27. Kim, B.S., Yoo, S.J.: Adaptive control of nonlinear pure-feedback systems with output constraints: integral barrier Lyapunov functional approach. Int. J. Control Autom. Syst. **13**(1), 249–256 (2015)

28. Krstic, M., Kanellakopoulos, I., Kokotovic, P.V.: Nonlinear and Adaptive Control Design. Wiley, New York (1995)

29. Zhao, K., Song, Y.D., Zhang, Z.R.: Tracking control of MIMO nonlinear systems under full state constraints: a single-parameter adaptation approach free from feasibility conditions. Automatica **55**(9), 52–60 (2019)

Toward Human-in-the-Loop PID Control Based on CACLA Reinforcement Learning

Junpei Zhong[1(✉)] and Yanan Li[2]

[1] Nottingham Trent University, Nottingham NG11 8NS, UK
zhong@junpei.eu
[2] University of Sussex, Falmer, Sussex BN1 9RH, UK

Abstract. A self-tuning PID control strategy using a reinforcement learning method, called CACLA (Continuous Actor-critic Learning Automata) is proposed in this paper with the example application of human-in-the-loop physical assistive control. An advantage of using reinforcement learning is that it can be done in an online manner. Moreover, since human is a time-variant system. The demonstration also shows that the reinforcement learning framework would be beneficial to give semi-supervision signal to reinforce the positive learning performance in any time-step.

Keywords: Human-in-the-loop · Reinforcement learning · Adaptive control

1 Introduction

As a result of the recent development of intelligent robotics, it can be seen that there are more scenarios that robotic application will have the following trends:

1. it will have physical or social interact with humans in industries, health-care and domestic uses;
2. more and more sensory information becomes available due to the rapid development and deployment of sensor hardware.

Both of above two trends can also become an overlapped question, which is: How we can develop adaptive method to have a better control policy of the robots, so that we can learn the profile of the individual difference of the users.

For instance, as one the classical control methods to achieve effective performance in matching the control criteria, the PID controllers have been used in various kinds robotic controllers, because of its structural simplicity and acceptable performances. Most of the conventional methods use the method of trial and error to tune the optimal PID constants. For instance, the first tuning rule of PID was proposed in [1]. Moreover, there are several tuning rules have been proposed. (see also [2]). Some knowledge learning methods have been proposed

© Springer Nature Switzerland AG 2019
H. Yu et al. (Eds.): ICIRA 2019, LNAI 11742, pp. 605–613, 2019.
https://doi.org/10.1007/978-3-030-27535-8_54

to adapt the uncertainties of the control plant, in the way to represent the continuous updating of the parameters as the knowledge. For instance, the fuzzy rules are used to mimic the human tuning procedures. In [3], a hybrid control system incorporating a fuzzy controller a PI controller in the steady-state is proposed. [4] suggested a fuzzy rule-based tuning method to adjust the PI gains. But both of the above methods cannot applied in such time-variant system, since the control rules and membership functions of fuzzy controller are hard-coded [5].

A few learning systems have also been developed to solve the parameter optimization problem in the time-variant systems by setting the system parameters based on neural network or fuzzy systems [6]. However, one assumption of using such learning methods is that the search space is continuous and differentially smooth. Thus for a complicated system, these methods usually have a low convergence speed. Although some non-linear search algorithms, such as the genetic algorithm (GA) [7], simulated annealing (SA) [8] and evolutionary programming (EP) [9,10] have been proposed for searching in a non-convex space, these methods are also difficult to apply in the human-in-the-loop learning settings, because most of them lack the ability to do on-line optimization.

Since the presence of human has been one of the factors in the control system, human-in-the-loop learning provide an effective way of obtaining the optimal values for the time-variant systems. By taking into account the human as part of the system itself, at one hand the human can act as a variable of the system. On the other hand, human can be involved in training, tuning and testing the data by providing feedbacks into the results. Therefore, obtaining learning robot skills by human-in-the-loop learning can be more efficient. By incorporating the human in the multi-agent system, the control and deployment of unmanned aerial vehicles (UAVs) show improvement [11]. [12] uses EMG signal as a measure of the human feedback to control exoskeleton robots. Particularly, reinforcement learning, as one of the semi-supervised learning method, is a friendly and straight-ward approach for the non-experienced users to give feedback for the robots without the explicit human demonstration. For instance, in the case of physical human-robot interaction (pHRI), it can be represented as a system that incorporates two sub-systems: the human and the robot. And we could simply these sub-systems as the same model: a mass-damper-spring system [13]. Nevertheless, the robotic sub-system should also learn the parameters of the human-mass-damper-spring system as a time-variant system, which will be the focus of our following research.

Thus, the purpose of this article is to present a solution of the human-in-the-loop system using an RL algorithm, aiming at two main requirements:

1. incorporate the knowledge added by the users to allow the agent to develop progressively its own knowledge;
2. dealing with continuous state and updates of the adaptabilities in an on-line manner.

2   Reinforcement Learning

In this paper, the reinforcement learning (RL) [14] is used to adaptively change the parameters of PID controller with part of the knowledge from the users and the environment, which is called semi-supervised learning. The general idea of RL is that the environment can always evaluate the exploitation results while the RL method is trying to exploit the environment. Different from the learning method unlike supervised learning, which the correct results will be given, or the "trial and error" that not any feedbacks are given.

2.1 Continuous Actor-Critic Automaton

Reinforcement learning (RL) is a framework for solving sequential decision problems, in which the model learns to take better decisions, which are called "actions" which represent the transit between each states while interacting with its environment. Such kinds of actions can be explicitly modelled as policies, or just a scalar value. Once the model performs an action, the state changes and the agent receives another values regarding to the current state. The underlying formalism of RL is that of Markov Decision Processes (MDP). An MDP is formally defined as a tuple, states S, actions A, models/transition models T, and rewards R. And the traditional MDP formulation usually employs the discrete grid world as the representation of both the state and actions.

In the case of adaptive PID control, for instance, the state can represent the combination of the parameters. Furthermore, there are values corresponding to each state. This value is called reward, which encodes information about the quality of the actual transition. The goal of the agent is to maximize the long-term expected total reward, which is equivalent to finding the optimal solution of an MDP.

In the MDP formulation, the set of actions T are defined as

$$T : S \times A \times S \to [0, 1] \tag{1}$$

where T determines the transition probabilities between states $(T(s, a, s_0) = p(s_0|a, s))$ is the probability from the current state s_0 from the next state s while the action a is executed. Then the reward signal is updated as

$$R : S \times A \to R \tag{2}$$

is a reward signal. It represents the signal that after transitioning from state S with an action A.

A policy, encoding how the model will behave is defined as

$$\pi : S \times A \to [0, 1] \tag{3}$$

Usually when using π, we always try to maximize the expected discounted reward:

$$\pi^* = \arg\max_{\pi} J(x) \tag{4}$$

$$= \arg\max_{\pi} E[\sum_{t=0}^{\infty} \gamma^t \times R[s_t, \pi_t(s_t)]] \tag{5}$$

where t denotes the time-steps and $0 \in (0, 1)$ is a discount factor.

By doing so, the Value V correspond to each state is also imported which represents the expected sum of rewards accumulated starting from state s, acting optimally the reach the final reward:

$$V_{t+1}^*(s) \leftarrow max \sum_{S=s}^{\infty} (s, a, s)[R(s, a, s) + \gamma V_i^*(s')] \tag{6}$$

The continuous actor-critic automata (CACLA) [15] follows the same principle of the MDP and general RL methods, but acts in the continuous space in both state and action representations. One significant change in algorithm while changing from discrete to continuous space is that the Values corresponding to each state are only updated while the temporal error γ is positive, which suggests that the latest performed (explorable) action leads to a larger reward than expected:

$$\delta_t = r_{t+1} + \gamma V_t(s_{t+1}) - V_t(s_t) \tag{7}$$

The CACLA is often implemented in neural networks as the universal approximators, for approximating both the critic and the actor values in the continuous domains.

3   Case Study: Robot-Assisted Recovery

3.1   Problem Formulation

In this paper, without loss of generality, we take a simplified example of using a assisted physical training robot for the upper-limb to test the CACLA based human-in-the-loop PID control. In this case, as shown in Fig. 1, which is a rehabilitation robot for the upper limb. To use it, the a human arm is holding to the robot while the robot is passively adapting the driven power to assist the human to recover the upper limb.

In this case, the dynamics of a planar physical training robot are given by

$$M_r(x)\ddot{x} + C_r(x, \dot{x}) \tag{8}$$

$$\dot{x} = u + f \tag{9}$$

where x is the position in the task space, $M_r(q)$ is the robot's inertia/mass matrix, $C_r(x, \dot{x})$ is the robot's Coriolis and centrifugal matrix, u is the robot's control input from its motors and f is the force applied by the human.

At the meanwhile, the dynamics of a human arm are given by

$$M_h(x)\ddot{x} + C_h(x, \dot{x}) \tag{10}$$

$$\dot{x} = u_h - f \tag{11}$$

where $M_h(x)$ is the human arm's inertia/mass matrix, $C_h(x, \dot{x})$ is the human arm's Coriolis and centrifugal matrix and u_h is the human's control input. Note

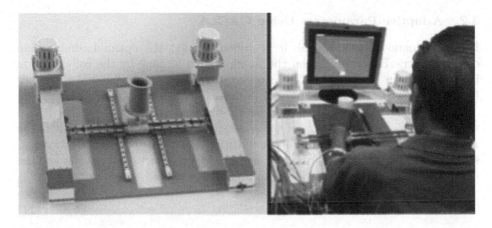

Fig. 1. An example of a rehabilitation robot for the upper limb, while the force of the human user should be taken into account. Adopted from [16]

that x is the common position in Eqs. 9 and 11 which is the position of the interaction point of the robot and human arm.

While the human and the robot are interacting together, we combine the Eqs. 9 and 11, and thus the dynamics of the combined system are as below:

$$M(x)\ddot{x} + C(x, \dot{x}) \tag{12}$$
$$\dot{x} = u + u_h \tag{13}$$

where the interaction force f disappears and

$$M(x) = M_r + M_h(x) \tag{14}$$
$$C(x, \dot{x}) = C_r(x, \dot{x}) + C_h(x, \dot{x}) \tag{15}$$

Therefore, the combined dynamics are determined by both the robot's and human's control inputs u and u_h. In this case, we need to the control policy to satisfy with two conditions:

- to track with trajectory with the desired positions with minimum errors;
- to fit with the desired requirement for the power executed by the human user, i.e. the human's control input u_h.

For this purpose, the human's unknown control input can be constructed based on certain periodic parameters, as follows

$$u_h = -K_{h1}(x - x_d) - K_{h2}\dot{x} \tag{16}$$

where K_{h1} and K_{h2} are the human's stiffness and damping parameters, respectively and x_d is the desired trajectory that is defined for a task. K_{h1} and K_{h2} are unknown parameters that can be time-varying during a tracking task.

3.2   Adaptive Parameters Using CACLA

In the scenario of PD control, it is difficult to get the optimal combination of parameters. Especially, when the manipulation is done by the collaboration between human and robot, it is necessary to adapt the individual difference between users or even the changes of impedance control paradigms.

The K_p and K_d are represented as a 2-dimensional input state space X in the CACLA network. The size of the state space is defined as $I_a \times I_b$, where the I indicates the index of the 2-dimensional state space. The neural activation $x_{a,b}$ state space is determined by the distance between the particular neuron and the represented parameters K_p and K_d in a Gaussian form:

$$x_{i_a,i_b} = e^{\frac{-distance}{2\sigma^2}} \tag{17}$$

where the distance is defined as

$$distance = \sqrt{(I_a - K_p)^2 + (I_b - K_d)^2} \tag{18}$$

Besides of the input, the CACLA network include two output units: the action and the critic. They are connected with:

$$action = XW_{act} \tag{19}$$

$$critic = XW_{cri} \tag{20}$$

where the X is the state space. the output of the action unit range from $[0, 2\pi)$, and the critic is usually below 1.

The update of the input space can be regarded as a movement of the combination of K_p and K_d. The movement is with a constant radius 1 but with different degree defined by the action output.

3.3   Case Study

A sine curve is chosen as the desired trajectory for the movement:

$$\hat{x} = 0.3 \times sin(t) \tag{21}$$

Referring to Eq. 9:

$$M = 5; \tag{22}$$

$$C = 0.1 \tag{23}$$

For the adaptive learning, iterations are employed to learn the optimal parameters online. In each iteration, a state of (K_p, K_d) is randomly selected in the state space. Then a update is made according to the output of action unit: it can be illustrated as a constant movement with the radius of 0.1 in the state space but with various degree of angle, which is the output of the action unit *action*. The iteration terminates while it reaches the pre-defined maximum number of iterations, or the signal of tracking the desired trajectory (with the pre-defined minimum error) is detected.

The detailed algorithm is as Algorithm 1:

Algorithm 1. CACLA Training

1: **procedure** ONE ITERATION(*withrandominitialspace*)
2:     **while** *error > threshold* or *iteration > maximum_iteration* **do**
3:             ▷ Repeat iteration for one sequence until threshold is achieved
4:         Output *action* and *critic*. (Eq. 20)
5:         W_{act} and W_{cri} updated
6:         **if** $\delta > 0$ (Eq. 7) **then**
7:             Agent moves
8:         **end if**
9:     **end while**
10: **end procedure**

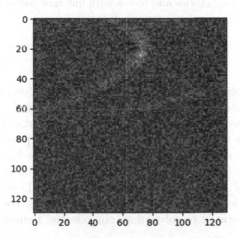

Fig. 2. Weighting matrix of the critic value. The optimal values of K_p and K_d can be obtained by the values on the axes divide by 10.

Figure 2 demonstrates the resulting values of the K_p and K_d. The green trace in the middle of the weighting matrix indicates the optimal values for K_p and K_d are around $(K_p = 8, K_d = 2)$. According to this, we select the values to see the performance of the system. As we can see in Fig. 3a, the trajectory of the robot basically follows the desired one. For comparison, we also select other combinations along the yellow trace of the weighting matrix. From Fig. 3b, a satisfying result can be also seen. More importantly, thanks to the continuous values of the weighting, we do not need to start training with every possible combination of the parameters, which is beneficial for the convex optimization problem with limited training samples from human.

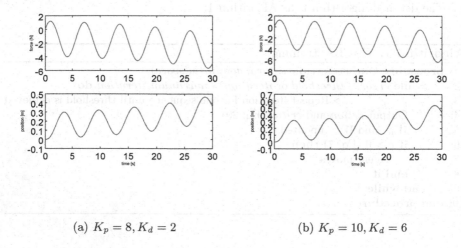

(a) $K_p = 8, K_d = 2$ (b) $K_p = 10, K_d = 6$

Fig. 3. The trajectories and forces with different parameter settings

4   Summary

In this paper, we propose to utilise a continuous reinforcement learning algorithm, named in both state and action space, to search for an optimal setting of the PID control system. Particularly, the system learns the parameters in an on-line time-variant manner, which is suitable to incorporate human-factors in the reinforcement learning loop. We also examine this learning mechanism in a 1-dimensional physical-assistive robot which include both human and robotic systems. The initial result shows that the adaptive PD control with this system can track the desired trajectory. At the next steps, the learning algorithm will be further elaborated to solve more complicated human-in-the-loop control systems.

References

1. Ziegler, J.G., Nichols, N.B.: Optimum settings for automatic controllers. Trans. ASME **64**(11), 759–765 (1942)
2. Åström, K.J., Hägglund, T., Astrom, K.J.: Advanced PID Control, vol. 461. ISA-The Instrumentation, Systems, and Automation Society Research Triangle ... (2006)

3. Sant, A.V., Rajagopal, K.: PM synchronous motor speed control using hybrid fuzzy-PI with novel switching functions. IEEE Trans. Magn. **45**(10), 4672–4675 (2009)
4. Jung, J.-W., Choi, Y.-S., Leu, V., Choi, H.: Fuzzy PI-type current controllers for permanent magnet synchronous motors. IET Electr. Power Appl. **5**(1), 143–152 (2011)
5. Li, Y., Ang, K.H., Chong, G.C.: PID control system analysis and design. IEEE Control Syst. Mag. **26**(1), 32–41 (2006)
6. Orelind, G., Wozniak, L., Medanic, J., Whittemore, T.: Optimal PID gain schedule for hydrogenerators-design and application. IEEE Trans. Energy Convers. **4**(3), 300–307 (1989)
7. Porter, B., Jones, A.: Genetic tuning of digital PID controllers. Electron. Lett. **28**(9), 843–844 (1992)
8. Roa-Sepulveda, C., Pavez-Lazo, B.: A solution to the optimal power flow using simulated annealing. Int. Electr. Power Energy Syst. **25**(1), 47–57 (2003)
9. Eiben, Á.E., Hinterding, R., Michalewicz, Z.: Parameter control in evolutionary algorithms. IEEE Trans. Evol. Comput. **3**(2), 124–141 (1999)
10. Lieslehto, J.: PID controller tuning using evolutionary programming. In: Proceedings of the 2001 American Control Conference (Cat. No. 01CH37148), vol. 4, pp. 2828–2833. IEEE (2001)
11. Orsag, M., et al.: Human-in-the-loop control of multi-agent aerial systems. In: 2016 European Control Conference (ECC), pp. 2139–2145. IEEE (2016)
12. Peternel, L., Noda, T., Petrič, T., Ude, A., Morimoto, J., Babič, J.: Adaptive control of exoskeleton robots for periodic assistive behaviours based on EMG feedback minimisation. PloS one **11**(2), e0148942 (2016)
13. Albu-Schäffer, A., Ott, C., Hirzinger, G.: A unified passivity-based control framework for position, torque and impedance control of flexible joint robots. Int. J. Robot. Res. **26**(1), 23–39 (2007)
14. Sutton, R.S., Barto, A.G., et al.: Introduction to Reinforcement Learning, vol. 135. MIT Press, Cambridge (1998)
15. van Hasselt, H., Wiering, M.: Reinforcement learning in continuous action spaces. In: IEEE International Symposium on Approximate Dynamic Programming and Reinforcement Learning, pp. 272–279 (2007)
16. Hussain, A., et al.: Self-paced reaching after stroke: a quantitative assessment of longitudinal and directional sensitivity using the H-man planar robot for upper limb neurorehabilitation. Front. Neurosci. **10**, 477 (2016)

Wearable and Assistive Devices and Robots for Healthcare

A Preliminary Study on Surface Electromyography Signal Analysis for Motion Characterization During Catheterization

Tao Zhou[1,2], Olatunji Mumini Omisore[1], Wenjing Du[1], Wenke Duan[1], Yuan Zhang[2(✉)], and Lei Wang[1(✉)]

[1] Shenzhen Institutes of Advanced Technology, Chinese Academy of Sciences, Shenzhen, China
wang.lei@siat.ac.cn
[2] School of Information Science and Engineering, University of Jinan, Jinan, China
yzhang@ujn.edu.cn

Abstract. Surface Electromyography (sEMG) signal has been widely applied in solving many mechanical control problems such as prosthetic control, medical rehabilitation and sports science. Similarly, this is becoming relatively applicable for interventional surgery where robotic catheter systems are being proposed for safe vascular catheterization. In this paper, two basic features are investigated for characterization of users' hand movements during vascular catheterization. For this purpose, controlled experiments were setup to acquire sEMG signals from six different muscles of nine volunteers who were asked to perform four basic movements namely, *move-out*, *move-in*, *turn-in*, *turn-out*; used during intravascular catheterization. Two features namely, Average Electromyography and Root Mean Square, were defined over an acquired database of sEMG signals from the nine subjects. The features were utilized to characterize and analyze the different motions in the hand movements dataset. Analysis of the processed signal shows that both features are highly comparable in terms of mean amplitude for all movements across the nine subjects. A significant difference ($p = 0.048$) was observed in the thumb abductor muscle, and just between *move-in* and *turn-in* movements.

Keywords: Vascular intervention · sEMG signal analysis · AEMG/RMS · Signal-based catheterization · Medical robotics

1 Introduction

For several decades, cardiovascular related diseases have been a leading cause of death in the world [1]. Traditional treatment methods for such diseases include open-heart surgery in which patient's cardiac region is opened wide enough to allow surgeons to carry out surgery on the internal structure of the heart.

© Springer Nature Switzerland AG 2019
H. Yu et al. (Eds.): ICIRA 2019, LNAI 11742, pp. 617–628, 2019.
https://doi.org/10.1007/978-3-030-27535-8_55

However, this method requires longer post-surgical hospital stays accompanied with intense pain and other problems, such as exposure of surgical site to infections, which would impede patient's recovery and sometimes causes post-surgery death [2].

Alternatively, catheterization has become a popular method adopted for the treatment of cardiovascular diseases [3]. This involves navigation of flexible endovascular tools, such as guidewire and catheter, through the blood vessels leading to the heart in order to allow surgeons access to the heart and carry out the surgery. This technique, known as Minimally Invasive Vascular Surgery (MIVS), has more advantages over the traditional open-heart surgery. For instance, it causes little or no hemorrhage, less surgical and post-surgical pain, and quicker recovery [4]; nonetheless, due to the necessity of X-ray imaging needed for visualization, surgeons are exposed to high-ionizing radiation energy and orthopedic spine injury from heavy shielded garments worn to resist radiation during operation. So the demand for corresponding robot-aided system arises, spontaneously. Minimally Invasive Vascular Surgical Robotics (MIVSR) permit the surgeons to be released from heavy radiation, and chronic orthopedic neck and back pain. Further, such robots and increase the accuracy of surgical operations; thus, it has received high attention and interest in the field of MIVS [5].

In recent years, research advances on MIVSR have focused on the development of motion control for fast and accurate catheterization procedures. Wang et al. [6] introduce a novel interventional surgical robotic system which simulates hand motion of surgeons to operate on guidewire. Similarly, a fuzzy-PID controller was proposed for interventional robotic surgery to solve the problem of tracking error from master to slave manipulators in [7]. Omisore et al. present an adaptive backlash compensation based on motion control and force modulation for a novel robotic catheter system [8]. Although, these could relieve surgeons during cardiac catheterization; however, integration of force sensing capabilities and feedback system are yet to be proposed for effectiveness and safety on the part of patients. Pacchierotti et al. [9] present a novel cutaneous approach to providing haptic feedback for palpation in robot-assisted surgery. The study includes a method for estimating visual and haptic force feedback on robotic surgical system in [10]. Lee et al. [11] present two isometric force generation tasks performed with a hand-held robotic tool that provides in-situ augmentation of force sensation. The robotic systems in these studies have two degree of freedom (2-DoF), but none of them focused on modeling the distinct for vascular catheterization.

Recently, application of signal-based control have been found in robotics. Raurale et al. [12] carry out the identification of real-time active hand movements EMG signals based on wrist-hand mobility for simultaneous control of prosthesis robotic hand. A simple and effective approach to govern robot arm motion in real-time using upper limb EMG signals is presented in Liu et al. [13]. Mahendran et al. [14] present a novel artificial neural network approach to control an intelligent wheelchair using myoelectric signals. However, the studies

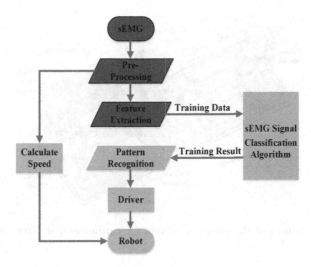

Fig. 1. Signal-based modeling for vascular catheterization.

have only focused on serial-link and parallel-link types robots in which distinct link components are directly controlled with unique joints. Such robotic systems do not feature the basic motions utilized for vascular catheterization. Thus, the studies are quite different from the case of intravascular surgery whereby robotic catheter system drives thin, long and highly flexible endovascular tools with distinct motion actions. The societal and ethical needs require that surgeons rely on using of their hands during MIVS with interventional robotic systems [15]. Thus, motion characterization is very vital for effective vascular catheterization. A modified principal component analysis (PCA) is presented to select a sensitive and principal muscle subset for improving the exibility of subjects' manipulations [16].

The rest of this paper is organized as follows. Materials and methodology are presented in Sect. 2. Results and discussion are given in Sect. 3. Conclusion and future works are summarized in Sect. 4.

2 Materials and Methodology

2.1 Proposed Framework for sEMG Catheterization

Figure 1 shows the overall diagram, the model is envisaged for sEMG signal-based motion characterization during vascular catheterization. The conceptual model includes five major parts namely, acquisition, pre-processing, feature extraction, classification, and robot control mapping. However, our focus in this study is to characterize four hand motions of the nine volunteers based on the two unique features. The characterization is approached with the signals acquired from six different muscles of the volunteers while making hand movements for vascular catheterization. Accurate classification of the distinct movements made by a

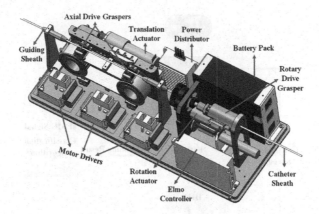

Fig. 2. Model of the catheter system for cardiovascular intervention.

surgeon is very important for an effective signal-based catheterization. Thus, acquisition and pre-processing of the signals should be done correctly, while better feature extraction must be ensured for good classification results. Thus, we focused the three phases highlighted with deep blue color in Fig. 1. CAD model of the second generation catheter system designed for cardiac interventions in our lab is illustrated as Fig. 2. The vascular robot is smarter and light-weighted than the first generation [8,17]. Both generations of the vascular surgical systems have 2-DoF; thus, the major operations are *move-in*, *move-out*, *turn-in* and *turn-out*. The first two are typically for axial translations while the latter are for axial rotation actions.

2.2 Subjects

Nine healthy subjects (seven men and two women, all right-handed, no neuromuscular diseases) from Shenzhen Institutes of Advanced Technology took part in the experiments. The mean age and body mass index of the subjects are 28.22 ± 5.63 years and $23.33 \pm 2.80 \, kg/m^2$, respectively. A brief explanation was given about the experimental purpose, duration and procedure ahead of the experiments. All participants signed the consent forms as approved by the Institutional Review Board of Shenzhen Institutes of Advanced Technology (Reference No. SIAT-IRB-190215-H0291).

2.3 Data Collection and Experimental Procedure

During the experiments, the participants were asked to perform the four kinds of movements namely: *move-out*, *move-in*, *turn-in* and *turn-out* for the purpose of signal acquisition. The four movements are the key motions performed by the interventionists during MIVS. Each movement was performed one hundred times as a sequence, and two sequences by each subject. Each time, a separate sEMG recording was captured from six muscles. Thus, 8 sEMG recordings were captured for each subject. Before experiment, each subject was guided and trained to perform the four movements several times to make sure that s/he can make the movements, effectively. During the experiment, the subjects are well observed to make sure all the electrodes are in their right positions with firm contact with the subject's skin. To ensure a common pace between consecutive movements in all the subjects, each subject was asked to follow an audio rhythm while performing the movements. Further, the subjects are made to rest for five minutes between two different movements so as to restore innervation of the muscles for each of the four movements. The muscles of interested are *Extensor Muscle* (ETM), *Interosseous Muscle 2* (IM2), *Thumb Abductor Muscle* (TAM), *Elbow Muscle* (ELM), *Interosseous Muscle 1* (IM1) and *Posterior Muscle* (PTM), which were chosen after many arbitral trials from one subject before expanding the investigation. To acquire sEMG signal of each muscle, six pairs of surface electrodes (disposable Ag/AgCl, 10 mm diameter, LT-301, China) were placed on the subject's forearm, as shown in Fig. 3. Before each experiment, sites of the muscles on the subject's skin were cleaned with alcohol in order to obtain high quality signals. The center-to-center distance between two electrodes for each channel was around 20 mm. Finally, signals were acquired at 1000 Hz sampling rate using a configurable electromyography (EMG) system (BioNomadix, BIOPAC Systems, Inc., Goleta, CA, USA). The experimental view is shown in Fig. 4. The sEMG activity recorded from the interested muscles of one of the subjects during the four movements is illustrated in Fig. 5.

2.4 Signal Processing

There are some unwanted components in the acquired signals from all subjects, so they can not be used directly. Thus, the three processes done are explained below:

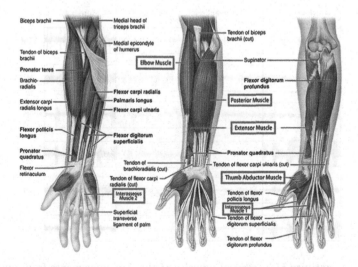

Fig. 3. The six muscles of interest; adapted from [18].

Fig. 4. The experimental view.

Filtering: As found in literature review [19], the common range of sEMG signals is 10 to 500 Hz. Thus, a 10–500 Hz band-pass filter was applied to make sure that all components of the signals were in the range. All the signals may be affected by power frequency. Afterwards, a 50 Hz-notch filter was applied to eliminate power frequency disturbances that could be present in the signal. Both filters were designed by the signal processing toolbox in MATLAB 2014b.

Normalization: sEMG normalization adopted in this study is the maximum value (MV) normalization approach [20]. The normalization method involves finding

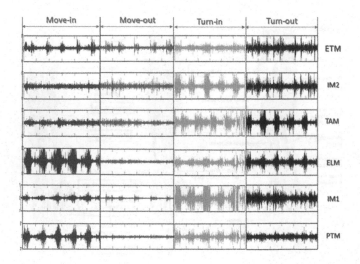

Fig. 5. sEMG activity of interested muscles of the four movements from one subject.

the peak value of the sEMG signal and normalize the rest of the data as a percentage of the peak value (%MV). The aim of normalization is to establish a baseline for comparing signals from distinct subjects.

Feature Extraction: Sequel to the filtering of unwanted components in the acquired signals and normalization, the features essential for classification were extracted.

(1) Average electromyogram (AEMG) value of the sEMG is regarded as an important indicator for a selected length of EMG signal. This is because it has no relationship with the length of time when comparing two signals. As a consequence, AEMG was calculated from the signals to reflect the innervation input during each of the movement. The AEMG value for the normalized sEMG signal was obtained with (1) where N is the number of data points.

$$AEMG = \frac{\sum_{i=1}^{N} |Data\,[i]|}{N} \tag{1}$$

(2) Root-mean-square (RMS) calculation of the sEMG is considered to provide insight on the amplitude of the sEMG signals since it gives a measure of the power of the signal. RMS of an acquired signal can be expressed as in (2) where T is a certain time period.

$$RMS = \sqrt{\frac{\sum_{i=0}^{T} Data\,[i]^2}{T}} \tag{2}$$

2.5   Statistical Analysis

Statistical analysis were performed by using one-way analysis of variance (ANOVA) to check whether AEMG and RMS are features with significant differences across all the subjects, and all the statistical results were obtained at a statistical significance level of $p = 0.05$ (95% confidence level).

3   Results and Discussion

In this section, results obtained for both AEMG and RMS features are analyzed to determine if both features can be used for proper classification of unique movements made by a surgeon during interventional surgery. This include statistical analysis performed to verify if the features have significant contributions.

3.1   Similar Pattern Between AEMG and RMS Features

First, visual inspection was observed by plotting the pre-processed signals that were acquired from each of the six muscles during the four movements in the nine subjects. The plots of mean values of both AEMG and RMS features in the nine subjects are shown in Fig. 6. For all the four movements, it was observed that ETM, TAM, ELM, and IM1 have clearer differences in their mean amplitude values for both the AEMG (Fig. 6(a)) and RMS (Fig. 6(b)) features, unlike in the cases of IM2 and PTM. In the latter cases, only *move-out* seems to have obvious difference while the remaining three motions are comparably similar. Although, *move-in* also shows a little distinction, when compared to *turn-in* and *turn-out*, in PTM. Notwithstanding, it is difficult to classify the two movements, distinctively, as all muscle activities in the four movements have their significant differences within a very small range of 0.2–0.3 mv.

Furthermore, other characteristics were employed to analyze the sEMG signal of the four movements. As presented in Fig. 6(a), it was observed that IM2, IM1 and PTM have stronger innervation during *move-out*; thus, it can be concluded that the muscles have higher contributions for the movement while TAM and ELM are comparably lower and TAM is the least. Similar conclusion can also be drawn in the case of other movements. For instance, in *move-in*, ETM and ELM have the highest contributions due to their strong innervation; however, for movement classification, TAM and IM1 shows distinct AEMG values for the movement. Thus, the muscles are said to be better indices for classification. It can be seen that IM1 can be uniquely used for classification of *move-in* but better results are expected when combined with TAM. Moreover, it is important to emphasize that TAM can be uniquely used for identification of *move-in*; however, it is not sufficient for classification purpose as the AEMG value of the muscle is lower compared to those of the other five muscles, and TAM has the weakest innervation in the four movements. Thus, classification of the movement should be based on astute combination of the several muscles.

The RMS feature was processed and analyzed in a similar way to AEMG feature. Due to the page limit, mean values of the RMS feature was used to validate across all the nine subjects, as plotted in Fig. 6(b). It was observed that both features exhibit the same patterns in the six muscles during the four

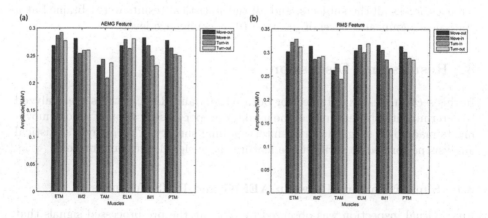

Fig. 6. The AEMG and RMS features of different movements in each muscle.

movements. Thus, it can be assumed that both AEMG and RMS are strongly correlated features in the different movements. However, the latter has slightly different range, of 0.24–0.33 mv, where the muscular activities are significantly different. Thus, it can be concluded that the RMS feature is slightly because the activity of each muscle during the four movements has a little higher amplitude than the corresponding cases of the AEMG feature.

3.2 Statistical Analysis of AEMG and RMS Features

For proper statistical analysis of the AEMG and RMS features, box-plots of the mean values observed from the six muscles during the four movements are plotted, as shown in Figs. 7 and 8, respectively. The movements are paired in all combinations of two movements, and the correlations between each pair were analyzed using one-way analysis of variance (ANOVA) with a significant threshold (p-value) of 0.05. As a matter of fact, only the *move-in* and *turn-in* movements show results with p-values lesser than 0.05 for the AEMG feature, as shown in Fig. 7(c). Thus, there exists a significant difference between the pair of

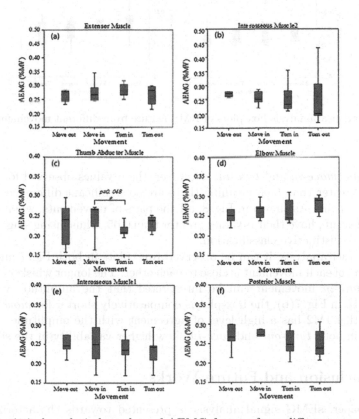

Fig. 7. Statistical analysis box-plots of AEMG feature from different movements in each muscle.

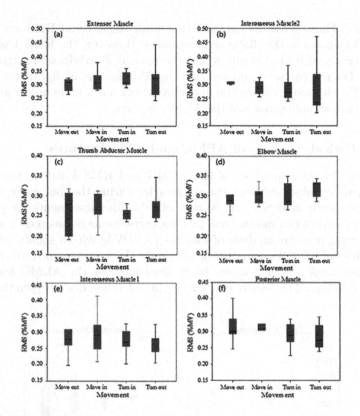

Fig. 8. Statistical analysis box-plots of RMS feature from different movements in each muscle.

movements (*move-in* and *turn-in*). However, the p-values observed for all other pairs are greater than 0.05 meaning there are no significant differences between the motion pairs. As shown in Fig. 8, all the pairs of movements, when observed on RMS feature, have their p-values greater than 0.05. Thus, using single muscles cannot give distinctive classification.

By further analysis, it can be observed from plots in both Fig. 7 and 8 that, the median of each movement is close to each other. The longer whiskers observed in the *move-in* movement can be interpreted that the amplitude vary more widely [21]. In Fig. 7(b), the box-plot is comparatively shorter for *move-out*, this suggests that IM2 has a high level of agreement with the amplitude. The long whiskers in both *turn-out* and *turn-in* show higher variability in the signals.

4   Conclusion and Future Works

In this paper, sEMG signal analysis is presented towards characterization of interventionist's hand motions during vascular catheterization. The analysis includes comparing two basic features which were derived from sEMG signals of nine subjects whom were trained to perform the four basic hand movements used for vascular catheterization. All muscular activities were recorded under controlled experiments. Upon the pre-processing and feature extraction phases, it was observed from results of the analysis that both AEMG and RMS features are highly comparable in terms of mean amplitude for all movements across the subjects. Meanwhile, TAM exhibits a significant difference ($p = 0.048$) between *move-in* and *turn-in* movements. A major finding from this study is the consistent existence of similar patterns between AEMG and RMS amongst all the nine subjects. In the future, deep learning methods like convolutional neural network will be applied for feature extraction and classification of the distinct movements with sEMG signals from trained surgeons.

Acknowledgments. We thank all the nine volunteers during data collection. This work was supported in part by the National Natural Science Foundation of China (Grants No. 61572231, No. U1713219), the Outstanding Youth Innovation Research Fund of SIAT-CAS (No. Y8G0381001) and The Enhancement Project for Shenzhen Biomedical Electronics Technology Public Service Platform.

References

1. Roth, G.A., et al.: Global and regional patterns in cardiovascular mortality from 1990 to 2013. Circulation **132**(17), 1667–1678 (2015)
2. Segal, C.G., Waller, D.K., Tilley, B., Piller, L., Bilimoria, K.: An evaluation of differences in risk factors for individual types of surgical site infections after colon surgery. Surgery **156**(5), 1253–1260 (2014)
3. Lahham, S., et al.: Ultrasound-guided central venous access: which probe is preferred for viewing the subclavian vein using a supraclavicular approach? Am. J. Emerg. Med. **34**(9), 1761–1764 (2016)
4. Guo, J., Cheng, Y., Guo, S., Du, W.: A novel path planning algorithm for the vascular interventional surgical robotic doctor training system. In: 2017 IEEE International Conference on Mechatronics and Automation (ICMA), pp. 45–50. IEEE (2017)
5. Bao, X., et al.: Operation evaluation in-human of a novel remote-controlled vascular interventional robot. Biomed. Microdevices **20**(2), 34 (2018)
6. Wang, Y., Guo, S., Gao, B., Peng, W., Li, G.: Study on motion following with feedback force disturbance in interventional surgical robot system. In: 2016 IEEE International Conference on Mechatronics and Automation (ICMA), pp. 485–489. IEEE (2016)
7. Guo, J., Jin, X., Guo, S., Du, W.: Study on the tracking performance of the vascular interventional surgical robotic system based on the fuzzy-PID controller. In: 2017 IEEE International Conference on Mechatronics and Automation (ICMA), pp. 29–34. IEEE (2017)
8. Omisore, O.M., et al.: Towards characterization and adaptive compensation of backlash in a novel robotic catheter system for cardiovascular interventions. IEEE Trans. Biomed. Circ. Syst. **12**(4), 824–838 (2018)
9. Pacchierotti, C., Prattichizzo, D., Kuchenbecker, K.J.: Cutaneous feedback of fingertip deformation and vibration for palpation in robotic surgery. IEEE Trans. Biomed. Eng. **63**(2), 278–287 (2016)

10. Haouchine, N., Kuang, W., Cotin, S., Yip, M.C.: Vision-based force feedback estimation for robot-assisted surgery using instrument-constrained biomechanical 3D maps. IEEE Robot. Autom. Lett. **3**(3), 2160–2165 (2018)
11. Lee, R., Klatzky, R.L., Stetten, G.D.: In-situ force augmentation improves surface contact and force control. IEEE Trans. Haptics **10**(4), 545–554 (2017)
12. Raurale, S.A., Chatur, P.N.: Identification of real-time active hand movements EMG signals for control of prosthesis robotic hand. In: 2014 International Conference on Computation of Power, Energy, Information and Communication (ICCPEIC), pp. 482–487. IEEE (2014)
13. Liu, H.-J., Young, K.-Y.: Robot motion governing using upper limb EMG signal based on empirical mode decomposition. In: 2010 IEEE International Conference on Systems Man and Cybernetics (SMC), pp. 441–446. IEEE (2010)
14. Mahendran, R.: EMG signal based control of an intelligent wheelchair. In: 2014 International Conference on Communications and Signal Processing (ICCSP), pp. 1267–1272. IEEE (2014)
15. Yang, G.-Z., et al.: The grand challenges of science robotics. Sci. Robot. **3**(14), eaar7650 (2018)
16. Zhou, X.-H., Bian, G.-B., Xie, X.-L., Hou, Z.-G., Hao, J.-L.: PCA-based muscle selection for interventional manipulation recognition. In: 2016 IEEE International Conference on Robotics and Biomimetics (ROBIO), pp. 921–926. IEEE (2016)
17. Omisore, O.M., ShiPeng, H., LingXue, R., Lei, W.: A teleoperated robotic catheter system with motion and force feedback for vascular surgery. In: 2018 18th International Conference on Control, Automation and Systems (ICCAS), pp. 172–177. IEEE (2018)
18. Cellcode.us: arm muscle identification. https://cellcode.us/quotes/arm-muscle-identification.html. Accessed 23 Feb 2019
19. Du, W., Omisore, O.M., Li, H., Ivanov, K., Han, S., Wang, L.: Recognition of chronic low back pain during lumbar spine movements based on surface electromyography signals. IEEE Access **6**, 65027–65042 (2018)
20. Halaki, M., Ginn, K.: Normalization of EMG signals: to normalize or not to normalize and what to normalize to? In: Computational Intelligence in Electromyography Analysis-A Perspective on Current Applications and Future Challenges. InTech (2012)
21. Wikipedia: Box-plot. https://en.wikipedia.org/wiki/Box_plot. Accessed 20 Feb 2019

Design and Control of a Novel Series Elastic Actuator for Knee Exoskeleton

Chenglong Qian[1], Aibin Zhu[2(✉)], Jiyuan Song[1], Huang Shen[3],
Xiaodong Zhang[2], and Guangzhong Cao[4]

[1] Shaanxi Key Laboratory of Intelligent Robots, Xi'an, China
[2] Institute of Robotics and Intelligent Systems,
Xi'an Jiaotong University, Xi'an 710049, China
abzhu@mail.xjtu.edu.cn
[3] Key Laboratory of Education Ministry for Modern Design
and Rotor-Bearing System, Xi'an, China
[4] Shenzhen Key Laboratory of Electromagnetic Control,
Shenzhen University, Shenzhen 518060, China
gzcao@szu.edu.cn

Abstract. The Series Elastic Actuator (SEA), as the power source of the exoskeleton robot, can greatly improve the flexibility of the exoskeleton robot, thus, improving the comfort and safety of human-computer interaction. In this paper, a SEA-based power-assisted driving system for the knee joint has been designed. The power-assisted driving system can be equal to a series of springs between the motor and the human body joint, controlling the torque output by controlling the spring displacement. In order to improve the accuracy of SEA position control, an RBF neural network control method has been proposed to realize the stable position control, by compensating the nonlinear characteristics of the load such as gravity and friction. Experimental results show that the actuator has a good position following and compliance, while safe interaction between the exoskeleton and the human body is realized.

Keywords: Series elastic actuator · Exoskeleton · RBF neural network · Impedance control

1 Introduction

As a highly coordinated booster device with the human body, exoskeleton robot can help people to work in various complex environments and has become an emerging research hotspot. On one hand, in terms of Medical treatment, the Lower extremity exoskeleton rehabilitation robot, ReWalk, developed by Argo Medical Technologies in the United States, has realized the rehabilitation training of Lower limbs of human body [1]. A lot of medical research shows that task-oriented training plays an important role in neuro rehabilitation today [2]. On the other hand, from the perspective of military equipment development, exoskeleton robot can reduce the energy consumption of the soldiers; thus, increasing their combat effectiveness. The power-assisted mechanical garment – BLEEX, developed by the university of California, Berkeley, is a typical representative [3].

© Springer Nature Switzerland AG 2019
H. Yu et al. (Eds.): ICIRA 2019, LNAI 11742, pp. 629–640, 2019.
https://doi.org/10.1007/978-3-030-27535-8_56

Walking robot is a kind of human-machine interaction robot, so its comfort and safety should be the primary consideration in its design. Existing rigid exoskeletons still have much to be strengthened and improved. For example, the robot joint cannot be as flexible as the biological joint: when the two send conflicts, the dislocation movement of the robot joint and the biological joint will cause the wearer to deviate from their natural motion mode. In 1995, Gill A. Pratt et al. conducted research on series elastic actuator (SEA) [4]. SEA added elastic elements between the motor and the load as torque transfer mechanism. Compared with the traditional rigid mechanism, it can directly calculate the load force by measuring the deformation of the spring connected with the load. This control method can realize more accurate torque control by transforming torque control into spring-shape control. As a force output drive device with flexible and bionic drive capabilities, the series elastic driver can achieve better human-machine interaction performance requirements by increasing the internal flexibility of the drive system [5]. However, the accuracy and robustness of position control are decreased because SEA is affected by nonlinear factors such as gravity, friction and damping. At present, the commonly used SEA control methods do not combine the SEA's own structural characteristics, which greatly limit the application of SEA characteristics.

In order to improve the human-machine comfort and coordination of the exoskeleton assisted robot, a series elastic actuator of knee joint has been proposed in this paper. The output of torque was controlled by the deformation of the spring to achieve accurate torque control. Through RBF neural network learning, the position control feedforward curve is obtained, which can compensate for the influence of various nonlinear factors.

2   Design of Series Elastic Actuator

This paper designed a knee joint mechanical structure, based on a series of elastic actuators, is shown in Fig. 1. There are three degrees of freedom in the integrated knee mechanism: the first degree of freedom is the realization of the rotational motion of the SEA mechanism driven by a motor in the sagittal plane of the knee joint, the second degree of freedom is the rotational motion of the disc elastic mechanism in the transverse plane of the knee joint, and the third degree of freedom is the linear motion of the linear gas buffer structure in the axial direction of the thigh.

Fig. 1. A novel series elastic actuator.

The flexion and extension motion of the knee joint is driven by a crank slider mechanism with a series elastic actuator, which is flexible with high follow-up. Due to the limitation of exoskeleton space and weight, the SEA knee joint structure makes full use of the space in the sagittal plane. By installing the driving motor and transmission mechanism in the space parallel to the sagittal plane, the size in the horizontal direction is greatly reduced compared with the traditional structure. So that the exoskeleton can be further fitted to the human body; and helpful to further improve the miniaturization, lightweight and high power density of the knee joint structure. The structure is shown in Fig. 2.

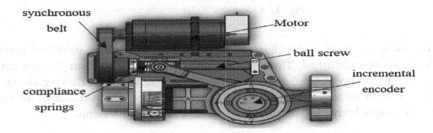

Fig. 2. A novel series elastic actuator based on crank slider mechanism.

The joint of the lower leg was designed with a disc elastic mechanism. Through the elastic characteristics of the spring, it can realize the internal and external rotation of the knee joint. Its structure is shown in Fig. 3.

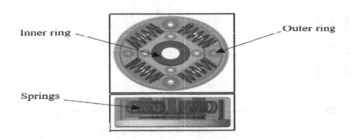

Fig. 3. Disk elastic mechanism.

During walk, the exoskeleton needs to repeatedly collide with the ground, and the impact often causes the vibration of the mechanical system, thus reducing the stability of the system and the comfort of human- machine interaction. Therefore, we designed a linear gas buffer structure. In the gait cycle, the linear gas buffer structure can reduce the impact of the ground on the exoskeleton, along the direction of the thigh, every time the foot lands. The structure is shown in Fig. 4.

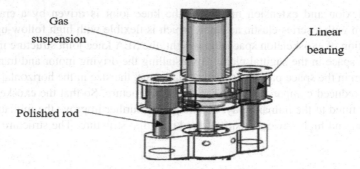

Fig. 4. Linear gas buffer structure.

By using the bionic 3d gait analysis system, the rigid body model of human walking can be established. Thus, when people wear the mechanism, we can get a range of motion data from all directions of the body. The measured data are shown in the Fig. 5. It can be seen from the Fig. 5 that after wearing the exoskeleton of the knee joint, the human body can still meet the normal motion requirements.

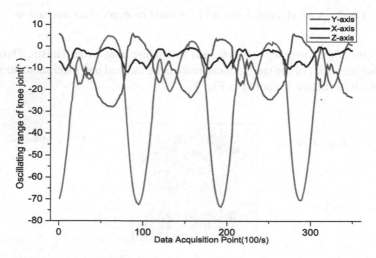

Fig. 5. Oscillating rang of knee joint.

The design has the following advantages over conventional exoskeleton structure:

(1) Flexible drive. By measuring the compression of the elastic element, combined with Hooke's law, the load imposed by the torque can be calculated. Since the required torque affects the load indirectly, the influence of nonlinear factors such as load variation and friction are reduced.

(2) Modular design. The knee exoskeleton mechanism integrates drive, transmission, sensing and communication into a modular joint; equivalent to a small complete system. Through this modular design, the knee joint structure can be quickly

combined with other structures to form a new system. This greatly reduces the production cost of the products and shortens the product development cycle.

(3) Precise torque control. Precise joint torque is controlled by position control. It is very difficult to control the joint torque directly, but it is much simpler to change the force to control the position of the two ends of the spring through the series elastic mechanism.

(4) Better robustness and stability. Because the series elastic mechanism adds elastic elements between the motor and the load, the physical properties of the system itself are compliant. On one hand, the elastic structure can reduce the negative influence of nonlinear factors such as inertia and friction on force control; on the other hand, the structure can better resist the system shock caused by external load change and impact [6, 7].

3 SEA Control

3.1 SEA Controlling Model

The SEA has high force control accuracy and low impedance characteristics, which makes it have a good application prospect in the human-computer interaction environment [8]. In the design of the series elastic actuator, the elastic element is embedded between the motor and the load. Compared with the traditional rigid torque sensor, the actuator itself has flexibility and its structure can be simplified as shown in Fig. 6.

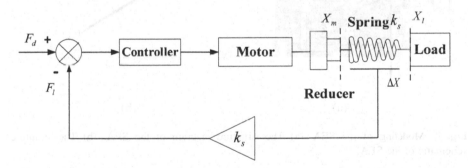

Fig. 6. Schematic diagram of a series elastic actuator.

From the diagram above we can derive the following equations:

$$F_1 = k_s(X_m - X_l) \tag{1}$$

$$F_m - F_1 = X_m M_m s^2 \tag{2}$$

Setting $s = j\omega$ and solving for F_m, in terms of F_l and X_l, we have:

$$F_m = F_l - \frac{M_m}{k_s}\omega^2 F_l - M_m\omega^2 X_l \qquad (3)$$

As can be seen above, the motor force has three components: the first, F_l, is the force applied through the elasticity to the load; the second, $\frac{M_m}{k_s}\omega^2 F_l$, is the force required to accelerate the motor's mass in order to change the deformation of the elasticity; the third, $M_m\omega^2 X_l$, is the force required to accelerate the motor's mass so as to track the motion of the load [4].

In order to design the control system, we also need to build the model between the motor's mass and the joint Angle. The series elastic actuator outputs a force, F_l, that is converted to torque on the joint by a slider-crank mechanism. The Modeling of the SEA is shown in Fig. 7. In which, Fig. 7(a) is the actual structure diagram, and Fig. 7(b) is the simplified schematic.

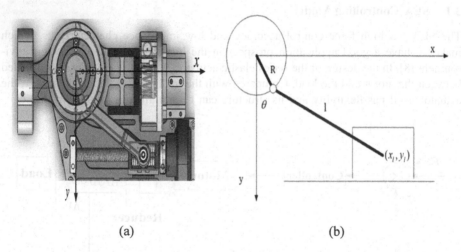

(a)   (b)

Fig. 7. Modeling of the SEA. (a) The structure diagram of the SEA. (b) The simplified schematic of the SEA.

From the Fig. 7b, we can derive the following equations:

$$(R\sin\theta - x_l)^2 + (R\cos\theta - y_l)^2 = l^2 \qquad (4)$$

From the above equations, we can get the relationship between the slider trajectory x_l and the joint angle θ as shown in Fig. 8.

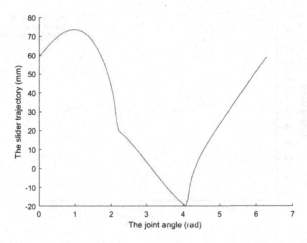

Fig. 8. The relationship between the slider trajectory and the joint angle.

In this design, because the trajectory of the slider is limited to 4–56 mm, the trajectory of the slider and the joint Angle can be approximated as a linear relationship. Meanwhile, in order to simplify the calculation process, we can approximate the relationship between the angular displacement of motor and knee joint angle to be linear, as shown in Fig. 9.

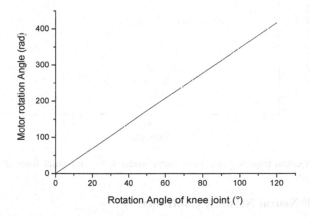

Fig. 9. The linear relationship between motor and joint angle.

Precise torque control of the load can be realized by controlling the position of SEA elastic element. However, since the position control cycle of SEA is larger than the traditional position closed-loop control cycle, the SEA is easy to be affected by the load change, resulting in the decrease in the robustness of the system. The traditional PID control is difficult to compensate for the nonlinear torque. Taking sinusoidal force as an example, the torque and the position trajectories under the interference of 10% nonlinear load are shown in the Figs. 10 and 11, respectively.

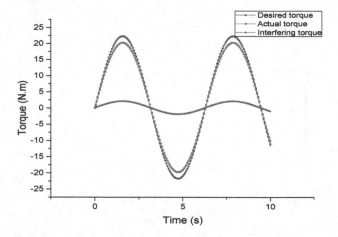

Fig. 10. Torque trajectory tracking curve under 10% sinusoidal force disturbance.

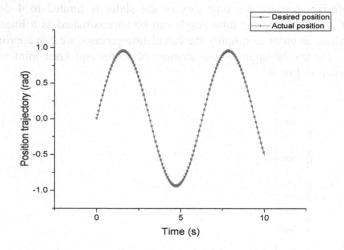

Fig. 11. Position trajectory tracking curve under 10% sinusoidal force disturbance.

3.2   The RBF Neural Network Controller

From the above two figures, the traditional PID control is not robust enough to compensate for the unknown nonlinear disturbances. In order to compensate these unknown nonlinear disturbances, we need to design a nonlinear controller for online learning. The RBF neural network controller [9, 10] is a nonlinear adaptive controller and is based on the reference compensation technology. For the torque control based on the series elastic joints, the feedforward curve of position control is learned to compensate for the influence of various nonlinear factors on the system control. The structure of the RBF neural network controller is shown in Fig. 12.

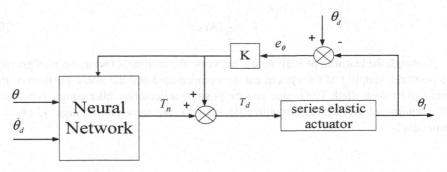

Fig. 12. Structure of the neural network controller.

The joint position following error, based on SEA, was defined as:

$$e_\theta = \theta_d - \theta_l \tag{5}$$

Wherein, θ_d is the expected Angle of the load, and θ_l is the actual Angle of the load. Neural network controller can be expressed as

$$T_d = T_n + Ke_\theta \tag{6}$$

K is the proportional coefficient of the controller, and T_n is the output of compensating torque calculated by the RBF neural network. A triple-input single-output neural network is established, and the RBF neural network algorithm [11] is:

$$h_j = \exp(-\frac{\left\|x(k) - c_j\right\|^2}{2b_j^2}) \tag{7}$$

$$f = \sum_{j=1}^{m} w_j h_j \tag{8}$$

Where $x(k)$ is the input of the network, and $h = [h_1, h_2, \cdots, h_m]$ is the output of the Gauss base function, w is the weight of the network, and m denotes the number of the neurons. Let the function of the desired compensating torque be $f(\theta, \dot{\theta}_d, e_\theta)$ when the joint is at Angle θ, the model control error as in:

$$Ke_\theta = T_d - T_n = T_d - f(\theta, \dot{\theta}_d, e_\theta) \tag{9}$$

Therefore, the training error of the RBF neural network controller is set as Ke_θ. When the training error converges to 0, the output torque T_n of the RBF neural network model is equal to the actual required torque. The objective function of optimization is set to:

$$F = \frac{1}{2}(Ke_\theta)^2 \tag{10}$$

Through the learning of RBF neural network, the nonlinear factors such as gravity, friction and damping of the system can be compensated and the stable position of the joint can be controlled. The torque and the position trajectories, after compensating the 10% nonlinear load interference with RBF network, are shown in the Figs. 13 and 14, respectively.

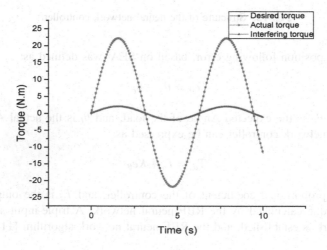

Fig. 13. RBF network is used to track the torque trajectory after nonlinear compensation.

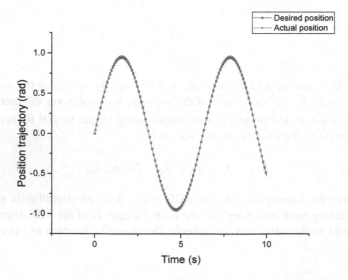

Fig. 14. RBF network is used to track the position trajectory after nonlinear compensation.

From the above two figures, using RBF network to compensate nonlinear distur- bance online can improve the torque tracking effect, and the degree of improvement is related to the disturbance size. It is good, especially, for the torque compensation effect. Therefore, it can be believed that this controller can effectively compensate the influ- ence of nonlinear load on the control and improve the system robustness.

In order to verify the effectiveness of the algorithm, tests were conducted. During the knee joint movement, with the change of joint Angle, the influencing factors such as gravity, friction and our additional disturbing forces on the system changed but the system still had good follow-through due to the existence of compensation mechanism as shown in Fig. 15. Even in the regions, where there is a sharp change in the direction of the acceleration, namely the wave trough position in the Fig. 15, the actual trajectory still has a maximum error of 3.8°. Based on the previous testing experience, these results attributed to the impact of motor performance.

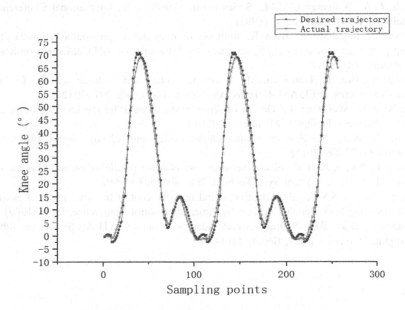

Fig. 15. Desired and actual knee joint trajectories.

4 Conclusion

In this paper, a new series elastic actuator for knee exoskeleton was developed. According to this structure, a compensation control strategy based on RBF neural network is proposed, which takes the walking gait of healthy human body as the reference for the position control of the lower limb exoskeleton robot and adjusts the compensation torque according to the rules obtained from the RBF neural network learning. By adjusting the stiffness of the elastic element and the structural parameters of the RBF neural network, the modular knee exoskeleton can be applied to a variety of complex situations.

Acknowledgment. The authors greatly appreciate the financial support from national key development plan project of intelligent robot, ministry of science and technology of China (No. 2017YFB1300505), National Natural Science Foundation of China (No. U1813212).

References

1. Esquenazi, A., Talaty, M., et al.: The ReWalk powered exoskeleton to restore ambulatory function to individuals with thoracic-level motor-complete spinal cord injury. Am. J. Phys. Med. Rehabil. **91**(11), 911–921 (2012)
2. Duschau-Wicke, A., Zitzewitz, J.V., et al.: Path control: a method for patient-cooperative robot-aided gait rehabilitation. IEEE Trans. Neural Syst. Rehabil. Eng. **18**(1), 38–48 (2010)
3. Zoss, A.B., Kazerooni, H., Chu, A.: On the mechanical design of the Berkeley Lower Extremity Exoskeleton (BLEEX). In: IEEE/RSJ International Conference on Intelligent Robots and Systems. IEEE (2005)
4. Pratt, G.A., Williamson, M.M.: Series elastic actuators. In: International Conference on Intelligent Robots & Systems (1995)
5. Schütz, S., Nejadfard, A., Bern, K.: Influence of loads and design parameters on the closed-loop performance of series elastic actuators. In: IEEE International Conference on Robotics & Biomimetics (2017)
6. Kong, K., Bae, J., Tomizuka, M.: A compact rotary series elastic actuator for human assistive systems. IEEE/ASME Trans. Mechatron. **17**(2), 288–297 (2012)
7. Yu-Xian, G., Wei-Ying, L.: Design of series elastic actuator for the knee joint of assistive limb. Machinery Design & Manufacture (2014)
8. Rong, X., et al.: Novel series elastic actuator design and velocity control. Electr. Mach. Control **19**, 83–88 (2015)
9. Lin, F.J., Wai, R.J., et al.: Neural-network controller for parallel-resonant ultrasonic motor drive. IEEE Trans. Control Syst. Technol. **7**(4), 494–501 (1999)
10. Zhang, T., Ge, S.S., et al.: Adaptive neural network control for strict-feedback nonlinear systems using back stepping design. In: American Control Conference. IEEE (1999)
11. Jinkun, L., et al.: RBF Neural Network Adaptive Control MATLAB Simulation, 4th edn. Tsinghua University Press, Beijing (2014)

Comparison of Different Schemes for Motion Control of Pneumatic Artificial Muscle Using Fast Switching Valve

Shenglong Xie, Binrui Wang$^{(\boxtimes)}$, and Dijian Chen

School of Mechanical and Electrical Engineering,
China Jiliang University, Hangzhou, China
wangbinrui@163.com

Abstract. This paper investigates the mathematical model and control schemes for tracking control of pneumatic artificial muscle (PAM) using fast switching valves. Three control schemes are proposed and compared to achieve high accuracy trajectory tracking. The static model of PAM is established using the isometric experimental data, and the dynamic model of PAM is derived based on the polytropic equation. Then, the hysteresis model and its inverse model of PAM is established by using Prandtl–Shlinskii (PI) model, in which the air mass flow rate through the fast switching valve is evaluated using the Sanville equation. Sequentially, the trajectory tracking control schemes of PAM are derived by means of feedforward, feedback, and feedforward/feedback control schemes, which are implemented in the environment of MATLAB/Simulink. The results indicate that the feedforward/feedback control scheme can achieve better performance and accuracy.

Keywords: Pneumatic artificial muscle · Fast switching valve · Hysteresis model · PI model · Feedforward/feedback control

1 Introduction

The emergence of cross-subjects in recent years promotes the research and application technology of robotics. The end actuator, which connects with target object directly, is the core part of robot. The actuator can be divided into two driving mode according to its rigidity: rigid driven (like servo-actuator) and soft driven (like tether and pneumatic muscle actuator). The pneumatic artificial muscle (PAM) possess several advantages over the servo-motor, such as simple structure, compactness, high power-to-weight ratio, etc. [1], which has been widely used in medical rehabilitation robots, bionic robots, and orthotics. However, its hysteresis [2], threshold pressures [3], creep [4], compliance [5], and low bandwidth [6] makes the design of the controller complicated. Especially, since the hysteresis may cause energy loss and reduce the contracting force, there are tracking errors in PAMs. Therefore, there is a demand to establish a precise hysteresis model to improve the dynamic behavior of a PAM [7].

Two types of electro-pneumatic valves are usually used to control the fluid flow of a PAM, i.e. the continuously acting servo/proportional valves and the on–off switching

© Springer Nature Switzerland AG 2019
H. Yu et al. (Eds.): ICIRA 2019, LNAI 11742, pp. 641–653, 2019.
https://doi.org/10.1007/978-3-030-27535-8_57

valves [8]. Although the servo/proportional valve has high control accuracy, it is expensive and tends to be bulky compared to the on–off switching (or fast switching) valve. Therefore, the trajectory control methods of PAM utilizing fast switching valves have been extensively studied in recent years. Li [9] proposed a novel position control scheme for a lightweight forceps manipulator using pneumatic artificial muscles (PAMs), the outer position feedback loop is PD controller and a feedforward block, and the inner pressure feedback loop is PI controller. The experiment results are satisfied. But the reference pressure of PAM needs to be derived according the structure of the robot, which limits the popularization of this method. Robinson [10] developed a PID control and fuzzy logic control with model-based feedforward compensation to improve the accuracy and smooth motion requirements for a two degree-of-freedom manipulator actuated by PAMs. But it does not consider the dynamic characteristics of PAM that better accounts for nonlinearities, such as hysteresis. To account for the hysteresis during the movement of PAM. Ito [11, 12] researched the motion control of a parallel manipulator with two degrees of freedom, which is driven by three PAMs. Where a stop model is used to account for the hysteresis in the contracting of PAM. Vo-Minh et al. [13] used a Maxwell-slip model as a lumped-parametric quasistatic mode to approach to the force/length hysteresis of a PAM. This model can analysis the behaviors like the hysteresis phenomena in mechanical friction. Lin [14] researched the hysteresis modeling and tracking control of PAM by using PI model and Bouc-Wen model, and taken different feedback control schemes combined with a feedforward controller based on PI model for hysteresis compensation to reduce the tracking error of PAM. But they all use servo/proportional valve to drive the PAM. However, Zhang [15, 16] et al. used high-speed on-off valves to research the control of PAMs. But they assume that the spool displacement changes linearly during the on and off process and does not consider the hysteresis characteristics of PAM. Therefore, it has to further investigate the precision tracking control of PAM using fast switching valves.

This paper deals with the trajectory tracking control of PAM using the fast switching valve. The rest of this paper is organized as follows. In Sect. 2 the experimental system is briefly introduced. In Sect. 3, the static model, dynamic model, and hysteresis model of the PAM are systematically derived. Then, three control schemes are proposed to achieve high accuracy trajectory tracking control of the PAM, and the simulations are carried out in the environment of MATLAB/Simulink in Sect. 4 before conclusions are drawn in Sect. 5.

2   System Description and Experimental Apparatus

2.1   Overview of the Control System

Figure 1 shows the schematic diagram of the control system of the pneumatic artificial muscle. The air compressor connects the fast switching valve with throttle valve and reservoir. The fast switching valve 1 is inlet valve, called inlet valve for short; the fast switching valve 2 is exhaust valve, called exhaust valve for short. In the absence of solenoid excitation, the valve keeps closed by return spring, and it opens when the solenoid is energized by DC voltage. The working process is as follows. Initially, the

PAM connects with the external environment, and the internal pressure of PAM is equal to atmospheric pressure. When the inlet valve is open, the compressed air flows into the PAM while the exhaust valve is closed, resulting in the contraction of the PAM. When the PAM reaches the desired position, the inlet and exhaust valves are closed at the same time, then the PAM keeps the compressed air inside and maintains the current state. When inlet valve is closed and exhaust valve is open, the compressed air is discharged through the exhaust valve. During this process, fast switching valves are controlled by PWM signals. In the beginning, the inlet valve is fully opened to let the PAM quickly reach the desired position; when it is approaching to the desired position, the duty cycle of PWM is reduced proportionally to the displacement deviation. When the displacement deviation is smaller than a given value, the duty cycle of PWM is set zero to avoid the PAM oscillating around the desired position. The components used in the experiment are given in Table 1.

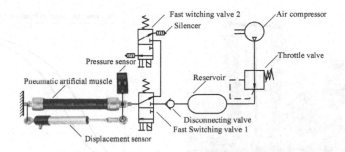

Fig. 1. Schematic of the experimental apparatus.

Table 1. Components of the experimental apparatus.

Component	Type	Company
PAM	DMSP-20-500N-RM-CM	Festo
Displacement sensor	TEX 0150 415 002 205	Novotechnik
Force sensor	DBBP-200	BONGSHIN
Pressure sensor	SDE1-D10-G2-WQ4-L-PU-M8-G5	Festo
Fast switching valve	MHE2-MS1H-3/2G-QS-4-K	Festo
Data acquisition card	PCI-6254	National instruments

2.2 Isometric Apparatus

The isometric setup is illustrated in Fig. 2. The aim of this experiment is to find the experimental model of the contracting force between the length and internal pressure of PAM. In isometric experiment, both end caps of the test muscle are fixed to a stiff metal plate, and one is fixed to the base via the force sensor. The PAM is constrained at a serial length, while the pressure is increased from 0 to 6 bar. Figure 3 shows the variations of contracting force F const versus internal pressure P at different constrained lengths x.

Fig. 2. Isometric experimental apparatus.

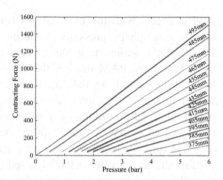

Fig. 3. Variations of F_{const} vs. P at different lengths x.

Fig. 4. Hysteresis experimental apparatus.

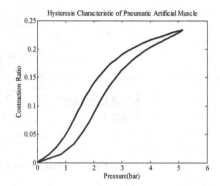

Fig. 5. Pressure/length hysteresis loop of PAM.

2.3   Hysteretic Apparatus

Figure 4 is the pressure/length hysteretic apparatus. In the setup, one end cap of PAM is fixed to the stiff metal plate, and another one is free to move, the PAM is contracting when the pressure is increased from 0 to 6 bar, which is recorded by the pressure sensor, and the displacement sensor records the length of PAM. Figure 5 shows the pressure/length hysteresis characteristics obtained from the experiment. Obviously, the contraction ratio of PAM is different between the stretching and contraction given the same pressure.

3   Mathematical Model

3.1   Static Model of PAM

The static model of a PAM gives a nonlinear relationship between the contracting force, the applied pressure, and the PAM length. There are several methods for developing static models of a PAM, such as geometry analysis, the principle of energy conservation, and empirical method. These models always rely on simplifying assumptions, for example, neglecting of the rugby-ball shape forms at either end of the PAM or the thickness of the PAM bladder, *etc*. These assumptions results in the inconsistency of predicted result and practical measurement, and make the precise position control of pneumatic muscle hard to be achieved. Therefore, in this paper, the static model is established by means of isometric experiment.

It can be seen from Fig. 3 that for a given length the variation of P vs. F_{const} is nearly linear, but the slopes are varied for x. It indicates that the contracting force can be formulated as a linear function of the internal pressure and length [17]

$$F_{\text{const}} = a(x)P + b(x) \tag{1}$$

where $a(x)$ and $b(x)$ are the slope and the intercept, respectively. $a(x)$ and $b(x)$ can be evaluated as follows

$$\begin{cases} a(x) = \displaystyle\sum_{i=0}^{2} a_i x^i \\ b(x) = \displaystyle\sum_{j=0}^{3} b_j x^j \end{cases} \tag{2}$$

where a_i and b_j are the coefficients of the polynomial function.

These coefficients can be obtained by using the least squares curve fitting tools in MATLAB, and are given as follows

$$\begin{cases} a(x) = 0.000953x^2 + 0.7979x - 370.7 \\ b(x) = 0.0004561x^3 - 0.5668x^2 + 234.6x - 32560 \end{cases} \tag{3}$$

Substituting Eq. (3) into Eq. (1), one can obtain the static model of PAM. Based on this model, the variation of the length of the PAM vs. its internal pressure can be obtained once given the load and internal pressure.

3.2 Dynamic Model of PAM

Since the PAM is constructed by an elastic nylon material rubber covered by a mesh of inextensible threads, it can be assumed that during charging and discharging process are in isothermal and adiabatic states. The relationship of the mass of air, muscle volume, and internal pressure obeys as follows [18]

$$\dot{P} = \frac{k}{V} \left(\dot{m}RT - P\dot{V} \right) \tag{4}$$

where P and V are the inner pressure and volume of PAM; m is the air mass inside the PAM; k is the polytropic exponent.

Assuming that the volume of PAM is constant during charging and discharging, then $P\dot{V} \equiv 0$ and the internal pressure can be obtained by taking integration of Eq. (4).

3.3   Hysteresis Model of PAM

In this section, the Prandtl-Ishlinskii (PI) model [19] is adopted to derive the hysteresis of the PAM. The elementary operator of the PI model is linear play operator, which can be mathematically illustrated by Fig. 6. Its ith linear play operator can be expressed as

$$y_i(k) = \max\{x(k) - r_i, \min\{x(k) + r_i, y_i(k - 1)\}\} \tag{5}$$

while the initial condition is

$$y_i(0) = \max\{x(0) - r_i, \min\{x(0) + r_i, y_{i0}\}\} \tag{6}$$

The output of PI model is

$$y(k) = \sum_{i=1}^{n} \omega_i y_i(k) = \omega^T H_r[x(k), y_0] \tag{7}$$

where H_r denotes the linear play operator; $\omega = [\omega_1, \cdots, \omega_n]^T$ is the weighting vector; $r = [r_1, \ldots, r_n]^T$ is the threshold vector; x and y are the input and output of the operator, respectively; y_0 is the initial state; k is the sampling number of the operator; and n is the number of the linear play operator.

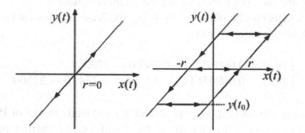

Fig. 6. The linear paly operator.

To determine the parameters of PI model, the threshold vector r is firstly determined by the following equation

$$r_i = \frac{i}{n+1} \max\{|x(t)|\} \qquad i = 1, \cdots, n \tag{8}$$

Then, using the least square method (LSM) the weighting vector ω is determined. The Eq. (7) can be rewritten as

$$y(k) = \sum_{i=1}^{n} \omega_i y_i(k) = H_r^T[x(k), y_i(k - 1)]\omega = \varphi^T(k)\theta \tag{9}$$

Then, one can obtain

$$\begin{cases} K(k) = \frac{P(k-1)\varphi(k)}{1+\varphi^T(k)P(k-1)\varphi(k)} \\ \theta(k) = \theta(k-1) + K(k)[y(k) - \varphi^T(k)\theta(k-1)] \\ P(k) = [I - K(k)\varphi^T(k)]P(k-1) \end{cases} \tag{10}$$

The initial value is given as follows

$$\begin{cases} P(0) = \alpha I \\ \theta(0) = \varepsilon \end{cases} \tag{11}$$

where α is a positive real number and ε is a zero vector.

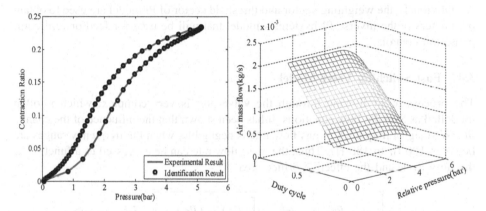

Fig. 7. Fitting result of PI model.   **Fig. 8.** Air mass flow of fast switching valve.

Figure 7 shows the comparison of the pressure/length hysteresis characteristics obtained from the experiment and the PI model using the identified parameters. The result clearly shows that the PI model can effectively characterize the hysteresis loop. From Eq. (5), the inverse model of PI model can be formulated as

$$x_i'(k) = \max\{y(k) - r_i', \min\{y(k) + r_i', x_i'(k-1)\}\} \tag{12}$$

$$x(k) = \sum_{i=1}^n \omega_i'\max\{y(k) - r_i', \min\{y(k) + r_i', x_i'(k-1)\}\} \tag{13}$$

Correspondingly, the inverse hysteresis model can then be formulated as follows.

$$x(k) = H^{-1}(y(k)) = \omega'^T H_r'[y(k), x_0] \tag{14}$$

where H'_r denotes the inverse PI operator; $\omega\prime = [\omega'_1, \ldots, \omega'_1]^T$ is the weighting vector; $r\prime = [r'_1, \ldots, r'_1]^T$ is the threshold vector; x_0 is the initial state. The parameters of the inverse hysteresis model can be given as

$$
\begin{cases}
\omega'_1 = \dfrac{1}{\omega_1} \\[2mm]
\omega'_i = \dfrac{-\omega_i}{\left(\omega_1 + \sum\limits_{j=2}^{i} \omega_j\right)\left(\omega_1 + \sum\limits_{j=2}^{i-1} \omega_j\right)} & i = 2, \cdots, n \\[6mm]
r'_i = \sum\limits_{j=1}^{i} \omega_j(r_i - r_j) & i = 1, \cdots, n \\[4mm]
x'_i(0) = \sum\limits_{j=1}^{i-1} \omega_j y_i(0) + \sum\limits_{j=i}^{n} \omega_j y_j(0) & i = 1, \cdots, n
\end{cases}
\tag{15}
$$

Obviously, the weighting vector and threshold vector of PI model are used to obtain parameters of the inverse PI hysteresis model that will be used for feedforward compensation control.

3.4   Fast Switching Valve Model

The process of air flowing through the valve port is very complex, which is often modelled as Sanville flow equations. It has been shown that the influence of the change of PWM signal frequency to gas flow rate is negligible, when the frequency ranges are between 100 Hz to 180 Hz. Thus, the mass flow rate can be expressed as a function of the duty cycle and the effective orifice area.

$$
\dot{m} =
\begin{cases}
dA_m \dfrac{p_u}{\sqrt{T_u}} \sqrt{\dfrac{2k}{R(k-1)}\left[\left(\dfrac{p_d}{p_u}\right)^{\frac{2}{k}} - \left(\dfrac{p_d}{p_u}\right)^{\frac{k+1}{k}}\right]} & \dfrac{p_d}{p_u} > 0.528 \\[6mm]
dA_m \dfrac{p_u}{\sqrt{T_u}} \left(\dfrac{2}{k+1}\right)^{\frac{1}{k-1}} \sqrt{\dfrac{2k}{R(k+1)}} & \dfrac{p_d}{p_u} \leq 0.528
\end{cases}
\tag{16}
$$

where $\dot{m}$ is the air mass flow rate of fast switching valve; p_u is the upstream pressure; p_d is the downstream pressure; T_u is the upstream temperature; k is the ratio of specific heat; d is duty cycle of PWM signals; A_m is the effective orifice area of fast switching valve. In reference [20], the effective orifice area A_m of the MHE2-MS1H-3/2G-M7-K fast switch valve is 1.8194×10^{-6} m^2. Figure 8 illustrates the air mass flow of fast switching valve between the duty cycle and relative pressure.

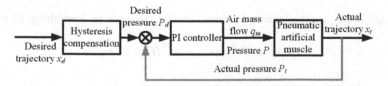

Fig. 9. Feedforward control scheme for pneumatic artificial muscle.

4 Motion Control Approach and Simulation

4.1 Feedforward Control

The feedforward control scheme is illustrated in Fig. 9. There are three steps for the design of feedforward compensation control. The first step is to determine the parameters of the hysteresis model, which is based on the linear or nonlinear identification method, as presented in Sect. 3. While the second step is to estimate the inverse hysteresis model for controller design. The third step is to develop the feedforward control scheme. The corresponding Simulink control scheme is shown in Fig. 10.

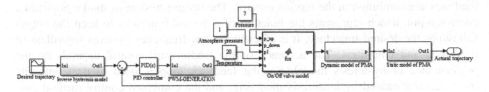

Fig. 10. Simulink model for feedforward control scheme.

4.2 Feedback Control

In the feedback control scheme, the nonlinearities are always treated as uncertainties, and the feedback controller will force the output to follow the desired trajectory based on the tracking error between the desired trajectory and the feedback output. The feedback loop is always a PID controller, which is given as

$$u(t) = K_p e(t) + K_i \int_0^t e(\tau) d\tau + K_d \frac{de(t)}{dt} \tag{17}$$

where $e(t)$ is error signal; $u(t)$ is output signal; K_p is proportional gain; K_i is integral gain; K_d is derivative gain.

The feedback control scheme is illustrated in Fig. 11. The feedback controller (PID controller) is used to provide high gain feedback which can overcome creep and vibration caused by hysteresis at low frequencies [21]. The corresponding Simulink control scheme is shown in Fig. 12.

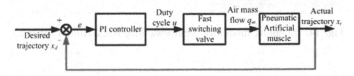

Fig. 11. Feedback control scheme for PAM.

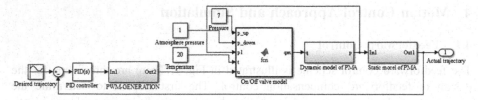

Fig. 12. Simulink model for feedback control scheme.

4.3 Feedforward/Feedback Control

To compensate the nonlinear hysteresis of the PAM, the input feedforward and output feedback are combined in the motion control. The inverse hysteresis model provides a control input, which represents the function of a desired trajectory to keep the output following the desired trajectory. It is efficient for low-frequency systems regardless of the creep and vibrations. The accuracy of the feedforward control depends on the performance of hysteresis model. So, the feedback loop is used to deal with the tracking error caused by hysteresis modeling, and the combined control method provides a high gain feedback and overcome creep and vibrations in the systems.

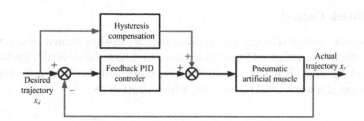

Fig. 13. Feedforward/feedback control scheme for PAM.

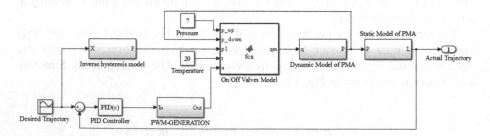

Fig. 14. Simulink model for feedforward/feedback control scheme.

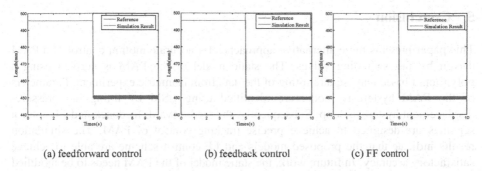

(a) feedforward control   (b) feedback control   (c) FF control

Fig. 15. Step response of PAM from initial length.

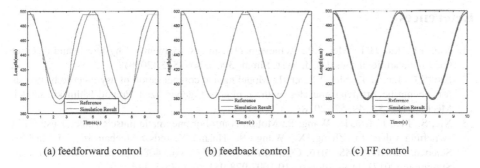

(a) feedforward control   (b) feedback control   (c) FF control

Fig. 16. Sinusoid response of PAM from initial length.

The feedforward/feedback (FF for short) control scheme is illustrated in Fig. 13. Hysteresis compensation based on inverse PI model is built into the control system through feedforward processing. The controller of the contraction ratio uses a proportional-integral (PID) controller. The corresponding Simulink control scheme is shown in Fig. 14.

Figures 15 and 16 show the simulation results of step and sinusoid trajectory tracking responses. Figure 15 is the step response of the PAM from initial length (500 mm), from which it can be seen that the PAM does not start from the initial length, because there are errors in the static model of the PAM. Figure 16 is the sinusoid response of PAM from initial length (500 mm). It can be found that the control accuracy of feedforward scheme is worse than the feedback and FF schemes. The wave crest is pared in the max length of PAM in Fig. 16(a) and (b). It is caused by the errors in the static model. While the trajectory is smooth in the wave crest in Fig. 16 (c), which indicates that the FF control scheme has better capability compared to the feedback control scheme. Numerical results show that the maximal residual in Fig. 16 (c) is 1%. It indicates that the FF control method can achieve satisfactory accuracy.

5 Conclusion

This paper presents three alternative approaches for accurate motion control of a PAM driven by fast switching valves. The static model of the PAM is derived using a polynomial based least square fitting of the data from isometric experiment. Parameters of the PAM hysteresis model are identified using LSM by fitting the pressure-displacement hysteresis loop. Subsequently, the feedforward, feedback and FF control schemes are designed to achieve precise tracking control of PAM. The simulation results indicate that the proposed models and FF control scheme are able to achieve satisfactory accuracy. In future work, the static model of the PAM needs to be modified in order to improve its accuracy, and experimental study will be carried out.

References

1. Xie, S.L., Liu, H.T., Mei, J.P.: Achievements and developments of hysteresis and creep of pneumatic artificial muscles. J. Syst. Simul. **30**(3), 809–823 (2018)
2. Xie, S.L., Liu, H.T., Mei, J.P., et al.: Modeling and compensation of asymmetric hysteresis for pneumatic artificial muscles with a modified generalized Prandtl-Ishlinskii model. Mechatronics **52**, 49–57 (2018)
3. Xie, S., Mei, J., Liu, H., Wang, P.: Motion control of pneumatic muscle actuator using fast switching valve. In: Zhang, X., Wang, N., Huang, Y. (eds.) Mechanism and Machine Science, ASIAN MMS 2016, CCMMS 2016. LNEE, vol. 408, pp. 1439–1451. Springer, Singapore (2017). https://doi.org/10.1007/978-981-10-2875-5_114
4. Vo-minh, T., Kamers, B., Ramon, H., et al.: Modeling and control of a pneumatic artificial muscle manipulator joint–part I: modeling of a pneumatic artificial muscle manipulator joint with accounting for creep effect. Mechatronics **22**(7), 923–933 (2012)
5. Daerden, F., Lefeber, D.: Pneumatic artificial muscles: actuators for robotics and automation. Eur. J. Mech. Environ. Eng. **47**(1), 11–21 (2002)
6. Caldwell, D.G., Medrano, G., Goodwin, M.: Control of pneumatic muscle actuators. IEEE Control Syst. **15**(1), 40–48 (1995)
7. Davis, S., Caldwel, D.G.: Braid effects on contractile range and friction modeling in pneumatic muscle actuators. Int. J. Robot. Res. **25**(4), 359–369 (2006)
8. Taghizadeh, M., Ghaffari, A., Najafi, F.: Modeling and identification of a solenoid valve for PWM control applications. Comptes Rendus Mecanique **337**(3), 131–140 (2005)
9. Li, H., Kawashima, K., Tadano, K., et al.: Achieving haptic perception in forceps manipulator using pneumatic artificial muscle. IEEE/ASME Trans. Mechatron. **18**(1), 74–85 (2013)
10. Robinson, R.M., Wereley, N.M., Kothera, C.S., et al.: Model-based feedforward control of a robotic manipulator with pneumatic artificial muscles. In: ASME Conference on Smart Materials, Adaptive Structures and Intelligent Systems, pp. 461–471. ASME, Georgia (2012)
11. Ito, A., Kiyoto, K., Furuya, N.: Motion control of parallel manipulator using pneumatic artificial actuators. In: IEEE International Conference on Robotics and Biomimetics, pp. 460–465. IEEE, Tianjin (2010)
12. Ito, A., Washizawa, N., Kiyoto, K., et al.: Control of pneumatic actuator in consideration of hysteresis characteristics. In: IEEE International Conference on Robotics and Biomimetics, pp. 2541–2546. IEEE, Phuket (2011)

13. Vo-minh, T., Tjahjowidodo, T., Ramon, H., et al.: A new approach to modeling hysteresis in a pneumatic artificial muscle using the Maxwell-slip model. IEEE/ASME Trans. Mechatron. **16**(1), 177–186 (2011)

14. Lin, C.J., Lin, C.R., Yu, S.K., et al.: Hysteresis modeling and tracking control for a dual pneumatic artificial muscle system using Prandtl-Ishlinskii model. Mechatronics **28**, 35–45 (2015)

15. Chen, Y., Zhang, J.F., Yang, C.J., et al.: Design and hybrid control of the pneumatic force-feedback systems for Arm-Exoskeleton by using on/off valve. Mechatronics **17**(6), 325–335 (2007)

16. Zhang, J.F., Yang, C.J., Chen, Y., et al.: Modeling and control of a curved pneumatic muscle actuator for wearable elbow exoskeleton. Mechatronics **18**(8), 448–457 (2008)

17. Pujana, A.A., Mendizabal, A., Arenas, J., et al.: Modelling in Modelica and position control of a 1-DoF set-up powered by pneumatic muscles. Mechatronics **20**(5), 535–552 (2010)

18. Xie, S.L., Mei, J.P., Liu, H.T.: Achievements and trends of research on McKibben pneumatic artificial muscles. Comput. Integr. Manuf. Syst. **24**(5), 1065–1081 (2018)

19. Kuhnen, K., Janocha, H.: Inverse feedforward controller for complex hysteretic nonlinearities in smart-material systems. Control Intell. Syst. **29**(3), 74–83 (2001)

20. Xie, S.L., Liu, H.T., Mei, J.P., et al.: Simulation of tracking control of pneumatic artificial muscle based on fast switching valves. Trans. Chin. Soc. Agric. Mach. **48**(1), 368–374+385 (2017)

21. Xie, S.L., Mei, J.P., Liu, H.T.: Kinematics modeling and simulation of trajectory tracking control of a foot-plate-based lower-limb rehabilitation robot. J. Tianjin Univ. (Sci. Technol.) **51**(5), 443–452 (2018)

Recognition of Pes Cavus Foot Using Smart Insole: A Pilot Study

Zhanyong Mei[1], Kamen Ivanov[2,3], Ludwig Lubich[4], and Lei Wang[2(✉)]

[1] College of Cyber Security, Chengdu University of Technology, Chengdu 610059, China
zhanyongm99@163.com

[2] Shenzhen Institutes of Advanced Technology, Chinese Academy of Sciences, Shenzhen 518055, China
{kamen,wang.lei}@siat.ac.cn

[3] Shenzhen College of Advanced Technology, University of Chinese Academy of Sciences, Shenzhen 518055, China

[4] Faculty of Telecommunications, Technical University of Sofia, Sofia 1000, Bulgaria
lvl@tu-sofia.bg

Abstract. The presence of pes cavus, a high-arched foot, is a potential reason for some neuromuscular problems. Active research efforts are being made to devise portable systems for monitoring and early detection of foot deviations. In line with that, we have developed instrumented insoles that incorporate force and inertial sensors and used them to capture data from sixty-four subjects; among them, there were forty-four subjects with normal feet arches and twenty subjects exhibiting pes cavus. We applied a 1D convolutional neural network to extract features and classify data. The trained model allowed for a recognition rate of more than 96%. The presented use case could inspire further research on using smart footwear for pes cavus screening and progression monitoring.

Keywords: Pes cavus · Smart insole · Plantar pressure · 1D CNN

1 Introduction

Individuals with pes cavus exhibit a higher foot arch compared to those with normal feet. Surveys show that pes cavus is present in around 8–15% of the world population [1]. This condition leads to neuromuscular problems, including unstable gait, foot pain, and ankle sprains [1, 2]. Its early recognition and appropriate assessment are essential for successful treatment and management [2]. So far, morphological parameters were always used to serve the classification of the foot type. Those were obtained using techniques of visual non-quantitative inspection, anthropometric measurement, footprint parameter measurement, and radiographic evaluation [3]. However, these methods are to be practiced by podiatrists and require repetitive training.

Efforts are being made for devising instruments and methods to automate data capture and foot function analysis. The evaluation of the foot locomotion characteristics

© Springer Nature Switzerland AG 2019
H. Yu et al. (Eds.): ICIRA 2019, LNAI 11742, pp. 654–662, 2019.
https://doi.org/10.1007/978-3-030-27535-8_58

is then performed based on kinematic and kinetic parameters. Existing instrumentation includes pressure distribution measurement systems and 3D force plates for obtaining kinetic parameters, and inertial sensors or visual capturing systems to retrieve kinematic ones. However, these systems require time-consuming procedures, and many of them are not applicable to serve regular evaluation or are not accessible to the general public due to high costs. The desire is to introduce portable measurement devices that could support foot type evaluation. As pes cavus progresses with the time, such automated devices could allow for regular screening and early detection of foot abnormalities [21]. Each foot type is associated with a specific pattern of plantar pressure distribution during the gait cycle [5]. In particular, the peak of vertical ground reaction force and the footprint areas during the stance phase were found different between a flat foot and pes valgus [4]. Also, the peak pressures under the five metatarsophalangeal joints and the minimum velocity of the center of pressure during the terminal stance phase [6] differ between a normal foot and pes cavus [5, 6]. The maximum force under the medial arch, the force-time integral under the hallux, the pressure-time integral under the fifth metatarsal head and their normalized values are also different between a normal foot and pes cavus [10]. As to automated methods for foot type classification, so far, artificial neural networks, adaptive neuro-fuzzy inference systems, and K-means algorithms were applied [14–16].

As inertial sensors are easy to incorporate into wearable devices, they can serve gait analysis and applications involving gait and activity recognition [11, 12, 22]. Loco-motion characteristics of pes cavus also were explored using accelerometers. Ledoux et al. [7] studied the difference in the calcaneal acceleration at heel strike between a normal foot and pes planus using an accelerometer. Pes cavus foot exhibited a higher acceleration in comparison with the normal foot [9]. Ogon et al. [8] found that acceleration amplitudes and angular rates of subjects with pes cavus are lower com-pared to respective ones of subjects with pes planus. Based on such differences, recognition systems could be constructed.

However, to date, no classifier was demonstrated that could effectively recognize pes cavus based on the combination of simultaneously captured inertial data and/or single point force sensors. To address this gap, we used data from a custom prototype incorporating inertial and force sensing. We hypothesized that the combination of simultaneously recorded multimodal sensor data could reflect better the specifics of pes cavus and allow for better recognition. Deep learning has been successfully used in different subdomains of biomedical data processing, including image processing, speech recognition, and natural language processing. Thus, we applied a 1D convo-lutional neural network (1D CNN) to extract gait features for the recognition of pes cavus from data acquired using our prototype.

2 Data Collection

2.1 Smart Insole Implementation

The sensor insole prototype consists of a Bluetooth Low Energy- enabled electronic control module, which connects to nine force sensors, and has an integrated inertial sensor. The module is based on a wireless system-on-chip of type nRF52832, and contains an inertial sensor of type BMI160 incorporating triaxial accelerometer and gyroscope. Selected force sensors are of type FlexiForce A301 and were attached to a specially designed thin and flexible printed circuit board, with locations matching the main weight-bearing positions of the foot, namely, the hallux, the five metatarsus heads, the lateral foot arch, the medial and lateral heel areas. All data were sampled at 100 Hz and transferred wirelessly to a personal computer. Each control module was attached on the top of the frontal part of the shoe. An assembled instrumented shoe is shown in Fig. 1a.

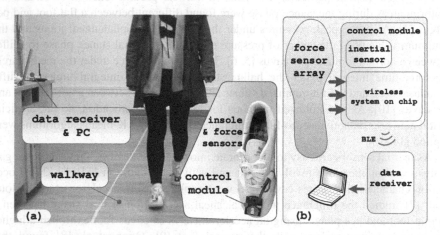

Fig. 1. (a) our smart insole prototype (b) experimental setting.

2.2   Experiment Configuration

Sixty-four volunteers participated in the experiment. Of them, forty-four with normal feet and twenty with pes cavus (Table 1). A podiatrist determined the foot type of each subject. Before executing the experiment, each volunteer was informed about the experimental procedure, signed an informed consent form, and filled a questionnaire about demographic characteristics, general health, and feet status. The data collection procedure was conducted in accordance with the Declaration of Helsinki and was approved by the ethics committee of the University of Technology of Chengdu. To perform a trial, the subject had to walk at a self-selected speed straight ahead for seven meters, wearing instrumented shoes of an appropriate size. Sudden changes in gait were not allowed. Each subject performed twenty trials. Each trial was recorded by a camera. Trial recordings which had missing data due to wireless transmission losses were excluded from the further analysis. Thus, 1130 records of right foot were processed. The characteristics of the subjects are presented in Table 1. The experimental configuration is shown in Fig. 1(b). A representative example of the waveforms of signals captured during a trial is provided in Fig. 2.

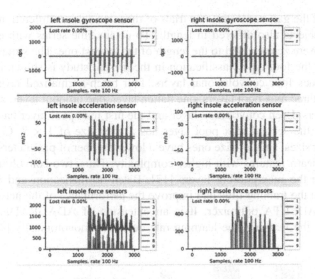

Fig. 2. Waveforms of signals captured during a trial.

Table 1. Characteristics of subjects

Foot type	Gender (male/female)	Height (cm ± SD)	Weight (kg ± SD)	Foot size (No[1] ± SD)
Normal (44)	31/13	169.1 ± 8.3	61.7 ± 10.3	40.1 ± 2.6
Pes cavus (20)	15/5	169.9 ± 5.9	61.0 ± 9.2	39.8 ± 2.2
Total (64)	46/18	169.3 ± 7.6	61.6 ± 10.7	40.0 ± 2.5

[1]Shoe size according to the Continental European system

3 1D CNN

Classical methods for foot type classification are always based on hand-crafted features extracted from plantar pressure. Possibly, these features do not fully reflect the characteristics of the different foot types. Consequently, the classifier may not reach the best performance because the most discriminative features were not found. Deep learning-based methods have a strong ability to learn features. For instance, 1D CNN has been successfully applied to human action recognition [11, 12]. Also, anterior cruciate ligament deficiency was recognized based on plantar pressure data passed to a 2D CNN [13].

In the present work, a 1D CNN deep learning method was used for feature learning and classification of the two types of foot. The typical CNN has a structure that involves convolution layers, a pool layer, and fully connected layers. The stack of convolution and pooling layers allows the automatic feature extraction, from low-level to high-level representations.

Because of the gait variability, the trials of the same subject differed in length; trials of different subjects also differed in length. To obtain time series with equal lengths, shorter series were zero padded to the length of the longest one. The structure of the 1D CNN used for the foot type classification in the present study is shown in Fig. 3. The network includes four convolutional layers, four batch-normalized layers, four activation layers, three max pool layers, one flatten layer, one dropout layer, and three fully connected layers. Each convolution layer and the first max pool layer have a filter size of 1×7, and the second max pool layer has a filter size of 1×7. Compared with filters of larger sizes, smaller-size ones have a lower number of parameters to learn, and they can also learn features with higher complexity. Thus, two convolution layers are stacked before the max-pooling layers [17]. Batch normalization and dropout were used to shorten the training time and improve the performance of the network [18, 19]. We used ADADELTA optimizer. It is an extension of ADAGRAD, and with the progression of the learning, the learning rate decreases monotonically [20].

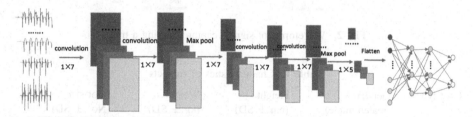

Fig. 3. The architecture of the proposed 1D CNN. It consists of two convolution layers, one max pool layer, two convolutional layers, a max pool layer, one flatten layer, and three fully connected layers. After every convolutional layer, there is a batch normalization layer.

4   Results

We tested the described network with the inertial and force sensor data separately, as well as taken together. To train the network, 80% of the samples were used, while the rest of them served for the testing. We trained the 1D CNN with 100 training epochs. The accuracies obtained by the 1D CNN are listed in Table 2. The best accuracy was obtained in two cases - when all modalities were used, and also for force data only. The training and validation losses are shown in Fig. 4. The confusion matrices are shown in Fig. 5.

For comparison with traditional methods, a random forest classifier with default parameter settings was tested as it is the best one to classify gait-related features [23]. The classifier took calculated input features. These were the maximum, minimum, mean, range, zero crossing rate, root-mean-square value, variance, standard variance, skewness, and kurtosis, obtained for each series. In Table 3, the performance of the random forest classifier is given. When applied to both inertial and force data, the classifier has shown the best accuracy. When using single-modality data, the accuracy of the classifier using force data was better than one only using inertial data.

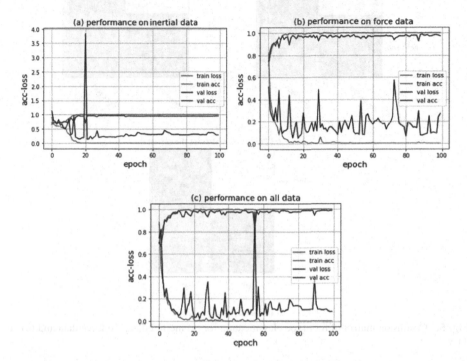

Fig. 4. Accuracy and loss for three kinds of sensor data passed during each epoch. (a) accuracy and loss on inertial data, (b) accuracy and loss on the force data, (c) accuracy and loss on all data.

Table 2. Performance of the 1D-CNN

	Foot type	Inertial data	Force data	All data
Accuracy	Normal	99.44%	100%	100%
	Pes cavus	85.42%	100%	100%
	Total	96.46%	100%	100%

Table 3. Performance of the random forest classifier

	Foot type	Inertial data	Force data	All data
Accuracy	Normal	98.31%	97.75%	99.42%
	Pes cavus	75%	83.33%	86.79%
	Total	93.36%	94.69%	96.46%

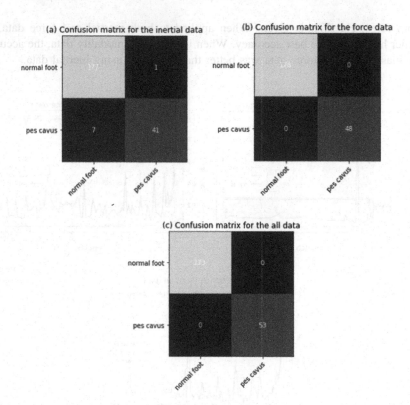

Fig. 5. Confusion matrix of foot type classification for (a) inertial data, (b) force data and (c) all data.

5 Discussion and Conclusion

The 1D CNN demonstrated high performance in the processing of smart insole data. The accuracies for the test data set of force data and all data reached 100%, respectively. Among the three tested variants, the force data and full data showed the best performance; this result could be evidence that the plantar pressure distribution pattern is a reliable indicator of the foot arch abnormalities. Inertial data also proved to be suitable for pes cavus detection. To date, there is no parameter described that can serve for the evaluation of pes cavus and flat foot at heel strike [7, 9]. Our results from inertial data classification indicate that the 1D CNN was able to find discriminative parameters. Even though only a single inertial sensor was used, the accuracy in discrimination between the two types of foot reached 96.46%. Increasing the number of sensors and improving sensor placement may allow for better accuracy. When we pooled inertial data and force data, the achieved accuracy was equal with the one from force data only. Multi-modal features could serve for the reliable discrimination of the foot types. As to the random forest method with handcrafted features, its performance was not as good as the one of 1D CNN for all the three data inputs.

Overall, the 1D CNN proved to be an appropriate choice for processing force and inertial sensor data. In the application of foot type classification, it allowed for reaching a good discriminative performance. Results imply that the smart insole, in combination with the proposed method, can be used for screening and progression monitoring of pes cavus.

Acknowledgments. This project was supported in parts by the Key Project 2017GZ0304 of the Science and Technology Department of Sichuan province and the Key Program of Joint Funds of the National Natural Science Foundation of China, grant U1505251.

References

1. Eleswarapu, A., Yamini, B., Bielski, R.J.: Evaluating the cavus foot. Pediatr. Ann. **45**(6), 218–222 (2016)
2. Burns, J., Crosbie, J., Hunt, A., Ouvrier, R.: The effect of pes cavus on foot pain and plantar pressure. Clin. Biomech. **20**(9), 877–882 (2005)
3. Razeghi, M., Batt, M.E.: Foot type classification: a critical review of current methods. Gait Posture **15**(3), 282–291 (2002)
4. Fan, Y.F., Fan, Y.B., Li, Z.Y., Lv, C.S., Luo, D.L.: Natural gaits of the non-pathological flat foot and high-arched foot. PLoS ONE **6**(3), 1–5 (2011)
5. Buldt, A.K., Forghany, S., Landorf, K.B., Levinger, P., Murley, G.S., Menz, H.B.: Foot posture is associated with plantar pressure during gait: a comparison of normal, planus and cavus feet. Gait Posture **62**, 235–240 (2018)
6. Buldt, A.K., Forghany, S., Landorf, K.B., Murley, G.S., Levinger, P., Menz, H.B.: Centre of pressure characteristics in normal, planus and cavus feet. J. Foot Ankle Res. **11**(1), 3 (2018)
7. Ledoux, W.R., Hillstrom, H.J.: Acceleration of the calcaneus at heel strike in neutrally aligned and pes planus feet. Clin. Biomech. **16**(7), 608–613 (2001)
8. Ogon, M., Aleksiev, A.R., Pope, M.H., Wimmer, C., Saltzman, C.L.: Does arch height affect impact loading at the lower back level in running? Foot Ankle Int. **20**(4), 263–266 (1999)
9. Grech, C., Formosa, C., Gatt, A.: Shock attenuation properties at heel strike: implications for the clinical management of the cavus foot. J. Orthop. **13**(3), 148–151 (2016)
10. Hillstrom, H.J., et al.: Foot type biomechanics part 1: structure and function of the asymptomatic foot. Gait & Posture. **37**(3), 445–451 (2013)
11. Hammerla, N.Y., Halloran, S., Plotz, T.: Deep, convolutional, and recurrent models for human activity recognition using wearables. In: Proceedings of the Twenty-Fifth International Joint Conference on Artificial Intelligence, April 2016
12. Ronao, C.A., Cho, S.B.: Human activity recognition with smartphone sensors using deep learning neural networks. Expert Syst. Appl. **59**(15), 234–244 (2016)
13. Xu, G.X., Wang, Z.F., Huang, H.S., Li, W.X.: A model for medical diagnosis based on plantar pressure, February 2018. https://arxiv.org/pdf/1802.10316.pdf
14. Barton, J.G., Lees, A.: Development of a connectionist expert system to identify foot problems based on under-foot pressure patterns. Clin. Biomech. **10**(7), 385–391 (1995)
15. Xu, S., Zhou, X., Sun, Y.N.: A novel gait analysis system based on adaptive neuro-fuzzy inference system. Expert Syst. Appl. **37**(2), 1265–1269 (2010)
16. De Cock, A., Willems, T., Witvrouw, E., Vanrenterghem, J., De Clercq, D.: A functional foot type classification with cluster analysis based on plantar pressure distribution during jogging. Gait Posture **23**(3), 339–347 (2006)

17. Simonyan, K., Zisserman, A.: Very deep convolutional networks for large-scale image recognition. In: Proceedings of the Twenty-Fifth International Joint Conference on Artificial Intelligence (2016)
18. Li, X., Chen, S., Hu, X.L., Yang, J.: Understanding the disharmony between dropout and batch normalization by variance shift, January 2018. https://arxiv.org/pdf/1801.05134.pdf
19. Ioffe, S., Szegedy, C.: Batch normalization: accelerating deep network training by reducing internal covariate shift, February 2015. https://arxiv.org/pdf/1502.03167v3.pdf
20. Ruder, S.: An overview of gradient descent optimization algorithms, June 2017. https://arxiv.org/abs/1609.04747
21. Wicart, P.: Cavus foot, from neonates to adolescents. Orthop. Traumatol.: Surg. Res. **98**(7), 813–828 (2012)
22. Sprager, S., Juric, M.B.: Inertial sensor-based gait recognition: a review. Sensors **15**(9), 22089–22127 (2015)
23. Schneider, O.S., MacLean, K.E., Altun, K., Karuei, I., Wu, M.M.: Real-time gait classification for persuasive smartphone apps: structuring the literature and pushing the limits. In: Proceedings of the 2013 International Conference on Intelligent User Interfaces, pp. 19–22, March 2013

Nonlinear Systems and Control

Controller Design by Using Simultaneous Perturbation Stochastic Approximation with Changeable Sliding Window

Qing Lu$^{(\boxtimes)}$ and Jun Zhou

Institute of Precision Guidance and Control,
Northwestern Polytechnical University, Xi'an 710072, Shaanxi, China
lamaxiya1990@163.com

Abstract. Many searching problems use simultaneous perturbation stochastic approximation (SPSA) method so as to get optimal parameters nowadays. This paper proposes a model free control (MFC) method based on SPSA with changeable sliding window. The controller here is founded based on an improved SPSA algorithm whose sampling window is updated according to the variation of the system. As a kind of MFC method, the key advantage of this approach is that it can complete the controller design task by using the input and output data of the system instead of establishing a complex model for it. In order to improve the efficiency of the control method, a changeable sliding window is used here to estimate the parameters. After that convergence analysis for the improved SPSA method is also provided in this paper. Simulation results for hypersonic vehicle tracking problem demonstrate that compare with traditional SPSA algorithm this improved method can significantly improve the feasibility and efficiency.

Keywords: SPSA · Model free control · Changeable window ·
Hypersonic vehicle

1 Introduction

Many systems we study today are very complex, as a result it is becoming more and more difficult for us to modeling the systems. Under these circumstances, designing controller for complex systems whose accurate models are unavailable would benefit a lot. The main feature of MFC is that only input and output data is needed for MFC method [1].

As a method of MFC, Neural networks (NN) are widely used in identification and controller design for unknown systems [2]. On the basis of NN, a virtual reference feedback tuning (VRFT) controller was designed by Esparza [3]. Radac and Precup designed a MFC approach to apply in non-linear system for trajectory tracking [4]. However, some necessary assumptions must be made if we want to use the methods above in practical systems. For example, system structure of the system is often already known, the parameter of the system is of unknown. In practical systems, the assumptions above are often difficult to be satisfied which makes it difficult for existing

© Springer Nature Switzerland AG 2019
H. Yu et al. (Eds.): ICIRA 2019, LNAI 11742, pp. 665–676, 2019.
https://doi.org/10.1007/978-3-030-27535-8_59

MFC methods to apply in practical systems. This provides the motivation for new MFC approaches.

By using SPSA method an objective function can be optimized efficiently [5]. SPSA method was firstly applied in controller design for a water treatment system by Spall in order to tune the parameters of NN controller [6]. After that the SPSA method has been widely used in many practical systems, for example real-time traffic signal control system [7], flexible robot arm control [8].

This paper proposed a MFC method so as to solve tracking problems for a practical system by using SPSA method. The most significant contribution is that the amount of data used in the SPSA method varies during the solving process. The modified SPSA methodology can be more efficient and accurate compared to traditional algorithm.

The reminder of this paper is as follows. An introduction of SPSA and its features is outlined in Sect. 2. Section 3 designs a modified SPSA algorithm with changeable sliding windows. A novel MFC strategy with modified SPSA is given in Sect. 4. Simulations and analysis for the new algorithm are shown in Sect. 5, and conclusions are drawn in Sect. 6.

2   Overview of SPSA

Consider the optimization problem [9]

$$\min_{\theta \in \mathbf{R}^p} L(\theta)$$

where $\theta \in \mathbf{R}^p$ denotes the parameter to be determined $L : \mathbf{R}^p \to \mathbf{R}$ denotes the objective function. The procedure of optimization method is to do iterations from initial value of the unknown parameters and adjust the parameters per iteration so as to improve the objective function. The iteration procedure will come to an end until minimum θ^* of the gradient equation is obtained.

$$g_k(\theta_k) \equiv \partial L_k / \partial \theta_k = (\partial u_k^T / \partial \theta_k) \cdot (\partial L_k / \partial u_k) = 0 \qquad (1)$$

Assume only measurements of L_k available and no direct measurements of $g_k(\theta_k)$ are used, as are required in stochastic gradient methods. The update law is given by

$$\hat{\theta}_{k+1} = \hat{\theta}_k - a_k \hat{g}_k(\hat{\theta}_k) \qquad (2)$$

where some small positive value a_k is defined as the gain sequence at the k th iteration, the estimation of the gradient $g_k(\cdot) = \partial L(\theta_k)/\partial(\theta_k)$ can be denoted as $\hat{g}_k(\cdot)$. For iteration $k \to k+1$, take measurements at design levels:

$$y(\hat{\theta}_k + c_k \Delta_k) = L(\hat{\theta}_k + c_k \Delta_k) + \varepsilon_k^{(+)} \quad y(\hat{\theta}_k - c_k \Delta_k) = L(\hat{\theta}_k - c_k \Delta_k) + \varepsilon_k^{(-)} \qquad (3)$$

where $y(\cdot)$ denotes a measurement of $L(\cdot)$, $\varepsilon_k^{(\pm)}$ are measurement noise terms, c_k denotes a positive scalar and $\Delta_k = \left[\Delta_{k1}, \Delta_{k2}, \ldots, \Delta_{kp} \right]^T$ is vector of p mean-zero random variables which are independent with each other at k th iteration. Then the form of standard simultaneous perturbation for $\hat{g}_k(\cdot)$ can be denoted as:

$$
\hat{g}_k\left(\hat{\theta}_k\right) = \begin{bmatrix} y\left(\hat{\theta}_k + c_k\Delta_k\right) - y\left(\hat{\theta}_k - c_k\Delta_k\right) \Big/ 2c_k\Delta_{k1} \\ \vdots \\ y\left(\hat{\theta}_k + c_k\Delta_k\right) - y\left(\hat{\theta}_k - c_k\Delta_k\right) \Big/ 2c_k\Delta_{kp} \end{bmatrix} \tag{4}
$$

Note that $\hat{g}_k(\cdot)$ only requires two measurements of $L(\cdot)$ independent of p, and based on twice evaluate of objective function all the parameters can be simultaneously updated.

3 Modified SPSA Algorithm with Changeable Sliding Window

This section gives an overview of a changeable sliding window method and its convergence analysis.

3.1 Changeable Sliding Window

For traditional SPSA method, the function should be evaluated twice to update on parameter and sampling at m points so as to evaluate the objective function. As a result, the system will rapidly vary due to the fact that the parameter updating cycle is $2m$, it will be very difficult for real system to follow. Thus, traditional SPSA method must be improved.

Based on the one-side SPSA method in [10], the performance of SPSA method can be further improved. Objective function for k th iteration can be chosen as

$$
L'_k(\cdot) = \sum_{i=1}^{m_k} \omega_{ik}(y_{ik} - r_{ik})^2, \quad k = 0, 1, \cdots \tag{5}
$$

where m_k is the number of points used to calculate objective function at k th iteration, ω_{ik} is the weighting parameter, r_{ik} is the command, y_{ik} is the output of the system. m_k can be changed during control process so as to change the range of sliding window for SPSA data sampling. For example m_k can be chosen as

$$
m_k = f(\dot{r}_{ik}) \tag{6}
$$

where $\dot{r}_{ik}$ is the change rate of the command, $f(\cdot)$ is an unknown bounded function so as to let m_k change according to $\dot{r}_{ik}$. So we have

$$
L'_k(\cdot) = L_{kVar}(\cdot) + L_k(\cdot) \tag{7}
$$

where $L_{kVar}(\cdot)$ is the changeable part of objective function, $L_k(\cdot)$ is the unchangeable part of objective function.

3.2   The Convergence of the Method

This condition that for varying $L(\cdot)$, $\hat{\theta}_k$ will almost surely converge to the optimal solution θ^* must be fulfilled. Due to the time varying objective function and underlying system evolution the general convergence results such as [9] can not be directly applied here. Based on [5] error term can be denoted as

$$e_k\left(\hat{\theta}_k\right) = \hat{g}_k\left(\hat{\theta}_k\right) - E\left(\hat{g}_k\left(\hat{\theta}_k\right)\Big|\hat{\theta}_k\right) \tag{8}$$

According to Lemma 1 [5], for almost all $\omega \in \Omega$,

$$b_k\left(\hat{\theta}_k\right) = E\left(\hat{g}_k\left(\hat{\theta}_k\right) - g_k\left(\hat{\theta}_k\right)\Big|\hat{\theta}_k\right) = O(c_k^2)(c_k \to 0) \tag{9}$$

where $c_k^{-2}\|b_k\|$ is uniformly bounded. [11] considered a generalized Robbins-Monro algorithm form. This form can also be used here to rewrite the update law.

$$\hat{\theta}_{k+1} = \hat{\theta}_k - a_k\left[g_k\left(\hat{\theta}_k\right) + b_k\left(\hat{\theta}_k\right) + e_k\left(\hat{\theta}_k\right)\right] \tag{10}$$

Some assumptions which are very similar to those of a number of other authors should be introduced.

A1: $\forall k$ we have $a_k, c_k > 0$;   as $k \to \infty$ we   have $a_k \to 0, c_k \to 0$;   and
$\sum_{k=0}^{\infty} a_k = \infty, \sum_{k=0}^{\infty} \left(\frac{a_k}{c_k}\right)^2 < \infty$

A2: $\forall k$ we have $\alpha_0, \alpha_1, \alpha_2 > 0$ and $E\left(L\left(\hat{\theta}_k \pm \bar{\Delta}_k\right)^2\right) \le \alpha_1$, $E\left(\varepsilon_k^{(\pm)}\right)^2 \le \alpha_0$, we also have $E(\Delta_{kl}^{-2}) \le \alpha_2$ $(l = 1, 2, \cdots, p)$.

A3: $\forall k$ we have $\left\|\hat{\theta}_k\right\| < \infty$.

A4: The asymptotically stable solution of the differential equation $dx(t)/dt = -g(x)$ can be obtained as θ^*.

A5: Based on initial value x_0, the solution of $dx(t)/dt = -g(x)$ can be denoted as $x(t|x_0)$. Then we have $D(\theta^*) = \{x_0 : lim_{t \to \infty} x(t|x_0) = \theta^*\}$ (That is to say, the domain of attraction is $D(\theta^*)$). For almost all sample points, there exists a compact $S \subseteq D(\theta^*)$ and $\hat{\theta}_k \in S$.

For above assumptions we should note: Typical SA conditions are A1 and A2. In practice, the most difficult to verify is perhaps A3. A4 and A5 are motivated by considering a limiting form of the deterministic version of $\hat{\theta}_{k+1} = \hat{\theta}_k - a_k\hat{g}_k\left(\hat{\theta}_k\right)$ as $k \to \infty$.

Proposition 1: Let A1–A5 and Lemma 1 in [5] hold, Then as $k \to \infty$

$$for\ almost\ all\ \omega \in \Omega,\ we\ have\ \hat{\theta}_k \to \theta^* \tag{11}$$

Proof: According to [12], (11) holds if

$$\lim_{k \to \infty} P\left(\sup_{m \geq k} \left\| \sum_{i=k}^{m} a_i e_i \left(\hat{\theta}_i \right) \right\| \geq \eta \right) = 0 \quad for\ any\ \eta > 0 \tag{12}$$

Consider (12), where $\left\{ \sum_{i=k}^{m} a_i e_i \right\}_{m \geq k}$ is a martingale sequence, from an inequality in [13] we have.

$$P\left(\sup_{m \geq k} \left\| \sum_{i=k}^{m} a_i e_i \left(\hat{\theta}_i \right) \right\| \geq \eta \right) \leq \eta^{-2} E \left\| \sum_{i=k}^{\infty} a_i e_i \right\|^2 = \eta^{-2} \sum_{i=k}^{\infty} a_i^2 E \|e_i\|^2 \tag{13}$$

For $\hat{g}_k \left(\hat{\theta}_k \right)$ and according to (3), (4) and (7) we can get

$$E\left(\left\| \hat{g}_{kl} \left(\hat{\theta}_k \right) \right\|^2 \right) = E\left(\left\| \frac{L_k'(\cdot) + \varepsilon_k^{(+)} - \left(L_k'(\cdot) + \varepsilon_k^{(-)} \right)}{2 c_k \Delta_{kl}} \right\|^2 \right)$$

$$= \frac{1}{4} c_k^{-2} E(\Delta_{kl}^{-2}) E\left(\left\| L_k'(\cdot) + \varepsilon_k^{(+)} - \left(L_k'(\cdot) + \varepsilon_k^{(-)} \right) \right\|^2 \right) \tag{14}$$

The function $f(\cdot)$ is bounded in practice so we can get the assumption
A6: For some $\alpha_3 > 0$ and $\forall k$, $E(L_{kVar}(\cdot)^2) \leq \alpha_3$ $(l = 1, 2, \cdots, p)$
Based on A2 and A6, we can get

$$E\left(\left\| \hat{g}_{kl} \left(\hat{\theta}_k \right) \right\|^2 \right) = \frac{1}{4} c_k^{-2} E(\Delta_{kl}^{-2}) E\left(\left\| L_k'(\cdot) + \varepsilon_k^{(+)} - \left(L_k'(\cdot) + \varepsilon_k^{(-)} \right) \right\|^2 \right)$$

$$\leq \frac{1}{4} c_k^{-2} E(\Delta_{kl}^{-2}) \left\{ 4 E\left(\|L_k'(\cdot)\|^2 + \left\| \varepsilon_k^{(+)} \right\|^2 + \|L_k'(\cdot)\|^2 + \left\| \varepsilon_k^{(-)} \right\|^2 \right) \right\}$$

$$= c_k^{-2} E(\Delta_{kl}^{-2}) E\left(2\|L_k'(\cdot)\|^2 + \left\| \varepsilon_k^{(+)} \right\|^2 + \left\| \varepsilon_k^{(-)} \right\|^2 \right)$$

$$\leq c_k^{-2} E(\Delta_{kl}^{-2}) E\left(4\|L_{kVar}(\cdot)\|^2 + 4\|L_k(\cdot)\|^2 + \left\| \varepsilon_k^{(+)} \right\|^2 + \left\| \varepsilon_k^{(-)} \right\|^2 \right)$$

$$\leq c_k^{-2} \alpha_2 \left(4\alpha_1 + 4\alpha_3 + 2\alpha_0 \right) \tag{15}$$

According to (8) we have

$$\left\|e_k\left(\hat{\theta}_k\right)\right\|^2 = \sum_{l=1}^{p}\left(\hat{g}_{kl}\left(\hat{\theta}_{kl}\right) - E\left(\hat{g}_{kl}\left(\hat{\theta}_{kl}\right)\middle|\hat{\theta}_{kl}\right)\right)^2 \tag{16}$$

so $E\left\|e_k\left(\hat{\theta}_k\right)\right\|^2 \leq pE\left(\left\|\hat{g}_{kl}\left(\hat{\theta}_k\right)\right\|^2\right) \leq pc_k^{-2}\alpha_2\left(4\alpha_1 + 4\alpha_3 + 2\alpha_0\right)$, Then from (13) and A1, the proof is completed.

4 Model Free Control Using Modified SPSA with Changeable Sliding Window

Instead of establishing an accurate model for the system, the control function can be determined by model free control who only uses the system I/O data. Here we use the form of traditional PID control whose parameters must be determined [14]. In this paper, the structure of PID is given at first [15], then modified SPSA method must be introduced into the control procedure. Traditional PID control is used here.

$$u(k+1) = \theta_P(k+1)\delta(k) + \theta_I(k+1)\int\delta(k)dt + \theta_D(k+1)\dot{\delta}(k) \tag{17}$$

where $u(k+1)$ is the control command, $\delta_j(k)$ is the bias between real system state and standard state, $\theta_P(k+1), \theta_I(k+1), \theta_D(k+1)$ are parameters which can be obtained by modified SPSA method, that is to say $\theta^* = [\theta_P(k+1) \quad \theta_I(k+1) \quad \theta_D(k+1)]^T$. Considering the constraints on $u(k+1)$, the control command can finally be expressed as

$$u_f(k+1) = \begin{cases} u_{\max}\frac{u(k+1)}{|u(k+1)|} & \text{when } |u(k+1)| > u_{\max} \\ u(k+1) & \text{when } |u(k+1)| \leq u_{\max} \end{cases} \tag{18}$$

where $u_{\max}$ is the maximum value of the control command.

It has been proven in previous part of this paper that the modified SPSA method would surely convergence. We use a changeable number of previous measurements and controls up to y_k and u_{k-1} so as to get the required control u_k. In other words, the sliding window here is changeable. Here the sequence of output data of the system is

$$\{y_1, y_2, y_3, \cdots\} \tag{19}$$

with corresponding controls

$$\{u_0, u_1, u_2, \cdots\} \tag{20}$$

A suitable θ^* is needed here so as to minimize some objective function relating with the states of the system. The objective function is chosen as

$$H_k(\theta_k) = \sum_{l=-1}^{m_k} (y(k-l) - r_d(k-l))^2 \tag{21}$$

where m_k represents the number of output data of the system i.e. the scale of sliding window, which is changeable during the control process as shown in Fig. 1. $y(k-l)$ is the real measurement of the system, $r_d(k-l)$ is the nominal state. The efficiency of the algorithm can be further improved by introducing a top threshold $m_{k\,max}$ and a bottom threshold $m_{k\,min}$ for m_k. When $m_k < m_{k\,min}$, there is no need for iteration and the current controller parameters were considered to be able to accommodate the instruction change. At the same time the condition $m_k < m_{k\,max}$ should be satisfied so as to avoid too slow iteration.

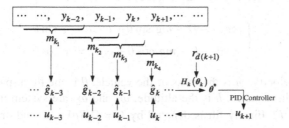

Fig. 1. Flow chart of the control method

The control parameter θ_k must be estimated based on SPSA method, the estimation can be done according to (2), where the simultaneous perturbation approximation of $g_k(\hat{\theta}_{k-1})$ can be denoted as $\hat{g}_k(\hat{\theta}_{k-1})$. Then we have l th component of $\hat{g}_k(\hat{\theta}_{k-1})$, $l = 1, 2, \cdots, p$

$$\hat{g}_{kl}\left(\hat{\theta}_{k-1}\right) = \hat{H}_k^{(+)} - \hat{H}_k^{(-)} \Big/ 2c_k \Delta_{kl} \tag{22}$$

where $\hat{H}_k^{(\pm)}$ are estimated values of $H_k(\hat{\theta}_{k-1} \pm c_k \Delta_k)$ using the observe sequence of I/O data. $\{c_k\}$ is a sequence of positive numbers and some regularity conditions must also be satisfied (typically $c_k \to 0$ or $c_k = c \forall k$). For SPSA method we need only two measurements to approximate $g_k(\cdot)$. Finally we can get the optimal parameter $\theta^* = [\theta_P(k+1) \quad \theta_I(k+1) \quad \theta_D(k+1)]^T$ when the iteration process comes to an end. By using Δ_k and a corresponding new pair of measurements, we can average several gradient approximations in high noise conditions which can ensure high performance of the method. Combining with the traditional PID controller control command can be obtained.

The most significant contribution of the modified method is that it can adapt the scale of sliding window according to the update frequency of the system so as to improve tracking performance. Some important points were proposed by Spall J C so as to achieve good performance [16]. θ_0 which is the initial value of θ_k should be chosen near θ^* so that the control algorithm can allow for a graceful transition to a more nearly optimal controller. Generating the elements of Δ_k according to Bernoulli ± 1 distribution is easy and theoretically valid. The gain sequence $\{a_k\}, \{c_k\}$ can be selected by using the principles proposed in [17].

5   Simulations and Analysis

A study of hypersonic vehicle model which is a nonlinear system is presented in this section. Traditional SPSA method for MFC was involved for comparison.

Consider the longitudinal flight control of hypersonic aircraft with constant velocity and altitude. Thrust can be ignored during reentry phase, the impact of the earth oblateness and the influence of the earth self-rotation on aerodynamics can also be neglected. We found complete 3-DOF model as follows:

$$\begin{cases} m\dot{v} = -D - mg \sin\theta + \omega_1, \dot{h} = v \sin\theta \\ mv\dot{\theta} = L - mg \cos\theta + \omega_2, \dot{x} = v \cos\theta \end{cases} \tag{23}$$

where v is the velocity, m is the mass of the vehicle, θ is the flight-path angle, x is the longitudinal flight distance, h is the altitude, ω_1 and ω_2 are system noises that satisfy $\omega_1, \omega_2 \sim N(0, \sigma^2 I)$. Finally lift is denoted by $L = C_L S \rho V^2 / 2$, and drag is denoted by $D = C_D S \rho V^2 / 2$, where ρ is the atmospheric density and S is the reference area. The aerodynamic coefficients C_D, C_L here can be denoted by angle of attack α, so we have $C_D = f_D(\alpha)$, $C_L = f_L(\alpha)$ where $f_D(\cdot)$ and $f_L(\cdot)$ are nonlinear functions. Therefore, the system consists of one control (the angle of attack α) and two outputs (the velocity v and the flight-path angle θ). The system is nonlinear and time-varying, constraints on α and vehicle states which present an additional challenge in developing a controller for the system should also be considered.

An objective function is used here in order to track one output.

$$H(t_k) = \left[e_{state}^T(t_k) e_{state}(t_k) \right]^{\frac{1}{2}} \tag{24}$$

where $e_{state}(t_k) = h - h_d$ is the error of system states at t_k, h_d is the nominal state we need to track. A changeable sliding window SPSA method combining with PID theory was used to model the controller, the sampling number is changing during the control process. Final command of α can be denoted as

$$\alpha_c = \begin{cases} \alpha_{max}(\alpha_{PID})/(|\alpha_{PID}|) & \text{when } |\alpha_{PID}| > \alpha_{max} \\ \alpha_{PID} & \text{when } |\alpha_{PID}| \leq \alpha_{max} \end{cases} \tag{25}$$

where α_{max} is the allowed maximum value of angle of attack, α_{PID} is the result from PID controller.

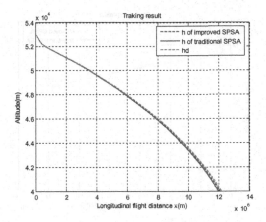

Fig. 2. Tracking performance

Initial states of the vehicle are shown in Table 1.

Table 1. Initial states

v(m/s)	θ(°)	h(m)	x(m)
6000	0	53000	0

The initial parameters of the controller can be chosen as Table 2.

Table 2. Initial controller parameters

$\theta_P(0)$	$\theta_I(0)$	$\theta_D(0)$	$m_{k\,max}$	$m_{k\,min}$
5	2	0.3	30	3

5.1 Compare with Traditional SPSA Method

Traditional SPSA method was also used to solve this problem. Their performance results are shown as follows. Simulation results for tracking monotonously changing altitude are as shown in Fig. 2 and Fig. 3, where h represents real altitude hd represents altitude command.

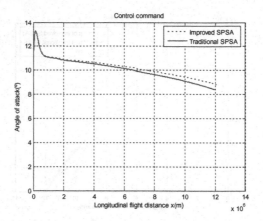

Fig. 3. Control command

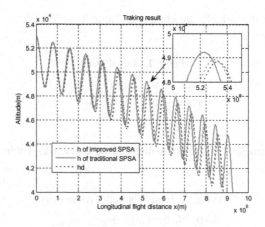

Fig. 4. Tracking performance

From simulation results we can see that for the case of monotonously changing altitude, both methods can achieve good tracking performance. However, traditional SPSA method has some degree of delay. Wavy trajectory is introduced for tracking test so as to further prove the effectiveness and feasibility of the modified SPSA method.

As shown in Figs. 4 and 5, changeable sliding window method can still achieve very good performance for the case of wavy trajectory. On the other hand, deal to the slow solving process traditional SPSA method can not complete the tracking task.

5.2 Robust of This Modified Method

In order to further illustrate the robustness of the modified algorithm, 500 simulations under the condition of random −15%~+15% pull-off of the aerodynamic coefficient are carried out. The maximum tracking deviation is recorded and the statistics are in Table 3:

Table 3. Initial controller parameters

Tracking error (m)	>300.0	150–300	50–150	<50
Number of trajectories	11	89	157	243

The simulation results show traditional PID control using modified SPSA algorithm can well complete the tracking tasks and has strong robustness. High tracking accuracy can also be ensured in the presence of pull-off. In addition, through the simulation of the time records we found that the convergence time of the proposed model-free tracking guidance method is within 1 s, so that the fast and real-time condition can be fulfilled.

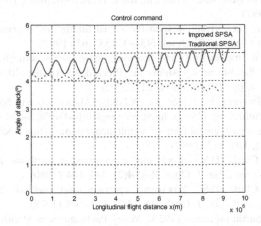

Fig. 5. Control command

6 Conclusion

This paper proposed a MFC algorithm considering the problem of controlling nonlinear stochastic systems with unknown system model. A changeable sliding window is used in this paper to make the approach different from traditional SPSA method.

The feasibility of the approach is illustrated by simulations. It was found that effective control performance can be achieved in some challenging problems at much lower cost than traditional SPSA method. However, there remain several questions in this approach. In our future work, we will try to found a selection criterion for m_k so as to achieve better control performance. A new stability analysis for MFC method only using I/O measurement data would be an important topic to be explored. The optimization tool can also be improved so that a global solution can be obtained.

References

1. Hou, Z., Jin, S.: A novel data-driven control approach for a class of discrete-time nonlinear systems. IEEE Trans. Control Syst. Technol. **19**(6), 1549–1558 (2011)
2. Chen, F.C., Khalil, H.K.: Adaptive control of a class of nonlinear discrete-time systems using neural networks. IEEE Trans. Autom. Control **40**(5), 791–801 (1995)
3. Esparza, A.: Application of neural networks to virtual reference feedback tuning controller design. In: Advanced Fuzzy and Neural Control, pp. 145–150 (2007)
4. Radac, M.B., Precup, R.E.: Data-based two-degree-of-freedom iterative control approach to constrained non-linear systems. IET Control Theory Appl. **9**(7), 1000–1010 (2015)
5. Spall, J.C.: Multivariate stochastic approximation using a simultaneous perturbation gradient approximation. IEEE Trans. Autom. Control **37**(3), 332–341 (1992)
6. Spall, J.C., Cristion, J.A.: A neural network controller for systems with unmodeled dynamics with applications to wastewater treatment. IEEE Trans. Syst. Man Cybern. Part B Cybern. **27** (3), 369–375 (1997)
7. Spall, J.C., Chin, D.C.: Traffic-responsive signal timing for system-wide traffic control. Transp. Res. Part C Emerg. Technol. **5**(3–4), 153–163 (1997)
8. Maeda, Y.: Real-time control and learning using neuro-controller via simultaneous perturbation for flexible arm system. In: Proceedings of the 2002 American Control Conference, vol. 4, pp. 2583–2588. IEEE (2002)
9. Benveniste, A., Priouret, P., Tivier, M.: Adaptive Algorithms and Stochastic Approxima-tions. Springer, Heidelberg (1990). https://doi.org/10.1007/978-3-642-75894-2
10. Spall, J.C.: A one-measurement form of simultaneous perturbation stochastic approximation. Automatica **33**(1), 109–112 (1997)
11. Kushner, H.J., Clark, D.S.: Stochastic approximation methods for constrained and unconstrained systems. Eur. J. Oper. Res. **4**(2), 143–144 (1980)
12. Kushner, H.J., Clark, D.S.: Stochastic approximation methods for constrained and unconstrained systems. Eur. J. Oper. Res. **4**(2), 143–144 (1978)
13. Doob, J.L.: Stochastic processes (1953). Wiley Publications in Statistics
14. Zhong, J., Fan, J., Zhu, Y., et al.: One Nonlinear PID Control to Improve the Control Performance of a Manipulator Actuated by a Pneumatic Muscle Actuator. Adv. Mech. Eng. **2014**(8), 1–19 (2014)
15. Ishizuka, S., Kajiwara, I.: Online adaptive PID control for MIMO systems using simultaneous perturbation stochastic approximation. J. Adv. Mech. Des. Syst. Manufact. **9** (2) (2015). Paper No. 14-00390
16. Spall, J.C.: Adaptive stochastic approximation by the simultaneous perturbation method. IEEE Trans. Autom. Control **45**(10), 1839–1853 (2000)
17. Spall, J.C.: Implementation of the simultaneous perturbation algorithm for stochastic optimization. IEEE Trans. Aerosp. Electron. Syst. **34**(3), 817–882 (1998)

Robust Adaptive Force Tracking Impedance Control for Robotic Capturing of Unknown Objects

Guotao Li, Hailin Huang, and Bing Li[⊠]

Department of Mechanical Engineering and Automation,
Harbin Institute of Technology, Shenzhen 518055, China
libing.sgs@hit.edu.cn

Abstract. The manipulation for space known objects has been studied extensively, however, the case for unknown objects still needs further investigation because there is little information to assist measurement and manipulation. This paper proposes a robust adaptive force tracking impedance controller for robotic capturing of space unknown objects, which has a great adaptability to the environmental parameters of the objects, a force tracking capability of capturing different types of space objects, and robustness to uncertainties. First, the position control based impedance control scheme is given. Second, an environmental parameters adaptive law is designed to estimate the environmental location and the stiffness of the grasped object. Third, by using the nonlinear high-gain tracking differentiator (HGTD) and linear extended state observer (LESO), a robust adaptive dynamic surface position controller for a space robot is proposed to guarantee a good position tracking performance of the controller and the robustness to system's parametric uncertainties. At last, numerical simulations are conducted to demonstrate the position/force tracking control performance of the proposed impedance control scheme.

Keywords: Force tracking impedance control · Robust adaptive control · Dynamic surface control

1 Introduction

Space unknown or non-cooperative objects generally refer to space debris or malfunctioned aircrafts that are difficult to conduct the on-orbit robotic manipulation control [1, 2]. The manipulation control for space cooperative objects has been studied extensively [3, 4], however, the case for unknown objects is quite different because the object itself cannot be equipped with any artificial markers or sensors to assist measurement and manipulation. Robotic capturing of space unknown objects is one of the most challenge problems in the space on-orbit missions.

Grasping a space unknown object is typically divided into several sequential stages: approach, pre-grasping, grasping, and post-grasping stage [5]. Due to the unknown parameters of the space unknown objects, large inertial force may generate inevitably on the robotic manipulators in the grasping and post-grasping stage, which may cause the severe damage on both robots and the space objects. To address these problems,

H. Yu et al. (Eds.): ICIRA 2019, LNAI 11742, pp. 677–688, 2019.
https://doi.org/10.1007/978-3-030-27535-8_60

several control methods [6–9] have been studied in recent years. But these literatures mainly discuss manipulation control in the pre-grasping stages without considering the impacts of the contact between the robots and the targets, which is always unknown and changing in the grasping process. In this situation, impedance control in the robotic manipulation process of space unknown objects becomes very important and necessary to address the contact problems. This research topic has also received many research attentions in recent years [11–14]. However, the aforementioned researches on impedance control for space grasping have not mentioned some performances that are necessary for capturing space objects, such as the force tracking performance and adaptability to the contact environment. In the area of force tracking performance, several researchers have studied the force tracking impedance control in recent years. Seraji [15] proposed two efficient position based force tracking impedance controller without the information of the stiffness and location of the object. Jung [16] presented a simple robust force tracking impedance control scheme considering the uncertainties of dynamics by using an adaptive control concept. Xu [17] proposed a sliding mode-based position/force control for a piezoelectric-bimorph microgripper by varying the corresponding gains or parameters. Based on the analysis, this paper will focus on proposing a high-performance impedance control scheme for grasping unknown space targets. The corresponding key technologies are impedance control, nonlinearity, adaptive control and dynamic surface control. We will discuss them in the following parts.

As we all know, high nonlinearity, Coriolis and centripetal effects, unknown disturbances and parameter uncertainties may result in the inaccuracy of motion control of space robots and even cause the instability of the robotic system. Great efforts have been made to solve the aforementioned problems such as sliding mode control, backstepping method and dynamic surface control, and so on. In these control approaches, the backstepping technique has been widely applied in various applications. However, the backstepping method has the "explosion of complexity" problem due to the repeated differentiation of the virtual immediate control terms. The dynamic surface control (DSC) method was proposed to solve this problem in [18], and modified dynamic surface control approaches were proposed in [19] to improve control performance. In addition, the ESO based control methods [20] have been applied in various industrial applications considering the advantageous characteristics of the ESO.

In this paper, a robust adaptive position based force tracking impedance control scheme of space robots is proposed by incorporating LESO, HGTD and DSC. LESO is design to estimate unmeasurable disturbances, nonlinear HGTD is introduced to improve the position tracking performance, an adaptive law is designed to obtain the unknown environmental parameters to achieve the better force tracking and the target impedance model is used to adjust impedance control performance for grasping unknown targets.

The rests of the paper are given as follows: dynamics of grasping robots is modeled in Sect. 2. In Sect. 3, the unknown environment parameters adaptive law and the force-tracking method are proposed. In Sect. 4, LESO is designed to estimate the system uncertainties and disturbances, nonlinear HGTD is incorporated into controller design and robust adaptive dynamic surface position controller with LESO and HGTD is developed. In Sect. 5, simulations are conducted to illustrate the effectiveness of the proposed impedance controller. At last, we give a conclusion.

2 Dynamics

The dynamics of a robot manipulators can be written as [21]:

$$\mathbf{M(q)\ddot{q}} + \mathbf{C(q,\dot{q})\dot{q}} + \mathbf{F(q,\dot{q})} = \tau \tag{1}$$

where $\mathbf{M(q)}$ represents symmetric positive define inertia matrix of the robotic manipulator, $\mathbf{C(q,\dot{q})}$ denotes the Coriolis/centripetal matrix, $\mathbf{F(q,\dot{q})}$ is the vector of external uncertainties, $\tau = [\tau_1, \cdots, \tau_n]$ represents the control input vector, $\mathbf{q} = [q_1, \cdots, q_n]$ denotes the angles of the robot joints.

For simplicity, we often use $\mathbf{M}$, $\mathbf{C}$ and $\mathbf{F}$ to represent matrices $\mathbf{M(q)}$, $\mathbf{C(q,\dot{q})}$ and $\mathbf{F(q,\dot{q})}$. Consider the modeling parameter uncertainties and external disturbances, we define $\mathbf{M} = \mathbf{M_0} + \Delta\mathbf{M}$ and $\mathbf{C} = \mathbf{C_0} + \Delta\mathbf{C}$, where $\mathbf{M_0}$ and $\mathbf{C_0}$ are the nominal values of $\mathbf{M}$ and $\mathbf{C}$, respectively, and $\Delta\mathbf{M}$ and $\Delta\mathbf{C}$ are the corresponding uncertain parts, respectively. Then, the rigid robot system can be reformulated as

$$\ddot{\mathbf{q}} = \mathbf{M_0^{-1}}(\tau - \mathbf{C_0\dot{q}} - \mathbf{F}) - \mathbf{M_0^{-1}F}_u \tag{2}$$

where $\mathbf{F}_u = \Delta\mathbf{C\dot{q}} + \Delta\mathbf{M\ddot{q}}$ represents the lumped uncertainties of the robotic manipulator.

Let the state variables be defined as $\mathbf{x}_1 = \mathbf{q} = [q_1, q_2, \cdots, q_n]$, $\mathbf{x}_2 = \dot{\mathbf{q}} = [\dot{q}_1, \dot{q}_2, \cdots, \dot{q}_n]$, Eq. (2) can be rewritten as:

$$\begin{cases} \dot{\mathbf{x}}_1 = \mathbf{x}_2 \\ \dot{\mathbf{x}}_2 = \mathbf{b_0 u} + \mathbf{f} \end{cases} \tag{3}$$

where $\mathbf{u}$ is the control input defined by $\mathbf{u} = \tau$, $\mathbf{b_0}$ is defined by $\mathbf{b_0} = \mathbf{M_0^{-1}}$ and $\mathbf{f}$ is defined by $\mathbf{f} = \mathbf{M_0^{-1}}(-\mathbf{C_0\dot{q}} - \mathbf{F}) - \mathbf{M_0^{-1}F}_u$, which mainly consider the system parameter uncertainties and external disturbances.

3 Robust Adaptive Impedance Control for Grasping

3.1 Impedance Control of Unknown Targets Capturing

The overall position based impedance controller has been shown in Fig. 1, it is mainly composed of the target impedance, DSC position controller and unknown environment parameters estimator.

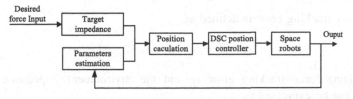

Fig. 1. The overall position based impedance control scheme

3.2   Force-Tracking Impedance Control

To avoid damaging space objects and space robots, an impedance controller is used to regulate the position and force signals by using the dynamics of target object and space robot. Since it is simple in control and has a good control performance, a second-order linear impedance model is used, which is given as

$$m_t(\ddot{x} - \ddot{x}_t) + b_t(\dot{x} - \dot{x}_t) + k_t(x - x_t) = f_e \tag{4}$$

where m_t, b_t, k_t denote the target impedance mass, damping, and stiffness, respectively, x_t and x represent the reference trajectory and the actual trajectory, respectively and f_e is the contact force of the robot by external environment.

As shown in Fig. 2, when robots and the environment are in contact, it will result in a reaction force f_e define as

$$f_e = k_e(x - x_e) \tag{5}$$

where x_e is the environment location and k_e denotes the environmental stiffness.

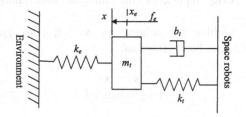

Fig. 2. Contact model of robots and environment

Then one can bring the reference force f_t into the target impedance control law in Eq. (4) [15], which yields that

$$m_t(\ddot{x} - \ddot{x}_t) + b_t(\dot{x} - \dot{x}_t) + k_t(x - x_t) = f_t - f_e \tag{6}$$

Since the reference position x_t is specified to contact with the environment by a constant and a constant contact force is produced, $\ddot{x}_t = \dot{x}_t = 0$ holds. Thus, the target impedance control dynamics can be rewritten as

$$m_t\ddot{x} + b_t\dot{x} + k_t(x - x_t) = f_t - f_e \tag{7}$$

The force tracking error is defined as

$$e_f = f_t - f_e = f_t - k_e(x_e - x) \tag{8}$$

Combining force tracking error e_f and the environment impedance model in Eq. (5), x can be expressed as

$$x = \frac{f_e}{k_e} + x_e = \frac{f_t - e_f}{k_e} + x_e \tag{9}$$

Substituting Eq. (9) into (7) and then using Laplace transformation yields

$$(m_t s^2 + b_t s + k_t + k_e)e_f = (m_t s^2 + b_t s + k_t)f_t + k_t k_e(x_e - x_t) \tag{10}$$

Due to the constant force f_t, the steady-state force-tracking error of can be obtained from Eq. (10) as

$$e_f = \frac{k_t[f_t + k_e(x_e - x_t)]}{k_t + k_e} \tag{11}$$

By defining the equivalent stiffness of the target impedance and the environment

$$k_{eq} = \left(\frac{1}{k_t} + \frac{1}{k_e}\right)^{-1} \tag{12}$$

The steady state force tracking error can be rewritten as follow

$$e_f = \frac{1}{k_{eq}}[\frac{f_t}{k_e} + x_e - x_t] \tag{13}$$

Regulating the steady state force tracking error e_f equal to zero, the relationship between the desired force and position, equivalent stiffness and the environment location is designed as follow

$$x_t = x_e + f_t/k_e \tag{14}$$

Thus, if the environmental location x_e and the environmental stiffness k_e are known, one can directly calculate the reference position x_t.

3.3   Adaptive Estimation of Unknown Environment Parameters

Since it is difficult to know the exact values of the environmental location x_e and the environmental stiffness k_e in practice, we design an adaptive law to estimate these two parameters. Based on Eq. (5), one can get the estimated environmental contact reaction force [23]

$$\hat{f}_e = \hat{k}_e(x - \hat{x}_e) \tag{15}$$

where $\hat{x}_e$ is the estimated value of x_e. Therefore, one can arrive at the error of environment reaction force

$$\tilde{e}_s = \hat{f}_e - f_e = [x \quad -1]\begin{bmatrix} \hat{k}_e - k_e \\ \hat{k}_e\hat{x}_e - k_ex_e \end{bmatrix} \tag{16}$$

So $\hat{k}_e$ and $\hat{x}_e$ will close to k_e and x_e, respectively, when $\tilde{e}_s = 0$ is satisfied. By defining the vector $\eta_e = [k_e \quad k_ex_e]^T$, one can get its estimated form $\hat{\eta}_e = [\hat{k}_e \quad \hat{k}_e\hat{x}_e]^T$. Then, Eq. (16) can be rewritten as

$$\tilde{e}_s = [x \quad -1]\tilde{\eta}_e \tag{17}$$

where $\tilde{\eta}_e = \hat{\eta}_e - \eta_e$ is the estimation error. The adaptive law is designed as

$$\dot{\hat{\eta}}_e = -\Gamma_e^{-1}[x \quad -1]^T\tilde{e}_s \tag{18}$$

where $\Gamma_e = \text{diag}[\gamma_{e1} \quad \gamma_{e2}]^T$ represents the matrix of control parameters.

The proof for stability of the adaptive law is as follows, we choose the Lyapunov function candidate as

$$V_e = \frac{1}{2}\tilde{\eta}_e^T\Gamma_e\tilde{\eta}_e \tag{19}$$

Differencing Eq. (19) with respect to time arrives at

$$\dot{V}_e = \tilde{\eta}_e^T\Gamma_e\dot{\hat{\eta}}_e \tag{20}$$

Substitute the adaptive law (18) into Eq. (20), we can get

$$\dot{V}_e = -\tilde{\eta}_e^T[x \quad -1]^T\tilde{e}_s = -\tilde{e}_s^T\tilde{e} = -(\hat{f}_e - f_e)^2 \tag{21}$$

Then, the estimated values of the environment location and environmental stiffness can be calculated by

$$\begin{cases} \dot{\hat{k}}_e = \gamma_{e1}x(\hat{f}_e - f_e) \\ \dot{\hat{x}}_e = -\frac{\hat{f}_e-f_e}{\hat{k}_e}(\gamma_{e2} + \gamma_{e1}x\hat{x}_e) \end{cases} \tag{22}$$

4   Dynamic Surface Position Control Design

4.1   LESO

The LESO can be used to estimate the unknown functions of the system with little input information [24, 25]. Here, by using the nominal values b_0 of the system in Eq. (3) mentioned in Sect. 2, the LESO is applied to observe the lumped unknown nonlinear function f. The second-order linear ESO can be written as

$$\begin{cases} \eta_1 = \hat{x}_1 - x_1 \\ \dot{\hat{x}}_1 = \hat{x}_2 - \kappa_1\eta_1 + b_0 u \\ \dot{\hat{x}}_2 = -\kappa_2\eta_1 \end{cases} \tag{23}$$

where $\hat{x}_1 = [\hat{x}_{11}, \cdots, \hat{x}_{n1}]$ is the estimated velocity of $\dot{q} = [\dot{q}_1, \dot{q}_2, \cdots, \dot{q}_n]$, $\hat{x}_2 = [\hat{x}_{12}, \cdots, \hat{x}_{n2}]$ is the estimated unknown nonlinear function of $f = [f_1, \cdots, f_n]$.

From [20, 26], one can know that the finite-time convergence of LESO is guaranteed immediately whose the observing error $\tilde{x}_i = \hat{x}_i - x_i, i = 1, 2$ satisfying the follow relationship

$$|\hat{x}_{ij} - x_{ij}| \leq \iota, i = 1, 2, j = 1, 2, \cdots, n \tag{24}$$

where $\hat{x}_{ij}$ denotes the estimated value of $x_{ij}, i = 1, 2, j = 1, \cdots, n$ and x_{2j} represents f_j.

4.2 Nonlinear High-Gain Tracking Differentiator

In order to achieve a better performance, the nonlinear high-gain tracking differentiator is used, which is given as

$$\begin{cases} \dot{\vartheta}_{i1}(t) = \vartheta_{i2}(t) \\ \dot{\vartheta}_{i2}(t) = R^2(-\rho_{i1}[\vartheta_{i1} - v(t)]^\alpha - \rho_{i2}[\vartheta_{i2}/R]^\beta) \end{cases} \tag{25}$$

where $[x]^\pi = |x|^\pi \text{sign}(x)$, $v(t)$ is the input signal, ϑ_{i1} and ϑ_{i2} are adopted to observe the signals and their derivative signals of the system, and α, β, R are the positive design parameters.

According to the reference [26], one can know that if the input signal $v(t)$ satisfies $\sup_{t\in[0,\infty)} |v(t)_i^{(j)}| < \infty$ for $j = 1, 2$, the differentiator in Eq. (25) is guaranteed to be convergent, and for $t > T$, the following inequality is satisfied

$$|\vartheta_{i1} - v(t)| \leq \varepsilon, |\vartheta_{i2} - \dot{v}(t)| \leq \varepsilon \tag{26}$$

where ε is always positive.

4.3 Robust Adaptive Dynamic Surface Position Control

By using the nonlinear HGTD, a robust adaptive dynamic surface position controller is designed bases on the LESO, which can be designed in the following steps.

First, we define the error surfaces of the ith link of the robots, as follows:

$$\begin{cases} e_{i1} = x_{i1} - x_{id} \\ e_{i2} = x_{i2} - \alpha_{i1} \end{cases} \tag{27}$$

Step 1. To obtain the derivative of x_{id}, the nonlinear high-gain tracking differentiator is designed as

$$\begin{cases} \dot{\vartheta}_{i11}(t) = \vartheta_{i12}(t) \\ \dot{\vartheta}_{i12}(t) = R^2(-\rho_{i11}[\vartheta_{i11} - x_{id}]^\alpha - \rho_{i12}[\vartheta_{i12}/R]^\beta) \end{cases} \tag{28}$$

with the filtering error bound $|\vartheta_{i12} - \dot{x}_{id}| \leq \varepsilon$.
For the stability of system, we design α_{i1} as

$$\alpha_{i1} = -k_{i1}e_{i1} - \hat{\theta}_{i1} \tanh(\frac{e_{i1}}{w}) + \vartheta_{i12} \tag{29}$$

The adaptive robust law of the corresponding parameter is designed as

$$\dot{\hat{\theta}}_{i1} = \gamma_{i1}(e_{i1} \tanh(\frac{e_{i1}}{w}) - \sigma_{i1}\hat{\theta}_{i1}) \tag{30}$$

Step 2. In order to calculate the derivative signal of α_{i1}, a HGTD is used in this step, which is designed as

$$\begin{cases} \dot{\vartheta}_{i21}(t) = \vartheta_{i22}(t) \\ \dot{\vartheta}_{i22}(t) = R^2(-\rho_{i21}[\vartheta_{i21} - \alpha_{i1}]^\alpha - \rho_{i22}[\vartheta_{i22}/R]^\beta) \end{cases} \tag{31}$$

with the filtering error bound $|\vartheta_{i22} - \dot{\alpha}_{i1}| \leq \varepsilon$.
Then the control input signal u_i can designed as

$$u_i = -k_{i2}e_{i2} - \hat{\theta}_{i2} \tanh(\frac{e_{i2}}{w}) - \hat{\phi}(\hat{x}_{2i} - \vartheta_{i22}) \tag{32}$$

And the parameter adaptive robust control laws can be designed as

$$\dot{\hat{\theta}}_{i2} = \gamma_{i2}(e_{i2} \tanh(\frac{e_{i2}}{w}) - \sigma_{i2}\hat{\theta}_{i2}) \tag{33}$$

$$\dot{\hat{\phi}}_i = \gamma_{\phi_i} e_{i2}(\hat{x}_{2i} - \vartheta_{i22}) \tag{34}$$

where $\hat{\phi}_i$ is the estimated parameter of $\phi_i = b_{i0}^{-1}$, $\hat{\theta}_{i2}$ is the estimated parameter of $\theta_{i2} = b_{i0}^{-1}(\iota + \varepsilon)$, and $\sigma_{i2}, \gamma_{i2}, \gamma_{\phi_i}$ are positive parameters.

4.4   Stability Analysis

In this section, the theorem is summarized.

Theorem 1. For the space serial n-link robots (1), if we design the control input signal as (32) with the law (29), LESO (23) and HGTD (28) and (31), then the proposed controller can be guaranteed to be semi-globally uniformly bounded.

Proof. The proof of the theorem is not provided here due to the space limit.

5 Simulation and Analysis

Numerical simulations are conducted to illustrate the control performance. As shown in Fig. 3, a two-link space robot is chosen as the robot and an unknown object is simplified to the contact environment located at x_e. The dynamics of the space robot can be written as follows:

$$\mathbf{M}(\mathbf{q}) = \begin{bmatrix} (m_1 + m_2)l_1^2 + m_2 l_2^2 + 2m_2 l_1 l_2 c_2 & m_2 l_2^2 + m_2 l_1 l_2 c_2 \\ m_2 l_2^2 + m_2 l_1 l_2 c_2 & m_2 l_2^2 \end{bmatrix}$$

$$\mathbf{C}(\mathbf{q}, \dot{\mathbf{q}})\,\dot{\mathbf{q}} = \begin{bmatrix} -m_2 l_1 l_2 s_2 \dot{q}_2^2 - 2m_2 l_1 l_2 s_2 \dot{q}_1 \dot{q}_2 \\ m_2 l_1 l_2 s_2 \dot{q}_2^2 \end{bmatrix},\ \mathbf{F}_f = \begin{bmatrix} F_{f_1} \\ F_{f_2} \end{bmatrix},\ \tau = \begin{bmatrix} \tau_1 \\ \tau_2 \end{bmatrix},\ \mathbf{d} = \begin{bmatrix} d_1 \\ d_2 \end{bmatrix}$$

where q_i is the position of the i-th joint, and s_i, c_i and c_{ij} represent $\sin(q_i)$, $\cos(q_i)$ and $\cos(q_i + q_j)$, respectively. The parameters and parametric uncertainties of system are set in Table 1. In detail, the parameters l_1 and l_2 are the lengths of the links, m_{10} and m_{20} are the end tip loads of joint 1 and 2, Δm_1 and Δm_2 denote the uncertainties portions of the end tip loads.

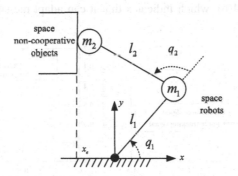

Fig. 3. Two-link robotic manipulator

Table 1. The parameters and parameter uncertainties of system

l_1(m)	l_2(m)	m_{10}(kg)	m_{20}(kg)	Δm_1(kg)	Δm_2(kg)
2	1	10	5	0.5	0.25

The proposed impedance control scheme is comprised of the environment parameter adaptive algorithm, the target impedance control model and robust adaptive dynamic surface position control. The initial parameter conditions of the proposed robust adaptive dynamic surface position controller are given as follows: $x_{i1}(0) = x_{i2}(0) = 0, \hat{x}_1(0) = \hat{x}_2(0) = 0, \vartheta_{ij1}(0) = \vartheta_{ij2}(0) = 0, j = 1, 2$. The parameters of the designed ESO are set to $\kappa_1 = [120, 135], \kappa_2 = [7500, 9500], \alpha_1 = [0.9, 0.9], \qquad \delta_1 = [0.0025, 0.0025], \qquad$ the parameters of HGTD are given as $R = [100, 100], \alpha = [0.5, 0.5], \beta = [0.66, 0.66], \rho_{ij1} = \rho_{ij2} = [1, 1], j = 1, 2$. Then, the parameters of the virtual and final control law are given as follows: $k_1 = [1500, 1190], k_2 = [1510, 1190], \gamma_1 = \gamma_2 = [0.5, 0.5], \sigma_1 = \sigma_2 = [0.5, 0.5], \omega = [3.8, 3.8], \gamma_\phi = [3.0, 3.0]$. The parameters of the environment parameter adaptive algorithm are set as follows: $\gamma_{e1} = \gamma_{e2} = 1000$.

5.1 Variable Environment Stiffness

Because grasping the unknown objects that may have a different stiffness, the simulation in this part is to illustrate how the proposed controller can adapt to the target objects with different environmental stiff nesses. Here, the environment location x_e is set to -0.5 m, the desired position in the y direction is set to 2 m, the desired force is set to $f_t = 200\,$N and the environment stiffness k_e satisfying

$$k_e = \begin{cases} 1000 & \text{if } t \le 0.5 \text{ s} \\ 500 & \text{if } t > 0.5 \text{ s} \end{cases} \tag{35}$$

As shown in Fig. 4(a), the force tracking result of the proposed impedance controller indicates that the proposed control scheme has a good robustness performance when abrupt changes in the environment stiffness occurs. In addition, the variation of the contact position x_t of the end-effects of robots for the proposed controller has been depicted in the Fig. 4(b), which indicates that it can adapt the stiffness properly.

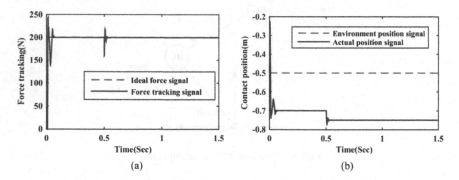

Fig. 4. The case with variable environment stiffness (a) force tracking (b) contact position.

5.2 Variable Environment Location

When grasping the space unknown objects, it is apparently that the environmental location of the target objects is changing. The simulation in this part is to illustrate the robustness of the proposed controller to the variation of the environment location. The environment stiffness is set to be 1000 Nm/m, the desired y-axis position is set to be 2 m, the desired force is set to $f_t = 200\,$N and the environment location x_e satisfying

$$x_e = \begin{cases} -0.5 & \text{if } t \le 0.5 \text{ s} \\ -0.5 + 0.1 \sin[2\pi(t - 0.5)] & \text{if } t > 0.5 \text{ s} \end{cases} \tag{36}$$

Force tracking with variable environment location are depicted in Fig. 5(a), which indicates that the proposed controller is robust to the variation of the environment location. The variation of the contact position for the proposed controller has been depicted in the Fig. 5(b), which indicates that the contact position of robots can adapt itself properly.

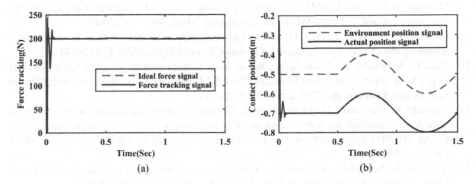

Fig. 5. The case with variable environment location (a) force tracking (b) contact position.

6 Conclusion

A robust adaptive force tracking impedance controller for robotic grasping unknown objects was proposed in this paper. An adaptive law was first designed to estimate the unknown environment location and stiffness in practice. Using the nonlinear HGTD, an LESO-based robust adaptive dynamic surface position controller was proposed. Finally, numerical simulations were conducted to illustrate the control performance of the proposed impedance controller.

Acknowledgement. This work was supported by the National Key Research and Development Program of China [Grant no. 2017YFB1302200], the Joint Funds of the National Natural Science Foundation of China [Grant no. U1613201], and the Key Research and Development Program of Guangdong Province [Grant no. 2019B090915001].

References

1. Xu, W., Peng, J., Liang, B., et al.: Hybrid modeling and analysis method for dynamic coupling of space robots. IEEE Trans. Aerosp. Electron. Syst. **52**(1), 85–98 (2016)
2. Huang, P., Zhang, F., Meng, Z., et al.: Adaptive control for space debris removal with uncertain kinematics, dynamics and states. Acta Astronaut. **128**, 416–430 (2016)
3. Nagamatsu, H., Kubota, T., Nakatani, I.: Capture strategy for retrieval of a tumbling satellite by a space robotic manipulator. In: IEEE Proceedings of International Conference on Robotics and Automation, vol. 1, pp. 70–75. IEEE (1996)
4. Huang, P., Xu, Y., Liang, B.: Tracking trajectory planning of space manipulator for capturing operation. Int. J. Adv. Robot. Syst. **3**(3), 31 (2006)
5. Huang, P., Cai, J., Meng, Z., et al.: Novel method of monocular real-time feature point tracking for tethered space robots. J. Aerosp. Eng. **27**(6), 04014039 (2014)

6. Aghili, F.: Pre- and post-grasping robot motion planning to capture and stabilize a tumbling/drifting free-floater with uncertain dynamics. In: IEEE International Conference on Robotics and Automation, pp. 5461–5468. IEEE (2013)
7. Aghili, F.: A prediction and motion-planning scheme for visually guided robotic capturing of free-floating tumbling objects with uncertain dynamics. IEEE Trans. Robot. 28(28), 634–649 (2012)
8. Mccourt, R.A., Silva, C.W.D.: Autonomous robotic capture of a satellite using constrained predictive control. IEEE/ASME Trans. Mechatron. 11(6), 699–708 (2006)
9. Floresabad, A., Wei, Z., Ma, O., et al.: Optimal control of space robots for capturing a tumbling object with uncertainties. J. Guidance Control Dyn. 37(6), 1–4 (2014)
10. Oki, T., Nakanishi, H., Yoshida, K.: Whole-body motion control for capturing a tumbling target by a free-floating space robot. In: IEEE/RSJ International Conference on Intelligent Robots and Systems, pp. 2256–2261. IEEE (2007)
11. Yoshida, K., Nakanishi, H., Inaba, N., et al.: Contact dynamics and control strategy based on impedance matching for robotic capture of a unknown satellite. In: Proceedings of 15th CISM-IFToMM Symposium on Robot Design, Dynamics and Control-Romansy, St-Hubert, Canada (2004)
12. Yoshida, K., Nakanishi, H., Ueno, H., et al.: Dynamics, control and impedance matching for robotic capture of a unknown satellite. Adv. Robot. 18(2), 175–198 (2004)
13. Uyama, N., Nakanishi, H., Nagaoka, K., et al.: Impedance-based contact control of a free-flying space robot with a compliant wrist for unknown satellite capture. In: 2012 IEEE/RSJ International Conference on Intelligent Robots and Systems (IROS), pp. 4477–4482. IEEE (2012)
14. Huang, P., Wang, D., Meng, Z., et al.: Impact dynamic modeling and adaptive target capturing control for tethered space robots with uncertainties. IEEE/ASME Trans. Mechatron. 21(5), 2260–2271 (2016)
15. Seraji, H., Colbaugh, R.: Force tracking in impedance control. Int. J. Robot. Res. 16(1), 97–117 (1997)
16. Jung, S., Hsia, T.C., Bonitz, R.G.: Force tracking impedance control of robot manipulators under unknown environment. IEEE Trans. Control Syst. Technol. 12(3), 474–483 (2004)
17. Xu, Q.: Adaptive discrete-time sliding mode impedance control of a piezoelectric microgripper. IEEE Trans. Robot. 29(29), 663–673 (2013)
18. Swaroop, D., Hedrick, J.K., Yip, P.P., et al.: Dynamic surface control for a class of nonlinear systems. Autom. Control IEEE Trans. 45(10), 1893–1899 (2000)
19. Wang, M., Ren, X., Chen, Q., et al.: Modified dynamic surface approach with bias torque for multi-motor servomechanism. Control Eng. Pract. 50, 57–68 (2016)
20. Han, J.Q.: From PID to active disturbance rejection control. IEEE Trans. Ind. Electron. 56(3), 900–906 (2009)
21. Zhang, W.H., Ye, X., Jiang, L., et al.: Output feedback control for free-floating space robotic manipulators base on adaptive fuzzy neural network. Aerosp. Sci. Technol. 29(1), 135–143 (2013)
22. Wie, B.: Space Vehicle Dynamics and Control, 2nd edn. American Institute of Aeronautics and Astronautics Inc., Reston (1998)
23. Erickson, D., Weber, M., Sharf, I.: Contact stiffness and damping estimation for robotic systems. Int. J. Robot. Res. 22(1), 41–58 (2003)
24. Xia, Y., Shi, P., Liu, G.P., et al.: Active disturbance rejection control for uncertain multivariable systems with time-delay. IET Control Theory Appl. 1(1), 75–81 (2007)
25. Gao, Z.: On discrete time optimal control: a closed-form solution. In: Proceedings of International Conference on Control Conference, Boston, USA, June, pp. 52–58 (2004)
26. Levant, A.: Higher-order sliding modes, differentiation and output-feedback control. Int. J. Control 76(9), 924–941 (2010)

Robust Controller Design for Non-linear System with Perturbation Compensation

Saad Jamshed Abbasi[✉], Wang Jie, Hamza Khan,
and Min Cheol Lee

Department of Mechanical Engineering, Pusan National University,
Busan, South Korea
saadjamshed93@gmail.com

Abstract. The control of non-linear systems has been a research topic of interest for many years. It is not feasible to control such systems using linear control because of uncertainties. Non-linear control, like Sliding Mode Control (SMC), is robust against these uncertainties. Integration of SMC with Sliding Perturbation Observer (SPO) is a more robust controller with a perturbation compensation technique. Chattering is a drawback of SMC due to high switching gain, which can be reduced by altering the structure of the sliding surface of SMC by multiplying the gain with the velocity error. Integration of this proportional derivative gain PDSMC with SPO introduces a more robust controller (PDSMCSPO) with a faster convergence to the desired state.

Keywords: Sliding Mode Control · Sliding Perturbation Observer · Proportional derivative sliding mode control

1 Introduction

Trajectory tracking is an essential requirement in robot manipulator movement applications. A robot manipulator is a non-linear system in nature and the control of such a system with modeling errors, parametric uncertainties, and external disturbances is a challenging task in the field of control engineering. SMC [1–4] is a robust control to tackle system uncertainties and external disturbances. SMC has two phases; reaching phase and sliding phase. The switching gain K should be greater than the perturbation to move the system to the desired states. This higher value of gain K increases the chattering as well as the breaking frequency of the low pass filter between the sliding surface and error during the sliding phase, because the high-frequency perturbation element affects the system during the sliding phase. SPO is a non-linear observer that utilizes partial state feedback (position) to estimate velocity and perturbation. SPO is a combination of a Sliding Observer (SO) and perturbation observer. Integration of SMC into SPO introduces a controller that is more robust against perturbations because of the perturbation compensation technique.

Different ideas have been discussed to remove chattering from the output of SMC [2]. In this research, a new approach is presented to reduce chattering from the system output, and when this PDSMC is integrated with SPO, the result is PDSMCPSO, whose convergence to the desired state is faster than conventional SMCSPO.

© Springer Nature Switzerland AG 2019
H. Yu et al. (Eds.): ICIRA 2019, LNAI 11742, pp. 689–700, 2019.
https://doi.org/10.1007/978-3-030-27535-8_61

Derivative gain is introduced in the structure of the sliding surface with a value between 0 and 1. During the reaching phase, this small gain is multiplied with perturbation and reduces its effect so a small switching gain K, which reduces chattering from system output, is needed. When the system reaches the sliding surface, the transfer function between the sliding surface and perturbation has more low pass filter characteristics compared to conventional SMC. PDSMCSPO is the result of the integration of PDSMC with SPO. This is a robust controller which uses the perturbation compensation technique to reduce chattering. PDSMCPSO convergences to the desired state faster than SMCSPO and the steady state error is also smaller than conventional SMCSPO [5–7].

This paper consists of 4 sections. First is the introduction. In the second section, control theory is presented, and the difference between the proposed and conventional methods are discussed. The third section consists of simulation and experiment results, and in the last section, conclusions are mentioned.

2   Control Theory

In this section, the dynamics of a hydraulic system after that SMC, SPO, our proposed scheme PDSMC, and its integration with SPO will be discussed first.

2.1   Dynamics of Hydraulic System

The hydraulic robot manipulator is shown in Fig. 1. The system consists of two hydraulic operated links, and one link is servo motor operated. The last link of the robot manipulator is used for simulation and experimental purposes. The dynamics of the 3rd link is extracted from the signal compression method [8].

Fig. 1. Hydraulic robot manipulator.

The schematic diagram of the third link of the robot manipulator is shown in Fig. 2, and its mathematical model is shown below.

$$(J + \Delta J) \cdot \ddot{\theta} + (B + \Delta B + \varphi) \cdot \dot{\theta} + 0.5 \cdot M \cdot g \cdot L \cdot sin\theta + D = F \cdot L \tag{1}$$

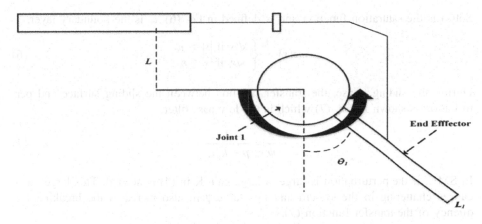

Fig. 2. Third link schematic diagram.

In Eq. (1) the perturbation is defined as.

$$\psi = \Delta J + \Delta B + D + \varphi \tag{2}$$

Equation (3) is the final form as shown below.

$$\ddot{\theta} = \frac{1}{J} \left(u - B * \dot{\theta} + \psi \right) \tag{3}$$

In the equation above J is inertia, B is the damping term and ψ is perturbation. J and B is obtained by the signal compression method. Their values are shown below in Table 1.

Table 1. System parameters

Serial no	Moment of inertia (kg m^2)	Damper (kg m^2/s)
1	303	15,355

2.2 Sliding Mode Control (SMC)

SMC is a non-linear controller. The main idea is to design a proper sliding surface as shown below in Eq. (4) where e is the error and c is a positive constant.

$$s = \dot{e} + c \cdot e \tag{4}$$

to verify the sliding condition $s \cdot \dot{s} \leq 0$ the gain K should be greater than the magnitude of perturbation in Eq. (5) below.

$$\dot{s} = -K \cdot \dot{s}at(s) + \psi \tag{5}$$

Sat(s) is the saturation function and is defined in Eq. (6). ε_c is the boundary layer.

$$sat(s) = \begin{cases} s/|s| \text{ if } |s| > \varepsilon_c \\ s/\varepsilon_c \text{ if } |s| \leq \varepsilon_c \end{cases} \tag{6}$$

During the sliding phase, the transfer function between the sliding surface and perturbation is shown in Eq. (7) which is the low pass filter.

$$\frac{s}{\psi} = \frac{1}{p + k/\varepsilon_c} \tag{7}$$

In SMC, if the perturbation is large, a large gain K in (4) is needed. This large value causes chattering in the system and this large gain also increases the breaking frequency of the transfer function (7).

2.3   PD Sliding Mode Control

The main idea is to multiply a small gain with the velocity error in the sliding surface. This small gain reduces chattering from the system output and reduces the breaking frequency of the transfer function between the sliding surface and perturbation. Equation (8) shows the structure of the sliding surface of PDSMC.

$$s = k_d \cdot \dot{e} + k_p \cdot e \tag{8}$$

k_p & k_d are the proportional and derivative gain where e is the error as defined in the section above. The value of $k_p > 0$, $0 < k_d < 1$. In PDSMC, during the reaching phase, the $\dot{s}$ dynamics is shown below.

During the reaching phase, the $\dot{s}$ dynamics become Eq. (9).

$$\dot{s} = -K' \cdot sat(s) + k_d \cdot \psi \tag{9}$$

In PDSMC, during the reaching phase $k_d < 1$, a small gain is multiplied with perturbation and reduces the effect of perturbation during the reaching phase which means that in PDSMC K' is small compared with SMC. So, there is less chattering in PDSMC compared with SMC, and it also reduces the breaking frequency of the transfer function between sliding surface and perturbation as shown in Eq. (10).

$$\frac{s}{\psi} = \frac{k_d}{p + K'/\varepsilon_c} \tag{10}$$

2.4   Sliding Perturbation Observer (SPO)

SPO is a non-linear observer that utilizes only partial state feedback to estimate the velocity and perturbation. Its structure is given in Eq. (11) and (12).

$$\dot{\hat{x}}_1 = \hat{x}_2 - k_1.sat(\tilde{x}_1) - \alpha_1.\tilde{x}_1$$
$$\dot{\hat{x}}_2 = -k_2.sat(\tilde{x}_1) + \alpha_3.\bar{u} - \alpha_2.\tilde{x}_1 \tag{11}$$
$$\dot{\hat{x}}_3 = \alpha_3^2.(\alpha_3.\hat{x}_2 + \bar{u} - \hat{x}_3)$$

$$\hat{\psi} = \alpha_3(\alpha_3 \cdot \hat{x}_2 - \hat{x}_3) \tag{12}$$

where $k_1, k_2, \alpha_3, \alpha_1, \alpha_2$ are constants and their values are greater than 0 and sat $(\hat{x}_1)$ is the saturation function which is defined below in Eq. (13).

$$sat(\tilde{x}_1) = \begin{cases} \tilde{x}_1/|\tilde{x}_1| & \text{if } |\tilde{x}_1| > \varepsilon_o \\ \tilde{x}_1/\varepsilon_0 & \text{if } |\tilde{x}_1| \le \varepsilon_o \end{cases} \tag{13}$$

2.5   Sliding Mode Control with Sliding Perturbation Observer (SMCSPO)

In this section the integration of SMC with SPO is briefly explained. SMCSPO is a robust control with a perturbation compensation technique.

The estimated sliding surface is given in Eq. (14) in order to enforce the sliding condition $s \cdot \dot{s} \le 0$. The control $\bar{u}$ is selected as.

$$\bar{u} = \frac{1}{\alpha_3}\left[-K \cdot sat(\hat{s}) + \tilde{x}_1\left\{ \frac{k_2}{\varepsilon_o} + \frac{c \cdot k_1}{\varepsilon_o} - \frac{k_1^2}{\varepsilon_o^2} \right\} + \ddot{x}_d - c(\hat{x}_2 - \dot{x}_d) - \hat{\psi} \right] \tag{14}$$

During the reaching phase, $\dot{\hat{s}}$ is shown below in Eq. (15).

$$\dot{\hat{s}} = -K \cdot sat(\hat{s}) - \frac{k_1}{\varepsilon_o}\tilde{x}_2 \tag{15}$$

The gain must satisfy $K > \frac{k_1^2}{\varepsilon_o}$ to verify the sliding condition.

2.6   Proportional Derivative Sliding Mode Control with Sliding Perturbation Observer (PDSMCSPO)

In this section, the proposed scheme PDSMC is integrated with SPO to obtain a more robust control with perturbation compensation. The estimated sliding surface is shown below in Eq. (16).

$$\hat{s} = k_d \cdot \dot{\hat{e}} + k_p \cdot \hat{e} \tag{16}$$

In the relation above, $\hat{e} = \hat{x} - x_d$ was the estimated error. $k_p \& k_d$ were proportional and the derivative gain of the proportional-integral-derivative controller (PID). It was assumed that $k_p > 1, 0 < k_d < 1$. The actual sliding surface is defined as below.

$$\tilde{s} = \hat{s} - s \tag{17}$$

The $\tilde{s}$ is obtained as Eq. (18)

$$\tilde{s} = k_d \cdot \dot{\tilde{x}}_1 + k_p \cdot \tilde{x}_1 \tag{18}$$

The control $\bar{u}$ was selected such that it satisfied the condition $\hat{s} \cdot \dot{\hat{s}} \leq 0$ during the reaching phase. To satisfy this condition, $\dot{\hat{s}}$ should be equal to $\dot{\hat{s}} = -K \cdot sat(\hat{s})$. After taking the derivative of Eq. (16) and using Eq. (11), the following equation was obtained as Eq. (19)

$$\dot{\hat{s}} = k_d \cdot \alpha_3 \cdot \bar{u} - \tilde{x}_1 \left\{ \frac{k_d \cdot k_2}{\varepsilon_o} + \frac{k_p \cdot k_1}{\varepsilon_o} - \frac{k_d \cdot k_1^2}{\varepsilon_o} \right\} - \left\{ \frac{k_d \cdot k_1}{\varepsilon_o} \right\} \tilde{x}_2$$
$$+ k_p \{\hat{x}_2 - \dot{x}_d\} - k_d \cdot \ddot{x}_d + k_d \cdot \hat{\psi} \tag{19}$$

After solving further, control $\bar{u}$ is obtained as.

$$\bar{u} = \frac{1}{\alpha_3} \left[-\frac{K'}{k_d} sat(\hat{s}) + \tilde{x}_1 \left\{ \frac{k_p \cdot k_1}{k_d \cdot \varepsilon_o} + \frac{k_2}{\varepsilon_o} - \frac{k_1^2}{\varepsilon_o} \right\} - \frac{k_p}{k_d} \{\hat{x}_2 - \dot{x}_d\} - \hat{\psi} + \ddot{x}_d \right] \tag{20}$$

After putting Eqs. (20) into (19) the actual $\hat{s}$ is obtained as Eq. (21).

$$\dot{\hat{s}} = -\frac{K'}{\varepsilon_c} \cdot \hat{s} - \frac{k_d \cdot k_1}{\varepsilon_o} \cdot \tilde{x}_2 \tag{21}$$

In the equation above, it can be seen that during the reaching phase, the $\dot{\hat{s}}$-dynamics were affected by the state estimation error $\tilde{x}_2$. To enforce the sliding condition, K' should follow Eq. (22).

$$K' > \frac{k_d \cdot k_1^2}{\varepsilon_o} \tag{22}$$

When the system reached the sliding surface or the prescribed manifold $|\hat{s}| \leq \varepsilon_c$, the actual s dynamics were obtained as shown below in Eq. (23).

$$\dot{s} + \frac{K}{\varepsilon_c} s = \tilde{x}_1 \left\{ \frac{k_d \cdot k_2}{\varepsilon_o} - \left(\frac{K}{\varepsilon_c} - \frac{k_1}{\varepsilon_o} \right) \left(k_p - \frac{k_1 \cdot k_d}{\varepsilon_o} \right) \right\} - \tilde{x}_2 \left\{ \frac{K \cdot k_d}{\varepsilon_c} + k_p \right\} - k_d \cdot \hat{\psi} \tag{23}$$

2.7   Design Procedure

This section presents the general design procedure for PDSCMSPO. When the condition $|\hat{s}| \leq \varepsilon_c, |\tilde{x}_1| \leq \varepsilon_o$ had been achieved, it was assumed that $c = K/\varepsilon_c$ and $c = k_p/k_d$. The controller and observer dynamics took place in the following form.

$$
\begin{bmatrix} \dot{\tilde{x}}_1 \\ \dot{\tilde{x}}_2 \\ \dot{\tilde{x}}_3 \\ \dot{s} \end{bmatrix} = \begin{bmatrix} -k_1/\varepsilon_o & 1 & 0 & 0 \\ -k_2/\varepsilon_o & \alpha_3^2 & -\alpha_3 & 0 \\ 0 & \alpha_3^3 & -\alpha_3^2 & 0 \\ k_d k_2/\varepsilon_o - \left(\frac{K}{\varepsilon_c} - \frac{k_1}{\varepsilon_o}\right)\left(k_p - \frac{k_1 \cdot k_d}{\varepsilon_o}\right) & \left(\frac{K \cdot k_d}{\varepsilon_o} + k_p + \alpha_3^2\right) & k_d \cdot \alpha_3 & \frac{-K}{\varepsilon_c} \end{bmatrix} \begin{bmatrix} \tilde{x}_1 \\ \tilde{x}_2 \\ \tilde{x}_3 \\ s \end{bmatrix} + \begin{bmatrix} 0 \\ 0 \\ 1 \\ 0 \end{bmatrix} \frac{\dot{\psi}}{\alpha_3}
$$

(24)

It seems like a conventional Luenberger Observer. The pole placement method is used to find the parameters of the control scheme by comparing it with the desired poles.

$$
[\lambda + K/\varepsilon_c]\left[\lambda^3 + (k_1/\varepsilon_0)\lambda^2 + (k_2/\varepsilon_0)\lambda + \alpha_3^2(k_2/\varepsilon_0)\right] = 0
$$

(25)

After comparing the coefficient of characteristic equations of (24) and (25) we get the following relation as shown in Eq. (26).

$$
\frac{k_1}{\varepsilon_o} = 3\lambda_d, \frac{k_2}{\varepsilon_o} = \lambda_d, \alpha_3 = \sqrt{\frac{\lambda_d}{3}}, \frac{K}{\varepsilon_c} = \lambda_d, \frac{k_p}{k_d} = \lambda_d
$$

(26)

2.8   Comparison of SMC and PDSMC

In SMC during the reaching phase as Eq. (5), the gain K should be greater than perturbation. Greater the perturbation, larger the gain and greater the breaking frequency of the low pass filter between the sliding surface and perturbation as shown in Eq. (7). In PDSMC shown in Eq. (9), during the reaching phase, the small gain k_d is multiplied with the perturbation and reduces the effect of perturbation and requires a small switching gain K in PDSMC. Because of this, the breaking frequency of the low pass filter between the sliding surface and perturbation Eq. (10) is smaller than Eq. (7). This means that during the sliding phase, PDSMC is insensitive to high-frequency perturbation.

2.9   Comparison Characteristics of SMCSPO and PDSMCSPO

The reaching time (t_r) in PDSMCPSO is smaller than the conventional method. As it is known, the mathematical presentation of t_r is given in (27).

$$
t_r \leq \frac{s_o}{\eta}
$$

(27)

In PDSMCSPO, the starting point or initial point of the sliding surface is smaller than SMCSPO. So, the convergence of PDSMCPOS is faster than SMCPSO, which is presented in the next section. The graph of the transfer function between the sliding surface and perturbation is shown in Fig. 3. It can be seen that the blue line shows the result of PDSMCPS and the red line SMCPSO. It is clearly visible that the attenuation of perturbation during the sliding phase in PDSMCPS is much better than the conventional method in all frequency ranges.

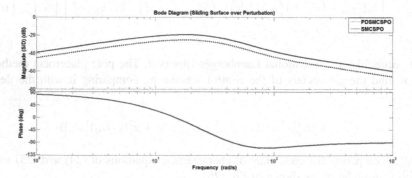

Fig. 3. Bode plot of sliding surface over perturbation. (Color figure online)

Similarly, in PDSMCSPO, the bode plot of the transfer function between the error and perturbation is shown in Fig. 4. It can be seen that our proposed scheme has better attenuation than the conventional one. The blue line shows the bode plot of PDSMCSPO which attenuates the disturbance signal more than SMCSPO, shown with the red line, but in the high-frequency range, the attenuation of both schemes is the same.

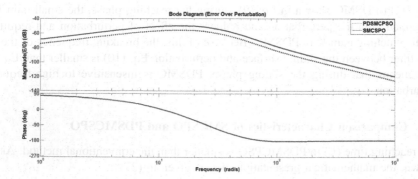

Fig. 4. Bode plot of error over perturbation (Color figure online)

3   Simulation and Experimental Results

3.1   SMC and PDSMC

Simulations were done with Matlab/Simulink. The system parameters are shown in Table 2.

Table 2. SMC and PDSMC parameters

Serial no	SMC	PDSMC
1	K = 550	K = 275
2	C = 16	$k_p = 8, k_d = 0.5$
3	D = 500	D = 500
4	Step input	Step input

A step input is given to the system, and more chattering is observed in the output of SMC compared with PDSMC because of the high gain K in (3). The blue line shows the output of PDSMC, whereas the red line shows the output of SMC with chattering (Fig. 5).

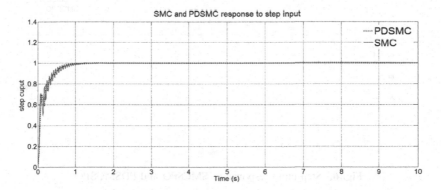

Fig. 5. Step input response

As it was mentioned earlier, PDSMC is insensitive to high-frequency perturbation during the sliding phase because of the low breaking frequency.

3.2   SMCSPO and PDSCMSPO

System parameters are shown in Table 3 for both algorithms. A step input is given to the system (Fig. 6).

Table 3. SMCSPO and PDSMCSPO parameters

Serial no	SMCSPO	PDSMCSPO
1	$\lambda = 30$	$\lambda = 30$
2	$\varepsilon_o, \varepsilon_c = 1$	$\varepsilon_o, \varepsilon_c = 1$
3	$\frac{k_1}{\varepsilon_o} = 90$	$\frac{k_1}{\varepsilon_o} = 90$
4	$\frac{k_2}{\varepsilon_o} = 2700$	$\frac{k_2}{\varepsilon_o} = 2700$
5	$\alpha_3 = 3.16$	$\alpha_3 = 3.16$
6	$\frac{K}{\varepsilon_c} = 30$	$\frac{K}{\varepsilon_c} = 30$
7	$\frac{k_p}{k_d} = 30, k_d = 0.5, k_p = 15$	$c = \frac{k_p}{k_d} = 30$
8	Input = step	Input = step

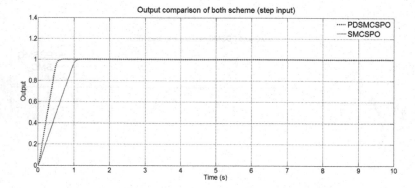

Fig. 6. Step input response of SMCSPO and PDSMCSPO

It can be seen that PDSMCSPO response is faster than SMCSPO.

3.3   Experimental Results

SMCSPO and PDSMCSPO is implemented on a real system. The experiment is implemented on the 3rd link of the robotic manipulator. A sinewave input is given to the system with a frequency of I rad/s. it can be seen that trajectory error of our proposed scheme (blue line) is smaller than SMCSPO (red line) (Fig. 7).

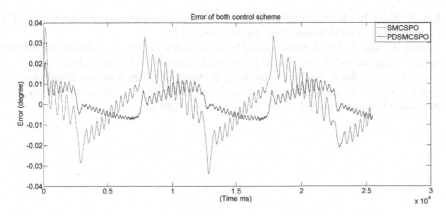

Fig. 7. Step input response of SMCSPO and PDSMCSPO

4   Conclusions

In this study, the robustness and convergence time characteristics corresponding to the trajectory tracking problem has been discussed. The derivative gain term is introduced in the sliding surface structure that reduces the gain K of conventional SMC. The small gain K results in the reduction of chattering from the system output, sliding surface, and controller output. This small value of gain K also reduces the breaking frequency of the low pass filter between the sliding surface and perturbation during the sliding phase. The results after the integration of this PDSMC into SPO (PDSMCSPO) have improved the system's response with better convergence time, as compared to SMCSPO. At the same time, it is worthy of mentioning that both algorithms (proposed and conventional) are the same.

Acknowledgment. Basic Science Research Program through the National Research Foundation of Korea (NRF) funded by the Ministry of Education (1345253125).

References

1. Elmali, W.-K.H., Olgac, N.: Sliding mode control with perturbation estimation (SMCPE). Int. J. Control **56**, 923–941 (1993)
2. Moura, J.T., Elmali, H., Olgac, N.: Sliding mode contorl with slididng pertrubation observer. J. Dyn. Syst. Meas. Control **119**, 657–665 (1997)
3. Butt, Q., Bhatti, A.: Estimation of gasoline–engine parameters using high order sliding mode control. IEEE Trasns. Ind. Electron. **55**, 3908–3916 (2008)
4. Kallu, K.D., Lee, M.C.: Sensor less force estimation of the end effector of two link manipulator using sliding mode control with sliding perturbation observer. Electronics (2018)
5. Abbasi, S.J., Lee, M.C.: Efficient control of nonlinear system using modified sliding mode control. In: Proceeding of the Society of Instrument and Control Engineers (SICE), Nara, Japan, 22–25 November 2018

6. Liu, X., Jiang, W.: Nonlinear adaptive control for dynamics dead zone uncertainties in robotic system. Int. J. Control Autom. Syst. **15**, 875–882 (2017)
7. Farooq, U., Gu, J.: Fuzzy model based bilateral control design of nonlinear tele-operating system using method of state convergence. IEEE Access **4**, 4119–4135 (2016)
8. Jin, S.Y., et al.: Study on the identification of dynamic system with non-linear term using signal compresson method and correleation coeffcient. In: Conference of the Socirty of Mechanical Engineering, vol. 1, no. 1, pp. 519–523 (1993)

Trajectory Tracking Control of a 7-Axis Robot Arm Using SMCSPO

Wang Jie, Saad Jamshed, Dong-Jun Kim, Bao Yulong,
and Min-Cheol Lee

School of Mechanical Engineering, Pusan National University,
Busan, South Korea
{wj,mclee}@pusan.ac.kr

Abstract. Multi-axis-robots have been wildly used in industry for soldering, plasma cutting with an indirect contact without high disturbance. However, recently, the multi axis robot is designed for a direct contact work which may generate a large reaction force from environment. The complex dynamics and high payload can lead to the control instability. In this paper, we proposed a method focusing on the trajectory tracking control for an electrical motor actuated 7-axis robot which is the sliding mode control with sliding perturbation observer. Sliding perturbation observer is used to estimate the dynamic uncertainties, errors occurred in modeling, the main payload and the disturbance from environment. Stability analysis is derived by the Lyapunov stability. The tracking performance is demonstrated by a real experiment.

Keywords: 7-axis robot arm · Sliding mode control ·
Sliding perturbation observer

1 Introduction

Robot arms have been developed with multi-axis which have a number of advantages such as the boarder work space, more capacity of payload, and more flexible. Much research and applications have been developed in many different areas, e.g. a surgical robot [1], an industrial soldering/welding robot in manufacturing [2], and a remote dismantling robot [3]. Many existing robots are designed for indirect contact with the objective or direct contact only obtained a small payload/disturbance. The trajectory tracking control for these kinds of robot is simple to design and has a fine performance. In an investigation of the previous research, many basic controllers are used for these robots, e.g. an adaptive PID controller is designed for a multi-axis welding robot [4], and Fuzzy control logic is designed for a 6-axis articulated robot [5]. However, for some direct contact work with high payload, the design for a good and robust controller is required on the multi-axis robot because of the complex dynamics and high disturbance. In order to assembly some heavy part, we designed a dual arm robot, each arm has a 7-axis joint with its own weight 28 kg. The goal for this robot is to assemble a maximal 3 kg product. Because its own heavy weight, complex dynamics and objective high payload, a robust controller is needed.

© Springer Nature Switzerland AG 2019
H. Yu et al. (Eds.): ICIRA 2019, LNAI 11742, pp. 701–708, 2019.
https://doi.org/10.1007/978-3-030-27535-8_62

Sliding mode control (SMC) is the most used controller type for the complex dynamics constituted system, which only needs to design an upper boundary for the uncertainties and the disturbance. The designed sliding surface and convergent driving force can ensure the stability. Recently, much research is aimed to improve the performance of the sliding mode control by a combination with other control algorithms. A self-adaptive fuzzy sliding mode control is designed for the multi-axis manipulator [6]. A terminal sliding mode control which changes the original linear sliding surface to a nonlinear fast shape sliding surface is developed for a 3aixs hydraulic robot [7]. Also, in order to compensate the disturbance and reduce the chattering happened during the convergence to sliding surface, torque sensor based or disturbance estimator based compensators are proposed with the SMC. Besides disturbance estimators, sliding perturbation observer (SPO) [8] has an outstanding performance for the low frequency motion. Many researchers have demonstrate the performance of SPO [9, 10].

In this research, the sliding mode control with sliding perturbation observer (SMCSPO) is used and designed to control the 7-aixs robot system for trajectory tracking. The main contribution is the application on a multi-axis robot system with sliding mode control and sliding perturbation observer, even though the controller is not designed as a novel type. In order to apply the controller SMCSPO, a dynamic identification for this 7-axis robot is also involved in this paper.

This paper is organized as following, the 7-axis robot system and its dynamic modeling are introduced first in Sect. 2, the controller SMCSPO for this robot is descried and proposed in Sect. 3, an experiment result is shown in Sect. 4, and we conclude this work in Sect. 5.

2 Dynamics Analysis of the 7-Axis-Robot

The 7-axis-robot is shown in Fig. 1 with 7 rotation joints. In the modeling linearization, each link is seemed decoupled with each other as a simple second order system shown as:

$$\ddot{x}_i = \frac{1}{J_i}u_i - \frac{D_i}{J_i}\dot{x}_i - \Psi_i$$

$$\Psi_i = \text{Nonlinear \& Coupled Terms} + \frac{F_{di}}{m} + \text{Model Assumption Errors} \quad (1)$$

$$i = 1, \ldots, 7.$$

where $\mathbf{x} \triangleq [\mathbf{X}_1 \cdots \mathbf{X}_7]^T$ is the state vector and $\mathbf{X}_i \triangleq [x_i, \dot{x}_i]^T$. For a second order system in (1), J_i is considered as the inertia of the system, D_i contains the damping term and Ψ is defined as the perturbation which contains modeling errors, nonlinear terms, coupled terms, some simplified calculation error, and main disturbances from the environment. The perturbation Ψ will be estimated by the SPO.

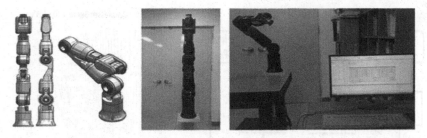

Fig. 1. A 7-axis robot manipulator

Signal compression method [11] is used to identify the dynamics. An equivalent impulse signal is generated to implement on an objective system as the desired trajectory. The equivalent impulse signal is obtained by passing a time delay filter from a designed impulse signal. The expanded impulse signal is available to apply on the real system. Then, the response output is filtered by the inverse of the time delay filter. The result after the inverse time delay filter is supposed as the real response which is from the origin impulse signal to the linear system. The system can be modeled when we change the model dynamics to match the correlation with the output signal from real experiment. This logic and the expanded signal are shown in Fig. 2. It obtained from the designed impulse signal in Eq. (1) passed by an time delay filter with following function in Eq. (2):

$$
\begin{aligned}
&P(n) = 60 \exp[-(\frac{n}{a})^{12}],\ 0 \leq n \leq N/2 - 1\\
&P(n) = 0,\ n = N/2\\
&P(n) = P(N - n),\ N/2 + 1 \leq n \leq N - 1
\end{aligned}
\tag{2}
$$

$$
\begin{aligned}
&H(n) = \exp[-\frac{12n^2}{b}j],\ 0 \leq n \leq N/2 - 1\\
&H(n) = 0,\ n = N/2\\
&H(n) = H(N - n),\ N/2 + 1 \leq n \leq N - 1
\end{aligned}
\tag{3}
$$

The highest correlation and corresponding dynamics of link 5 is shown in Fig. 3. The other links are identified using same way by comparing the correlation coefficient. Dynamics identification result are show in Table 1.

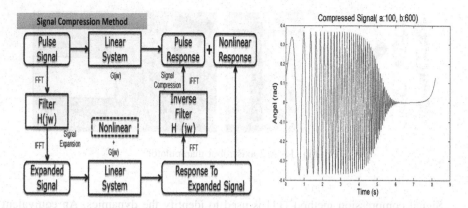

Fig. 2. Signal compression method logic and expanded signal.

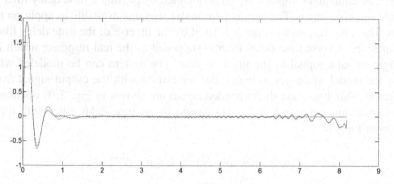

Fig. 3. Correlation of real system response with modeled system response result of link 5.

Table 1. Dynamic parameters

	ζ	ω_n	2nd order model
1	0.642	6.864	$\frac{4.711}{s^2+8.813s}$
2	1.521	2.937	$\frac{0.8626}{s^2+8.934s}$
3	0.324	7.628	$\frac{5.819}{s^2+4.943s}$
4	0.61	5.521	$\frac{3.048}{s^2+6.736s}$
5	0.346	12.469	$\frac{15.55}{s^2+8.629s}$
6	0.37	13.21	$\frac{17.45}{s^2+9.775s}$
7	0.35	12.502	$\frac{15.63}{s^2+8.751s}$

3   Controller Design

In this section, the controller for the robot is proposed with an ASSUMPTION that the perturbations have an upper bound by a known continuous function of the state $\Gamma_i \geq \Psi_i$: The state space with a new state variable x_{3j} can be represented as

$$
\begin{aligned}
\dot{x}_{1i} &= x_{2i} \\
\dot{x}_{2i} &= a_{3i}\bar{u}_i + \Psi_i \\
\dot{x}_{3i} &= \alpha_{3i}\dot{x}_{2i} - \dot{\Psi}_i/\alpha_{3j} \\
y_i &= x_{1i}.
\end{aligned}
\tag{4}
$$

The new state variable x_{3i} is defined as

$$
x_{3i} = \alpha_{3i}x_{2i} - \Psi_i/\alpha_{3i}.
\tag{5}
$$

The sliding perturbation observer (SPO) equations for a i-th link can be described as follows:

$$
\dot{\hat{x}}_{1i} = \hat{x}_{2i} - k_{1i}\,\mathrm{sat}(\tilde{x}_{1i}),
$$

$$
\dot{\hat{x}}_{2i} = \alpha_3\bar{u}_i - k_{2i}\,\mathrm{sat}(\tilde{x}_{1i}) + \hat{\Psi}_i
$$

$$
\dot{\hat{x}}_{3i} = \alpha_{3i}^2(\bar{u}_i + \alpha_{3i}\hat{x}_{2i} - \hat{x}_{3i})
$$

$$
\hat{\Psi}_i = \alpha_{3i}(\alpha_{3i}\hat{x}_{2i} - \hat{x}_{3i}).
\tag{6}
$$

The stability of SPO is proved in [7]. The perturbation estimation is used to design a robust controller. In here, we use sliding mode control with its combination of SPO. The sliding function of estimation is defined as:

$$
\hat{s}_i = \dot{\hat{e}}_i + c_{1i}\hat{e}_i.
\tag{7}
$$

where $c_{1i} > 0$, $\hat{e}_i = \hat{x}_{1i} - x_{1di}$ is the estimated position tracking error and $[x_{1di}\dot{x}_{1di}]^T$ is the desired motion for the "i-th" degree of freedom. $s_j = \dot{e}_j + c_{1j}e_j$, $e_i = x_i - x_{di}$ is the error between the desired trajectory and the actual trajectory in tracking. The error estimation of the sliding function is defined as $\tilde{s}_i = \hat{s}_i - s_i$. Using (24) and (30) its value can be computed as

$$
\tilde{s}_i = \dot{\tilde{x}}_{1i} + c_{i1}\tilde{x}_{1i}.
\tag{8}
$$

Where $K_i > \Gamma_i(\mathbf{x}, t) + \eta_i$ and

$$\text{sat}(\hat{s}_i) = \begin{cases} \hat{s}_i/|\hat{s}_i|, & if\,|\hat{s}_i| \geq \varepsilon_{ci} \\ \hat{s}_i/\varepsilon_{ci}, & if\,|\hat{s}_i| \leq \varepsilon_{ci} \end{cases}. \tag{9}$$

where ε_{ci} is positive. $\dot{\hat{s}}_i$ can be obtained as

$$\dot{\hat{s}}_i = \alpha_{3i}\bar{u}_i - [k_{2i}/\varepsilon_{0i} + c_{i1}(k_{1i}/\varepsilon_{0i}) - (k_{1i}/\varepsilon_{0i})^2]\tilde{x}_{1i} - (k_{1i}/\varepsilon_{0i})\tilde{x}_{2i} - \ddot{x}_{1id} + c_{1i}(\hat{x}_{2i} - \dot{x}_{1id}) + \hat{\Psi}_i. \tag{10}$$

In order to enforce (10) when $\tilde{x}_{2i} = 0$, a control law is selected as

$$\bar{u}_i = \frac{1}{\alpha_{3i}}\{-K_i\text{sat}(\hat{s}_i) + [\frac{k_{2i}}{\varepsilon_{0i}} + c_{i1}\frac{k_{1i}}{\varepsilon_{0i}} - (\frac{k_{1i}}{\varepsilon_{0i}})^2]\tilde{x}_{1i} + \ddot{x}_{1id} - c_{1i}(\hat{x}_{2i} - \dot{x}_{1id}) - \hat{\Psi}_i\}. \tag{11}$$

In the control input of SMCSPO (10), the resulting $\hat{s}_i$-dynamics including the effects of $\tilde{x}_{2i}$ becomes

$$\dot{\hat{s}}_i = -K_i\,\text{sat}(\hat{s}_i) - (k_{1i}/\varepsilon_{0i})\tilde{x}_{2i}. \tag{12}$$

To satisfy $\dot{\hat{s}}\hat{s} \leq 0$ when $|\hat{s}_i| \geq \varepsilon_{ci}$, the robust control gains must be chosen such that

$$K_i \geq k_{1i}^2/\varepsilon_{0i}. \tag{13}$$

4 Experiment

The trajectory tracking experiment is proceed by the Windows OS RTX based (real time operating system, 3 ms sampling time). The desired reference trajectory is shown in the first figure of Fig. 4. Others figures in Fig. 4 present the tracking error of each link.

The Experimental results show that the tracking error of each link except link 5 is less than 1° with a small chatting, which demonstrates the good control performance of SMCSPO. The key to improve the control performance is the system sampling time, which restrict the designed parameter of SMCSPO [7]. The selection of controller parameter is discussed in the [8].

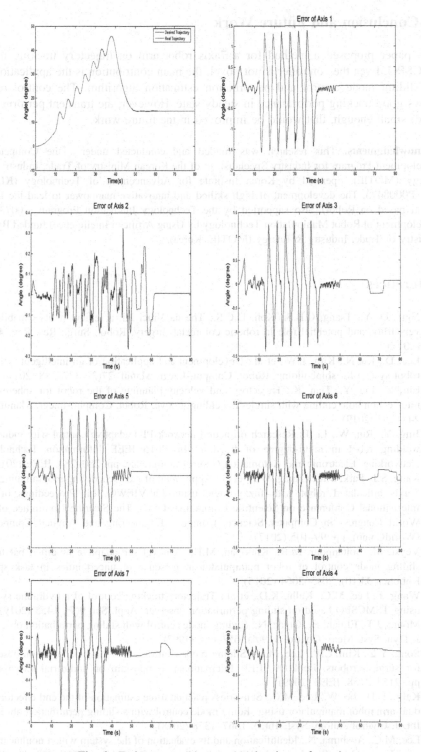

Fig. 4. Trajectory tracking result (planning and error)

5   Conclusion and Future Work

This paper proposed a method for a 7axis robot arm on trajectory tracking using SMCSPO. Even the controller is not novel, the main contribution is the application of the sliding mode control and perturbation estimation algorithm. The control result shows good tracking performance in steady state. However, the transient performance is not small enough, that would be improved in the future work.

Acknowledgments. This research was funded and conducted under 「the Competency Development Program for Industry Specialists」 of the Korean Ministry of Trade, Industry and Energy (MOTIE), operated by Korea Institute for Advancement of Technology (KIAT). (No. P0008473, The development of high skilled and innovative manpower to lead the Innovation based on Robot), also supported by the Technology Innovation Program (10073147, Development of Robot Manipulation Technology by Using Artificial Intelligence) funded By the Ministry of Trade, Industry & Energy (MOTIE, Korea).

References

1. Ngu, J.C.Y., Tsang, C.B.S., Koh, D.C.S.: The da Vinci Xi: a review of its capabilities, versatility, and potential role in robotic colorectal surgery. Robot. Surg.: Res. Rev. **4**, 77 (2017)
2. Lee, D., Ku, N., Kim, T.W., et al.: Development and application of an intelligent welding robot system for shipbuilding. Robot. Comput.-Integr. Manuf. **27**(2), 377–388 (2011)
3. Liu, Y., Liu, Y., Tian, X.: Trajectory and velocity planning of the robot for sphere-pipe intersection hole cutting with single-Y welding groove. Robot. Comput.-Integr. Manuf. **56**, 244–253 (2019)
4. Jing, Y., Rui, W., Li, J.: Research on neural network PID adaptive control with industrial welding robot in multi-degree of freedom. In: 2016 IEEE Information Technology, Networking, Electronic and Automation Control Conference, pp. 280–284. IEEE (2016)
5. Kang, S.J., Park, S.K., Chung, W.J., et al.: Application of gain scheduling programming to a 6-axis articulated robot with fuzzy logic using LabVIEW®. In: Proceedings of the International Conference on Scientific Computing (CSC). The Steering Committee of the World Congress in Computer Science, Computer Engineering and Applied Computing (WorldComp), pp. 99–105 (2017)
6. Veysi, M., Soltanpour, M.R., Khooban, M.H.: A novel self-adaptive modified bat fuzzy sliding mode control of robot manipulator in presence of uncertainties in task space. Robotica **33**(10), 2045–2064 (2015)
7. Wang, J., Lee, M.C., Kallu, K.D., et al.: Trajectory tracking control of a hydraulic system using TSMCSPO based on sliding perturbation observer. Appl. Sci. **9**(7), 1455 (2019)
8. Moura, J.T., Elmali, H., Olgac, N.: Sliding mode control with sliding perturbation observer. J. Dyn. Syst. Meas. Control **119**(4), 657–665 (1997)
9. Song, Y.E., Kim, C.Y., Lee, M.C.: Sliding mode control with sliding perturbation observer for surgical robots. In: 2009 IEEE International Symposium on Industrial Electronics, pp. 2153–2158. IEEE (2009)
10. Kallu, K.D., Jie, W., Lee, M.C.: Sensorless reaction force estimation of the end effector of a dual-arm robot manipulator using sliding mode control with a sliding perturbation observer. Int. J. Control Autom. Syst. **16**(3), 1367–1378 (2018)
11. Lee, M.C., Aoshima, N.: Identification and its evaluation of the system with a nonlinear element by signal compression method. Trans. Soc. Instrum. Control Eng. **25**(7), 729–736 (1989)

Research on Control Algorithms
of Underactuated Gymnastic Robot's Leaping
Between Horizontal Bar

Wenkang Lian[1], Ying Li[2], Yu Liu[1(✉)], Yan Zhang[1], and Yong Liu[1]

[1] Harbin Institute of Technology, Harbin 150006, China
liuyunum@163.com
[2] Yingkou Vocational and Technical College, Yingkou, China

Abstract. This paper mainly studies the leaping movement of gymnastic robot between horizontal bar. There are two stages in the bar changing movement preparation stage and leap stage. The preparation stage refers to the swing-up stage of the gymnastic robot, which accumulates energy for leap through the swing of the active joint. The leap stage is the process in which a gymnastic robot is released from one horizontal bar to the other. Keeping the configuration unchanged, the gymnastic robot rotates uniformly around the whole center of mass after leaving the bar. In order to make the gymnastic robot turn appropriate angle to grasp the bar after leaping, the initial state of the robot during is planned by considering the constraints of leaving bar and grasping bar. In order to achieve the desire state of leaping, a swing-up controller based on subsection control is adopted in swing-up stage. With this approach the gymnastic robot can continuously swing up and accumulate energy under the constraints in the physical experiment, and reach the initial state required for leap periodically. Finally, we build the controller model in Matlab/Simulink and verify the proposed control strategy.

Keywords: Control strategy · Gymnastic robot · Swing up · Leaping

1 Introduction

Gymnastic robot on the bar is a typical example of underactuated, nonlinear and strong coupling complex system. Its control has high complexity and non-linearity which can be used to test the effectiveness of control theory and control method in such complex system control. The gymnastic robot designed in this paper is an under-actuated two-link robot. The control goal is to make the gymnastic robot realize the leap between the two horizontal bars, which is divided into the swing-up stage and the leap stage.

When studying the swing-up of gymnastic robot, researchers at home and abroad usually simplify it as Acrobot model, and propose many different control methods for this model. Hauser and Murray [1] use the non-linear approximation method to achieve the inverted balance control of two-link planar gymnastic robot. Takashima [2, 3] and Nakawak [4] modeled and experimented on the simplified Acrobot to achieve swing-up and inverted balance. In the 1990s, Spong summarized the underactuated problem and used partial feedback linearization method [5, 6] to increase the energy of the whole

© Springer Nature Switzerland AG 2019
H. Yu et al. (Eds.): ICIRA 2019, LNAI 11742, pp. 709–718, 2019.
https://doi.org/10.1007/978-3-030-27535-8_63

system and realize swing-up motion. However, this method is difficult to achieve the desired position accurately, and it is strongly dependent on the parameters and initial conditions. Xinxin proposed Lyapunov's direct method [7, 8] which achieves the Acrobot's swing-up and stabilize the system to the required orbit. However, the angle range and torque of active joint required by the control method are too large, which is difficult to achieve in the actual control of the gymnastics robot. In China, the research on underactuated gymnastic robots started relatively late. Professor Li of Chongqing University proposed a human-like intelligent control strategy [9, 10], which imitated human gymnastic movement and realized the swing of gymnastic robots. Professor Lai from Central South University mainly studies the underactuated two-joint and three-joint robots, and proposes an intelligent control [11] method for swing-up.

Few studies have been done on the leap motion of gymnastic robots. when Acrobot is in the air, the momentum equation is not integrable because of the nonzero initial angular momentum and the flying time is so short that it is difficult to control its attitude. The research on leaping motion at home and abroad is mainly focused on primate robots. Fukuda and Nishimura [12, 13] proposed a control method based on target dynamics to realize ladder motion of primate robots. Xinxin [7] presents a precise linearization method based on coordinate transformation, which realizes the global stabilization control of Acrobot in the air. However, the state variables and input variables after coordinate transformation are difficult to correspond to physical quantity, and it is difficult to apply in the actual control. Cheng proposed a virtual constraints based dynamic servo control [14, 15], and made a prototype of two-degree-of-freedom primate bionic robot. The active joint of the robot can rotate freely around the joint, which is difficult to apply to the actual control of gymnastic robot.

In order to leap between horizontal bar under the angular limitation and torque requirements, In this paper, first the state of gymnastic robot before leap is planned and then this paper proposes a method based on segmentation control, which can achieve the desired initial leaping state of the bar-changing under physical constraints.

2   Initial Leap State Planning

When the gymnastic robot is released from the first horizontal bar with its configuration unchanged in the air, the centroid the system do projectile motion, and the whole robot rotates around the center of mass uniformly, as shown in the following figure:

Assuming that the trajectory is symmetrical and θ_2 is unchanged in the air, the following constraints can be listed:

$$
\begin{aligned}
&y_{c0}(\theta_{10}, \theta_{20}) = y_{cf}(\theta_{1f}, \theta_{2f}) \\
&v_{cy0}(\theta_{10}, \theta_{20}, \dot{\theta}_{10}, \dot{\theta}_{20}) = t_f g/2 \\
&v_{cx0}(\theta_{10}, \theta_{20}, \dot{\theta}_{10}, \dot{\theta}_{20})t_f = d - 2x_{c0}(\theta_{10}, \theta_{20}) \\
&\theta_{1f} - \theta_{10} = \dot{\theta}_{1f} t_f \\
&\dot{\theta}_{20} = \dot{\theta}_{2f} = 0, \theta_{20} = \theta_{2f} = const, d = const
\end{aligned}
\tag{1}
$$

Where

$x_{c0} = M_1 l_{c1} \sin \theta_{10} + M_2 [l_1 \sin \theta_{10} + l_{c2} \sin(\theta_{10} + \theta_{20})]$

$y_{c0} = -M_1 l_{c1} \cos \theta_{10} - M_2 [l_1 \cos \theta_{10} + l_{c2} \cos(\theta_{10} + \theta_{20})]$

$x_{cf} = M_1 l_{c1} \sin \theta_{1f} + M_2 [l_1 \sin \theta_{1f} + l_{c2} \sin(\theta_{1f} + \theta_{2f})]$

$y_{cf} = -M_1 l_{c1} \cos \theta_{1f} - M_2 [l_1 \cos \theta_{1f} + l_{c2} \cos(\theta_{1f} + \theta_{2f})]$

$v_{cx0} = M_1 l_{c1} \dot\theta_{10} \cos \theta_{10} + M_2 [l_1 \dot\theta_{10} \cos \theta_{10} + l_{c2}(\dot\theta_{10} + \dot\theta_{20}) \cos(\theta_{10} + \theta_{20})]$

$v_{cx0} = M_1 l_{c1} \dot\theta_{10} \sin \theta_{10} + M_2 [l_1 \dot\theta_{10} \sin \theta_{10} + l_{c2}(\dot\theta_{10} + \dot\theta_{20}) \sin(\theta_{10} + \theta_{20})]$

t_f — — *time of leaping*

d — — *distance between horizontal bar*

$M_1 = \frac{m_1}{m_1 + m_2}, M_2 = \frac{m_2}{m_1 + m_2}$

In the above formula what we don't know are θ_{10}, θ_{1f}, $\dot\theta_{10}$ and t_f. Put constraints into MATLAB and use Fourth-order Runge-Kutta method to solve these variables. Under given conditions $\dot\theta_{2d} = 0, \theta_{2f} = pi/6, d = 0.5$, we get the solution

$$\left(\theta_{10}, \theta_{20}, \dot\theta_{10}, \dot\theta_{20}\right) = (1.0611, pi/6, 10.7901, 0).$$

In the coordinate system of Fig. 1, the initial leaping condition is converted to

$$\left(\theta_{10}, \theta_{20}, \dot\theta_{10}, \dot\theta_{20}\right) = (-0.5079, pi/6, 10.7901, 0)$$

The energy and the link 2 angle of initial leaping state are selected as the desired periodic trajectory. Simulink model is built in MATLAB for simulation, and its inertia parameters are derived from the Creo model (Fig. 2 and Table 1).

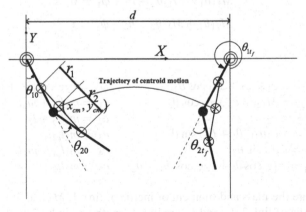

Fig. 1. Free flying phase of the

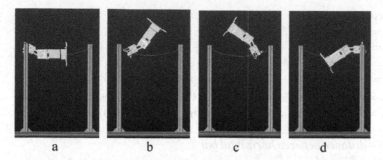

Fig. 2. Leaping of the Gymnastic robot

Table 1. Simulation parameters of gymnastic robot model

M_1	M_2	L_1	L_2	l_{c1}	l_{c2}	I_1	I_2	g
0.933	1.82	0.135	0.195	0.04	0.103	0.00127	0.0126	9.81

3   Controller Design

3.1   Dynamics Model of Gymnastic Robot

The equations of motion of the Acrobot shown in Fig. 3 are just the standard equations of motion of a two-link planar robot [7] except that there is no independent input to the first equation, i.e.

$$M_{11}\ddot{\theta}_1 + M_{12}\ddot{\theta}_2 + h_1 + \phi_1 = 0$$
$$M_{21}\ddot{\theta}_1 + M_{22}\ddot{\theta}_2 + h_2 + \phi_2 = \tau \tag{2}$$

Where

$$
\begin{aligned}
M_{11} &= c_1 + c_2 + 2c_3 \cos\theta_2 \\
M_{21} &= M_{12} = c_2 + c_3 \cos\theta_2 \\
M_{22} &= c_2 \\
h_1 &= -c_3\dot{\theta}_2(2\dot{\theta}_1 + \dot{\theta}_2)\sin\theta_2 \\
h_2 &= c_3\dot{\theta}_1^2 \sin\theta_2 \\
\phi_1 &= c_4 g \cos\theta_1 + c_5 g \cos(\theta_1 + \theta_2)
\end{aligned}
\qquad
\begin{aligned}
\phi_2 &= c_5 g \cos(\theta_1 + \theta_2) \\
c_1 &= m_1 l_{c1}^2 + m_2 l_1^2 + I_1 \\
c_2 &= m_2 l_{c2}^2 + I_2 \\
c_3 &= m_2 l_{c2} l_1 \\
c_4 &= m_1 l_{c1} + m_2 l_1 \\
c_5 &= m_2 l_{c2}
\end{aligned}
$$

M_1 and I_1 are the mass and moment of inertia of link 1. M_2 and I_2 are the mass and moment of inertia of link 2, L_1 and L_2 are link 1 length and link 2 length, θ_1 is the angle between the link 1 and the vertical direction, θ_2 is the angle between the link 1 and the link 2, τ is a joint input torque, and the center of mass of each link is located on the center line which passes through adjacent joints at a distance l_{ci}.

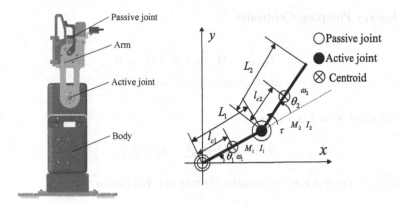

Fig. 3. The Gymnastic robot model

The attitude of Gymnastics robot in the air is difficult to control, instead, by planning the initial leap state, the Gymnastics robot can switch naturally and ultimately have the appropriate attitude to grasp. Based on this idea, it is sufficient to design a suitable swing-up control algorithm to achieve the desired leaping state. Gymnastics robot is an underactuated robot, which cannot achieve the stabilization of any trajectory points, while the leaping process only requires the initial leaping state. Therefore, as long as the controller is designed to enable the robot to reach the initial state required for leaping periodically, the Gymnastics robot can leaping from one bar to the other.

When Gymnastics robot swings periodically, it is similar to the periodic motion of a simple pendulum. When the single pendulum is released from a certain height, and regardless of the energy loss, the pendulum will periodically reach the initial release height. Similarly, it can be found that in Gymnastics robot, too. When $\dot{\theta}_2 = 0$, the motion of Gymnastics robot is the same as that of a pendulum. The system will continue to move periodically along a circular orbit, the radius of the orbit is determined by θ_2, and the highest point of the orbit is determined by the system mechanical energy E. At this point, the periodic orbit can be determined completely by $[\theta_2, E]$. If the output of the system is chosen as $y = [\theta_2, E]$, the desired periodic orbital equation can be described as

$$y = [\theta_{2d}, E_d] \tag{3}$$

Designing a controller which can stabilize the output to the desired value so that the Gymnastics robot can periodically reach the desired initial leaping conditions/state. Considering the physical constrain of the gymnastic robot, this paper proposes a segmentation control method, which can make the gymnastic robot reach the initial leaping state periodically under physical constrain.

3.2   Energy Pumping Controller

$$M_{11}\ddot{\theta}_1 + M_{12}\ddot{\theta}_2 + h_1 + \phi_1 = 0$$
$$M_{21}\ddot{\theta}_1 + M_{22}\ddot{\theta}_2 + h_2 + \phi_2 = \tau_2 \tag{4}$$

If we solve $\ddot{\theta}_2$ in Eq. (4) as

$$\ddot{\theta}_1 = -d_{11}^{-1}(d_{12}\ddot{q}_2 + h_1 + \phi_1) \tag{5}$$

Substitute the resulting expression (5) into (4). We obtain

$$\bar{M}_2\ddot{\theta}_2 + \bar{h}_2 + \bar{\phi}_2 = \tau \tag{6}$$

where

$$\bar{M}_2 = M_{22} - M_{21}M_{11}^{-1}M_{12}$$
$$\bar{h}_2 = h_2 - M_{21}M_{11}^{-1}h_1$$
$$\bar{\phi}_2 = \phi_2 - M_{21}M_{11}^{-1}\phi_1$$

The term M_{11} is positive and is bounded away from zero by the uniform positive definiteness of the robot's inertia matrix. Also, it can be seen that $\bar{M}_2 = M_{11}^{-1}\Delta$, where $\Delta = M_{11}M_{22} - M_{21}M_{12}$ is the determinant of the robot's inertia matrix. Hence M_{22} is also positive and bounded away from zero. Therefore, a feedback linearizing controller [16] can be defined for equation according to

$$\tau_2 = \bar{M}_2 v_2 + \bar{h}_2 + \hat{\phi}_2 \tag{7}$$

Where v_2 is an additional control input yet to be defined. The complete system can be written as

$$M_{11}\ddot{\theta}_1 + h_1 + \phi_1 = -M_{12}v_2$$
$$\ddot{\theta}_2 = v_2 \tag{8}$$

θ_2 can track any reference trajectory if choose the appropriate v_2, but, the chosen reference trajectory should enable Acrobat to swing up. According to the principle of energy pumping, we can select theta to track the following trajectory.

$$\theta_2^d = 2\alpha \arctan(\dot{\theta}_1)/\pi \tag{9}$$

At this time, the coupling torque generated during the swing-up process is the same direction as $\dot{\theta}_1$. So the total energy of the system is continuously increased. By introducing the reference trajectory, the swing angle of the link 2 is always within the allowable range, it is suitable for the physical constrain of the gymnastics robot. Then we choose the control term v_2 as

$$v_2 = \ddot{\theta}_2^d + k_d\left(\dot{\theta}_2^d - \dot{\theta}_2\right) + k_p\left(\theta_2^d - \theta_2\right) \tag{10}$$

Where k_p and k_d are positive gains. θ_2 can track θ_{2d} very well. However, it is difficult to obtain the jerk of the passive joint in the controller (10) by measurement, so the change controller as follows

$$v_2 = k_d\dot{\theta}_2 + k_p(\theta_2^d - \theta_2) \tag{11}$$

In the first stage of Gymnastics robot swing-up, the controller is used to accumulate the energy of the system. When the energy of the system approaches the required energy, the controller is switched to the orbit stabilization controller to stabilize the desired orbit.

3.3 Periodic Orbit Stabilization Controller

In order to make the system converge to the periodic orbit required by the initial leaping state, define the following Lyapunov function candidate [7]

$$V = \frac{1}{2}k_E\tilde{E}^2 + \frac{1}{2}k_D\dot{\theta}_2^2 + \frac{1}{2}k_p e_{\theta 2}^2 \tag{12}$$

Where $\tilde{E} = E - E_d, e_{\theta 2} = \theta_2 - \theta_{2d}, k_E, k_D, k_p$ are all positive gains. Taking the time derivative of V in (12) and using the fact $\dot{\tilde{E}} = \dot{\theta}_2\tau_2$ yield

$$\dot{V} = \dot{\theta}_2\left(k_E\tilde{E}\tau_2 + k_D\ddot{\theta}_2 + k_p e_{\theta 2}\right) \tag{13}$$

If we can choose τ_2 such that

$$k_E\tilde{E}\tau + k_D\ddot{\theta}_2 + k_p\theta_2 = -k_v\dot{\theta}_2 \tag{14}$$

Then

$$\dot{V} = -k_v\dot{\theta}_2^2$$
$$\lim_{t\to\infty} e_{\theta 2} = 0, \lim_{t\to\infty} \tilde{E} = 0$$

The proof we can get from Xinxin [7]. Substituting (5) into (14) yields

$$(k_E\tilde{E} + k_D\rho)\tau = -k_v\dot{\theta}_2 - k_p\theta_2 - k_D\frac{M_{21}(h_1 + \phi_1) - M_{11}(h_2 + \phi_2)}{\Delta} \tag{15}$$

where

$$\Delta = M_{11}M_{22} - M_{12}^2$$
$$\rho = \frac{M_{11}}{\Delta}$$

If $k_E \tilde{E} + k_D \rho \neq 0$, Then τ can be obtained from Eq. (15), and there is no singularity at this time. Choose ρ^* as follow

$$\rho^* = \min \rho(\theta_2) = \min_{\theta_2} \frac{c_1 + c_2 + 2c_3 \cos \theta_2}{c_1 c_2 - c_3^2 \cos^2 \theta_2} \tag{16}$$

If k_d meets the following conditions

$$k_D > 2k_E E_{top}/\rho^* \tag{17}$$

We can get

$$k_E \tilde{E} + k_D \rho \geq -2k_E E_{top} + k_D \rho^* > 0 \tag{18}$$

So when $k_D > 2k_E E_{top}/\rho^*$, $k_E \tilde{E} + k_D \rho \neq 0$. At this point v_2 is negative definite. Then the following control law is defined below:

$$\tau = \frac{-(k_v \dot{\theta}_2 + k_p \theta_2)\Delta - k_D(M_{21}(h_1 + \phi_1) - M_{11}(h_2 + \phi_2))}{k_E \tilde{E} \Delta + k_D M_{11}} \tag{19}$$

When the above controller is selected as the active torque input then the output $y \to [\theta_{2d}, E_d]$. Gymnastics robot periodically reaches the desired initial leaping state.

4 Verification of the Controller

In the swing-up stage, the gymnastics robot adopts the method of segmentation control. The first stage uses a feedback linearization based controller. When the gymnastic robot starts giant loop, switch to orbit stabilization controller to control the Off-Bar Attitude. In the first stage $k_p = 114.66, k_d = 15$. In the second stage $k_E = 200, k_V = 55$, $k_D = 20, k_p = 20$. The simulation results in MATLAB/Simulink are as follows (Figs. 4, 5 and 6):

when t = 30 s it can be seen from the simulation results that the Gymnastics robot has been calmed to the required periodic orbit for leaping movement. The active joint angle is between $[-1,1]$ rad and the maximum torque during the whole swinging process is about 4 N.m. The periodic track can be well maintained which provides a desired leaping state. This verifies the effectiveness of our controller.

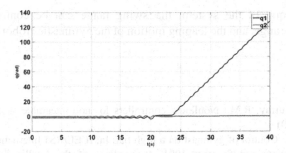

Fig. 4. The angle of link 1 and link 2

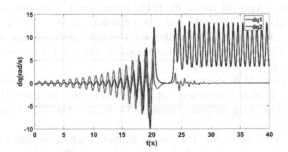

Fig. 5. The angle velocity of link 1 and link 2

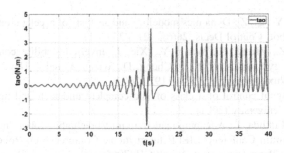

Fig. 6. Torque of the active joint

5 Conclusion

This paper proposes a segmentation control method for gymnastics robots, and successfully realizes the leap movement. In the first stage, a controller based on energy accumulation is used to continuously increase the mechanical energy of gymnastics robot through active joint swing. When the energy accumulates close to that of the required periodic orbit, switching to the orbital stabilization controller based on the Lyapunov method, the gymnastics robot system is stabilized to the required periodic trajectory of the leaping movement. By segmentation control method, while reducing the required torque of the system, the swing range can be controlled within the mechanical limit range, and the leaping motion of the gymnastics robot is well achieved.

References

1. Hauser, J., Murray, R.M.: Nonlinear controllers for non-integrable systems: the Acrobot example (1990)
2. Takashima, S.: Control of gymnast on a high bar. In: IEEE/RSJ International Workshop on Intelligent Robots and Systems 1991, Proceedings of the Intelligence for Mechanical Systems, IROS 1991, Osaka, 3–5 November 1991, pp. 1424–1429 (1991)
3. Takashima, S.: Dynamic modeling of a gymnast on a high bar-computer simulation and construction of a gymnast robot. In: IEEE International Workshop (1990). Author, F., Author, S., Author, T.: Book title, 2nd edn. Publisher, Location (1999)
4. Nakawaki, D., Sangwan, J., Miyazaki, F.: Dynamic modeling approach to gymnastic coaching. In: IEEE International Conference on Robotics and Automation, Leuven, 16–20 May 1998, pp. 1069–1076 (1998)
5. DeJong, G., Spong, M.W.: Swinging up the Acrobot: an example of intelligent control. In: 1994 American Control Conference, vol. 2, pp. 2158–2162. IEEE (1994)
6. Spong, M.W.: The swing up control problem for the Acrobot. IEEE Control Syst. Mag. **15** (1), 49–55 (1995)
7. Xin, X., Mita, T., Kaneda, M.: The posture control of a two-link free flying Acrobot with initial angular momentum. IEEE Trans. Autom. Control **49**(7), 1201–1206 (2004)
8. Xin, X., Kaneda, M.: The swing up control for the Acrobot based on energy control approach. In: 2002 Proceedings of the 41st IEEE Conference on Decision and Control. IEEE (2003)
9. Xue, F., Guo, Y., Li, Z.: Dynamics modeling and analysis of acceleration-driven three-joint gymnastics robot. Control Decis. **26**(6), 821–825 (2011)
10. Li, Z., Tan, Z., Zhang, H., Wang, Y., Xie, J.: Inverted stability control of three-joint horizontal bar gymnastics robot. In: Cheng, D., Wang, X. (eds.) The 23rd China Control Conference, Wuxi, China, pp. 1188–1192 (2004)
11. Lai, X.: Intelligent control of a class of non-complete underactuated mechanical systems. Central South University (2001)
12. Nakanishi, J., Fukuda, T.: A leaping maneuvre for a brachiating robot. In: Proceedings 2000 ICRA. Millennium Conference, IEEE International Conference on Robotics and Automation, Symposia Proceedings (Cat. No. 00CH37065), vol. 3, pp. 2822–2827. IEEE (2000)
13. Nakanishi, J., Fukuda, T., Koditschek, D.E.: Experimental implementation of a "target dynamics" controller on a two-link brachiating robot. In: Proceedings of the 1998 IEEE International Conference on Robotics and Automation (Cat. No. 98CH36146), vol. 1, pp. 787–792. IEEE (1998)
14. Cheng, H., Rui, C., Hao, L.: Motion planning for ricochetal brachiation locomotion of bio-primitive robot. In: 2017 IEEE 7th Annual International Conference on CYBER Technology in Automation, Control, and Intelligent Systems (CYBER), pp. 259–264. IEEE (2017)
15. Wan, D., Cheng, H., Ji, G., et al.: Non-horizontal ricochetal brachiation motion planning and control for two-link bio-primate robot. In: 2015 IEEE International Conference on Robotics and Biomimetics (ROBIO), pp. 19–24. IEEE (2015)
16. Slotine, J.J.E., Li, W.: Applied Nonlinear Control. Prentice Hall, Englewood Cliffs (1991)

Design and Simulation of a Push Recovery Strategy for Biped Robot

Dandan Hu, Ruoqiao Guan[(⊠)], and Peiran Yu

Robotics Institute, Civil Aviation University of China, Tianjin, China
183847023@qq.com

Abstract. Maintaining balance and recovering from unexpected thrust is an important performance for bipedal robots. In this paper, we use the simplified biped robot model to solve the ZMP point, the variable height inverted pendulum model and sliding mode controller to solve the CoM point. Then, a nonlinear element is designed to describe the stability criterion of robot attitude. Finally, the whole process of push recovery is simulated by computer and the results verify the effectiveness and rapidity of the proposed method.

Keywords: Biped robot · Variable height inverted pendulum model ·
Sliding mode controller · Push recovery

1 Introduction

The self-balancing method of biped robot has always been a research hotspot. However, there are few effective control strategies.

Kajita et al. simplified the complex robot model into a linear inverted pendulum model [1], which was not conducive to the accurate control of the robot. In al. [2], Koolen et al. proposed to replace the traditional simplified model with the variable-height model, which made it possible to dynamically capture CoM trajectory. In reference [3], Krause et al. used model predictive controller (MPC) to calculate CoM capture points, while Moosavian et al. used sliding mode controller [4].

In our work, motion constraints based on variable-height inverted pendulum model are added, the output of the sliding mode controller is used to solve the real time CoM trajectory, a stability criterion composed of two factors is defined and described by a nonlinear link.

2 A Simplified Model of the Robot Lower Limb

The foot movement of biped robot can be described as a 6-dof kinematics model driven by 1 hip, 2 knees and 2 ankles. Generally, the walking process of the robot is divided into the single-leg support stage and the two-legs support stage. In order to simplify the analysis and to facilitate the application of control, it is assumed that the robot only carries out planar motion, and then the single-leg 5 links model of the biped robot is established, as shown in Fig. 1.

© Springer Nature Switzerland AG 2019
H. Yu et al. (Eds.): ICIRA 2019, LNAI 11742, pp. 719–728, 2019.
https://doi.org/10.1007/978-3-030-27535-8_64

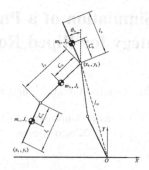

Fig. 1. 5 links model of lower limb of biped robot

2.1 Kinematics Model of Biped Robot Lower Limb

Since biped robot is driven by purpose, it is necessary to establish kinematics equation and find the inverse solution. In order to simplify the calculation, the leg model of the biped robot is simplified, and the simplified leg structure and swing diagram are shown in Fig. 2 [1].

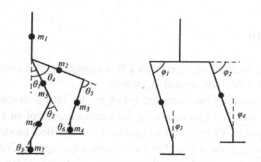

(a) Forward swing model   (b) lateral swing model

Fig. 2. Simplified leg swing model

The kinematics model of the lower limbs are as follows.

$$L = \sqrt{(x_a - x_h)^2 + (y_a - y_h)^2 + (z_a - z_h)^2} \tag{1}$$

$$\theta_1 = \arcsin \frac{l_c \sin(\pi - \arccos \frac{l_t^2 + l_c^2 - L^2}{2l_t l_c})}{L} + \arctan \frac{x_a - x_h}{z_h - l_a} \tag{2}$$

$$\theta_2 = \arcsin \frac{l_t \sin(\pi - \arccos \frac{l_t^2 + l_c^2 - L^2}{2l_t l_c})}{L} - \arctan \frac{x_a - x_h}{z_h - l_a} \tag{3}$$

$$\varphi_1 = \arctan \frac{z_h - z_a}{x_h - x_a} \tag{4}$$

$$\varphi_3 = \frac{\pi}{2} - \varphi_1 \tag{5}$$

Where θ_i ($i = 1, 2 \dots, 6$) in Fig. 2(a) represent the forward swing angles of lower limb joints and φ_j ($j = 1, 2, 3, 4$) in Fig. 2(b) represent lateral swing angles of lower limb joints. l_t, l_c is the length of thigh and calf separately and L is the total length of thigh and calf. (x_a, y_a, z_a) represents the coordinate of ankle joint and (x_h, y_h, z_h) represents the coordinate of hip joint.

2.2 Dynamics Model of Biped Robot

The biped robot in walking state is equivalent to a 3 driving force with 6 DoF underdriven system. At this time, each link of the robot has the expectation for velocity and acceleration, let the robot mass be $\mathbf{M}$, and the CoM be $\mathbf{c} = [x, y, z]^T$. According to the momentum and angular momentum theorem, the dynamic equation of robot walking motion is determined.

$$\begin{cases} \mathbf{P} = \mathbf{M}\dot{\mathbf{c}} \\ \mathbf{L} = \mathbf{c} \times \mathbf{P} = \mathbf{M}(\mathbf{c} \times \dot{\mathbf{c}}) \end{cases} \tag{6}$$

$$\mathbf{F} = -\mathbf{M} \begin{bmatrix} \ddot{x} \\ \ddot{y} \\ \ddot{z} \end{bmatrix} = \begin{bmatrix} \mathbf{F_x} \\ \mathbf{F_y} \\ \mathbf{F_z} \end{bmatrix} \mathbf{G}g \tag{7}$$

Where $\mathbf{P}$ and $\mathbf{L}$ respectively represent the momentum and angular momentum of the robot. $\mathbf{F}$ is the inertial force received by the robot, $\dot{\mathbf{c}}$ is the velocity of the robot's CoM and $\ddot{\mathbf{c}}$ is the acceleration of the robot's CoM. $\ddot{x}, \ddot{y}, \ddot{z}$ and $\mathbf{F_x}, \mathbf{F_y}, \mathbf{F_z}$ are the components of the acceleration of the CoM in the body coordinate system.

Assuming that the force acting on the biped robot facing the ground is $\mathbf{F}$, $\mathbf{F}$ intersects the contact surface at zero moment point ZMP, and the horizontal component of $\mathbf{F}$ at this point is 0, it can be obtained as follows.

$$(\mathbf{c} - \mathbf{P}) \times \mathbf{F} + (\mathbf{c} - \mathbf{P}) \begin{bmatrix} 0 \\ 0 \\ -\mathbf{G} \end{bmatrix} = \begin{bmatrix} 0 \\ 0 \\ \tau_z \end{bmatrix} \tag{8}$$

$$\begin{cases} \mathbf{P_x} = x - \frac{(z - \mathbf{p_z})}{\ddot{z} - g} \ddot{x} \\ \mathbf{P_y} = y - \frac{(z - \mathbf{p_z})}{\ddot{z} - g} \ddot{y} \end{cases} \tag{9}$$

Where $\mathbf{G}$ is the force of gravity on the robot, g is the gravitational acceleration and $\mathbf{P} = [\mathbf{p_x}, \mathbf{p_y}, \mathbf{p_z}]$ is the position of ZMP.

3   Variable Height Inverted Pendulum Model and Sliding Mode Control

In order to obtain the trajectory equation of the CoM, the kinematics model with complete motion constraints was proposed based on the variable-height inverted pendulum model [2] proposed by Koolen et al. According to Lyapunov stability criterion, sliding control is carried out on the tiny hyperplane of the phase plane of the model. In addition, on the basis of the research in literature [2], a more complete boundary function of control quantity was proposed, and then the trajectory of the center of mass capture point of the control flow and the model with variable height was obtained.

3.1   Variable-Height Inverted Pendulum Model

Considering that the bending and stretching of the knee will lead to changes in the height of the CoM of the robot, and the distance from the CoM to the ZMP is an important basis for judging whether the robot falls or not. In order to carry out the gait planning when the robot responds to external forces, on the basis of Chap. 1, the lower limbs of the biped robot are further equivalent to the two-dimensional inverted pendulum model, as shown in Fig. 3.

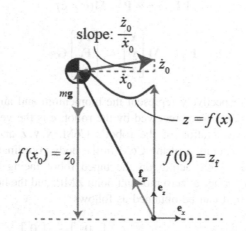

Fig. 3. 2D Inverted pendulum model with variable height

The walking action under this model is regarded as the continuous control of the falling state, and the kinematics model and motion constraint established are shown in Eqs. (10–11).

$$\mathbf{q}(x, t) = \begin{bmatrix} \mathbf{q_x}(x, t) \\ \mathbf{q_z}(x, t) \end{bmatrix} = \begin{bmatrix} x(0) + \dot{x}(0)t \\ z(0) + \dot{z}(0)t - \frac{1}{2}gt^2 \end{bmatrix} \tag{10}$$

$$\begin{cases} x_c(t)^2 + (z_c(t) - h_f)^2 \leq (L_1 + L_2)^2 \\ (x_c(t) - x_k)^2 + (z_c(t) - z_k)^2 \geq L_2^2 \\ [(x_{c0} + S) - (x_{k0} + 2S)]^2 + [(z_{c0} + H) \\ \qquad\qquad - (z_{k0} + 2H)]^2 \geq L_2^2 \\ (x_{c0} - x_{k0} - S)^2 + (z_{c0} - z_{k0} - H)^2 \geq L_2^2 \end{cases} \quad (11)$$

Where $\mathbf{q}(x, t)$ is the trajectory of the CoM, $\mathbf{q_x}(x, t)$ and $\mathbf{q_z}(x, t)$ respectively represents the trajectory component of the CoM on the X-axis and Z-axis, $x(0)$ and $\dot{x}(0)$ respectively represents the initial position and velocity of the CoM. S and H represent step width and step height respectively. h_f is pitch distance between feet and ankle joints. L_1 and L_2 represent the length of upper and lower legs respectively. Points c and k respectively represents crotch joint and knee joint of the robot.

3.2   Sliding Mode Controller

At present, the typical self-balancing control methods include intelligent PID control, fuzzy control, H_∞ control, sliding mode control, neural network, etc. The pros and cons are shown in Table 1.

Table 1. Pros and cons of typical self-balancing control methods

Method	Advantage	Disadvantage
Intelligent PID control	It makes up for the deficiency of linear PD and has parameter adaptability	The design process is complicated, requiring designers to have rich experience
Fuzzy control	High precision model is not needed. The control method is simple and robust	It lacks the ability to learn from itself and require experienced designers
H_∞ control	It has good robust control ability and anti-interference	When the object parameters and structure are uncertain, the design results are conservative
Sliding mode control	Different control laws are applied to different areas of the system phase space. It has strong robustness and adaptability to external disturbances	Chattering is easy to occur during zone switching
Neural network	It has the ability to approximate nonlinear function arbitrarily, without controlling object model analysis, self-learning ability and good control robustness. Has the parallel processing ability, the real-time is strong	The updating speed of the weight matrix of the network is high and the convergence is not easy to guarantee

Since the sliding mode controller has both robustness and self-adaptability, which requires little of the designer's experience and sample size, we chose the sliding mode control method to design the self-balancing controller of biped robot.

According to the principle of sliding control mode, a hyperplane $\boldsymbol{\sigma}(x)$ is defined in the phase plane of the higher-order nonlinear system [4], and a controller is designed by using Lyapunov direct method, so that all the points in the theoretical state space will slide to $\boldsymbol{\sigma}(x) = 0$. However, due to the highly discontinuous nature of the system state near $\boldsymbol{\sigma}(x) = 0$, the actual system state will have "chattering" phenomenon when approaching $\boldsymbol{\sigma}(x) = 0$, as shown in Fig. 4.

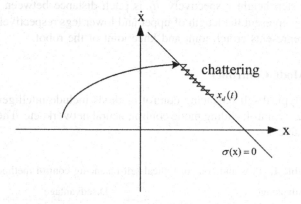

Fig. 4. Chattering phenomenon during state convergence

For this, use the property of exponential function to solve this problem.

$$\boldsymbol{\sigma}(x) = \boldsymbol{\sigma}_0 e^{-t} = \mathbf{PY} \tag{12}$$

At this time, although the discontinuity of the state still exists, its convergence rate under the continuous control law $\boldsymbol{\mu}$ increases exponentially. The selected Lyapunov function is as follows.

$$\begin{cases} \mathbf{V}(x) = \frac{1}{2}\boldsymbol{\sigma}(x)^T\boldsymbol{\sigma}(x) \\ \dot{\sigma}(x) = \frac{\partial \boldsymbol{\sigma}}{\partial x}\dot{x} \\ \dot{\mathbf{V}}(x) = \boldsymbol{\sigma}(x)^T\dot{\sigma}(x) = \boldsymbol{\sigma}(x)^T\frac{\partial \boldsymbol{\sigma}}{\partial x}\dot{x} < 0 \end{cases} \tag{13}$$

The designed continuous control law is as follows.

$$\boldsymbol{\mu} = -(\mathbf{PB}^*)^{-1}\mathbf{PA}^*\mathbf{Y} - \delta\mathbf{x}^T \tag{14}$$

Where $\mathbf{A}$ and $\mathbf{B}$ are the state matrix and control matrix of the system respectively, and δ is a sliding margin with positive value.

In order to avoid dealing with singularities in the phase plane of the nonlinear system, a boundary function is set for the control law, so that the final control law is as follows.

$$\mu(x) = \min(\max(U(x), 0), 1) \tag{15}$$

4   Centroid Stability Region and Overall Control Flow

According to literature [4], the distance from ZMP to the CoM is related to the walking stability of robot, and the distance from ZMP to the CoM capture point is defined.

$$\Delta Z(t) = \det \begin{bmatrix} \mathbf{q_x}(x,t) - \mathbf{p_x}(x,t) \\ \mathbf{q_y}(y,t) - \mathbf{p_y}(y,t) \\ \mathbf{q_z}(x,t) - \mathbf{p_z}(z,t) \end{bmatrix} \tag{16}$$

In our definition of criteria, the stability of the robot posture is determined by two factors. The weak stability criterion means that if $\forall \Delta Z(t) \in [0, L_1 + L_2]$, $\exists \Delta t \geq 0 \Rightarrow \Delta Z(t + \Delta t) \in [-z, z]$, the robot must be in static stable state. The value of z is determined by the parameters of robot. The strong stability criterion means that if the velocity and acceleration states of the robot $\mathbf{V} = [v, \dot{v}]$ are in the steady state domain $\mathbf{Q_1}$, the robot must be in dynamic stable state. Therefore, the overall stability criterion is described as follows.

$$\begin{cases} \mathbf{S} = \{x | \Delta Z \in [-z, z] \cap \mathbf{V} \in \mathbf{Q_1}\} \\ \mathbf{A} = \{x | \Delta Z \in [-z, z] \cap \mathbf{V} \notin \mathbf{Q_1}\} \\ \mathbf{U} = \{x | \Delta Z \notin [-z, z]\} \\ \mathbf{Q_1} = \{\mathbf{V} | v(x) \in v_{normal}(x) \cap \dot{v}(x) \in \dot{v}_{normal}(x)\} \end{cases} \tag{17}$$

Where $\mathbf{S}$ is the stable domain, $\mathbf{A}$ is the adjustable domain and $\mathbf{U}$ is the unstable state domain, $v_{normal}(x)$ and $\dot{v}_{normal}(x)$ respectively represent the normal speed and acceleration that the robot can maintain walking.

The nonlinear element used to describe the stability criterion and its connection with PD controller are shown in Fig. 5.

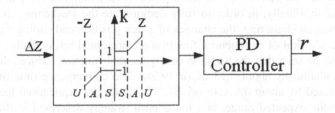

Fig. 5. The nonlinear link and its connection with PD controller

When the state **V** is in the stable domain **S**, the output coefficient $k = \pm 1$. When the state **V** is in the adjustable domain **A**, with the increase of, the coefficient also increases linearly to correct the robot attitude. When the state **V** is in the unstable domain **U**, we consider that the robot is falling or has fallen. At this time, in order to protect the robot actuator, the output coefficient $k = 0$. Then, we use the output coefficient k to dynamically adjust the proportional amplification coefficient of the PD controller, and then adjust the output of the robot steering gear, so that the robot can execute the push and recovery strategy. The overall control flow is shown in Fig. 6.

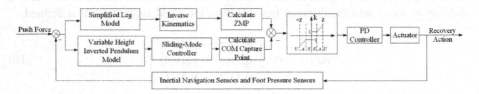

Fig. 6. Overall control flow

5 Simulation and Results

The simulation experiment is carried out on the basis of Gabriel's research [5]. The initial parameters of the robot in our laboratory are shown in Table 2.

Table 2. The initial parameters of the robot

Parameter	μ_{max}	x_0	z_0	t_f	z_{f0}	x_{d0}	z_{d0}
Value	25	−1.05	1.3	10	0.8	3.1	−1.2

It can be seen from Figs. 7 and 8 that after the robot is pushed, the CoM is adjusted at a fast initial speed and reduced acceleration. When the CoM stops changing, the robot returns to a stable standing state. Meanwhile, it can be seen from Fig. 9 that after the exponential function e-t is added, the control action enters the steady state within 2 s and the chattering of the sliding surface stops within 0.4 s. On the other hand, before entering the steady state, the value of the sliding surface function is always negative, and its first derivative is always positive. According to (13), the adjustment process is stable. Finally, in order to fully demonstrate the weakening effect of exponential function on chattering, the changes of z-axis position and sliding surface before and after the addition of exponential function are presented respectively, as shown in Fig. 10. It can be seen that the addition of exponential function reduces the amplitude of z-axis oscillation by about 0.13 m, or 19.7%. The convergence time of the sliding surface decreased by about 0.8 s, or 66.7%. Therefore, the exponential function limits chattering to the expected range, and the control strategy described in this paper has good performance and can enable the robot to effectively and quickly deal with part of the unexpected thrust.

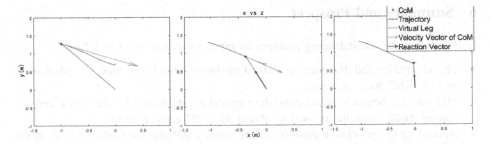

Fig. 7. Push recovery process

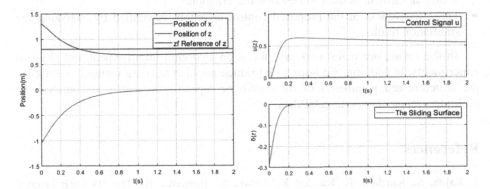

Fig. 8. The position of the CoM within 2 s

Fig. 9. Control signal and sliding surface within 2 s

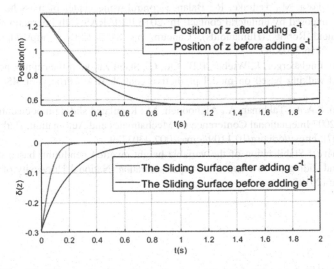

Fig. 10. The weakening effect of exponential function on chattering

6 Summary and Prospect

In this paper, the self-balancing problem of biped robot is studied as follows.

- The kinematics and dynamics models of the biped robot lower limb was conducted, and the ZMP were obtained;
- The variable-height inverted pendulum model is established for the robot, and the sliding mode controller is used to obtain the CoM capture point;
- According to the relative position of the robot ZMP and the CoM, as well as the robot speed and acceleration, the robot posture stability criterion is designed. The input of PD controller is adjusted according to the different stability domain, and a nonlinear element is used to describe the criterion.
- The effectiveness of the proposed control algorithm is verified by analyzing the simulation results.

In the future, our main work will focus on algorithm improvement and physical experiments. In addition, we hope to introduce machine learning method to optimize the structure and parameters of the controller depend on statistics and analysis of multiple groups of experimental data.

References

1. Kajita, S., Kanehiro, F., Kaneko, K., Yokoi, K., Hirukawa, H.: The 3D linear inverted pendulum mode: a simple modeling for a biped walking pattern generation. In: Proceedings 2001 IEEE/RSJ International Conference on Intelligent Robots and Systems. Expanding the Societal Role of Robotics in the Next Millennium (Cat. No. 01CH37180), Maui, HI, USA, vol. 1, pp. 239–246 (2001). https://doi.org/10.1109/iros.2001.973365
2. Koolen, T., Posa, M., Tedrake, R.: Balance control using center of mass height variation: limitations imposed by unilateral contact. In: 2016 IEEE-RAS 16th International Conference on Humanoid Robots (Humanoids), Cancun, pp. 8–15 (2016). https://doi.org/10.1109/humanoids.2016.7803247
3. Krause, M., Englsberger, J., Wieber, P.B., Ott, C.: Stabilization of the capture point dynamics for bipedal walking based on model predictive control. IFAC Proc. Vol. 45(22), 165–171 (2012)
4. Moosavian, S.A.A., Takhmar, A., Alghooneh, M.: Regulated sliding mode control of a biped robot. In: 2007 International Conference on Mechatronics and Automation, Harbin, pp. 1547–1552 (2007). https://doi.org/10.1109/icma.2007.4303779
5. García Chávez: Stabilization of the variable-height inverted pendulum based on input-state stability and sliding mode contact and input saturation. National University of Engineering, Lima, Peru (2018)

Nonlinear Dynamic Analysis of Inclined Impact Oscillator with a Harmonically External Excitation

Mei Wu and Ming Hu[⊠]

National and Local Joint Engineering Research Center of Reliability Analysis
and Testing for Mechanical and Electrical Products,
Zhejiang Sci-Tech University, Hangzhou 310018, China
huming@zstu.edu.cn

Abstract. The nonlinear dynamic of an inclined oscillator impacted on a harmonically external excitation is discussed. Different domains and boundaries of the system are defined, and the conditions of stick and grazing motions are studied. The specified periodic motions of such discontinuous systems are predicted. The sticking and grazing motion conditions are developed by flow switchability theory. The complex period motion and one-period motion are presented. The numerical solution of different periods of motions are also presented and the bifurcations of two kinds of conditions are observed. The obtained results are complicated than the previous studies. And there are still more periodic motions and the analytical bifurcation need to be investigated in the future.

Keywords: Inclined impact oscillator · Nonlinear dynamic analysis ·
Stick and grazing motion

1 Introduction

Impact oscillators have been widely investigated by researchers as a typical kind of discontinuous vibro-impact system. There will be clearance in all kinds of mechanical systems either by the structural design requirements or produced by the fatigue wear. These make the vibro-impact occurred during the operation and cause strong nonlinear vibration, such as gear rattle phenomenon, cotter recoil characteristics, and may even cause significant noise.

Several kinds of vibro-impact systems have been well studied recently. Czolczynski [1] investigated the cantilever beam with a mass at its end impacting against a harmonically moving frame. He presented an analytical method obtained stable periodic solutions to the equations of motion. Liu's analysis [2] showed how to use path-following techniques for non-smooth systems to determine the optimal control parameters in terms of energy expenditure. Gritli [3] developed an analytical

This work is supported by National Natural Science Foundation of China (51375485), National Natural Science Foundation of China and (51805488).

© Springer Nature Switzerland AG 2019
H. Yu et al. (Eds.): ICIRA 2019, LNAI 11742, pp. 729–740, 2019.
https://doi.org/10.1007/978-3-030-27535-8_65

expression of a stroboscopic controlled hybrid Poincarémap. He also presented the conditions to determining the fixed point of Poincarémap and studied its stability. These analysis mainly focused on the solution of the discontinuous dynamic system, but the complexity of the flow's local singularity to the separation boundary was not provided.

Sun and Fu [4, 5] investigated the quarter car suspension system and studied the singularity in discontinuous dynamical Systems with the G-functions introduced in Luo [6]. To investigate the local singularity of the separation boundary, Luo [6–10] established a general theory for discontinuous dynamical systems with connectable domains. He presented the flow switchability theory of discontinuous dynamical systems on time-varying domains, and applied such theory to different practical problems, such as the sliding motion and grazing motions in a periodically forced discontinuous dynamical system with incline line boundary, the grazing motion and stick motions for a periodically traveling belt with dry friction, and the dynamics of gear transmission systems.

The main goal of this paper is to study the conditions of stick and grazing motions in an inclined impact pair with periodically external excitation. Using Luo's flow switchability theory, different domains and boundaries of the motions are defined. The numerical simulations are given to illustrate the analytical results of the complex motions. The complex period motion and the special one-period motion are presented. The two conditions of bifurcation are also illustrated. From these results, the complicated dynamical behaviors of the inclined impact pair are presented. And there are still more periodic motions and the analytical bifurcation need to be investigated in the future.

2   Dynamic Model of the Inclined Impact Oscillator

2.1   Equations of Motion

To analysis the dynamic behavior of the inclined impact damper shown in Fig. 1, a dynamic system describing by displacement x(t) and X(t) considering the mechanical model of the free mass m moving within the primary mass M can be formulate as

$$\ddot{x} = -g \sin \theta \tag{1}$$

$$X = A \sin(\omega t + \varphi) \tag{2}$$

where g is the gravitational acceleration and t, A, ω and φ are the time, the amplitude, the frequency and the initial phase angle of the motion acting on the primary mass.

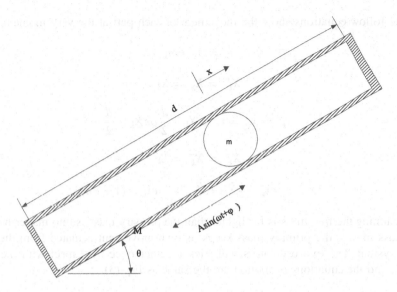

Fig. 1. Inclined impact damper: free mass m moving along the primary mass M

This system consists of incline angle θ imposed on primary system, inside length d which the free mass moves along, and this model doesn't consider friction. So, the corresponding displacement and velocity of the free mass, and the velocity and acceleration of the primary mass can be obtained as

$$\dot{X} = A\omega \, cos(\omega t + \varphi) \tag{3}$$

$$\ddot{X} = -A\omega^2 \, sin(\omega t + \varphi) \tag{4}$$

$$\dot{x} = \dot{x}_k^+ - g\left(t - t_k^+\right) \sin \theta \tag{5}$$

$$x = -\frac{1}{2}g\left(t - t_k^+\right)^2 \sin \theta + \dot{x}_k^+ \left(t - t_k^+\right) + x_k^+ \tag{6}$$

in which $t \in \left(t_k^+, t_{k+1}^-\right)$. The subscript "k" denotes the kth impact and the superscripts "+" and "−" denote the time before and after the impact.

Once the free mass moves to the either edge of the primary mass with different speed, which means $|x - X| = \frac{d}{2}$ and $\dot{x} \neq \dot{X}$, the impact occurred. This impacts among two masses can be described through the simple impact law with restitution coefficient e as follow.

$$e = -\frac{\dot{x}_k^+ - \dot{X}_k^+}{\dot{x}_k^- - \dot{X}_k^-} \tag{7}$$

The follow equations show the movement of each part at the very moment.

$$t_k^+ = t_k^- = t_k \tag{8}$$

$$X_k^+ = X_k^- = X_k \tag{9}$$

$$x_k^+ = x_k^- = x_k = X_k - \frac{d}{2} \, or \, X_k + \frac{d}{2} \tag{10}$$

$$\dot{X}_k^+ = \dot{X}_k^- = \dot{X}_k \tag{11}$$

$$\dot{x}_k^+ = -e\dot{x}_k^- + e\dot{X}_k^- + \dot{X}_k^+ = -e\dot{x}_k + (1+e)\dot{X}_k \tag{12}$$

Assuming the free mass is far lighter than the primary mass, so no matter how the free mass moves, the primary mass keeps its own movement actuated from the excitation system. The two oscillators will stick together once they meet with the same speeds, and the equations of motion are the same as Eq. (3).

2.2   Description of the Discontinuous Domains

If the two oscillators move respectively, they must be away from each other, which means they must away from the edges of the other one. If the impacts occur, the two oscillators must meet at edges with different speeds. And if the stick motion appears, they must meet at edges with the same speed.

Precisely because of these kinds of motion, this discontinuous dynamic system can be assumed to consist with two kinds of domains and boundaries. First kind is one free motion domain with two non-passable boundaries defined as follow.

$$\Omega_1 = \left\{ (x, \dot{x}) | x \in \left(X - \frac{d}{2}, X + \frac{d}{2} \right) \right\} \tag{13}$$

$$\partial\Omega_{1(-\infty)} = \left\{ (x, \dot{x}) | \varphi_{1(-\infty)} \equiv x - X = -\frac{d}{2}, \dot{x} \neq \dot{X} \right\} \tag{14}$$

$$\partial\Omega_{1(+\infty)} = \left\{ (x, \dot{x}) | \varphi_{1(+\infty)} \equiv x - X = \frac{d}{2}, \dot{x} \neq \dot{X} \right\} \tag{15}$$

Before the stick motion appears, all the motions are eventually back to Ω_1. The impacts between two masses occur at the non-passable boundaries, which means the two oscillators move back to the free motion each time after the impacts.

Second kind is three domains with two passable boundaries, which are defined as follow.

$$\Omega_1 = \left\{ (x, \dot{x}) | x \in \left(X_{cr} - \frac{d}{2}, X_{cr} + \frac{d}{2} \right) \right\} \tag{16}$$

$$\Omega_0 = \left\{ (x,\dot{x}) | x \in \left(-\infty, X_{cr} - \frac{d}{2} \right), x = X_{cr} - \frac{d}{2}, \dot{x} = \dot{X} \right\} \qquad (17)$$

$$\Omega_2 = \left\{ (x,\dot{x}) | x \in \left(X_{cr} + \frac{d}{2} + \infty \right), x = X_{cr} + \frac{d}{2}, \dot{x} = \dot{X} \right\} \qquad (18)$$

$$\partial\Omega_{02} = \left\{ (x,\dot{x}) | \varphi_{02} \equiv \dot{x} - \dot{X}_{cr} = 0, x - X_{cr} = -\frac{d}{2} \right\} \qquad (19)$$

$$\partial\Omega_{12} = \left\{ (x,\dot{x}) | \varphi_{12} \equiv \dot{x} - \dot{X}_{cr} = 0, x - X_{cr} = \frac{d}{2} \right\} \qquad (20)$$

If the stick motion exists, there will be three kinds of domains, represent for free motion and two sides of stick motions, and two kinds of motions transform, where stick motion start and vanish at left and right sides of the free motion domain.

2.3 Relative Motion Model

From the Eqs. (1)–(6), to simplify the expression and get the vector expression, the equations of relative motion model can be showed as follow.

$$\ddot{y} = \ddot{x} - \ddot{X} = A\omega^2 \sin(\omega t + \varphi) - g, t \in (t_k, t_{k+1}) \qquad (21)$$

$$\dot{y} = \dot{x} - \dot{X} = -A\omega \cos(\omega t + \varphi) - g(t - t_k) + \dot{y}_k^+ + A\omega \cos(\omega t_k + \varphi) \qquad (22)$$

$$y = x - X = -A \sin(\omega t + \varphi) - \frac{1}{2}g(t - t_k)^2 + \left[\dot{y}_k^+ + A\omega \cos(\omega t_k + \varphi) \right](t - t_k) + A \sin(\omega t_k + \varphi) + y_k^+ \qquad (23)$$

Bring the relative motion model into the domains and boundaries, here gets the relative ones.

$$\Omega_1 = \left\{ (y,\dot{y}) | y \in \left(-\frac{d}{2}, \frac{d}{2} \right) \right\} \qquad (24)$$

$$\Omega_0 = \left\{ (y,\dot{y}) | y = -\frac{d}{2}, \dot{y} = 0 \right\} \qquad (25)$$

$$\Omega_2 = \left\{ (y,\dot{y}) | y = \frac{d}{2}, \dot{y} = 0 \right\} \qquad (26)$$

$$\partial\Omega_{10} = \left\{ (y,\dot{y}) | \varphi_{10} \equiv \dot{y}_{cr} = 0, y_{cr} = -\frac{d}{2} \right\} \qquad (27)$$

$$\partial\Omega_{12} = \left\{ (y,\dot{y}) | \varphi_{12} \equiv \dot{y}_{cr} = 0, y_{cr} = \frac{d}{2} \right\} \qquad (28)$$

$$\partial\Omega_{1(-\infty)} = \left\{ (y,\dot{y})|\varphi_{1(-\infty)} \equiv y = -\frac{d}{2}, \dot{y} \neq 0 \right\} \tag{29}$$

$$\partial\Omega_{1(+\infty)} = \left\{ (y,\dot{y})|\varphi_{1(+\infty)} \equiv y = \frac{d}{2}, \dot{y} \neq 0 \right\} \tag{30}$$

Hence, the stick domains and boundaries become points at phase diagram.
The absolute and relative vectors in the relative coordinates can be described as

$$\mathbf{x}^{(\lambda)} = \begin{pmatrix} x^{(\lambda)} \\ \dot{x}^{(\lambda)} \end{pmatrix}, \mathbf{F}^{(\lambda)} = \dot{\mathbf{x}}^{(\lambda)} = \begin{pmatrix} \dot{x}^{(\lambda)} \\ F^{(\lambda)} \end{pmatrix} \tag{31}$$

$$\mathbf{y}^{(\lambda)} = \begin{pmatrix} y^{(\lambda)} \\ \dot{y}^{(\lambda)} \end{pmatrix}, \mathbf{H}^{(\lambda)} = \dot{\mathbf{y}}^{(\lambda)} = \begin{pmatrix} \dot{y}^{(\lambda)} \\ h^{(\lambda)} \end{pmatrix} \tag{32}$$

where $\lambda = 0, 1, 2$ give the corresponding left-stick, non-stick and right-stick domains.
For the left-stick motion,

$$F^{(0)}\left(\mathbf{x}^{(0)}, t\right) = -A\omega^2 \sin(\omega t + \varphi) \tag{33}$$

$$h^{(0)}\left(\mathbf{y}^{(0)}, t\right) = 0 \tag{34}$$

For the non-stick motion,

$$F^{(1)}\left(\mathbf{x}^{(1)}, t\right) = -g \tag{35}$$

$$h^{(1)}\left(\mathbf{y}^{(1)}, t\right) = -g + A\omega^2 \sin(\omega t + \varphi) \tag{36}$$

For the right-stick motion,

$$F^{(2)}\left(\mathbf{x}^{(2)}, t\right) = -A\omega^2 \sin(\omega t + \varphi) \tag{37}$$

$$h^{(2)}\left(\mathbf{y}^{(2)}, t\right) = 0 \tag{38}$$

So, the equations of motion are

$$\dot{\mathbf{y}}^{(\lambda)} = \mathbf{v}^{(\lambda)}\left(\mathbf{y}^{(\lambda)}, \mathbf{X}^{(\lambda)}, t\right), \dot{\mathbf{X}}^{(\lambda)} = \mathbf{F}^{(\lambda)}\left(\mathbf{X}^{(\lambda)}, t\right) \tag{39}$$

2.4   Grazing Dynamics and Stick Motion

To analysis the switching conditions of stick and grazing motions, this section will use the theory of flow switchability for discontinuous dynamical systems [9].

Introduce the normal vector of the relative boundary is

$$
\boldsymbol{n}_{\partial\Omega_{\alpha\beta}} = \nabla\varphi_{\alpha\beta} = \begin{pmatrix} \frac{\partial\varphi_{\alpha\beta}}{\partial y} \\ \frac{\partial\varphi_{\alpha\beta}}{\partial\dot{y}} \end{pmatrix}
\tag{40}
$$

From the Eqs. (27)–(30), the normal vectors to the relative stick boundaries and relative impact boundaries can be given by

$$
\boldsymbol{n}_{\partial\Omega_{1(-\infty)}} = \begin{pmatrix} 1 \\ 0 \end{pmatrix}, \boldsymbol{n}_{\partial\Omega_{1(+\infty)}} = \begin{pmatrix} 1 \\ 0 \end{pmatrix}
$$

$$
\boldsymbol{n}_{\partial\Omega_{10}} = \begin{pmatrix} 0 \\ 1 \end{pmatrix}, \boldsymbol{n}_{\partial\Omega_{12}} = \begin{pmatrix} 0 \\ 1 \end{pmatrix}
\tag{41}
$$

The zero-order and first-order G-functions for the relative boundaries are

$$
\left.\begin{aligned}
G^{(0,\alpha)}_{\partial\Omega_{\alpha\beta}}\left(\boldsymbol{y}^{(i)}_{t_{m\pm}}, \boldsymbol{x}^{(i)}_{t_{m\pm}}, t_{m\pm}\right) &= \boldsymbol{n}^T_{\partial\Omega_{\alpha\beta}} \cdot \boldsymbol{H}^{(i)}_{t_{m\pm}}\left(\boldsymbol{z}^{(i)}_{t_{m\pm}}, \boldsymbol{x}^{(i)}_{t_{m\pm}}, t_{m\pm}\right) \\
G^{(1,\alpha)}_{\partial\Omega_{\alpha\beta}}\left(\boldsymbol{y}^{(i)}_{t_{m\pm}}, \boldsymbol{x}^{(i)}_{t_{m\pm}}, t_{m\pm}\right) &= \boldsymbol{n}^T_{\partial\Omega_{\alpha\beta}} \cdot \boldsymbol{DH}^{(i)}_{t_{m\pm}}\left(\boldsymbol{z}^{(i)}_{t_{m\pm}}, \boldsymbol{x}^{(i)}_{t_{m\pm}}, t_{m\pm}\right)
\end{aligned}\right\}
\tag{42}
$$

Using G-functions, the switching conditions of either stick motion for flow passable boundary or grazing motion for impact boundary can be obtained as follow.

The onset conditions of stick motion from domain Ω_1 to Ω_2 are:

$$
G^{(0,1)}_{\partial\Omega_{12}} > 0 \text{ and } G^{(0,2)}_{\partial\Omega_{12}} > 0
\tag{43}
$$

The vanishing conditions of stick motion from domain Ω_1 to Ω_2 are:

$$
\begin{cases}
G^{(0,1)}_{\partial\Omega_{10}} = 0 \text{ and } G^{(0,0)}_{\partial\Omega_{10}} = 0 \\
G^{(1,1)}_{\partial\Omega_{10}} < 0 \text{ and } G^{(1,0)}_{\partial\Omega_{10}} < 0
\end{cases}
\tag{44}
$$

The onset conditions of stick motion from domain Ω_1 to Ω_0 are:

$$
G^{(0,1)}_{\partial\Omega_{10}} < 0 \text{ and } G^{(0,0)}_{\partial\Omega_{10}} < 0
\tag{45}
$$

The vanishing conditions of stick motion from domain Ω_0 to Ω_1 are:

$$
\begin{cases}
G^{(0,1)}_{\partial\Omega_{10}} = 0 \ and \ G^{(0,0)}_{\partial\Omega_{10}} = 0 \\
G^{(1,1)}_{\partial\Omega_{10}} > 0 \ and \ G^{(1,0)}_{\partial\Omega_{10}} > 0
\end{cases}
\tag{46}
$$

The grazing motion conditions for the stick boundary $\partial\Omega_{21}$ are:

$$
G^{(0,1)}_{\partial\Omega_{10}} = 0 \ and \ G^{(1,1)}_{\partial\Omega_{10}} < 0
\tag{47}
$$

or

$$
G^{(0,2)}_{\partial\Omega_{10}} = 0 \ and \ G^{(1,2)}_{\partial\Omega_{10}} > 0
\tag{48}
$$

The grazing motion conditions for the stick boundary $\partial\Omega_{01}$ are:

$$
G^{(0,1)}_{\partial\Omega_{10}} = 0 \ and \ G^{(1,1)}_{\partial\Omega_{10}} > 0
\tag{49}
$$

or

$$
G^{(0,0)}_{\partial\Omega_{10}} = 0 \ and \ G^{(1,0)}_{\partial\Omega_{10}} < 0
\tag{50}
$$

The grazing motion conditions for the impact boundary $\partial\Omega_{1(-\infty)}$ are:

$$
G^{(0,1)}_{\partial\Omega_{1(-\infty)}} = 0 \ and \ G^{(1,1)}_{\partial\Omega_{1(-\infty)}} > 0
\tag{51}
$$

The grazing motion conditions for the impact boundary $\partial\Omega_{1(-\infty)}$ are:

$$
G^{(0,1)}_{\partial\Omega_{1(+\infty)}} = 0 \ and \ G^{(1,1)}_{\partial\Omega_{1(+\infty)}} < 0
\tag{52}
$$

3   Numerical Simulations

To illustrate the motions of the inclined impact oscillator, the solution for the particle motions have been shown as Eqs. (21)–(23).

Consider parameters m = 0.00001, M = 1.0, e = 0.1, A = 2.0, g = 9.81, d = 1 with $\omega = 3$. From the analytical prediction, when $\theta = \frac{\pi}{6}$ and the initial condition is $t_0 = 0.8533$, $x_0 = -1.6711$, $\dot{x}_0 = -3.2964$, there can be a periodic motion of stick(on lower)-free motion-impact (on top)-impact (on lower) six times, which can be seen in Fig. 2.

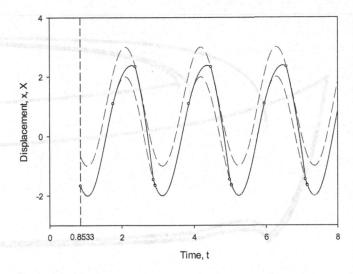

Fig. 2. Periodic motion ($\omega = 3$, $\theta = \frac{\pi}{6}$)

When $\theta = \frac{\pi}{2}$ and the initial condition is $t_0 = 0.9795$, $x_0 = -1.9589$, $\dot{x}_0 = -1.2098$, there can be a periodic motion of stick (on lower)-free motion-impact (on top) four times-stick (on top) -free motion –impact (on lower) six times, which can be seen in Fig. 3.

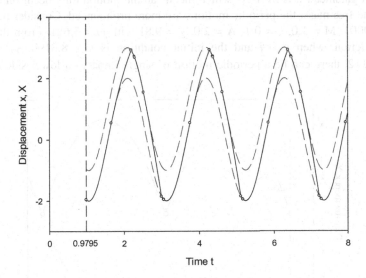

Fig. 3. Periodic motion ($\omega = 3$, $\theta = \frac{\pi}{2}$)

Switching points on the boundaries versus excitation frequency in a bifurcation diagram are shown in Fig. 4.

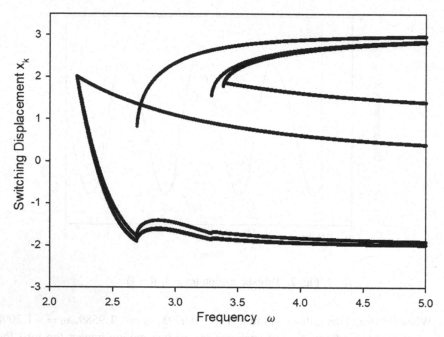

Fig. 4. Bifurcation varying with excitation frequency ω (m = 0.00001, M = 1.0, e = 0.1, A = 2.0, g = 9.81, d = 1)

When parameter d is over 10, which means all the motion only occur on the lower side of the free mass, the periodic motions are more pronounced. Consider parameters m = 0.00001, M = 1.0, e = 0.1, A = 2.0, g = 9.81 with $\omega = 3.621$. From the analytical prediction, when $\theta = \frac{\pi}{2}$ and the initial condition is $t_0 = 8.3190$, $x_0 = 0.5490$, $\dot{x}_0 = 8.5112$, there can be a periodic motion of single impact on lower side (Fig. 5).

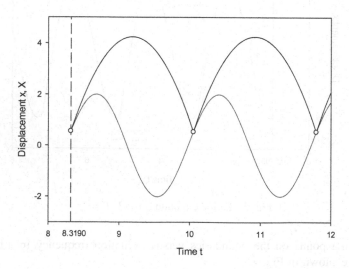

Fig. 5. Period-1 motion on the lower side ($\omega = 3.621$, $\theta = \frac{\pi}{2}$)

In this case, switching points on the boundaries versus excitation frequency in a bifurcation diagram are shown in Fig. 6.

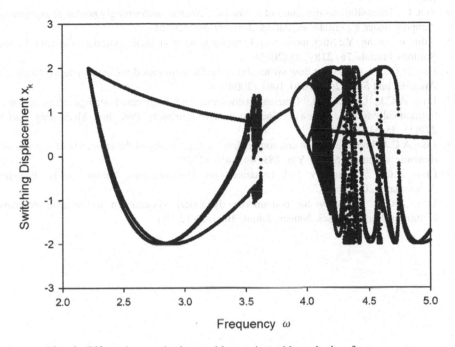

Fig. 6. Bifurcation on the lower side varying with excitation frequency ω

4 Conclusions

With a harmonically external excitation, discontinuous dynamics of inclined impact oscillator were investigated using flow switchability theory of discontinuous system in this paper. Different domains and boundaries were defined due to the discontinuity. The analytical conditions for motion switchability at the separation boundary were developed. The specified periodic motions of such discontinuous systems were predicted. It is noted that the present analysis can be extended to cover other kinds of dynamical systems. More complex motions of the systems are still being studied and will be investigated in the future, and actual scene experiments will be added to confirm them.

References

1. Czolczynski, K., Blazejczyk-Okolewska, B., Okolewski, A.: Analytical and numerical investigations of stable periodic solutions of the impacting oscillator with a moving base. Int. J. Mech. Sci. **115–116**, 325–338 (2016)
2. Liu, Y., Chávez, J.P.: Controlling coexisting attractors of an impacting system via linear augmentation. Phys. D Nonlinear Phenom. **348**, 1–11 (2017)

3. Gritli, H., Belghith, S.: Diversity in the nonlinear dynamic behavior of a one-degree-of-freedom impact mechanical oscillator under OGY-based state-feedback control law: order, chaos and exhibition of the border-collision bifurcation. Mech. Mach. Theory **124**, 1–41 (2018)

4. Sun, G.: Discontinuous dynamics of a class of oscillators with strongly nonlinear asymmetric damping under a periodic excitation. **2**(5), 99–110 (2016)

5. Xilin, F., Zhang, Y.: Stick motions and grazing flows in an inclined impact oscillator. Chaos, Solitons Fractals **76**, 218–230 (2015)

6. Luo, A.C.J.: A theory for flow switchability in discontinuous dynamical systems. Nonlinear Anal. Hybrid Syst. **2**(4), 1030–1061 (2008)

7. Luo, A.C.J., Chen, L.D.: Grazing phenomena and fragmented strange attractors in a harmonically forced, piecewise, linear system with impacts. Proc. Inst. Mech. Eng. Part K **220**(1), 35–51 (2006)

8. Luo, A.C.J.: Imaginary, sink and source flows in the vicinity of the separatrix of non-smooth dynamic system. J. Sound Vib. **285**, 443–456 (2005)

9. Luo, A.C.J.: Singularity and Dynamics on Discontinuous Vector Fields. Elsevier, Amsterdam (2006)

10. Luo, A.C.J.: A theory for non-smooth dynamical systems on connectable domains. Commun. Nonlinear Sci. Numer. Simul. **10**, 1–55 (2005)

Author Index